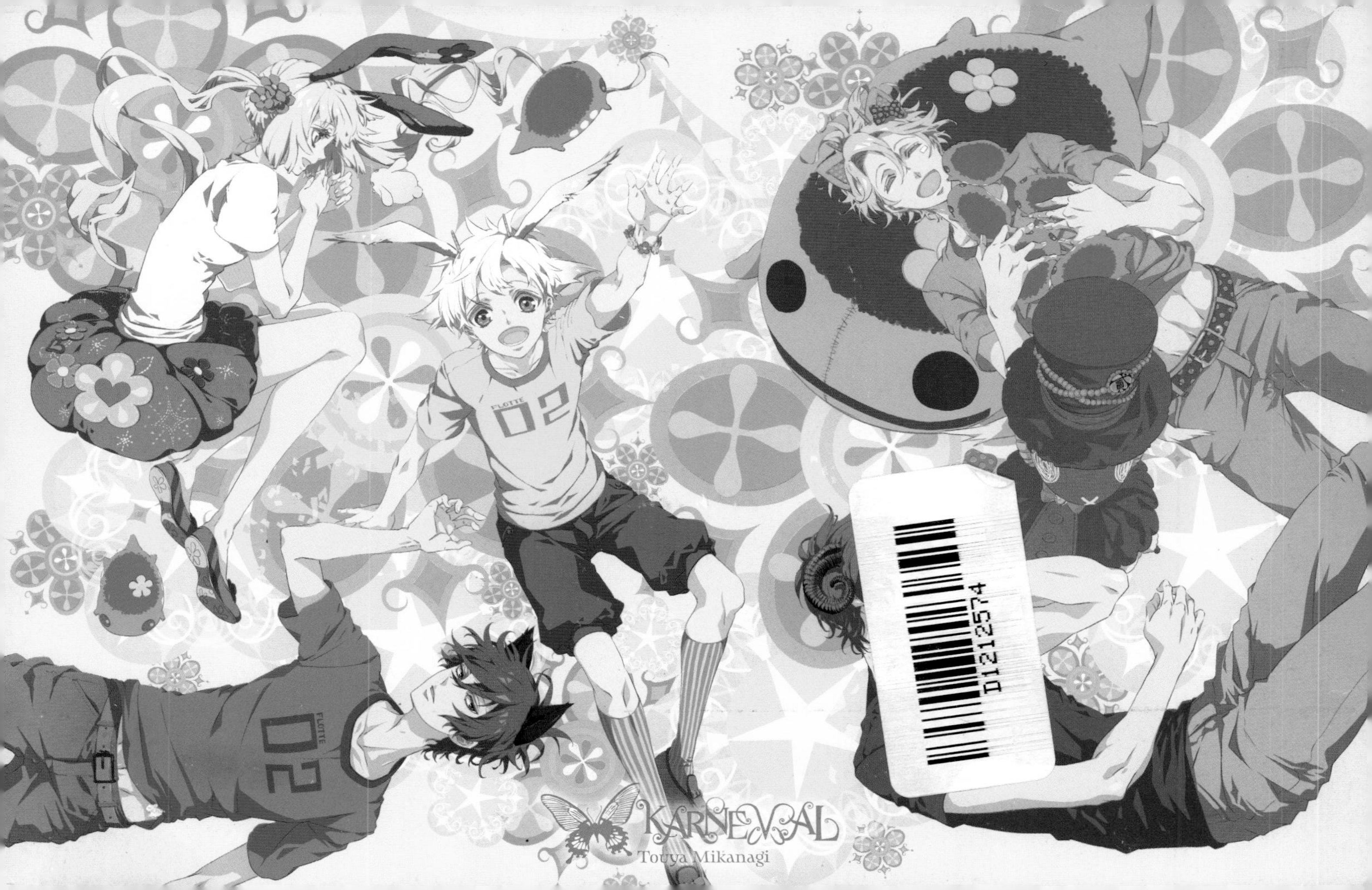
FLOTTE
02
FLOTTE
02
KARNEVAL
Touya Mikanagi

KARNEVAL

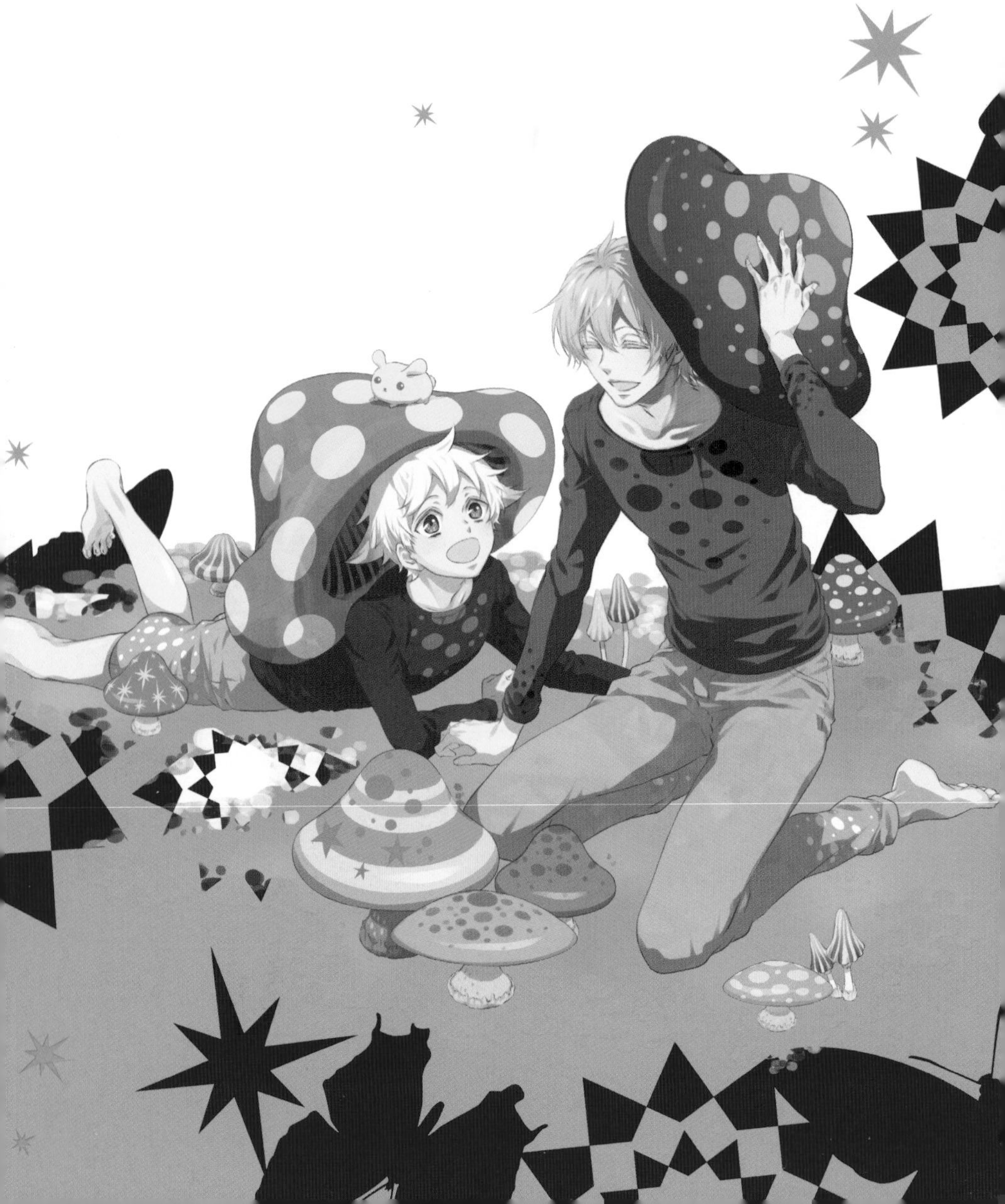

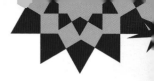

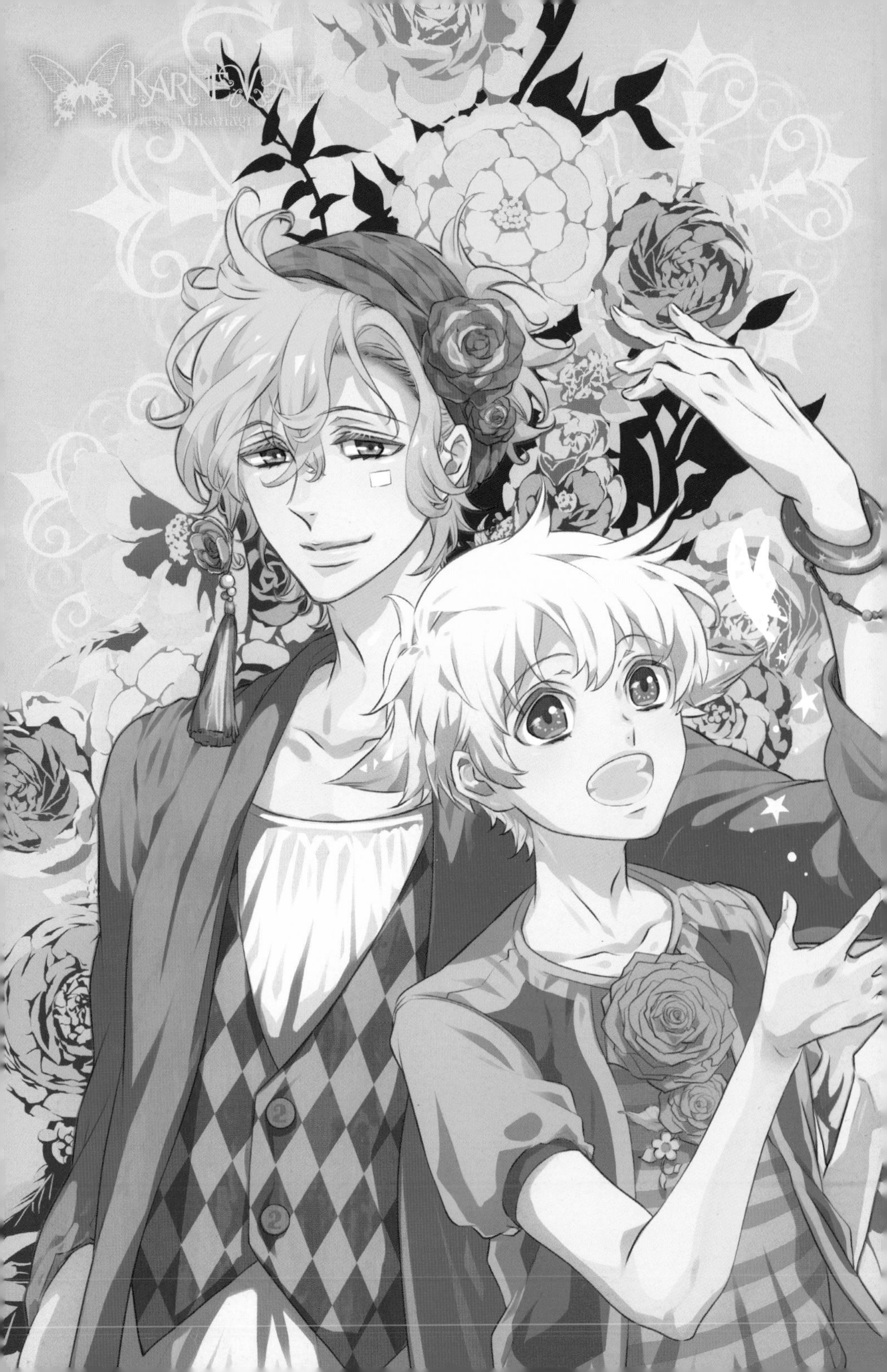
KARNEVAL

KARNEVAL

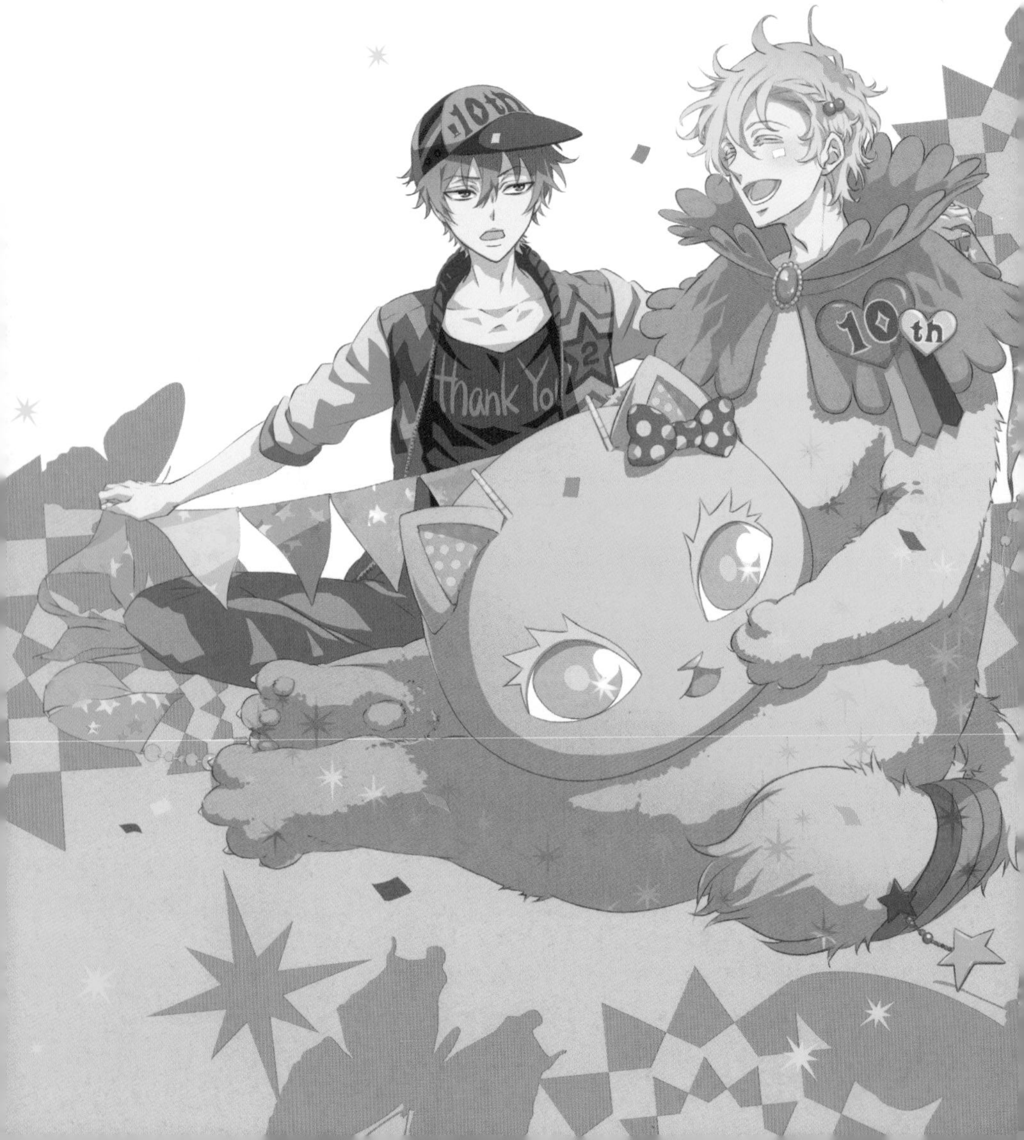
10th
thank Yo
2
10 th

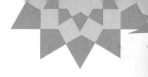

KARNEVAL 10

Touya Mikanagi

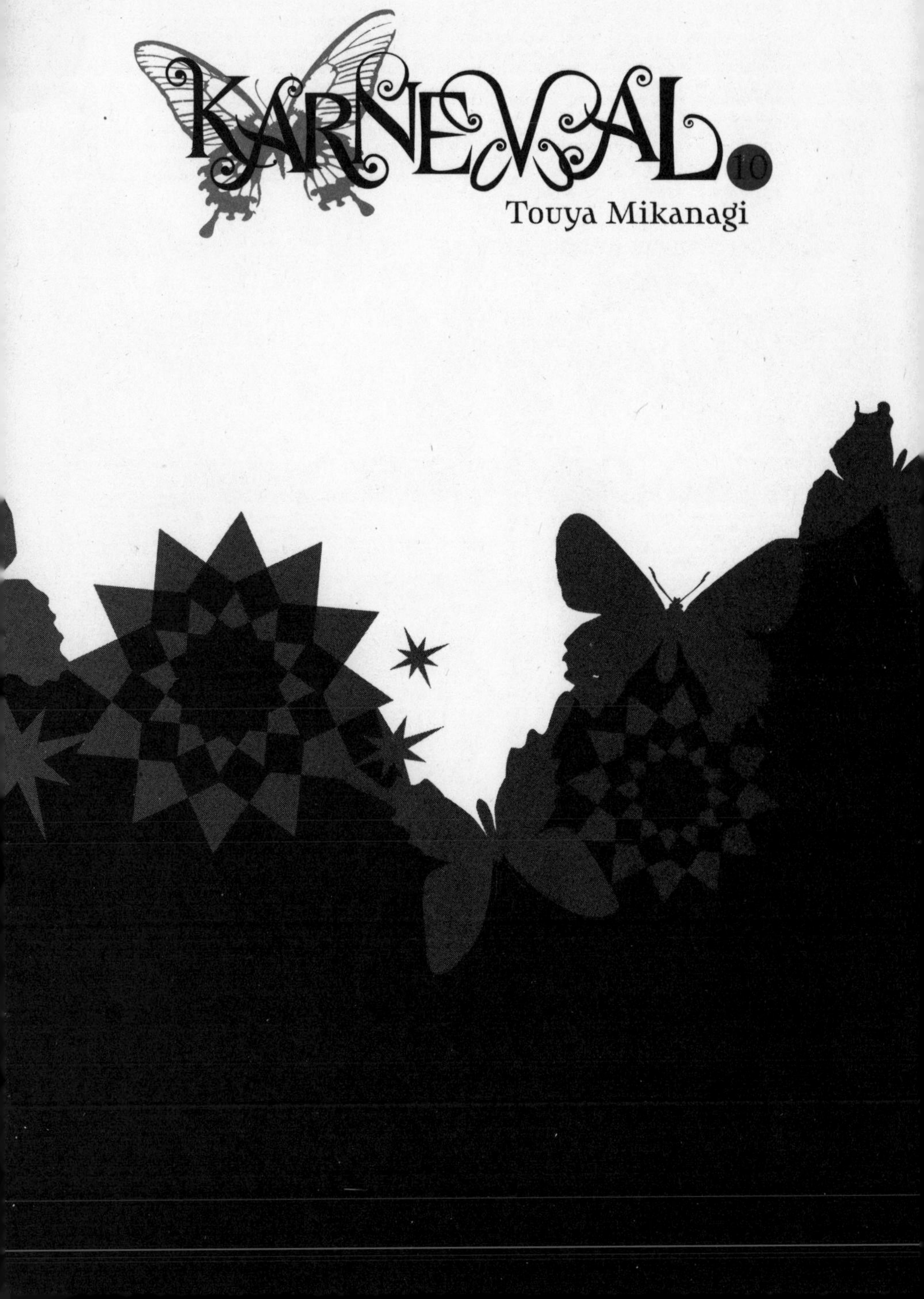

STORY

THE 2ND SHIP CREW MEMBERS, ALONG WITH DR. AKARI, GAREKI, AND JIKI, STOP BY A TOWN CALLED LEBERGANZE TO INVESTIGATE POSSIBLE CONNECTIONS TO VARUGA ACTIVITY. WHILE THERE, YOGI MEETS A YOUNG GIRL CALLED MANAI. IN THAT MOMENT, YOGI'S EMOTIONS COMPLETELY OVERFLOW, AND HE SUDDENLY KIDNAPS THE GIRL AND DISAPPEARS FROM SIGHT. AFTERWARD, THE CREW MEMBERS SEE A PHOTO OF THE GIRL AND DETERMINE SHE IS MIEUXMARIE, THE CROWN PRINCESS OF RIMHAKKA, A KINGDOM WHICH MANY YEARS AGO FELL UNDER VARUGA ATTACK AND WAS DESTROYED. TO MAKE MATTERS WORSE, IT APPEARS LIKELY THAT THE INCUNA CELLS' CONSCIOUSNESS WITHIN YOGI HAS SURFACED, SO HIRATO AND HIS TEAM RACE TO TRACK HIM DOWN. THANKS TO NAI'S POWERFUL ABILITY TO "HEAR" A PERSON'S CONSCIOUSNESS, THEY ARE SOON ABLE TO FIND YOGI AND MIEUXMARIE. YOGI IS IN A VERY CONFUSED STATE OF MIND AFTER REGAINING HIS MEMORIES, BUT HEARING NAI AND GAREKI CALLING OUT TO HIM, HE IS ABLE TO REGAIN HIS SENSES, ENABLING BOTH HIS AND MIEUXMARIE'S SAFE RECOVERY.

CHARACTERS OF KARNEVAL

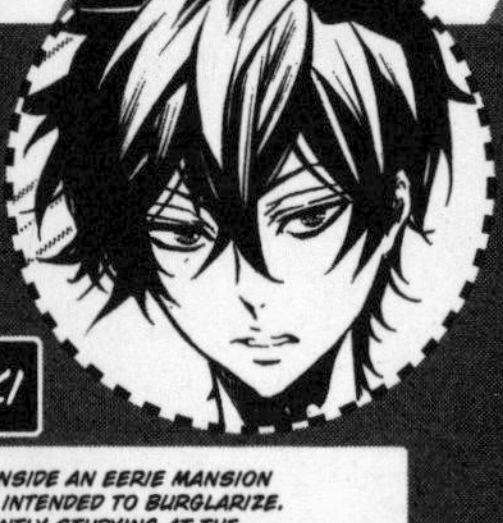

GAREKI

HE MET NAI INSIDE AN EERIE MANSION THAT HE HAD INTENDED TO BURGLARIZE. HE IS CURRENTLY STUDYING AT THE RESEARCH TOWER IN ORDER TO BECOME CIRCUS'S FIRST COMBAT MEDIC.

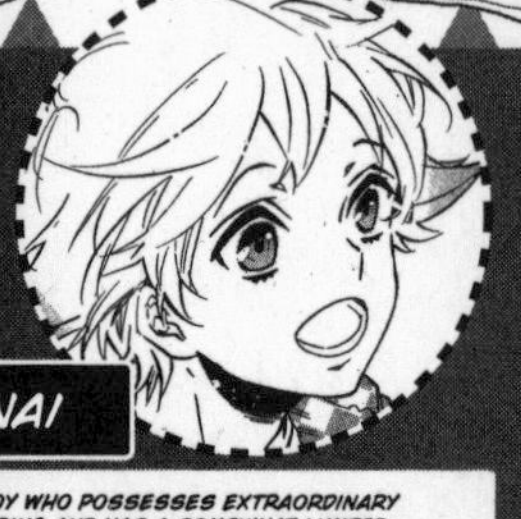

NAI

A BOY WHO POSSESSES EXTRAORDINARY HEARING AND HAS A SOMEWHAT LIMITED UNDERSTANDING OF HOW THE WORLD WORKS. HE IS CURRENTLY LIVING ABOARD CIRCUS'S 2ND SHIP ALONGSIDE KAROKU.

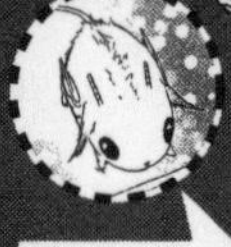

NIJI

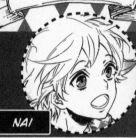

THE ANIMAL FROM WHICH NAI WAS CREATED. THEY EXIST ONLY IN THE RAINBOW FOREST, A HIGHLY UNUSUAL ECOSYSTEM THAT ALLOWED THE NIJI TO EVOLVE AS THEY DID.

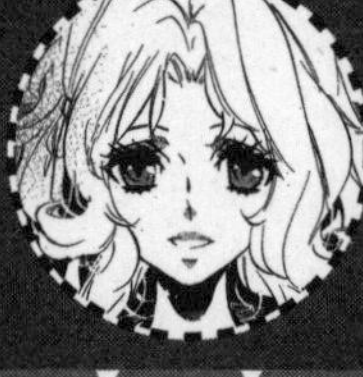

MANAI

THE FORMER PRINCESS OF RIMHAKKA, HER REAL NAME IS MIEUXMARIE. SHE IS YOGI'S YOUNGER SISTER. SHE IS A VERY KIND, RESILIENT GIRL.

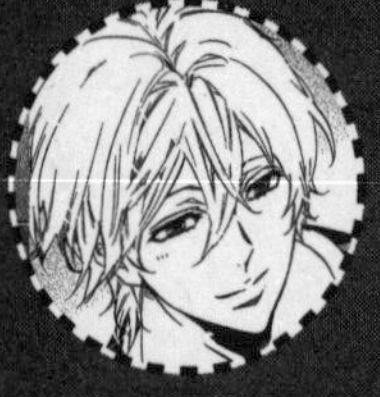

KAROKU

THE PERSON BELIEVED TO HAVE CREATED NAI. HE HAS RECOVERED HIS MEMORIES AND IS NOW LIVING ABOARD CIRCUS'S 2ND SHIP.

NATIONAL SUPREME DEFENSE FORCE "CIRCUS" 2ND SHIP

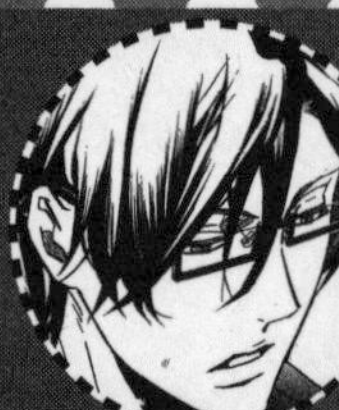

HIRATO

CAPTAIN OF CIRCUS'S 2ND SHIP. NAI, WHO BROUGHT HIM A BRACELET BELONGING TO CIRCUS, AND GAREKI ARE CURRENTLY UNDER HIS PROTECTION. HE AND TSUKITATCHI, CAPTAIN OF CIRCUS'S 1ST SHIP, ARE FORMER CLASSMATES.

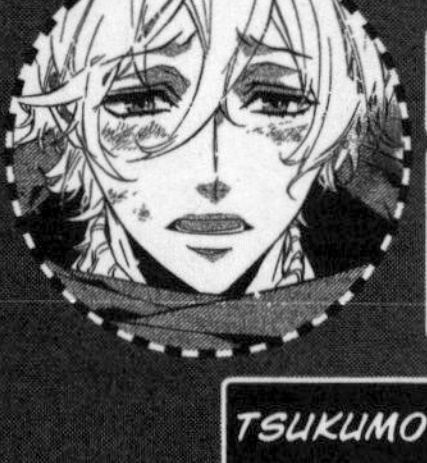

YOGI

CIRCUS'S 2ND SHIP COMBAT SPECIALIST. HE HAS A CHEERFUL, FRIENDLY PERSONALITY. HE WAS BORN THE CROWN PRINCE OF RIMHAKKA, A KINGDOM THAT WAS DESTROYED IN A VARUGA ATTACK.

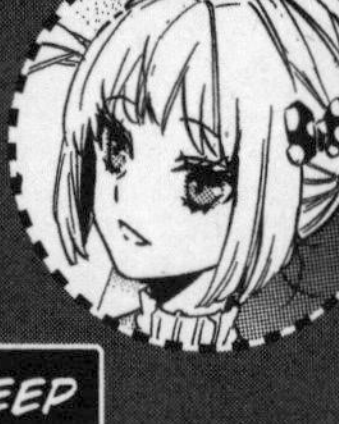

TSUKUMO

CIRCUS'S 2ND SHIP COMBAT SPECIALIST. A BEAUTIFUL GIRL WITH A COOL, SERIOUS PERSONALITY. RECENTLY, SHE SEEMS TO HAVE TAKEN UP SEWING STUFFED TOYS AS A PASTIME. SHE HATES BUGS.

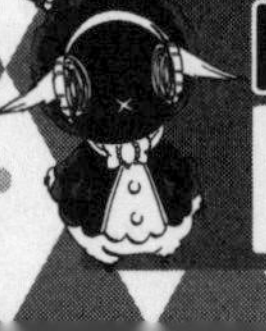

SHEEP

A CIRCUS DEFENSE SYSTEM. DESPITE THEIR CUTE APPEARANCE, THE SHEEP HAVE SOME VERY POWERFUL CAPABILITIES.

Q: WHAT IS CIRCUS?

A: THE EQUIVALENT OF THE REAL-WORLD POLICE. THEY CONDUCT THEIR LARGE-SCALE "OPERATIONS" UTILIZING COORDINATED, POWERFUL ATTACKS AND WITHOUT FOREWARNING TO ENSURE THEIR TARGETS WILL NOT ESCAPE ARREST!! AFTER SUCH AN OPERATION, CIRCUS PERFORMS A "SHOW" FOR THE PEOPLE OF THE CITY AS AN APOLOGY FOR THE FEAR AND INCONVENIENCE THEIR WORK MAY HAVE CAUSED. IN SHORT, "CIRCUS" IS A CHEERFUL(?) AGENCY THAT CARRIES OUT THEIR MISSION DAY AND NIGHT TO APPREHEND EVIL AND PROTECT THE PEACE OF THE LAND.

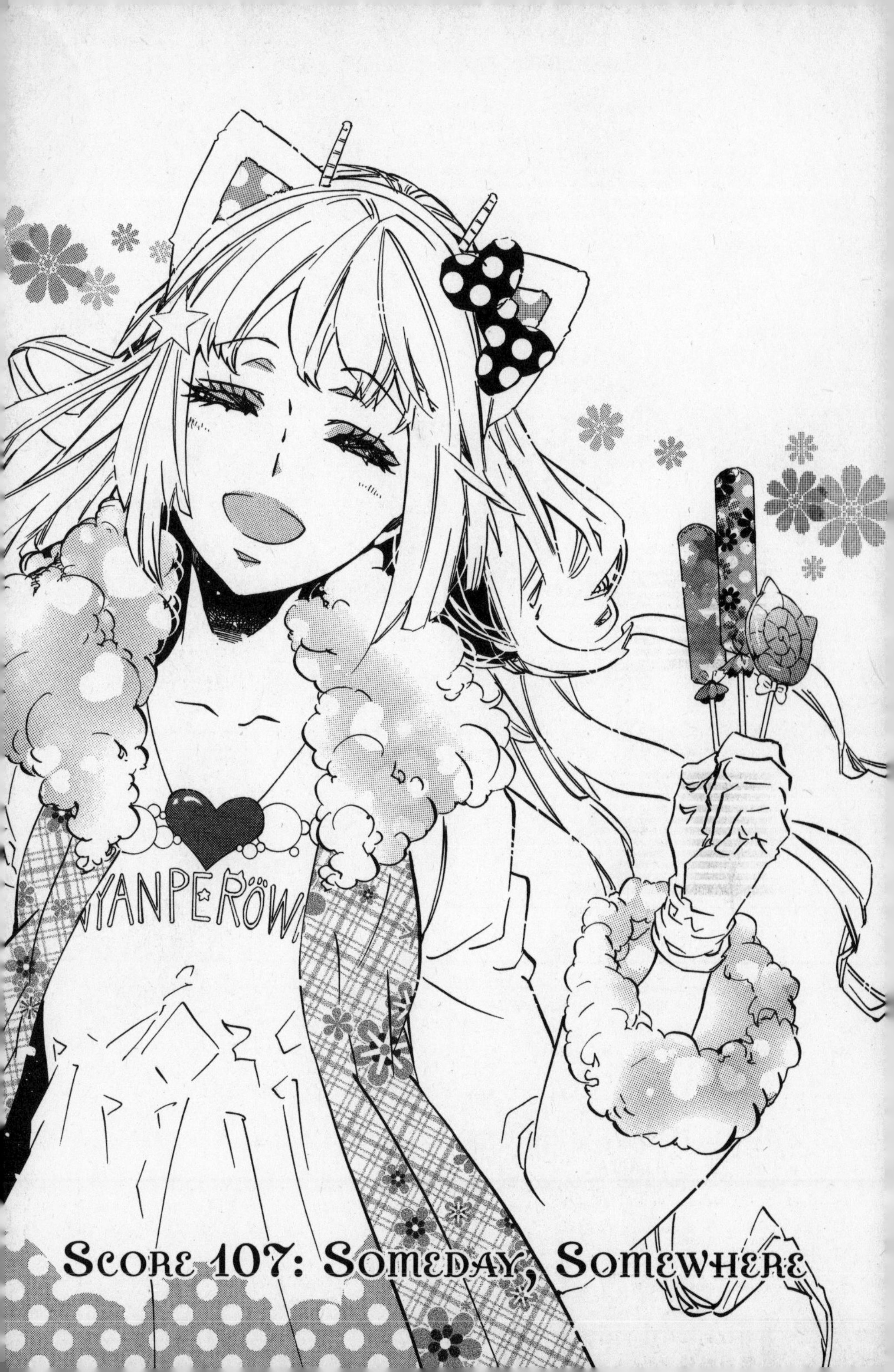
NYANPERÖW

Score 107: Someday, Somewhere

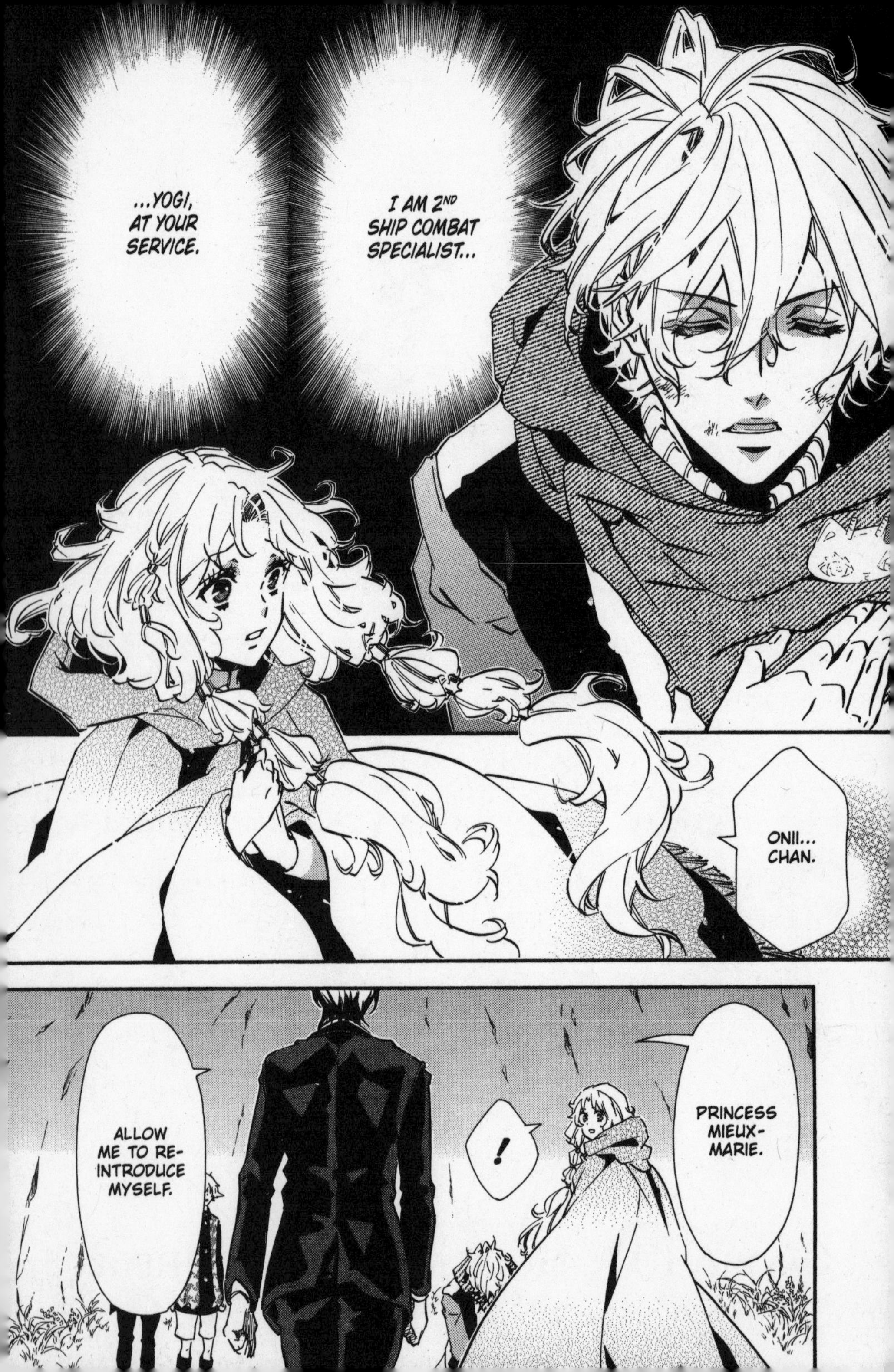
I AM 2ND SHIP COMBAT SPECIALIST...
...YOGI, AT YOUR SERVICE.
ONII... CHAN.
PRINCESS MIEUX-MARIE.
!
ALLOW ME TO RE-INTRODUCE MYSELF.

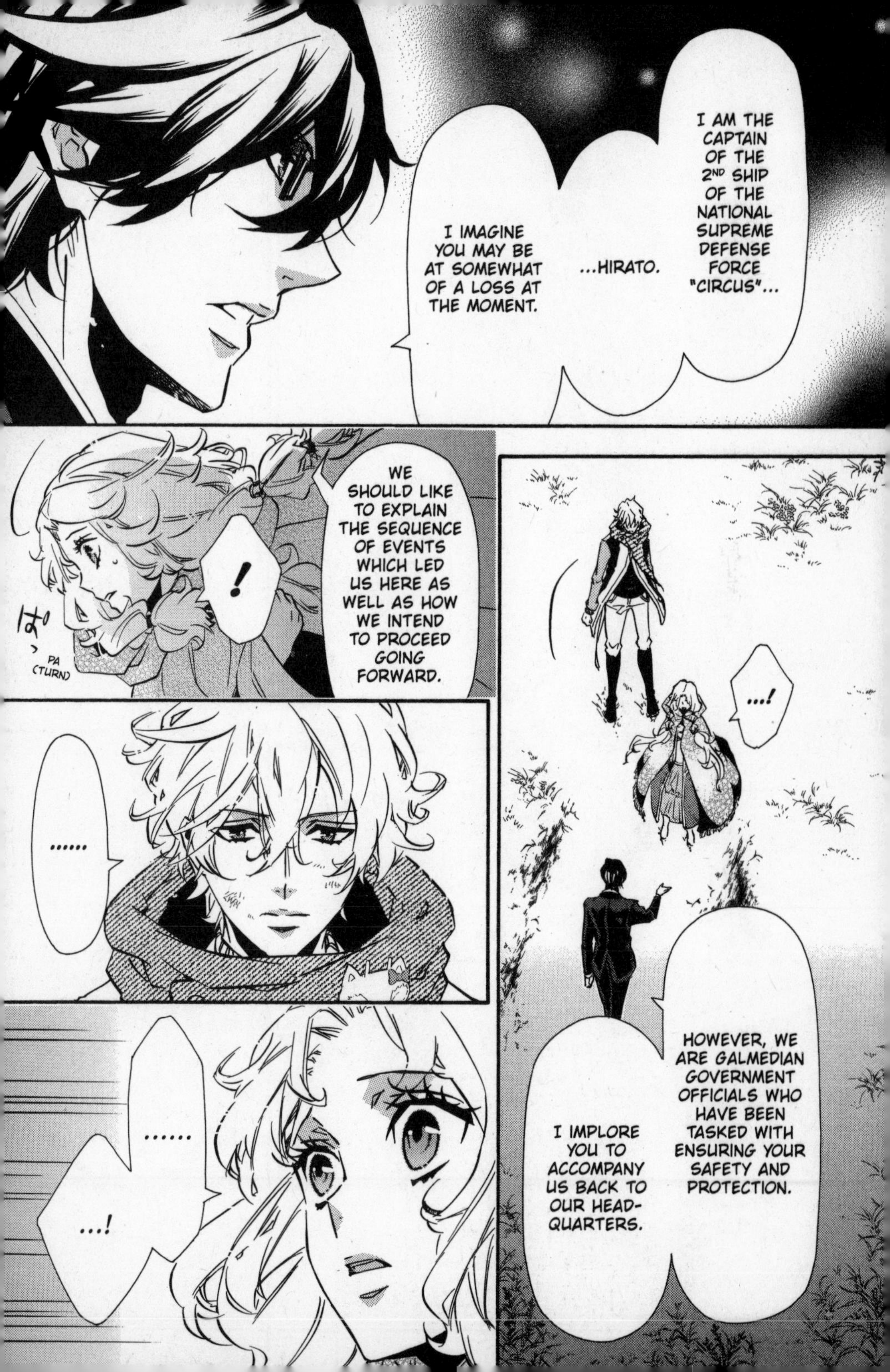
I AM THE CAPTAIN OF THE 2ND SHIP OF THE NATIONAL SUPREME DEFENSE FORCE "CIRCUS"...
...HIRATO.
I IMAGINE YOU MAY BE AT SOMEWHAT OF A LOSS AT THE MOMENT.
...!
HOWEVER, WE ARE GALMEDIAN GOVERNMENT OFFICIALS WHO HAVE BEEN TASKED WITH ENSURING YOUR SAFETY AND PROTECTION.
I IMPLORE YOU TO ACCOMPANY US BACK TO OUR HEAD-QUARTERS.
WE SHOULD LIKE TO EXPLAIN THE SEQUENCE OF EVENTS WHICH LED US HERE AS WELL AS HOW WE INTEND TO PROCEED GOING FORWARD.
!
ぱっ
PA (TURN)
......
......
...!

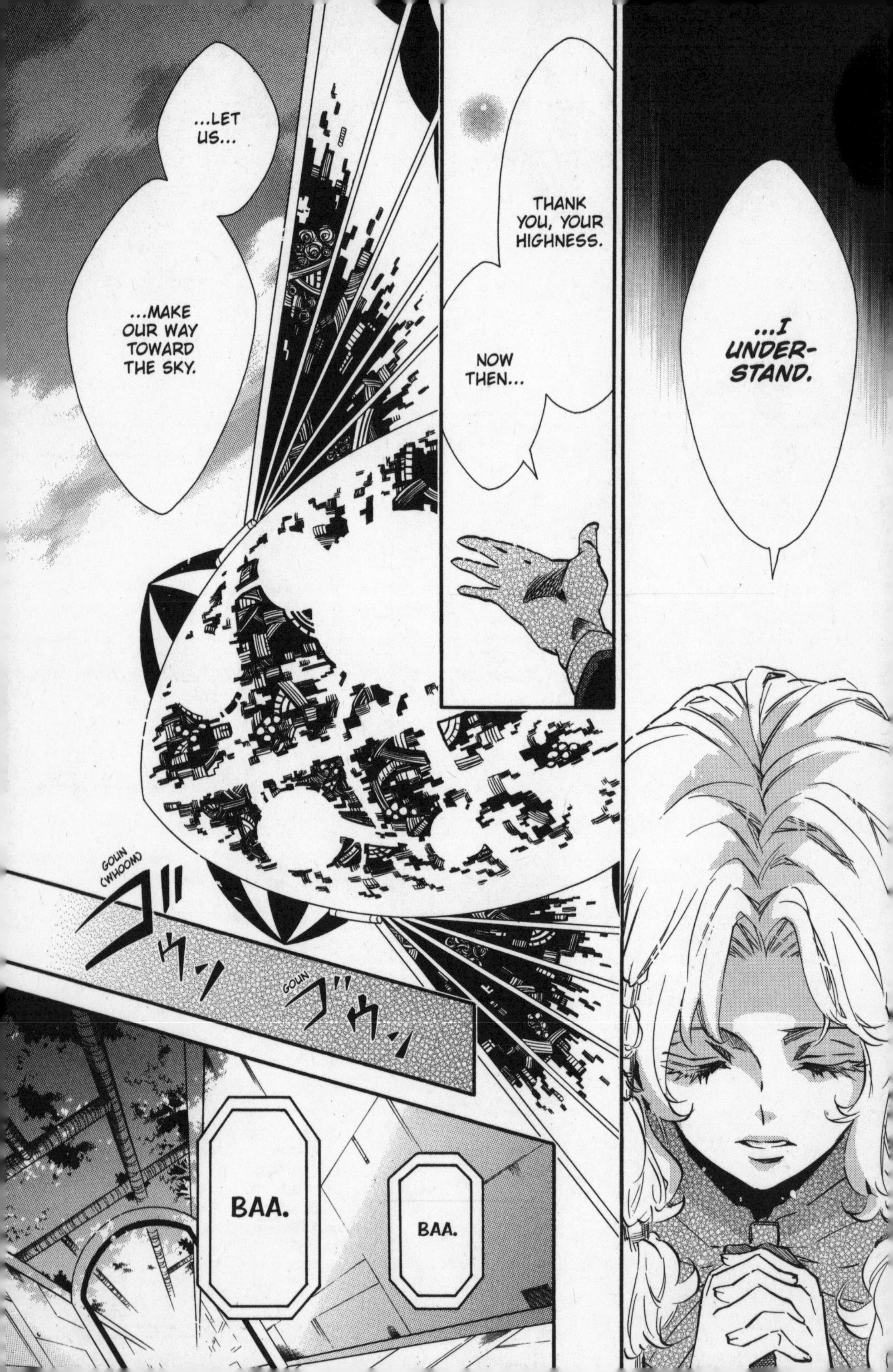
...I UNDERSTAND.
THANK YOU, YOUR HIGHNESS.
NOW THEN...
...LET US...
...MAKE OUR WAY TOWARD THE SKY.
GOUN (WHOOM)
GOUN
BAA.
BAA.

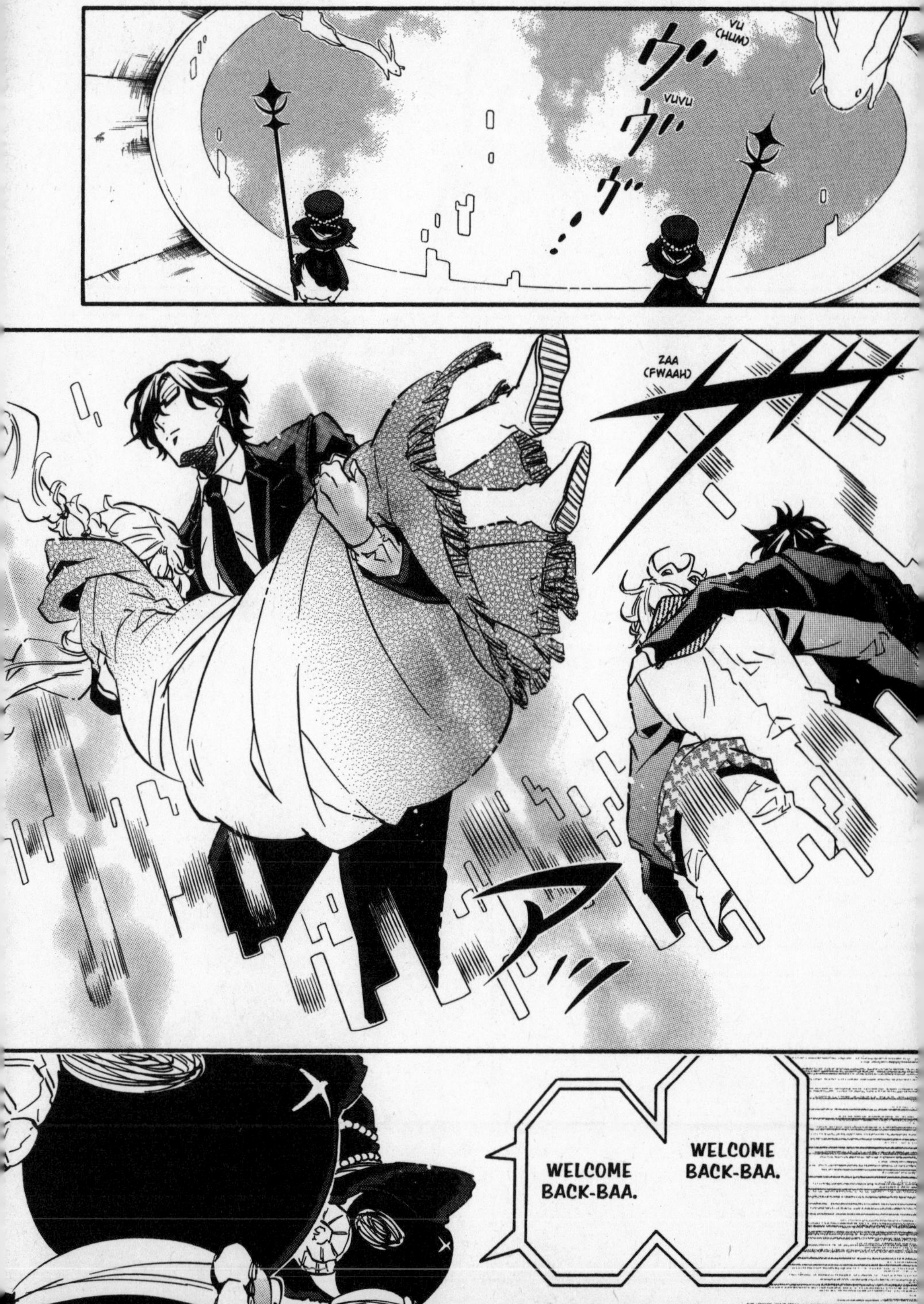
VU (HUM)
VUVU
ZAA (FWAAH)
WELCOME BACK-BAA.
WELCOME BACK-BAA.

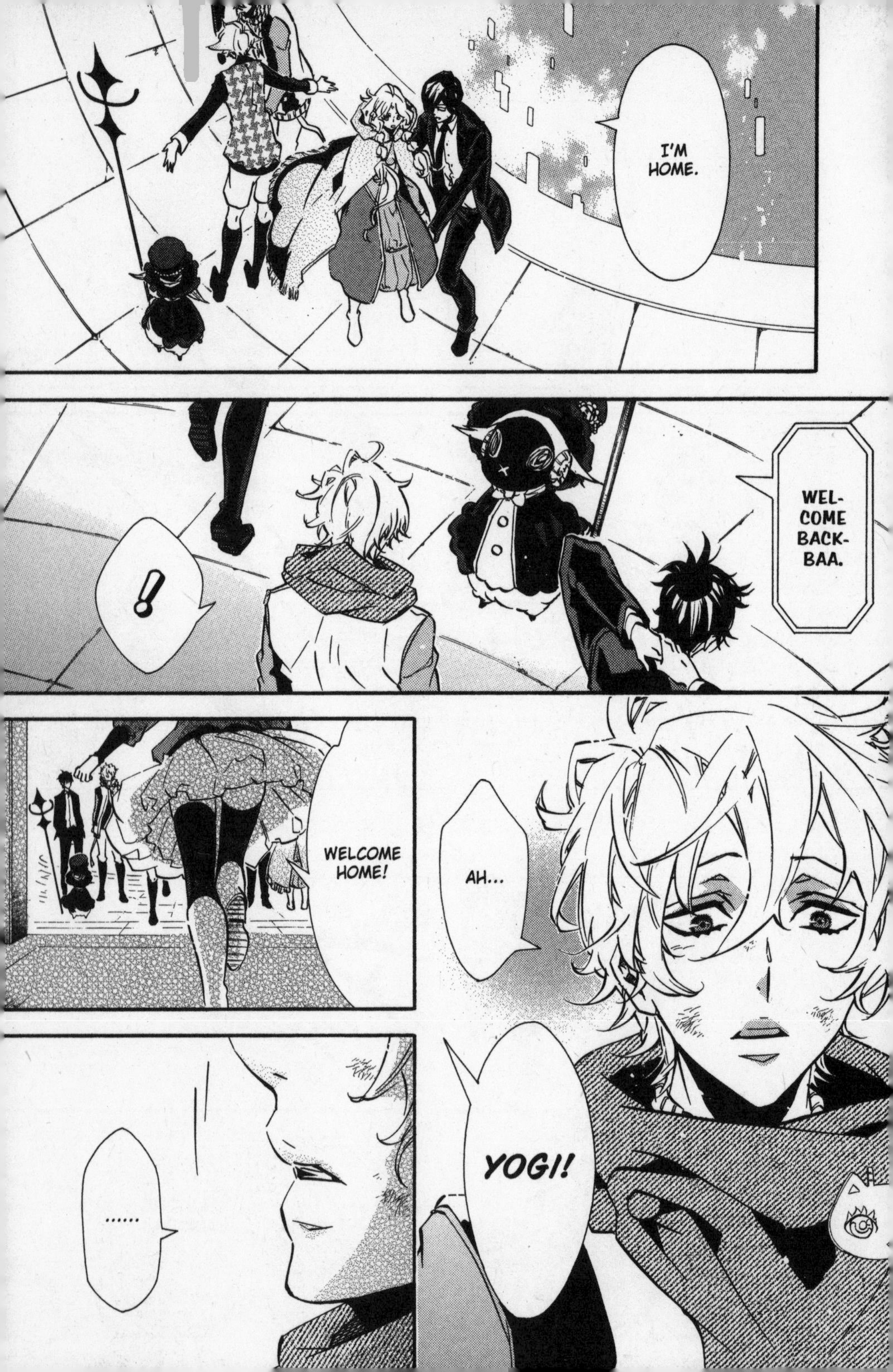
I'M HOME.
WEL-COME BACK-BAA.
!
AH...
YOGI!
WELCOME HOME!
......

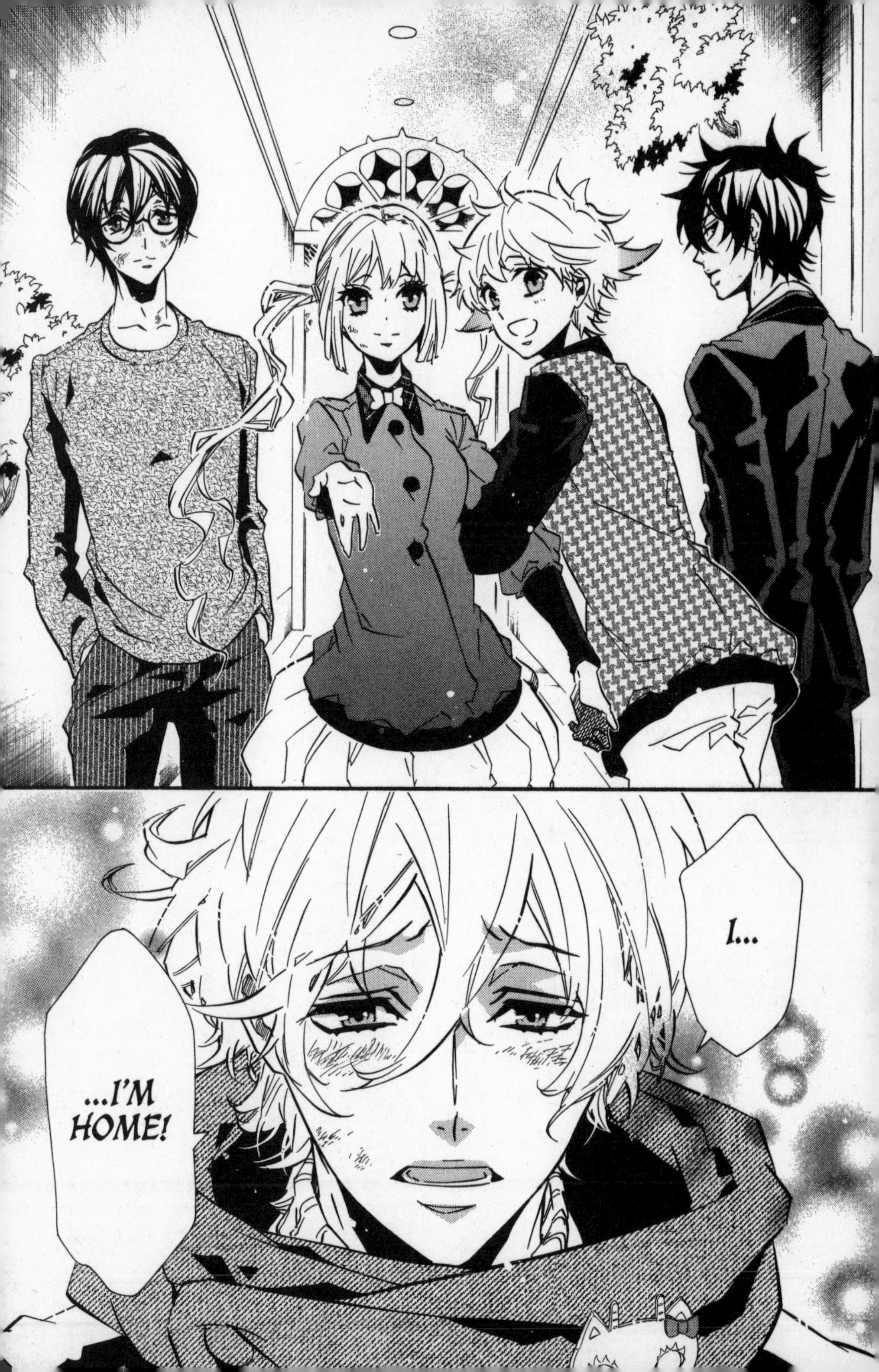
I...
...I'M HOME!

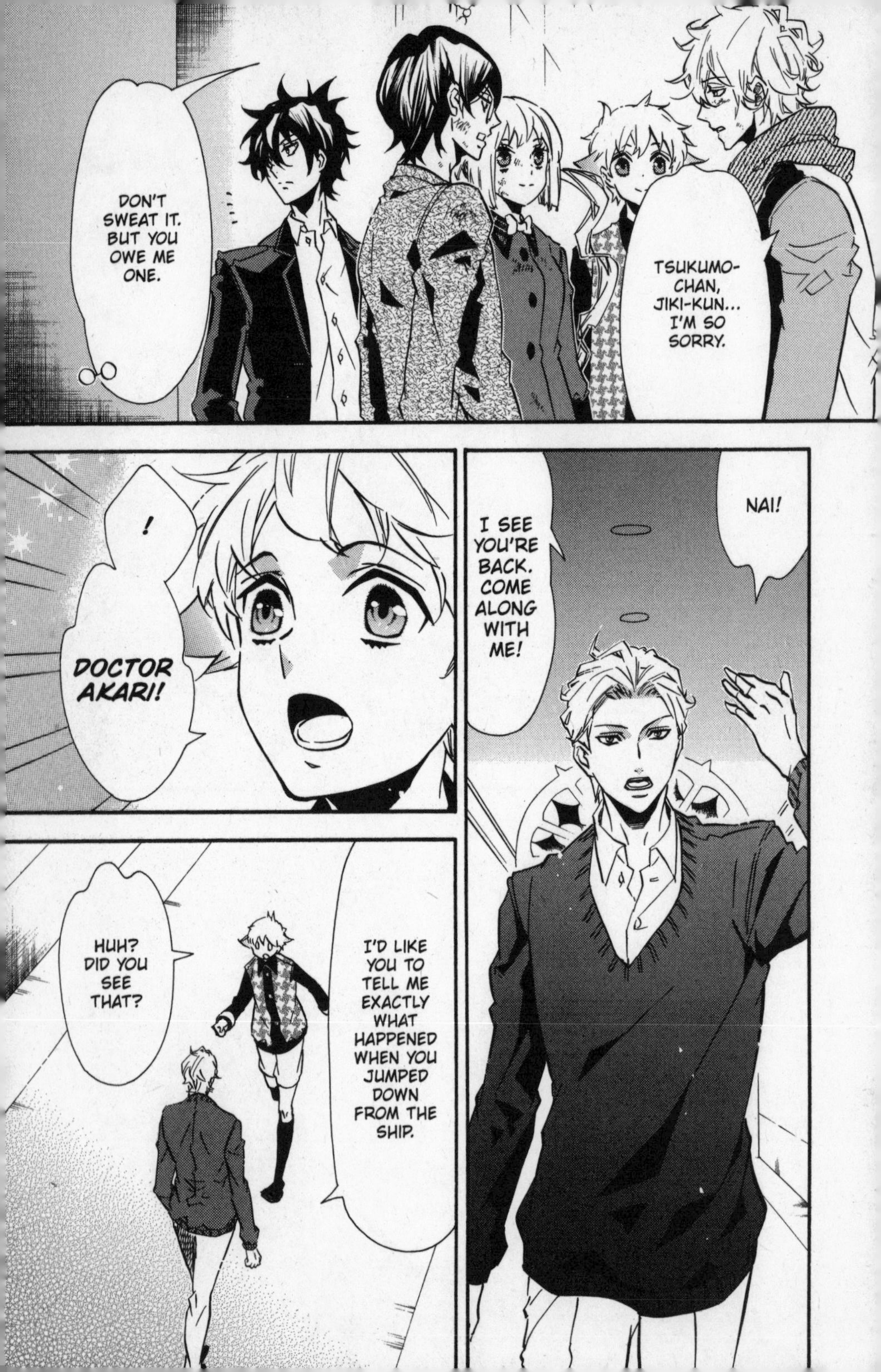
TSUKUMO-CHAN, JIKI-KUN... I'M SO SORRY.
DON'T SWEAT IT. BUT YOU OWE ME ONE.
NAI!
I SEE YOU'RE BACK. COME ALONG WITH ME!
!
DOCTOR AKARI!
I'D LIKE YOU TO TELL ME EXACTLY WHAT HAPPENED WHEN YOU JUMPED DOWN FROM THE SHIP.
HUH? DID YOU SEE THAT?

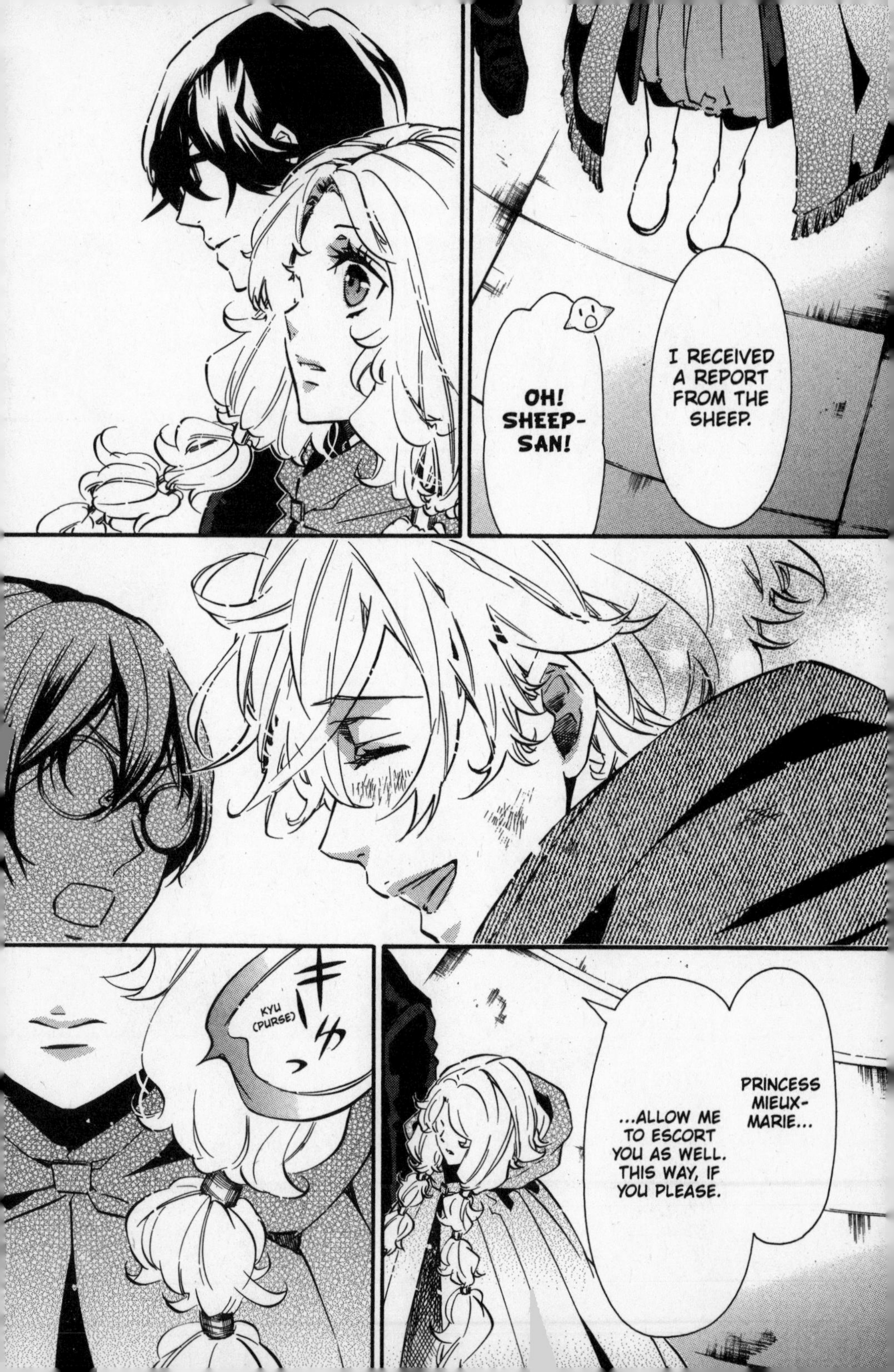
I RECEIVED A REPORT FROM THE SHEEP.
OH! SHEEP-SAN!
PRINCESS MIEUX-MARIE...
...ALLOW ME TO ESCORT YOU AS WELL. THIS WAY, IF YOU PLEASE.
KYU (PURSE)
キュッ

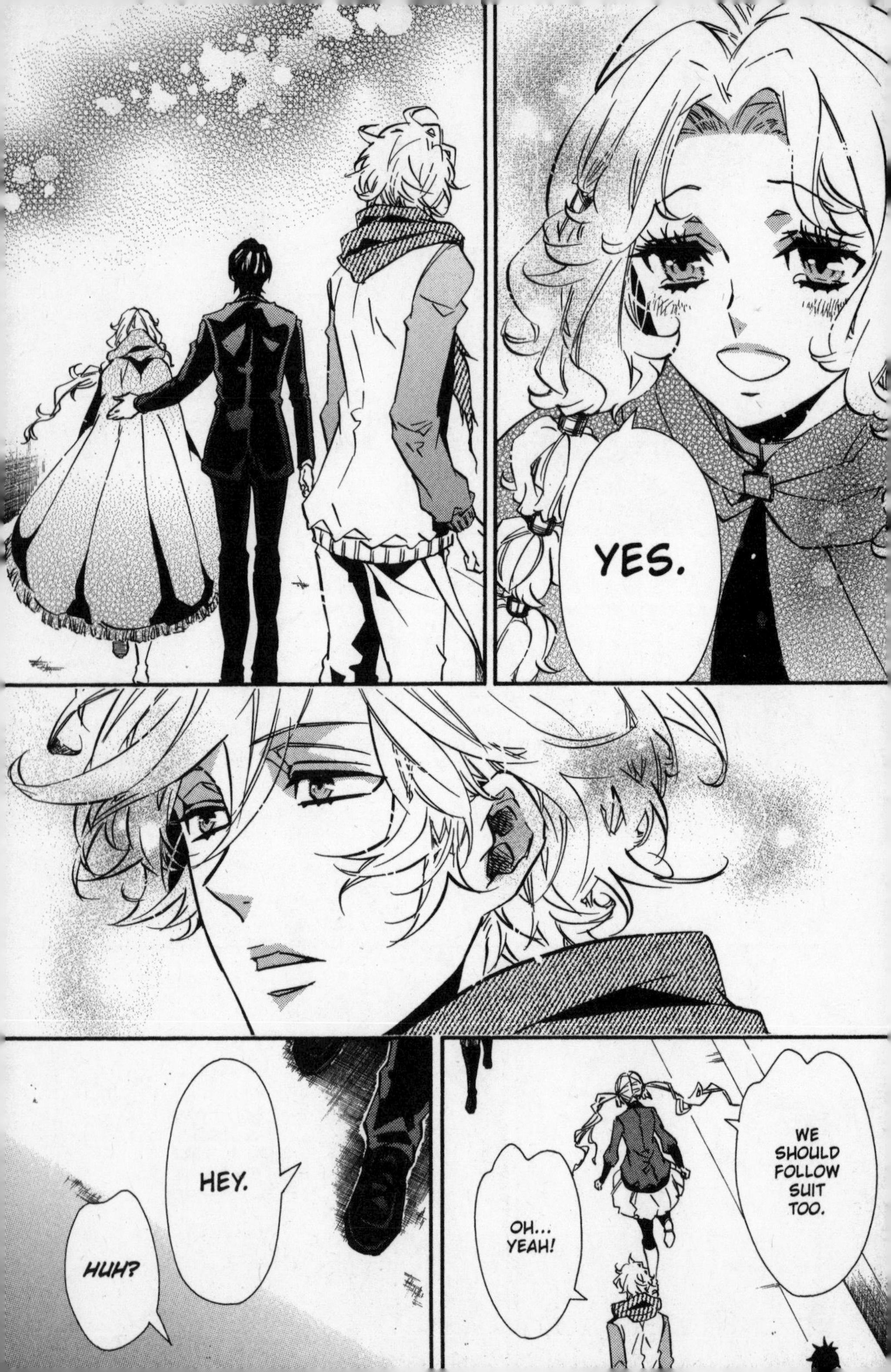
YES.
WE SHOULD FOLLOW SUIT TOO.
OH... YEAH!
HEY.
HUH?

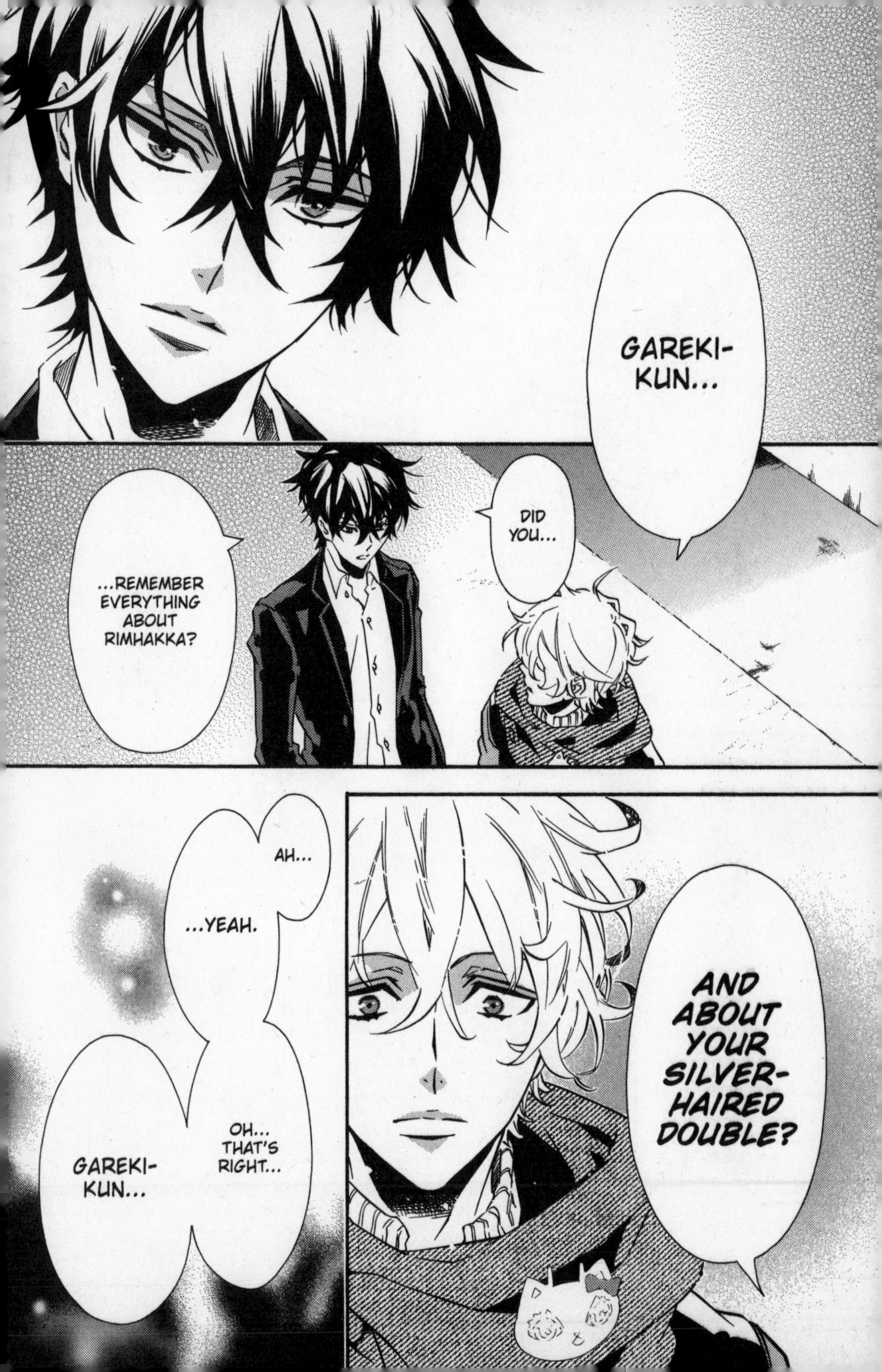
GAREKI-KUN...
DID YOU...
...REMEMBER EVERYTHING ABOUT RIMHAKKA?
AND ABOUT YOUR SILVER-HAIRED DOUBLE?
AH...
...YEAH.
OH... THAT'S RIGHT...
GAREKI-KUN...

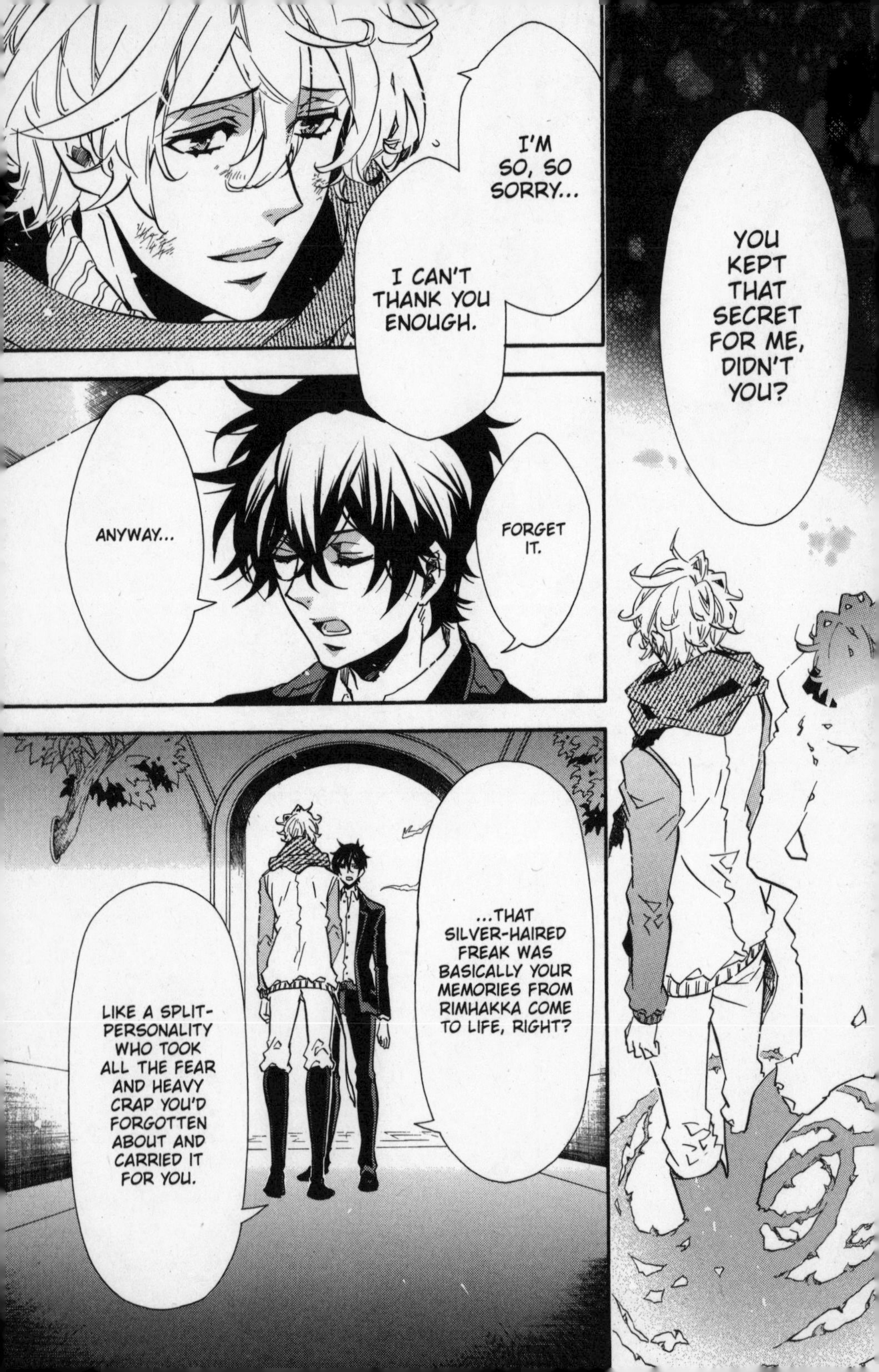
YOU KEPT THAT SECRET FOR ME, DIDN'T YOU?
I'M SO, SO SORRY...
I CAN'T THANK YOU ENOUGH.
FORGET IT.
ANYWAY...
...THAT SILVER-HAIRED FREAK WAS BASICALLY YOUR MEMORIES FROM RIMHAKKA COME TO LIFE, RIGHT?
LIKE A SPLIT-PERSONALITY WHO TOOK ALL THE FEAR AND HEAVY CRAP YOU'D FORGOTTEN ABOUT AND CARRIED IT FOR YOU.

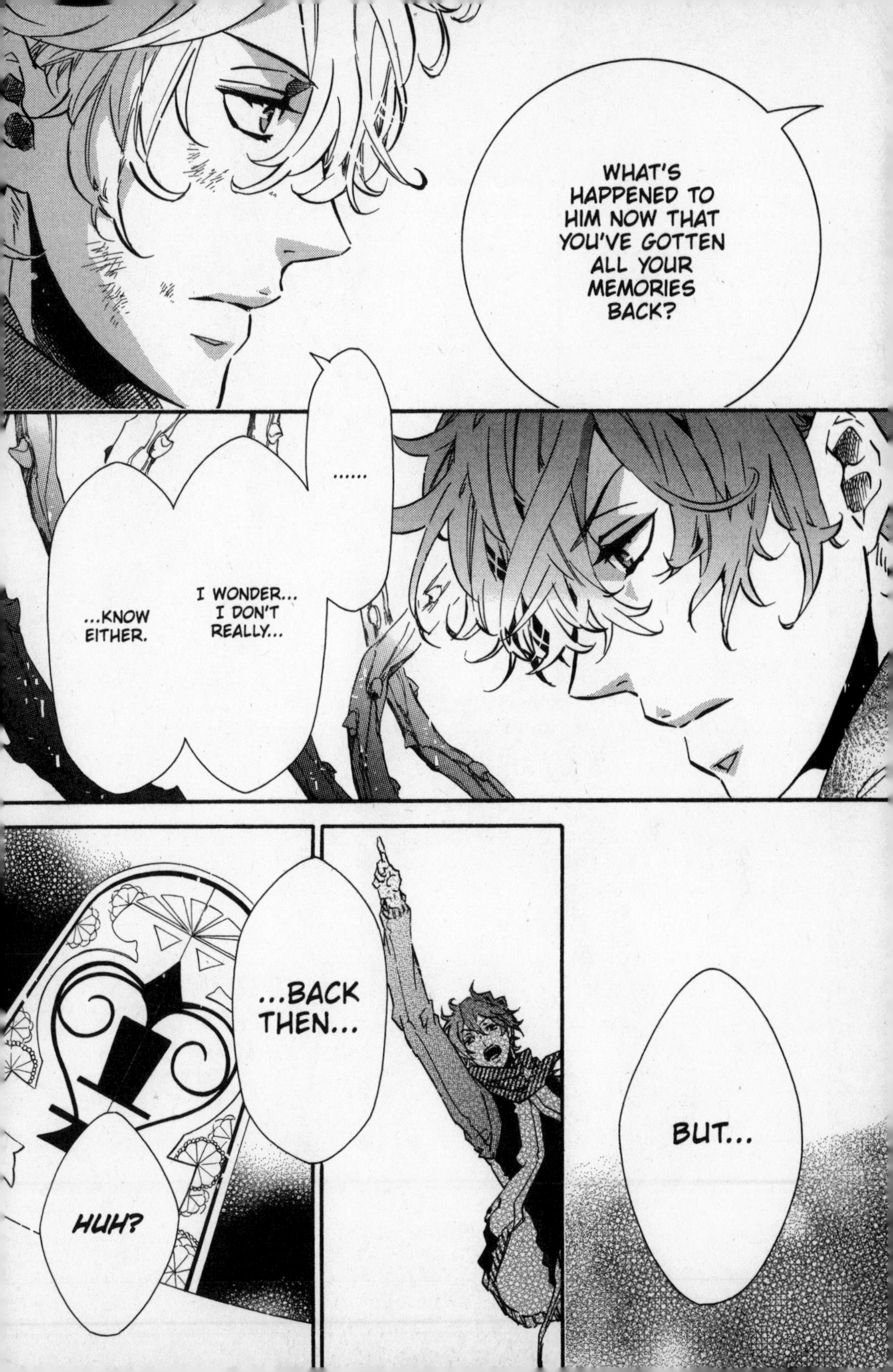
WHAT'S HAPPENED TO HIM NOW THAT YOU'VE GOTTEN ALL YOUR MEMORIES BACK?
......
I WONDER... I DON'T REALLY...
...KNOW EITHER.
BUT...
...BACK THEN...
HUH?

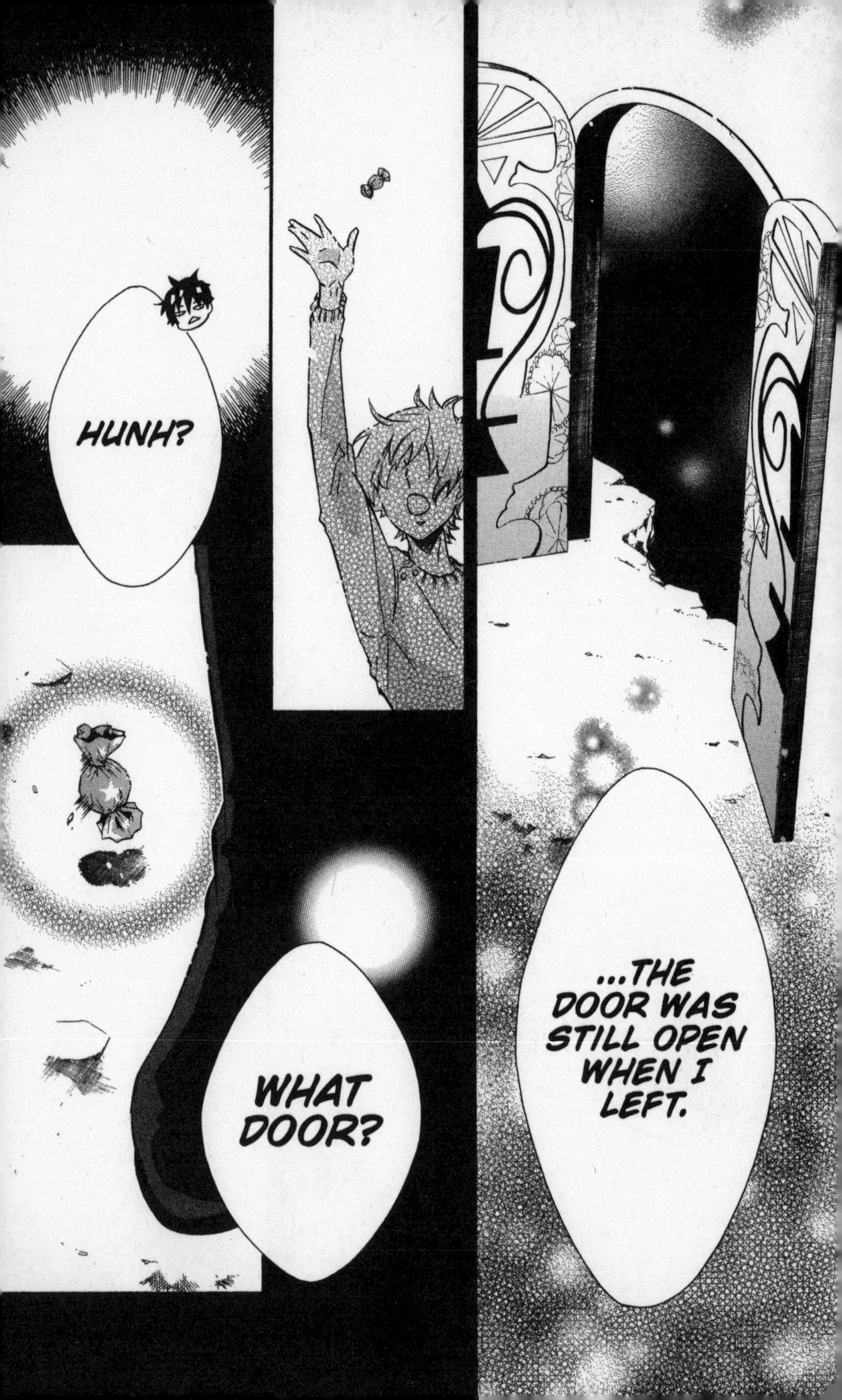
...THE DOOR WAS STILL OPEN WHEN I LEFT.
HUNH?
WHAT DOOR?

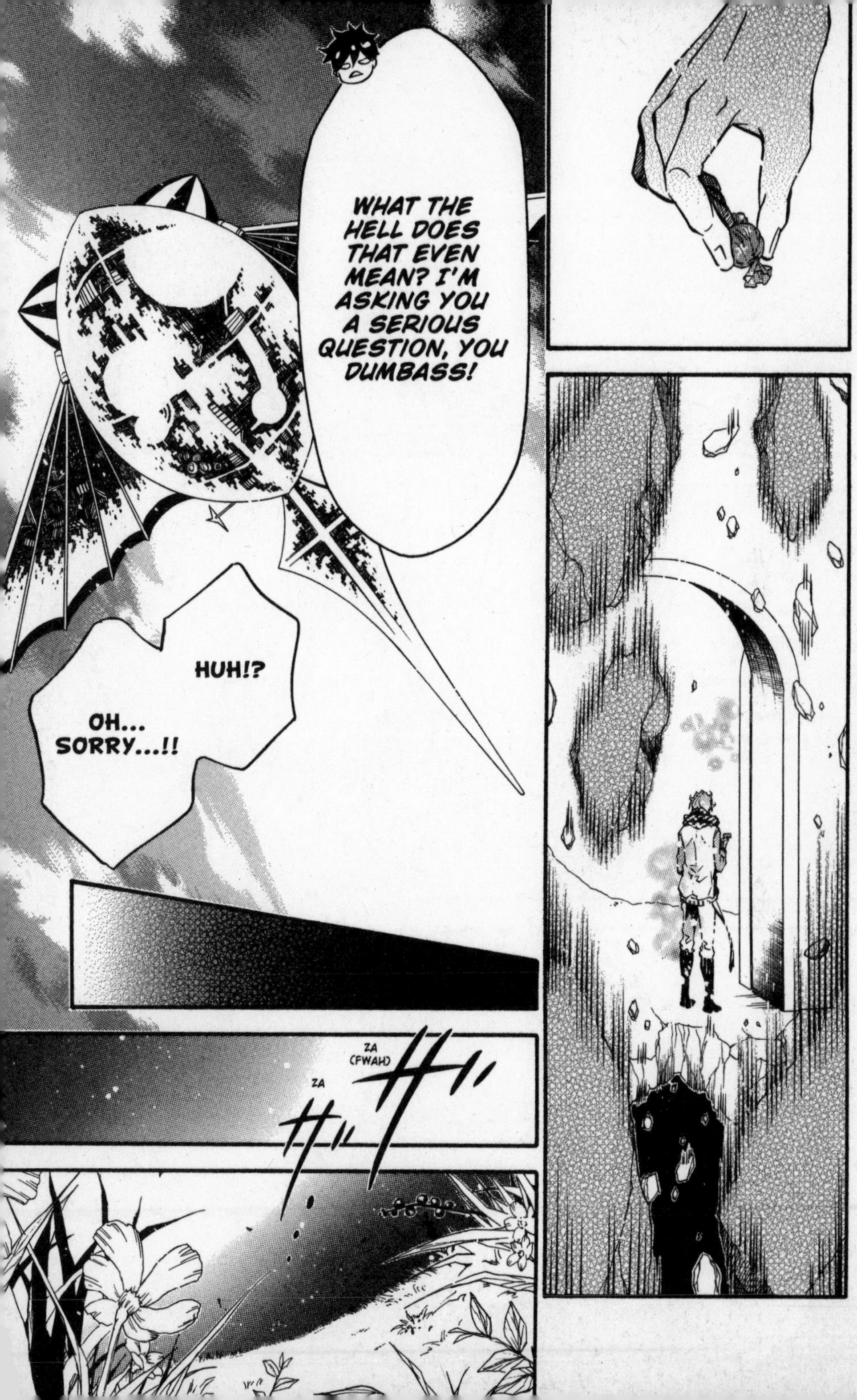
WHAT THE HELL DOES THAT EVEN MEAN? I'M ASKING YOU A SERIOUS QUESTION, YOU DUMBASS!
HUH!?
OH... SORRY...!!
ZA (FWAH)
ZA

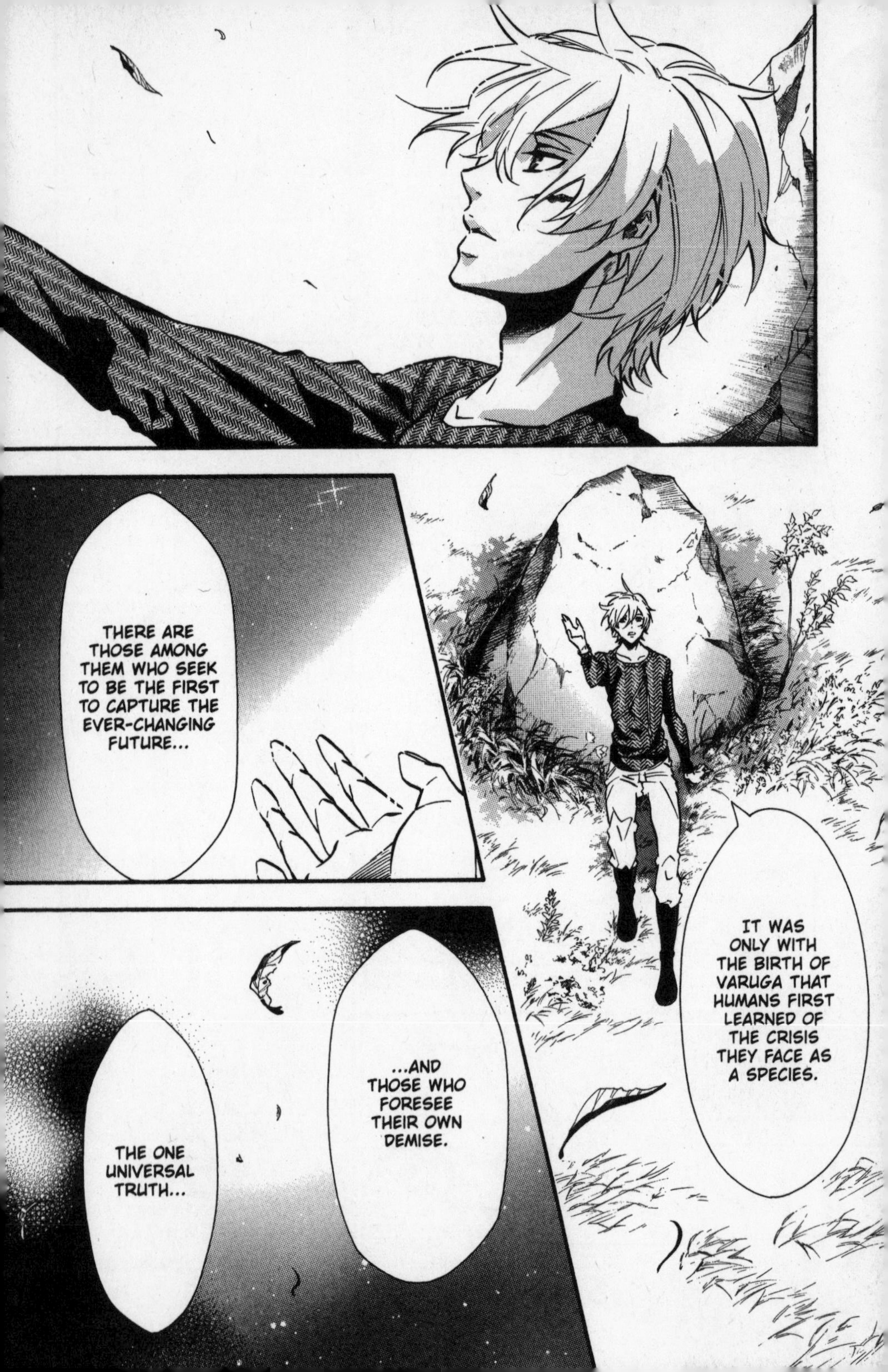
IT WAS ONLY WITH THE BIRTH OF VARUGA THAT HUMANS FIRST LEARNED OF THE CRISIS THEY FACE AS A SPECIES.
THERE ARE THOSE AMONG THEM WHO SEEK TO BE THE FIRST TO CAPTURE THE EVER-CHANGING FUTURE...
...AND THOSE WHO FORESEE THEIR OWN DEMISE.
THE ONE UNIVERSAL TRUTH...

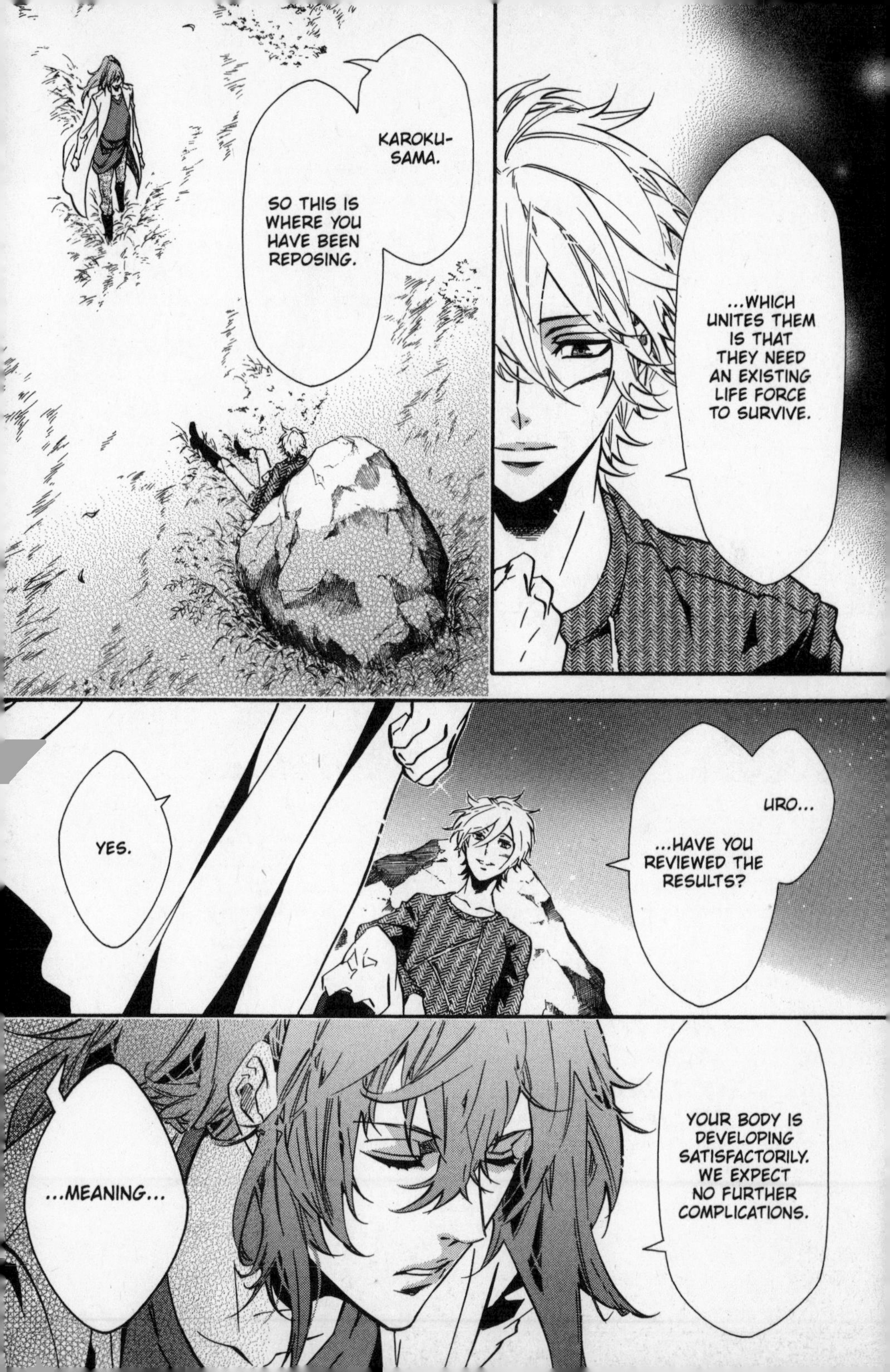
...WHICH UNITES THEM IS THAT THEY NEED AN EXISTING LIFE FORCE TO SURVIVE.
KAROKU-SAMA.
SO THIS IS WHERE YOU HAVE BEEN REPOSING.
URO...
...HAVE YOU REVIEWED THE RESULTS?
YES.
YOUR BODY IS DEVELOPING SATISFACTORILY. WE EXPECT NO FURTHER COMPLICATIONS.
...MEANING...

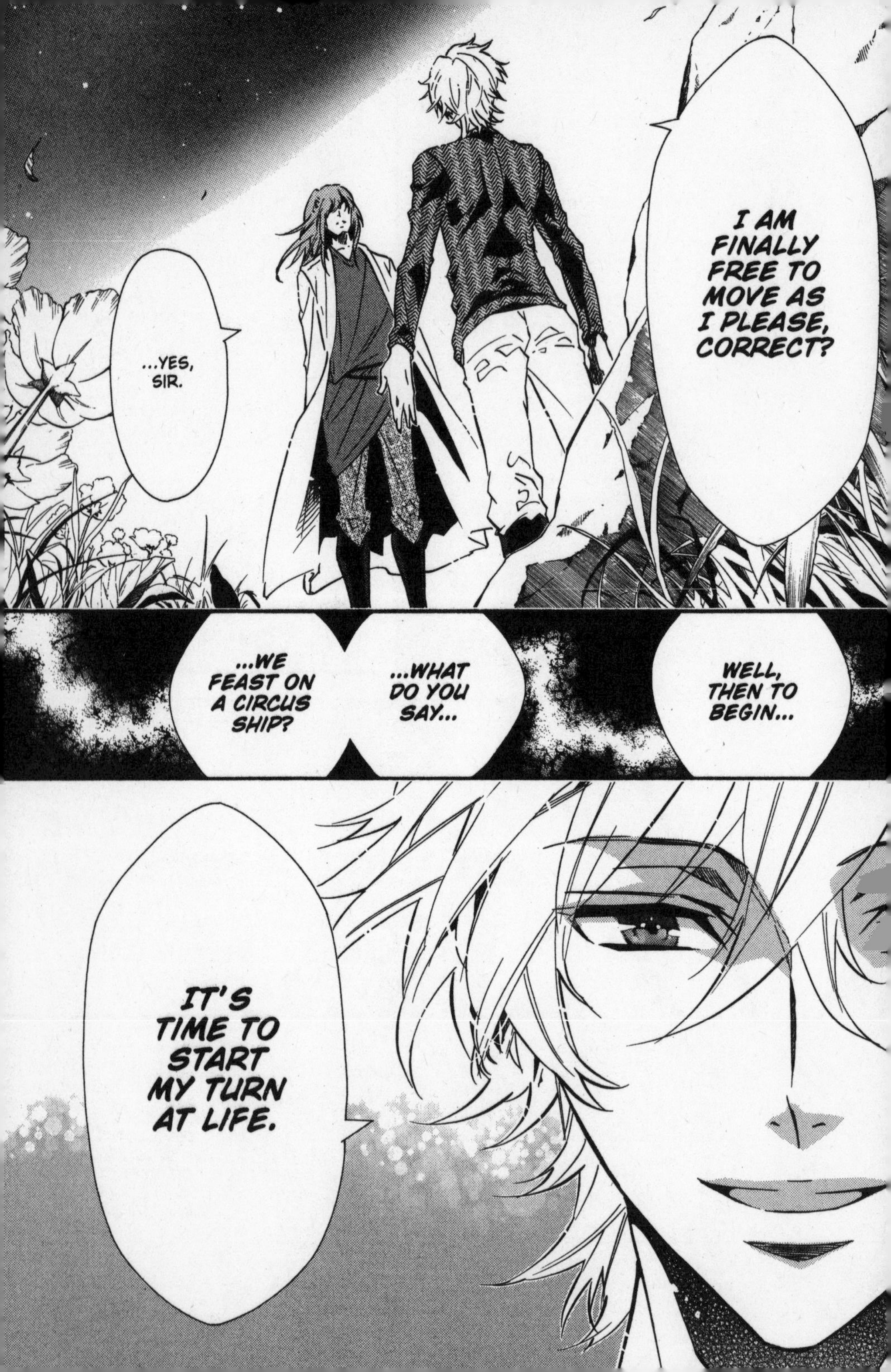
I AM FINALLY FREE TO MOVE AS I PLEASE, CORRECT?
...YES, SIR.
WELL, THEN TO BEGIN...
...WHAT DO YOU SAY...
...WE FEAST ON A CIRCUS SHIP?
IT'S TIME TO START MY TURN AT LIFE.

KARNEVAL

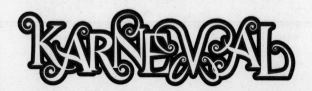

KARNEVAL

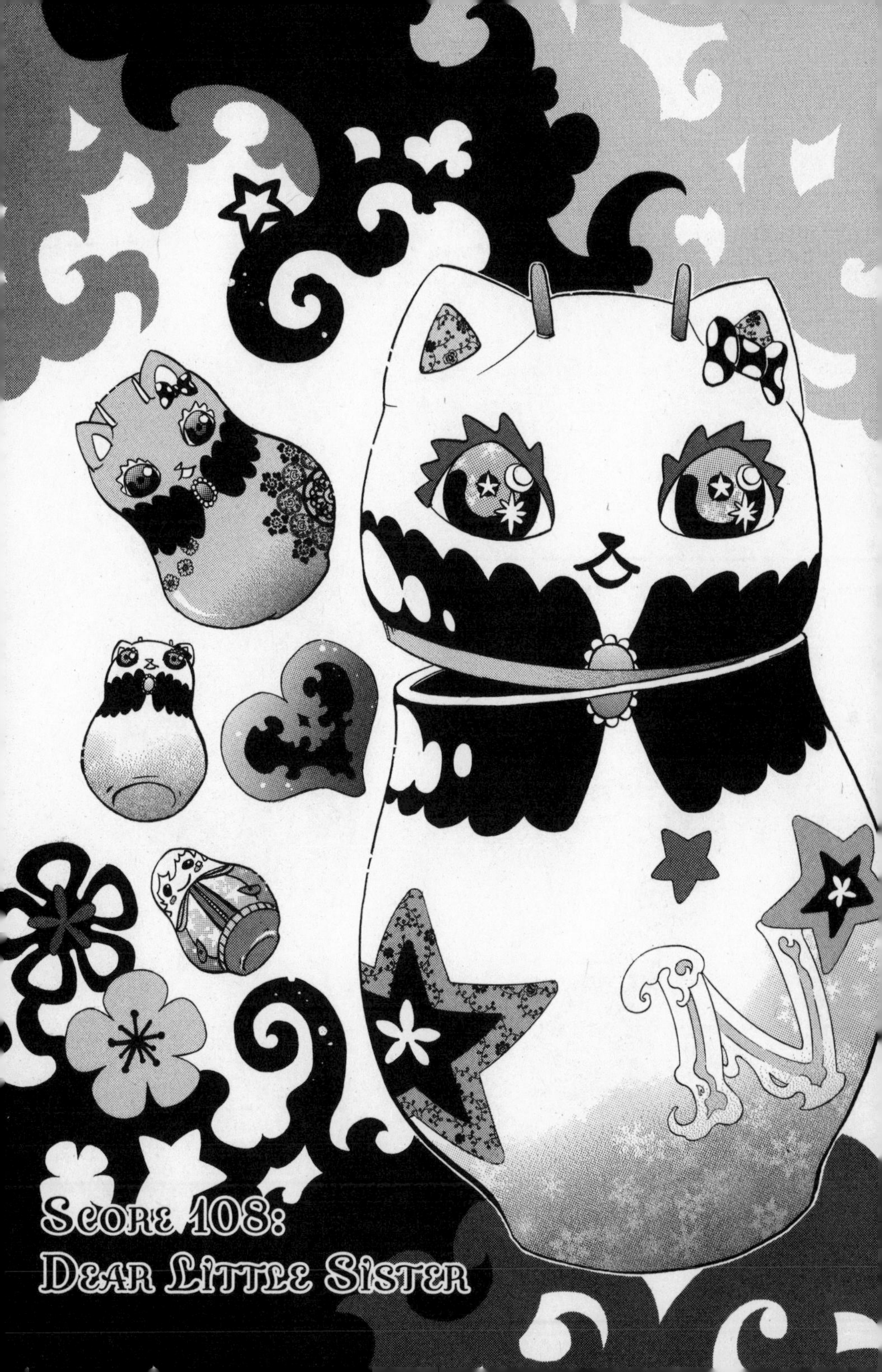
Score 108:
Dear Little Sister

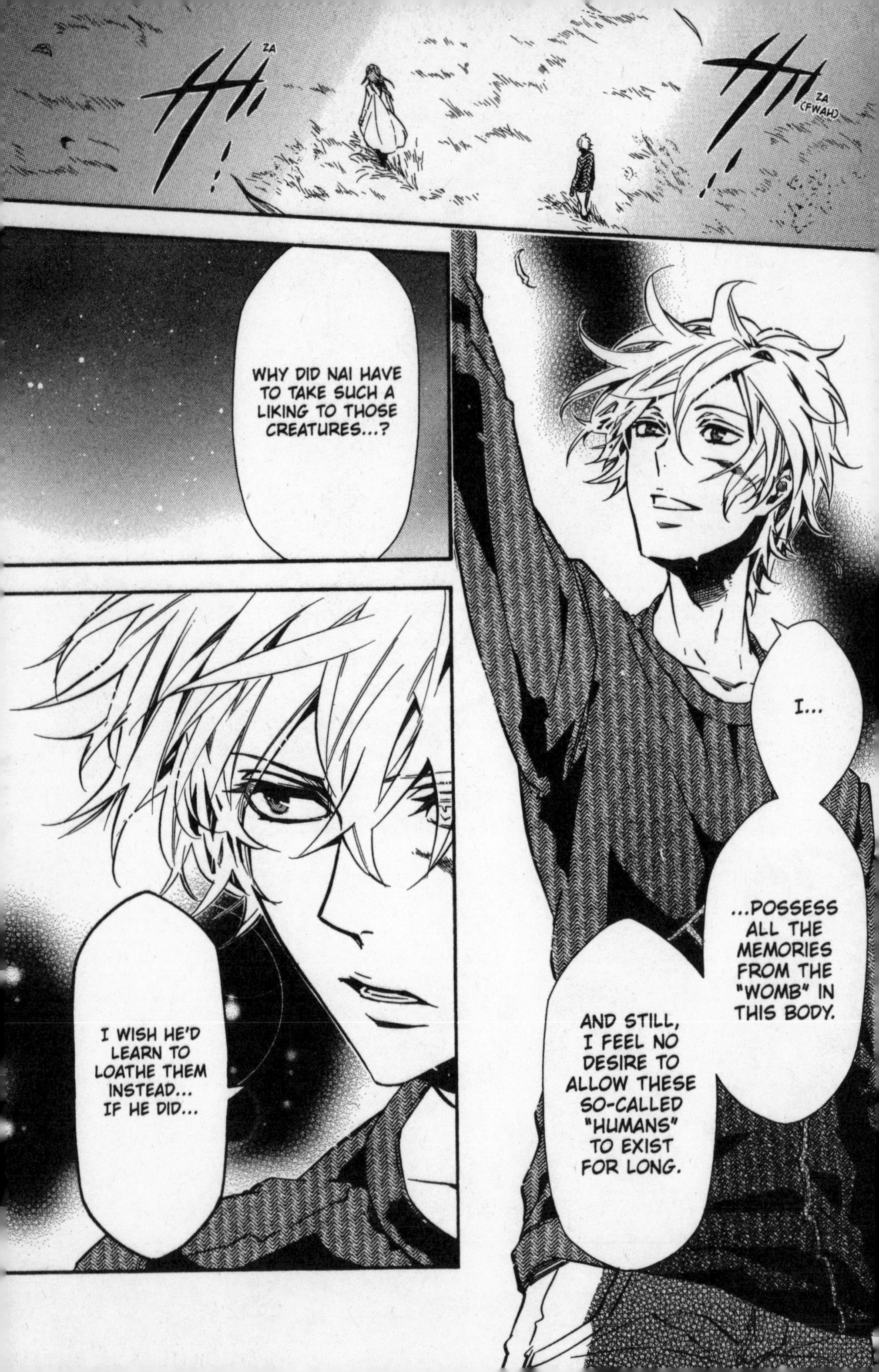
ZA (FWAH)
ZA
I...
...POSSESS ALL THE MEMORIES FROM THE "WOMB" IN THIS BODY.
AND STILL, I FEEL NO DESIRE TO ALLOW THESE SO-CALLED "HUMANS" TO EXIST FOR LONG.
WHY DID NAI HAVE TO TAKE SUCH A LIKING TO THOSE CREATURES...?
I WISH HE'D LEARN TO LOATHE THEM INSTEAD... IF HE DID...

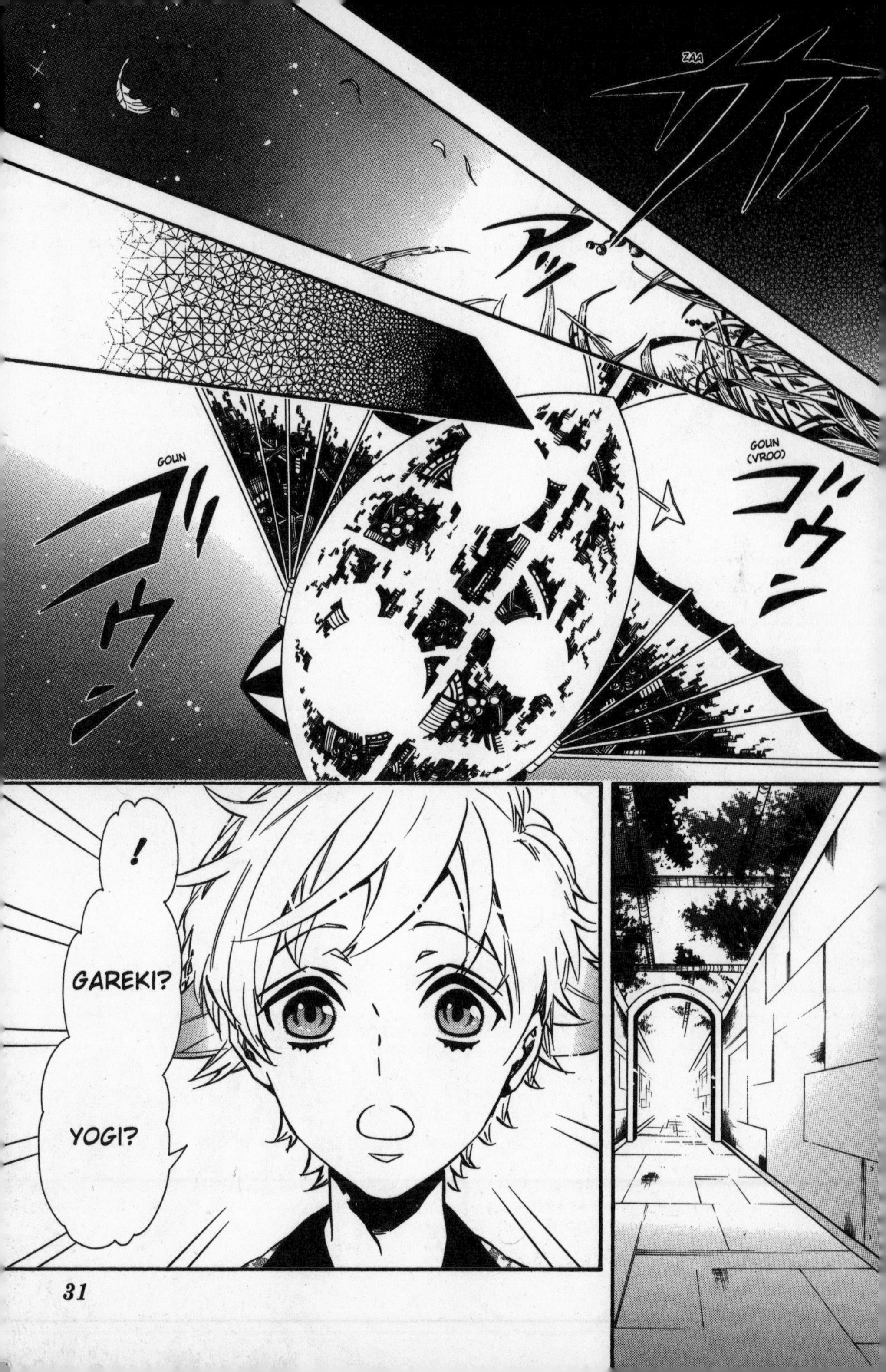
ZAA
GOUN (VROO)
GOUN
!
GAREKI?
YOGI?

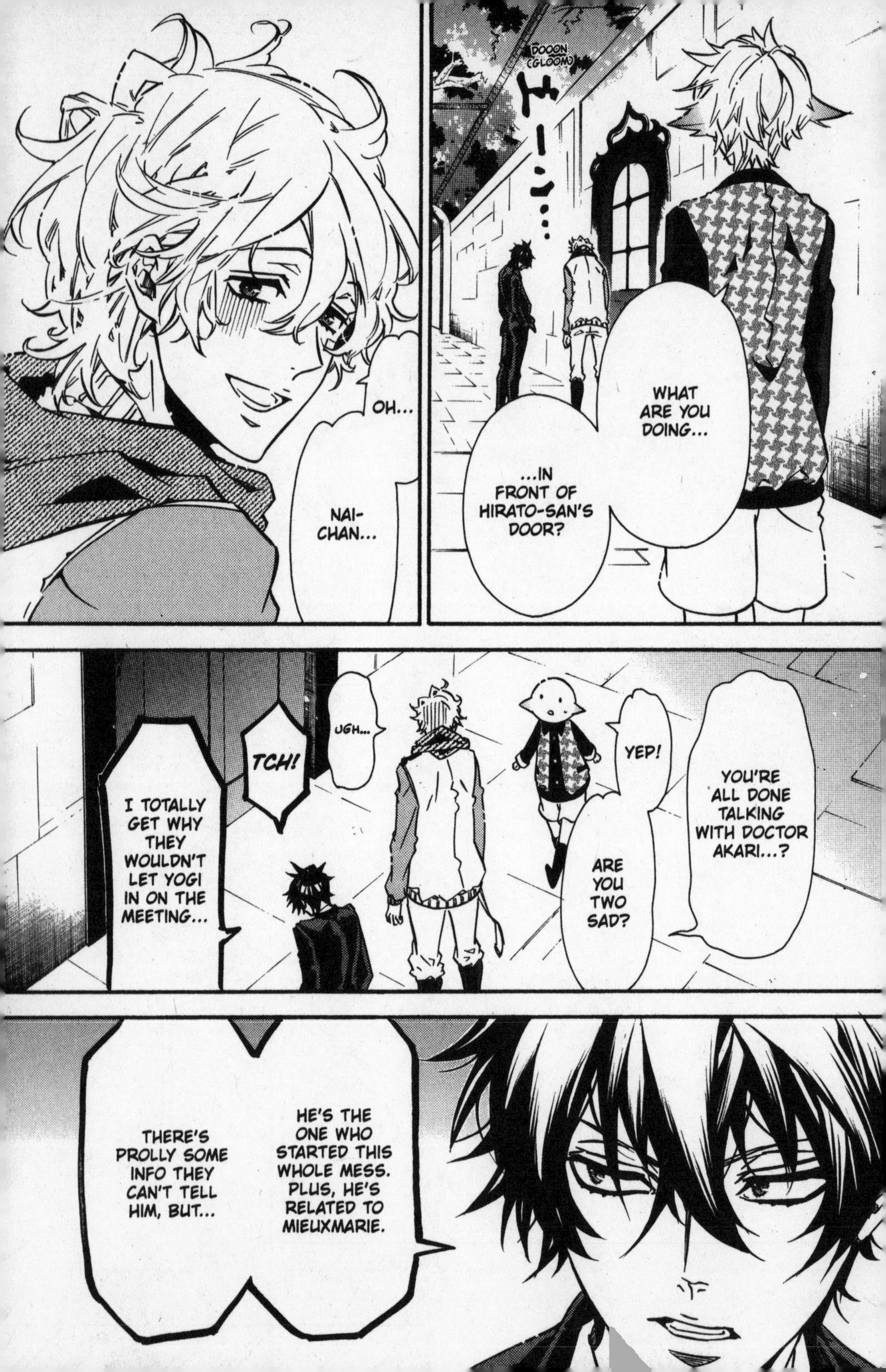
DOOON (GLOOM)
ドーン…
WHAT ARE YOU DOING...
...IN FRONT OF HIRATO-SAN'S DOOR?
OH...
NAI-CHAN...
YOU'RE ALL DONE TALKING WITH DOCTOR AKARI...?
YEP!
ARE YOU TWO SAD?
UGH...
TCH!
I TOTALLY GET WHY THEY WOULDN'T LET YOGI IN ON THE MEETING...
HE'S THE ONE WHO STARTED THIS WHOLE MESS. PLUS, HE'S RELATED TO MIEUXMARIE.
THERE'S PROLLY SOME INFO THEY CAN'T TELL HIM, BUT...

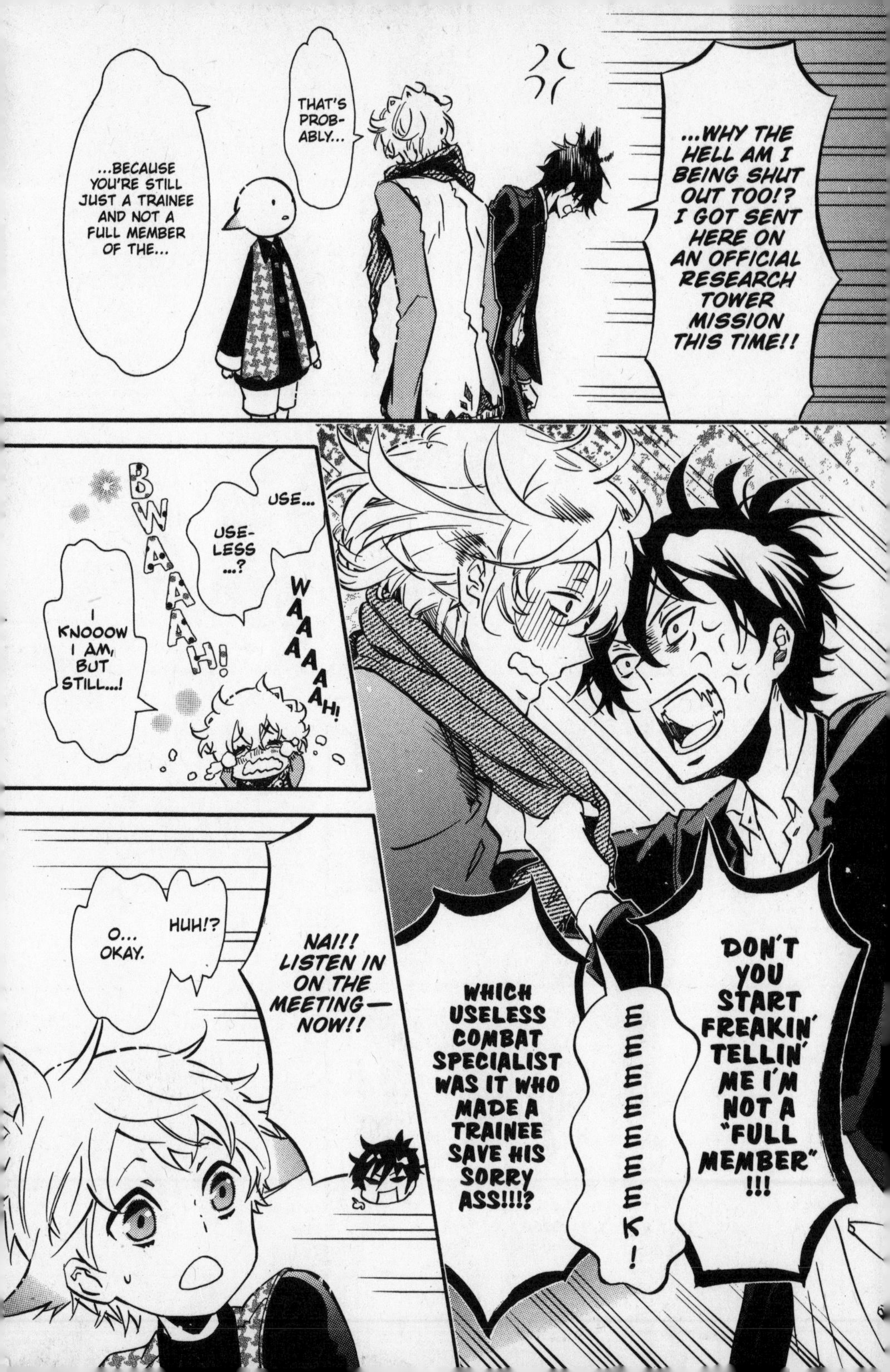
...WHY THE HELL AM I BEING SHUT OUT TOO!? I GOT SENT HERE ON AN OFFICIAL RESEARCH TOWER MISSION THIS TIME!!
THAT'S PROB-ABLY...
...BECAUSE YOU'RE STILL JUST A TRAINEE AND NOT A FULL MEMBER OF THE...
DON'T YOU START FREAKIN' TELLIN' ME I'M NOT A "FULL MEMBER"!!!
WHICH USELESS COMBAT SPECIALIST WAS IT WHO MADE A TRAINEE SAVE HIS SORRY ASS!!!?
EEEEEEEEK!
USE...
USE-LESS...?
BWAAAAH!
WAAAAAAH!
I KNOOOW I AM, BUT STILL...!
NAI!! LISTEN IN ON THE MEETING—NOW!!
HUH!?
O... OKAY.

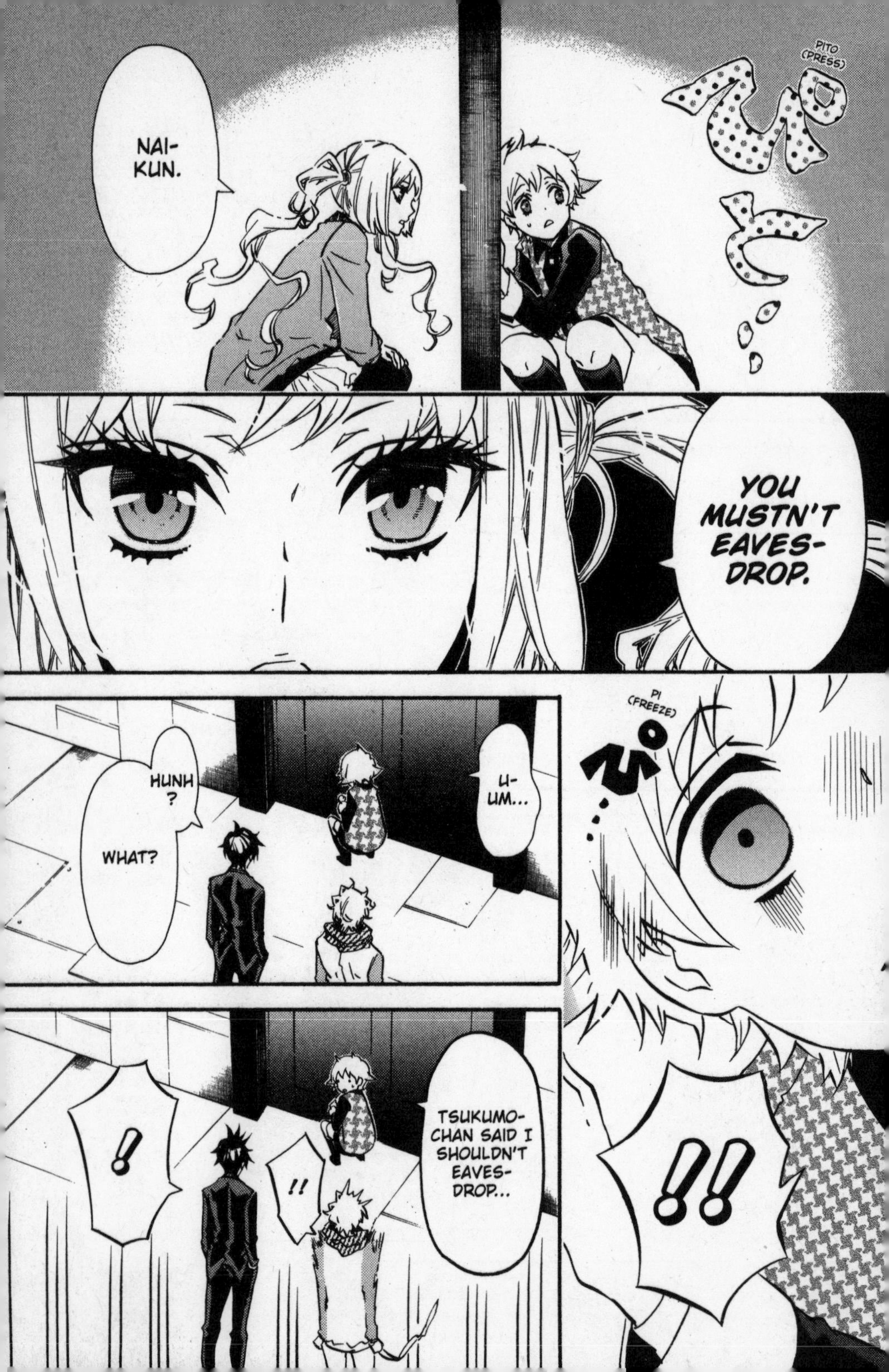
PITO (PRESS)
NAI-KUN.
YOU MUSTN'T EAVES-DROP.
PI (FREEZE)
!!
U-UM...
HUNH?
WHAT?
TSUKUMO-CHAN SAID I SHOULDN'T EAVES-DROP...
!!
!

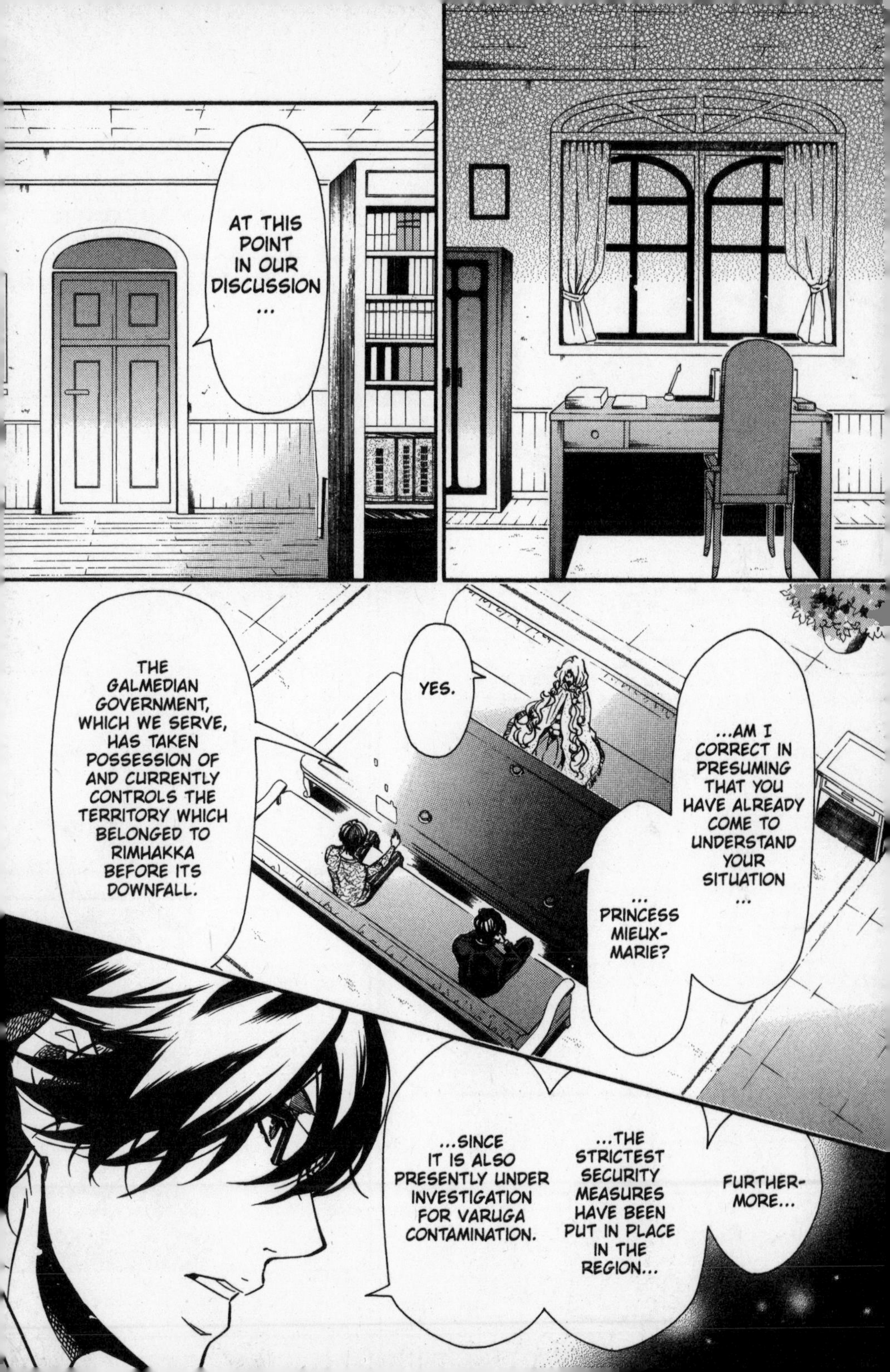

AT THIS POINT IN OUR DISCUSSION...
...AM I CORRECT IN PRESUMING THAT YOU HAVE ALREADY COME TO UNDERSTAND YOUR SITUATION...
...PRINCESS MIEUX-MARIE?
YES.
THE GALMEDIAN GOVERNMENT, WHICH WE SERVE, HAS TAKEN POSSESSION OF AND CURRENTLY CONTROLS THE TERRITORY WHICH BELONGED TO RIMHAKKA BEFORE ITS DOWNFALL.
FURTHER-MORE...
...THE STRICTEST SECURITY MEASURES HAVE BEEN PUT IN PLACE IN THE REGION...
...SINCE IT IS ALSO PRESENTLY UNDER INVESTIGATION FOR VARUGA CONTAMINATION.

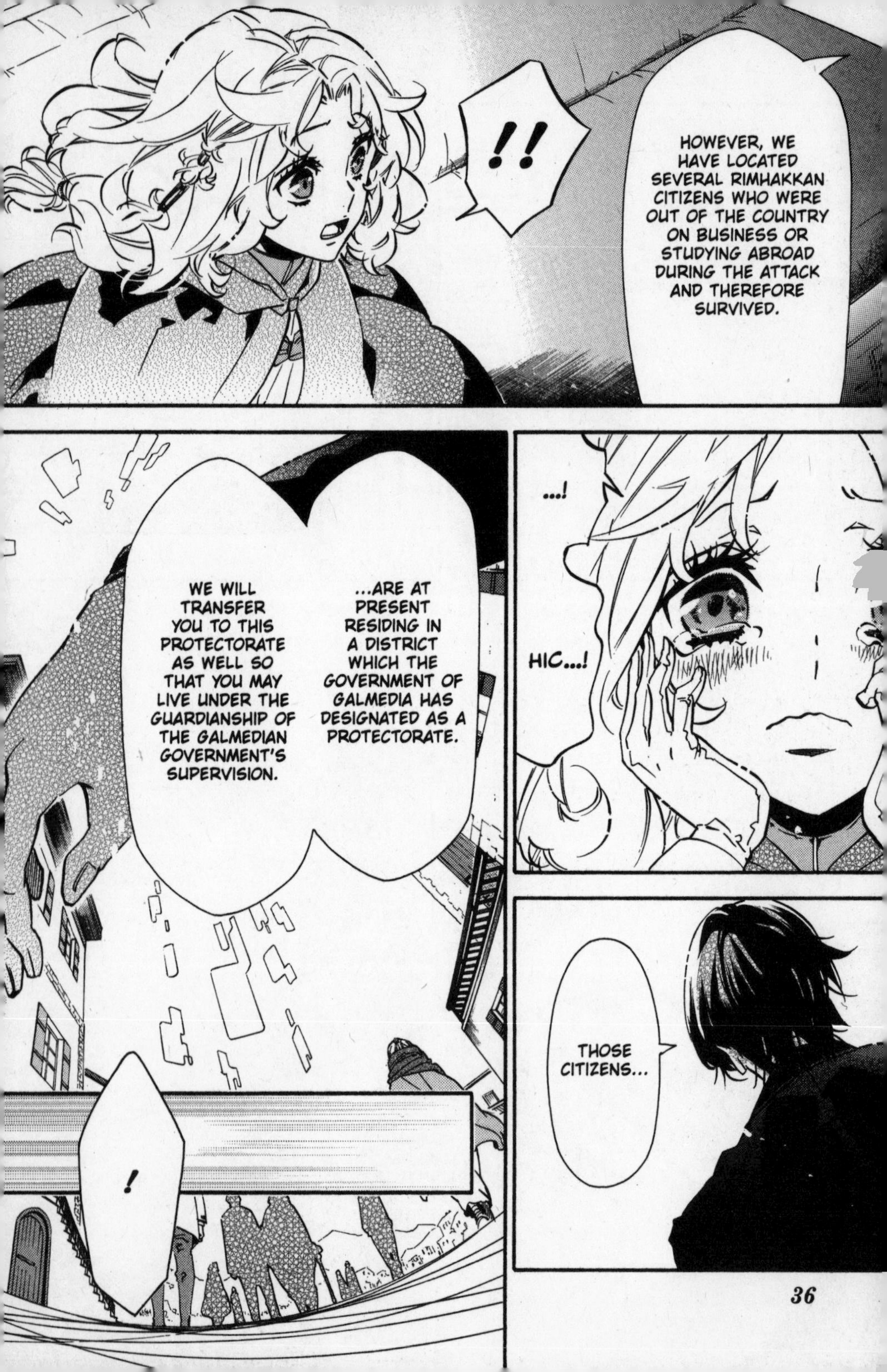
HOWEVER, WE HAVE LOCATED SEVERAL RIMHAKKAN CITIZENS WHO WERE OUT OF THE COUNTRY ON BUSINESS OR STUDYING ABROAD DURING THE ATTACK AND THEREFORE SURVIVED.
!!
...!
HIC...!
THOSE CITIZENS...
...ARE AT PRESENT RESIDING IN A DISTRICT WHICH THE GOVERNMENT OF GALMEDIA HAS DESIGNATED AS A PROTECTORATE.
WE WILL TRANSFER YOU TO THIS PROTECTORATE AS WELL SO THAT YOU MAY LIVE UNDER THE GUARDIANSHIP OF THE GALMEDIAN GOVERNMENT'S SUPERVISION.
!

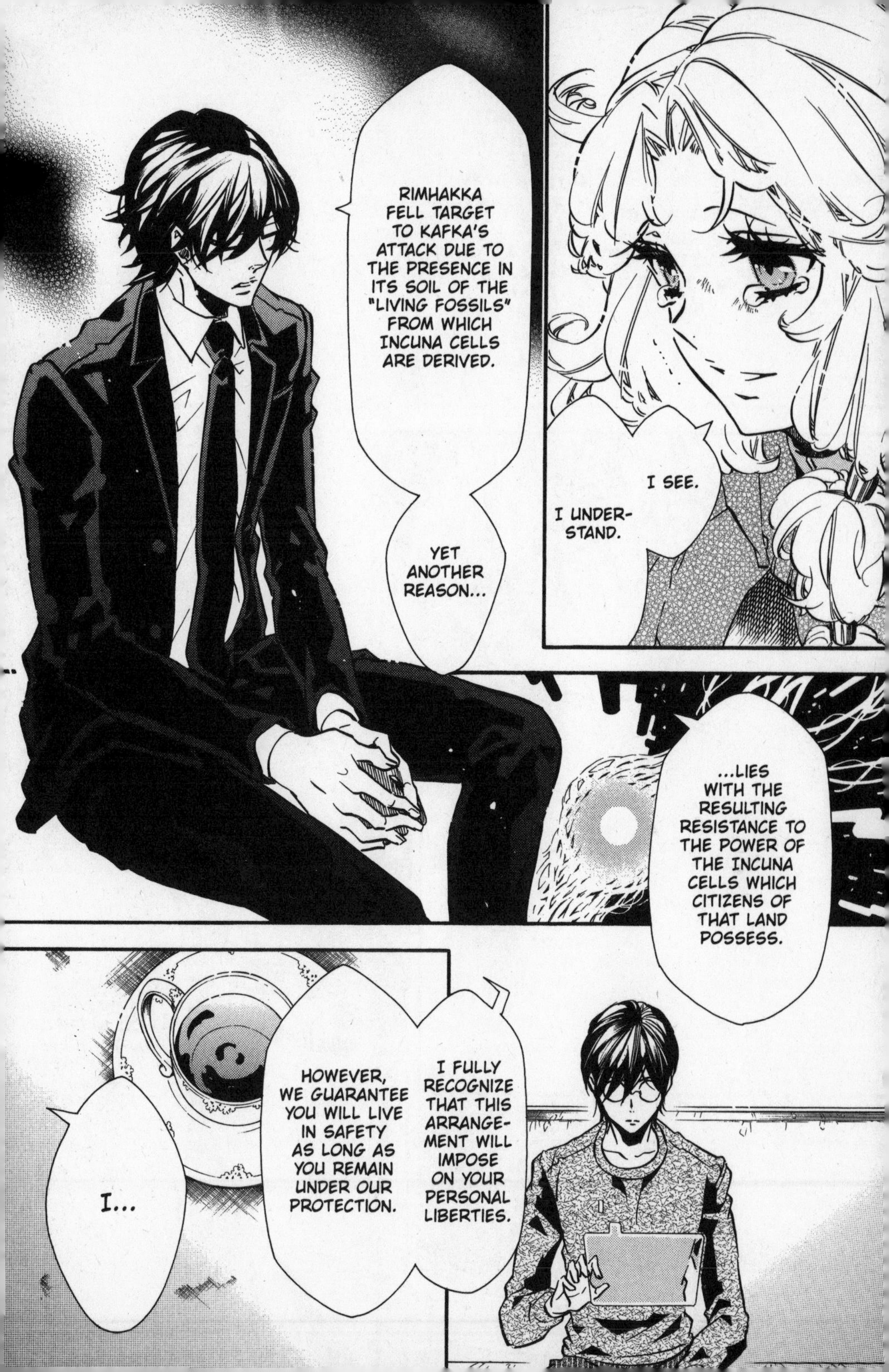
I SEE.
I UNDERSTAND.
RIMHAKKA FELL TARGET TO KAFKA'S ATTACK DUE TO THE PRESENCE IN ITS SOIL OF THE "LIVING FOSSILS" FROM WHICH INCUNA CELLS ARE DERIVED.
YET ANOTHER REASON...
...LIES WITH THE RESULTING RESISTANCE TO THE POWER OF THE INCUNA CELLS WHICH CITIZENS OF THAT LAND POSSESS.
I FULLY RECOGNIZE THAT THIS ARRANGEMENT WILL IMPOSE ON YOUR PERSONAL LIBERTIES.
HOWEVER, WE GUARANTEE YOU WILL LIVE IN SAFETY AS LONG AS YOU REMAIN UNDER OUR PROTECTION.
I...

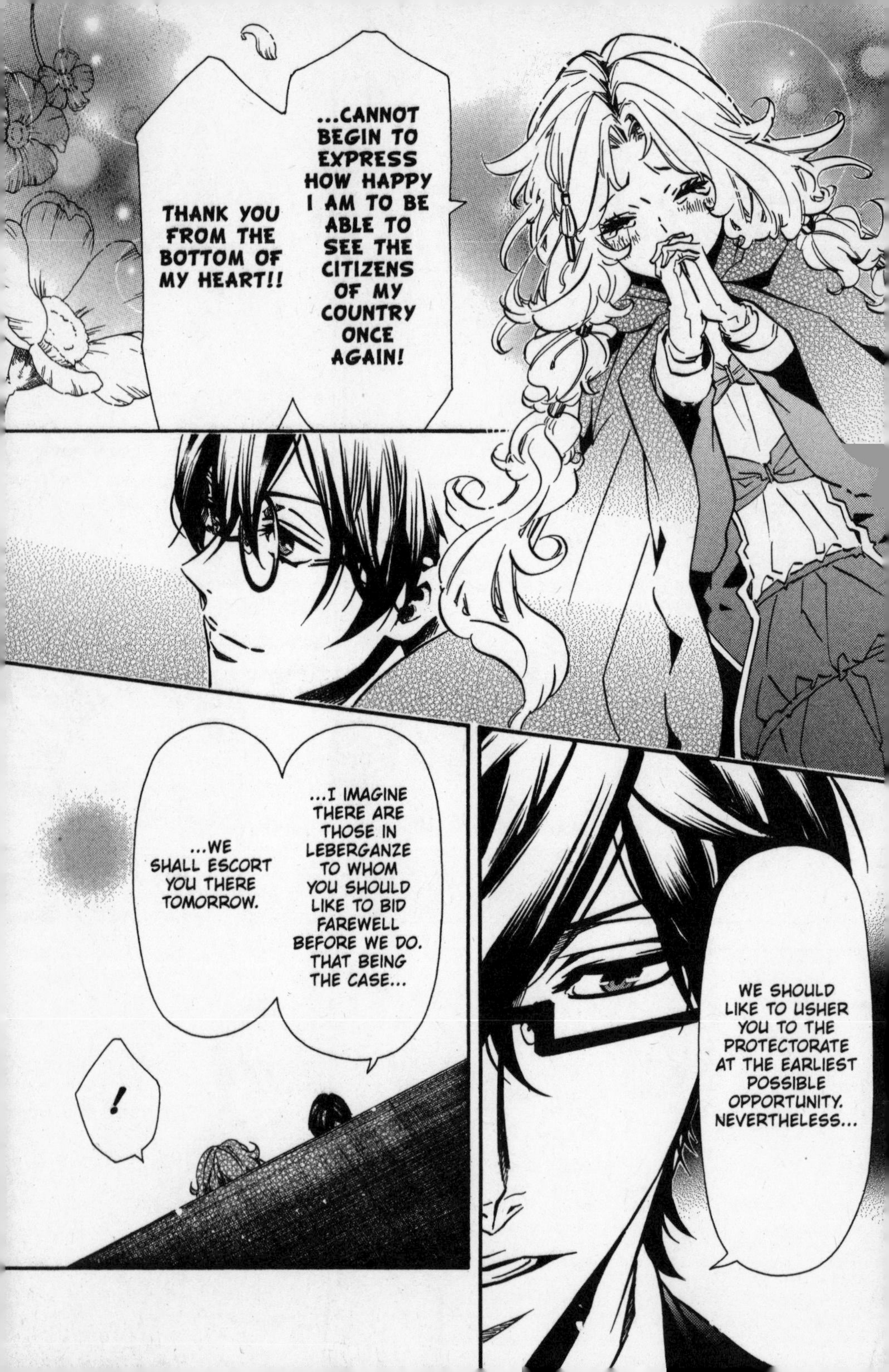
...CANNOT BEGIN TO EXPRESS HOW HAPPY I AM TO BE ABLE TO SEE THE CITIZENS OF MY COUNTRY ONCE AGAIN!
THANK YOU FROM THE BOTTOM OF MY HEART!!
WE SHOULD LIKE TO USHER YOU TO THE PROTECTORATE AT THE EARLIEST POSSIBLE OPPORTUNITY. NEVERTHELESS...
...I IMAGINE THERE ARE THOSE IN LEBERGANZE TO WHOM YOU SHOULD LIKE TO BID FAREWELL BEFORE WE DO. THAT BEING THE CASE...
...WE SHALL ESCORT YOU THERE TOMORROW.
!

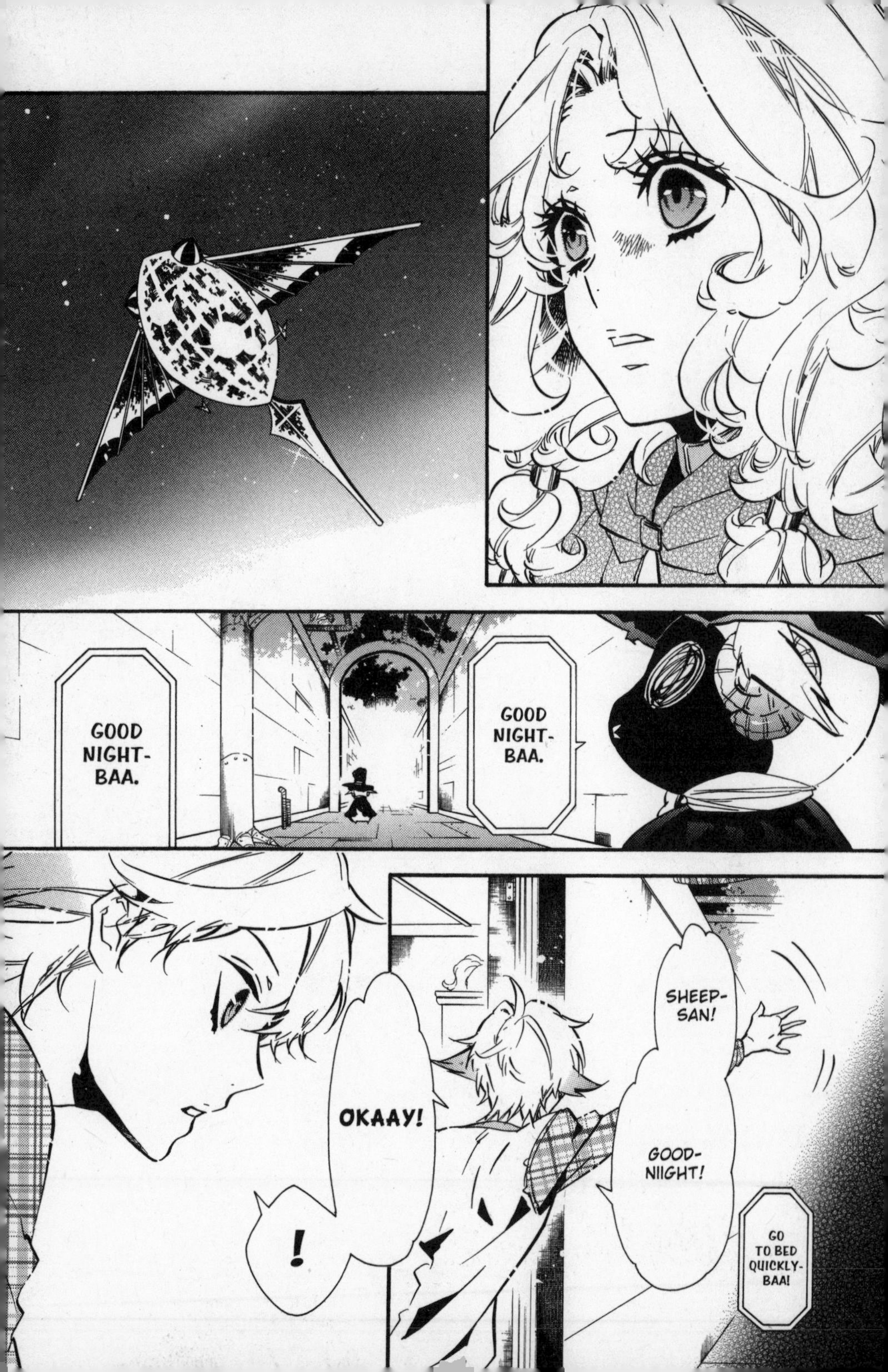
GOOD NIGHT-BAA.
GOOD NIGHT-BAA.
SHEEP-SAN!
GOOD-NIIGHT!
GO TO BED QUICKLY-BAA!
OKAAY!
!

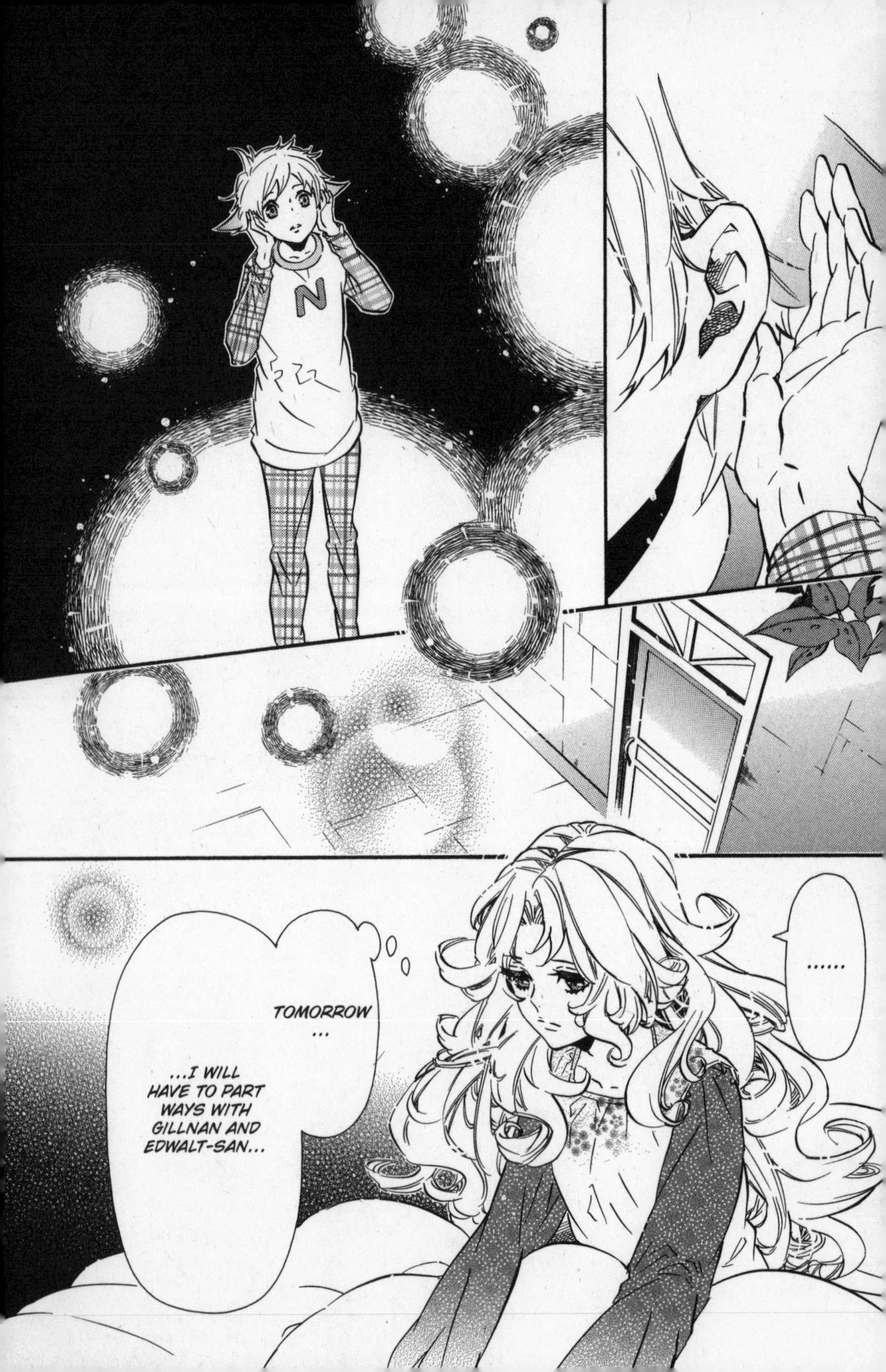
......
TOMORROW ...
...I WILL HAVE TO PART WAYS WITH GILLNAN AND EDWALT-SAN...

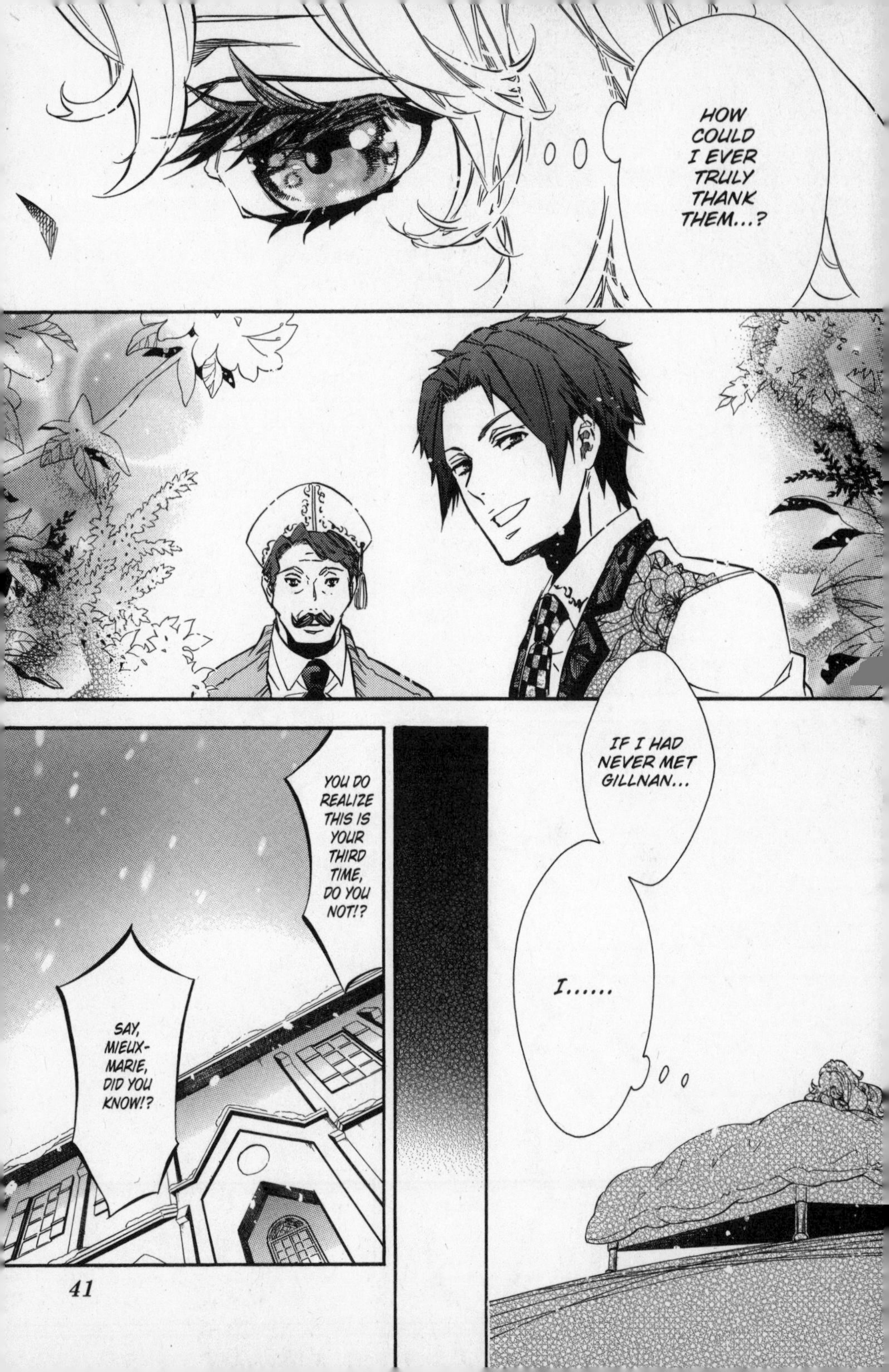
HOW COULD I EVER TRULY THANK THEM...?
IF I HAD NEVER MET GILLNAN...
I......
YOU DO REALIZE THIS IS YOUR THIRD TIME, DO YOU NOT!?
SAY, MIEUX-MARIE, DID YOU KNOW!?

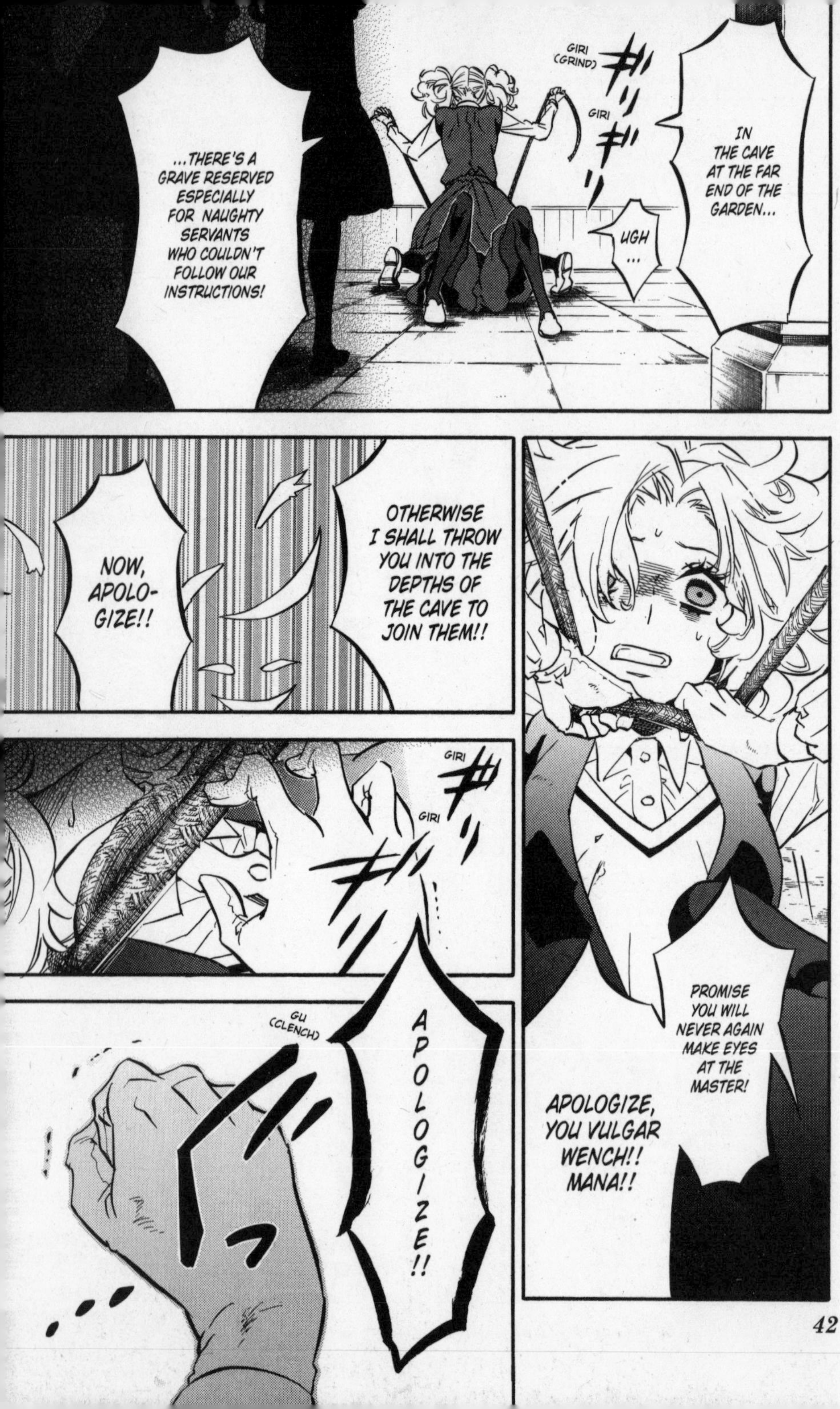
IN THE CAVE AT THE FAR END OF THE GARDEN...
GIRI (GRIND)
GIRI
UGH ...
...THERE'S A GRAVE RESERVED ESPECIALLY FOR NAUGHTY SERVANTS WHO COULDN'T FOLLOW OUR INSTRUCTIONS!
PROMISE YOU WILL NEVER AGAIN MAKE EYES AT THE MASTER!
APOLOGIZE, YOU VULGAR WENCH!! MANA!!
OTHERWISE I SHALL THROW YOU INTO THE DEPTHS OF THE CAVE TO JOIN THEM!!
NOW, APOLOGIZE!!
GIRI
GIRI
...
GU (CLENCH)
APOLOGIZE!!
...

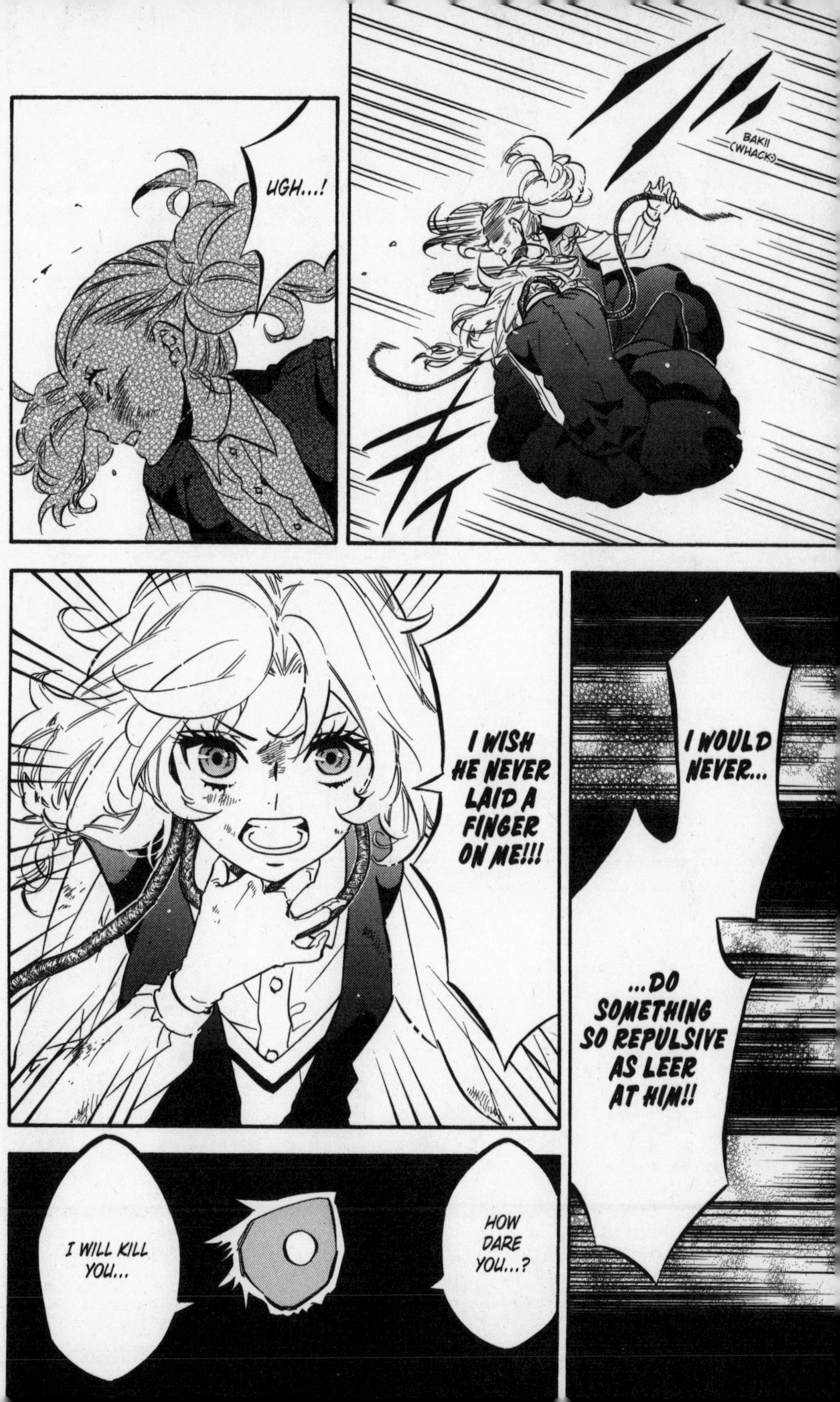
BAKII (WHACK)
UGH...!
I WOULD NEVER...
...DO SOMETHING SO REPULSIVE AS LEER AT HIM!!
I WISH HE NEVER LAID A FINGER ON ME!!!
HOW DARE YOU...?
I WILL KILL YOU...

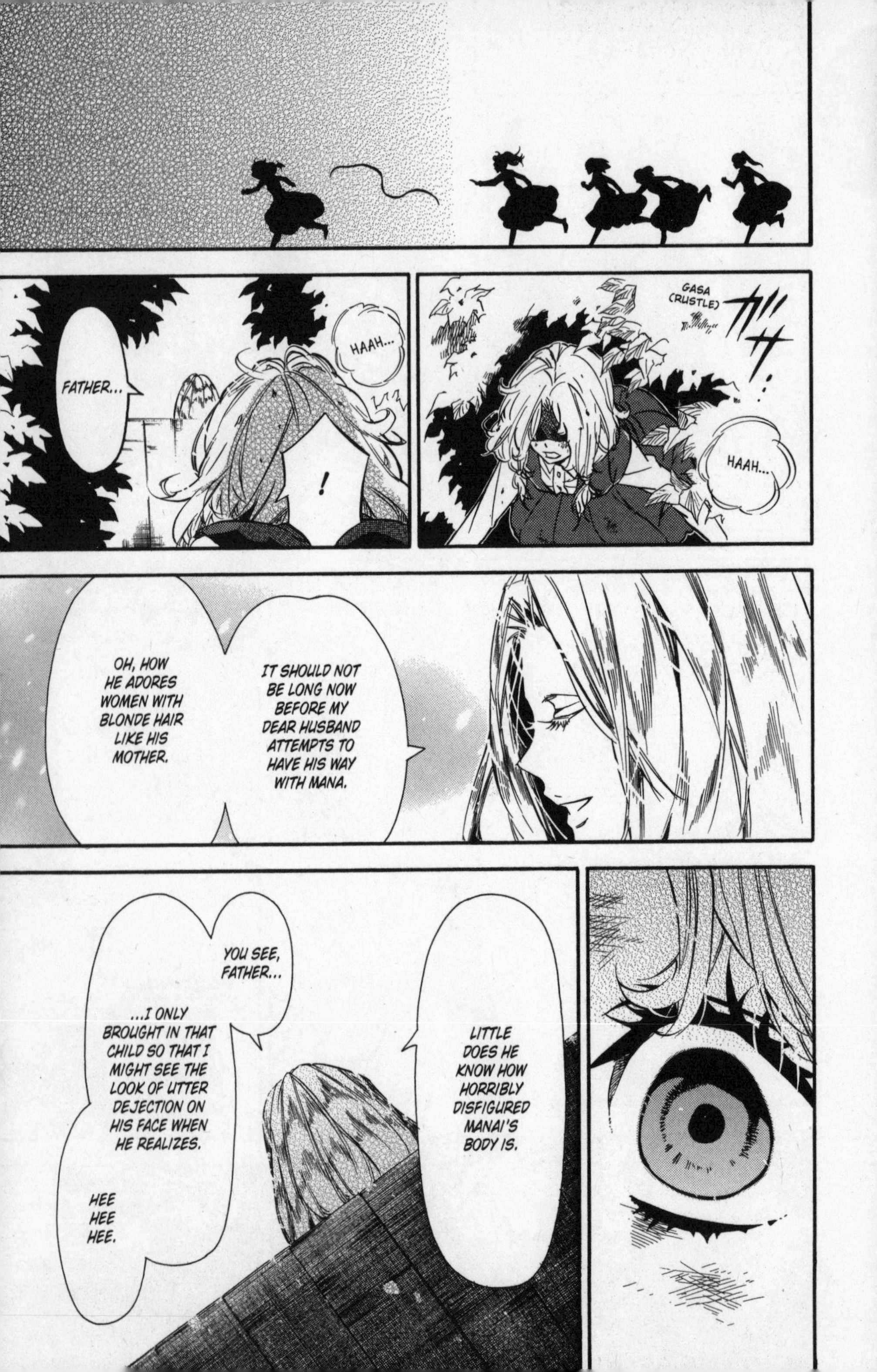
GASA (RUSTLE)
HAAH...
HAAH...
FATHER...
!
IT SHOULD NOT BE LONG NOW BEFORE MY DEAR HUSBAND ATTEMPTS TO HAVE HIS WAY WITH MANA.
OH, HOW HE ADORES WOMEN WITH BLONDE HAIR LIKE HIS MOTHER.
LITTLE DOES HE KNOW HOW HORRIBLY DISFIGURED MANAI'S BODY IS.
YOU SEE, FATHER...
...I ONLY BROUGHT IN THAT CHILD SO THAT I MIGHT SEE THE LOOK OF UTTER DEJECTION ON HIS FACE WHEN HE REALIZES.
HEE HEE HEE.

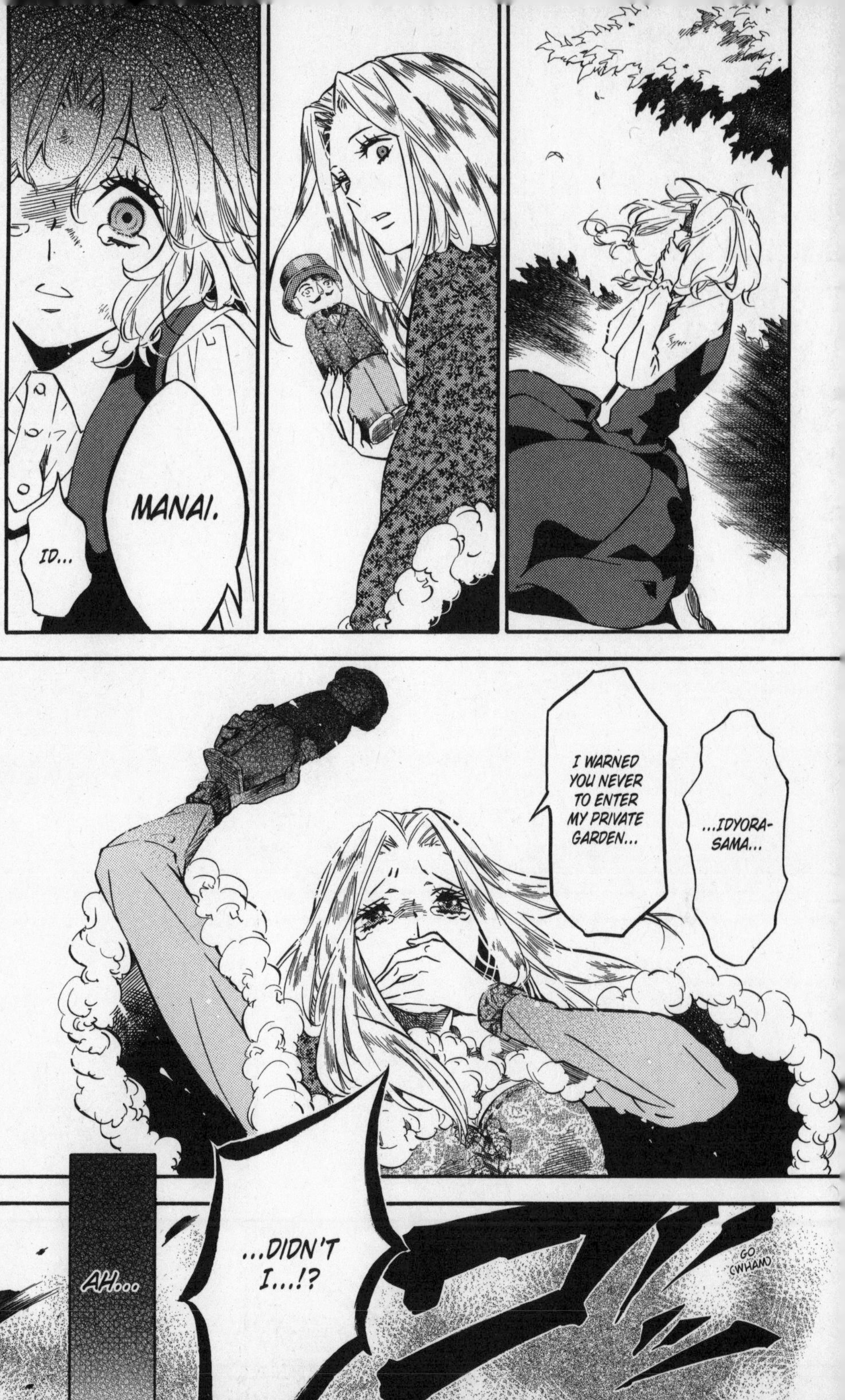
MANAI.
ID...
...IDYORA-SAMA...
I WARNED YOU NEVER TO ENTER MY PRIVATE GARDEN...
GO (WHAM)
...DIDN'T I...!?
AHooo

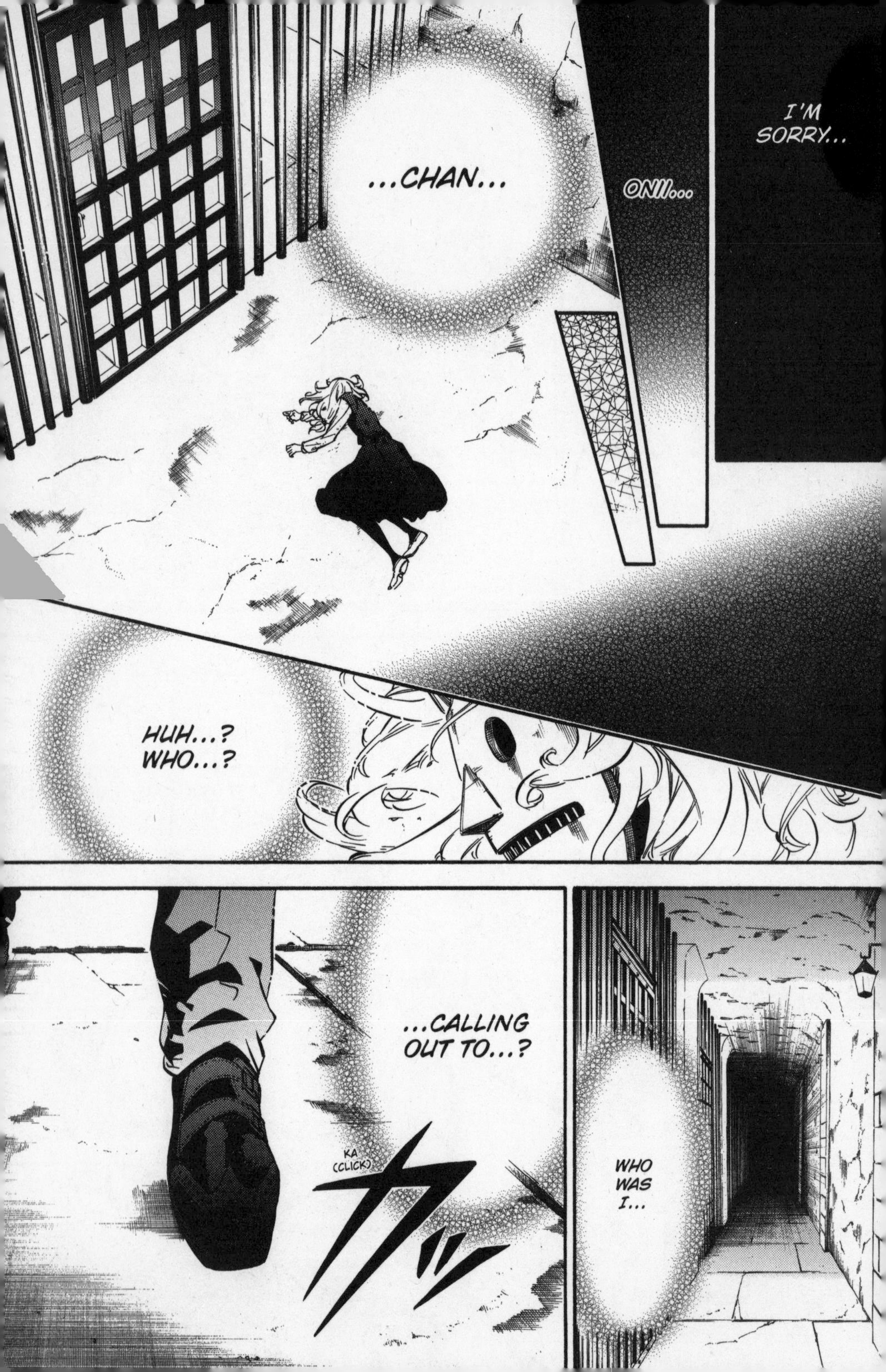
I'M SORRY...
ONII...
...CHAN...
HUH...? WHO...?
WHO WAS I...
...CALLING OUT TO...?
KA (CLICK)

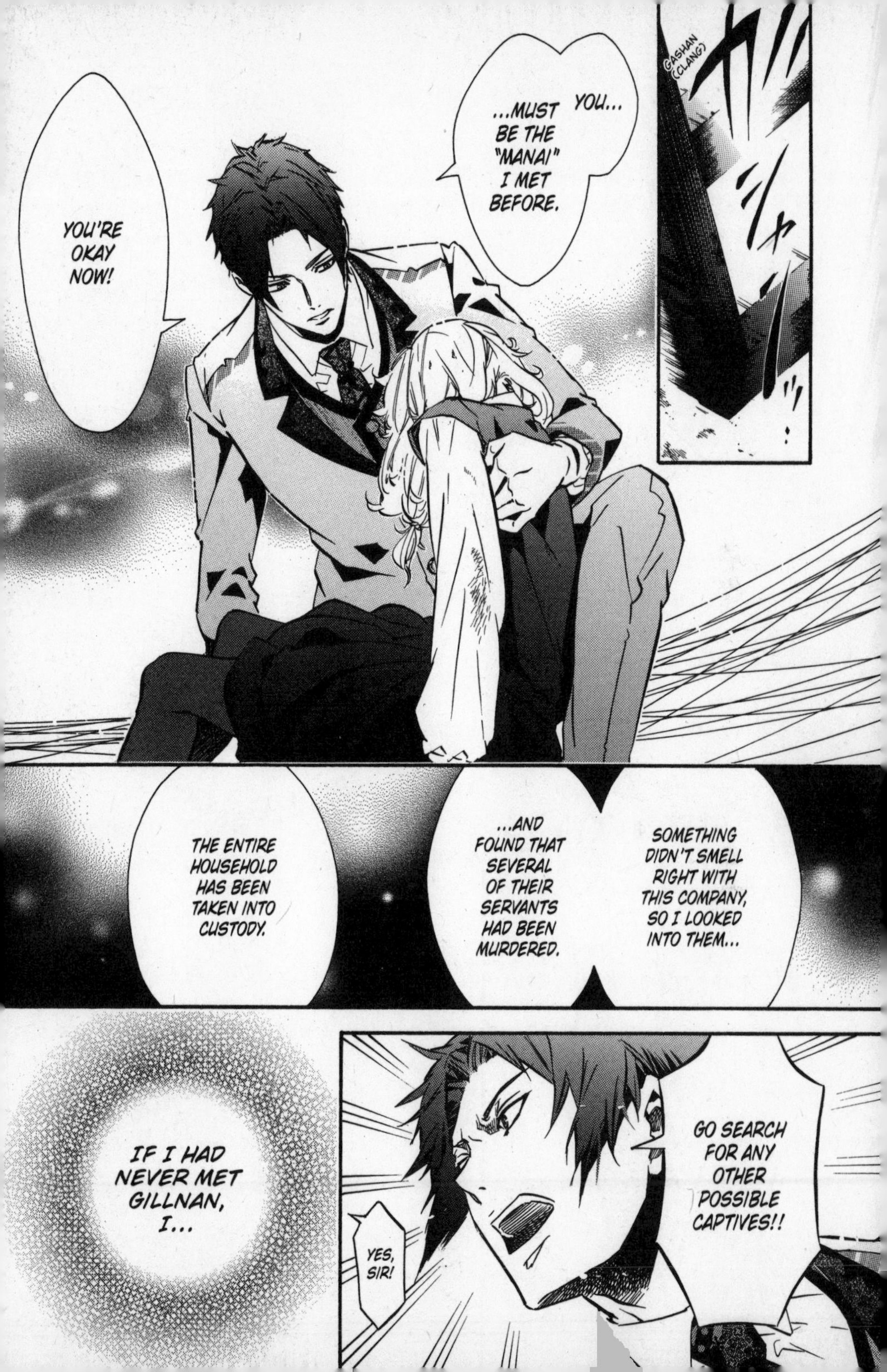
GASHAN (CLANG)
シャ
YOU... ...MUST BE THE "MANAI" I MET BEFORE.
YOU'RE OKAY NOW!
SOMETHING DIDN'T SMELL RIGHT WITH THIS COMPANY, SO I LOOKED INTO THEM...
...AND FOUND THAT SEVERAL OF THEIR SERVANTS HAD BEEN MURDERED.
THE ENTIRE HOUSEHOLD HAS BEEN TAKEN INTO CUSTODY.
GO SEARCH FOR ANY OTHER POSSIBLE CAPTIVES!!
YES, SIR!
IF I HAD NEVER MET GILLNAN, I...

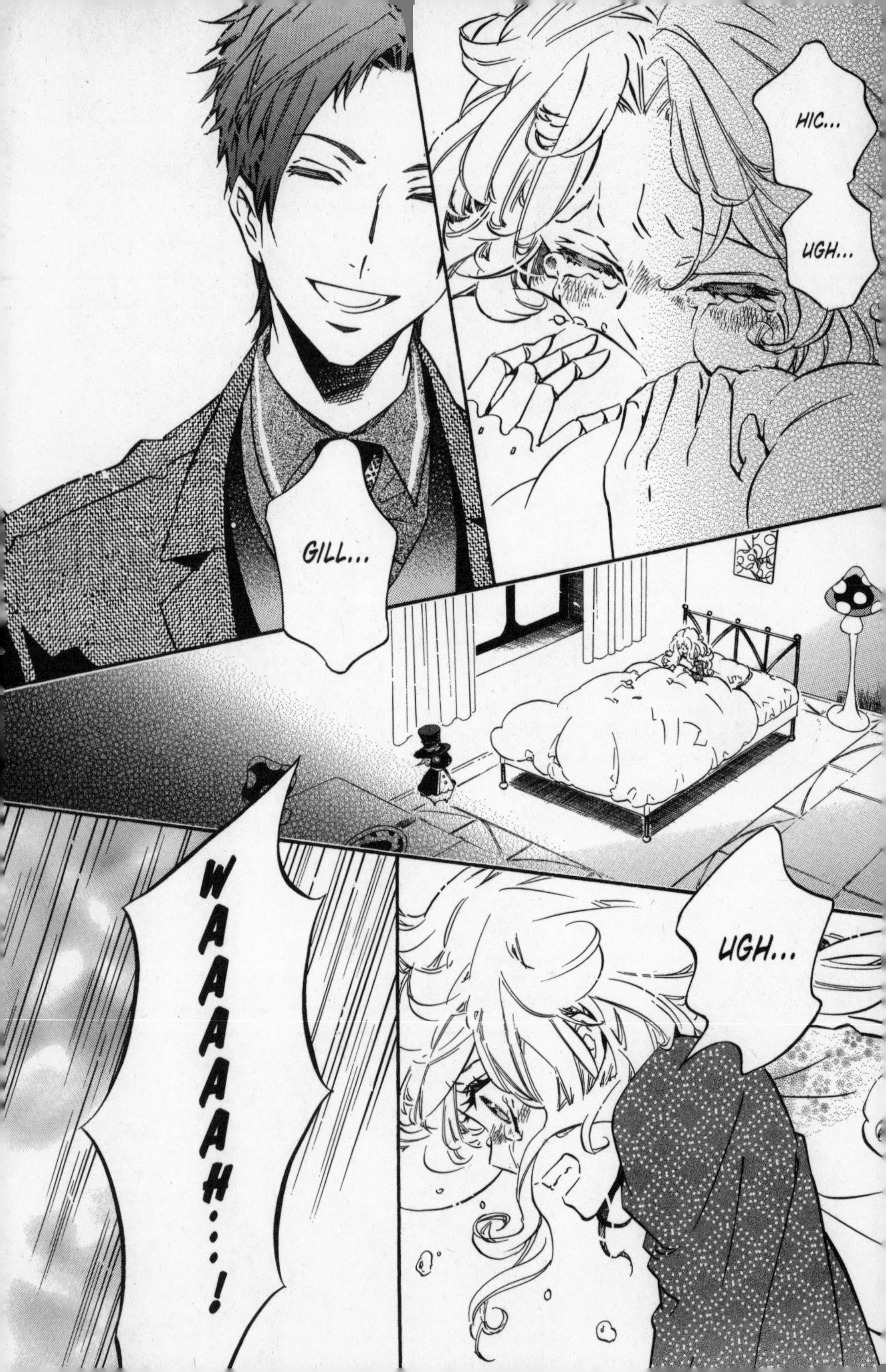
HIC...
UGH...
GILL...
UGH...
WAAAAAH...!

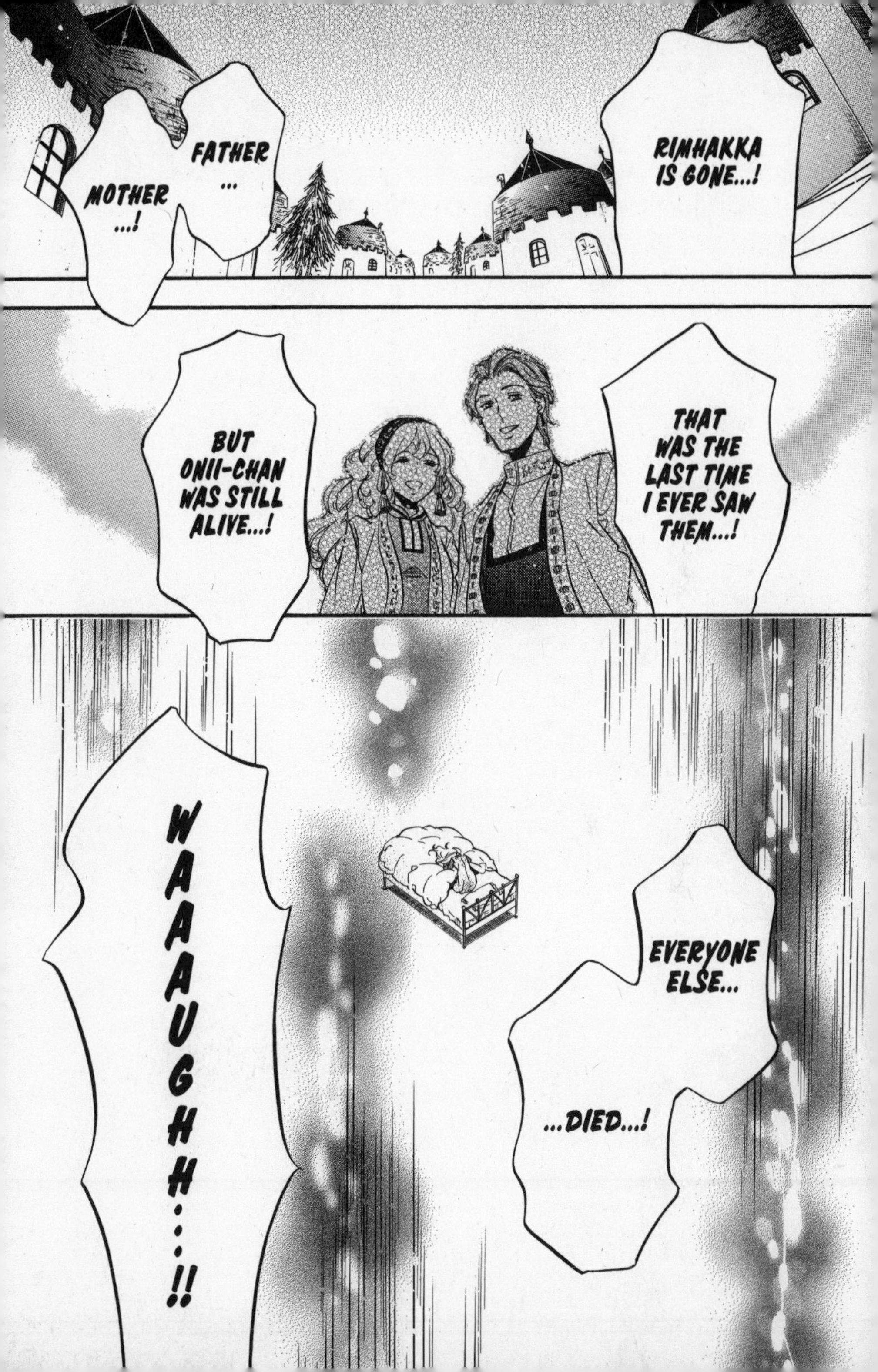
RIMHAKKA IS GONE...!
FATHER...
MOTHER...!
THAT WAS THE LAST TIME I EVER SAW THEM...!
BUT ONII-CHAN WAS STILL ALIVE...!
EVERYONE ELSE...
...DIED...!
WAAAAUGHHH...!!

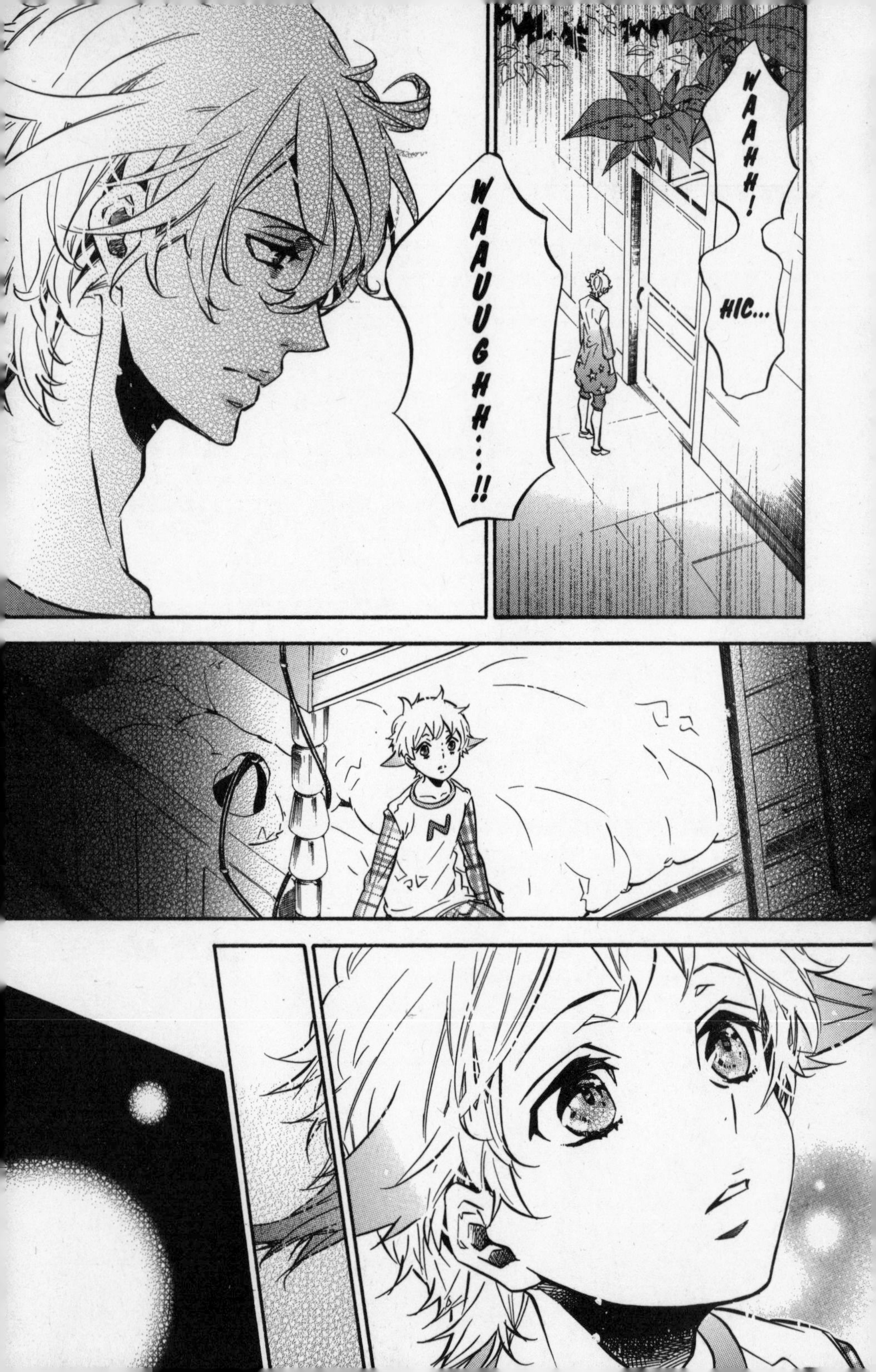
WAAAHH!
HIC...
WAAAUUGHH...!!

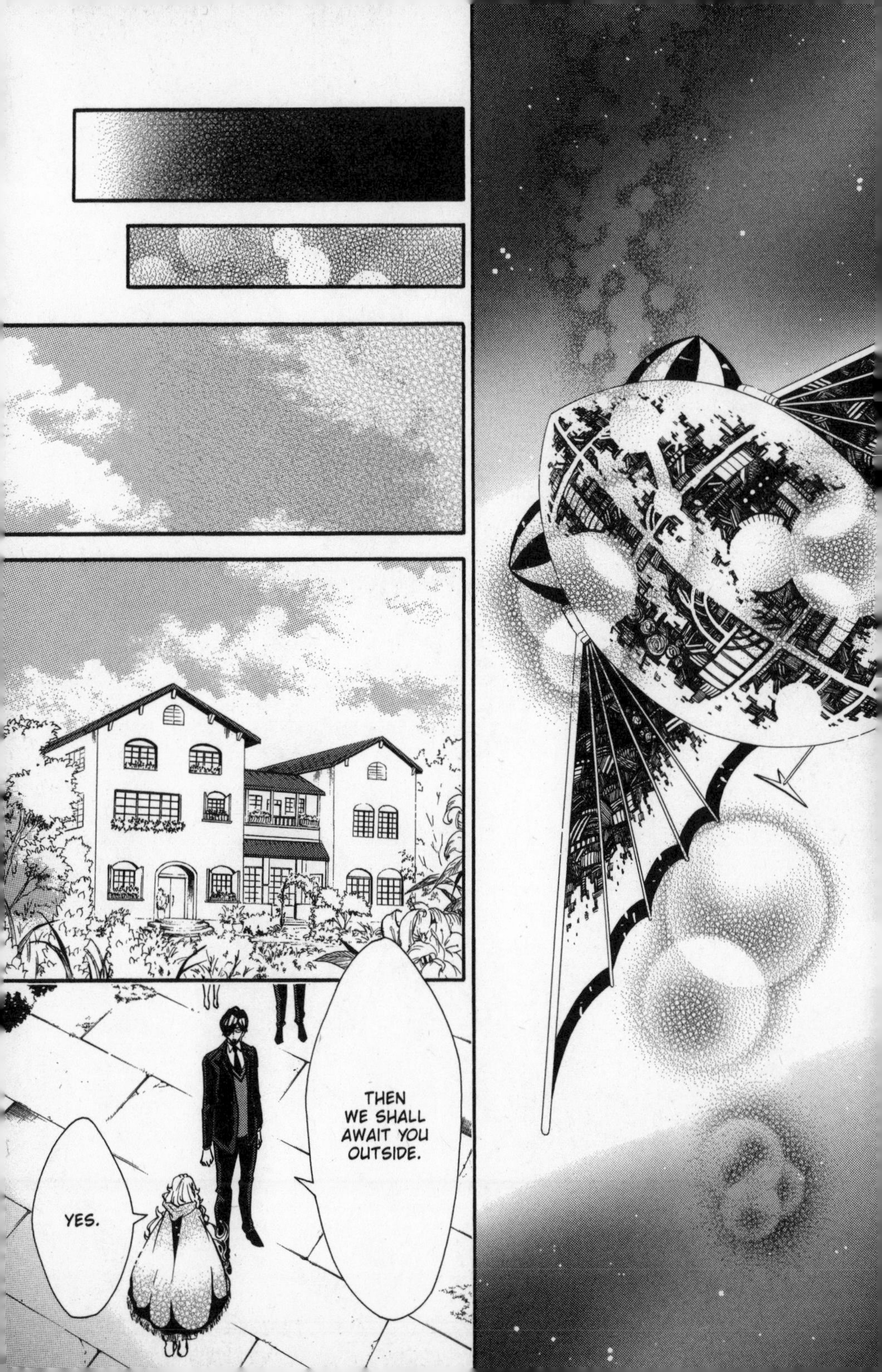
THEN WE SHALL AWAIT YOU OUTSIDE.
YES.

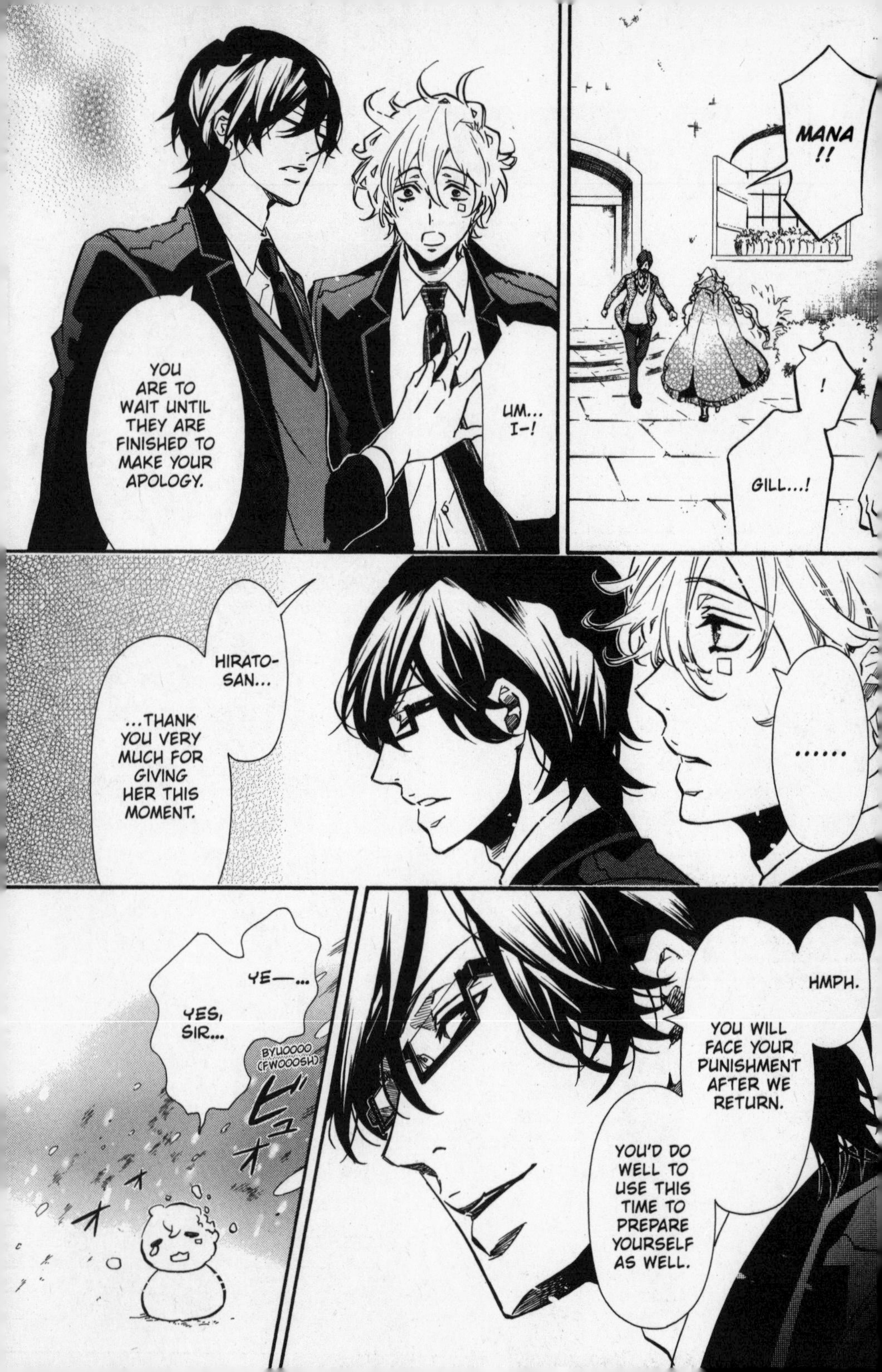
MANA !!
!
GILL...!
UM... I—!
YOU ARE TO WAIT UNTIL THEY ARE FINISHED TO MAKE YOUR APOLOGY.
......
HIRATO-SAN...
...THANK YOU VERY MUCH FOR GIVING HER THIS MOMENT.
HMPH.
YOU WILL FACE YOUR PUNISHMENT AFTER WE RETURN.
YOU'D DO WELL TO USE THIS TIME TO PREPARE YOURSELF AS WELL.
YE—...
YES, SIR...
BYUOOOO (FWOOOSH)
ビュオオオ

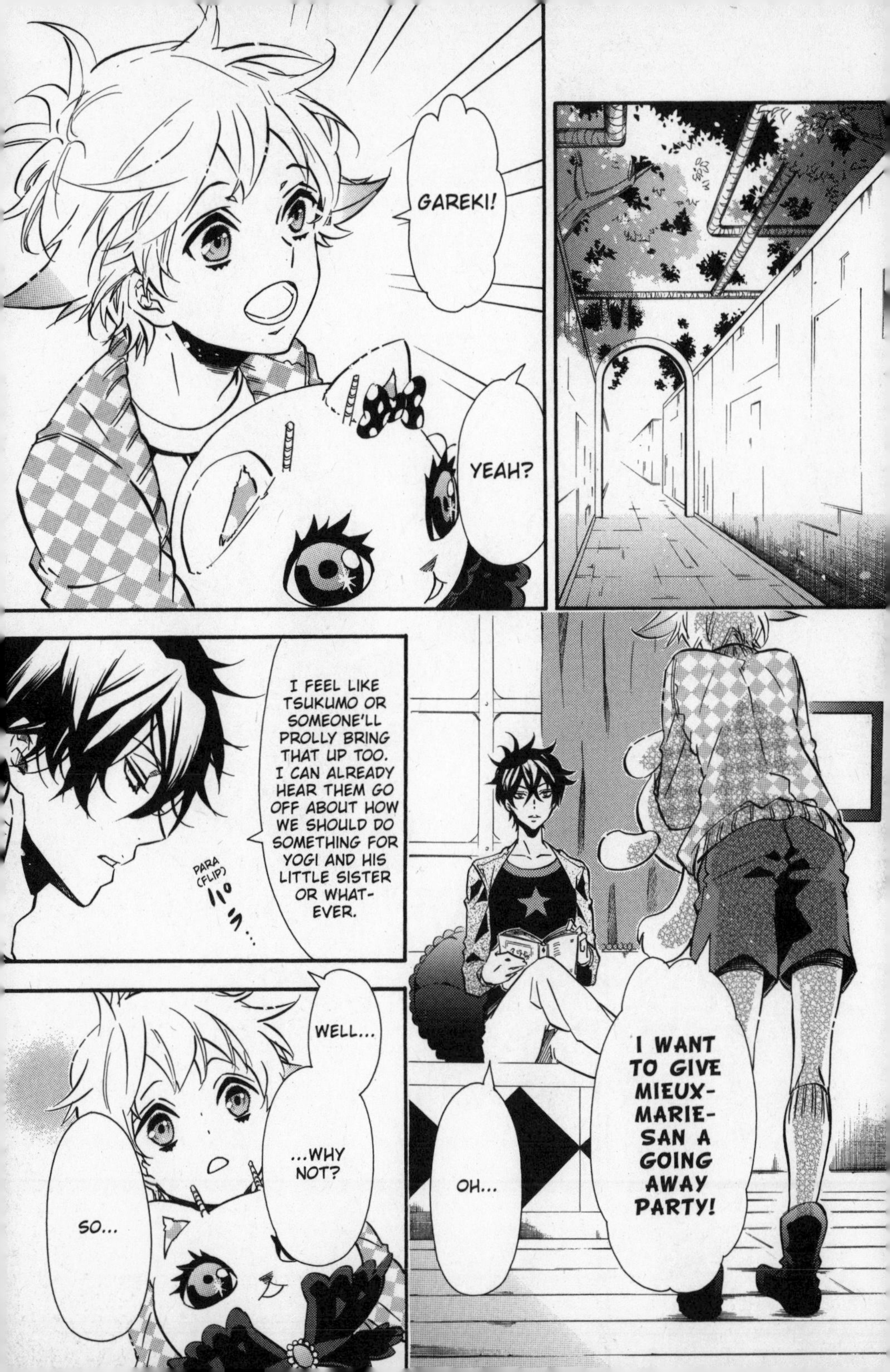
GAREKI!
YEAH?
I WANT TO GIVE MIEUX-MARIE-SAN A GOING AWAY PARTY!
OH...
I FEEL LIKE TSUKUMO OR SOMEONE'LL PROLLY BRING THAT UP TOO. I CAN ALREADY HEAR THEM GO OFF ABOUT HOW WE SHOULD DO SOMETHING FOR YOGI AND HIS LITTLE SISTER OR WHATEVER.
PARA (FLIP)
WELL...
...WHY NOT?
SO...

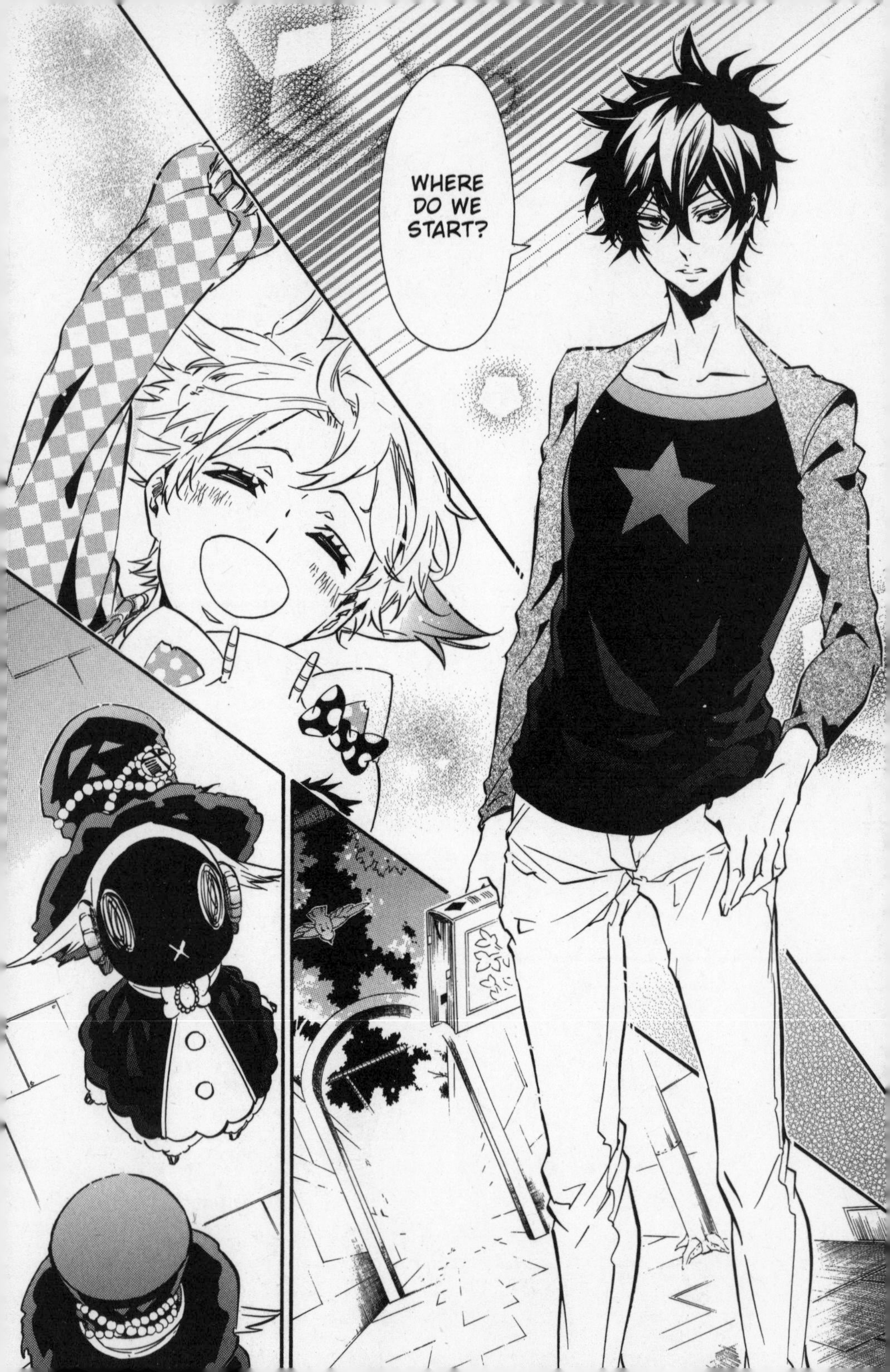
WHERE DO WE START?

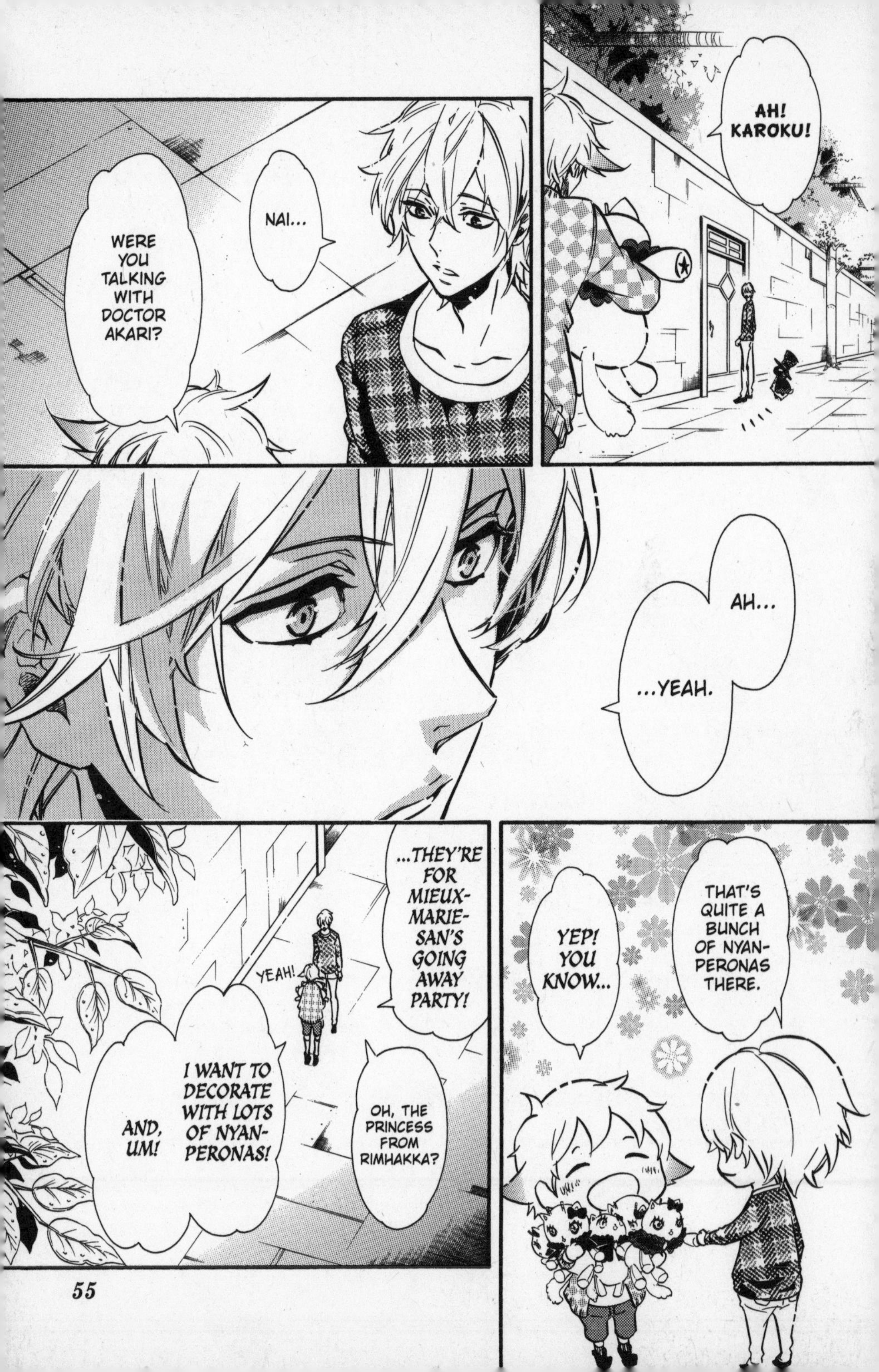
AH! KAROKU!
NAI...
WERE YOU TALKING WITH DOCTOR AKARI?
AH...
...YEAH.
THAT'S QUITE A BUNCH OF NYAN-PERONAS THERE.
YEP! YOU KNOW...
...THEY'RE FOR MIEUX-MARIE-SAN'S GOING AWAY PARTY!
OH, THE PRINCESS FROM RIMHAKKA?
YEAH!
I WANT TO DECORATE WITH LOTS OF NYAN-PERONAS!
AND, UM!

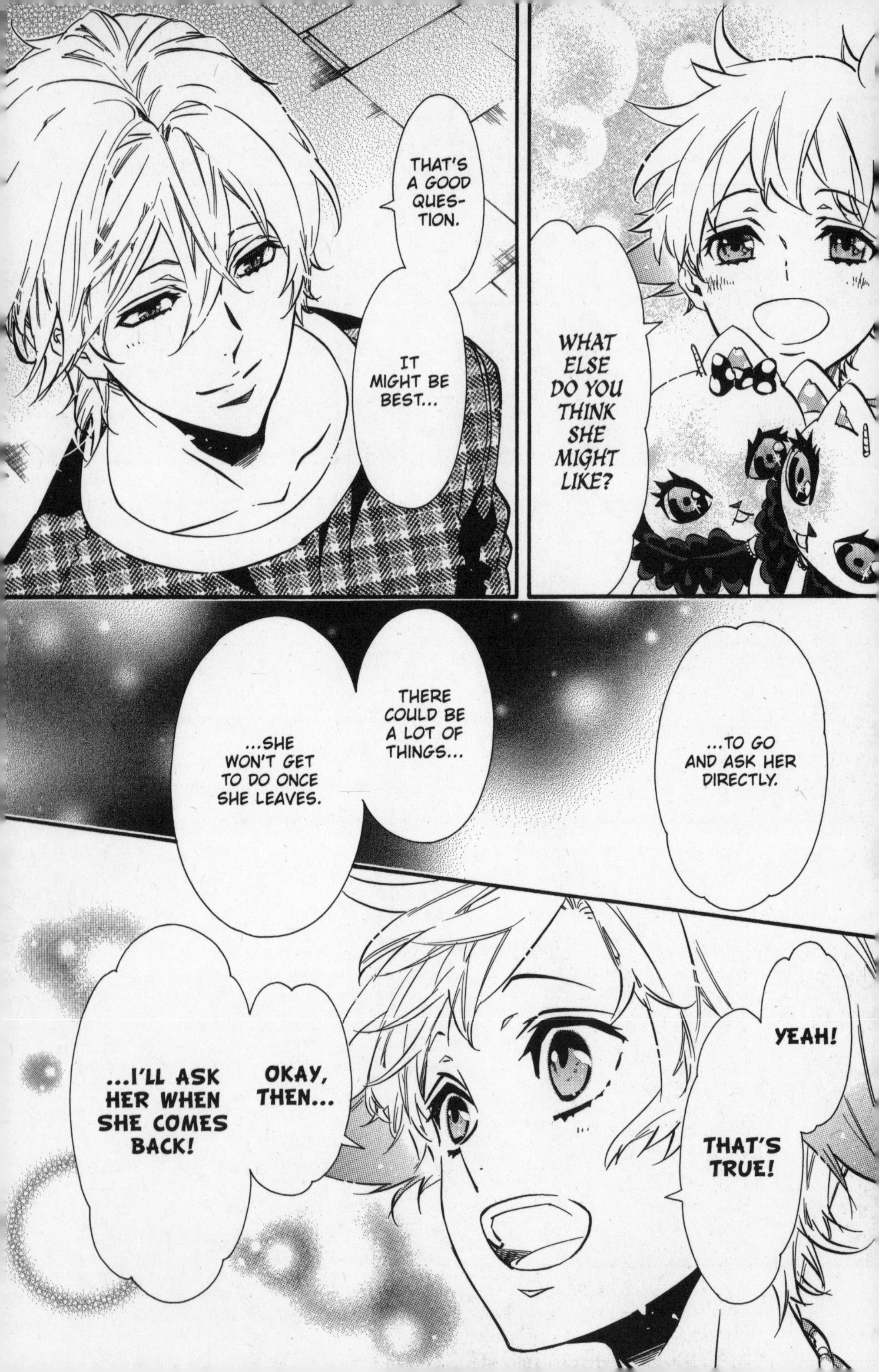
WHAT ELSE DO YOU THINK SHE MIGHT LIKE?
THAT'S A GOOD QUES-TION.
IT MIGHT BE BEST...
...TO GO AND ASK HER DIRECTLY.
THERE COULD BE A LOT OF THINGS...
...SHE WON'T GET TO DO ONCE SHE LEAVES.
YEAH!
THAT'S TRUE!
OKAY, THEN...
...I'LL ASK HER WHEN SHE COMES BACK!

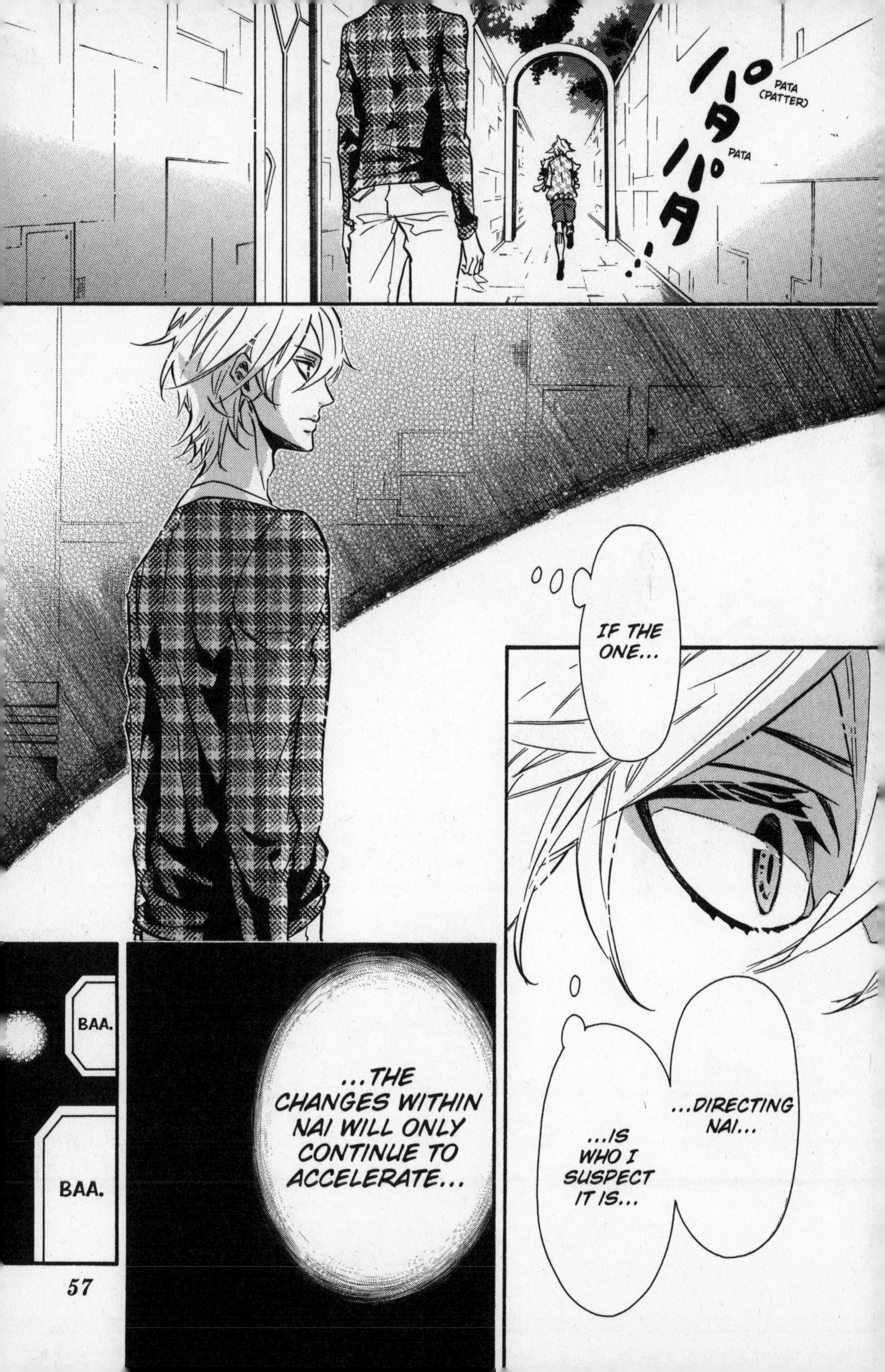
パタ
PATA
(PATTER)
パタ…
PATA
IF THE ONE...
...DIRECTING NAI...
...IS WHO I SUSPECT IT IS...
...THE CHANGES WITHIN NAI WILL ONLY CONTINUE TO ACCELERATE...
BAA.
BAA.

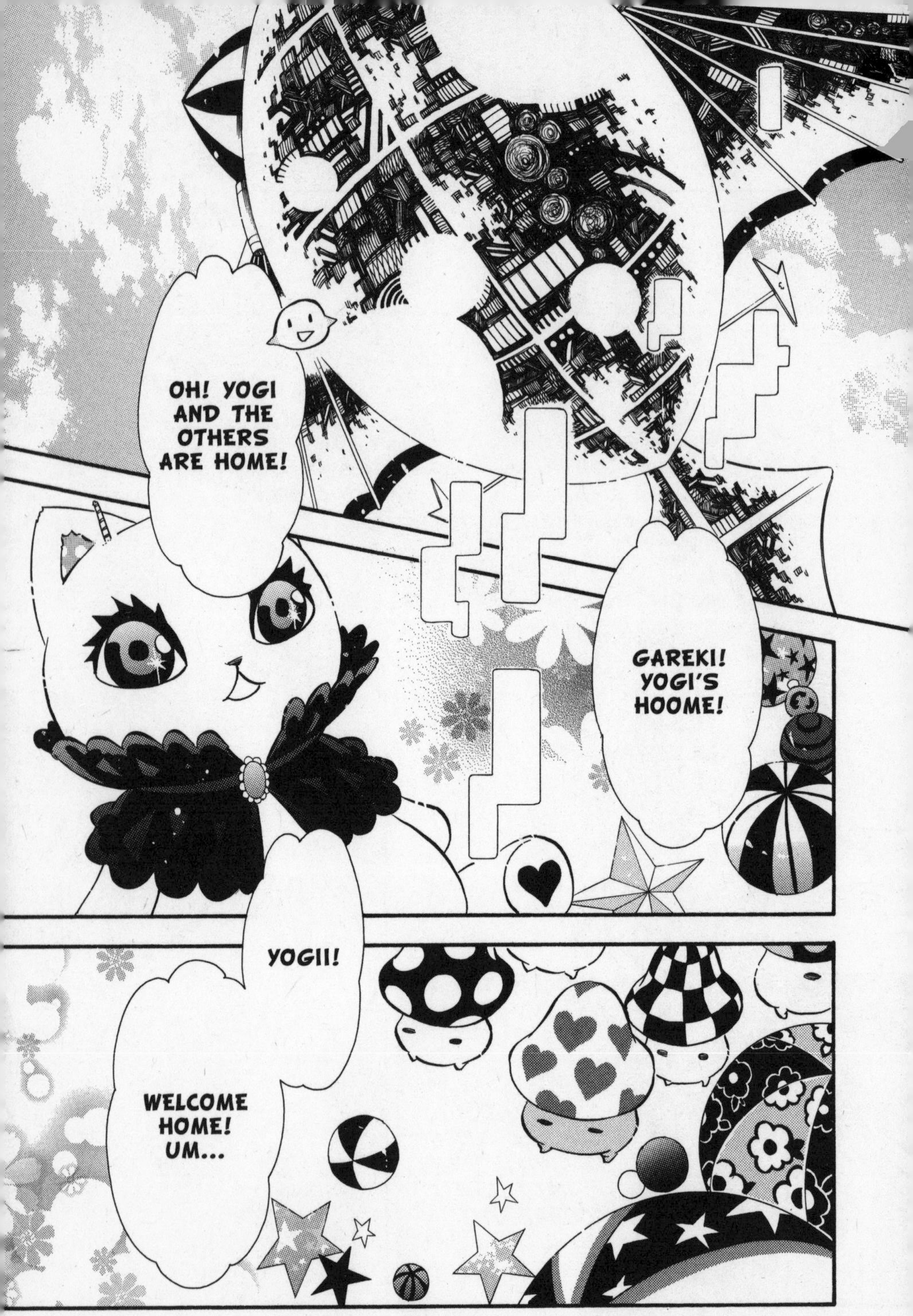
OH! YOGI AND THE OTHERS ARE HOME!
GAREKI! YOGI'S HOOME!
YOGII!
WELCOME HOME! UM...

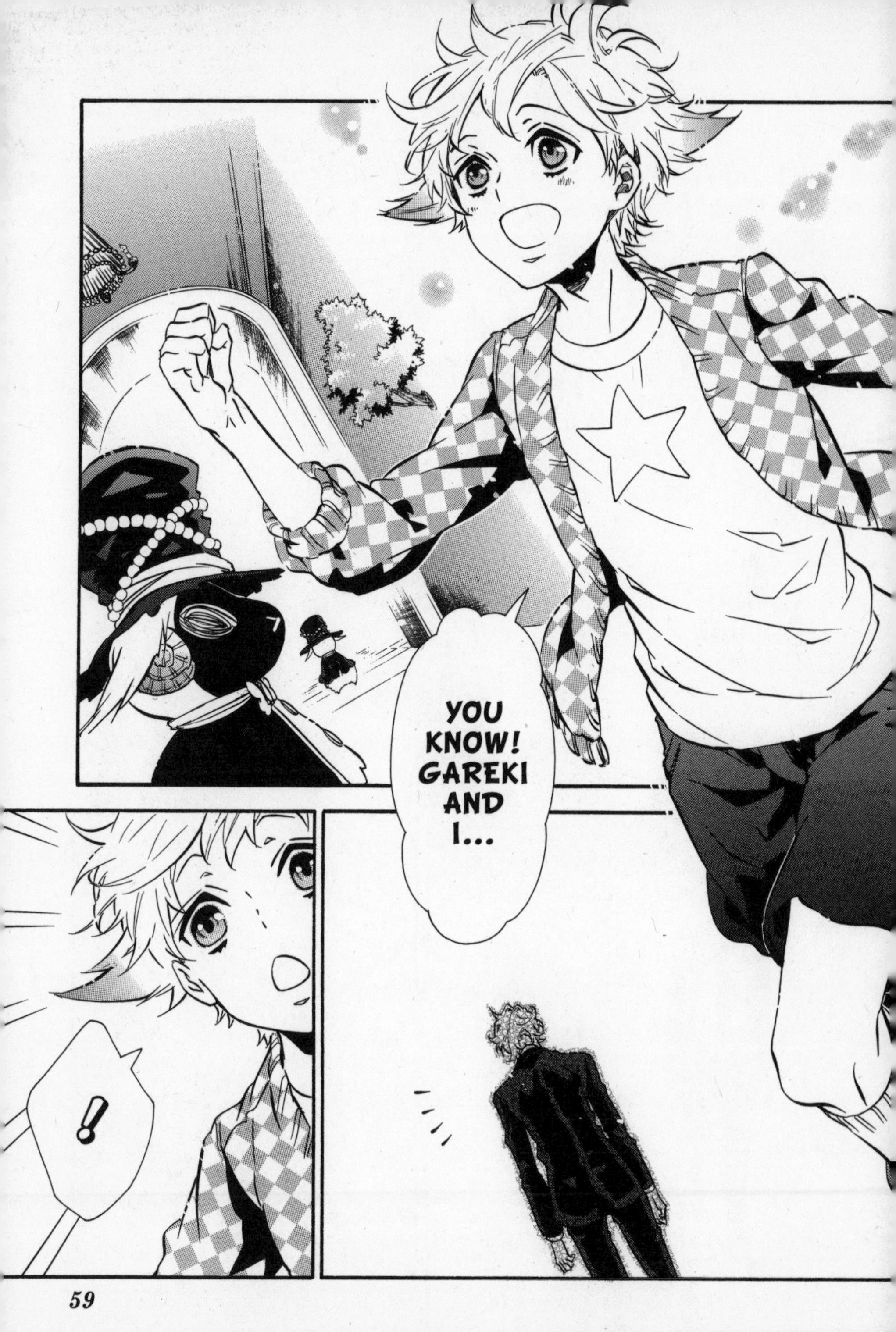
YOU KNOW! GAREKI AND I...
!

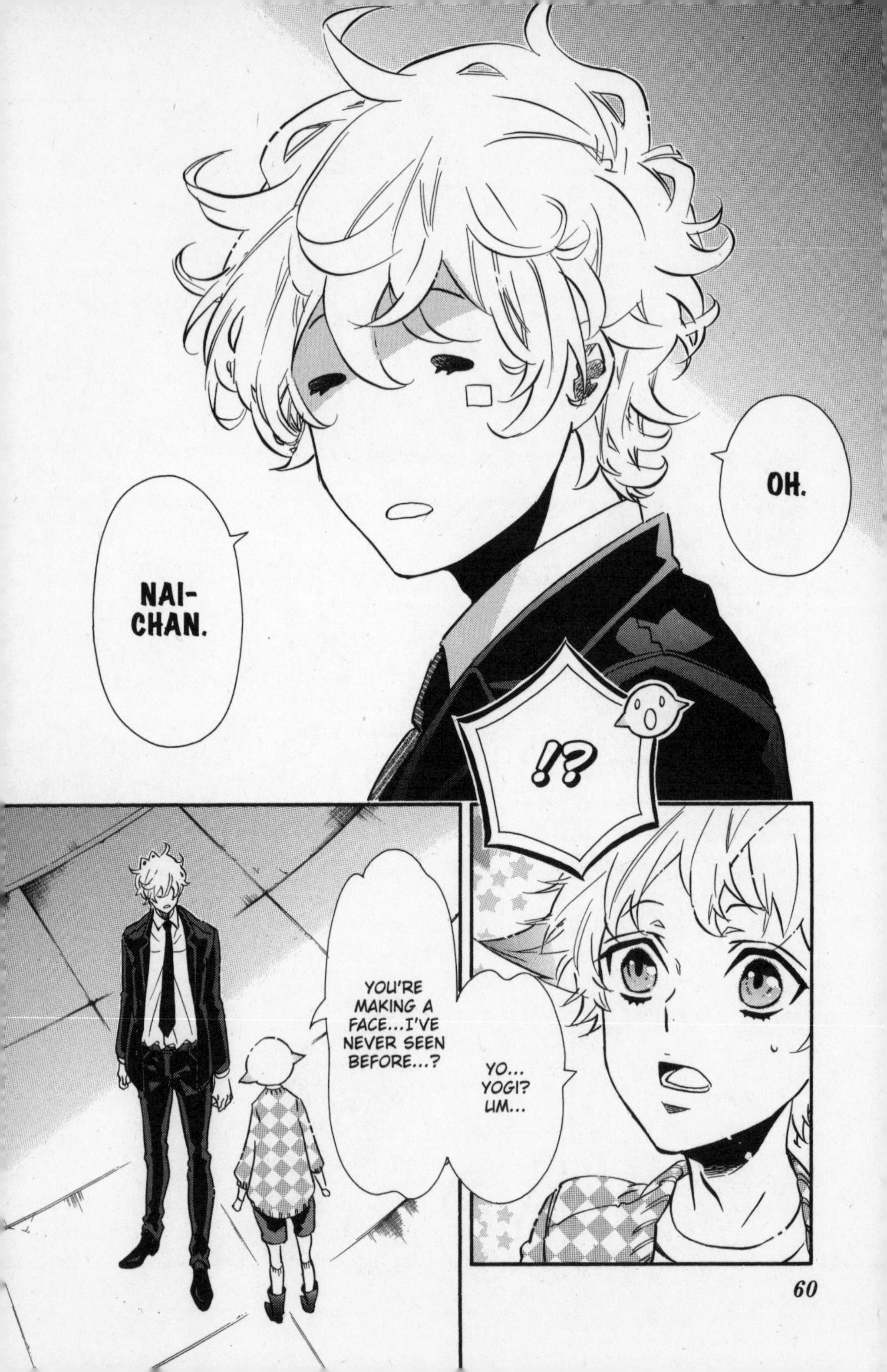
OH.
NAI-CHAN.
!?
YO... YOGI? UM...
YOU'RE MAKING A FACE...I'VE NEVER SEEN BEFORE...?

KARNEVAL

KARNEVAL

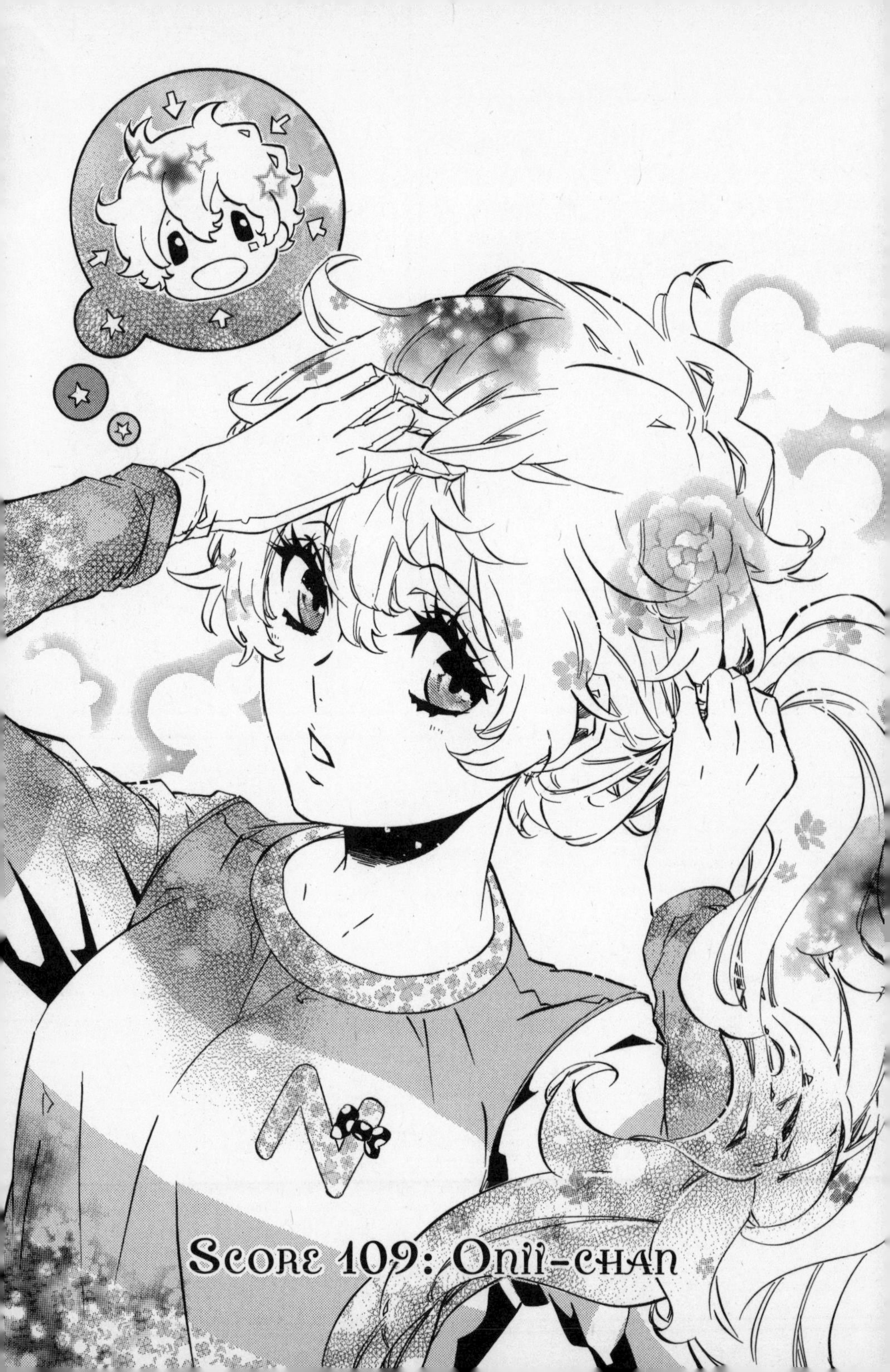
Score 109: Onii-chan

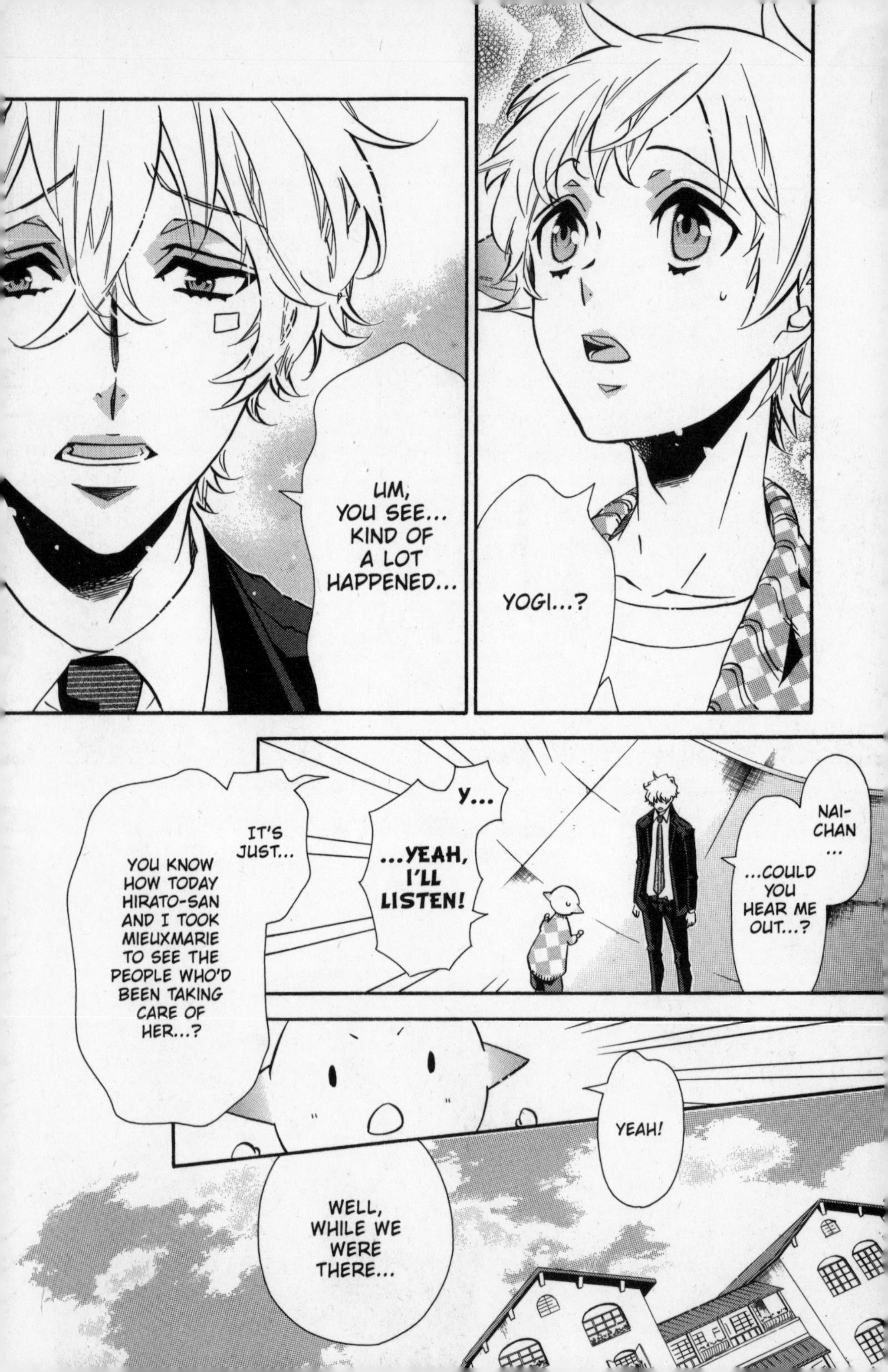
YOGI...?
UM, YOU SEE... KIND OF A LOT HAPPENED...
NAI-CHAN... ...COULD YOU HEAR ME OUT...?
Y...
...YEAH, I'LL LISTEN!
IT'S JUST...
YOU KNOW HOW TODAY HIRATO-SAN AND I TOOK MIEUXMARIE TO SEE THE PEOPLE WHO'D BEEN TAKING CARE OF HER...?
YEAH!
WELL, WHILE WE WERE THERE...

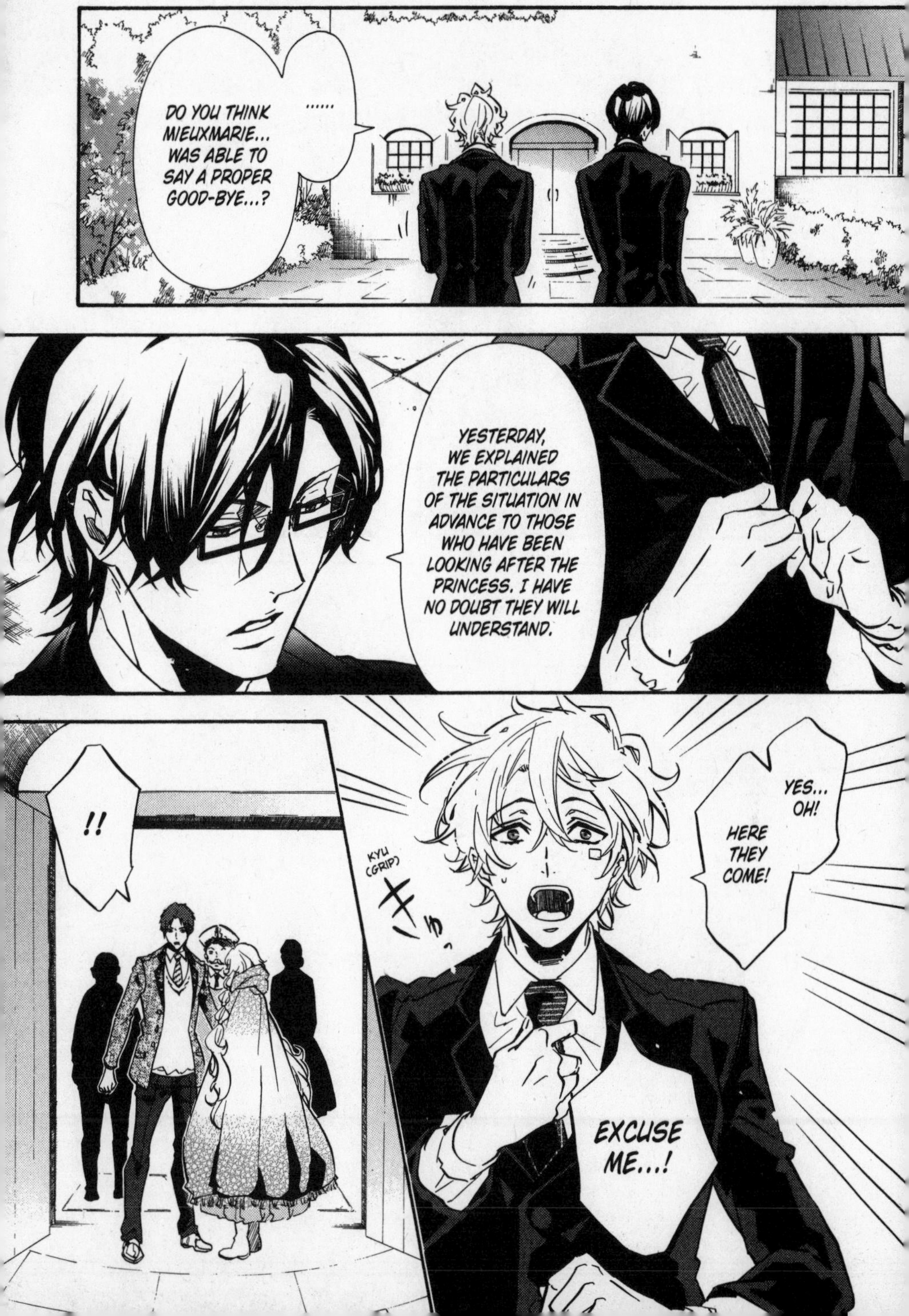
......
DO YOU THINK MIEUXMARIE... WAS ABLE TO SAY A PROPER GOOD-BYE...?
YESTERDAY, WE EXPLAINED THE PARTICULARS OF THE SITUATION IN ADVANCE TO THOSE WHO HAVE BEEN LOOKING AFTER THE PRINCESS. I HAVE NO DOUBT THEY WILL UNDERSTAND.
YES... OH!
HERE THEY COME!
KYU (GRIP)
EXCUSE ME...!
!!

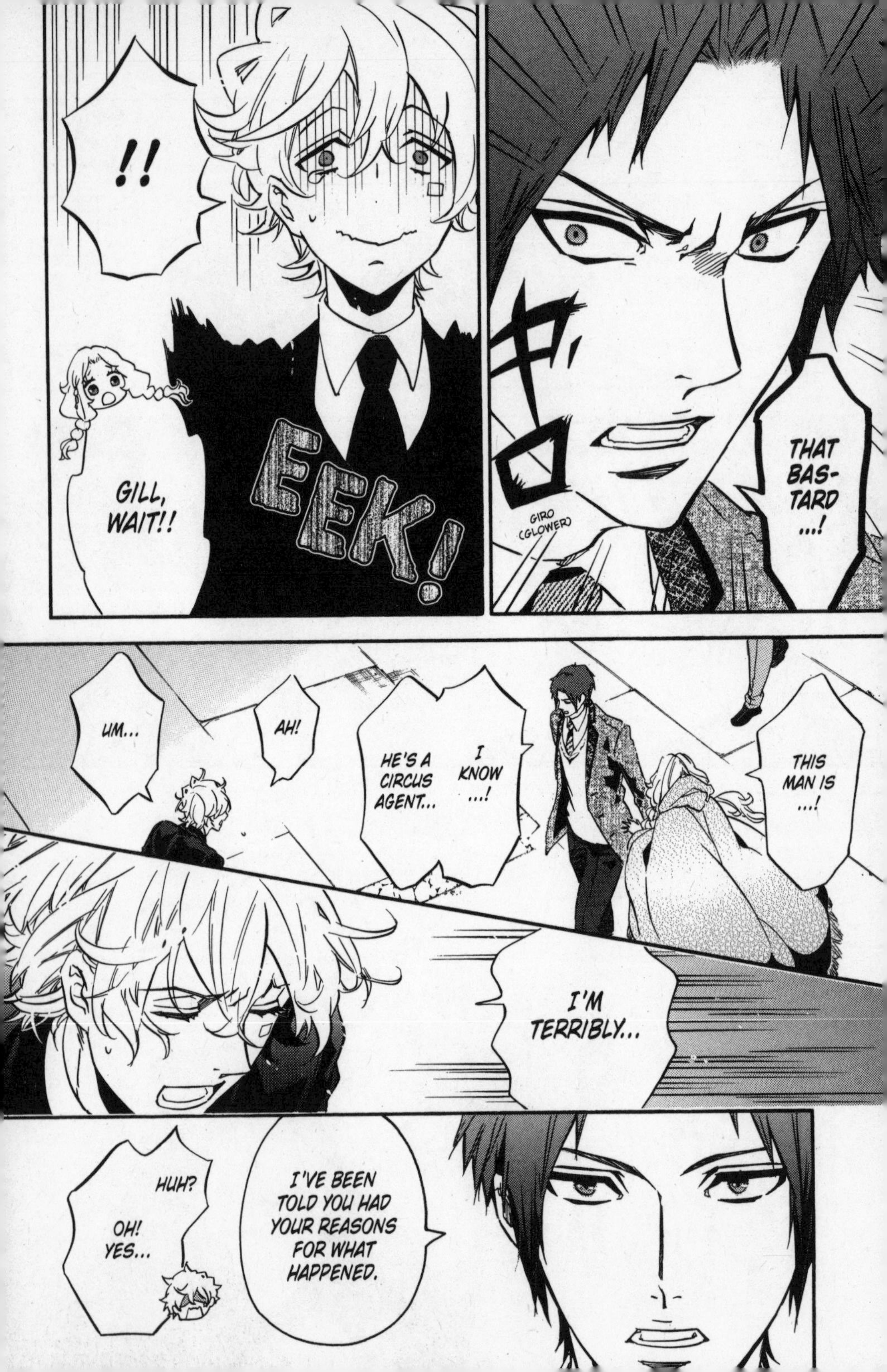
THAT BAS-TARD ...!
GIRO (GLOWER)
!!
EEK!
GILL, WAIT!!
THIS MAN IS ...!
I KNOW ...!
HE'S A CIRCUS AGENT...
AH!
UM...
I'M TERRIBLY...
I'VE BEEN TOLD YOU HAD YOUR REASONS FOR WHAT HAPPENED.
HUH?
OH! YES...

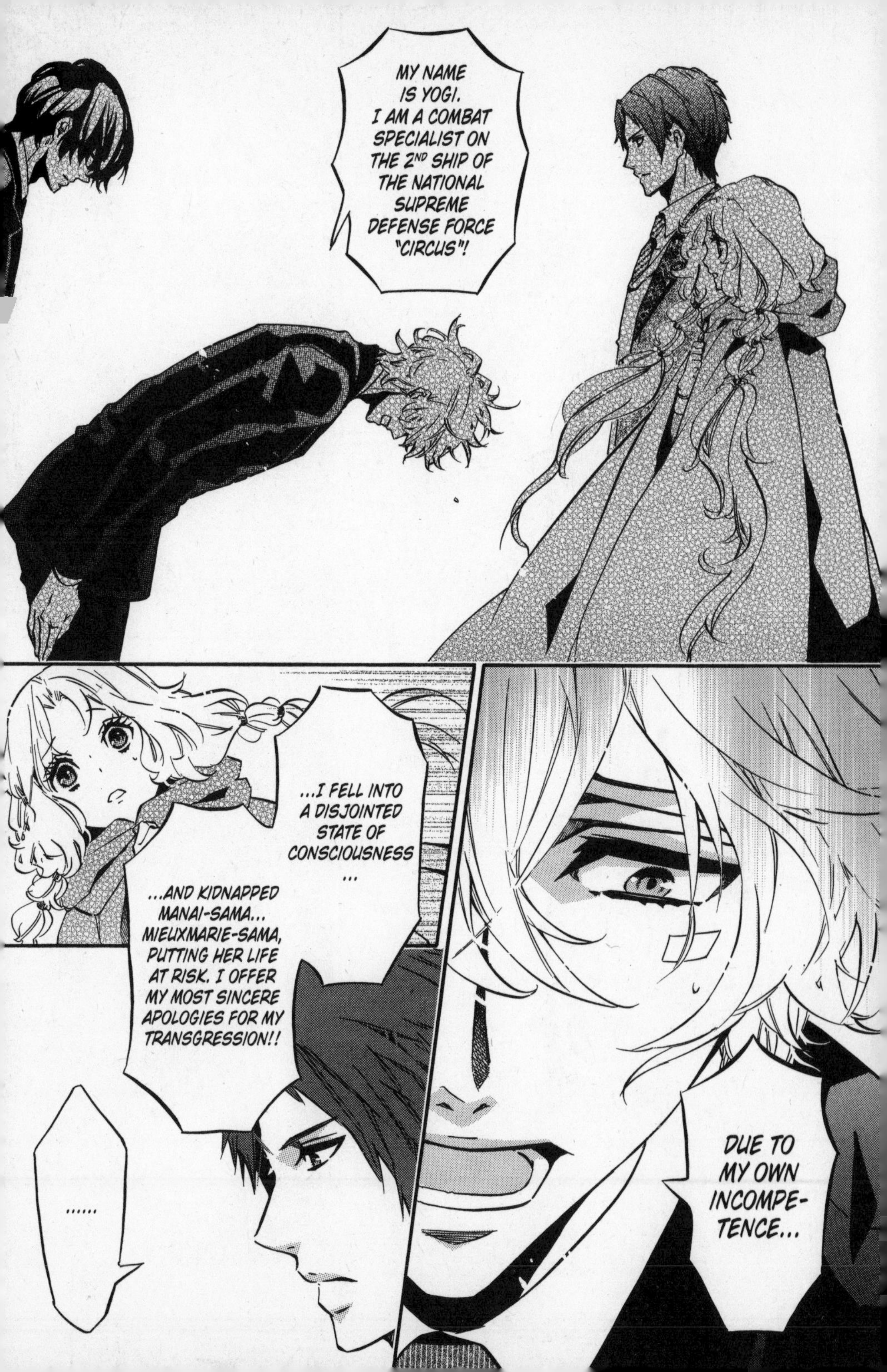
MY NAME IS YOGI. I AM A COMBAT SPECIALIST ON THE 2ND SHIP OF THE NATIONAL SUPREME DEFENSE FORCE "CIRCUS"!
DUE TO MY OWN INCOMPE-TENCE...
...I FELL INTO A DISJOINTED STATE OF CONSCIOUSNESS...
...AND KIDNAPPED MANAI-SAMA... MIEUXMARIE-SAMA, PUTTING HER LIFE AT RISK. I OFFER MY MOST SINCERE APOLOGIES FOR MY TRANSGRESSION!!
......

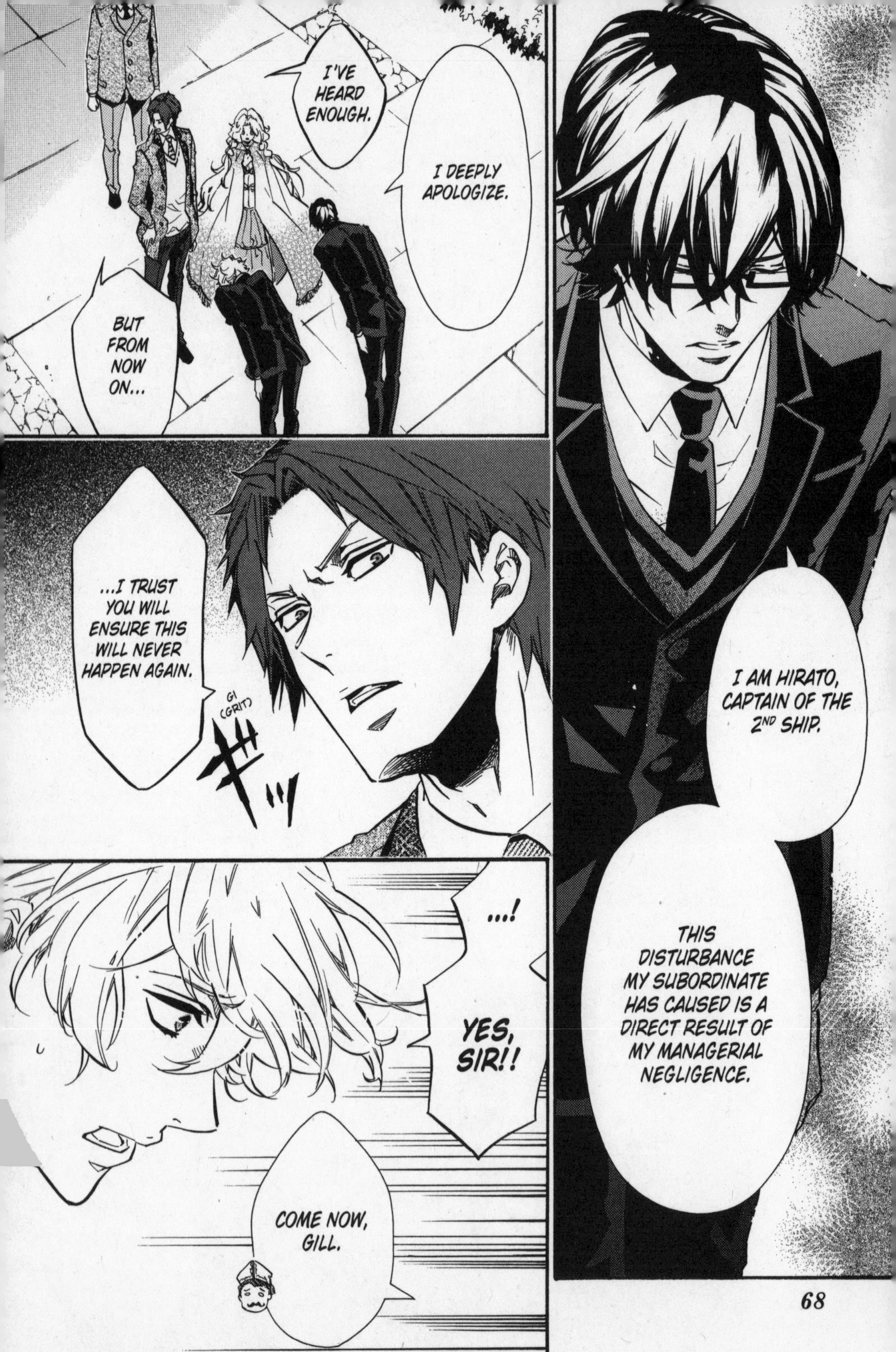
I AM HIRATO, CAPTAIN OF THE 2ND SHIP.
THIS DISTURBANCE MY SUBORDINATE HAS CAUSED IS A DIRECT RESULT OF MY MANAGERIAL NEGLIGENCE.
I DEEPLY APOLOGIZE.
I'VE HEARD ENOUGH.
BUT FROM NOW ON...
...I TRUST YOU WILL ENSURE THIS WILL NEVER HAPPEN AGAIN.
GI (GRIT)
...!
YES, SIR!!
COME NOW, GILL.

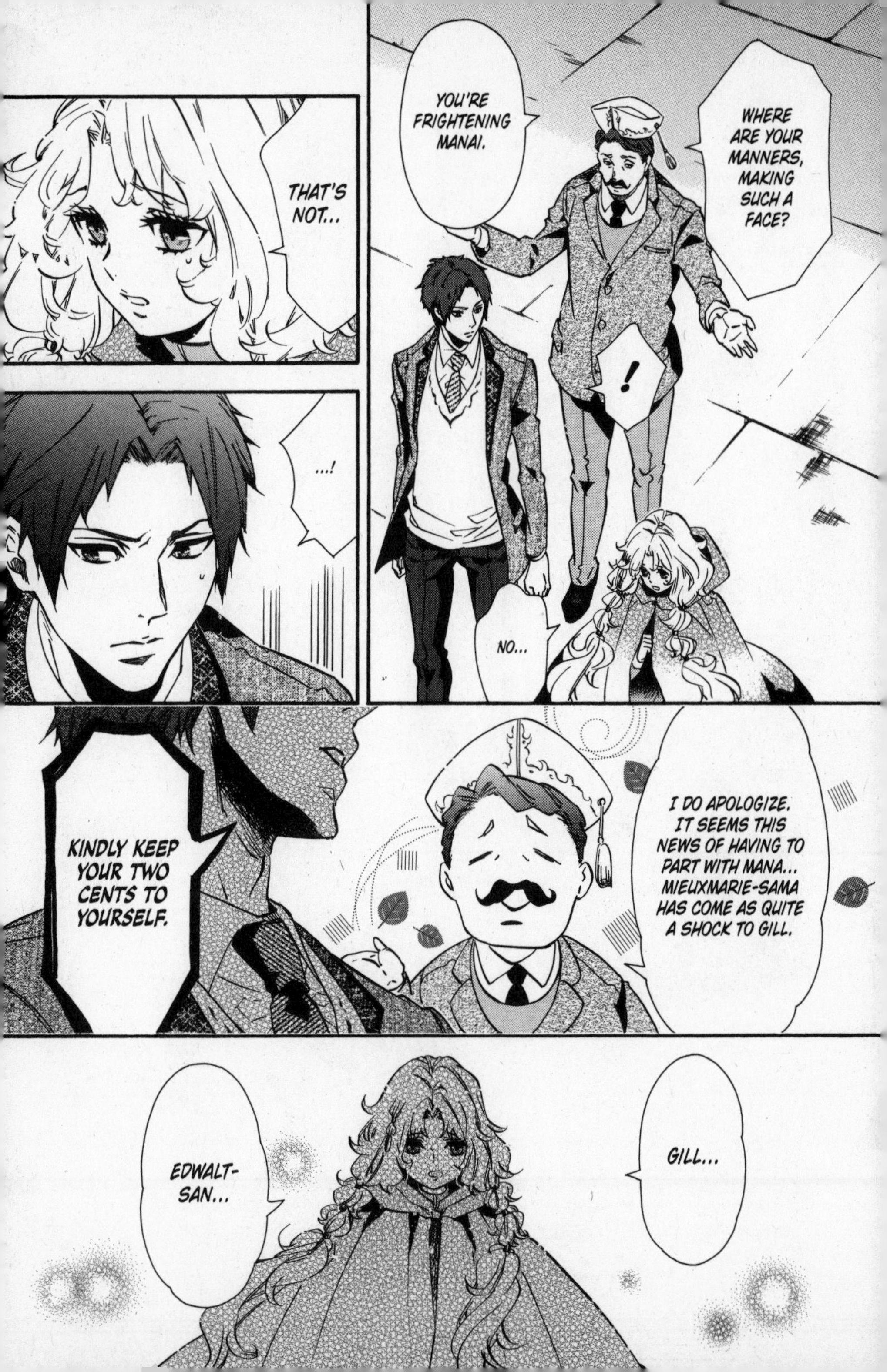
WHERE ARE YOUR MANNERS, MAKING SUCH A FACE?
YOU'RE FRIGHTENING MANAI.
!
NO...
THAT'S NOT...
...!
I DO APOLOGIZE. IT SEEMS THIS NEWS OF HAVING TO PART WITH MANA... MIEUXMARIE-SAMA HAS COME AS QUITE A SHOCK TO GILL.
KINDLY KEEP YOUR TWO CENTS TO YOURSELF.
GILL...
EDWALT-SAN...

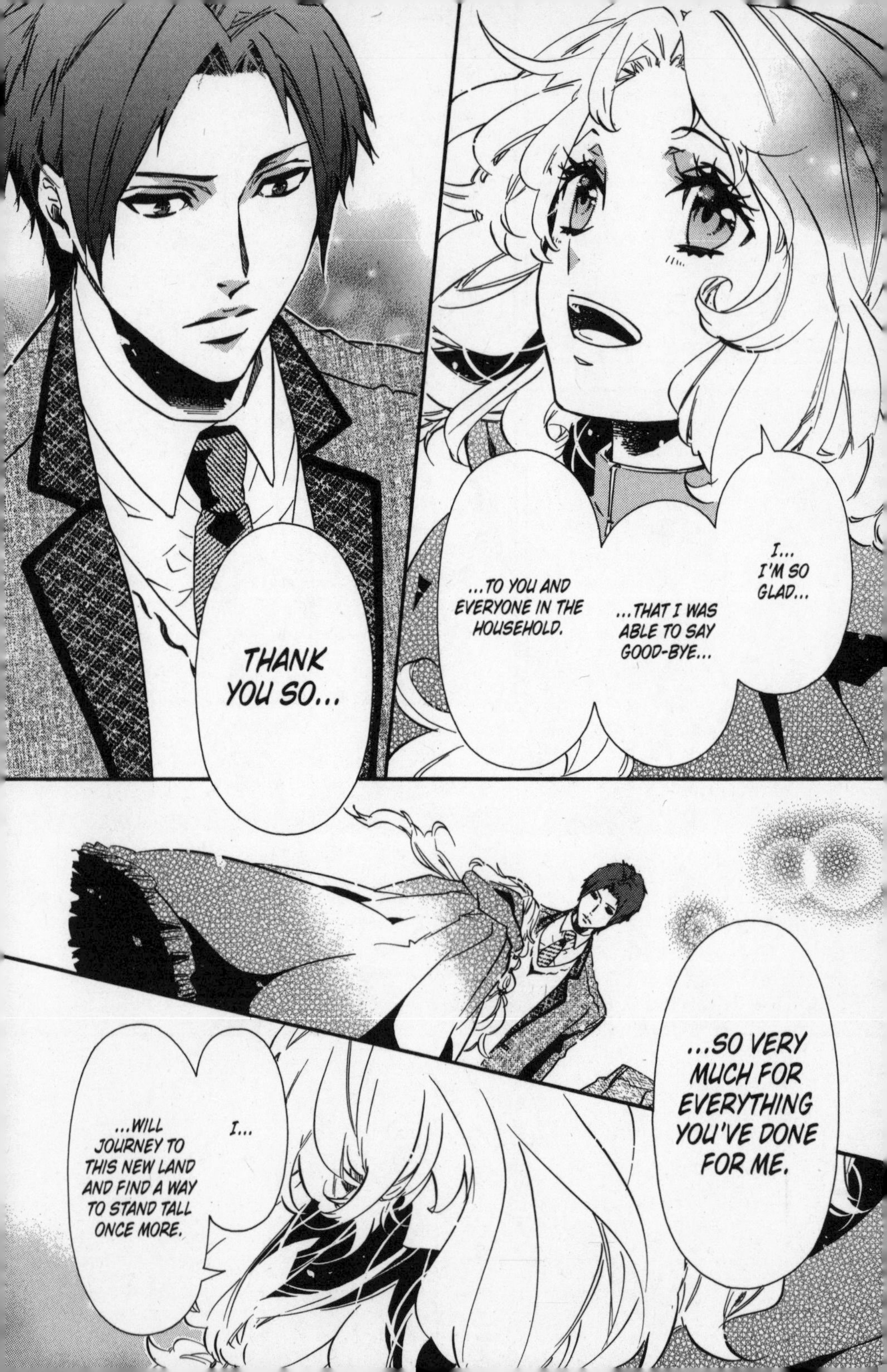
I... I'M SO GLAD...
...THAT I WAS ABLE TO SAY GOOD-BYE...
...TO YOU AND EVERYONE IN THE HOUSEHOLD.
THANK YOU SO...
...SO VERY MUCH FOR EVERYTHING YOU'VE DONE FOR ME.
I...
...WILL JOURNEY TO THIS NEW LAND AND FIND A WAY TO STAND TALL ONCE MORE.

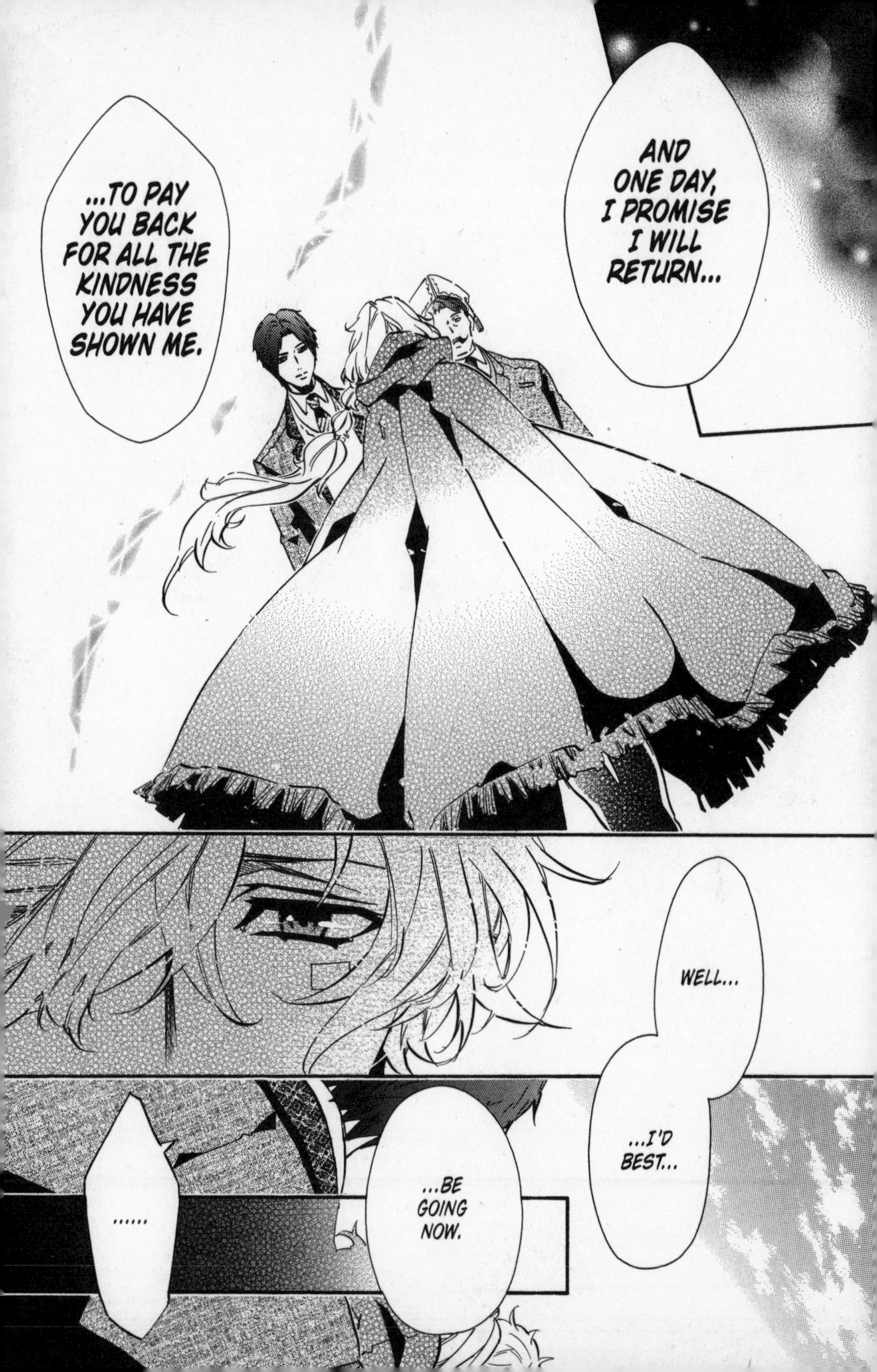
AND ONE DAY, I PROMISE I WILL RETURN...
...TO PAY YOU BACK FOR ALL THE KINDNESS YOU HAVE SHOWN ME.
WELL...
...I'D BEST...
...BE GOING NOW.
......

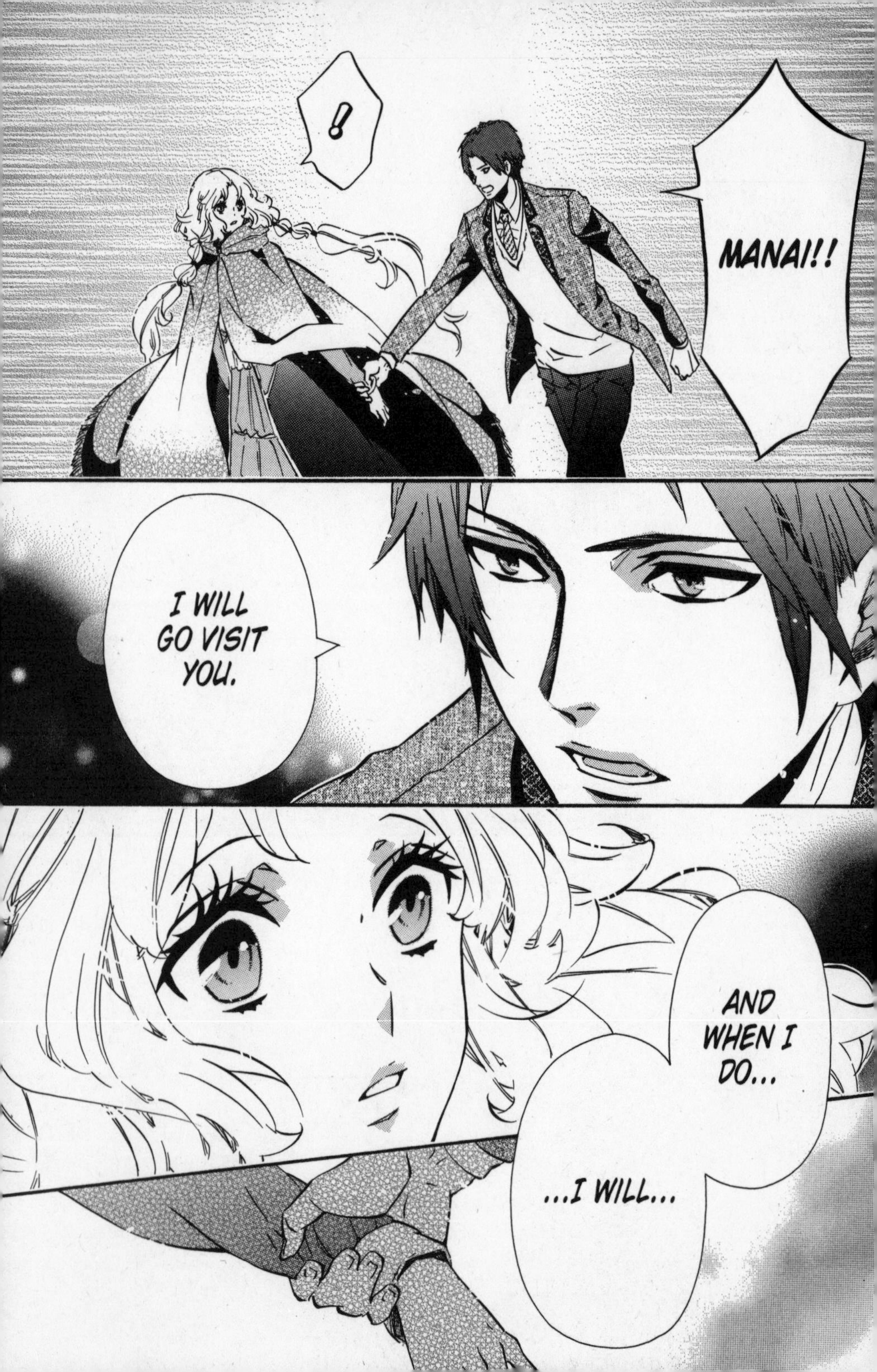
MANAI!!
!
I WILL GO VISIT YOU.
AND WHEN I DO...
...I WILL...

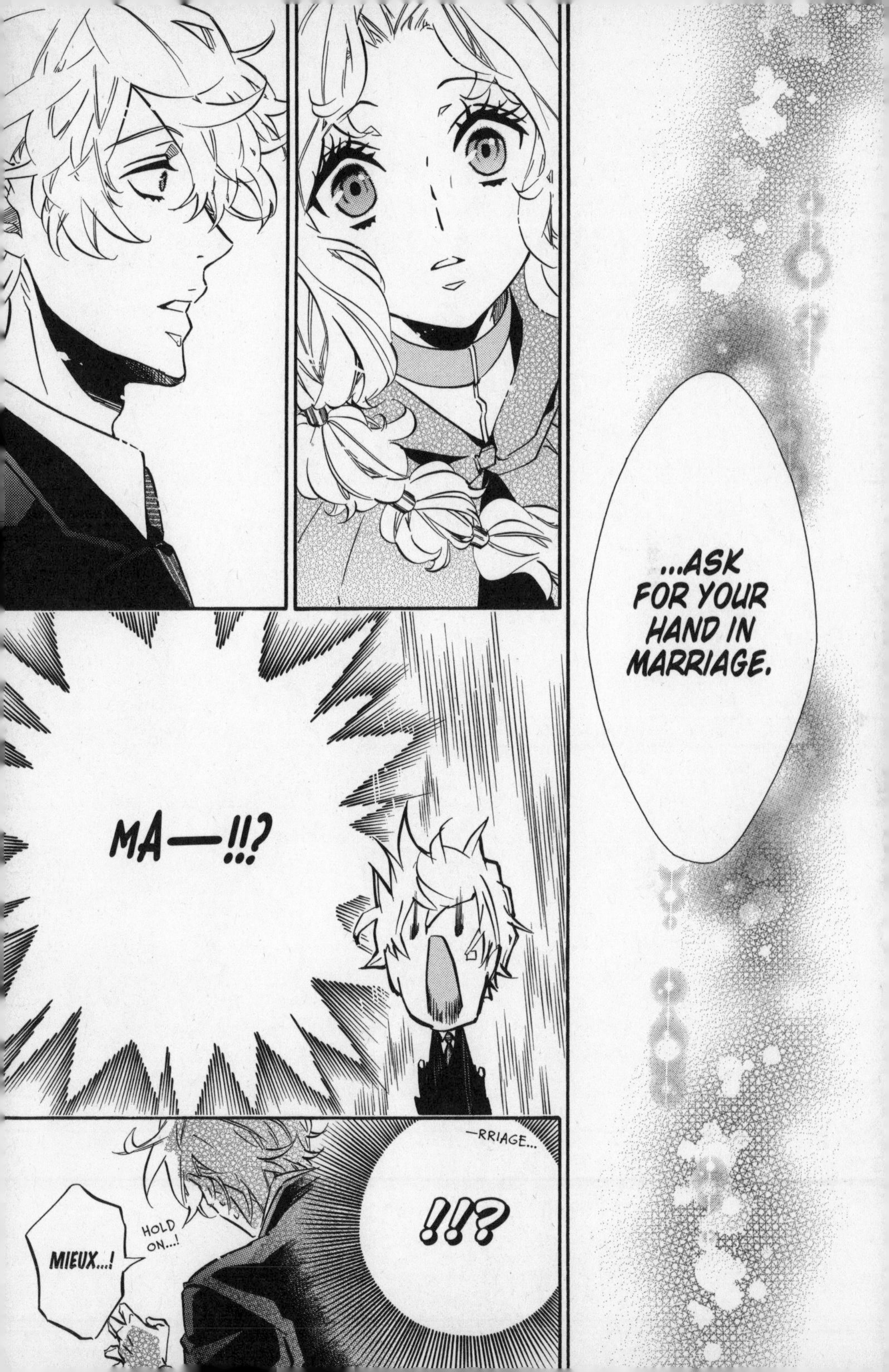
...ASK FOR YOUR HAND IN MARRIAGE.
MA—!!?
—RRIAGE...
!!?
HOLD ON...!
MIEUX...!

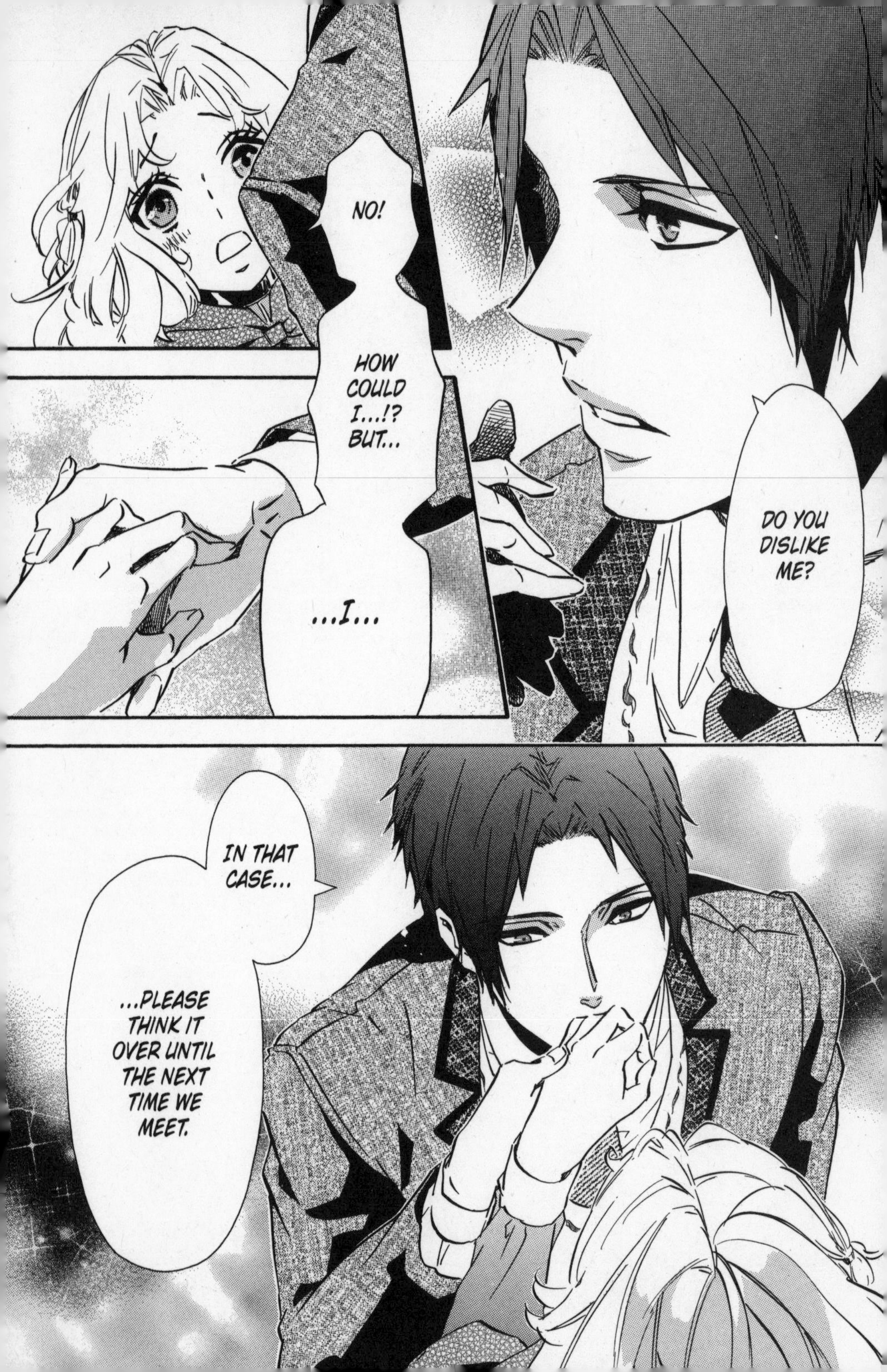
DO YOU DISLIKE ME?
NO!
HOW COULD I...!? BUT...
...I...
IN THAT CASE...
...PLEASE THINK IT OVER UNTIL THE NEXT TIME WE MEET.

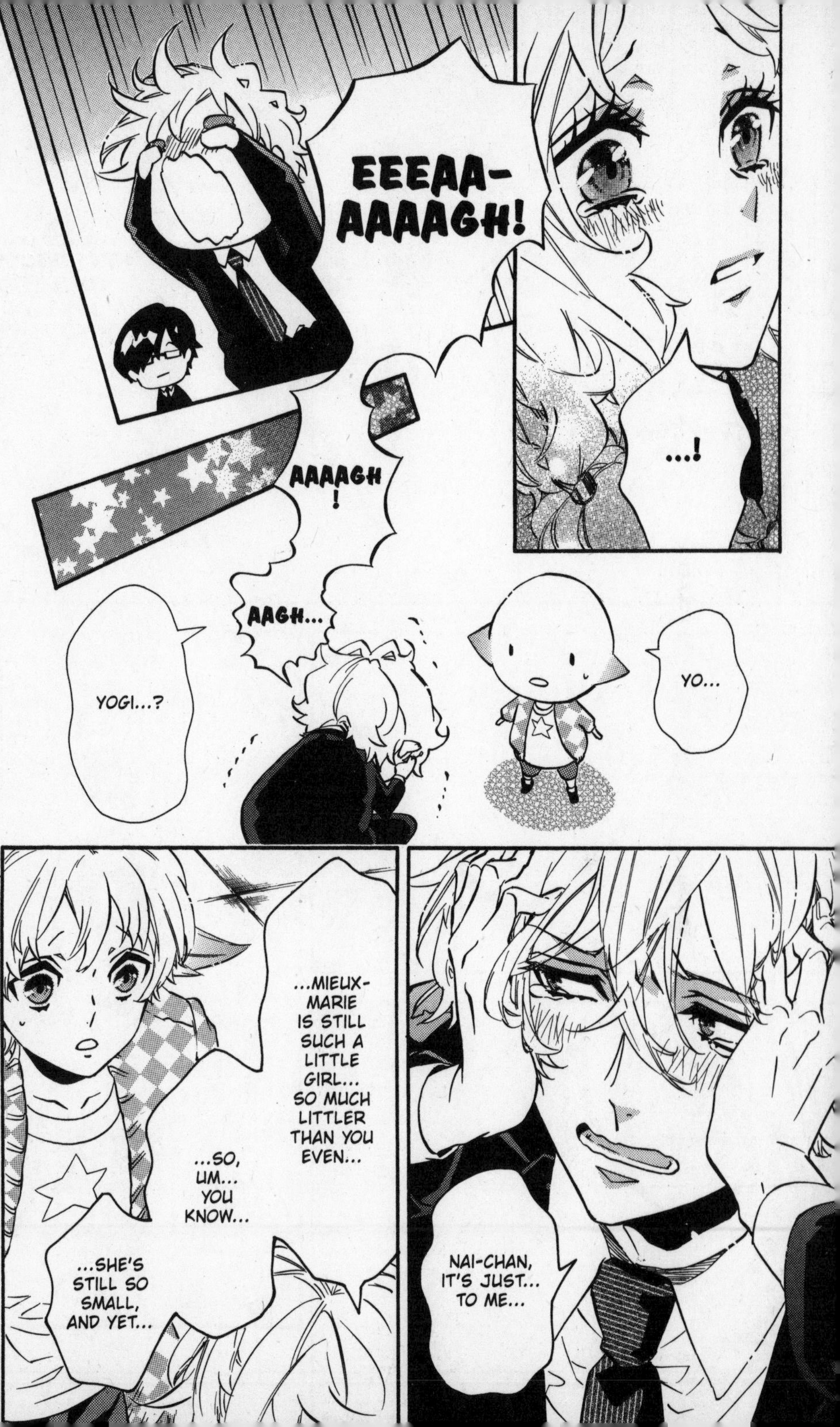

EEEAA-AAAAGH!
...!
AAAAGH!
AAGH...
YO...
YOGI...?
NAI-CHAN, IT'S JUST... TO ME...
...MIEUX-MARIE IS STILL SUCH A LITTLE GIRL... SO MUCH LITTLER THAN YOU EVEN...
...SO, UM... YOU KNOW...
...SHE'S STILL SO SMALL, AND YET...

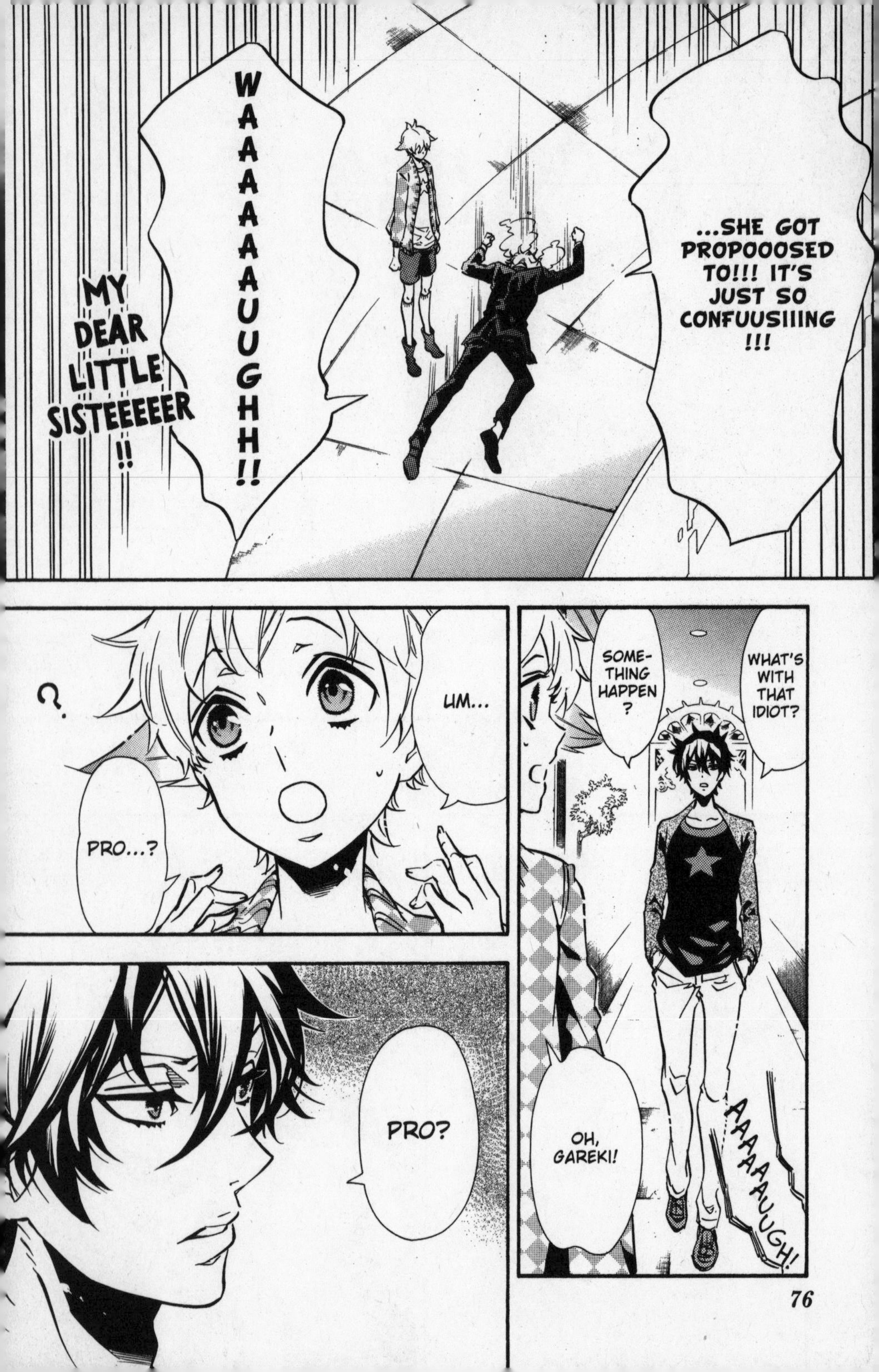
...SHE GOT PROPOOOSED TO!!! IT'S JUST SO CONFUUSIIING!!!
WAAAAAAAAUUGHH!!
MY DEAR LITTLE SISTEEEEER!!
WHAT'S WITH THAT IDIOT?
SOME-THING HAPPEN?
OH, GAREKI!
AAAAAAUUGH!
UM...
PRO...?
PRO?

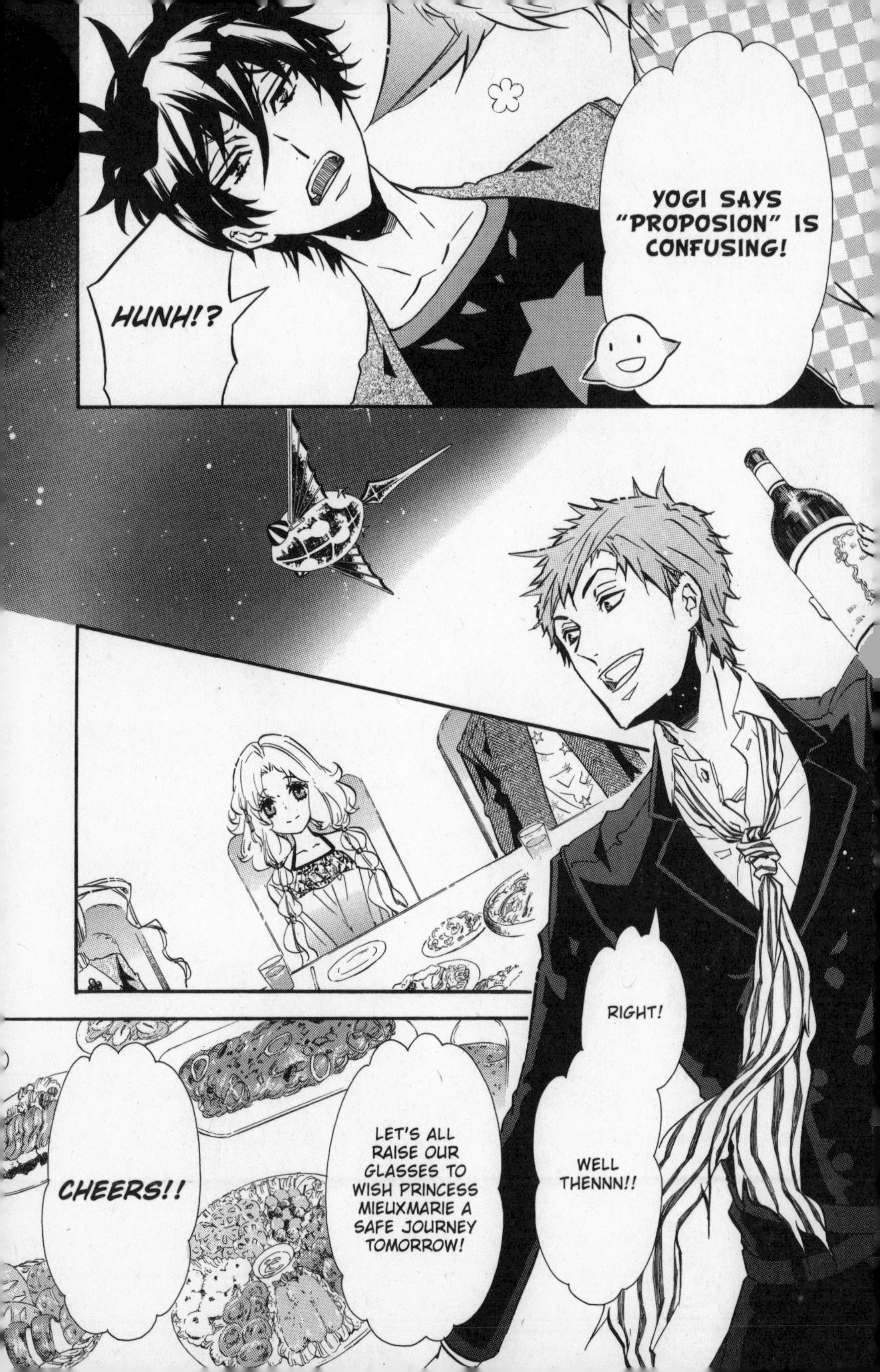
YOGI SAYS "PROPOSION" IS CONFUSING!
HUNH!?
RIGHT!
WELL THENNN!!
LET'S ALL RAISE OUR GLASSES TO WISH PRINCESS MIEUXMARIE A SAFE JOURNEY TOMORROW!
CHEERS!!

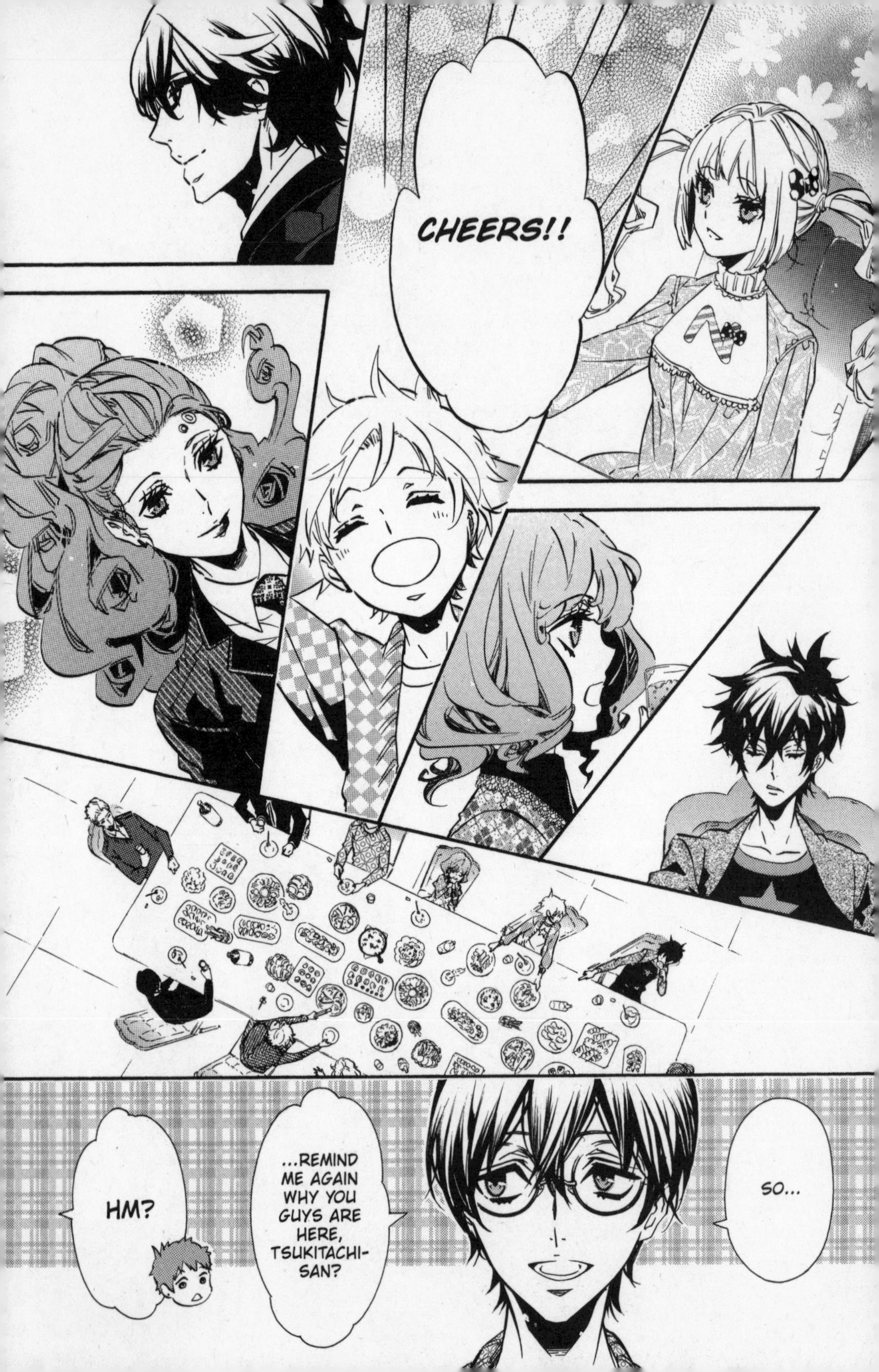
CHEERS!!
SO...
...REMIND ME AGAIN WHY YOU GUYS ARE HERE, TSUKITACHI-SAN?
HM?

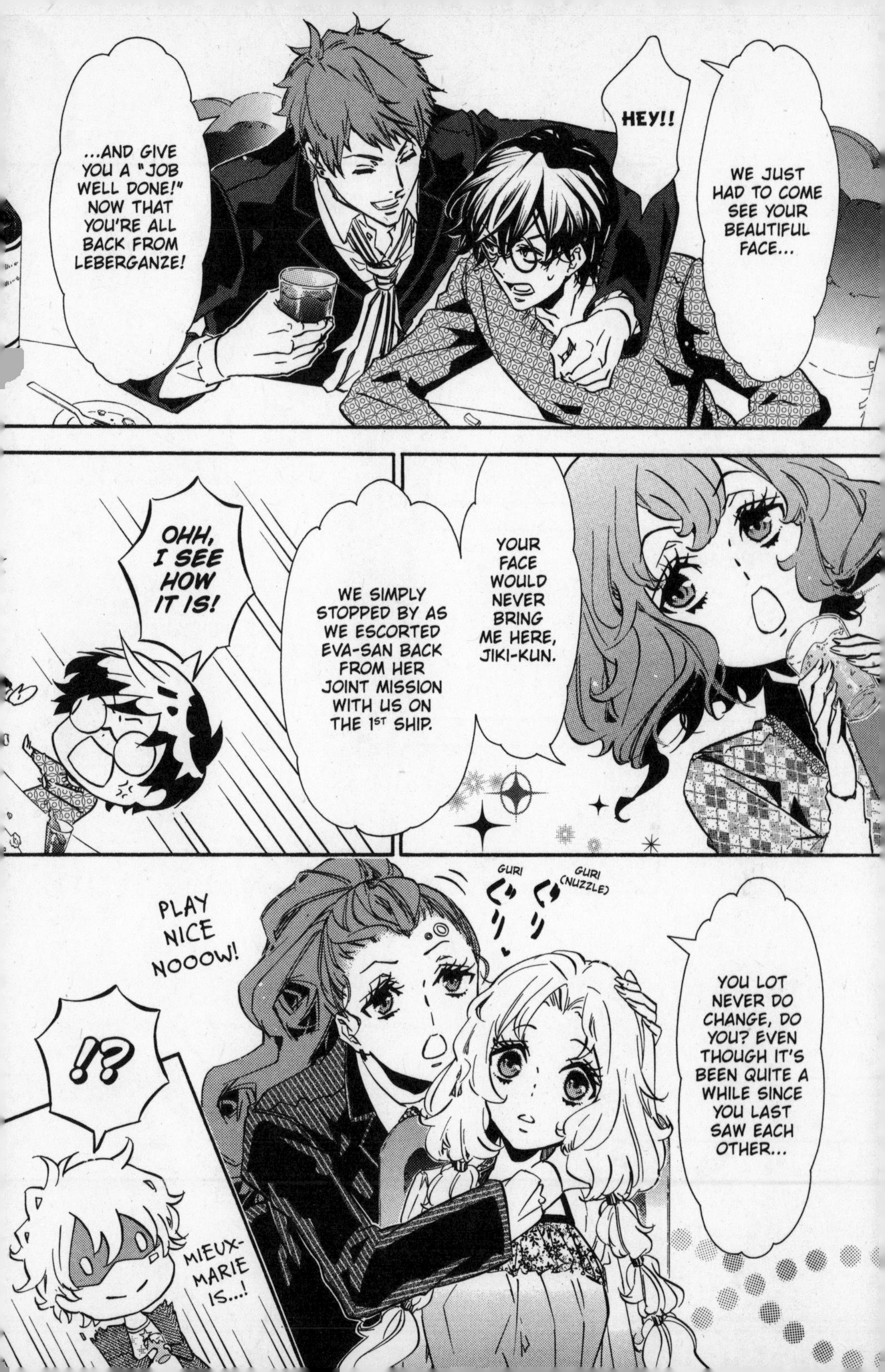
WE JUST HAD TO COME SEE YOUR BEAUTIFUL FACE...
HEY!!
...AND GIVE YOU A "JOB WELL DONE!" NOW THAT YOU'RE ALL BACK FROM LEBERGANZE!
YOUR FACE WOULD NEVER BRING ME HERE, JIKI-KUN.
WE SIMPLY STOPPED BY AS WE ESCORTED EVA-SAN BACK FROM HER JOINT MISSION WITH US ON THE 1ST SHIP.
OHH, I SEE HOW IT IS!
YOU LOT NEVER DO CHANGE, DO YOU? EVEN THOUGH IT'S BEEN QUITE A WHILE SINCE YOU LAST SAW EACH OTHER...
GURI GURI (NUZZLE)
PLAY NICE NOOOW!
!?
MIEUX-MARIE IS...!

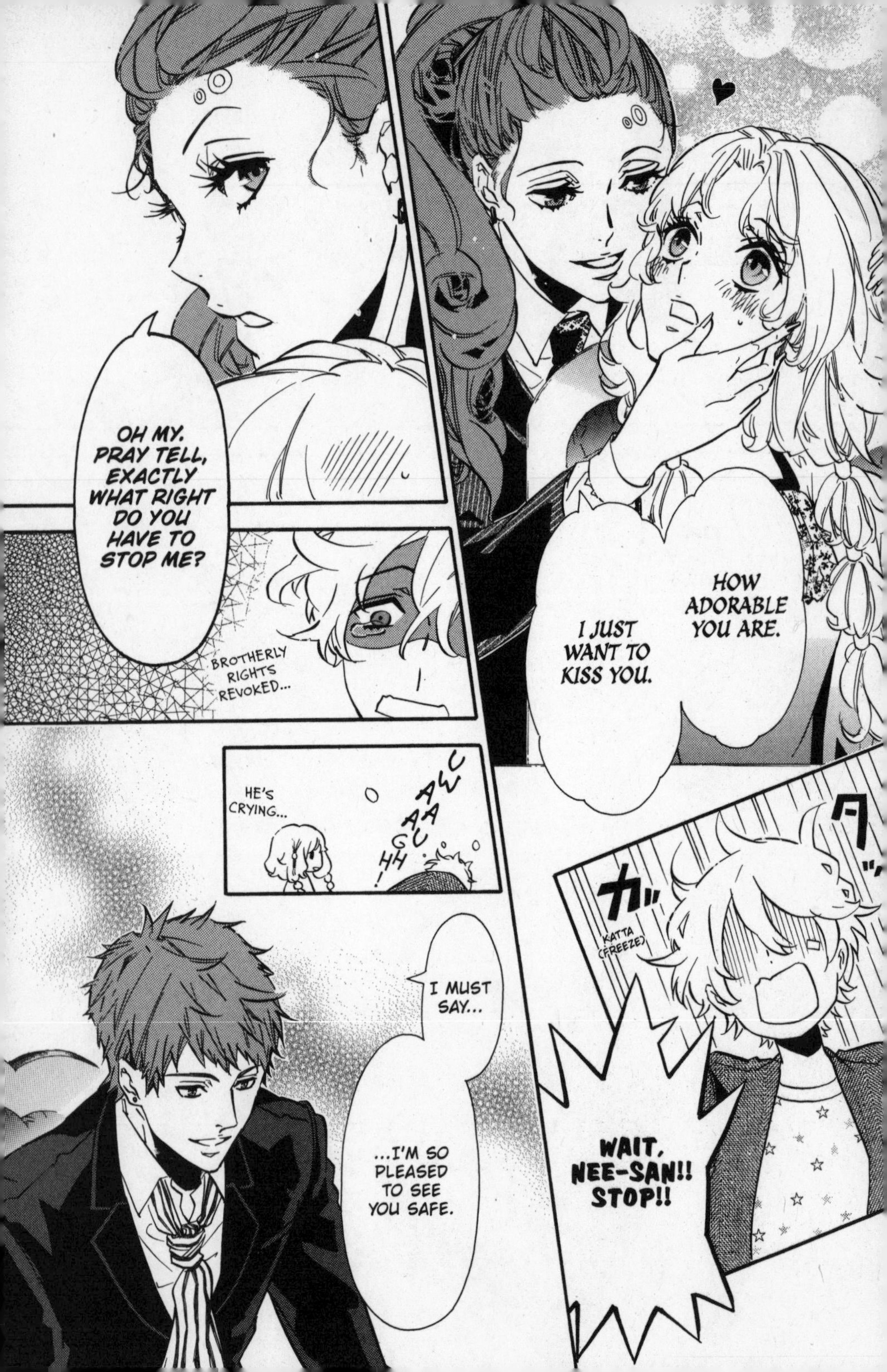
HOW ADORABLE YOU ARE.
I JUST WANT TO KISS YOU.
カッ
KATTA (FREEZE)
WAIT, NEE-SAN!! STOP!!
OH MY. PRAY TELL, EXACTLY WHAT RIGHT DO YOU HAVE TO STOP ME?
BROTHERLY RIGHTS REVOKED...
UWAAAAUGHH!
HE'S CRYING...
I MUST SAY...
...I'M SO PLEASED TO SEE YOU SAFE.

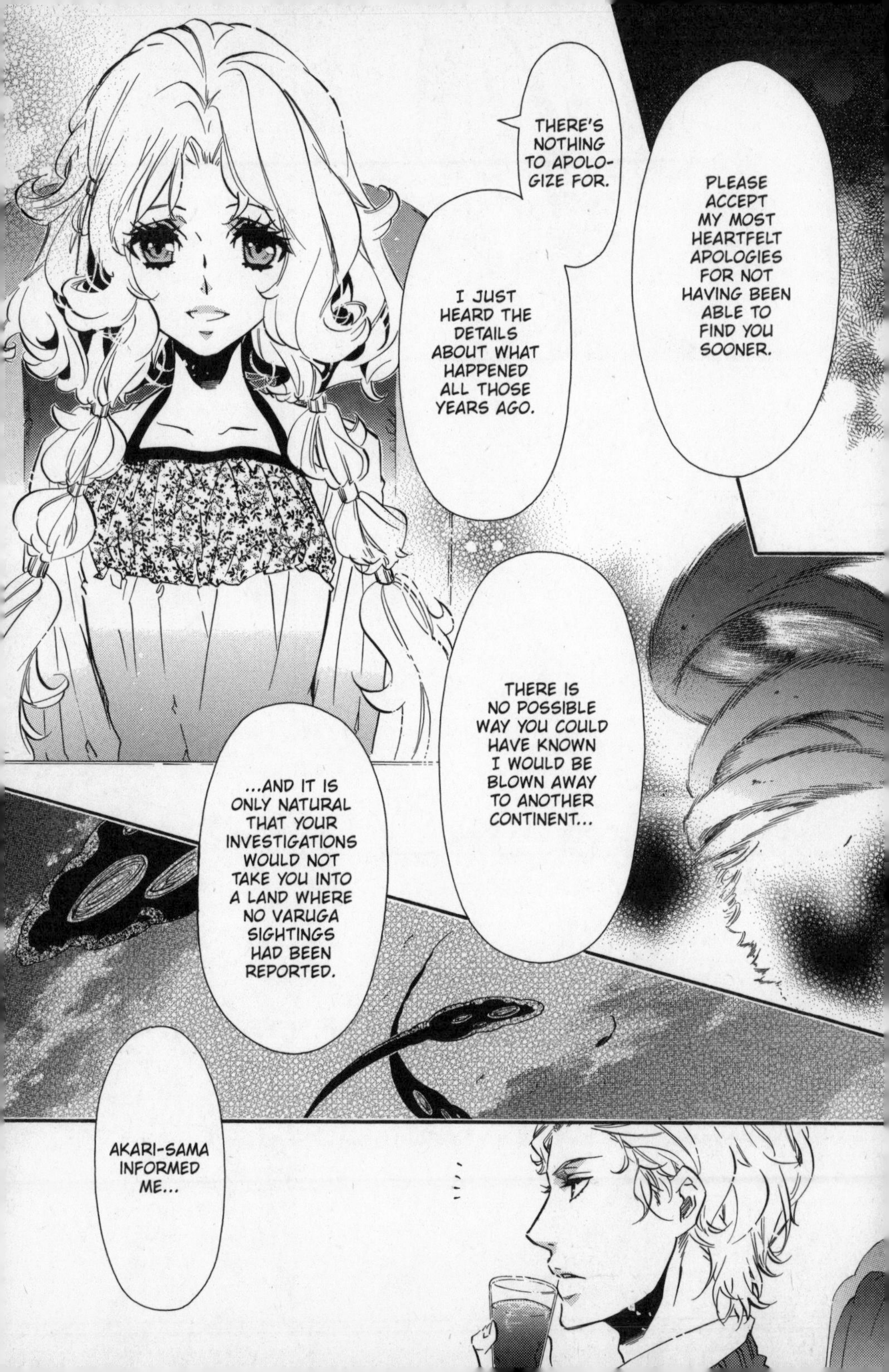
PLEASE ACCEPT MY MOST HEARTFELT APOLOGIES FOR NOT HAVING BEEN ABLE TO FIND YOU SOONER.
THERE'S NOTHING TO APOLOGIZE FOR.
I JUST HEARD THE DETAILS ABOUT WHAT HAPPENED ALL THOSE YEARS AGO.
THERE IS NO POSSIBLE WAY YOU COULD HAVE KNOWN I WOULD BE BLOWN AWAY TO ANOTHER CONTINENT...
...AND IT IS ONLY NATURAL THAT YOUR INVESTIGATIONS WOULD NOT TAKE YOU INTO A LAND WHERE NO VARUGA SIGHTINGS HAD BEEN REPORTED.
...
AKARI-SAMA INFORMED ME...

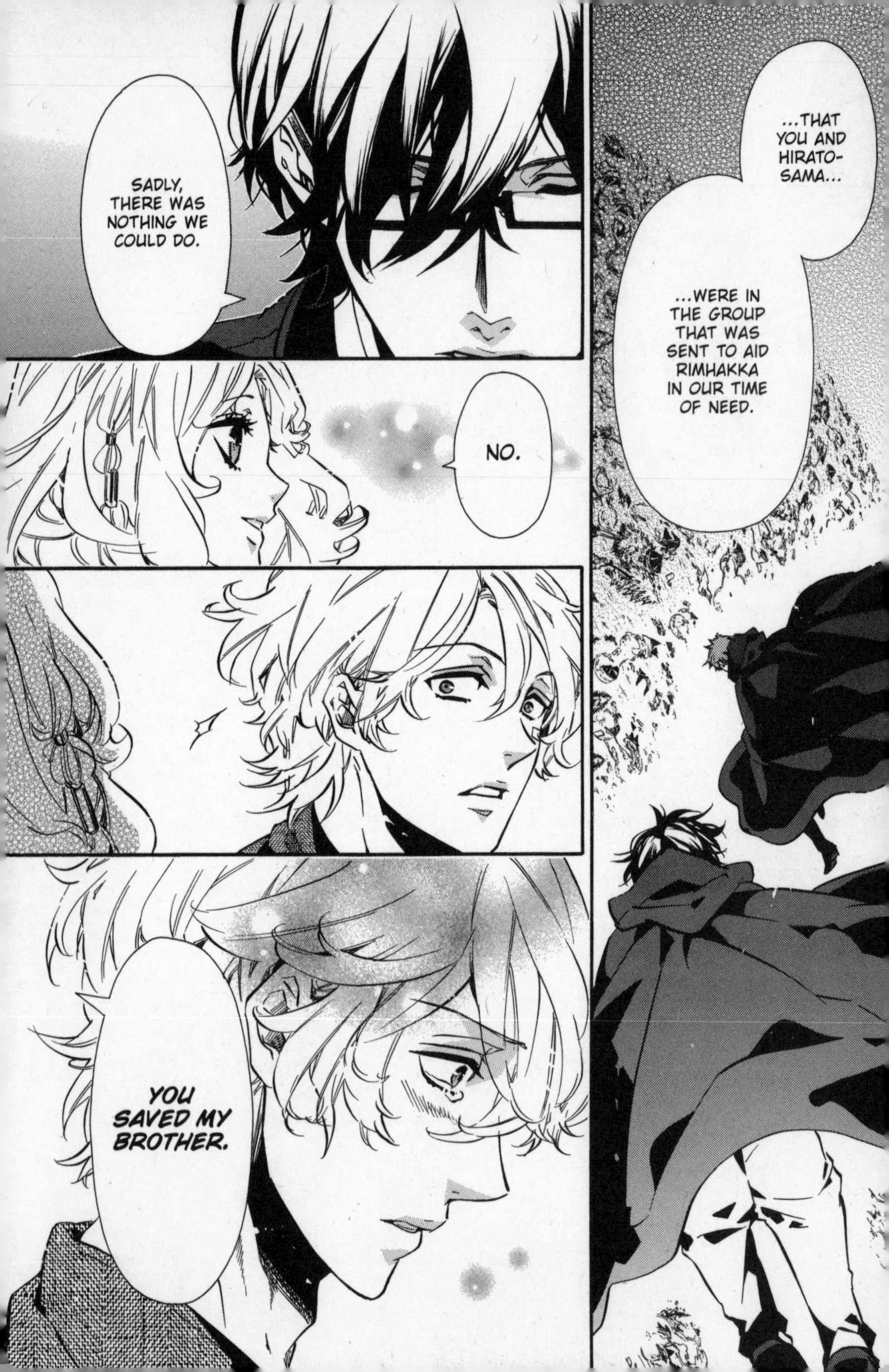
...THAT YOU AND HIRATO-SAMA...
...WERE IN THE GROUP THAT WAS SENT TO AID RIMHAKKA IN OUR TIME OF NEED.
SADLY, THERE WAS NOTHING WE COULD DO.
NO.
YOU SAVED MY BROTHER.

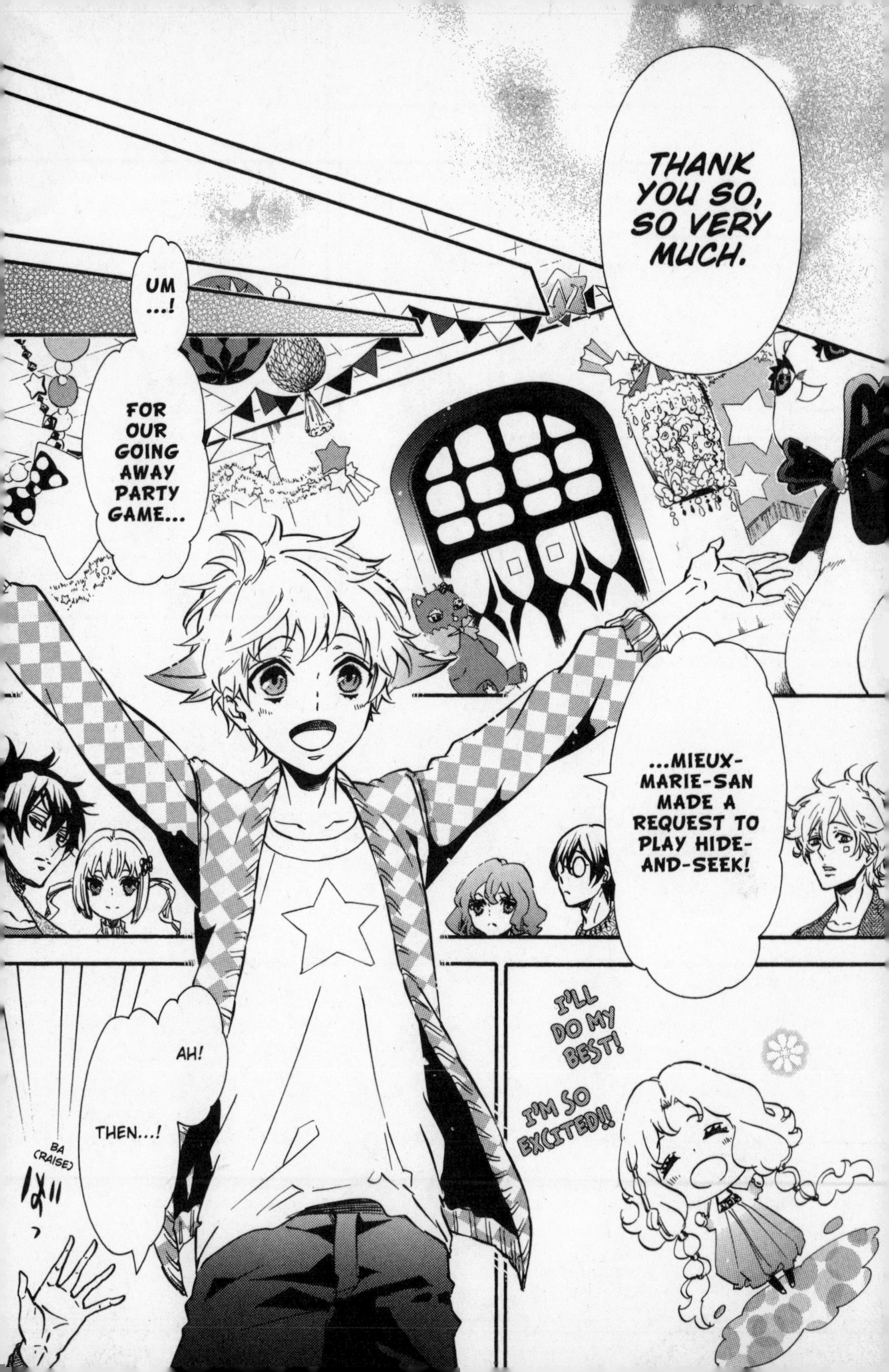
THANK YOU SO, SO VERY MUCH.
UM ...!
FOR OUR GOING AWAY PARTY GAME...
...MIEUX-MARIE-SAN MADE A REQUEST TO PLAY HIDE-AND-SEEK!
I'LL DO MY BEST!
I'M SO EXCITED!!
AH!
THEN...!
BA (RAISE)

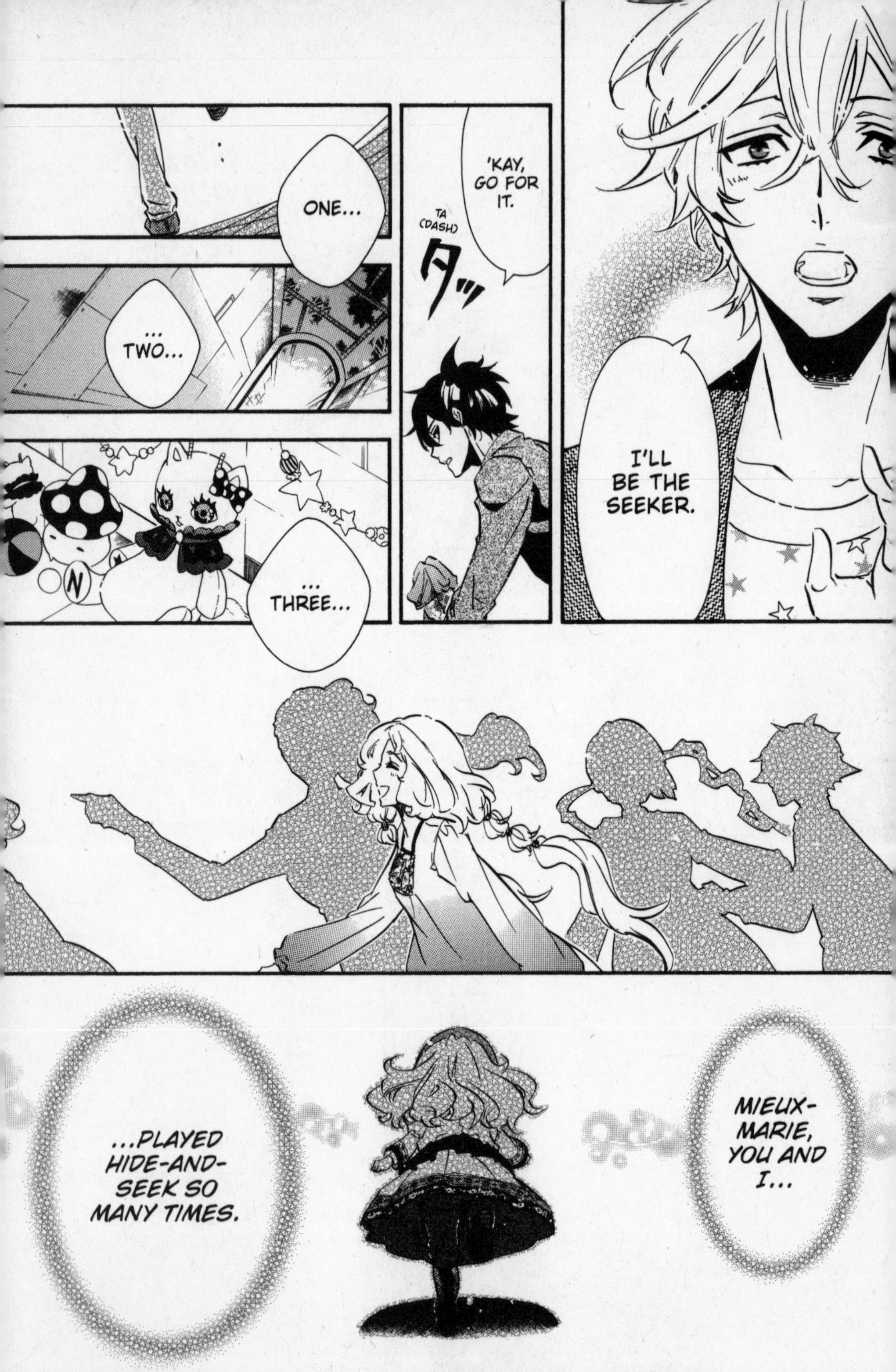
I'LL BE THE SEEKER.
'KAY, GO FOR IT.
TA (DASH)
タッ
ONE...
...TWO...
...THREE...
MIEUX-MARIE, YOU AND I...
...PLAYED HIDE-AND-SEEK SO MANY TIMES.

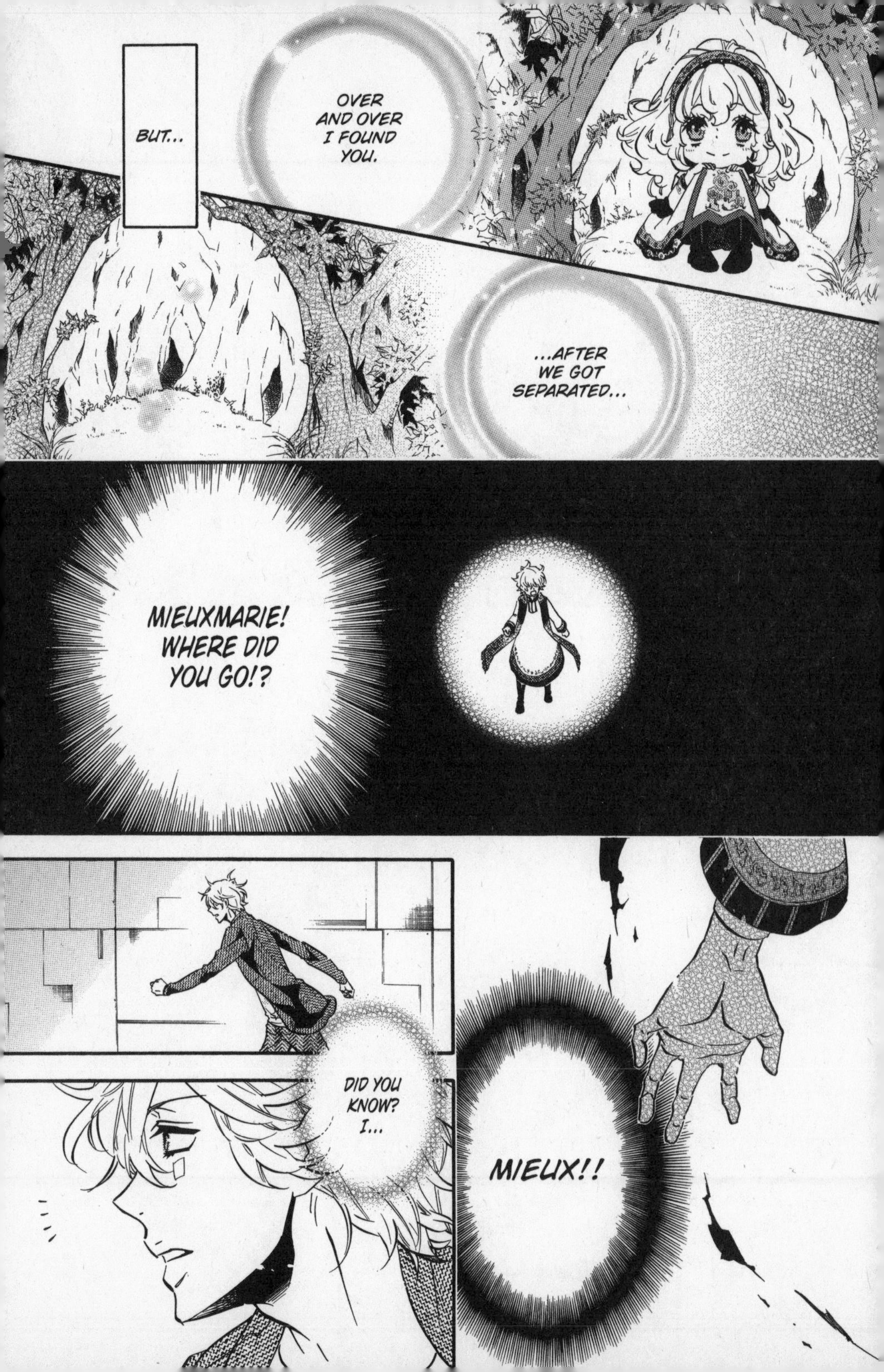
OVER AND OVER I FOUND YOU.
...AFTER WE GOT SEPARATED...
BUT...
MIEUXMARIE! WHERE DID YOU GO!?
MIEUX!!
DID YOU KNOW? I...

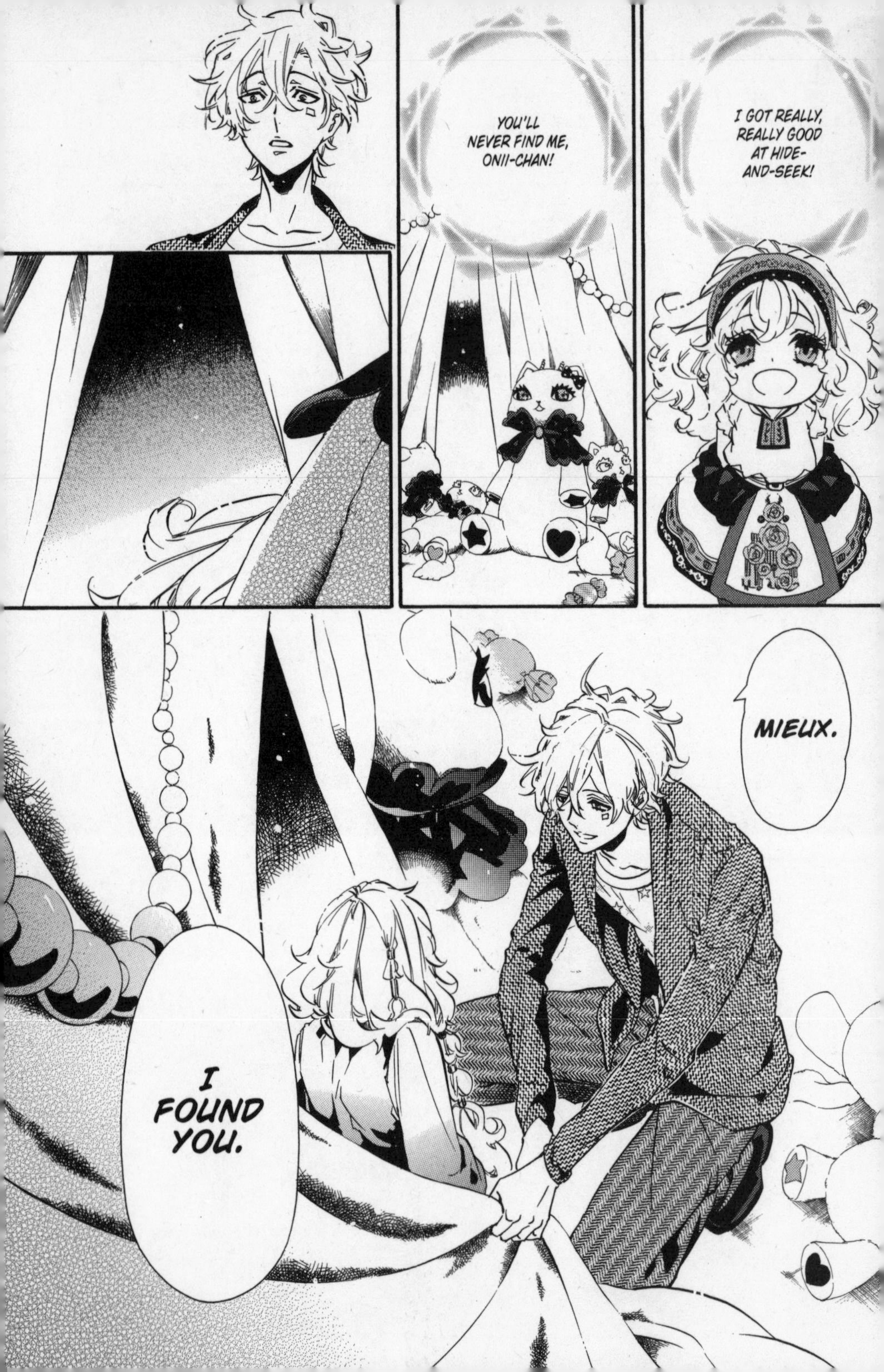
I GOT REALLY, REALLY GOOD AT HIDE-AND-SEEK!
YOU'LL NEVER FIND ME, ONII-CHAN!
MIEUX.
I FOUND YOU.

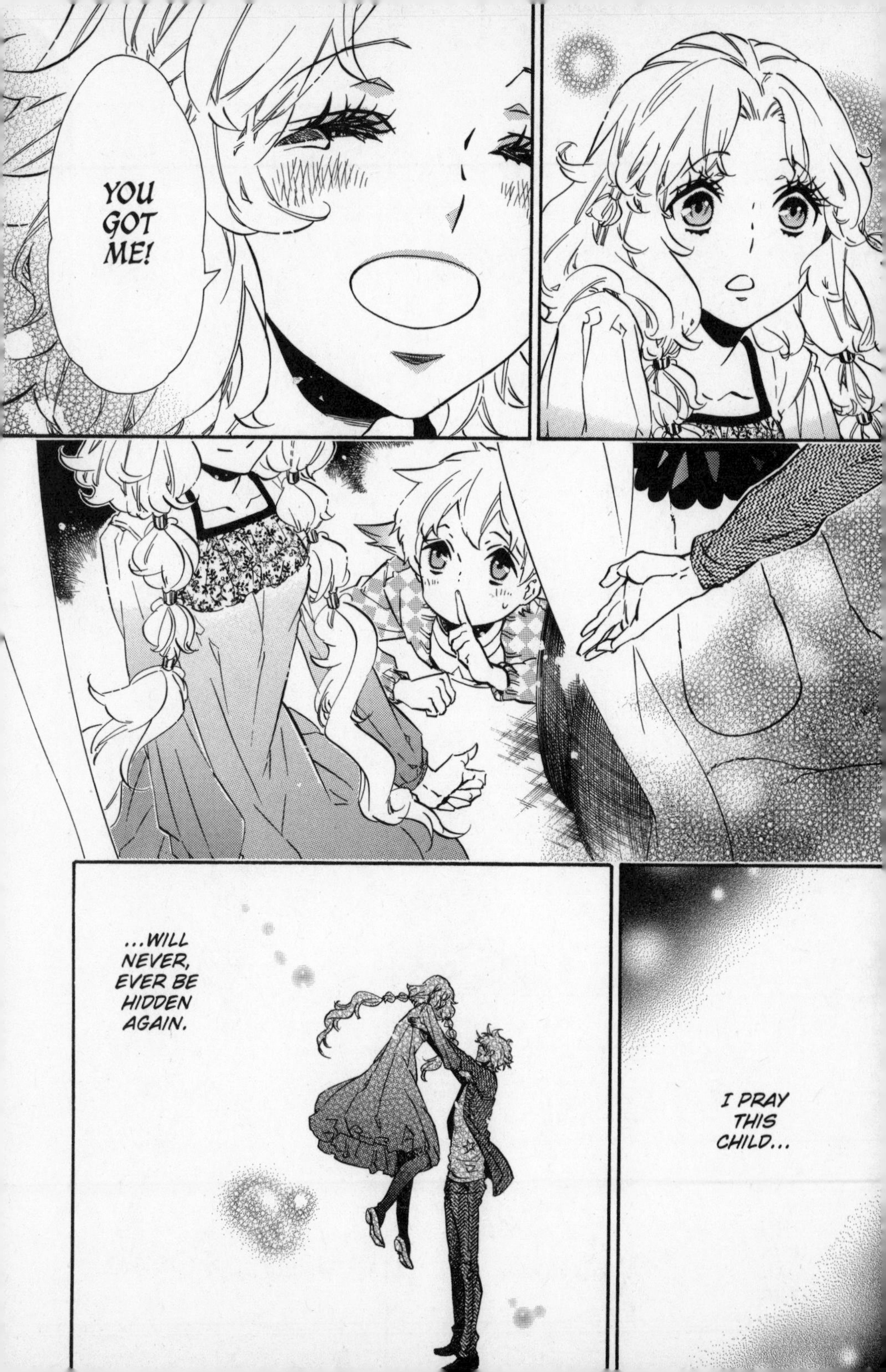
YOU GOT ME!
I PRAY THIS CHILD...
...WILL NEVER, EVER BE HIDDEN AGAIN.

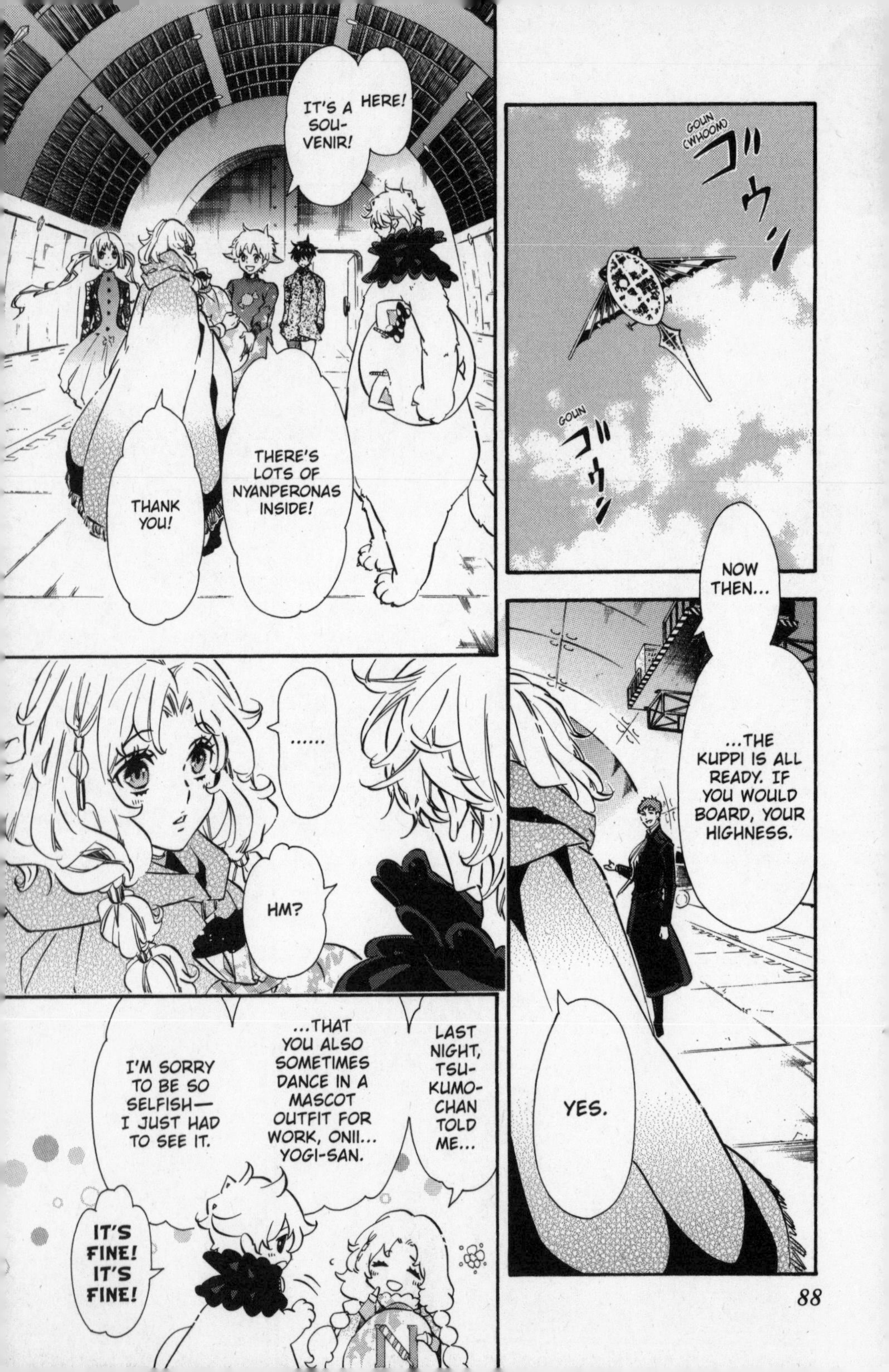
GOUN (WHOOM) ゴウン
GOUN ゴウン
NOW THEN...
...THE KUPPI IS ALL READY. IF YOU WOULD BOARD, YOUR HIGHNESS.
YES.
HERE!
IT'S A SOUVENIR!
THERE'S LOTS OF NYANPERONAS INSIDE!
THANK YOU!
......
HM?
LAST NIGHT, TSUKUMO-CHAN TOLD ME...
...THAT YOU ALSO SOMETIMES DANCE IN A MASCOT OUTFIT FOR WORK, ONII... YOGI-SAN.
I'M SORRY TO BE SO SELFISH— I JUST HAD TO SEE IT.
IT'S FINE! IT'S FINE!

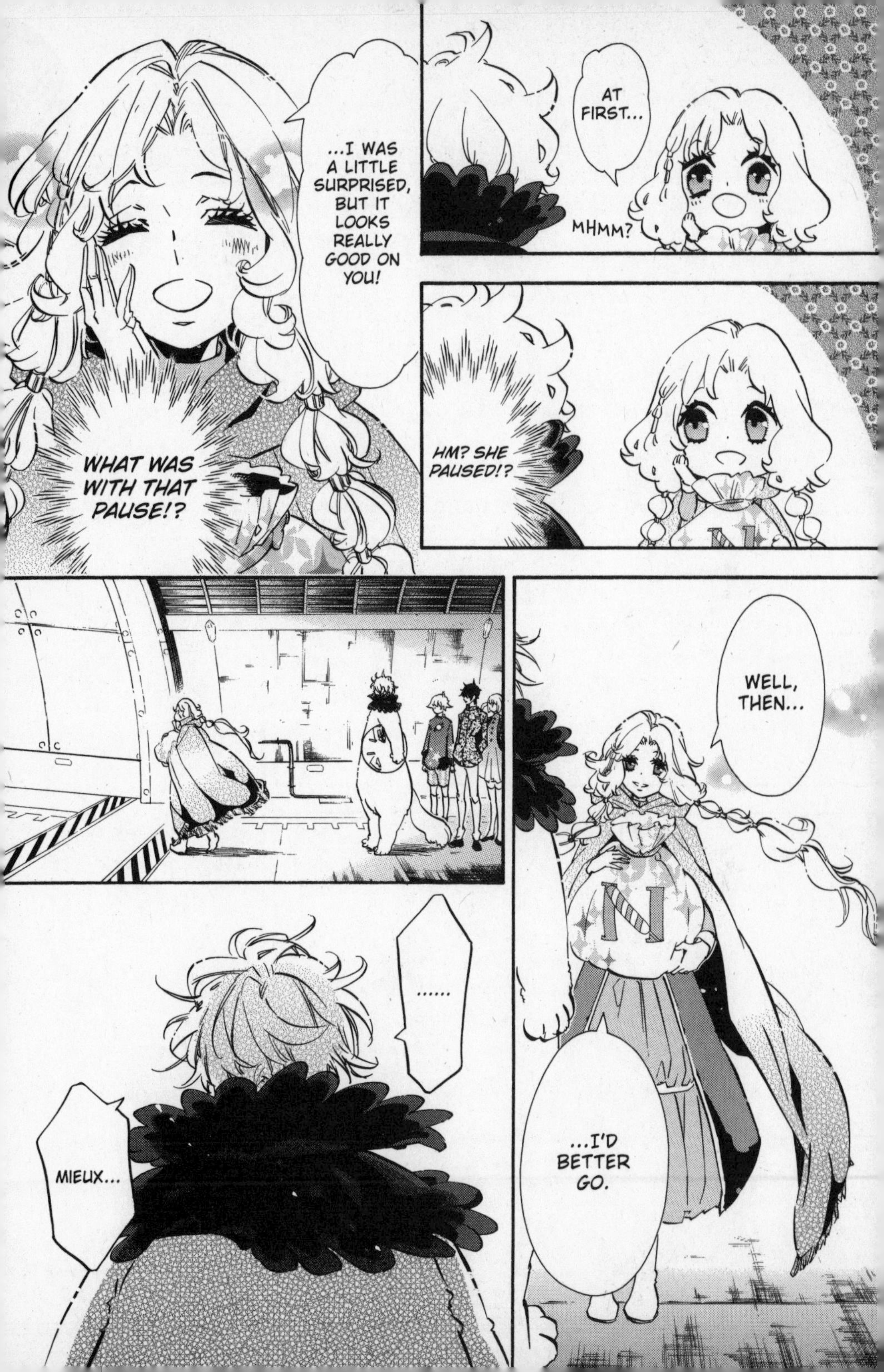
AT FIRST...
MHMM?
HM? SHE PAUSED!?
...I WAS A LITTLE SURPRISED, BUT IT LOOKS REALLY GOOD ON YOU!
WHAT WAS WITH THAT PAUSE!?
WELL, THEN...
...I'D BETTER GO.
......
MIEUX...

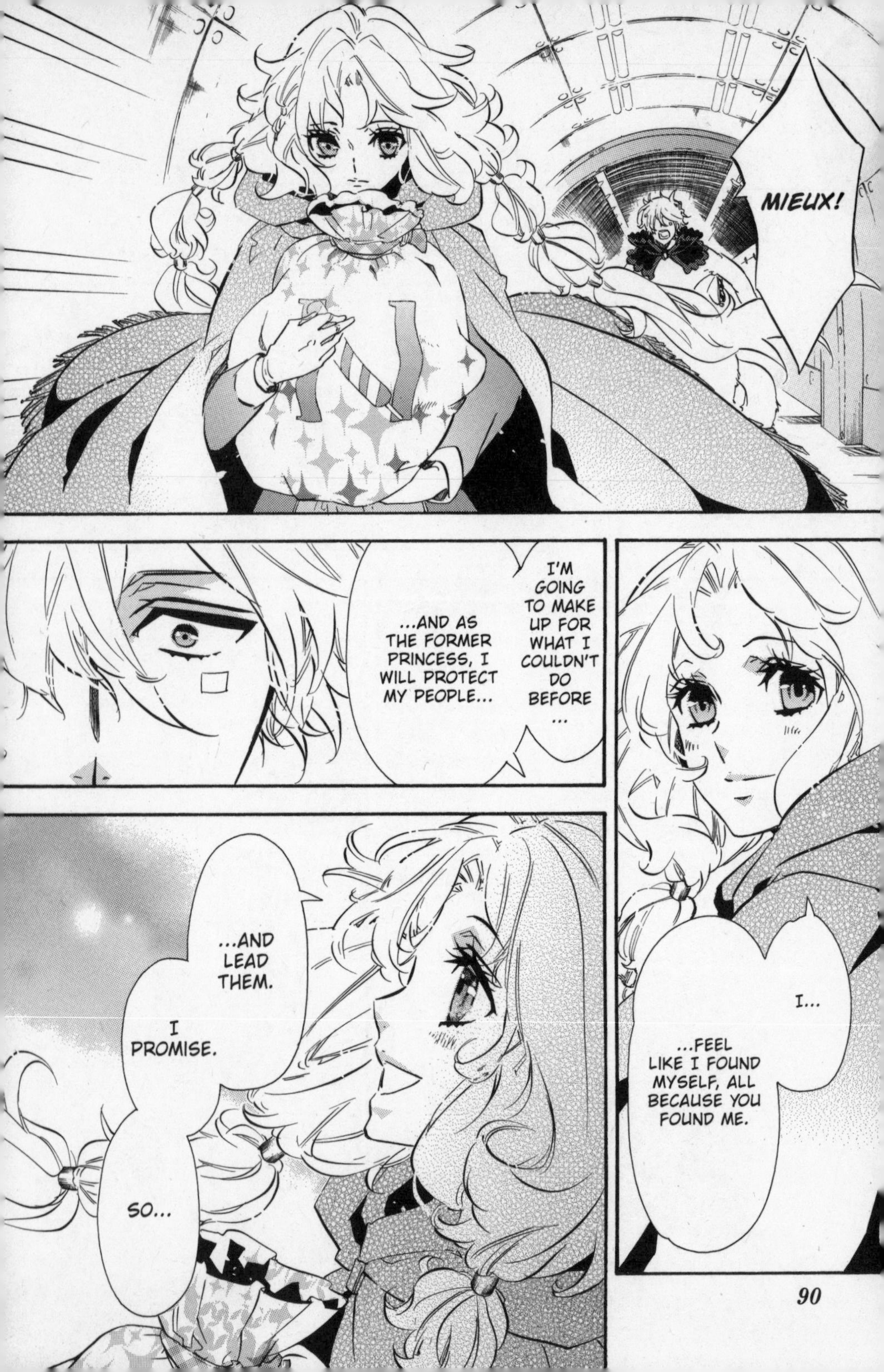
MIEUX!
I...
...FEEL LIKE I FOUND MYSELF, ALL BECAUSE YOU FOUND ME.
I'M GOING TO MAKE UP FOR WHAT I COULDN'T DO BEFORE...
...AND AS THE FORMER PRINCESS, I WILL PROTECT MY PEOPLE...
...AND LEAD THEM.
I PROMISE.
SO...

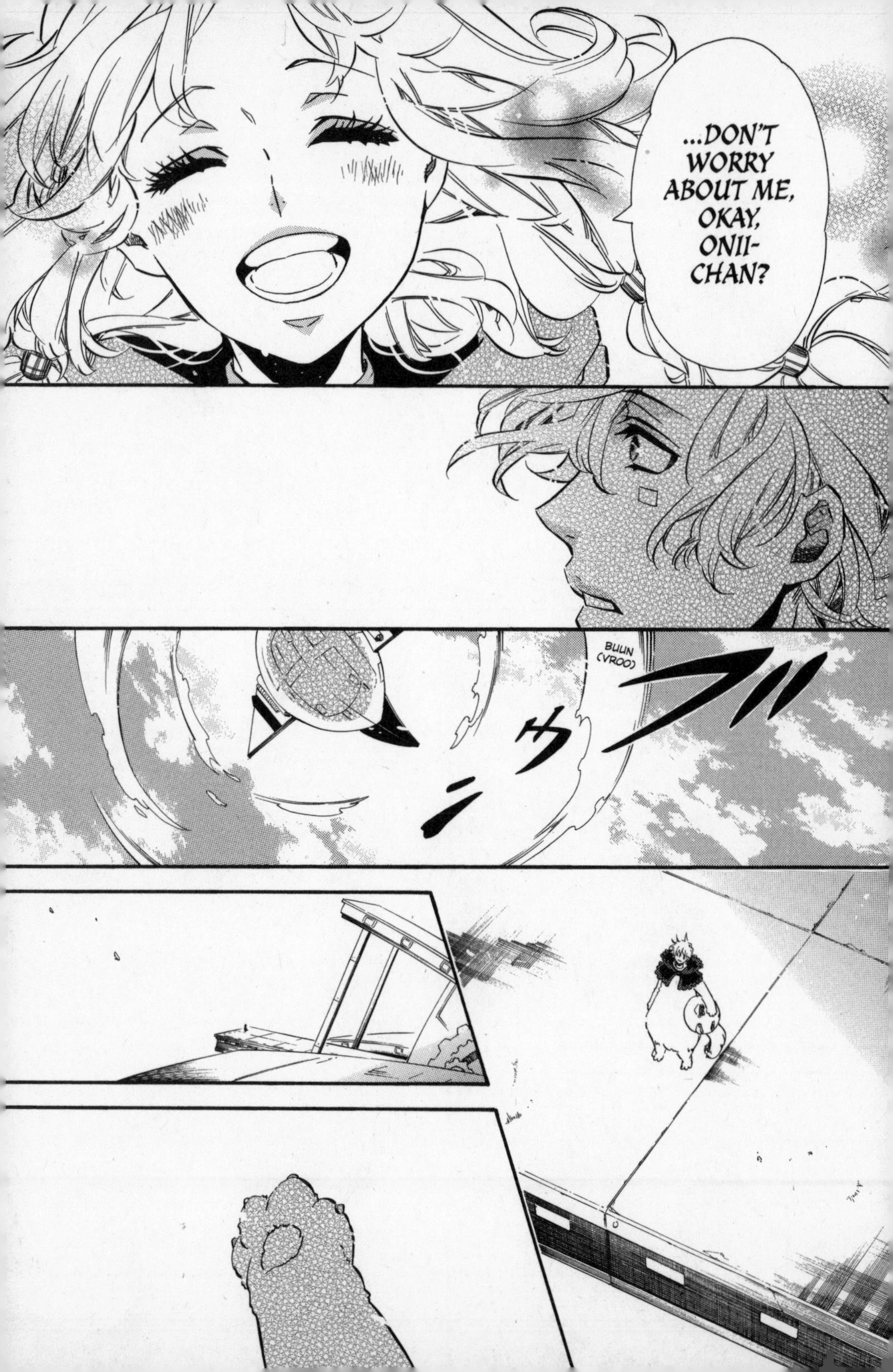
...DON'T WORRY ABOUT ME, OKAY, ONII-CHAN?
BUUN (VROO)

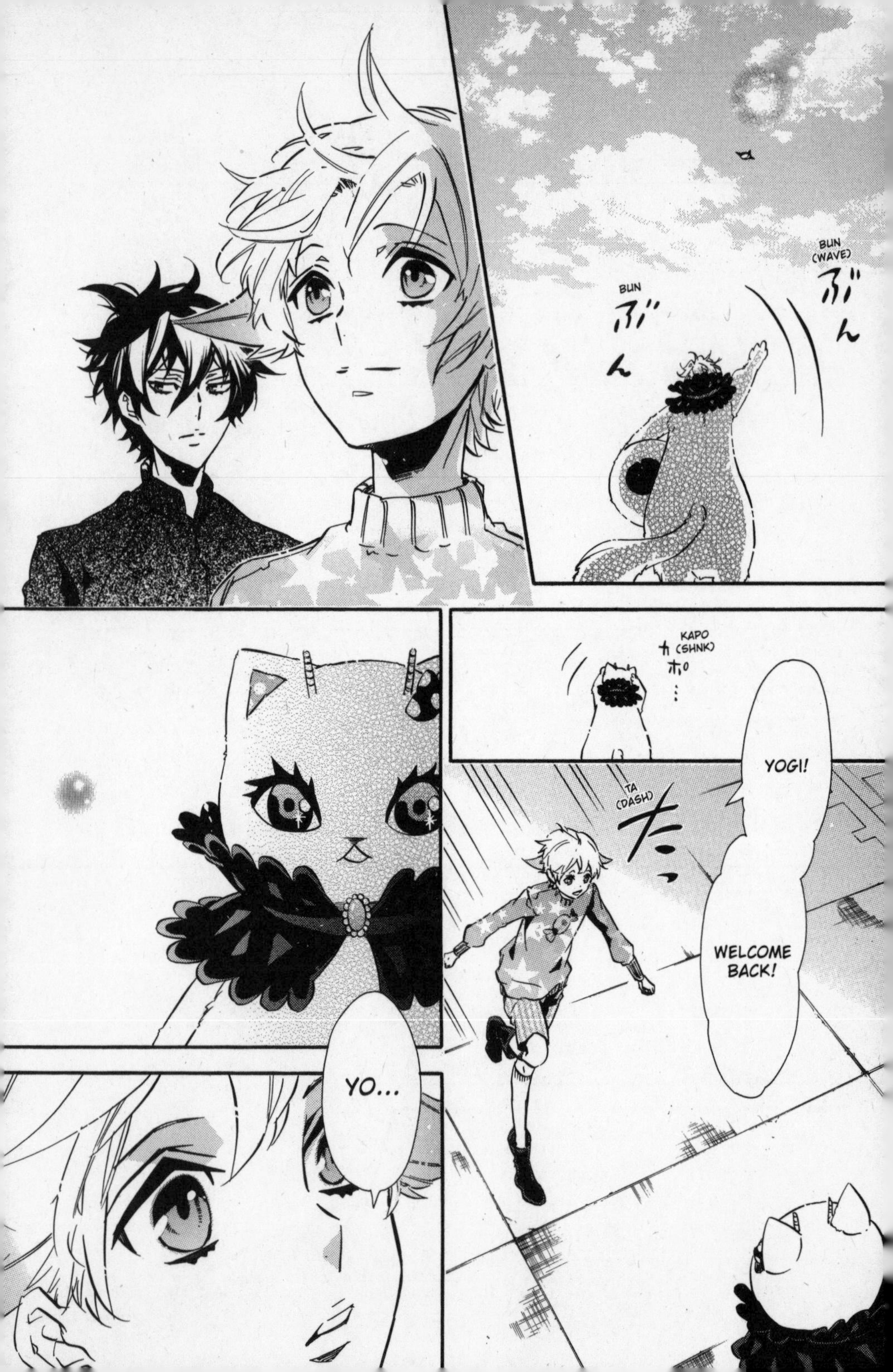

BUN (WAVE)
ぶん
BUN
ぶん
KAPO (SHNK)
カポ…
YOGI!
WELCOME BACK!
TA (DASH)
たっ
YO...

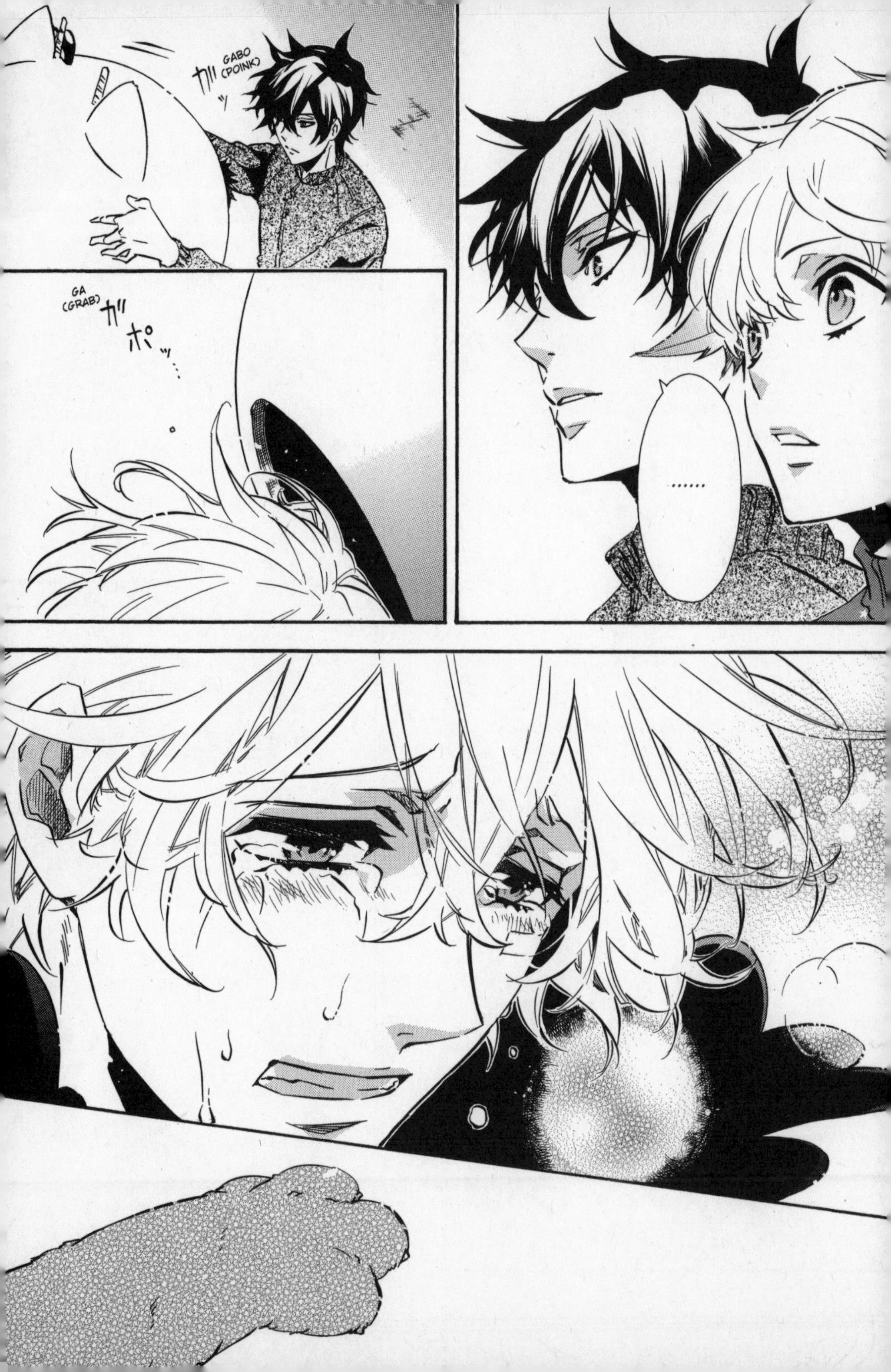
......
GABO (POINK)
GA (GRAB)
ガ
ポッ

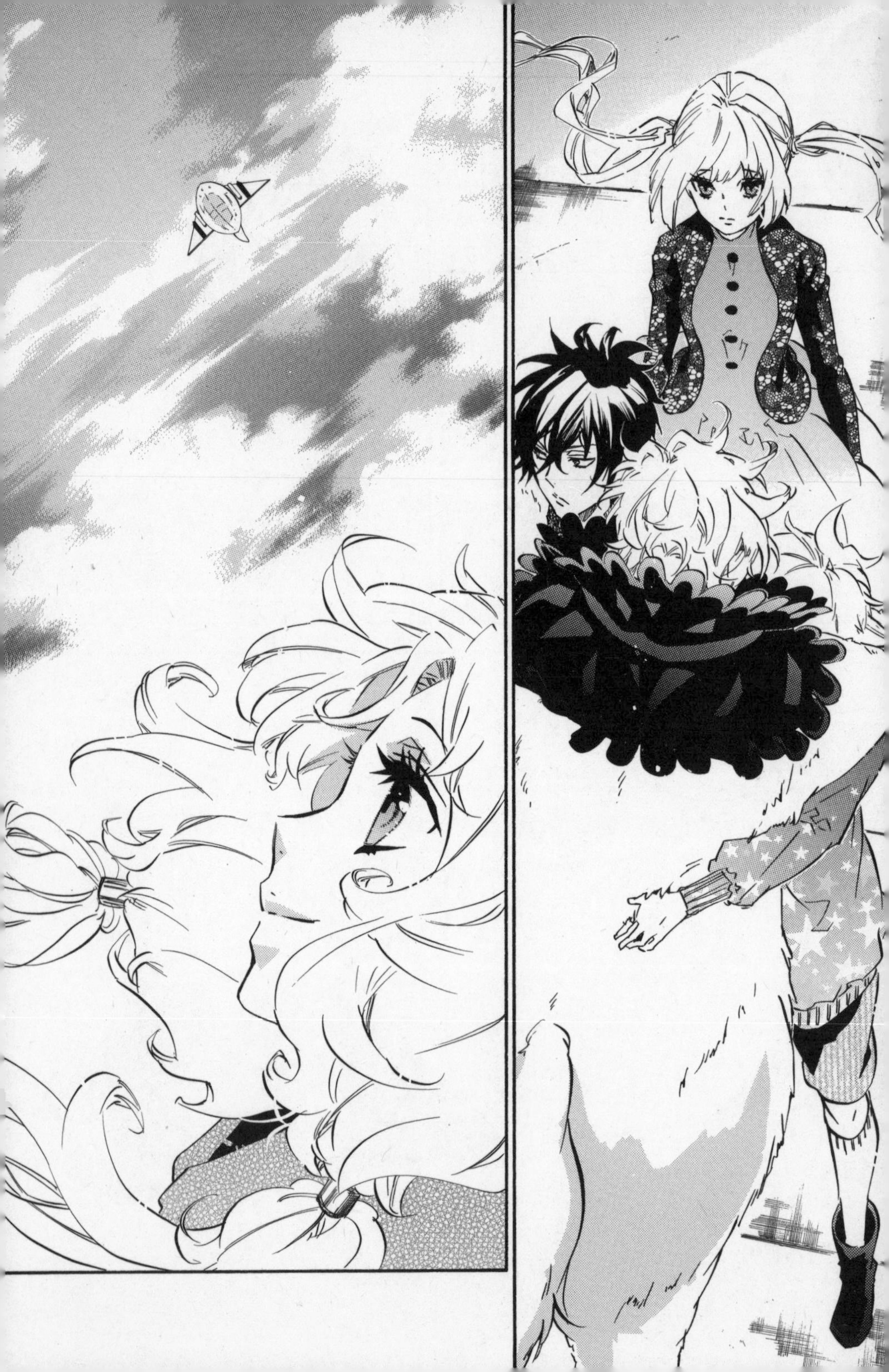

KARNEVAL

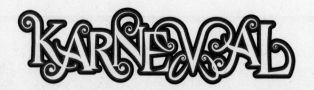

KARNEVAL

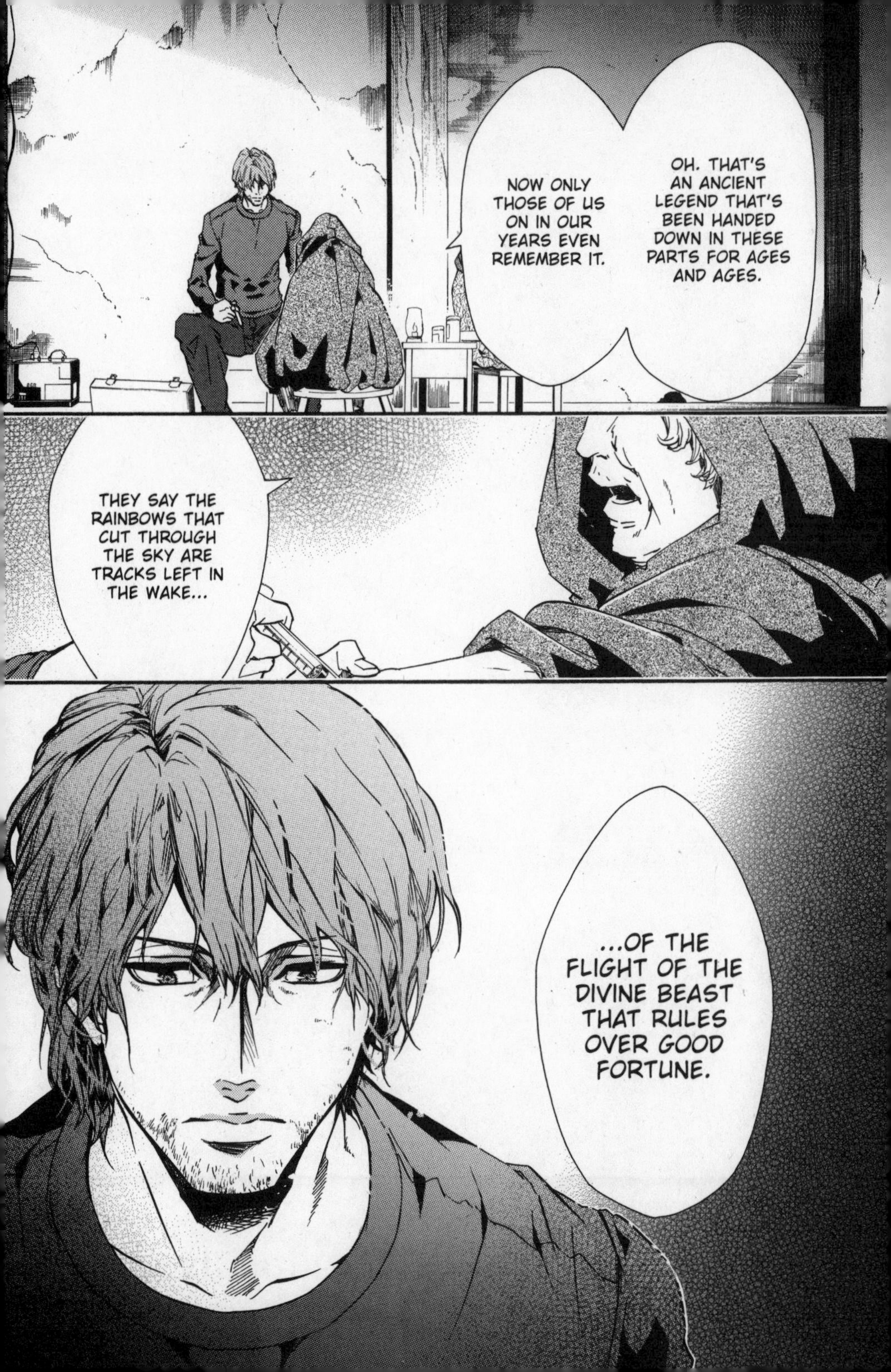
OH. THAT'S AN ANCIENT LEGEND THAT'S BEEN HANDED DOWN IN THESE PARTS FOR AGES AND AGES.
NOW ONLY THOSE OF US ON IN OUR YEARS EVEN REMEMBER IT.
THEY SAY THE RAINBOWS THAT CUT THROUGH THE SKY ARE TRACKS LEFT IN THE WAKE...
...OF THE FLIGHT OF THE DIVINE BEAST THAT RULES OVER GOOD FORTUNE.

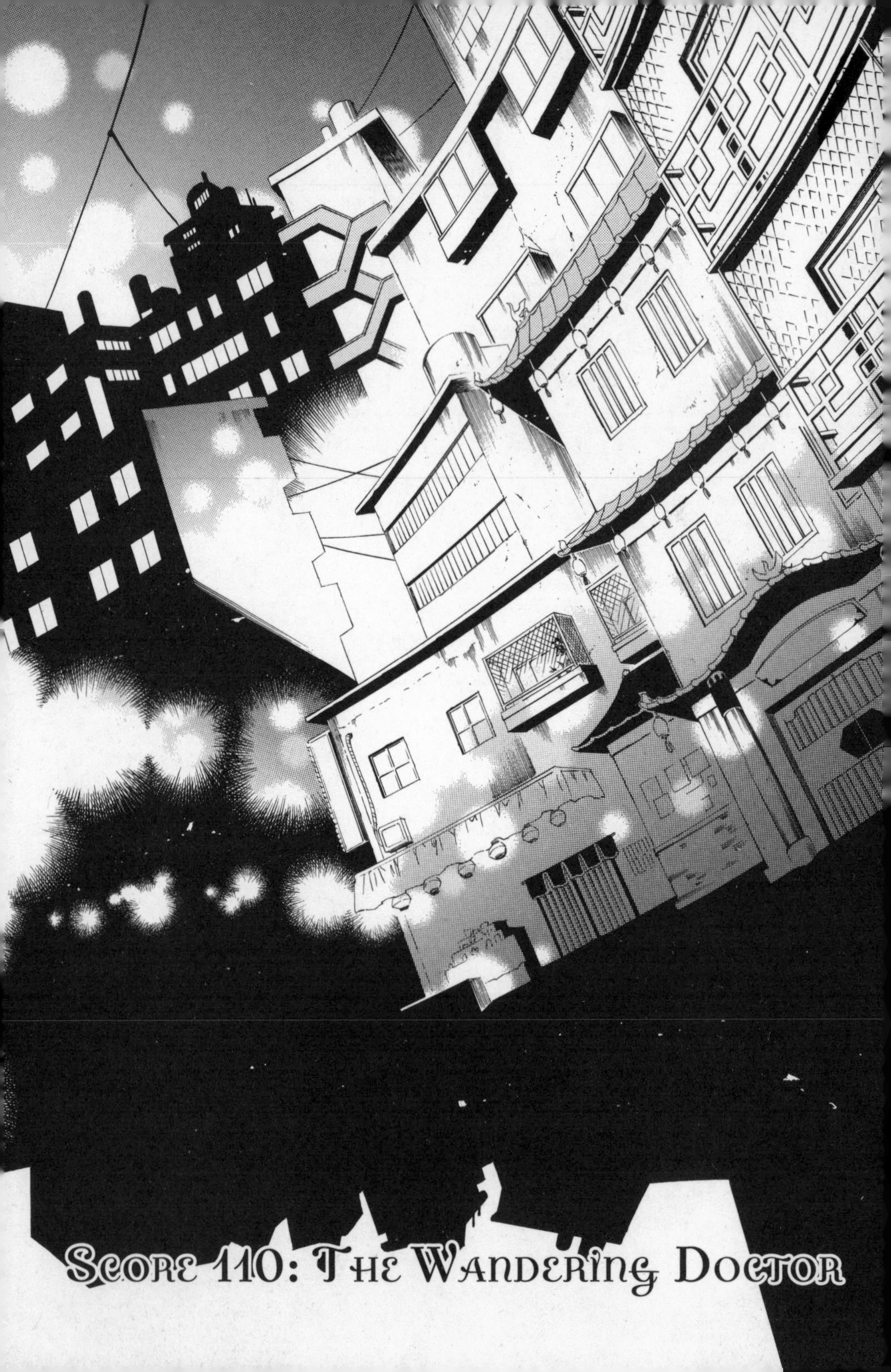

Score 110: The Wandering Doctor

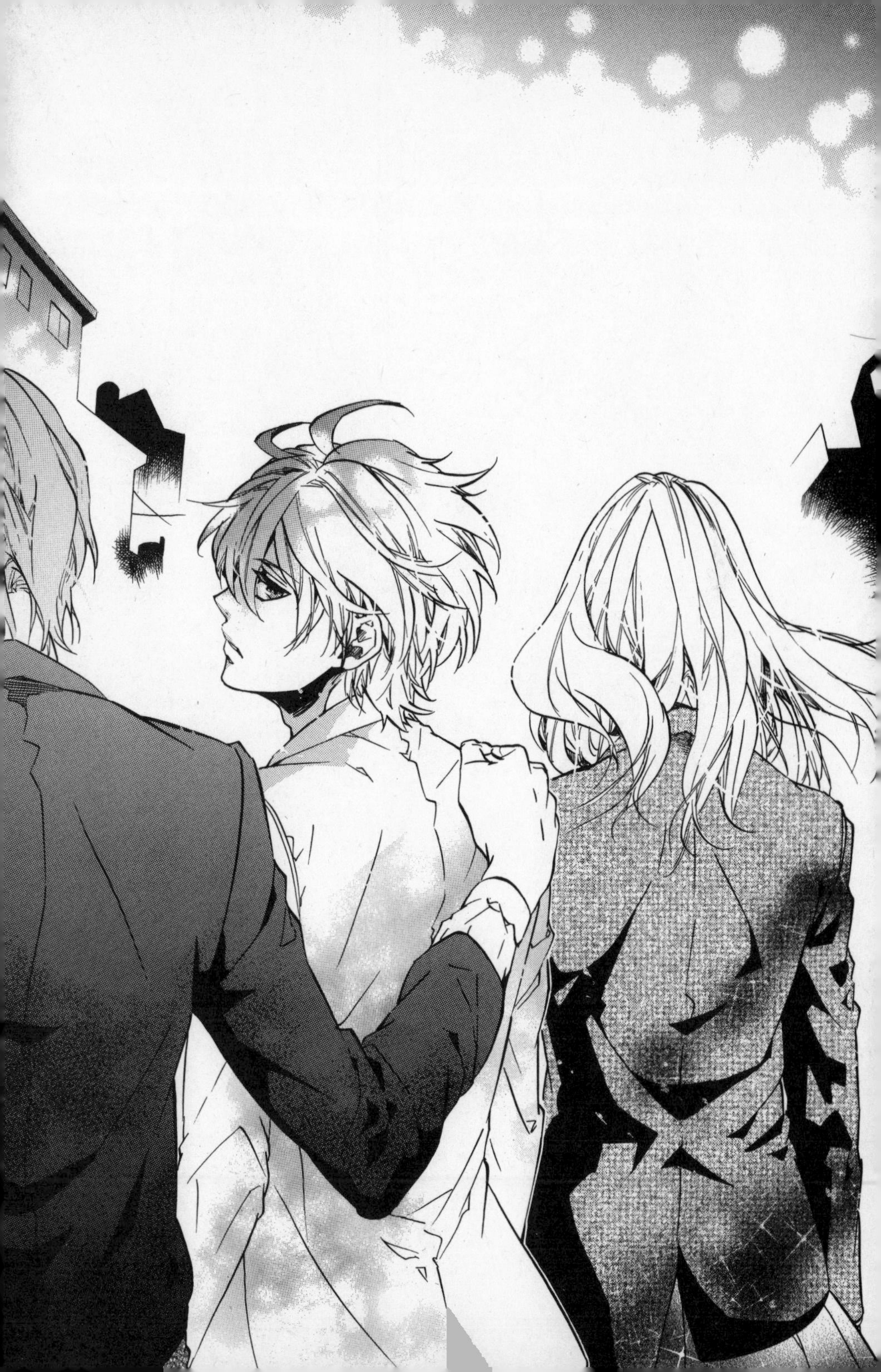

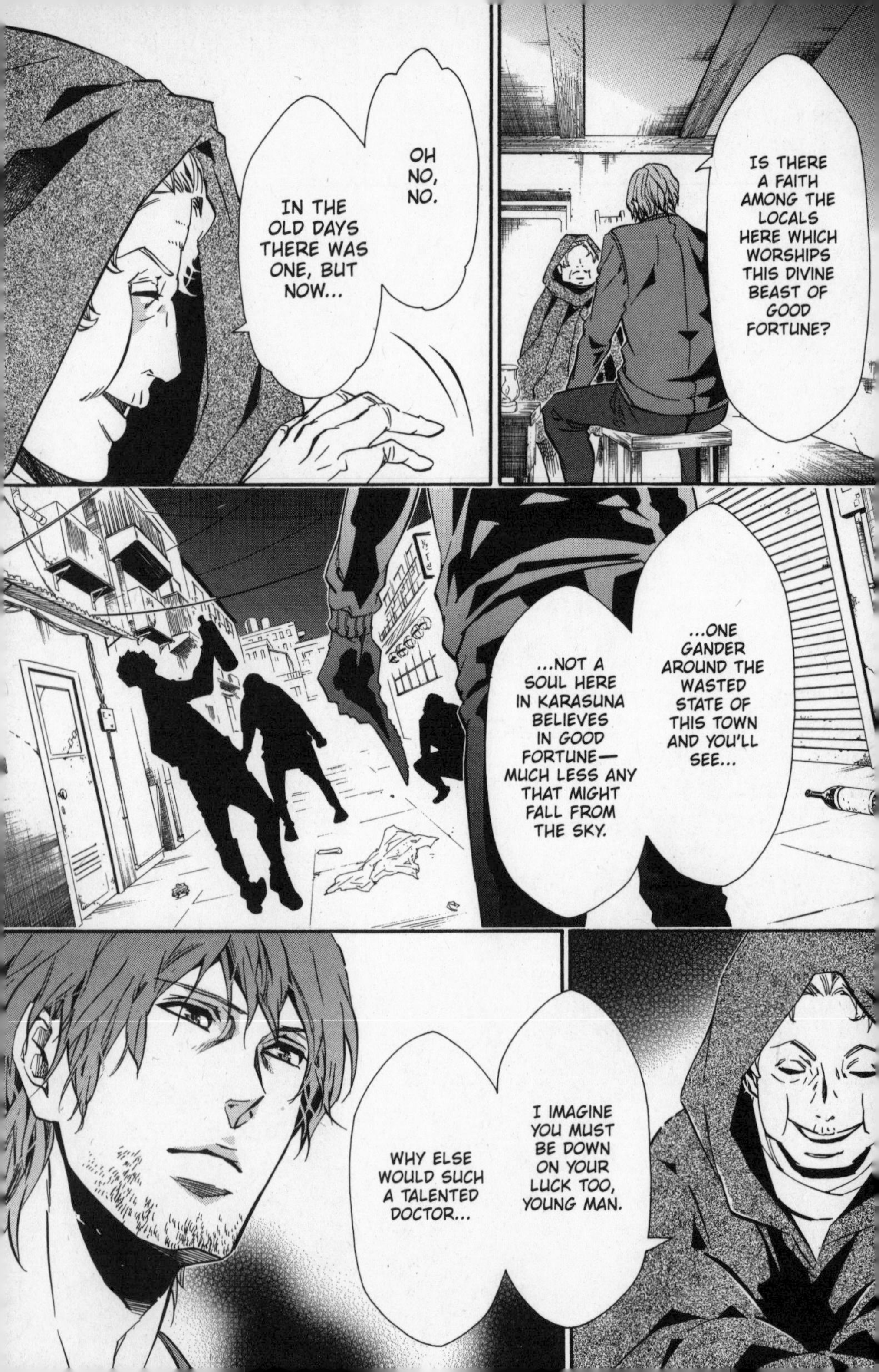
IS THERE A FAITH AMONG THE LOCALS HERE WHICH WORSHIPS THIS DIVINE BEAST OF GOOD FORTUNE?
OH NO, NO.
IN THE OLD DAYS THERE WAS ONE, BUT NOW...
...ONE GANDER AROUND THE WASTED STATE OF THIS TOWN AND YOU'LL SEE...
...NOT A SOUL HERE IN KARASUNA BELIEVES IN GOOD FORTUNE—MUCH LESS ANY THAT MIGHT FALL FROM THE SKY.
I IMAGINE YOU MUST BE DOWN ON YOUR LUCK TOO, YOUNG MAN.
WHY ELSE WOULD SUCH A TALENTED DOCTOR...

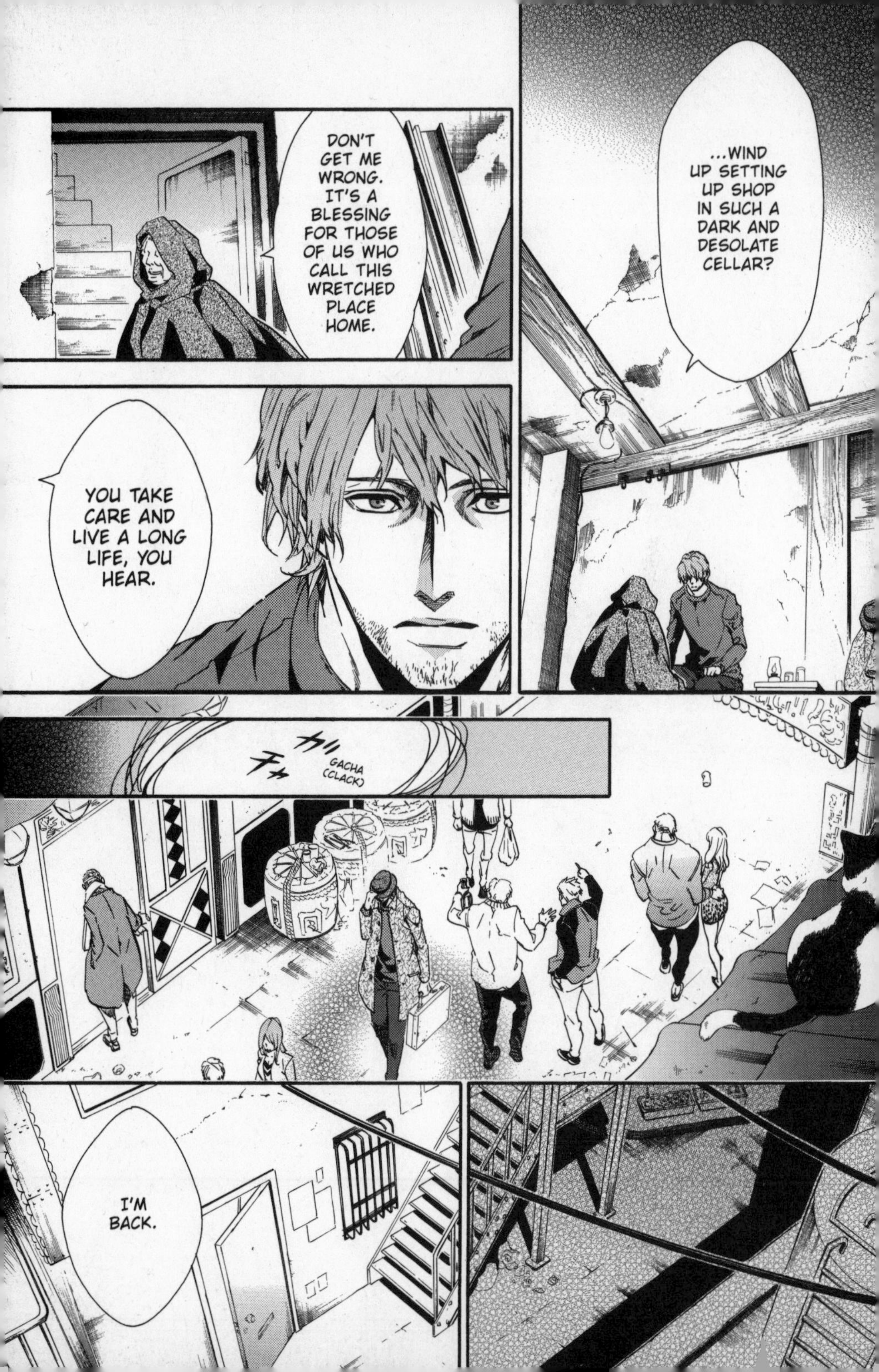
...WIND UP SETTING UP SHOP IN SUCH A DARK AND DESOLATE CELLAR?
DON'T GET ME WRONG. IT'S A BLESSING FOR THOSE OF US WHO CALL THIS WRETCHED PLACE HOME.
YOU TAKE CARE AND LIVE A LONG LIFE, YOU HEAR.
GACHA (CLACK)
I'M BACK.

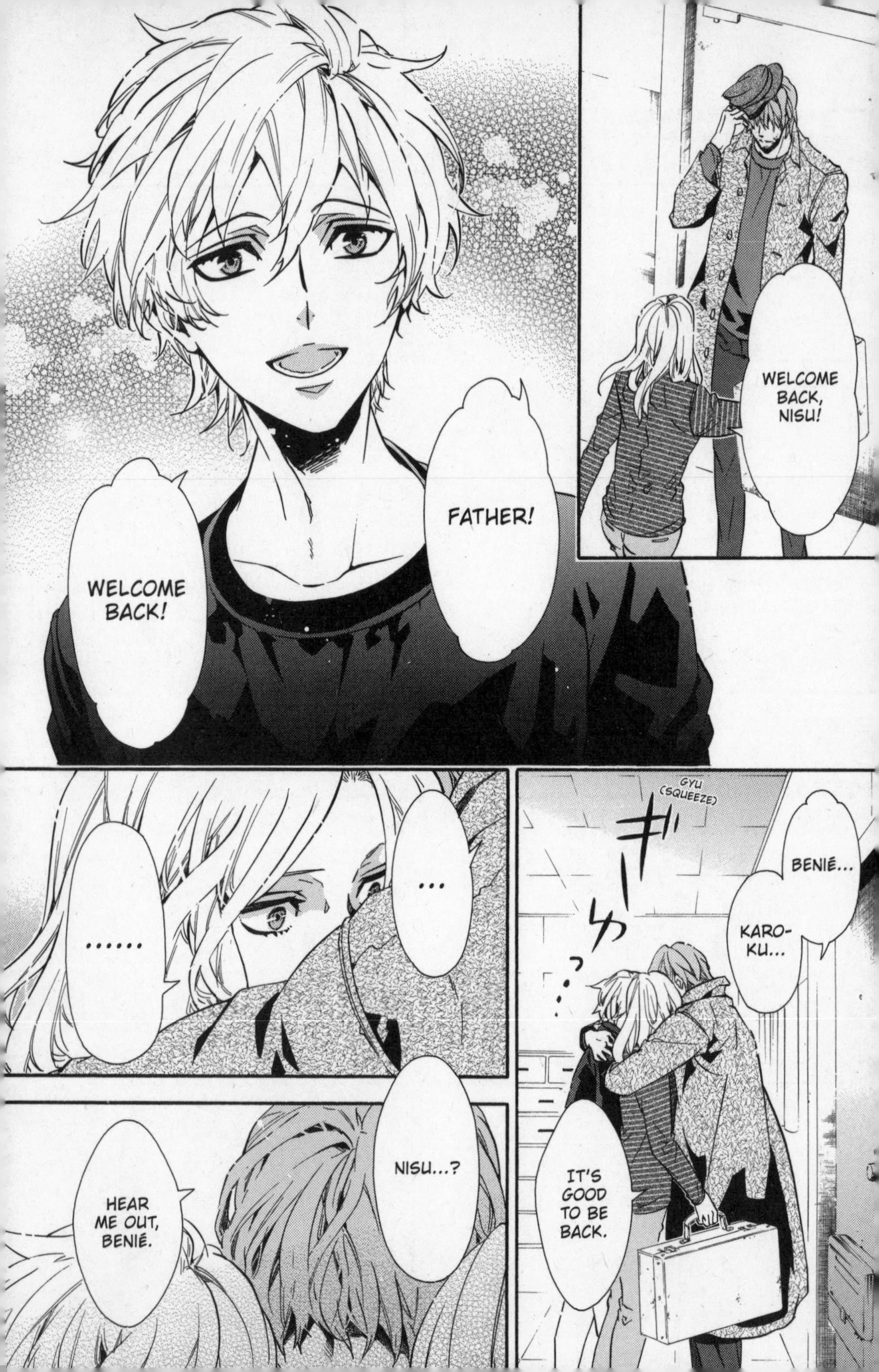

WELCOME BACK, NISU!
FATHER!
WELCOME BACK!
GYU (SQUEEZE)
BENIÉ...
KARO-KU...
IT'S GOOD TO BE BACK.
...
......
NISU...?
HEAR ME OUT, BENIÉ.

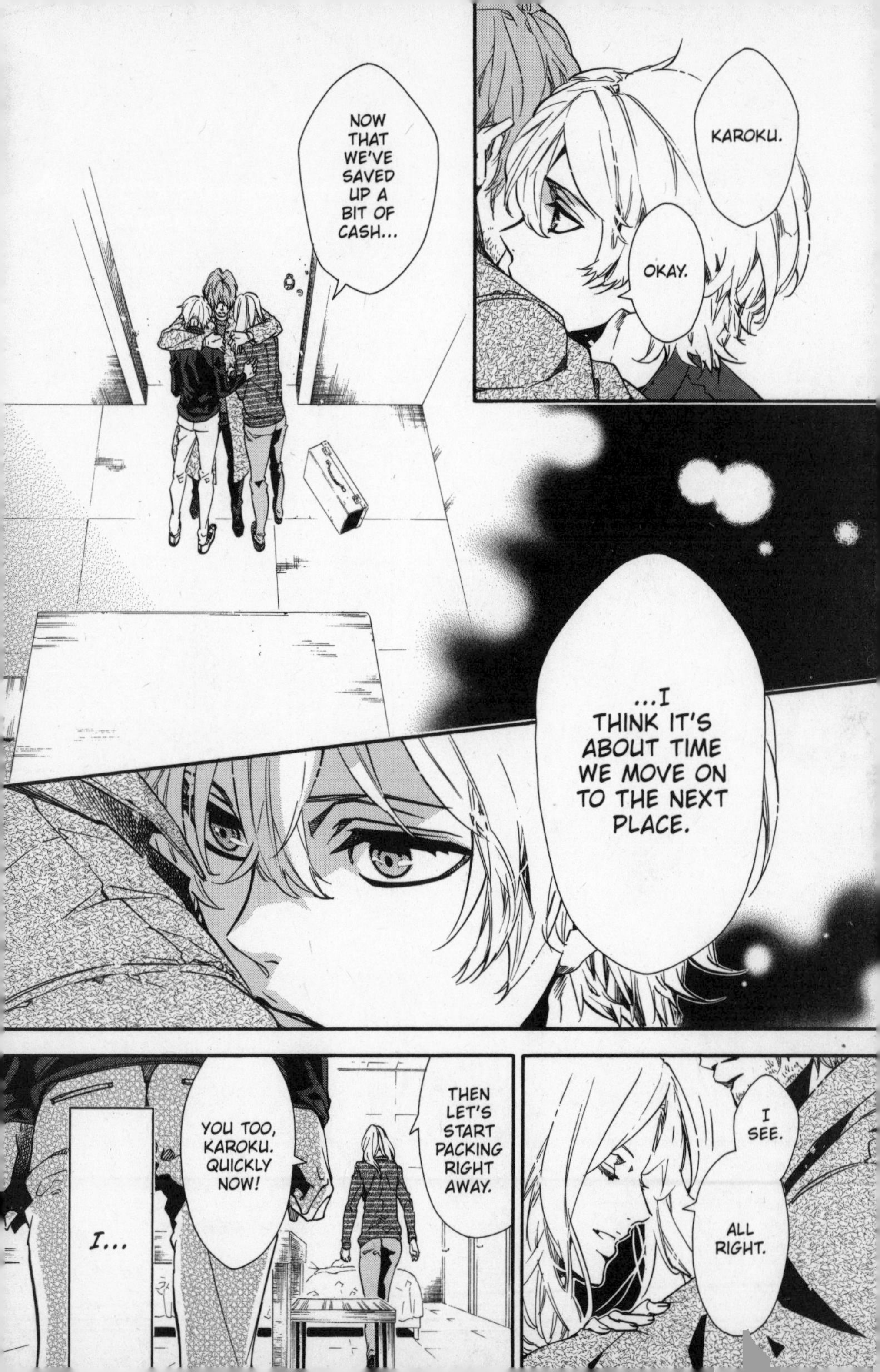
KAROKU.
OKAY.
NOW THAT WE'VE SAVED UP A BIT OF CASH...
...I THINK IT'S ABOUT TIME WE MOVE ON TO THE NEXT PLACE.
I SEE.
ALL RIGHT.
THEN LET'S START PACKING RIGHT AWAY.
YOU TOO, KAROKU. QUICKLY NOW!
I...

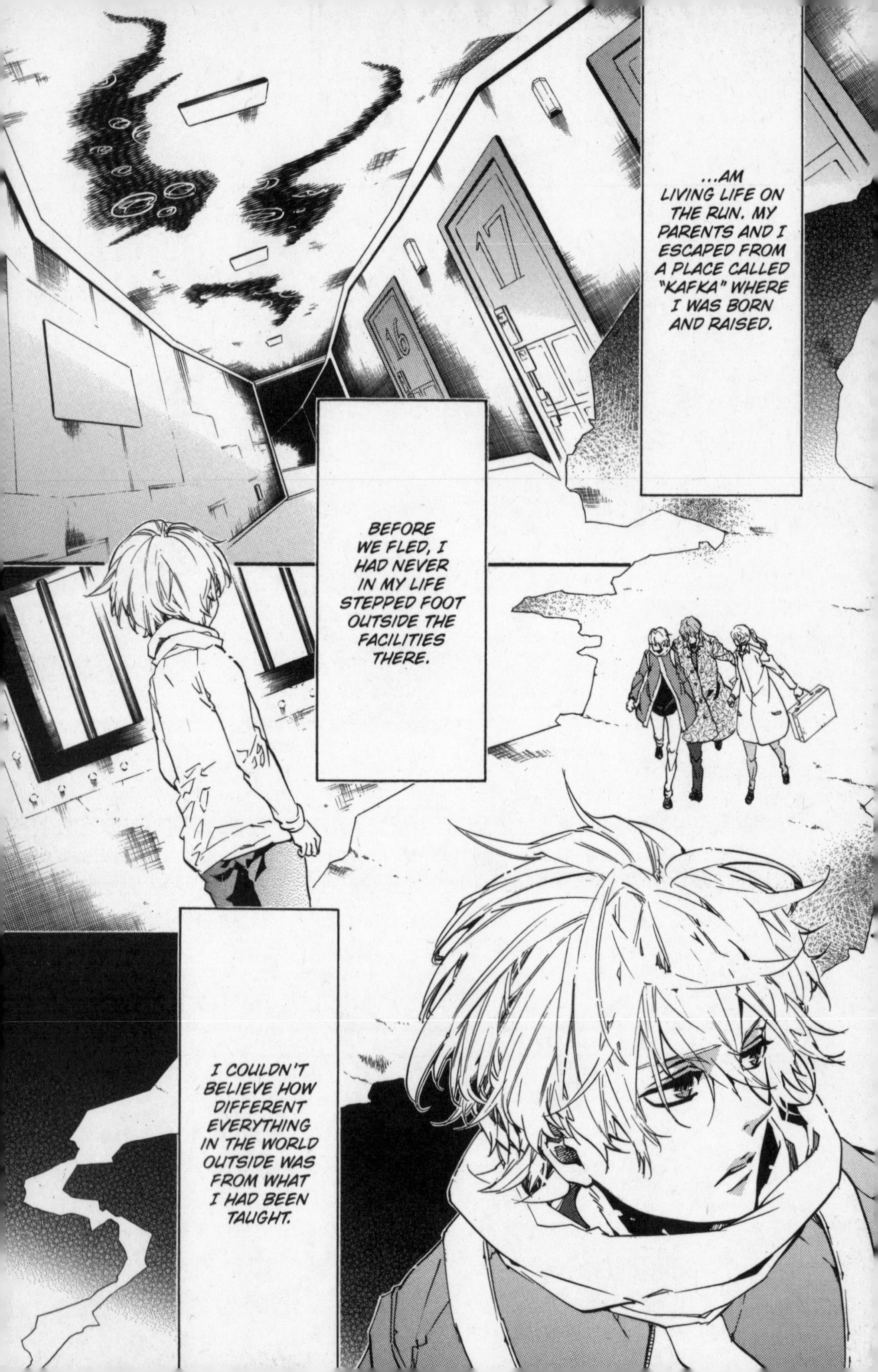
...AM LIVING LIFE ON THE RUN. MY PARENTS AND I ESCAPED FROM A PLACE CALLED "KAFKA" WHERE I WAS BORN AND RAISED.
BEFORE WE FLED, I HAD NEVER IN MY LIFE STEPPED FOOT OUTSIDE THE FACILITIES THERE.
I COULDN'T BELIEVE HOW DIFFERENT EVERYTHING IN THE WORLD OUTSIDE WAS FROM WHAT I HAD BEEN TAUGHT.

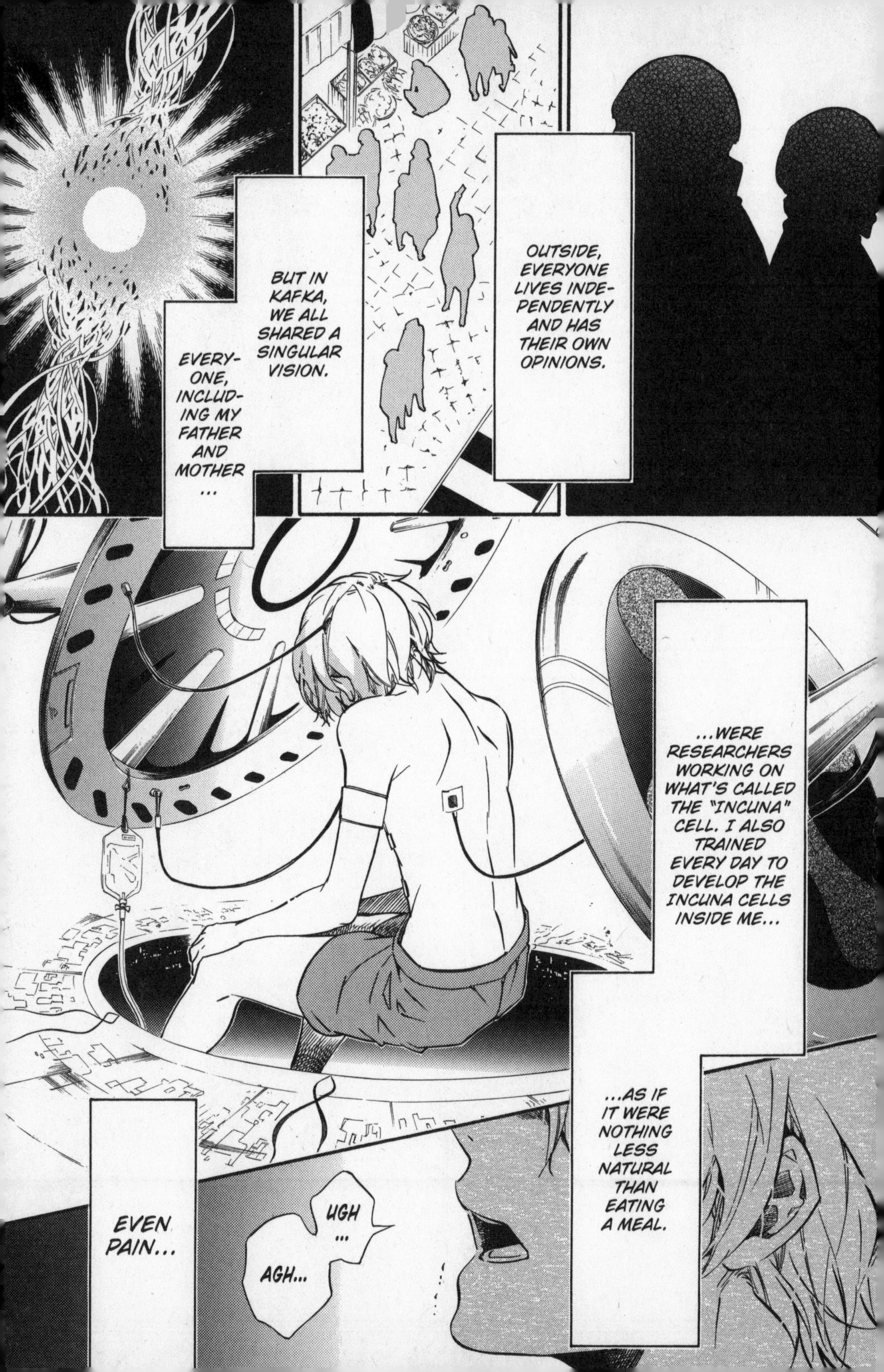
OUTSIDE, EVERYONE LIVES INDEPENDENTLY AND HAS THEIR OWN OPINIONS.
BUT IN KAFKA, WE ALL SHARED A SINGULAR VISION.
EVERYONE, INCLUDING MY FATHER AND MOTHER...
...WERE RESEARCHERS WORKING ON WHAT'S CALLED THE "INCUNA" CELL. I ALSO TRAINED EVERY DAY TO DEVELOP THE INCUNA CELLS INSIDE ME...
...AS IF IT WERE NOTHING LESS NATURAL THAN EATING A MEAL.
UGH...
AGH...
EVEN PAIN...

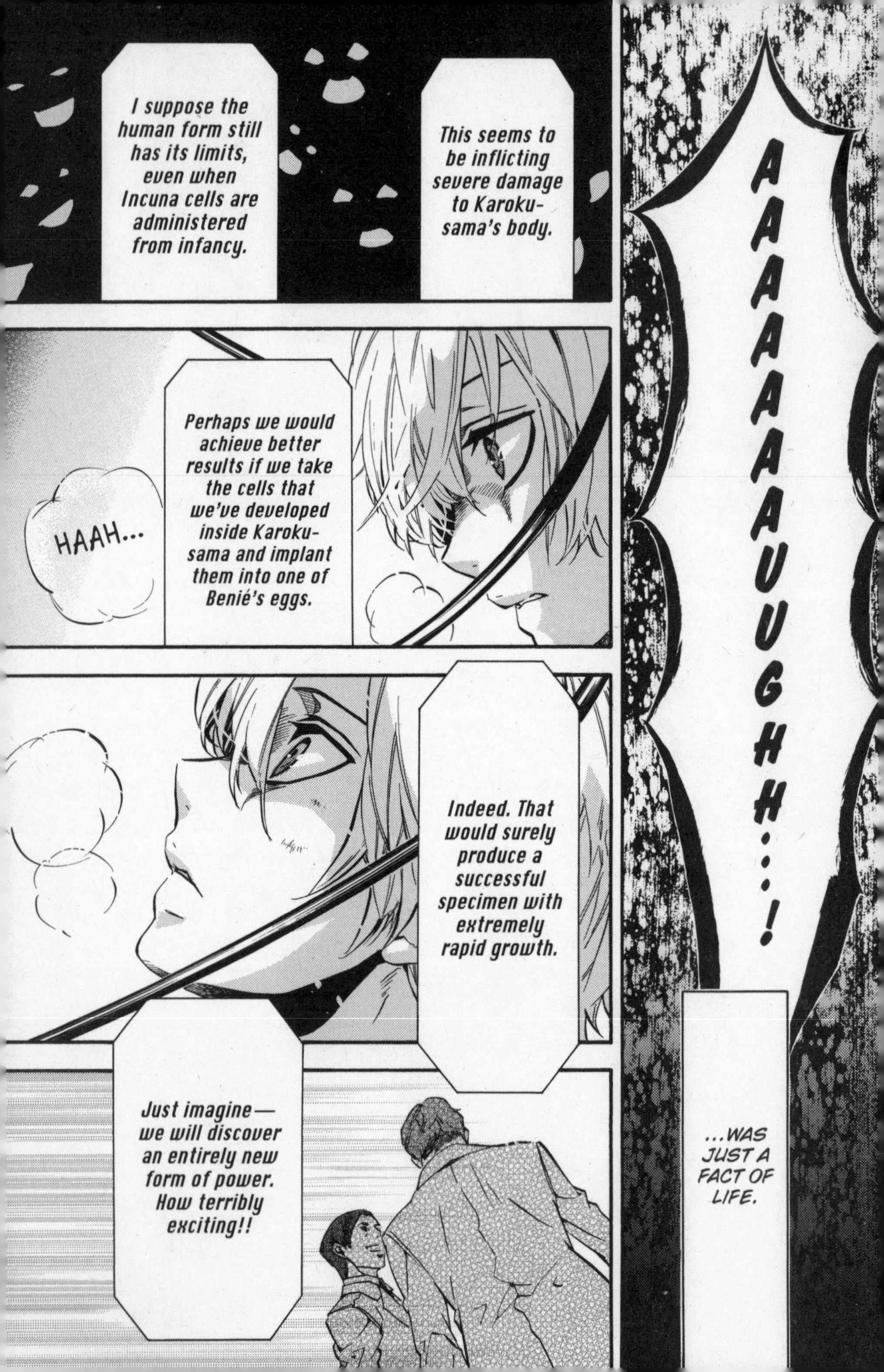
AAAAAAAUUGHH...!
...WAS JUST A FACT OF LIFE.
This seems to be inflicting severe damage to Karoku-sama's body.
I suppose the human form still has its limits, even when Incuna cells are administered from infancy.
Perhaps we would achieve better results if we take the cells that we've developed inside Karoku-sama and implant them into one of Benié's eggs.
HAAH...
Indeed. That would surely produce a successful specimen with extremely rapid growth.
Just imagine—we will discover an entirely new form of power. How terribly exciting!!

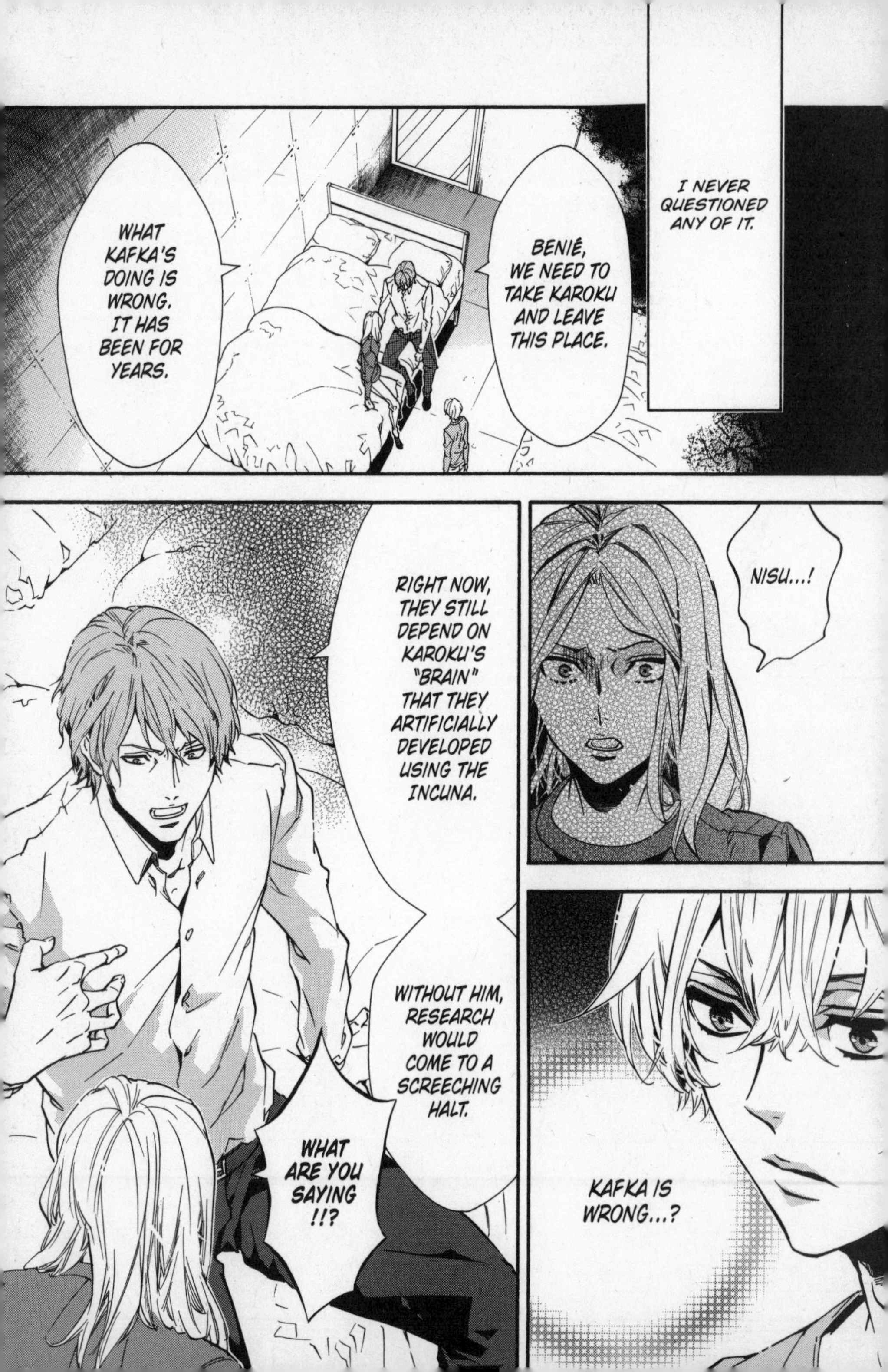
I NEVER QUESTIONED ANY OF IT.
BENIÉ, WE NEED TO TAKE KAROKU AND LEAVE THIS PLACE.
WHAT KAFKA'S DOING IS WRONG. IT HAS BEEN FOR YEARS.
NISU...!
KAFKA IS WRONG...?
RIGHT NOW, THEY STILL DEPEND ON KAROKU'S "BRAIN" THAT THEY ARTIFICIALLY DEVELOPED USING THE INCUNA.
WITHOUT HIM, RESEARCH WOULD COME TO A SCREECHING HALT.
WHAT ARE YOU SAYING !!?

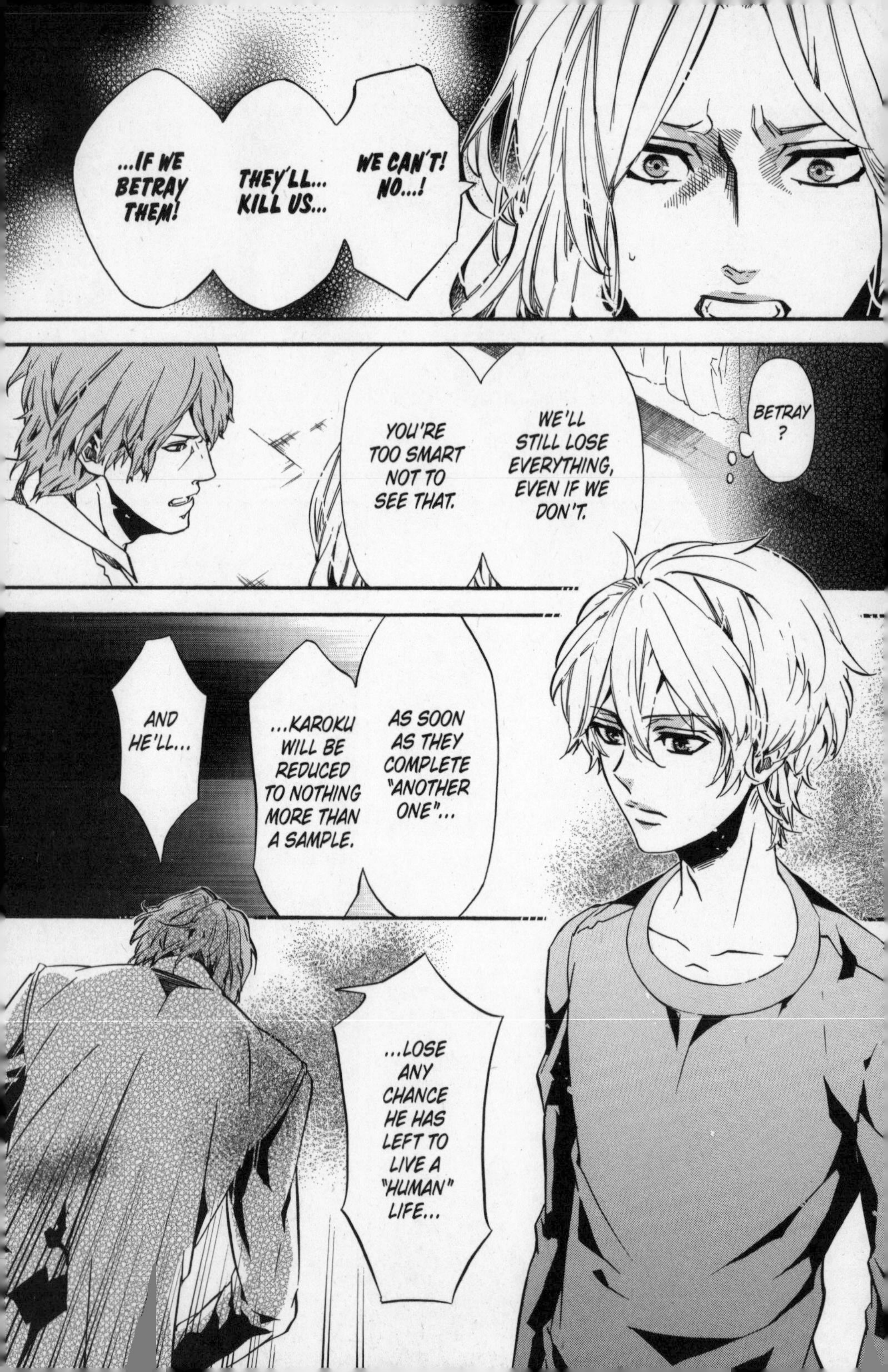
WE CAN'T! NO...!
THEY'LL... KILL US...
...IF WE BETRAY THEM!
BETRAY?
WE'LL STILL LOSE EVERYTHING, EVEN IF WE DON'T.
YOU'RE TOO SMART NOT TO SEE THAT.
AS SOON AS THEY COMPLETE "ANOTHER ONE"...
...KAROKU WILL BE REDUCED TO NOTHING MORE THAN A SAMPLE.
AND HE'LL...
...LOSE ANY CHANCE HE HAS LEFT TO LIVE A "HUMAN" LIFE...

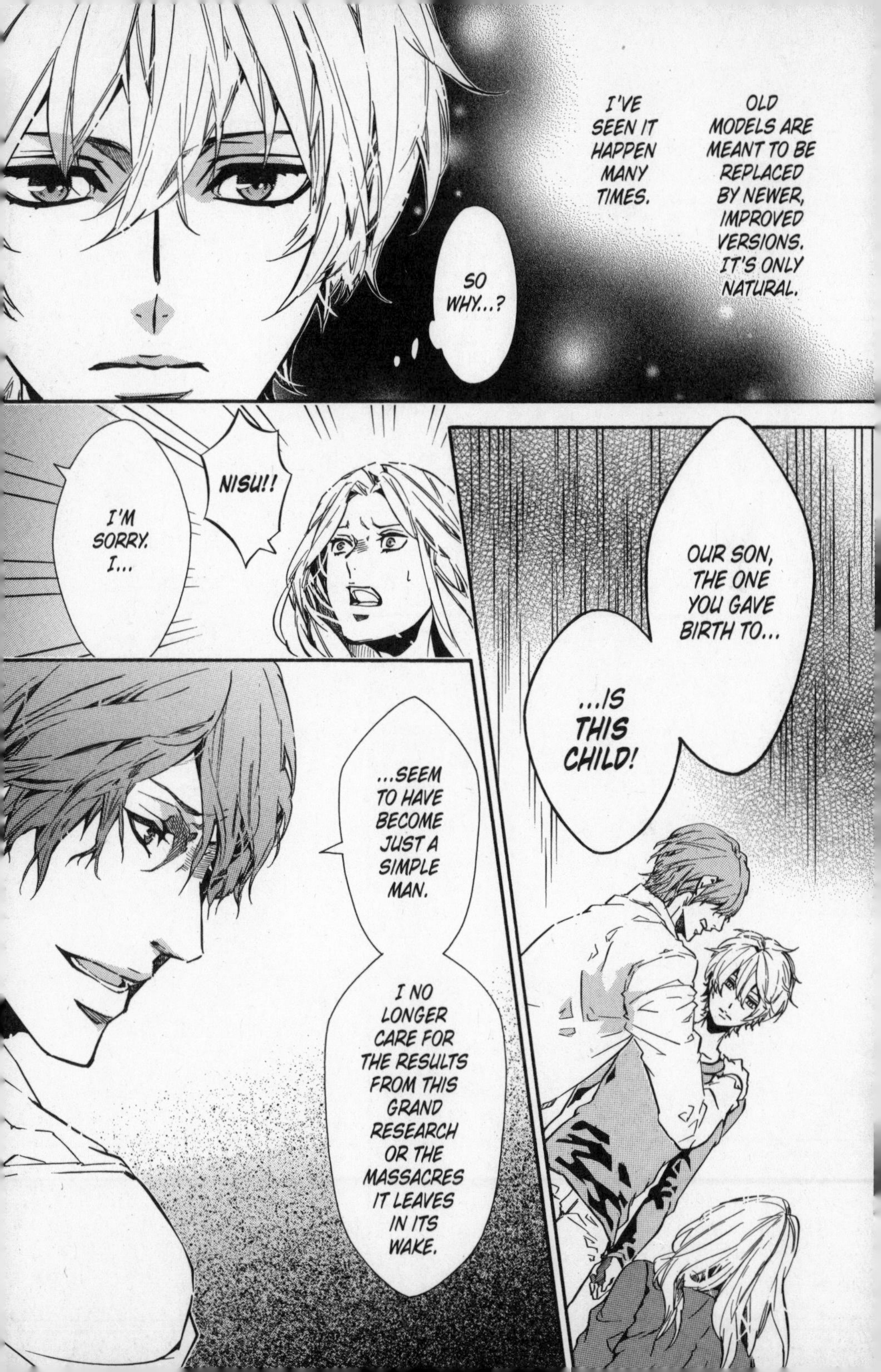
OLD MODELS ARE MEANT TO BE REPLACED BY NEWER, IMPROVED VERSIONS. IT'S ONLY NATURAL.
I'VE SEEN IT HAPPEN MANY TIMES.
SO WHY...?
OUR SON, THE ONE YOU GAVE BIRTH TO...
...IS **THIS CHILD!**
NISU!!
I'M SORRY. I...
...SEEM TO HAVE BECOME JUST A SIMPLE MAN.
I NO LONGER CARE FOR THE RESULTS FROM THIS GRAND RESEARCH OR THE MASSACRES IT LEAVES IN ITS WAKE.

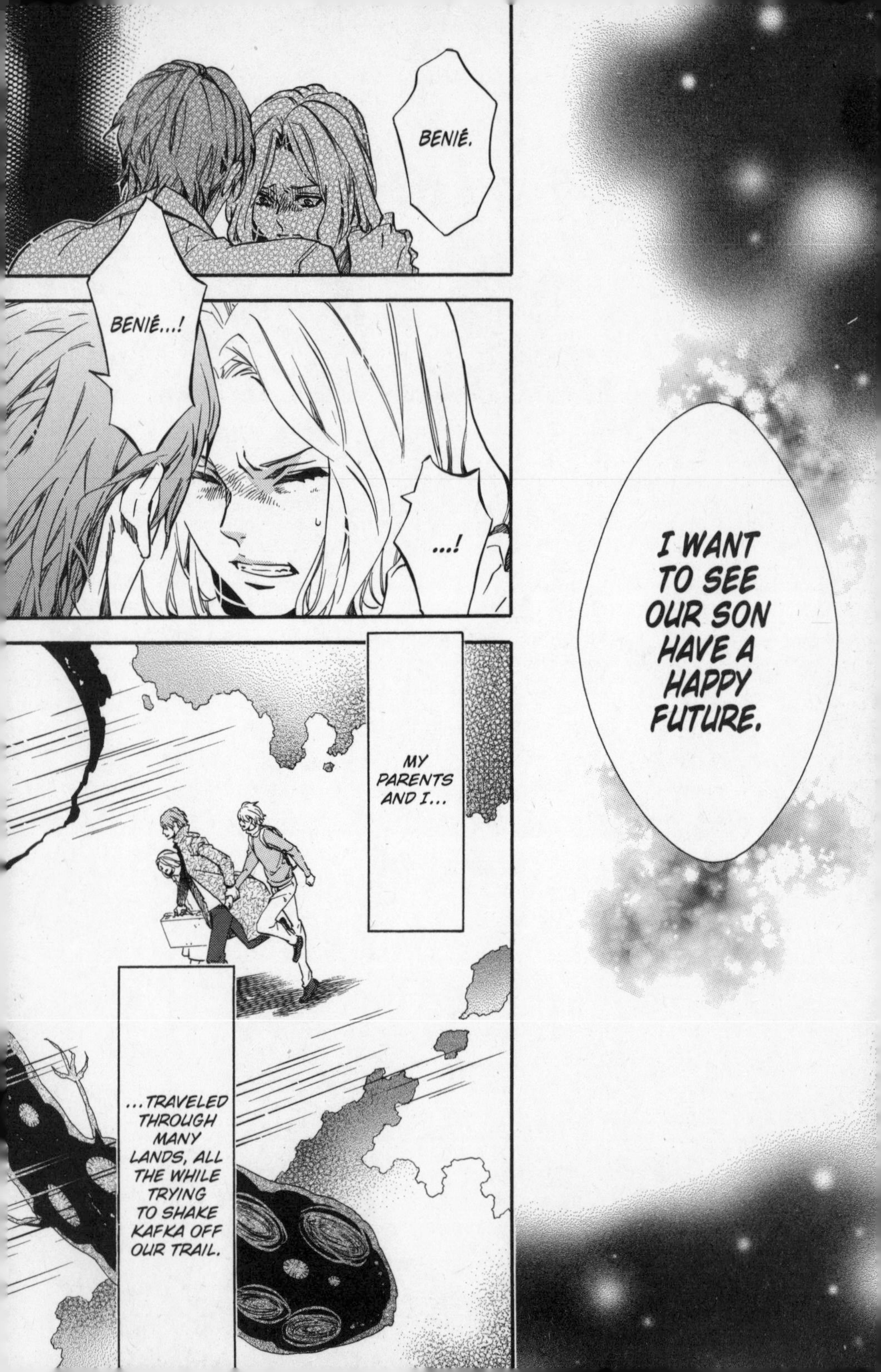
I WANT TO SEE OUR SON HAVE A HAPPY FUTURE.
BENIÉ.
BENIÉ...!
...!
MY PARENTS AND I...
...TRAVELED THROUGH MANY LANDS, ALL THE WHILE TRYING TO SHAKE KAFKA OFF OUR TRAIL.

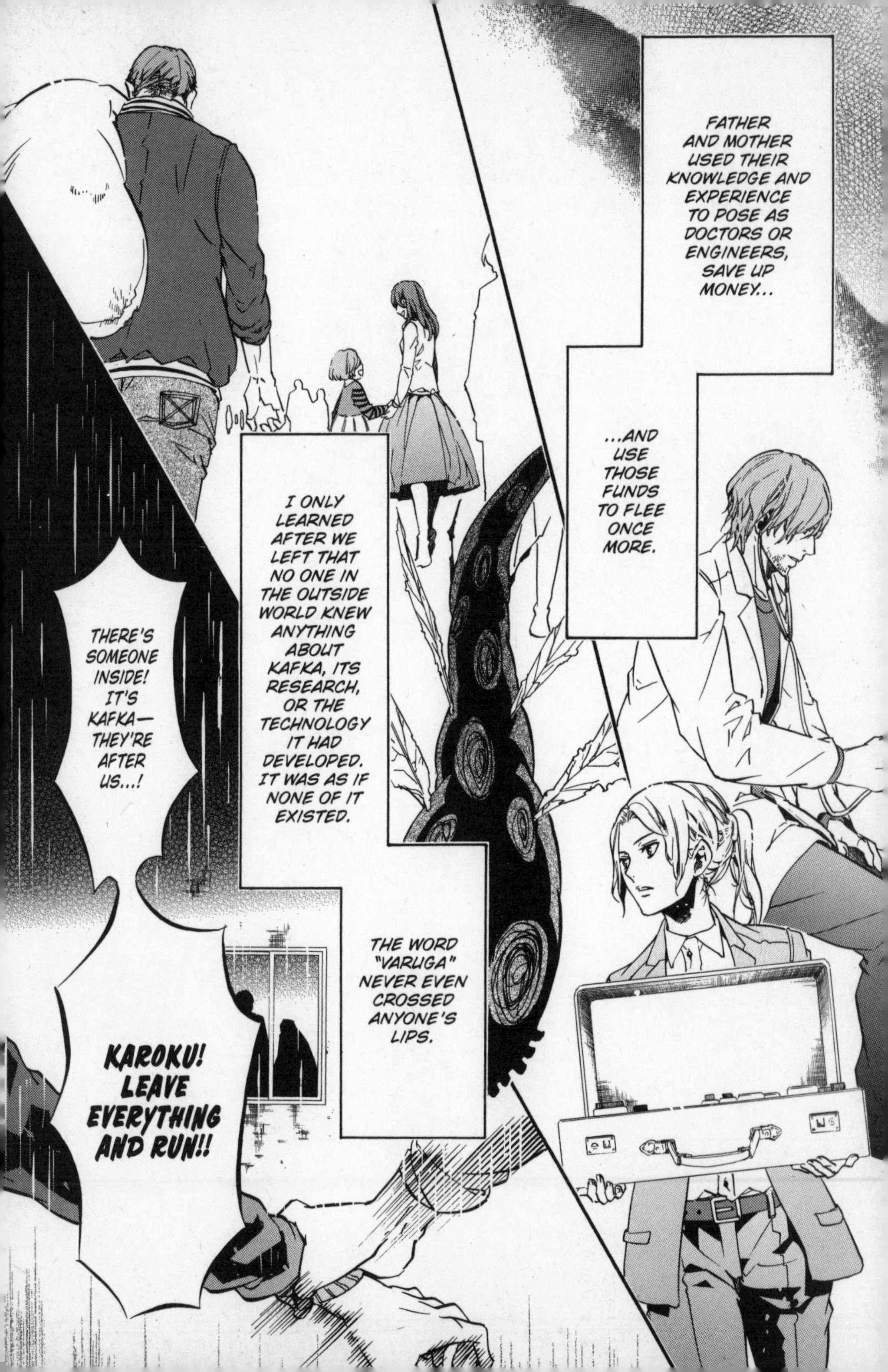

FATHER AND MOTHER USED THEIR KNOWLEDGE AND EXPERIENCE TO POSE AS DOCTORS OR ENGINEERS, SAVE UP MONEY...
...AND USE THOSE FUNDS TO FLEE ONCE MORE.
I ONLY LEARNED AFTER WE LEFT THAT NO ONE IN THE OUTSIDE WORLD KNEW ANYTHING ABOUT KAFKA, ITS RESEARCH, OR THE TECHNOLOGY IT HAD DEVELOPED. IT WAS AS IF NONE OF IT EXISTED.
THE WORD "VARUGA" NEVER EVEN CROSSED ANYONE'S LIPS.
THERE'S SOMEONE INSIDE! IT'S KAFKA—THEY'RE AFTER US...!
KAROKU! LEAVE EVERYTHING AND RUN!!

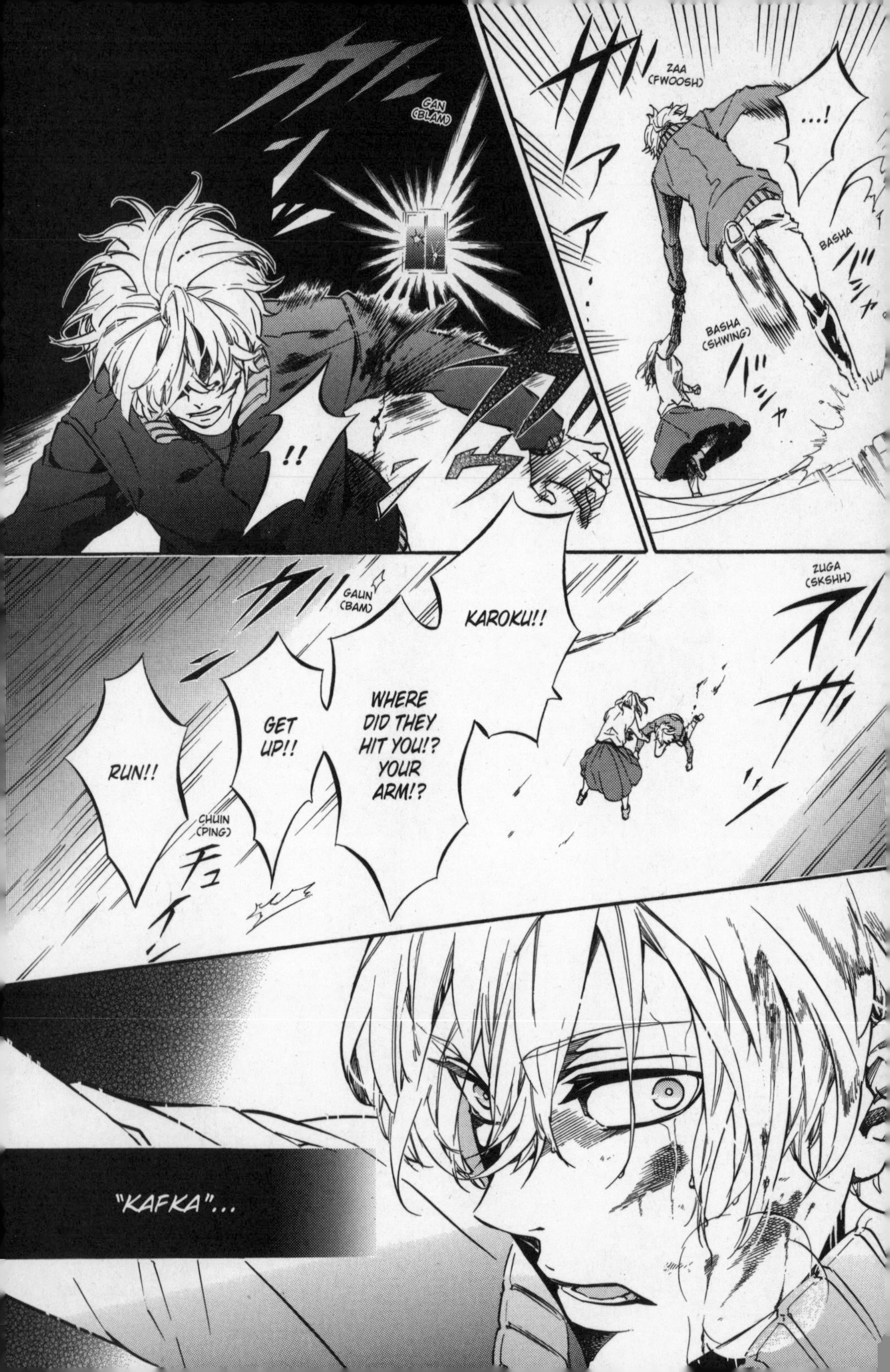
ZAA (FWOOSH)
...!
BASHA
BASHA (SHWING)
GAN (BLAM)
!!
ZUGA (SKSHH)
KAROKU!!
GAUN (BAM)
WHERE DID THEY HIT YOU!? YOUR ARM!?
GET UP!!
RUN!!
CHUIN (PING)
"KAFKA"...

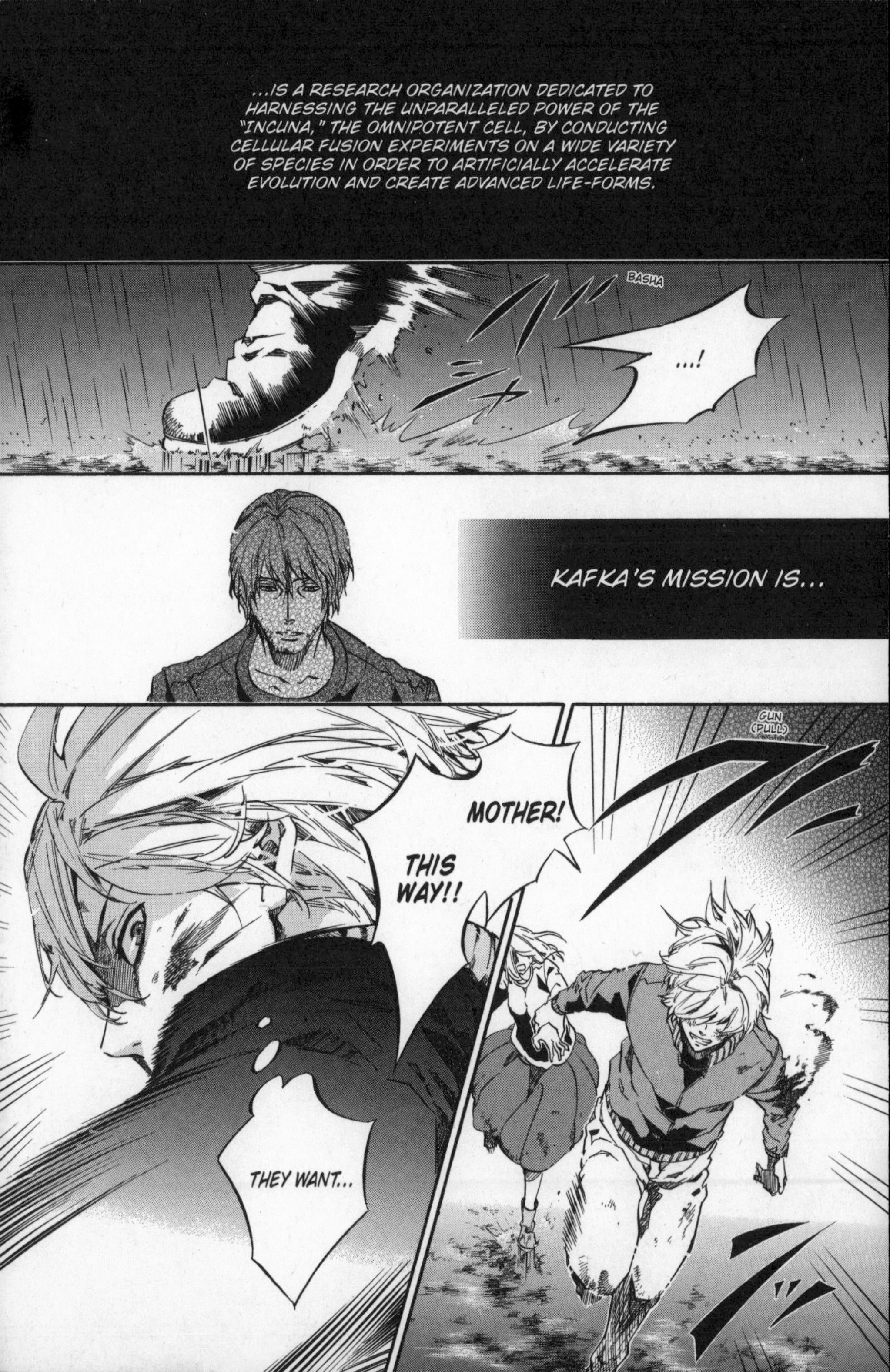
...IS A RESEARCH ORGANIZATION DEDICATED TO HARNESSING THE UNPARALLELED POWER OF THE "INCUNA," THE OMNIPOTENT CELL, BY CONDUCTING CELLULAR FUSION EXPERIMENTS ON A WIDE VARIETY OF SPECIES IN ORDER TO ARTIFICIALLY ACCELERATE EVOLUTION AND CREATE ADVANCED LIFE-FORMS.
BASHA
...!
KAFKA'S MISSION IS...
GUN (PULL)
MOTHER!
THIS WAY!!
THEY WANT...

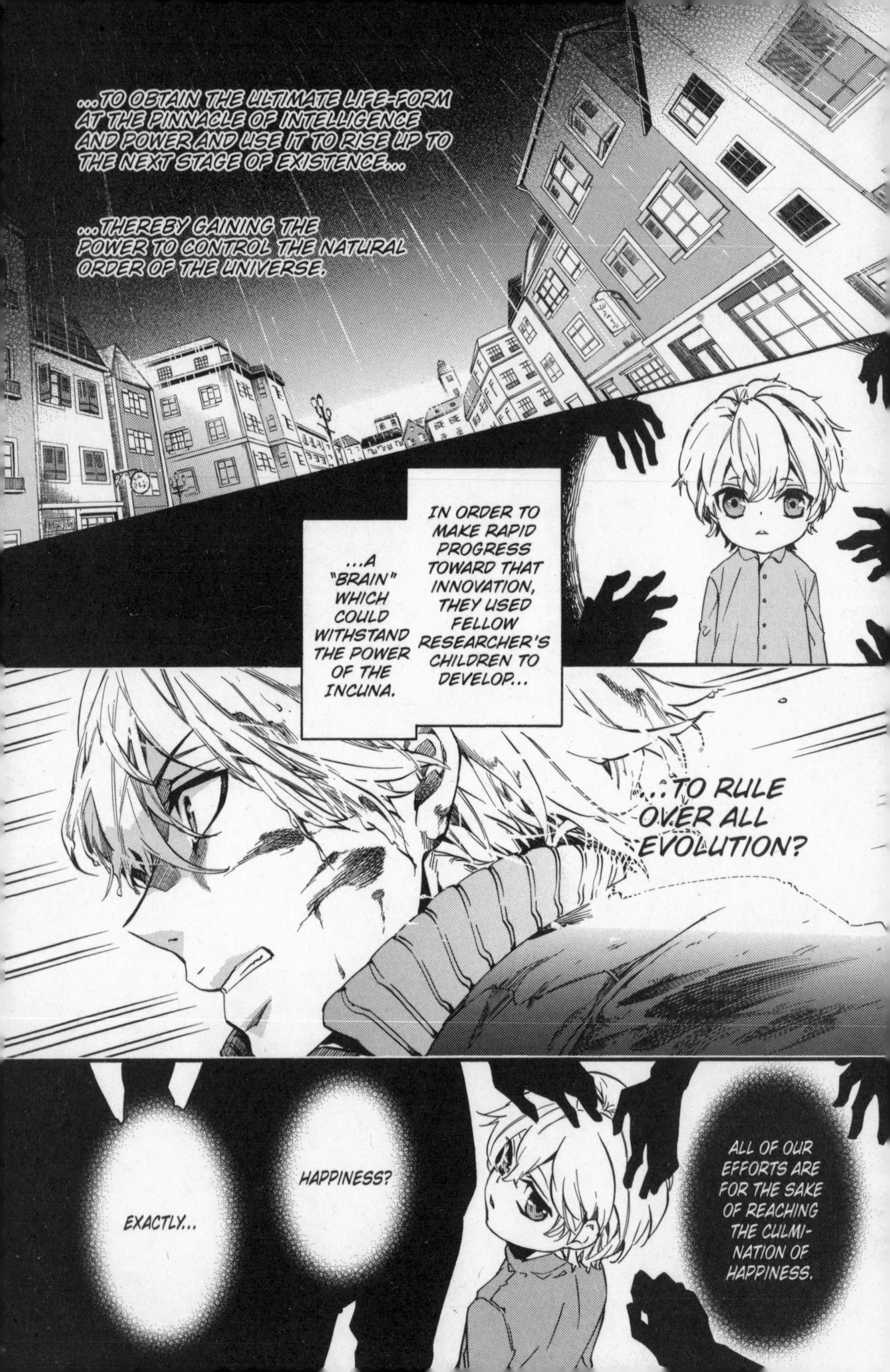
...TO OBTAIN THE ULTIMATE LIFE-FORM AT THE PINNACLE OF INTELLIGENCE AND POWER AND USE IT TO RISE UP TO THE NEXT STAGE OF EXISTENCE...
...THEREBY GAINING THE POWER TO CONTROL THE NATURAL ORDER OF THE UNIVERSE.
IN ORDER TO MAKE RAPID PROGRESS TOWARD THAT INNOVATION, THEY USED FELLOW RESEARCHER'S CHILDREN TO DEVELOP...
...A "BRAIN" WHICH COULD WITHSTAND THE POWER OF THE INCUNA.
...TO RULE OVER ALL EVOLUTION?
ALL OF OUR EFFORTS ARE FOR THE SAKE OF REACHING THE CULMI-NATION OF HAPPINESS.
HAPPINESS?
EXACTLY...

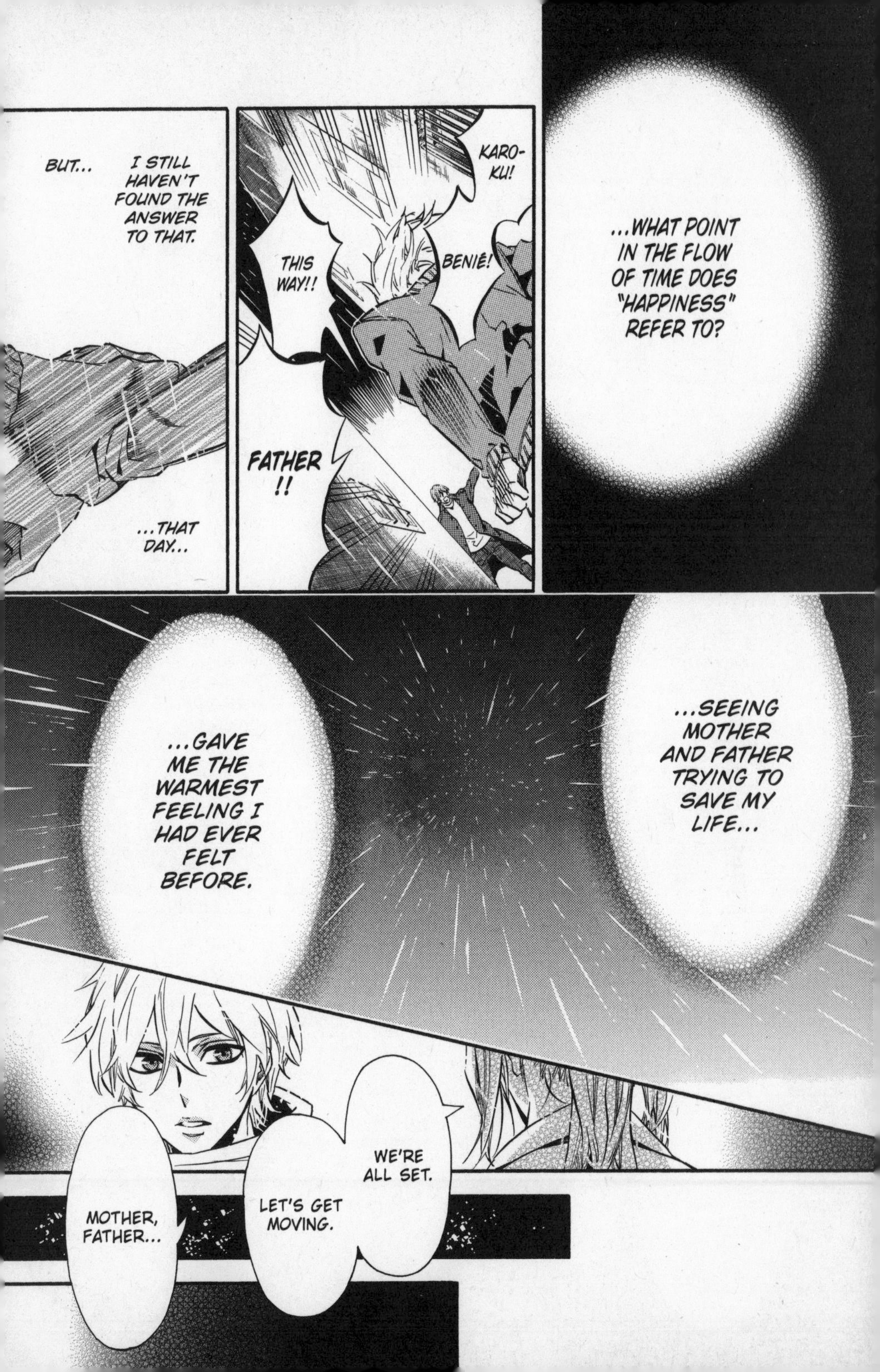
...WHAT POINT IN THE FLOW OF TIME DOES "HAPPINESS" REFER TO?
KARO-KU!
BENIÉ!
THIS WAY!!
FATHER !!
I STILL HAVEN'T FOUND THE ANSWER TO THAT.
BUT...
...THAT DAY...
...SEEING MOTHER AND FATHER TRYING TO SAVE MY LIFE...
...GAVE ME THE WARMEST FEELING I HAD EVER FELT BEFORE.
WE'RE ALL SET.
LET'S GET MOVING.
MOTHER, FATHER...

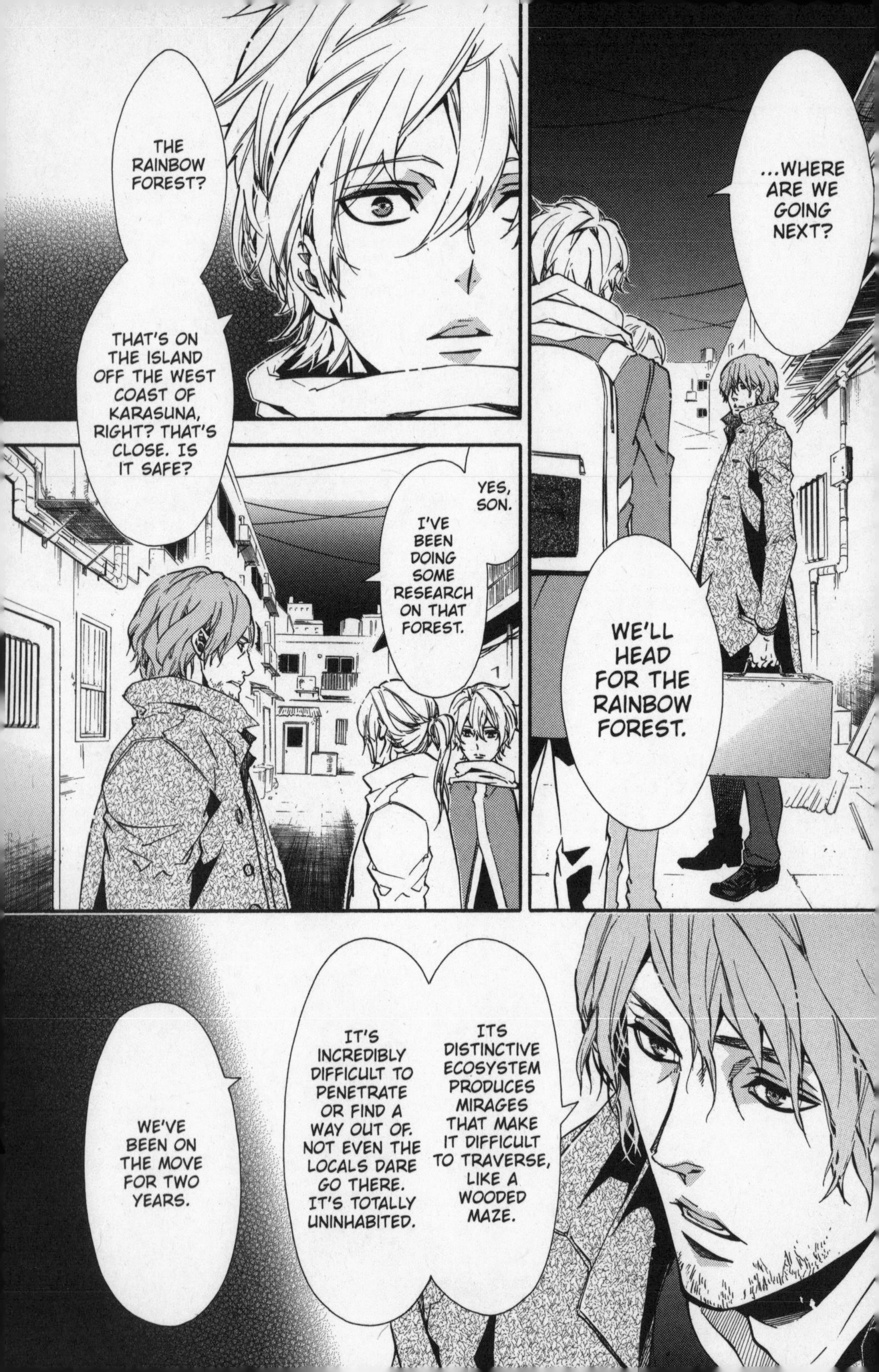
...WHERE ARE WE GOING NEXT?
WE'LL HEAD FOR THE RAINBOW FOREST.
THE RAINBOW FOREST?
THAT'S ON THE ISLAND OFF THE WEST COAST OF KARASUNA, RIGHT? THAT'S CLOSE. IS IT SAFE?
YES, SON.
I'VE BEEN DOING SOME RESEARCH ON THAT FOREST.
ITS DISTINCTIVE ECOSYSTEM PRODUCES MIRAGES THAT MAKE IT DIFFICULT TO TRAVERSE, LIKE A WOODED MAZE.
IT'S INCREDIBLY DIFFICULT TO PENETRATE OR FIND A WAY OUT OF. NOT EVEN THE LOCALS DARE GO THERE. IT'S TOTALLY UNINHABITED.
WE'VE BEEN ON THE MOVE FOR TWO YEARS.

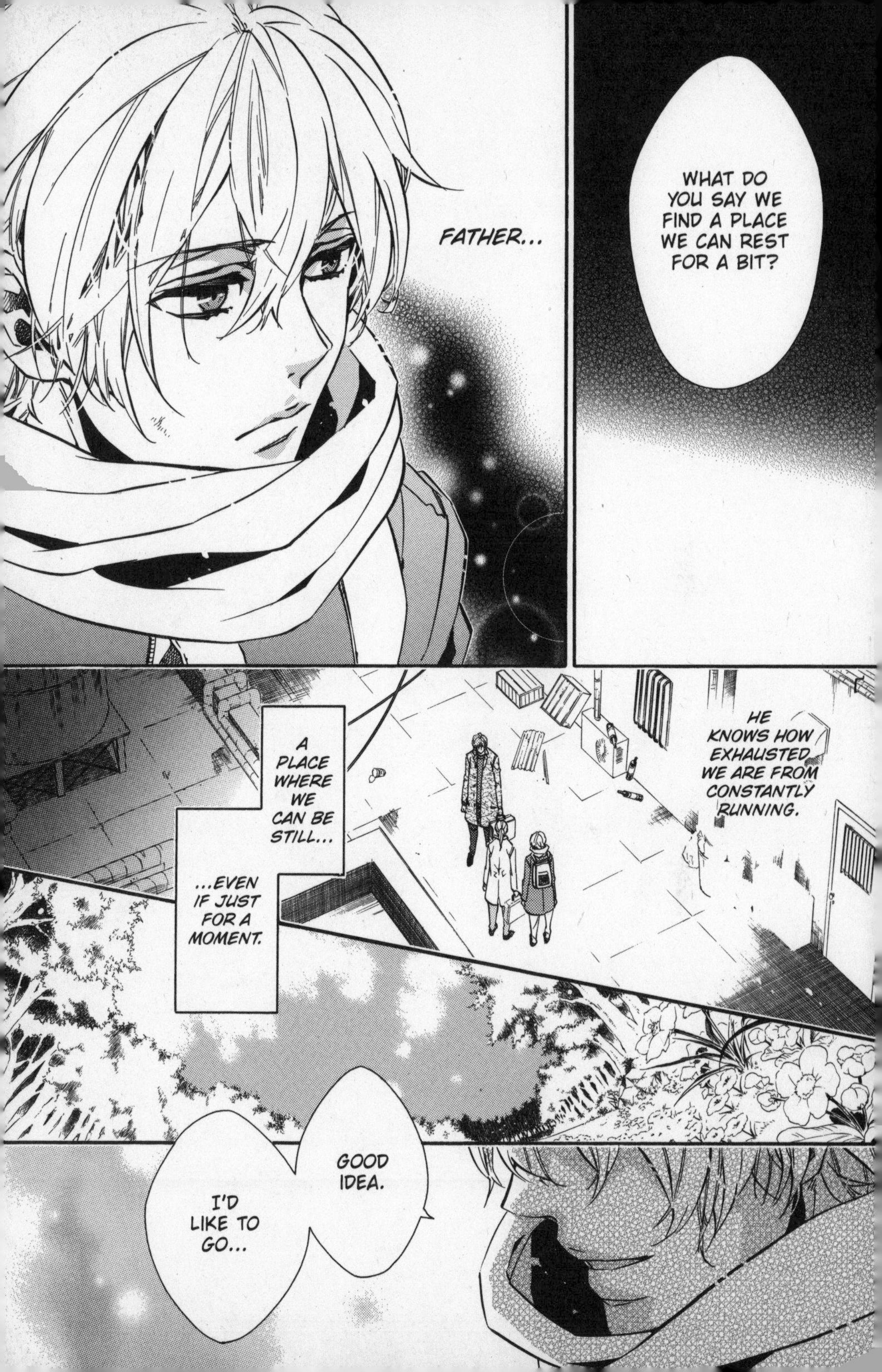
WHAT DO YOU SAY WE FIND A PLACE WE CAN REST FOR A BIT?
FATHER...
HE KNOWS HOW EXHAUSTED WE ARE FROM CONSTANTLY RUNNING.
A PLACE WHERE WE CAN BE STILL...
...EVEN IF JUST FOR A MOMENT.
GOOD IDEA.
I'D LIKE TO GO...

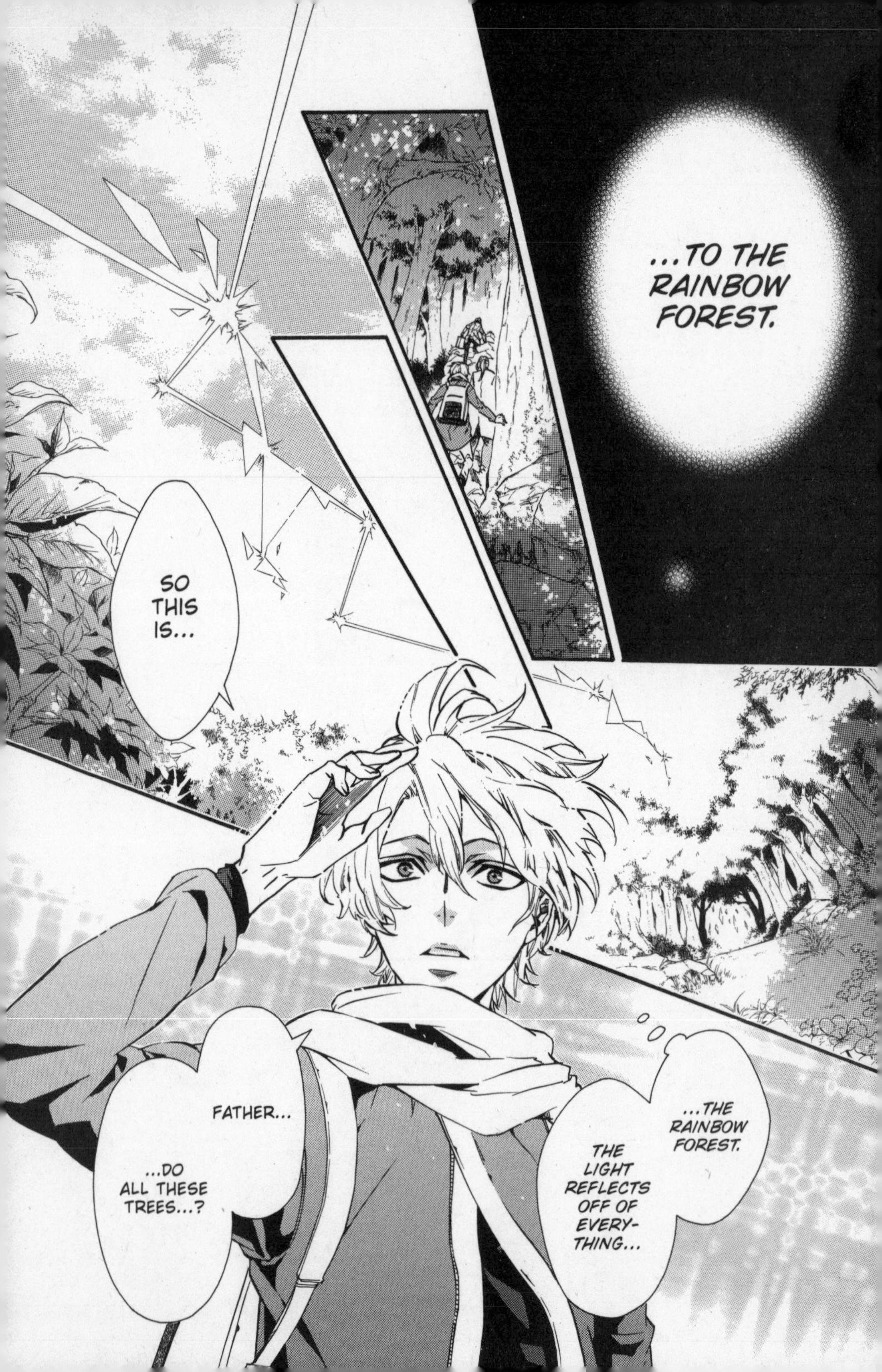
...TO THE RAINBOW FOREST.
SO THIS IS...
...THE RAINBOW FOREST.
THE LIGHT REFLECTS OFF OF EVERY-THING...
FATHER...
...DO ALL THESE TREES...?

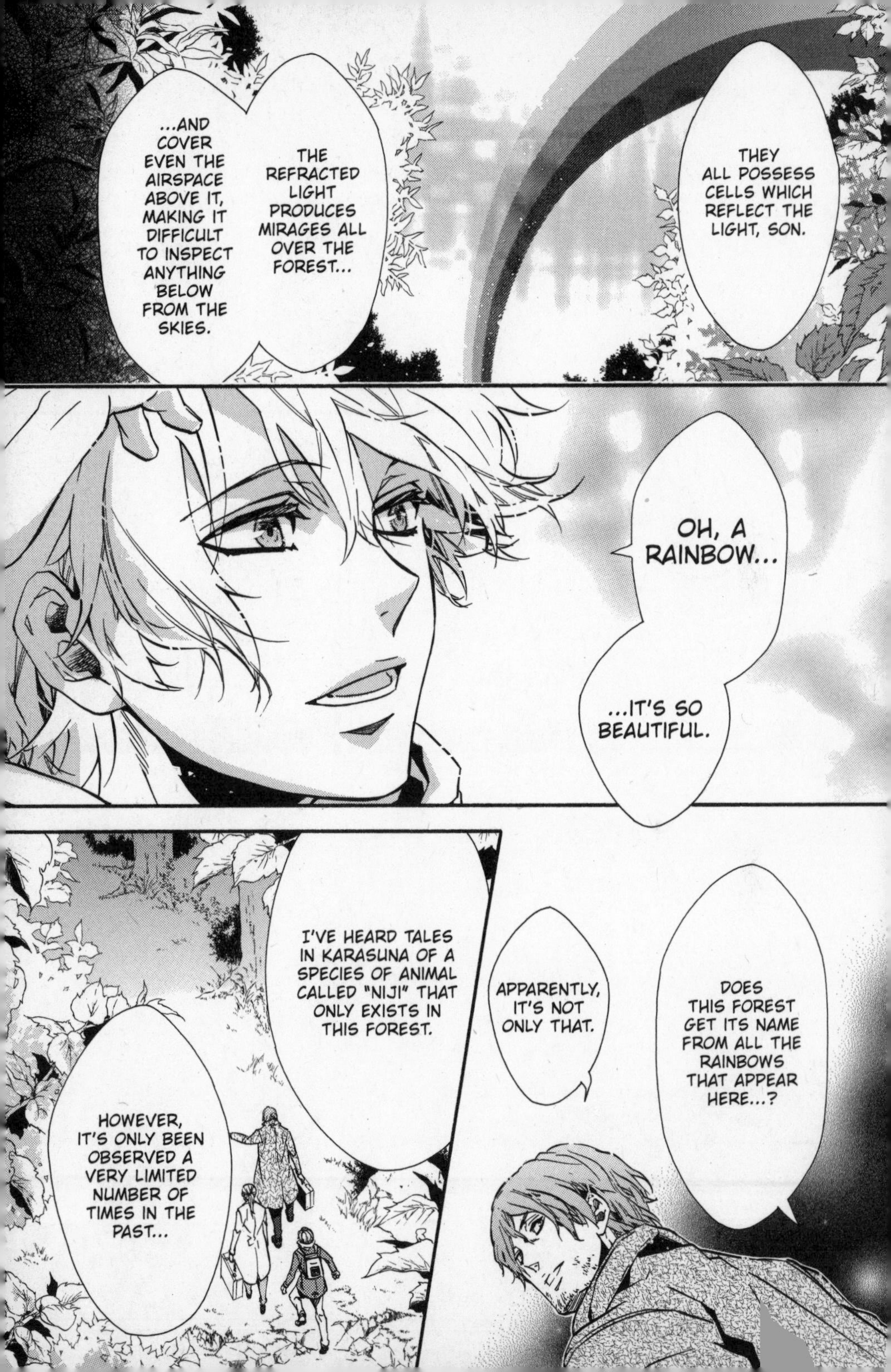
THEY ALL POSSESS CELLS WHICH REFLECT THE LIGHT, SON.
THE REFRACTED LIGHT PRODUCES MIRAGES ALL OVER THE FOREST...
...AND COVER EVEN THE AIRSPACE ABOVE IT, MAKING IT DIFFICULT TO INSPECT ANYTHING BELOW FROM THE SKIES.
OH, A RAINBOW...
...IT'S SO BEAUTIFUL.
DOES THIS FOREST GET ITS NAME FROM ALL THE RAINBOWS THAT APPEAR HERE...?
APPARENTLY, IT'S NOT ONLY THAT.
I'VE HEARD TALES IN KARASUNA OF A SPECIES OF ANIMAL CALLED "NIJI" THAT ONLY EXISTS IN THIS FOREST.
HOWEVER, IT'S ONLY BEEN OBSERVED A VERY LIMITED NUMBER OF TIMES IN THE PAST...

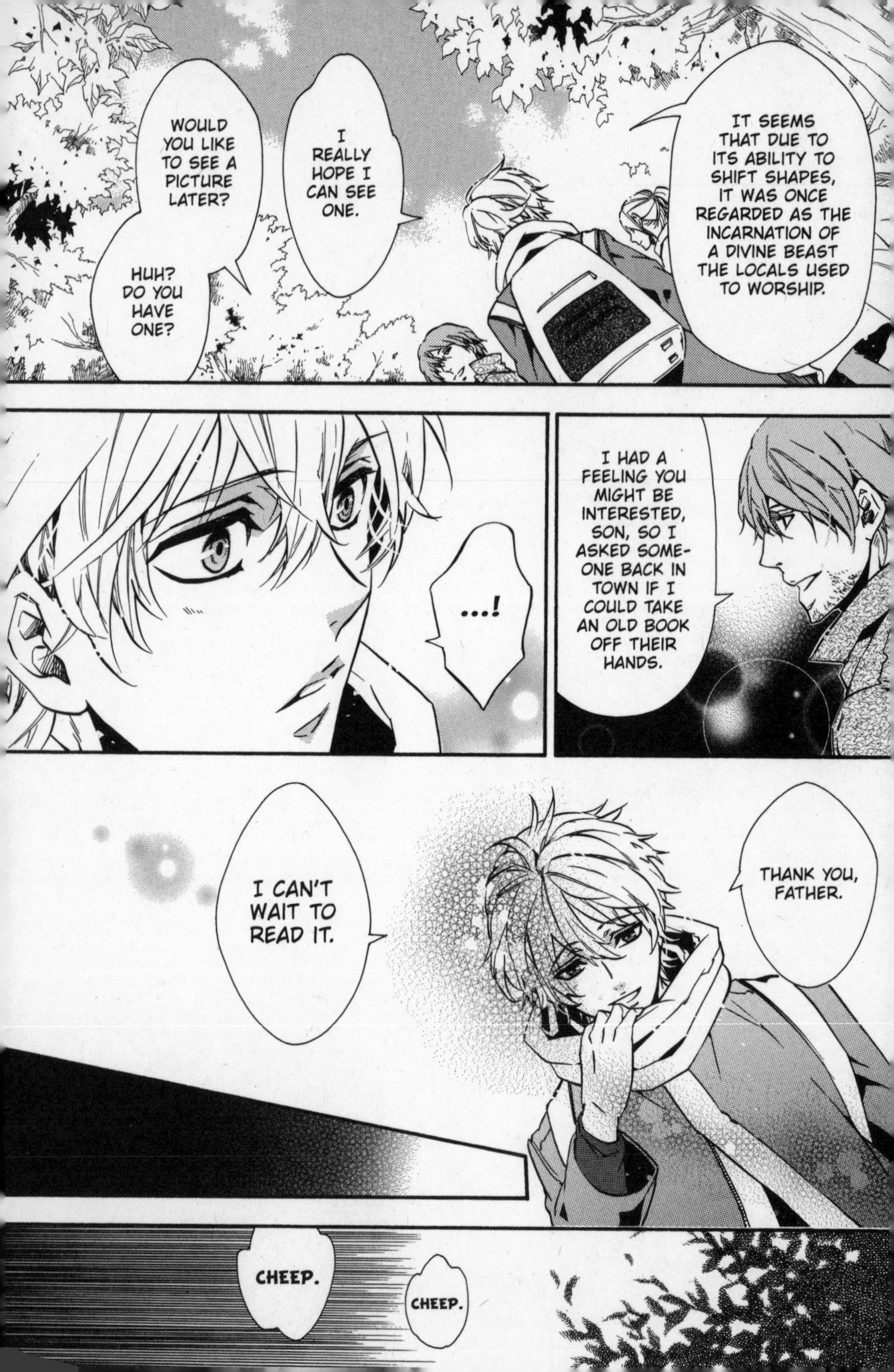
IT SEEMS THAT DUE TO ITS ABILITY TO SHIFT SHAPES, IT WAS ONCE REGARDED AS THE INCARNATION OF A DIVINE BEAST THE LOCALS USED TO WORSHIP.
I REALLY HOPE I CAN SEE ONE.
WOULD YOU LIKE TO SEE A PICTURE LATER?
HUH? DO YOU HAVE ONE?
I HAD A FEELING YOU MIGHT BE INTERESTED, SON, SO I ASKED SOME-ONE BACK IN TOWN IF I COULD TAKE AN OLD BOOK OFF THEIR HANDS.
...!
THANK YOU, FATHER.
I CAN'T WAIT TO READ IT.
CHEEP.
CHEEP.

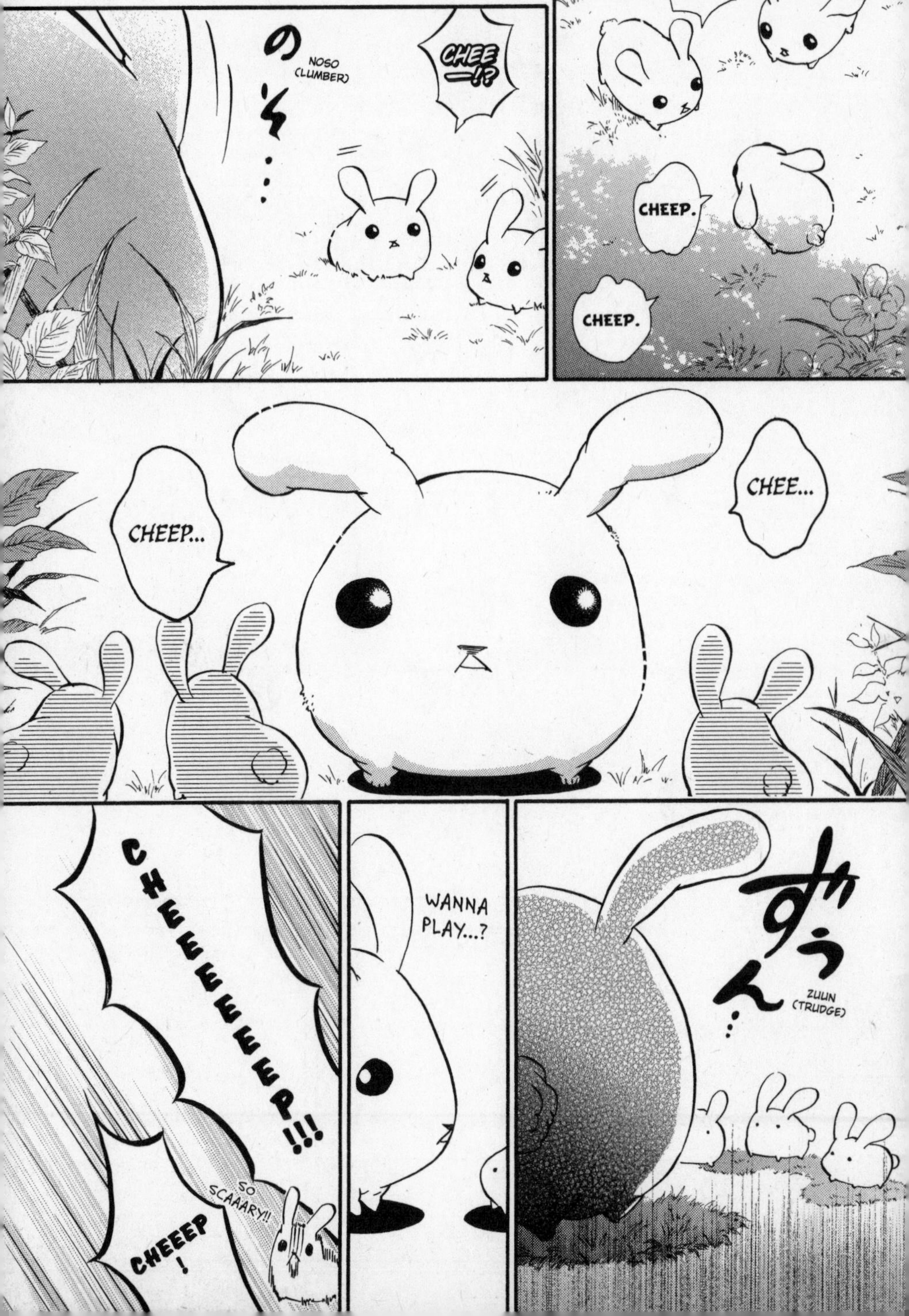
CHEEP.
CHEEP.
CHEEP.
CHEE—!?
のそ…
NOSO (LUMBER)
CHEE...
CHEEP...
ずうん…
ZUUN (TRUDGE)
WANNA PLAY...?
CHEEEEEEP!!!
SO SCAAARY!!
CHEEEP!

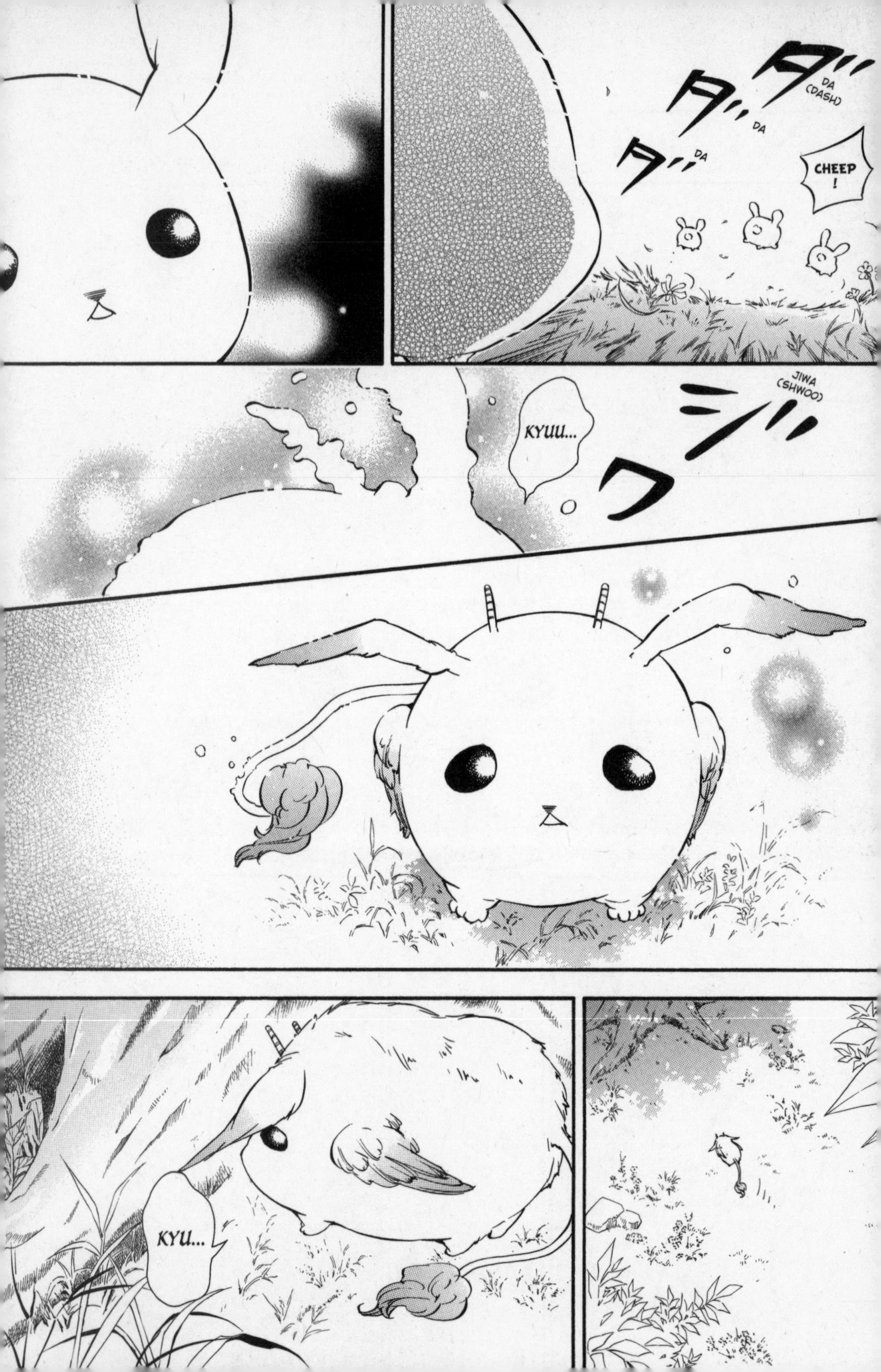
DA (DASH)
DA
DA
CHEEP!
JIWA (SHWOO)
KYUU...
KYU...

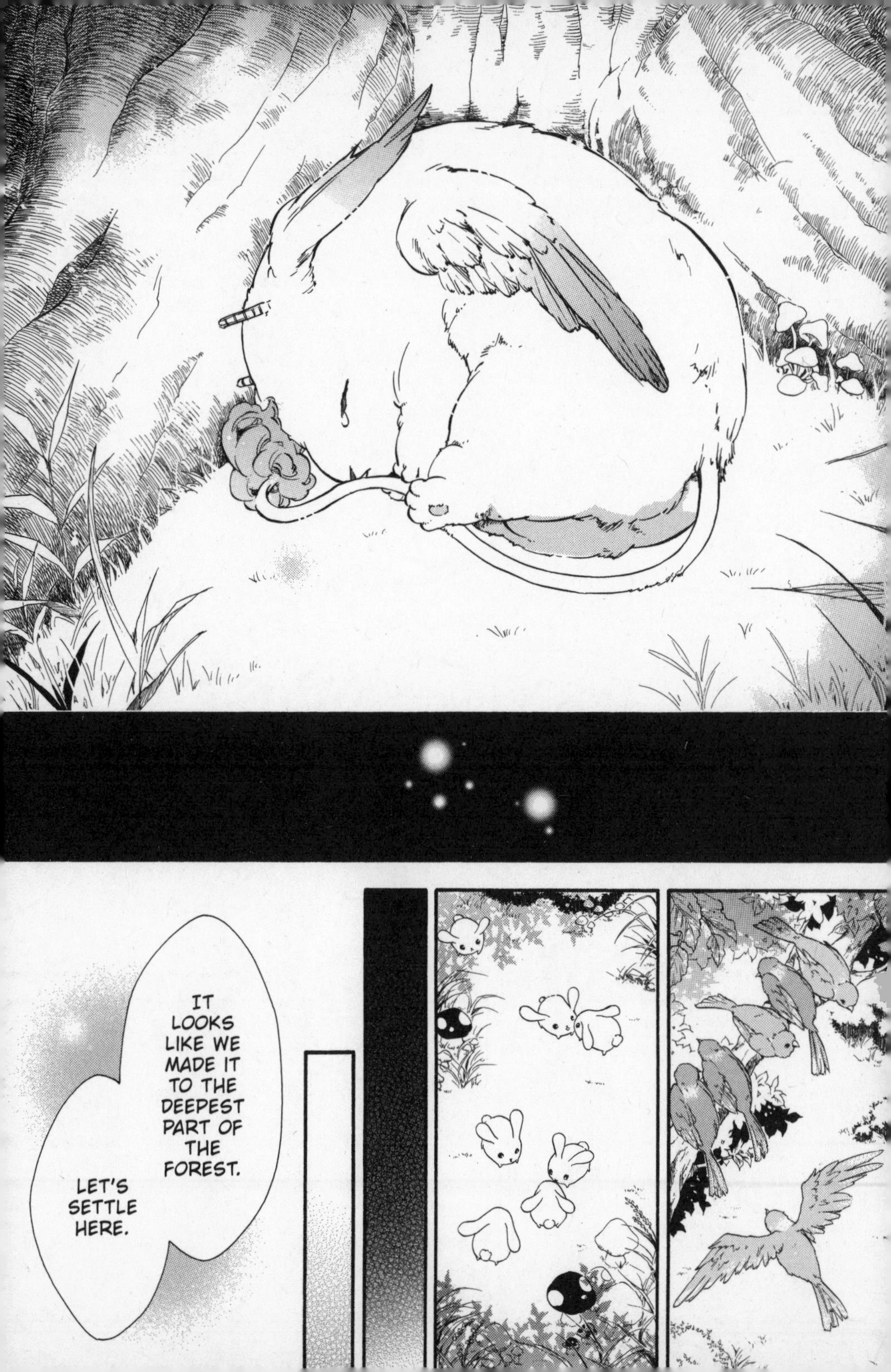
IT LOOKS LIKE WE MADE IT TO THE DEEPEST PART OF THE FOREST.
LET'S SETTLE HERE.

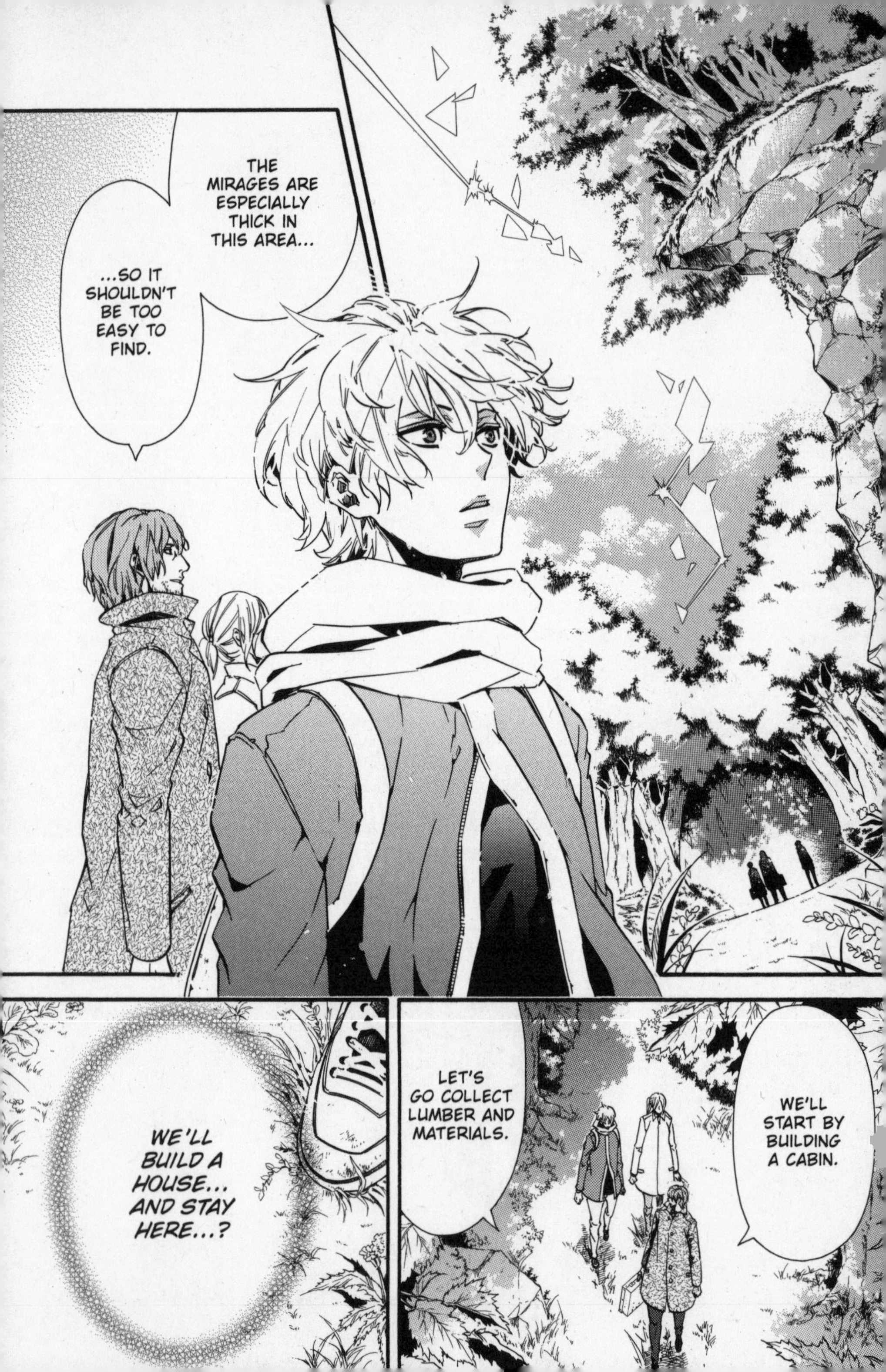
THE MIRAGES ARE ESPECIALLY THICK IN THIS AREA...
...SO IT SHOULDN'T BE TOO EASY TO FIND.
WE'LL START BY BUILDING A CABIN.
LET'S GO COLLECT LUMBER AND MATERIALS.
WE'LL BUILD A HOUSE... AND STAY HERE...?

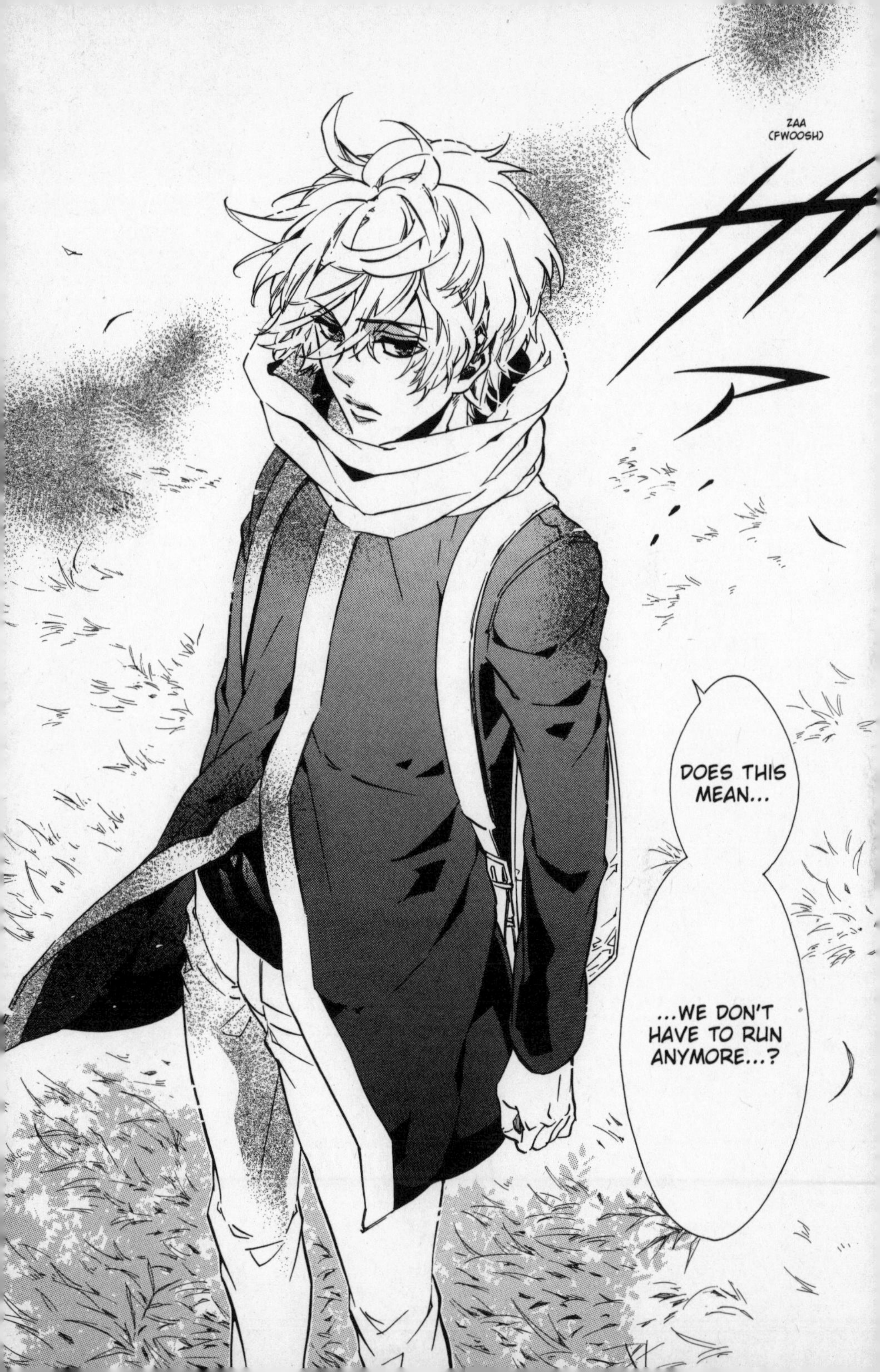
ZAA (FWOOSH)
DOES THIS MEAN...
...WE DON'T HAVE TO RUN ANYMORE...?

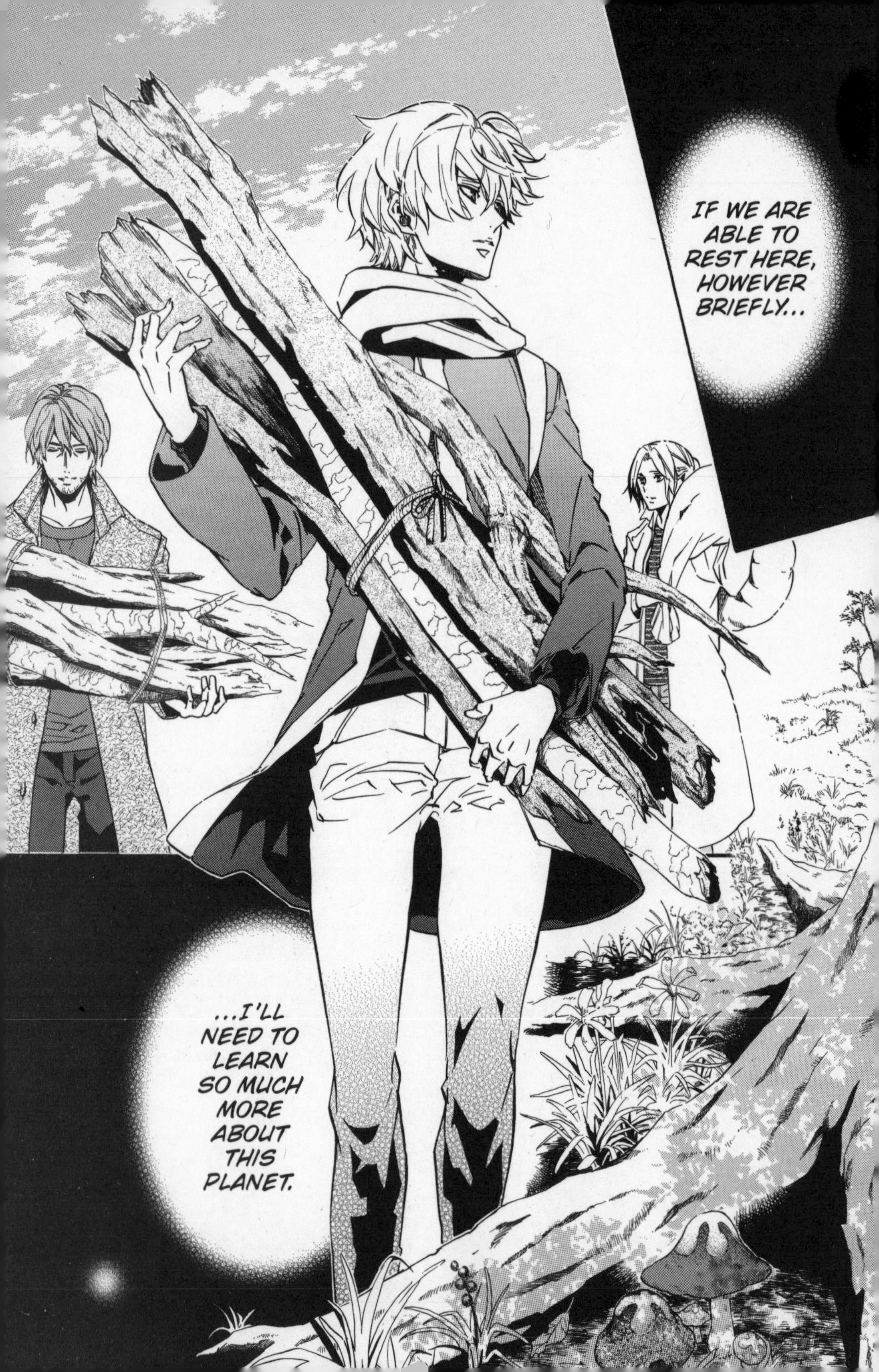
IF WE ARE ABLE TO REST HERE, HOWEVER BRIEFLY...
...I'LL NEED TO LEARN SO MUCH MORE ABOUT THIS PLANET.

KARNEVAL

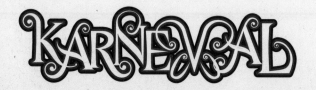

KARNEVAL

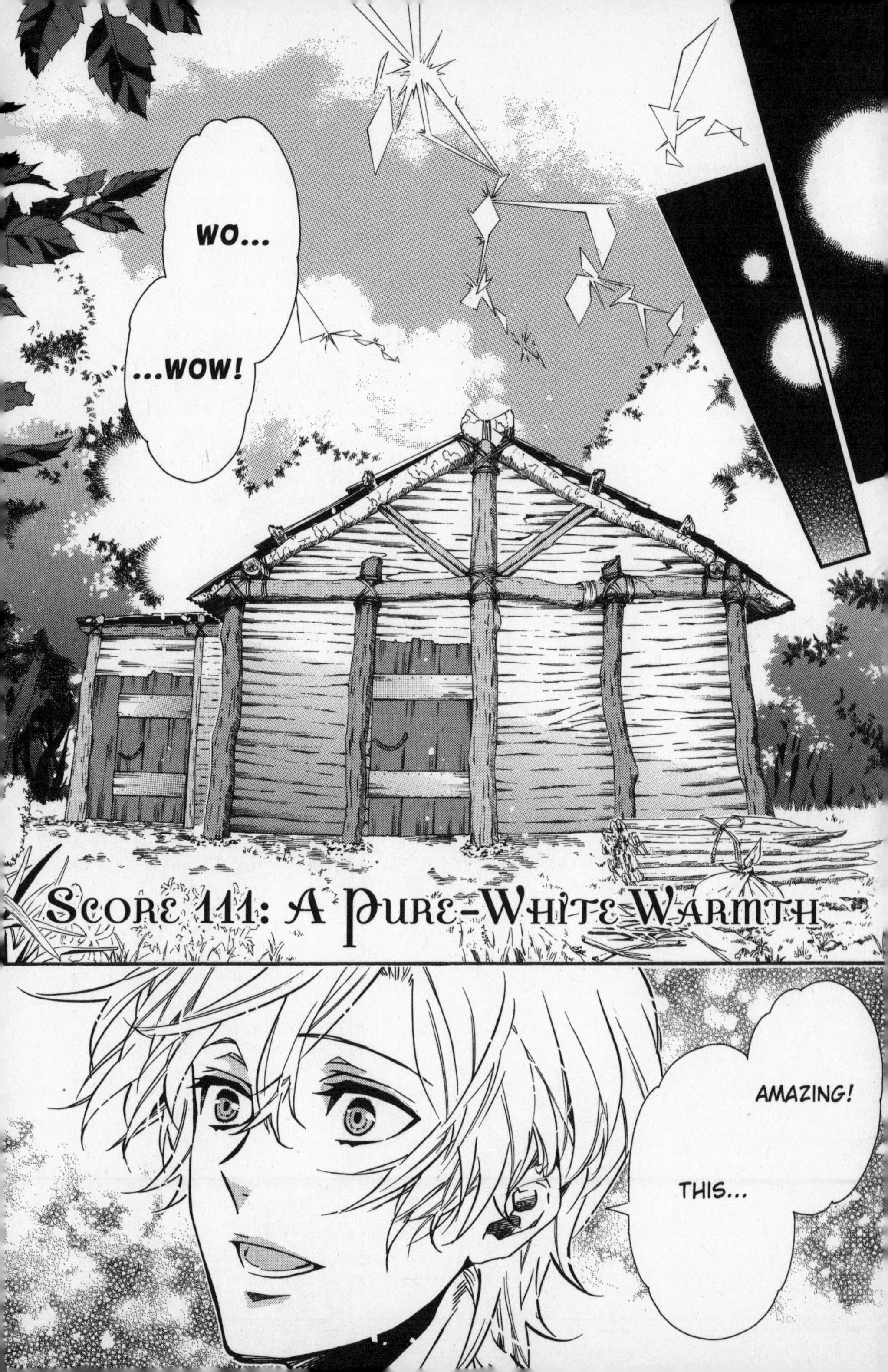
WO...
...WOW!
SCORE 111: A PURE-WHITE WARMTH
AMAZING!
THIS...

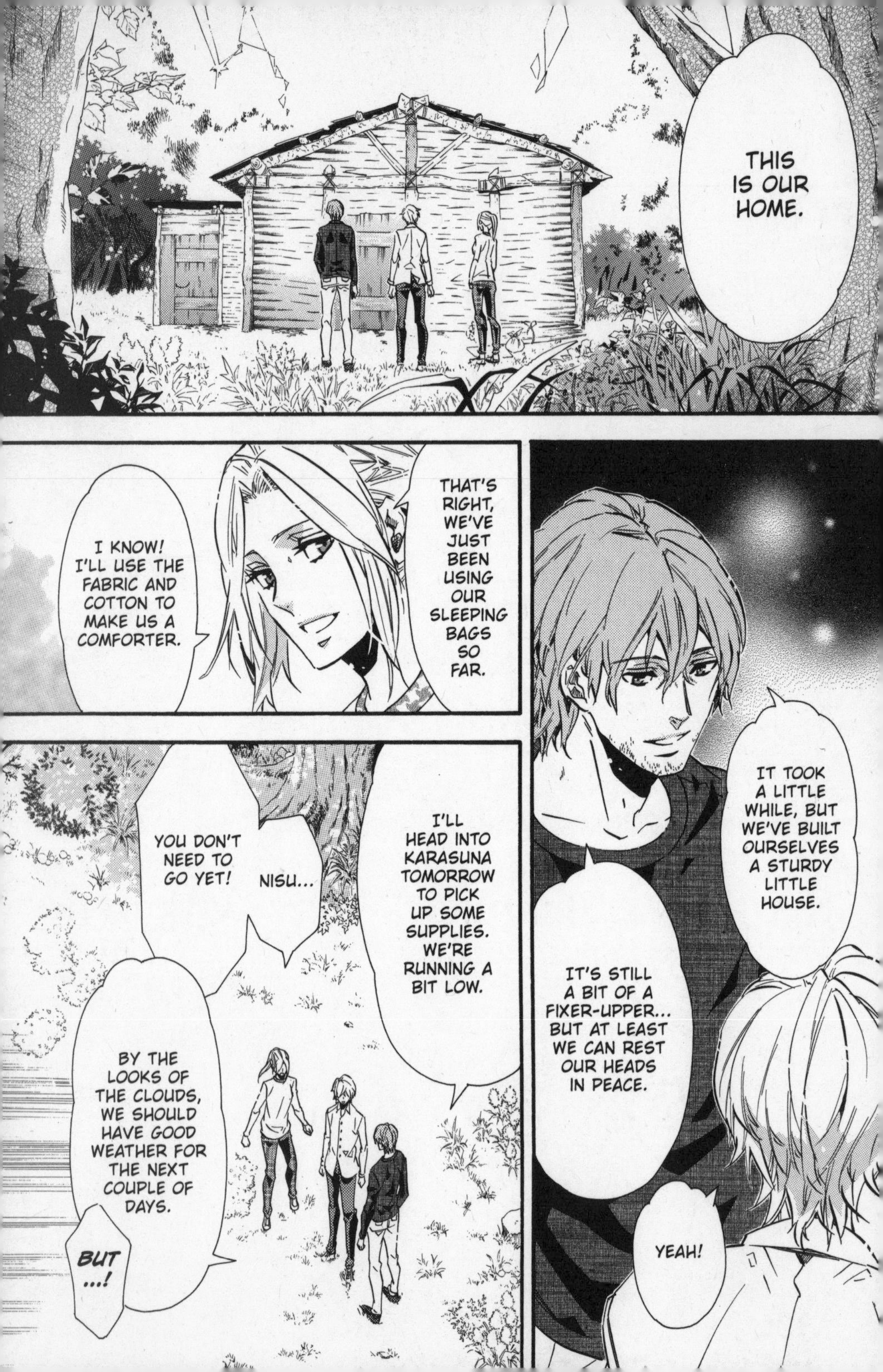
THIS IS OUR HOME.
IT TOOK A LITTLE WHILE, BUT WE'VE BUILT OURSELVES A STURDY LITTLE HOUSE.
IT'S STILL A BIT OF A FIXER-UPPER... BUT AT LEAST WE CAN REST OUR HEADS IN PEACE.
YEAH!
THAT'S RIGHT, WE'VE JUST BEEN USING OUR SLEEPING BAGS SO FAR.
I KNOW! I'LL USE THE FABRIC AND COTTON TO MAKE US A COMFORTER.
I'LL HEAD INTO KARASUNA TOMORROW TO PICK UP SOME SUPPLIES. WE'RE RUNNING A BIT LOW.
NISU...
YOU DON'T NEED TO GO YET!
BY THE LOOKS OF THE CLOUDS, WE SHOULD HAVE GOOD WEATHER FOR THE NEXT COUPLE OF DAYS.
BUT ...!

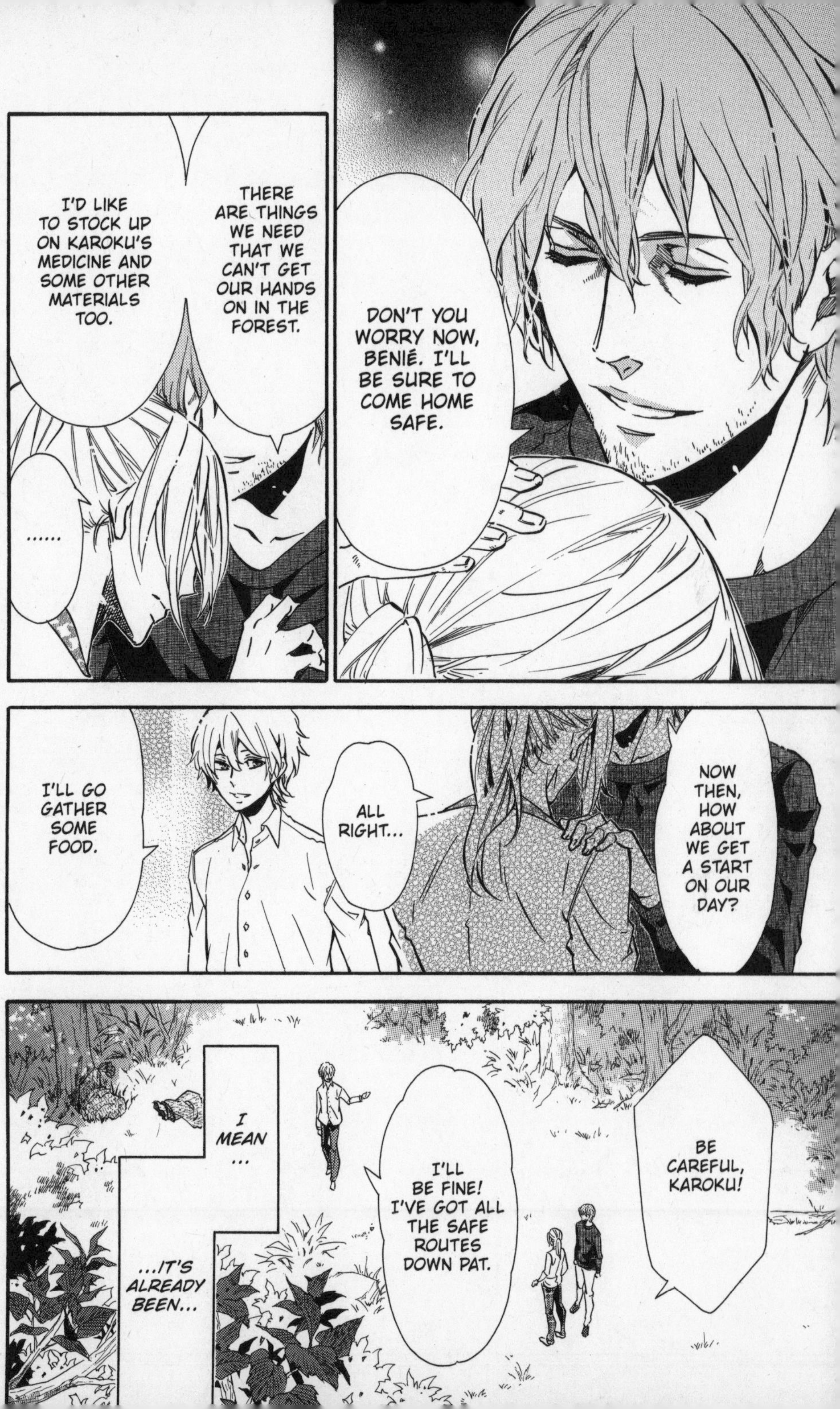
DON'T YOU WORRY NOW, BENIÉ. I'LL BE SURE TO COME HOME SAFE.
THERE ARE THINGS WE NEED THAT WE CAN'T GET OUR HANDS ON IN THE FOREST.
I'D LIKE TO STOCK UP ON KAROKU'S MEDICINE AND SOME OTHER MATERIALS TOO.
......
NOW THEN, HOW ABOUT WE GET A START ON OUR DAY?
ALL RIGHT...
I'LL GO GATHER SOME FOOD.
BE CAREFUL, KAROKU!
I'LL BE FINE! I'VE GOT ALL THE SAFE ROUTES DOWN PAT.
I MEAN...
...IT'S ALREADY BEEN...

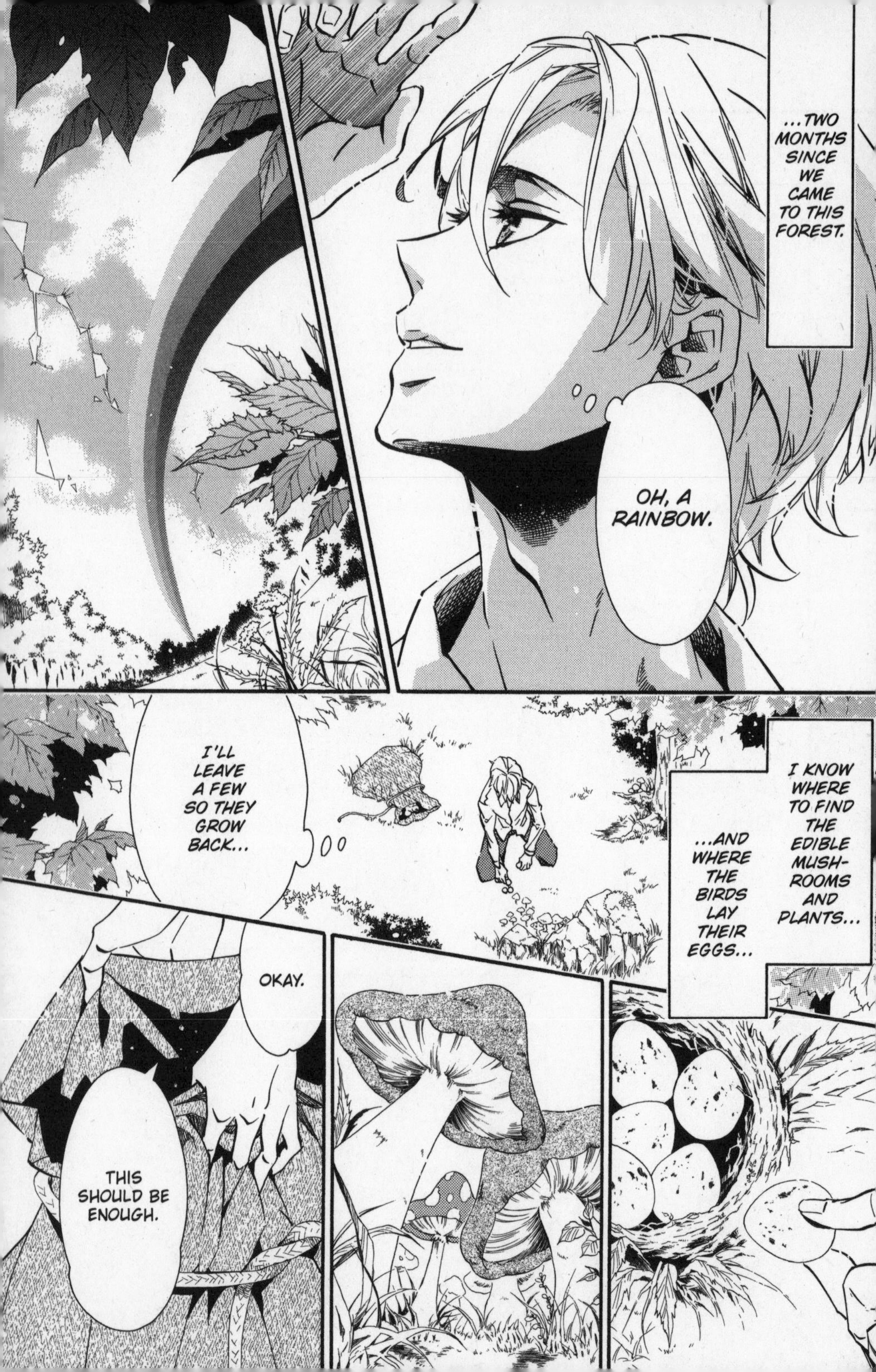
...TWO MONTHS SINCE WE CAME TO THIS FOREST.
OH, A RAINBOW.
I KNOW WHERE TO FIND THE EDIBLE MUSH-ROOMS AND PLANTS...
...AND WHERE THE BIRDS LAY THEIR EGGS...
I'LL LEAVE A FEW SO THEY GROW BACK...
OKAY.
THIS SHOULD BE ENOUGH.

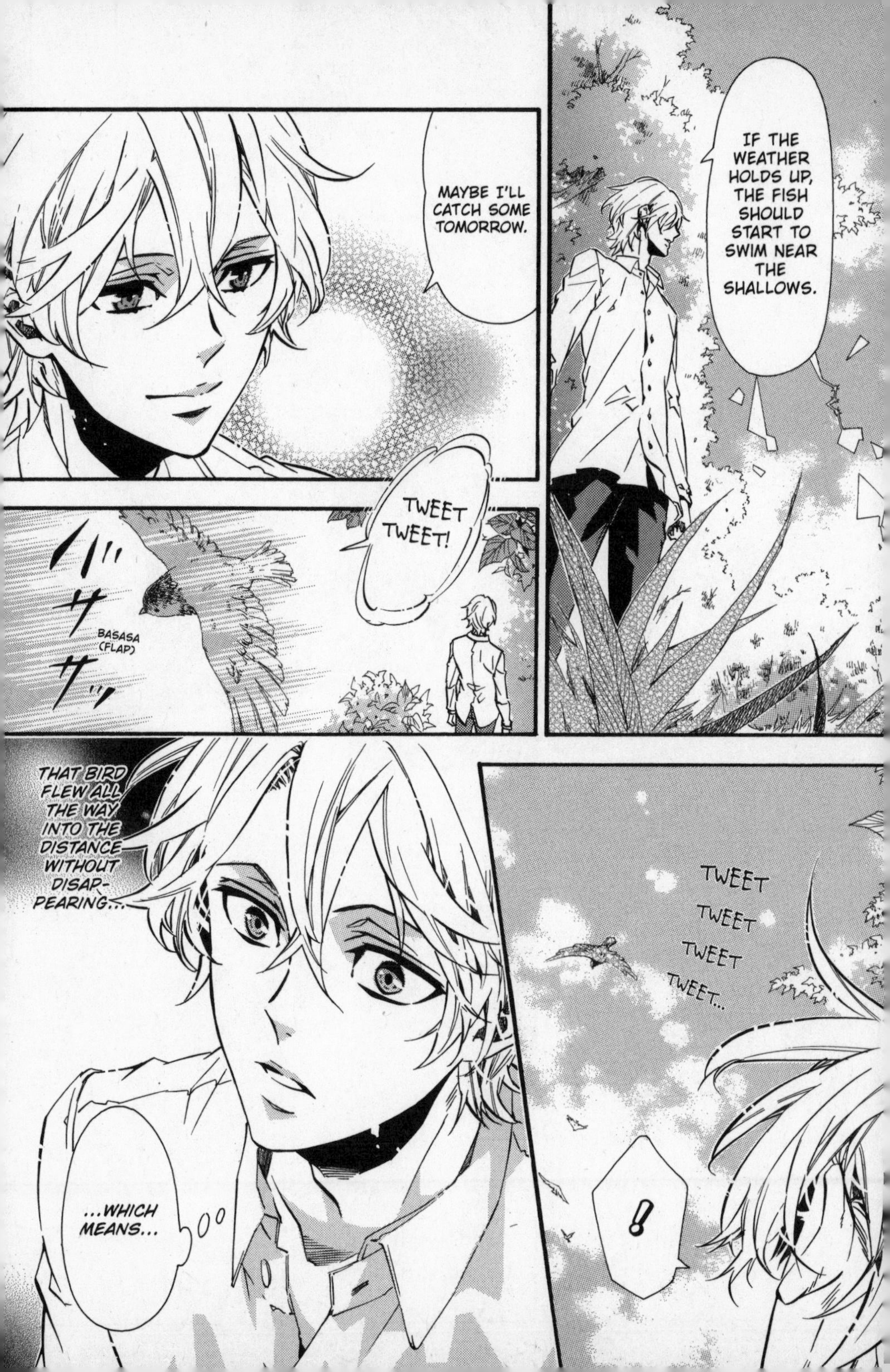
IF THE WEATHER HOLDS UP, THE FISH SHOULD START TO SWIM NEAR THE SHALLOWS.
MAYBE I'LL CATCH SOME TOMORROW.
TWEET TWEET!
BASASA (FLAP)
TWEET TWEET TWEET TWEET...
!
THAT BIRD FLEW ALL THE WAY INTO THE DISTANCE WITHOUT DISAP-PEARING...
...WHICH MEANS...

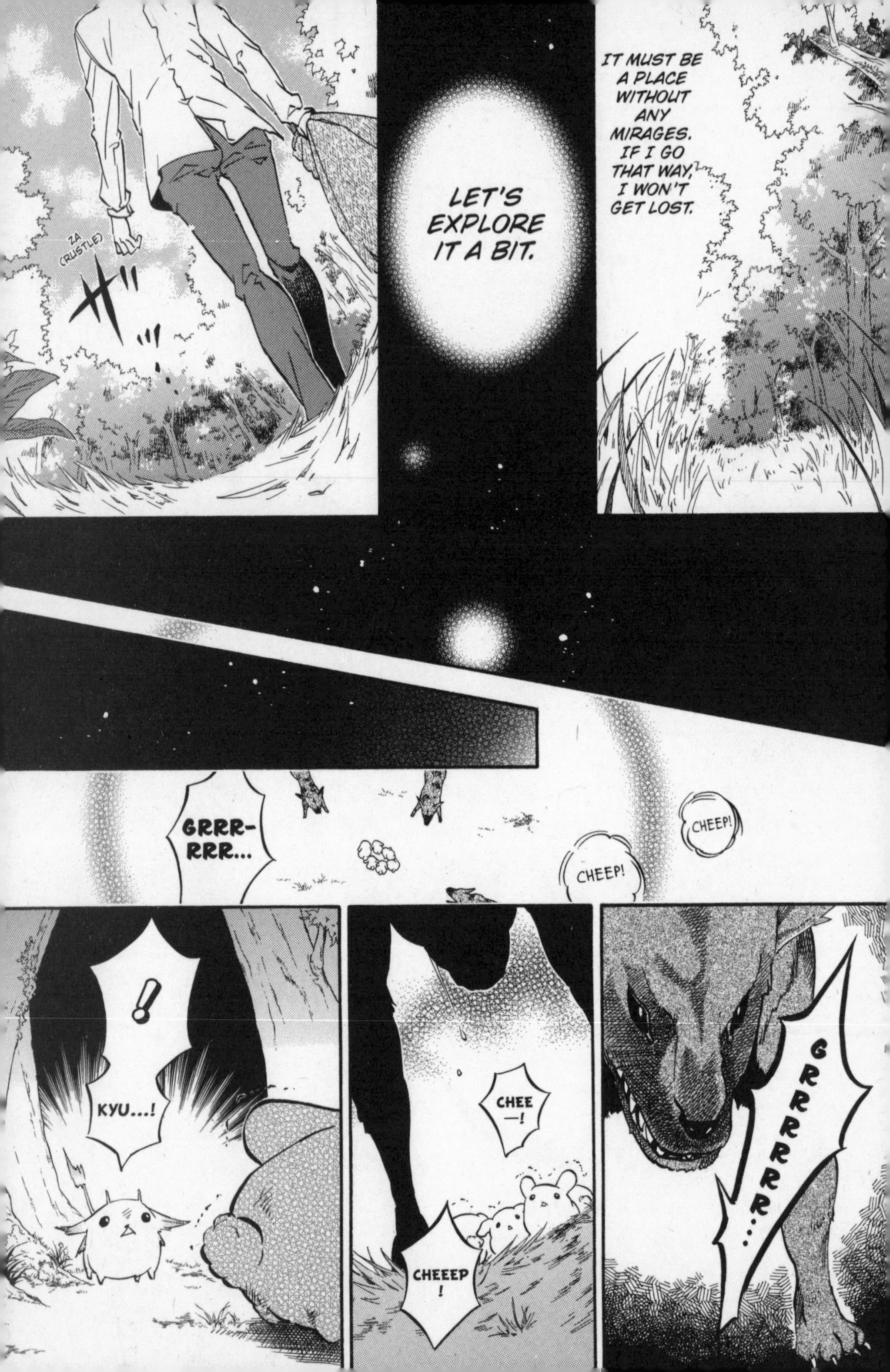
IT MUST BE A PLACE WITHOUT ANY MIRAGES. IF I GO THAT WAY, I WON'T GET LOST.
LET'S EXPLORE IT A BIT.
ZA (RUSTLE)
CHEEP!
CHEEP!
GRRR-RRR...
GRRRRRR...
CHEE—!
CHEEEP!
!
KYU...!

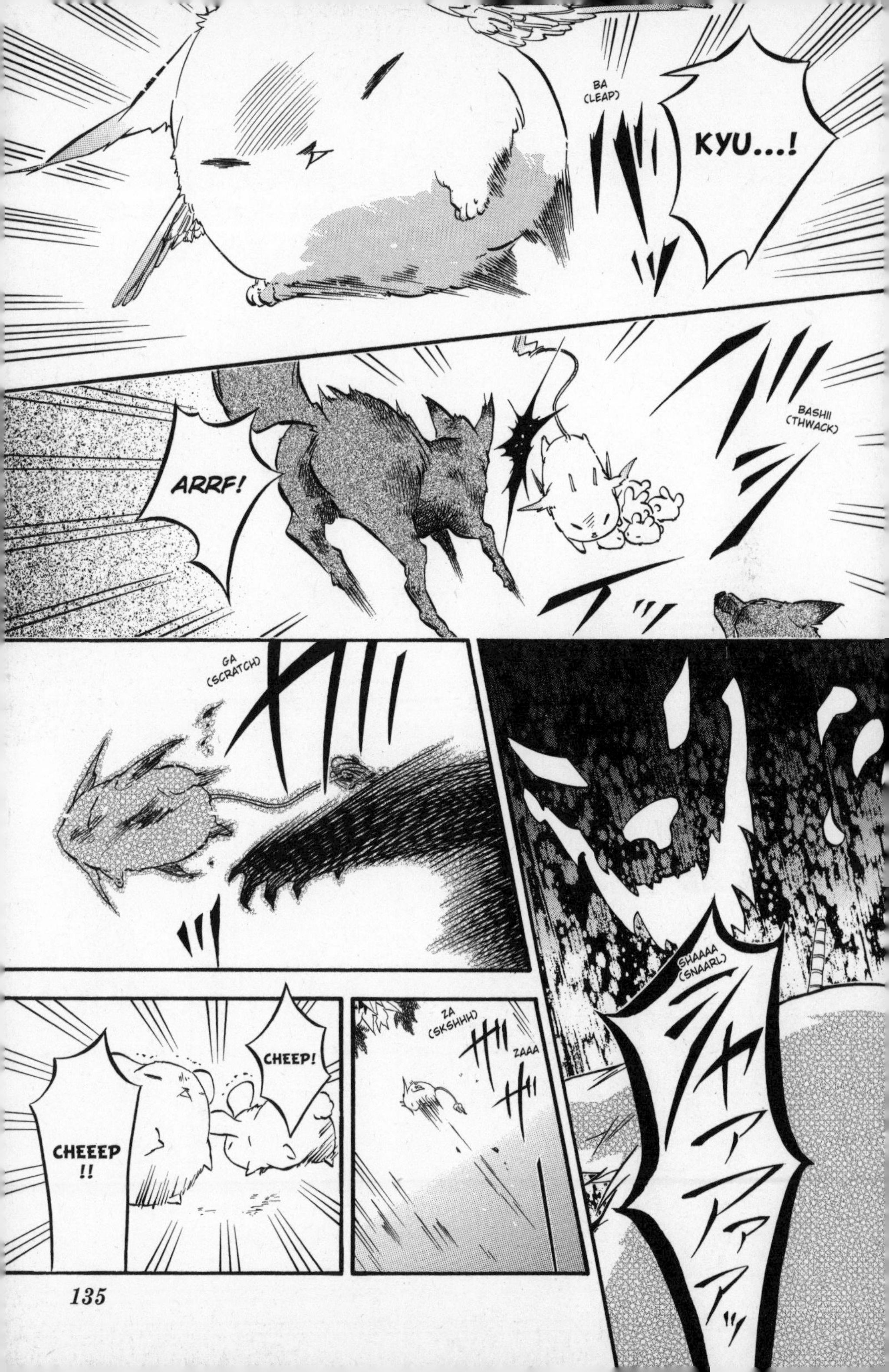
BA
(LEAP)
KYU...!
BASHII
(THWACK)
ARRF!
SHAAAA
(SNAARL)
GA
(SCRATCH)
ZA
(SKSHHH)
ZAAA
CHEEP!
CHEEEP
!!

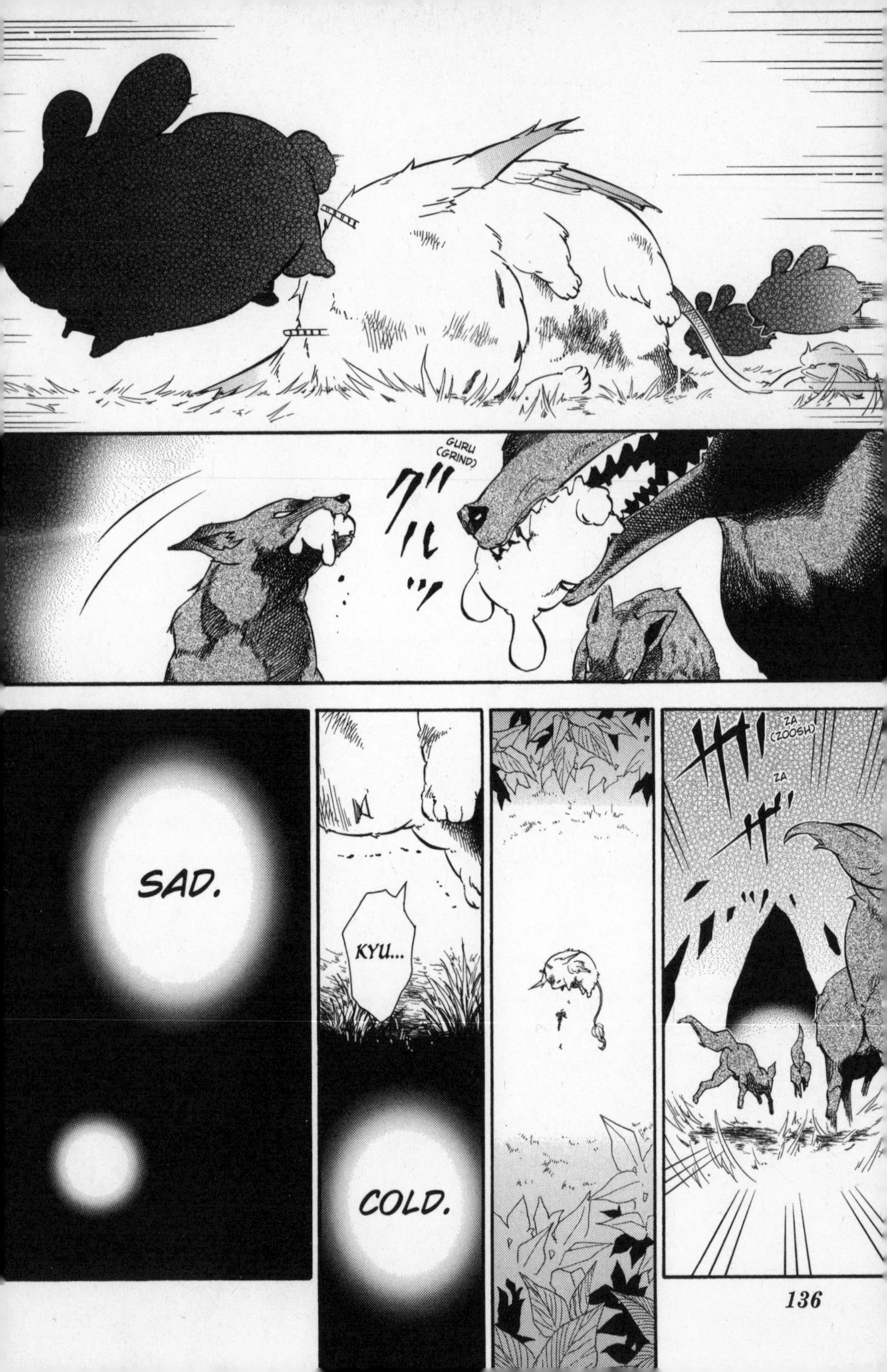
GURU (GRIND)
グルッ
ZA (ZOOSH)
ZA
KYU...
COLD.
SAD.

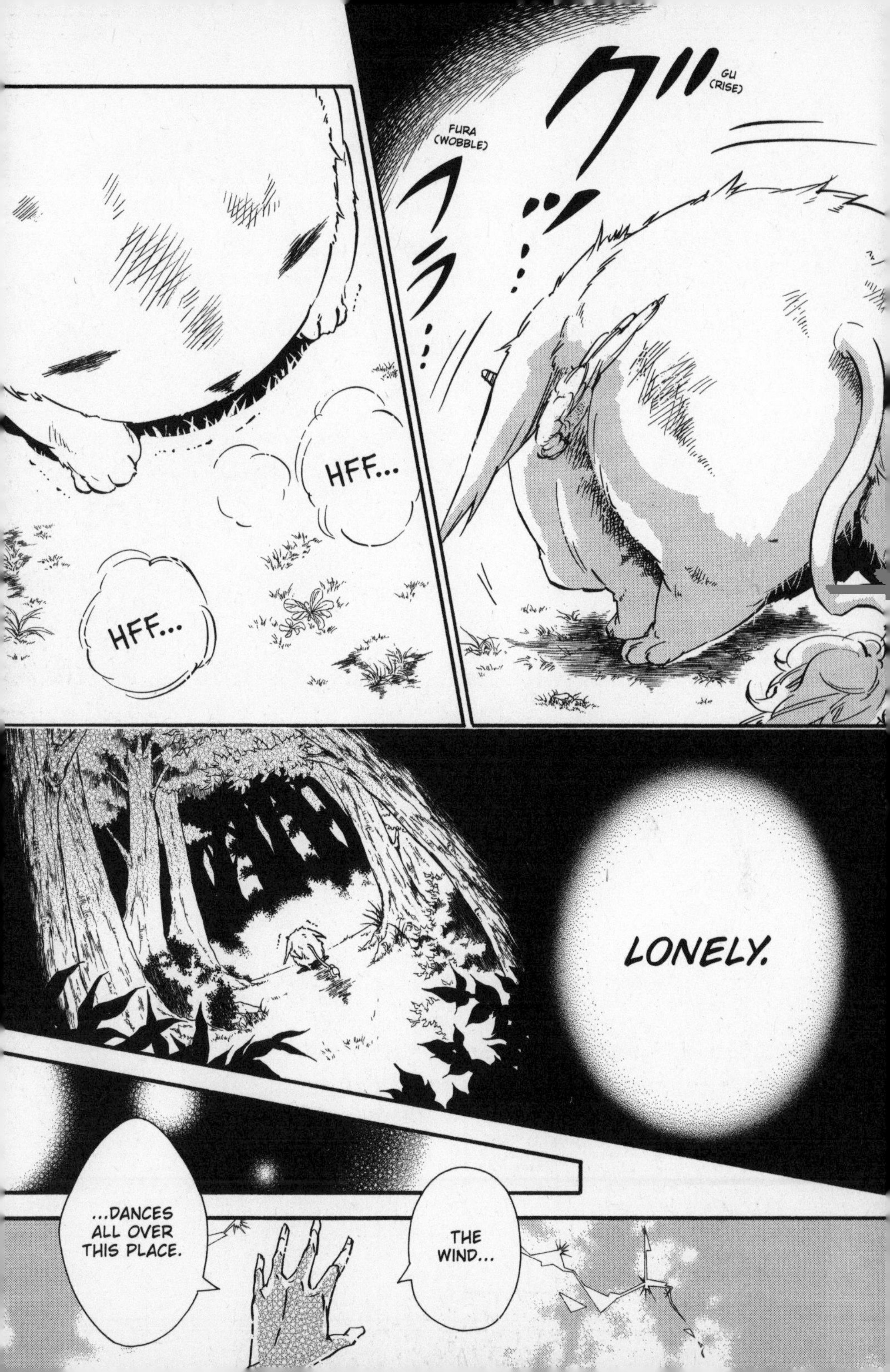
GU (RISE)
FURA (WOBBLE)
HFF...
HFF...
LONELY.
THE WIND...
...DANCES ALL OVER THIS PLACE.

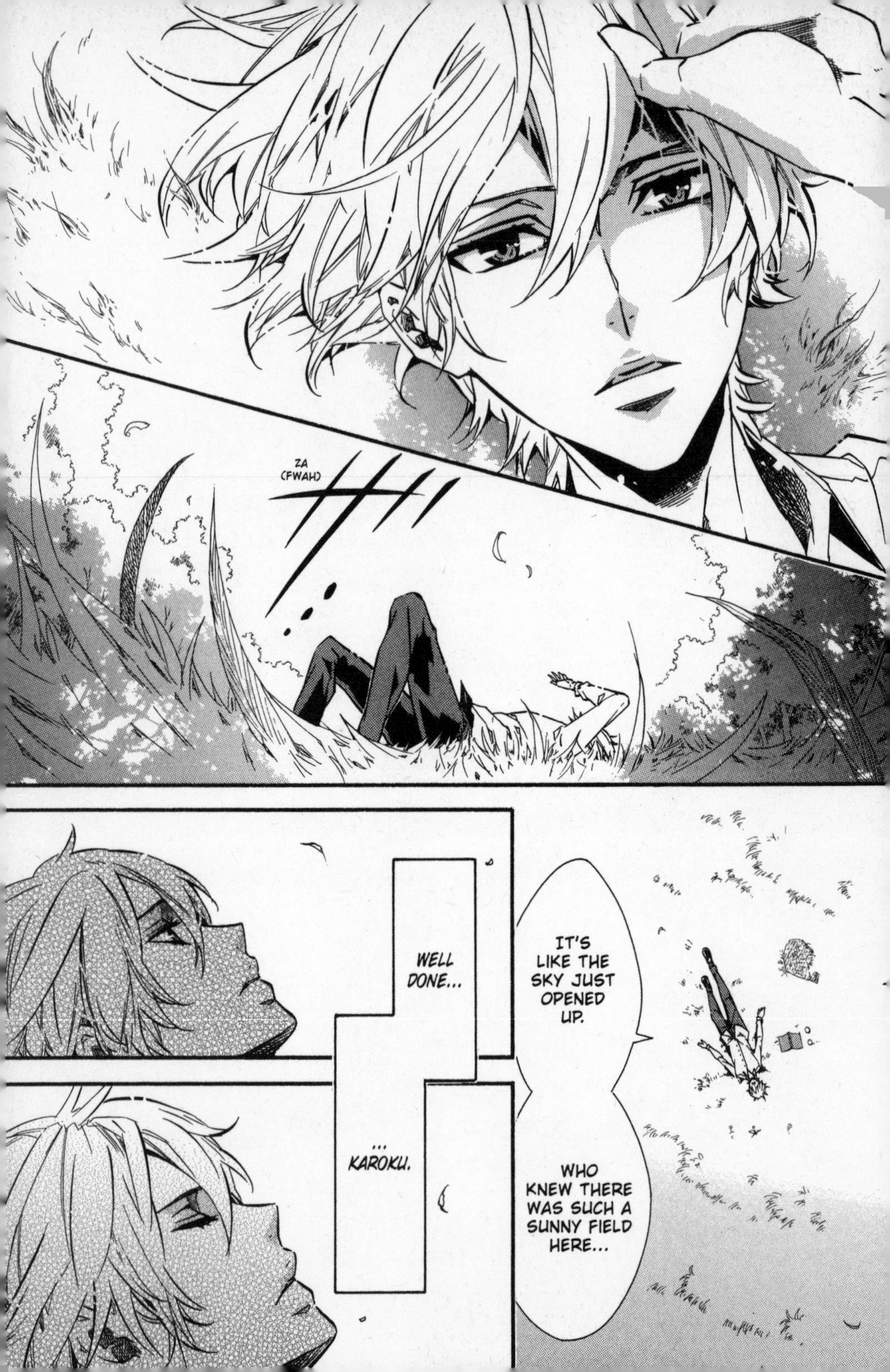
ZA (FWAH)
IT'S LIKE THE SKY JUST OPENED UP.
WHO KNEW THERE WAS SUCH A SUNNY FIELD HERE...
WELL DONE...
...KAROKU.

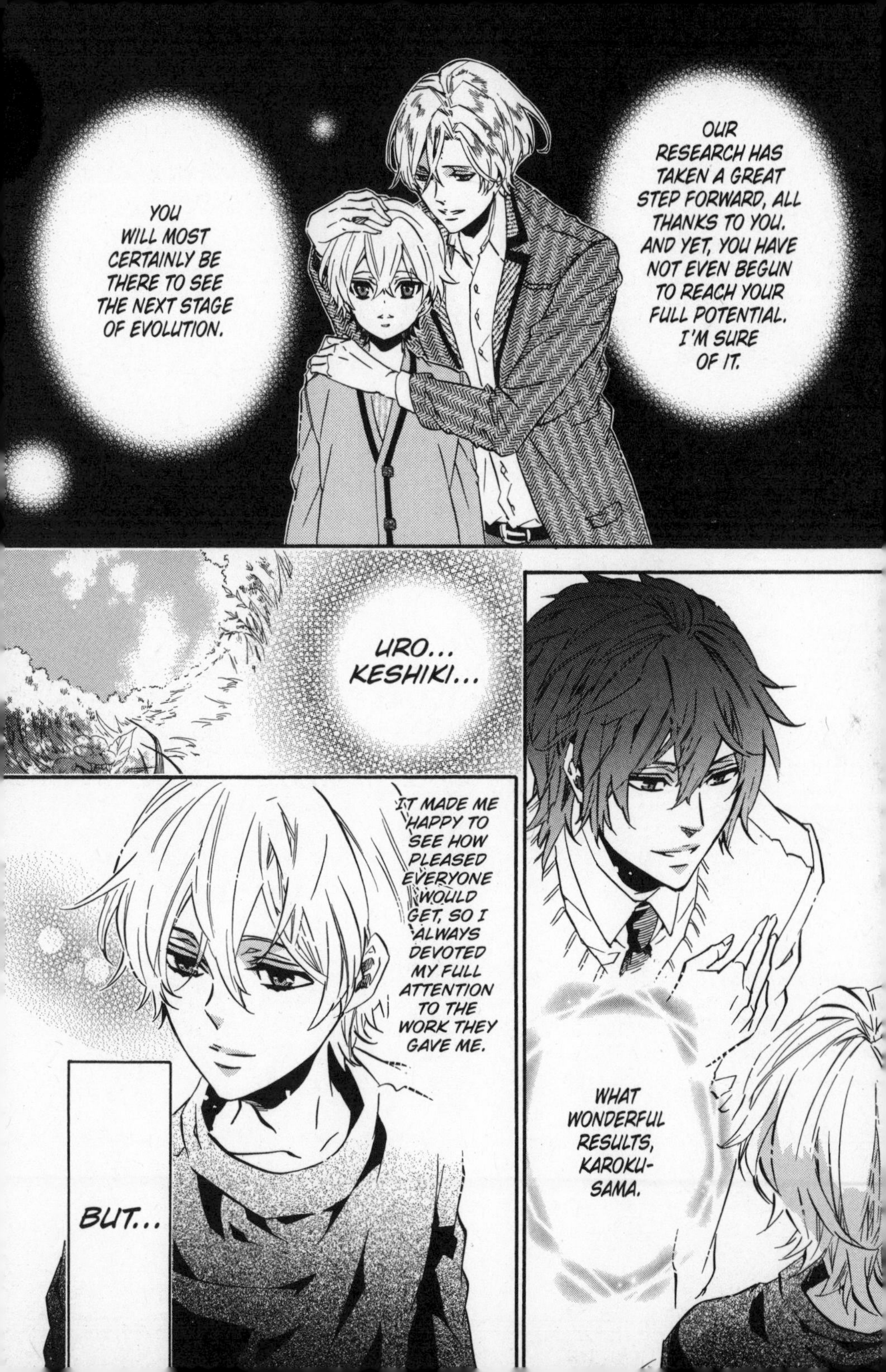
OUR RESEARCH HAS TAKEN A GREAT STEP FORWARD, ALL THANKS TO YOU. AND YET, YOU HAVE NOT EVEN BEGUN TO REACH YOUR FULL POTENTIAL. I'M SURE OF IT.
YOU WILL MOST CERTAINLY BE THERE TO SEE THE NEXT STAGE OF EVOLUTION.
WHAT WONDERFUL RESULTS, KAROKU-SAMA.
URO... KESHIKI...
IT MADE ME HAPPY TO SEE HOW PLEASED EVERYONE WOULD GET, SO I ALWAYS DEVOTED MY FULL ATTENTION TO THE WORK THEY GAVE ME.
BUT...

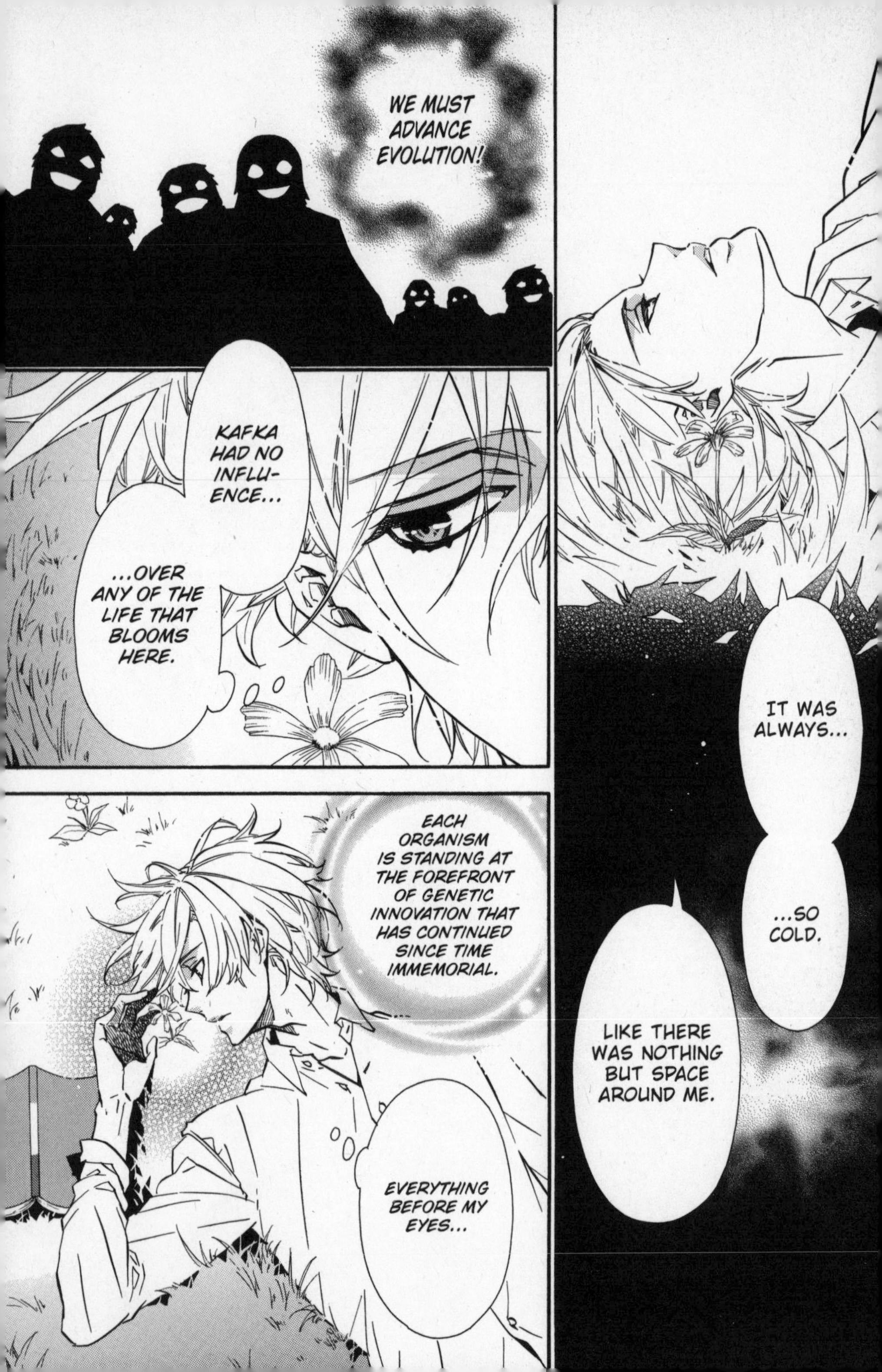
IT WAS ALWAYS...
...SO COLD.
LIKE THERE WAS NOTHING BUT SPACE AROUND ME.
WE MUST ADVANCE EVOLUTION!
KAFKA HAD NO INFLUENCE...
...OVER ANY OF THE LIFE THAT BLOOMS HERE.
EACH ORGANISM IS STANDING AT THE FOREFRONT OF GENETIC INNOVATION THAT HAS CONTINUED SINCE TIME IMMEMORIAL.
EVERYTHING BEFORE MY EYES...

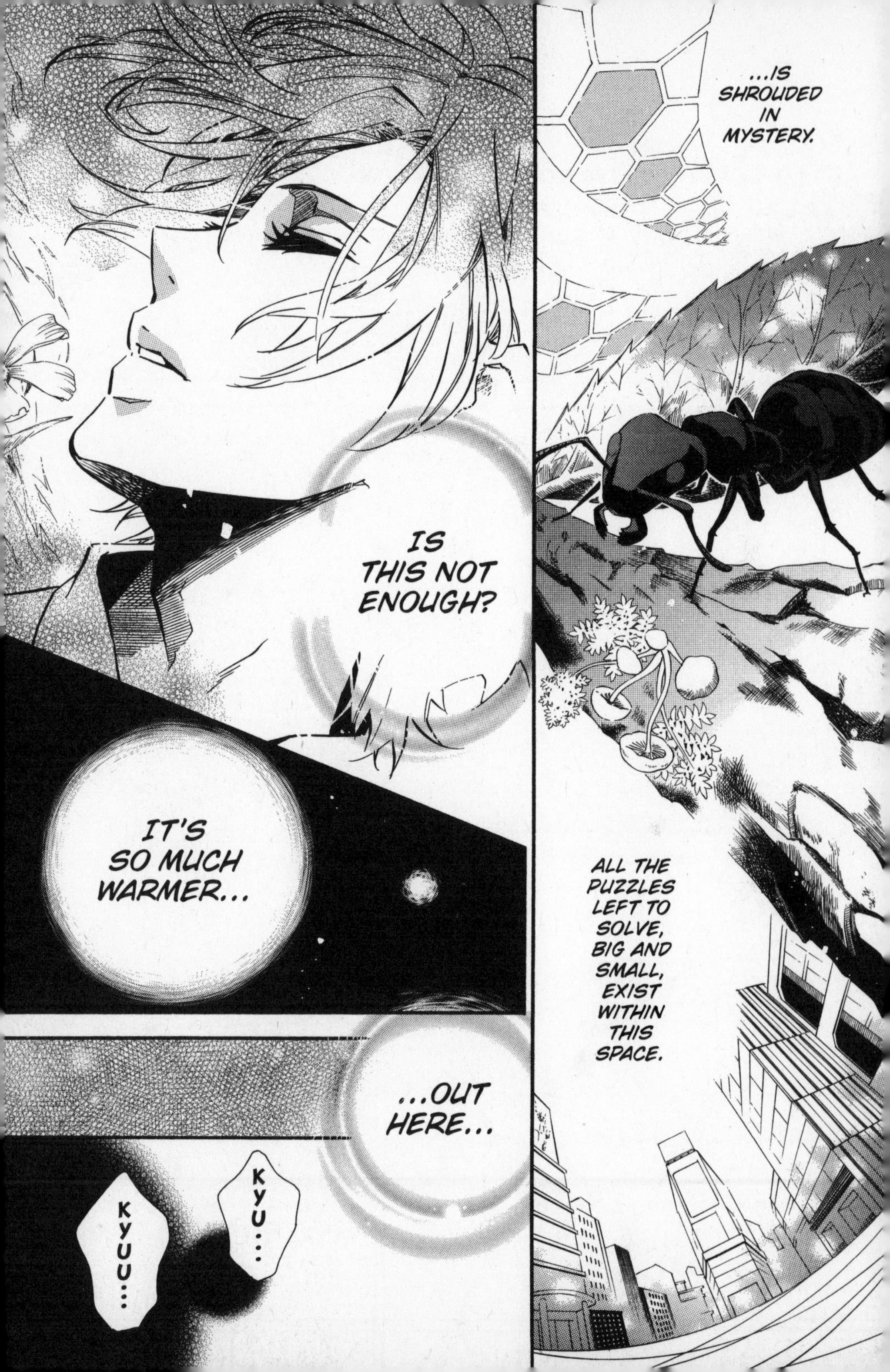
...IS SHROUDED IN MYSTERY.
ALL THE PUZZLES LEFT TO SOLVE, BIG AND SMALL, EXIST WITHIN THIS SPACE.
IS THIS NOT ENOUGH?
IT'S SO MUCH WARMER...
...OUT HERE...
KYU...
KYUU...

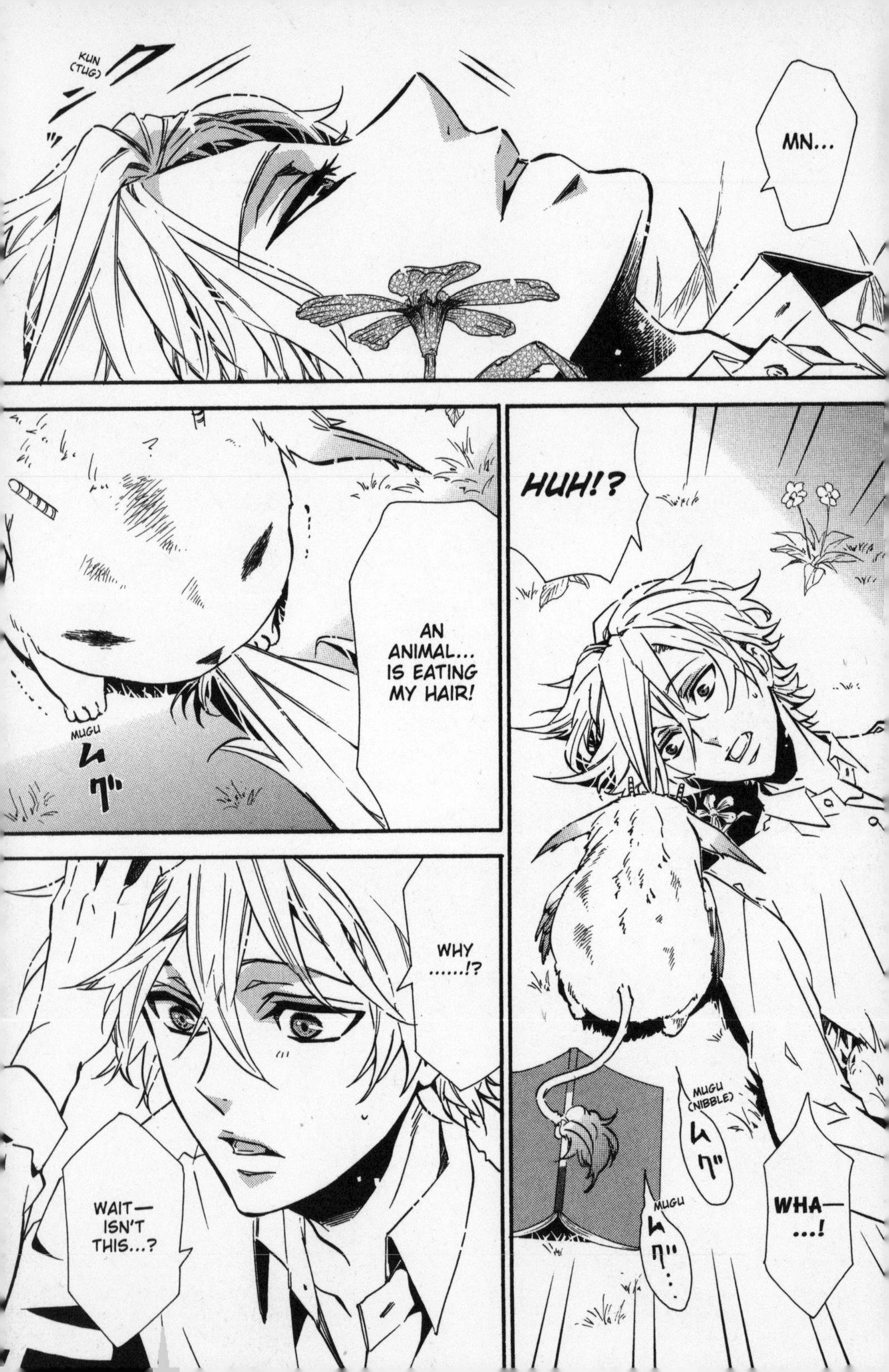
MN...
KUN (TUG)
クン
HUH!?
MUGU (NIBBLE)
ムグ
WHA— ...!
MUGU
ムグ…
AN ANIMAL... IS EATING MY HAIR!
MUGU
ムグ
WHY ......!?
WAIT— ISN'T THIS...?

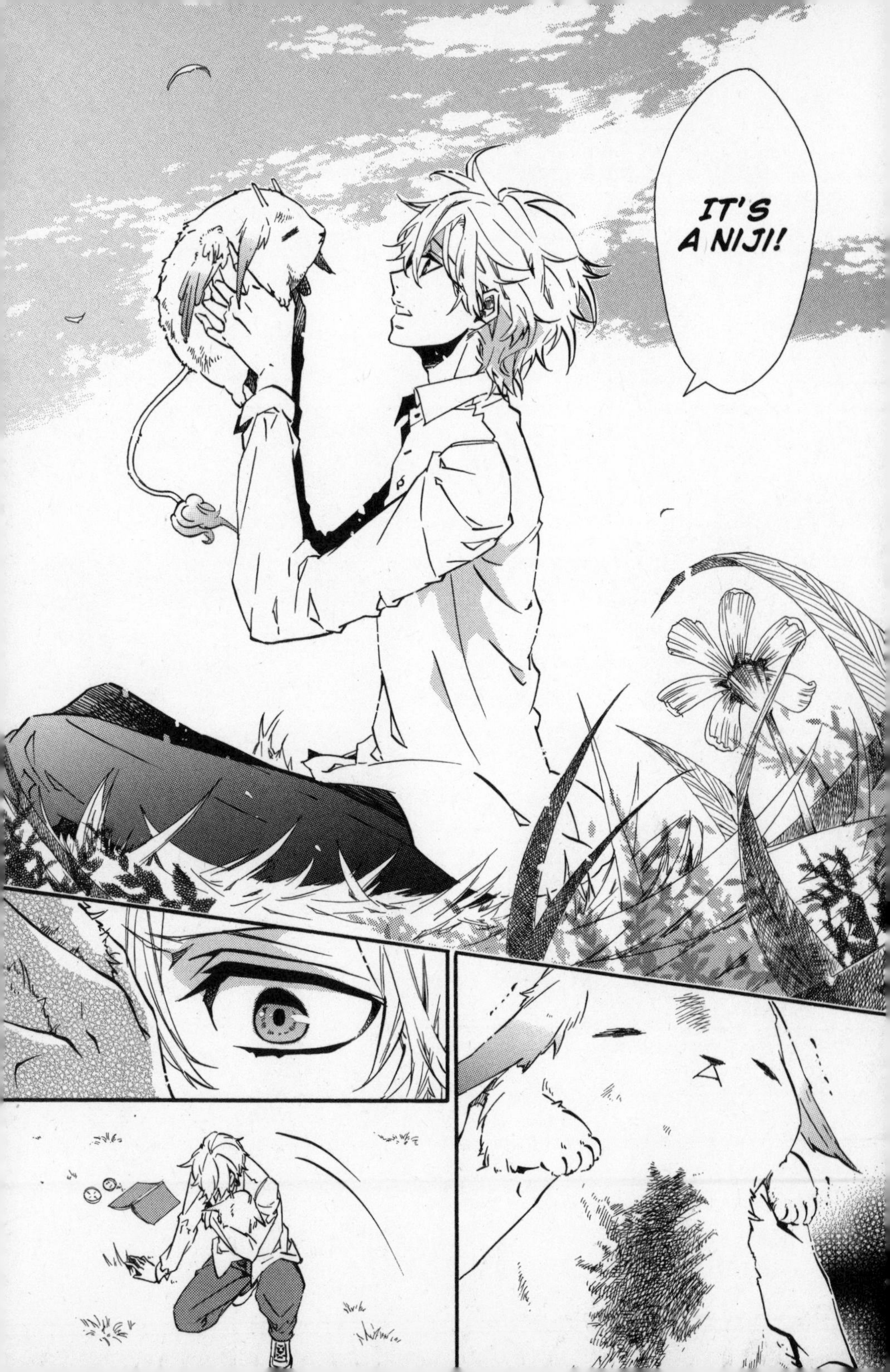
IT'S A NIJI!

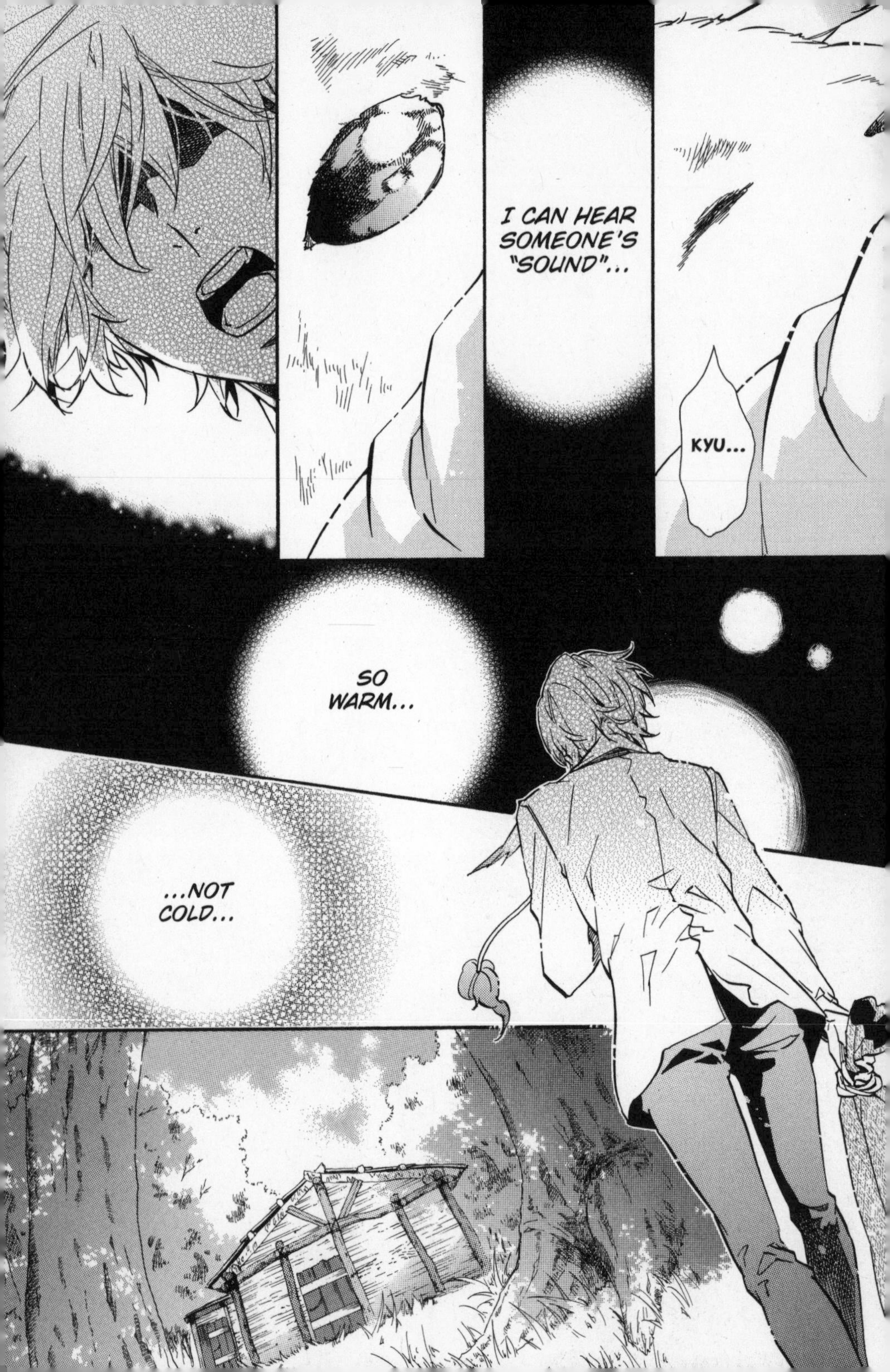
KYU...
I CAN HEAR SOMEONE'S "SOUND"...
SO WARM...
...NOT COLD...

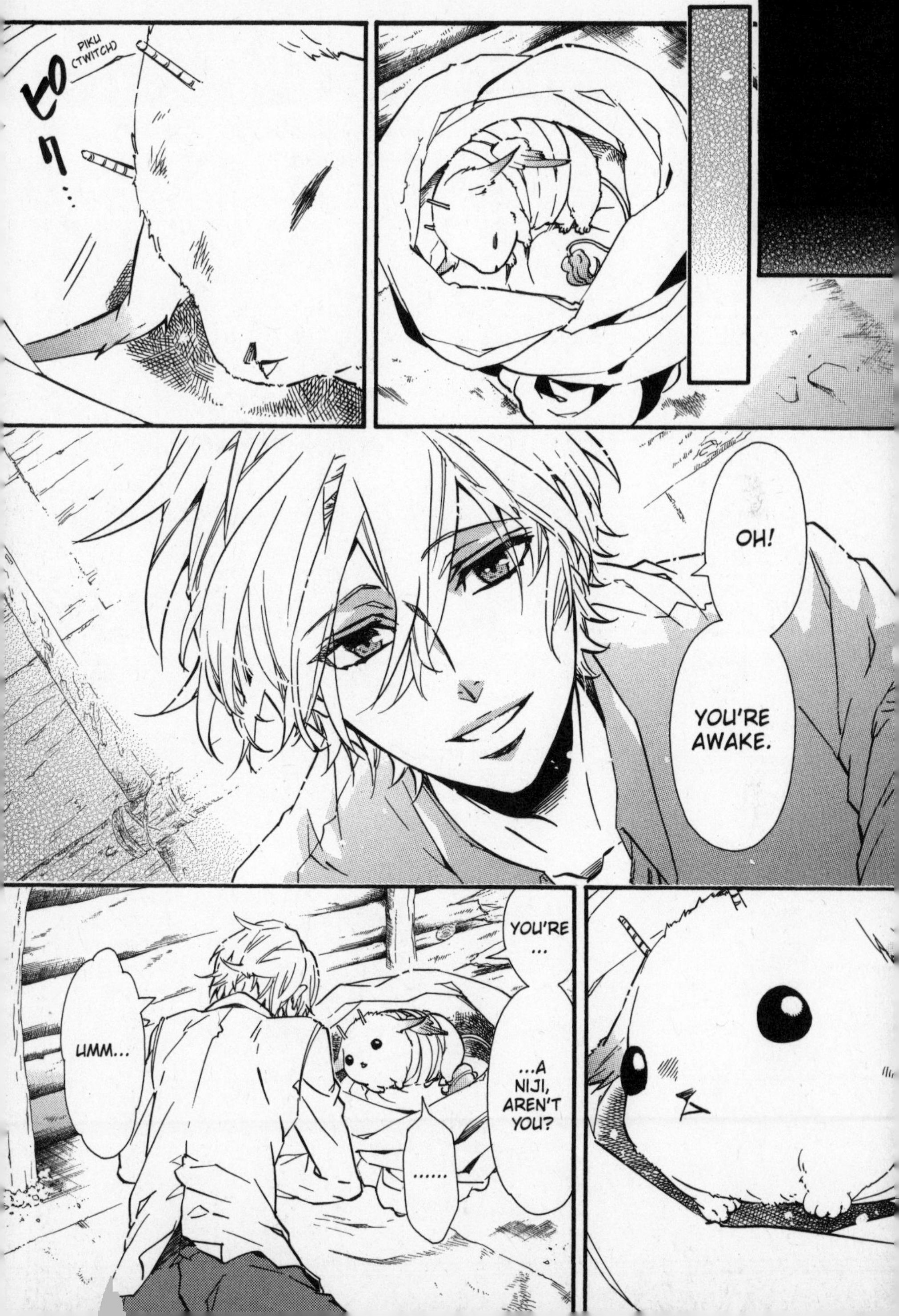
ピク…
PIKU (TWITCH)
OH!
YOU'RE AWAKE.
YOU'RE ...
...A NIJI, AREN'T YOU?
......
UMM...

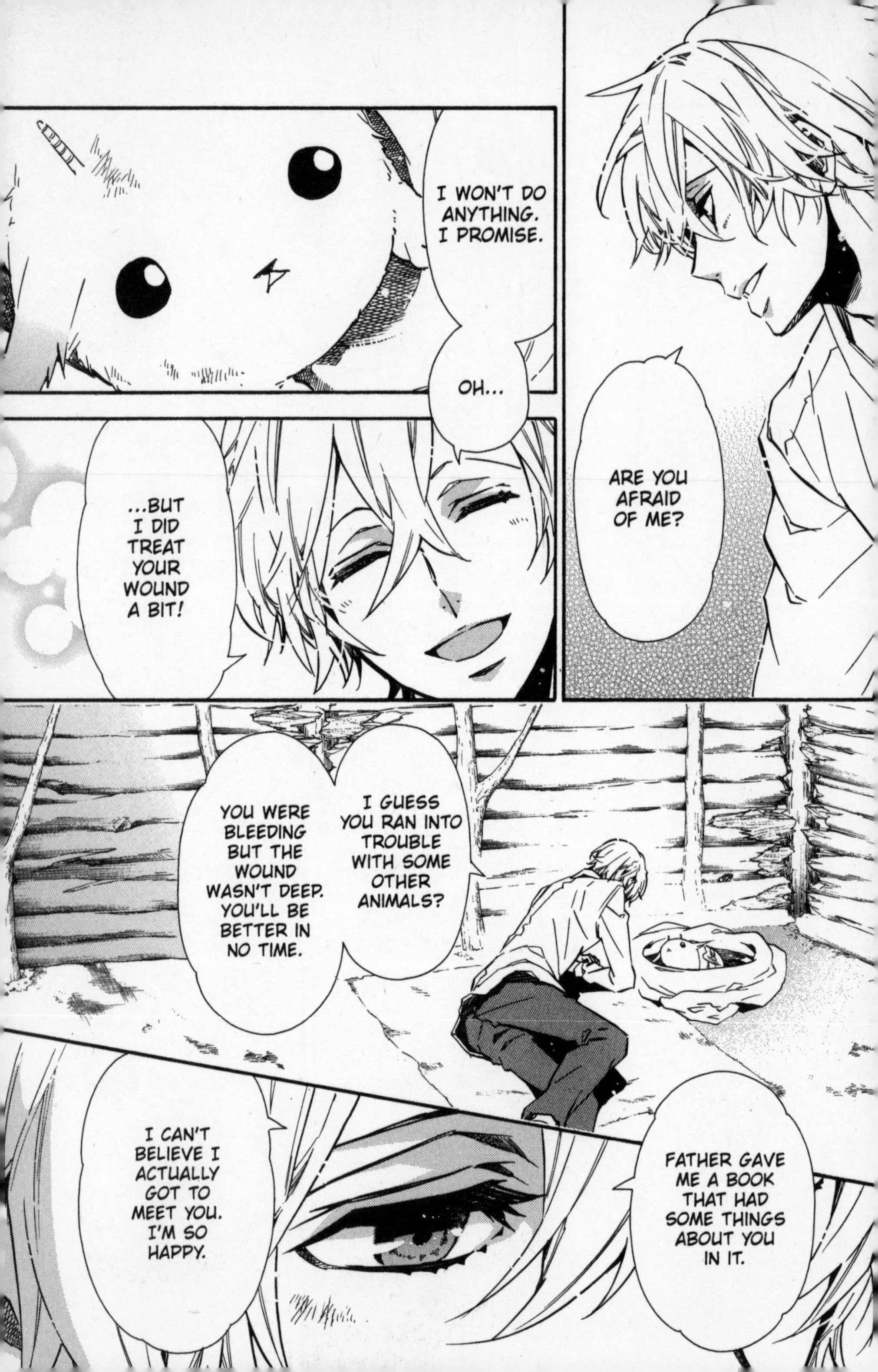
ARE YOU AFRAID OF ME?
I WON'T DO ANYTHING. I PROMISE.
OH...
...BUT I DID TREAT YOUR WOUND A BIT!
I GUESS YOU RAN INTO TROUBLE WITH SOME OTHER ANIMALS?
YOU WERE BLEEDING BUT THE WOUND WASN'T DEEP. YOU'LL BE BETTER IN NO TIME.
FATHER GAVE ME A BOOK THAT HAD SOME THINGS ABOUT YOU IN IT.
I CAN'T BELIEVE I ACTUALLY GOT TO MEET YOU. I'M SO HAPPY.

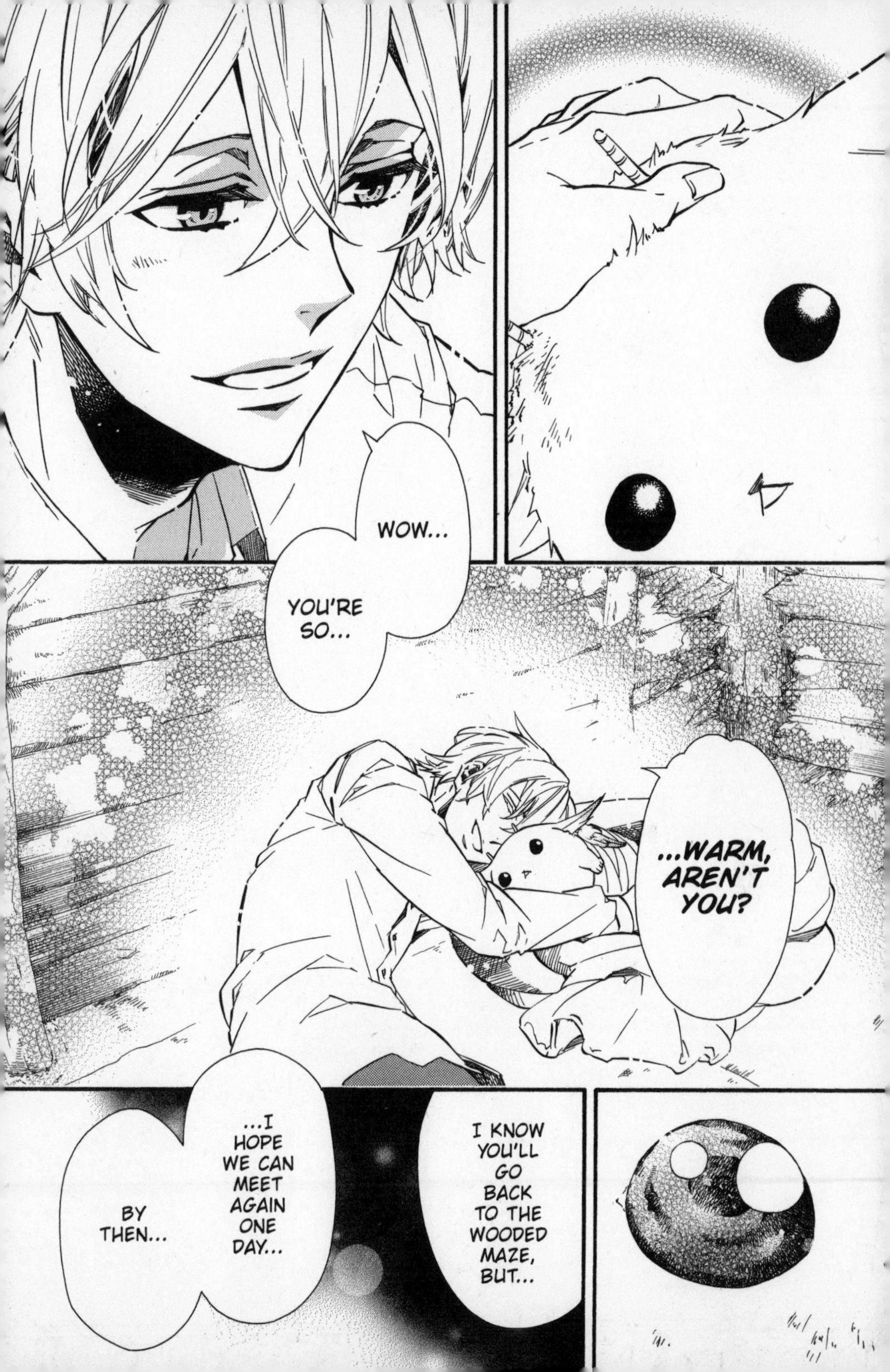
WOW...
YOU'RE SO...
...WARM, AREN'T YOU?
I KNOW YOU'LL GO BACK TO THE WOODED MAZE, BUT...
...I HOPE WE CAN MEET AGAIN ONE DAY...
BY THEN...

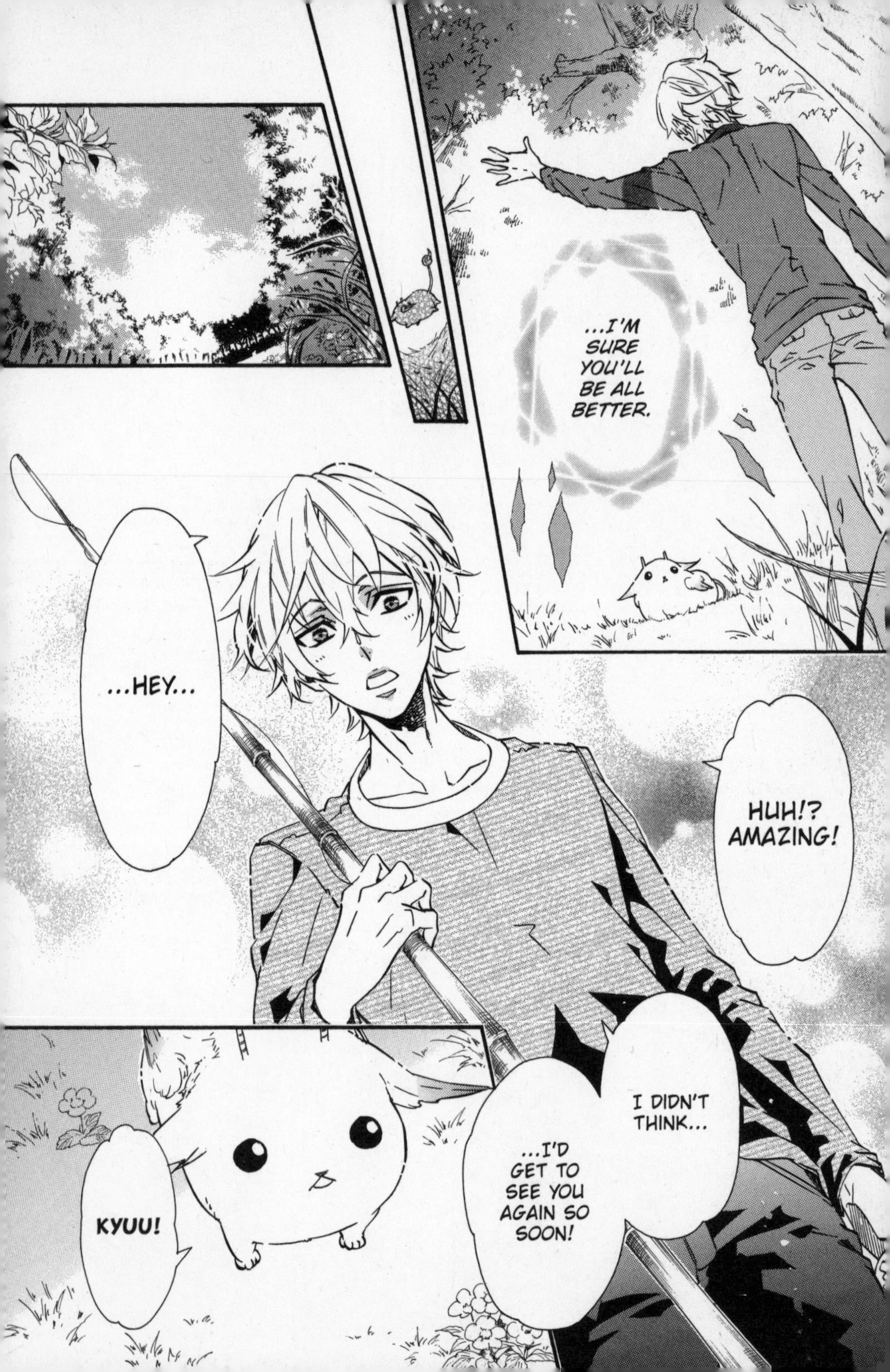
...I'M SURE YOU'LL BE ALL BETTER.
HUH!? AMAZING!
...HEY...
I DIDN'T THINK...
...I'D GET TO SEE YOU AGAIN SO SOON!
KYUU!

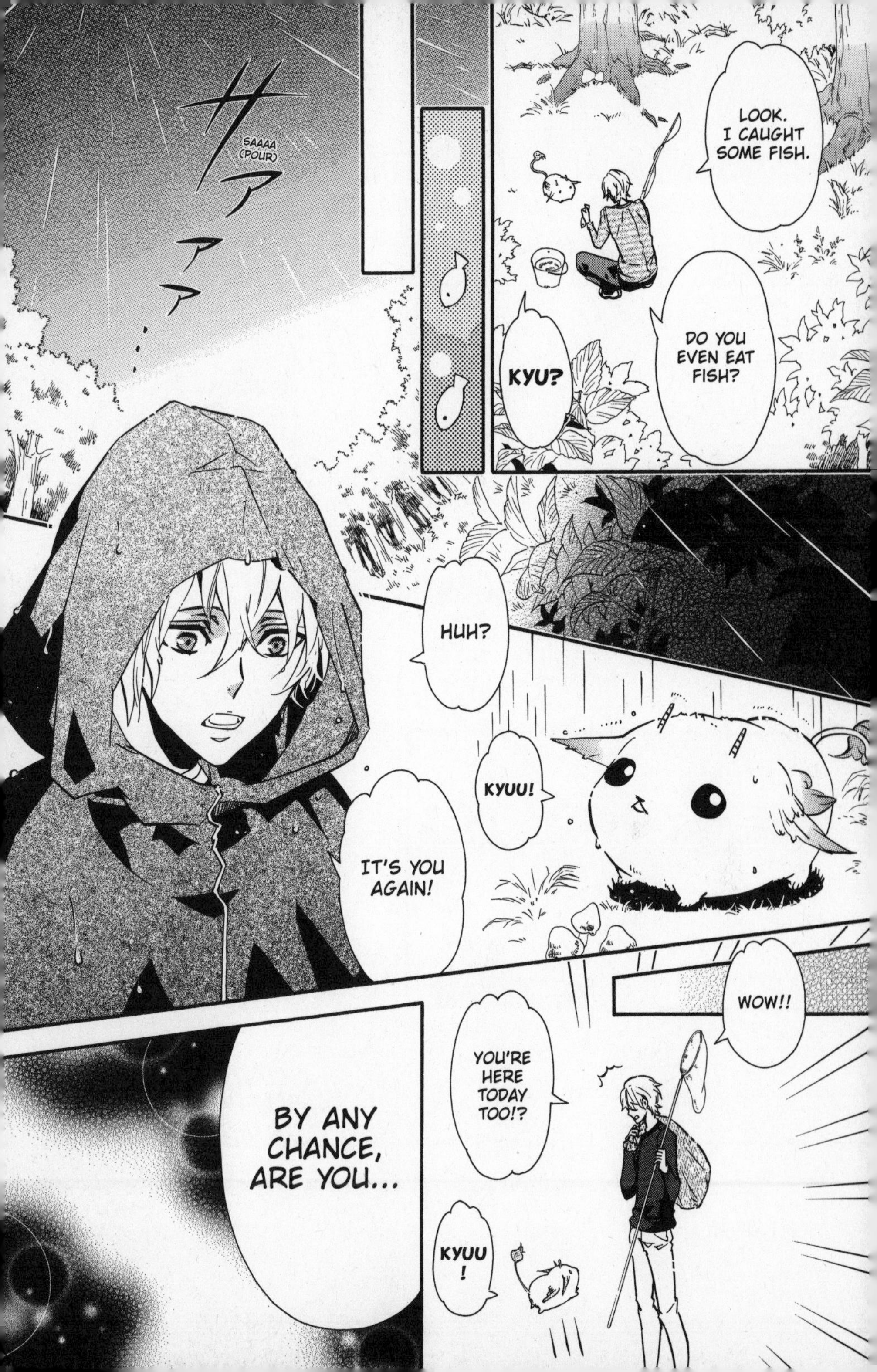
LOOK. I CAUGHT SOME FISH.
DO YOU EVEN EAT FISH?
KYU?
SAAAA (POUR)
HUH?
KYUU!
IT'S YOU AGAIN!
WOW!!
YOU'RE HERE TODAY TOO!?
KYUU!
BY ANY CHANCE, ARE YOU...

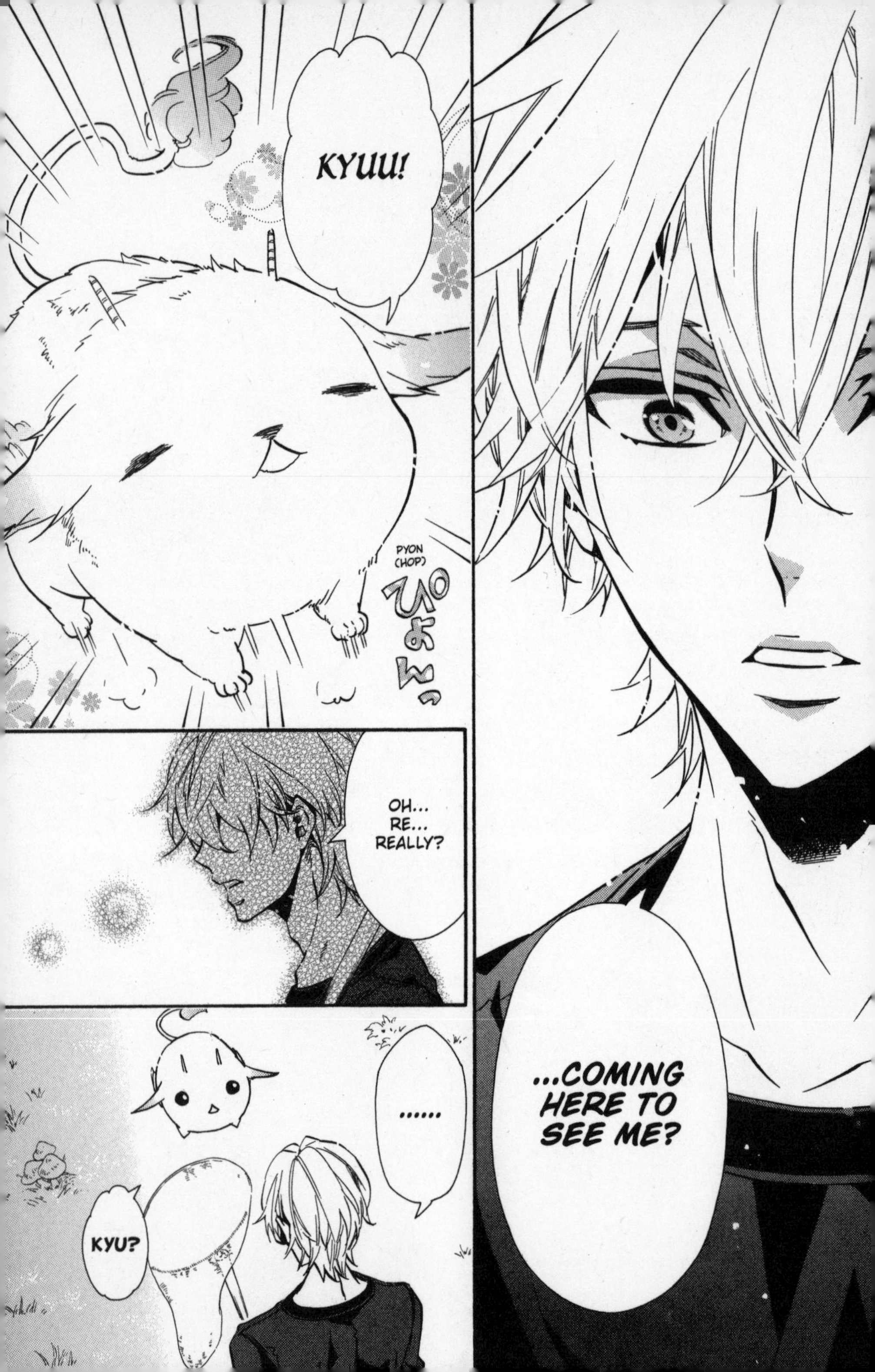
...COMING HERE TO SEE ME?
KYUU!
PYON (HOP)
ぴょんっ
OH... RE... REALLY?
......
KYU?

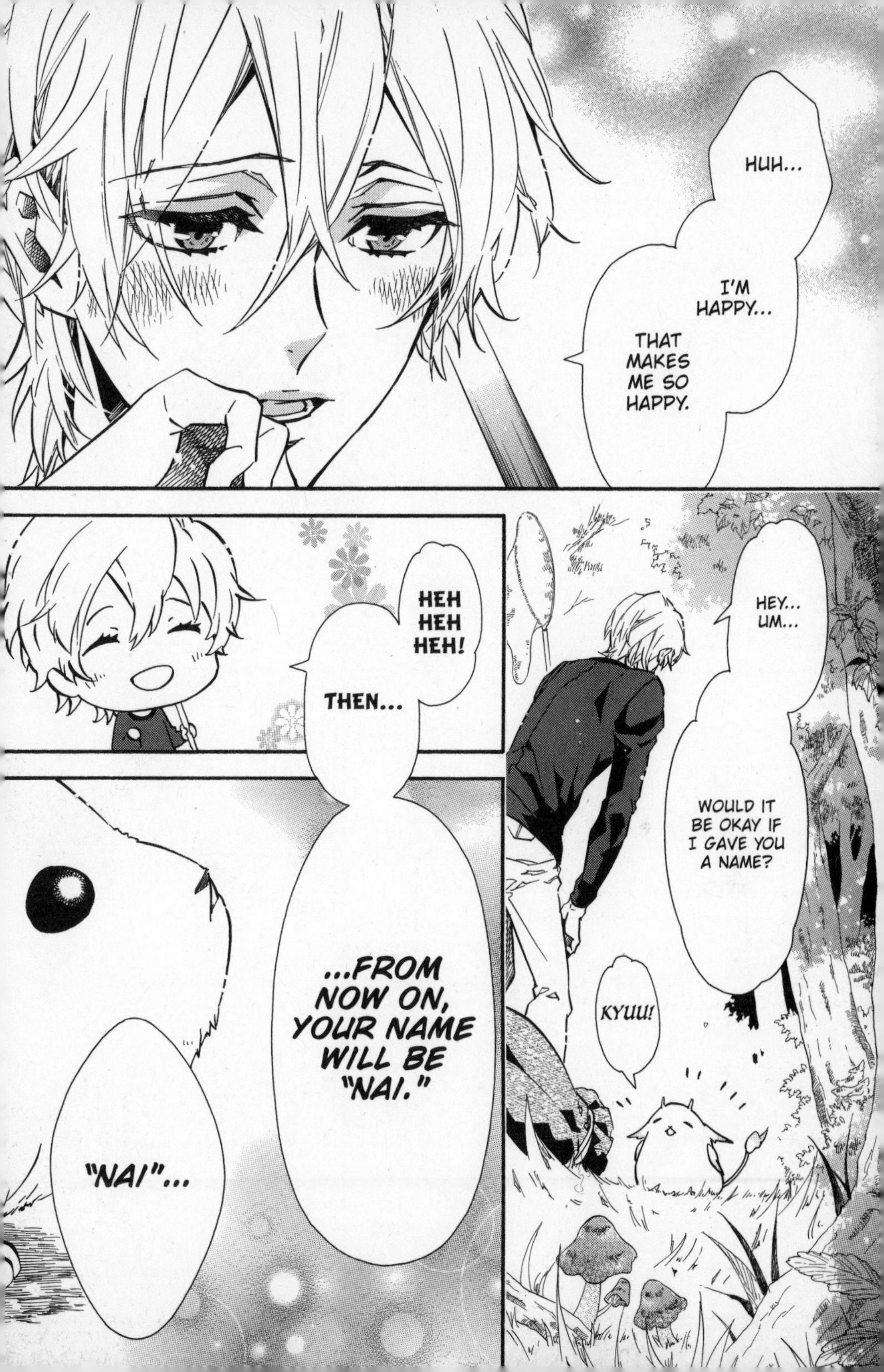
HUH...
I'M HAPPY...
THAT MAKES ME SO HAPPY.
HEY... UM...
WOULD IT BE OKAY IF I GAVE YOU A NAME?
KYUU!
HEH HEH HEH!
THEN...
...FROM NOW ON, YOUR NAME WILL BE "NAI."
"NAI"...

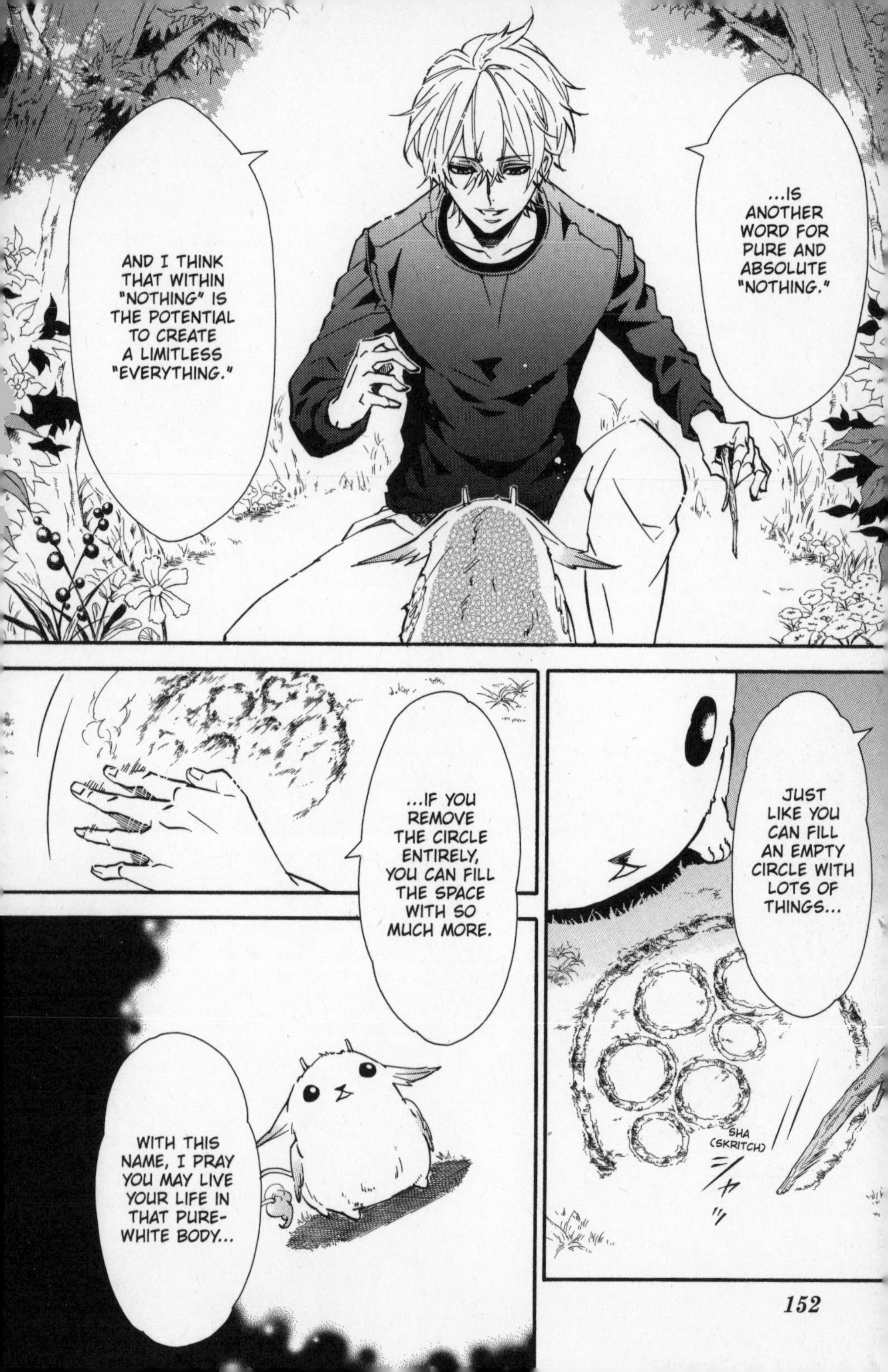
...IS ANOTHER WORD FOR PURE AND ABSOLUTE "NOTHING."
AND I THINK THAT WITHIN "NOTHING" IS THE POTENTIAL TO CREATE A LIMITLESS "EVERYTHING."
JUST LIKE YOU CAN FILL AN EMPTY CIRCLE WITH LOTS OF THINGS...
SHA (SKRITCH)
...IF YOU REMOVE THE CIRCLE ENTIRELY, YOU CAN FILL THE SPACE WITH SO MUCH MORE.
WITH THIS NAME, I PRAY YOU MAY LIVE YOUR LIFE IN THAT PURE-WHITE BODY...

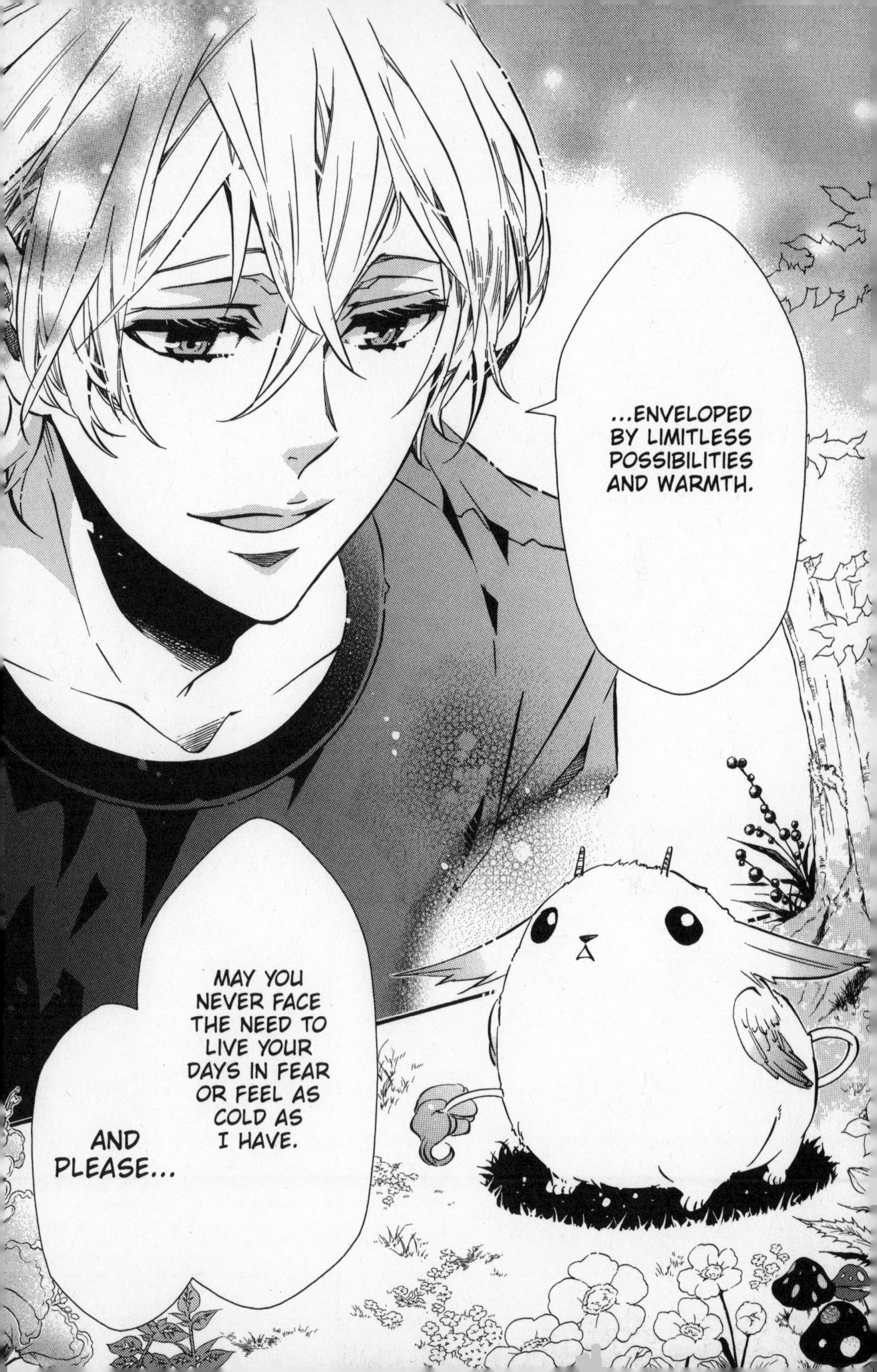
...ENVELOPED BY LIMITLESS POSSIBILITIES AND WARMTH.
AND PLEASE...
MAY YOU NEVER FACE THE NEED TO LIVE YOUR DAYS IN FEAR OR FEEL AS COLD AS I HAVE.

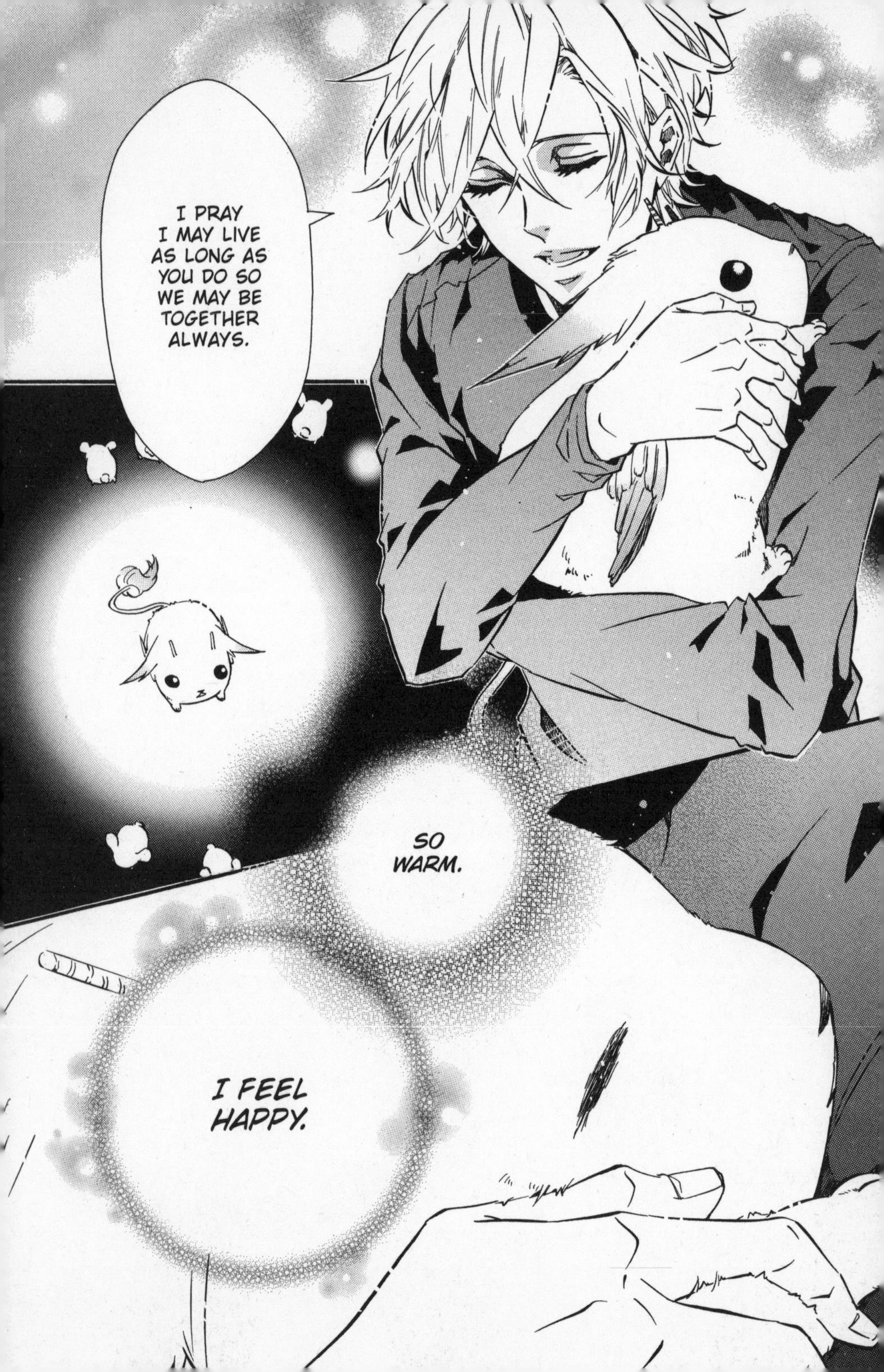
I PRAY I MAY LIVE AS LONG AS YOU DO SO WE MAY BE TOGETHER ALWAYS.
SO WARM.
I FEEL HAPPY.

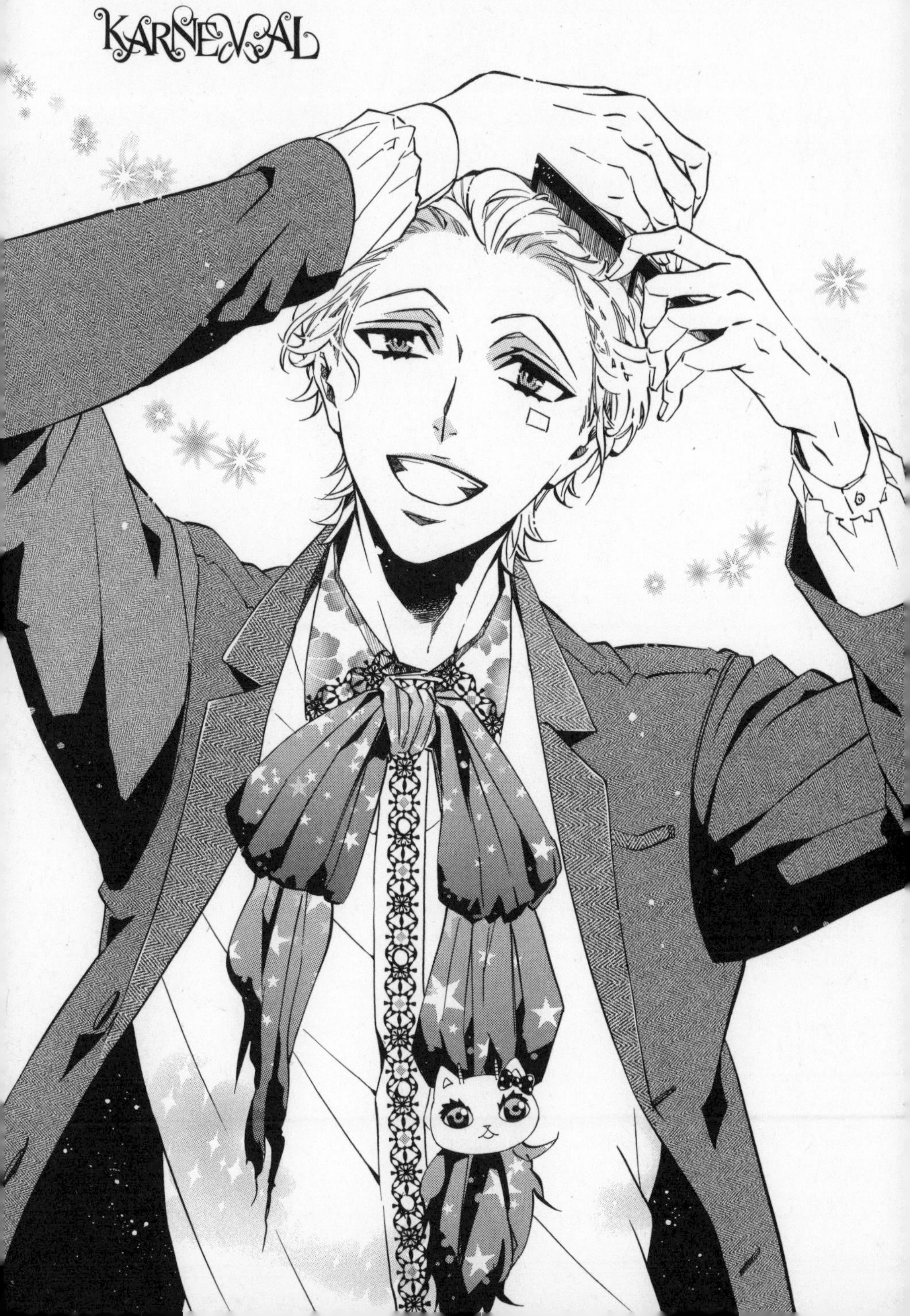
KARNEVAL

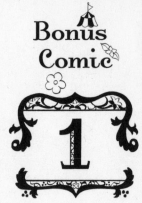

Bonus Comic 1

All of It

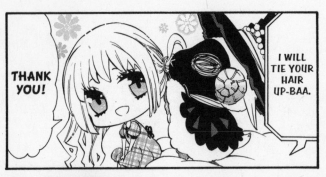

I WILL TIE YOUR HAIR UP-BAA.
THANK YOU!
SHEEEEP, COULD I HAVE SOME WOOOL? NYANPERONA'S STOMACH RIPPED AND HIS STUFFING FELL OUUUT!
BAA.
....
すぴーすぴー
I KNOW I'VE BEEN AWAY FOR A BIT, BUT YOU ALL SERIOUSLY GO WAY TOO EASY ON THEM.
IT'S OUR JOB-BAA.

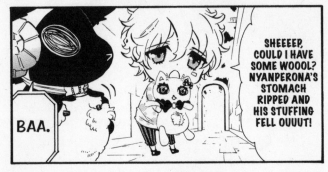

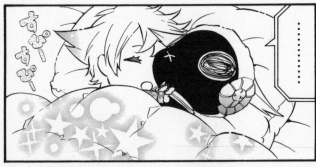

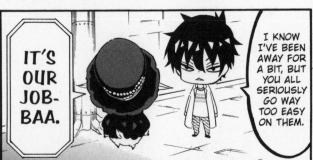

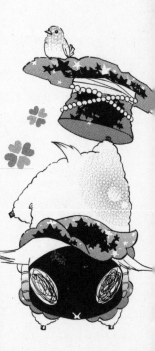

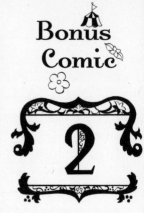

Bonus Comic 2

Out in Society

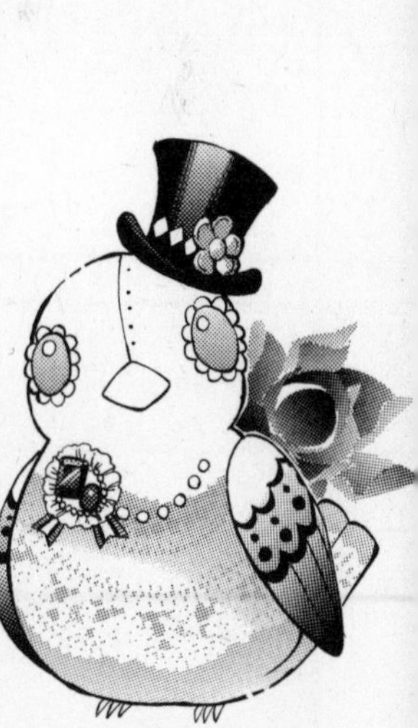

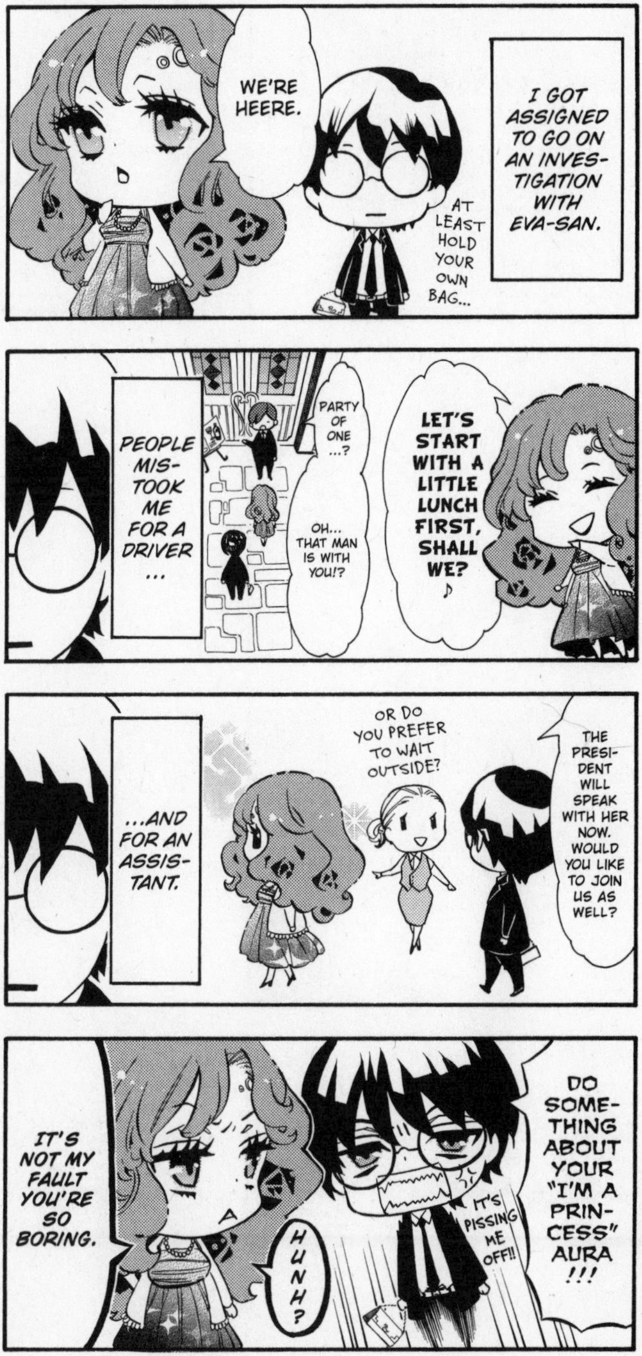

I GOT ASSIGNED TO GO ON AN INVESTIGATION WITH EVA-SAN.
AT LEAST HOLD YOUR OWN BAG...
WE'RE HEERE.
LET'S START WITH A LITTLE LUNCH FIRST, SHALL WE? ♪
PARTY OF ONE ...?
OH... THAT MAN IS WITH YOU!?
PEOPLE MISTOOK ME FOR A DRIVER ...
THE PRESIDENT WILL SPEAK WITH HER NOW. WOULD YOU LIKE TO JOIN US AS WELL?
OR DO YOU PREFER TO WAIT OUTSIDE?
...AND FOR AN ASSISTANT.
DO SOMETHING ABOUT YOUR "I'M A PRINCESS" AURA!!!
IT'S PISSING ME OFF!!
HUNH?
IT'S NOT MY FAULT YOU'RE SO BORING.

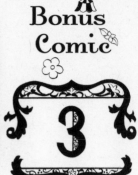

Bonus Comic 3

Taxi

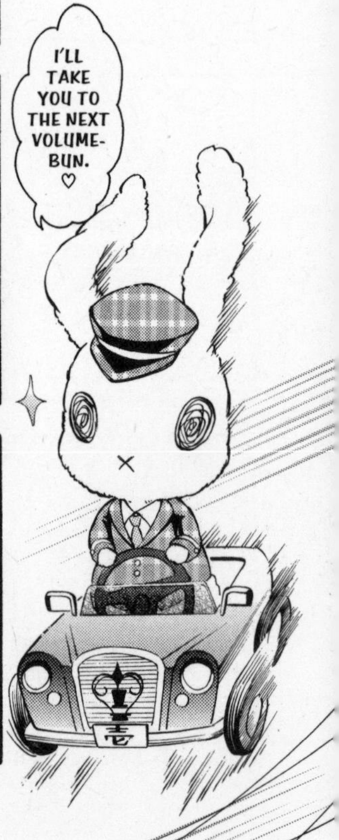

I'LL TAKE YOU TO THE NEXT VOLUME-BUN. ♡

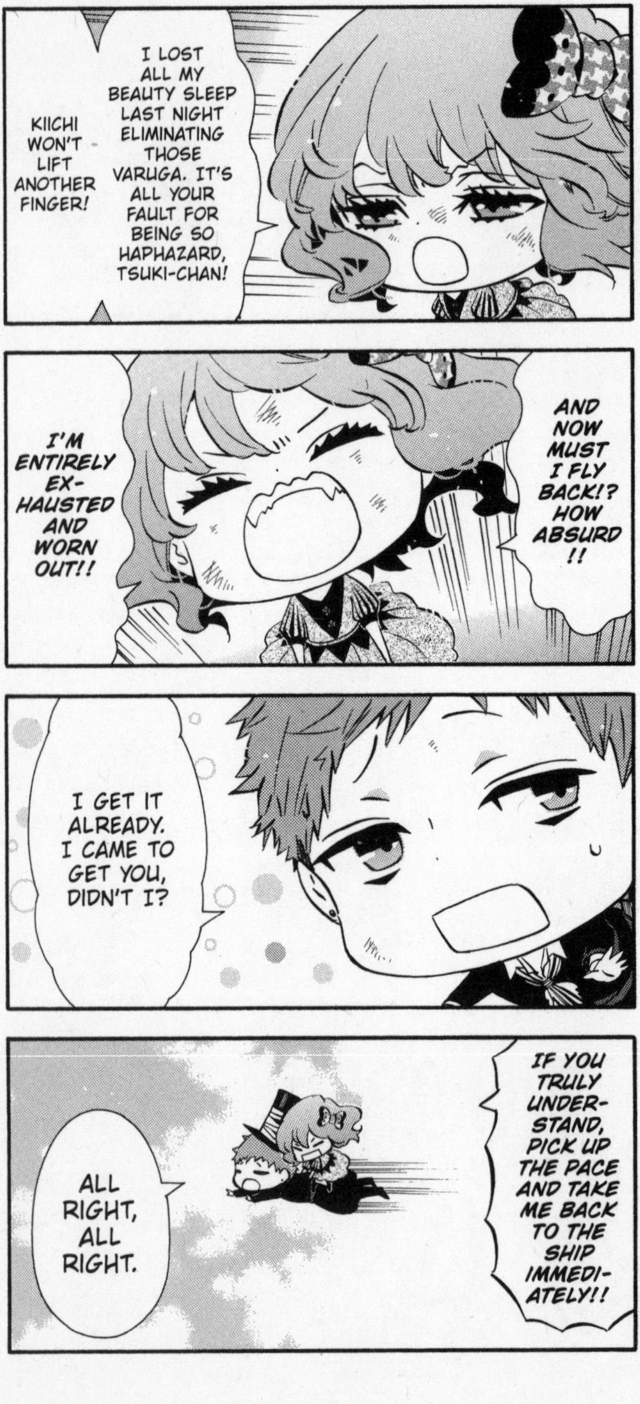

I LOST ALL MY BEAUTY SLEEP LAST NIGHT ELIMINATING THOSE VARUGA. IT'S ALL YOUR FAULT FOR BEING SO HAPHAZARD, TSUKI-CHAN!
KIICHI WON'T LIFT ANOTHER FINGER!
AND NOW MUST I FLY BACK!? HOW ABSURD!!
I'M ENTIRELY EX-HAUSTED AND WORN OUT!!
I GET IT ALREADY. I CAME TO GET YOU, DIDN'T I?
IF YOU TRULY UNDER-STAND, PICK UP THE PACE AND TAKE ME BACK TO THE SHIP IMMEDI-ATELY!!
ALL RIGHT, ALL RIGHT.

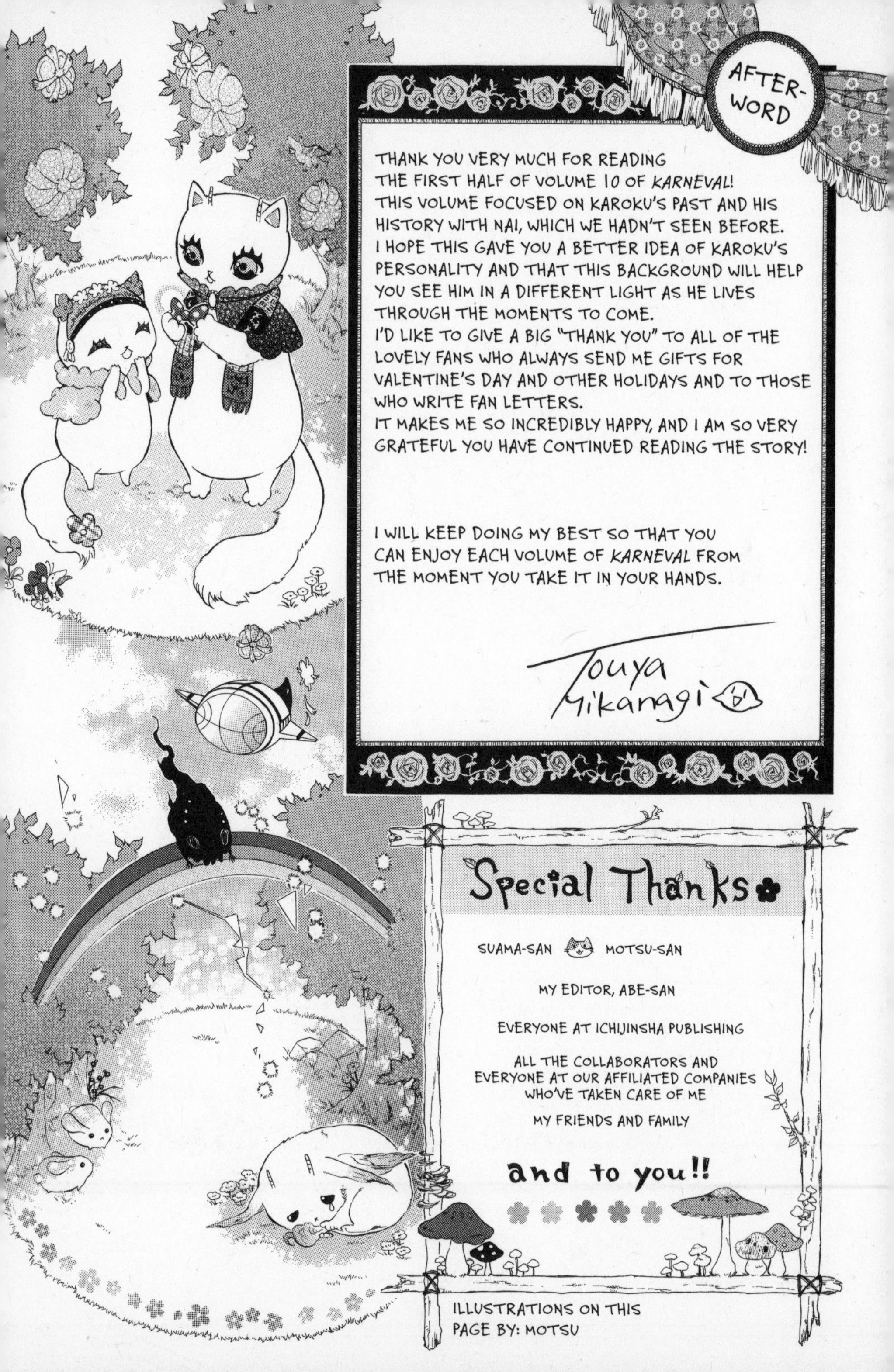

AFTER-WORD

THANK YOU VERY MUCH FOR READING THE FIRST HALF OF VOLUME 10 OF *KARNEVAL*! THIS VOLUME FOCUSED ON KAROKU'S PAST AND HIS HISTORY WITH NAI, WHICH WE HADN'T SEEN BEFORE. I HOPE THIS GAVE YOU A BETTER IDEA OF KAROKU'S PERSONALITY AND THAT THIS BACKGROUND WILL HELP YOU SEE HIM IN A DIFFERENT LIGHT AS HE LIVES THROUGH THE MOMENTS TO COME.

I'D LIKE TO GIVE A BIG "THANK YOU" TO ALL OF THE LOVELY FANS WHO ALWAYS SEND ME GIFTS FOR VALENTINE'S DAY AND OTHER HOLIDAYS AND TO THOSE WHO WRITE FAN LETTERS.

IT MAKES ME SO INCREDIBLY HAPPY, AND I AM SO VERY GRATEFUL YOU HAVE CONTINUED READING THE STORY!

I WILL KEEP DOING MY BEST SO THAT YOU CAN ENJOY EACH VOLUME OF *KARNEVAL* FROM THE MOMENT YOU TAKE IT IN YOUR HANDS.

Touya Mikanagi

Special Thanks

SUAMA-SAN MOTSU-SAN

MY EDITOR, ABE-SAN

EVERYONE AT ICHIJINSHA PUBLISHING

ALL THE COLLABORATORS AND EVERYONE AT OUR AFFILIATED COMPANIES WHO'VE TAKEN CARE OF ME

MY FRIENDS AND FAMILY

and to you!!

ILLUSTRATIONS ON THIS PAGE BY: MOTSU

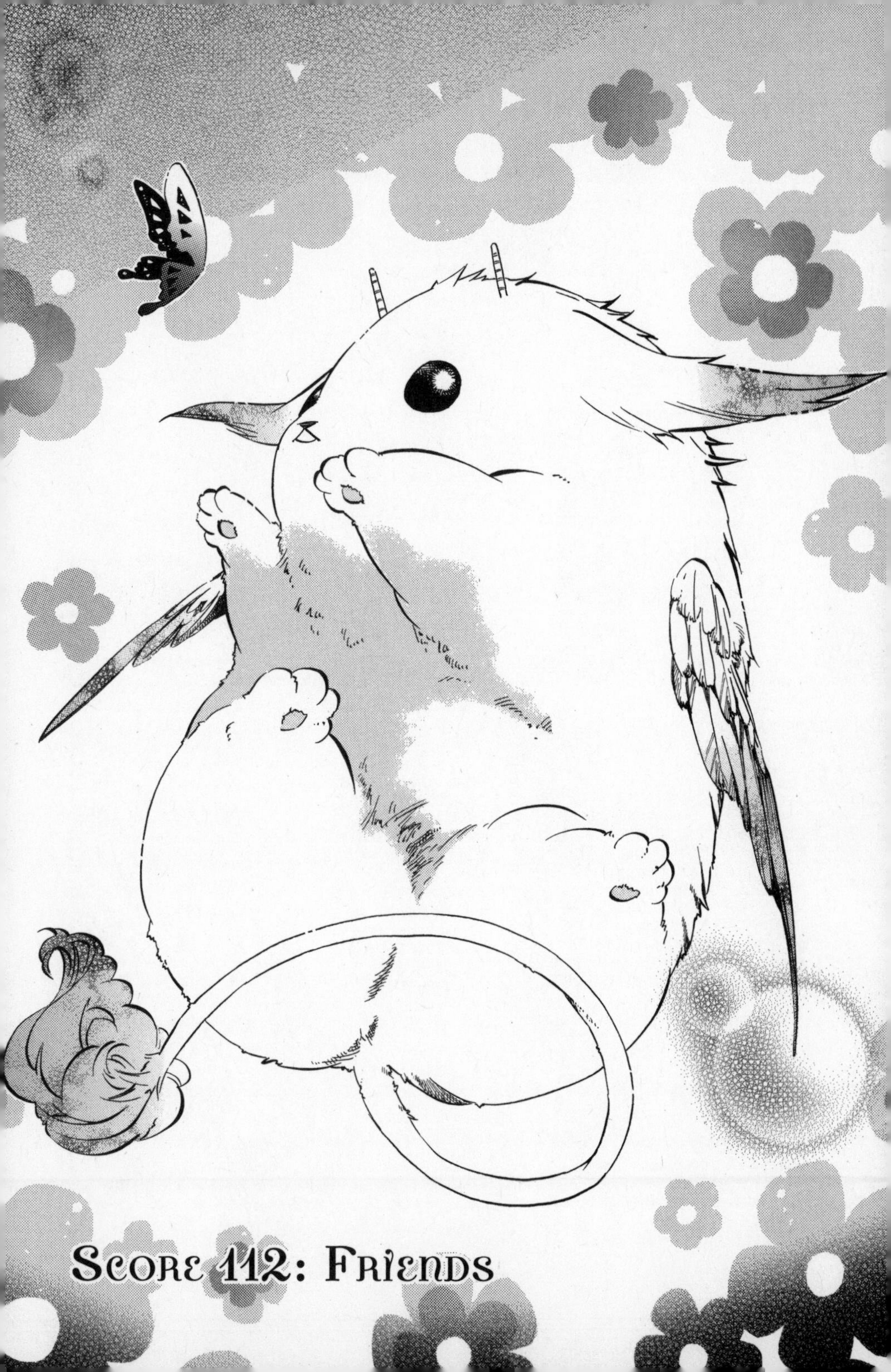

Score 112: Friends

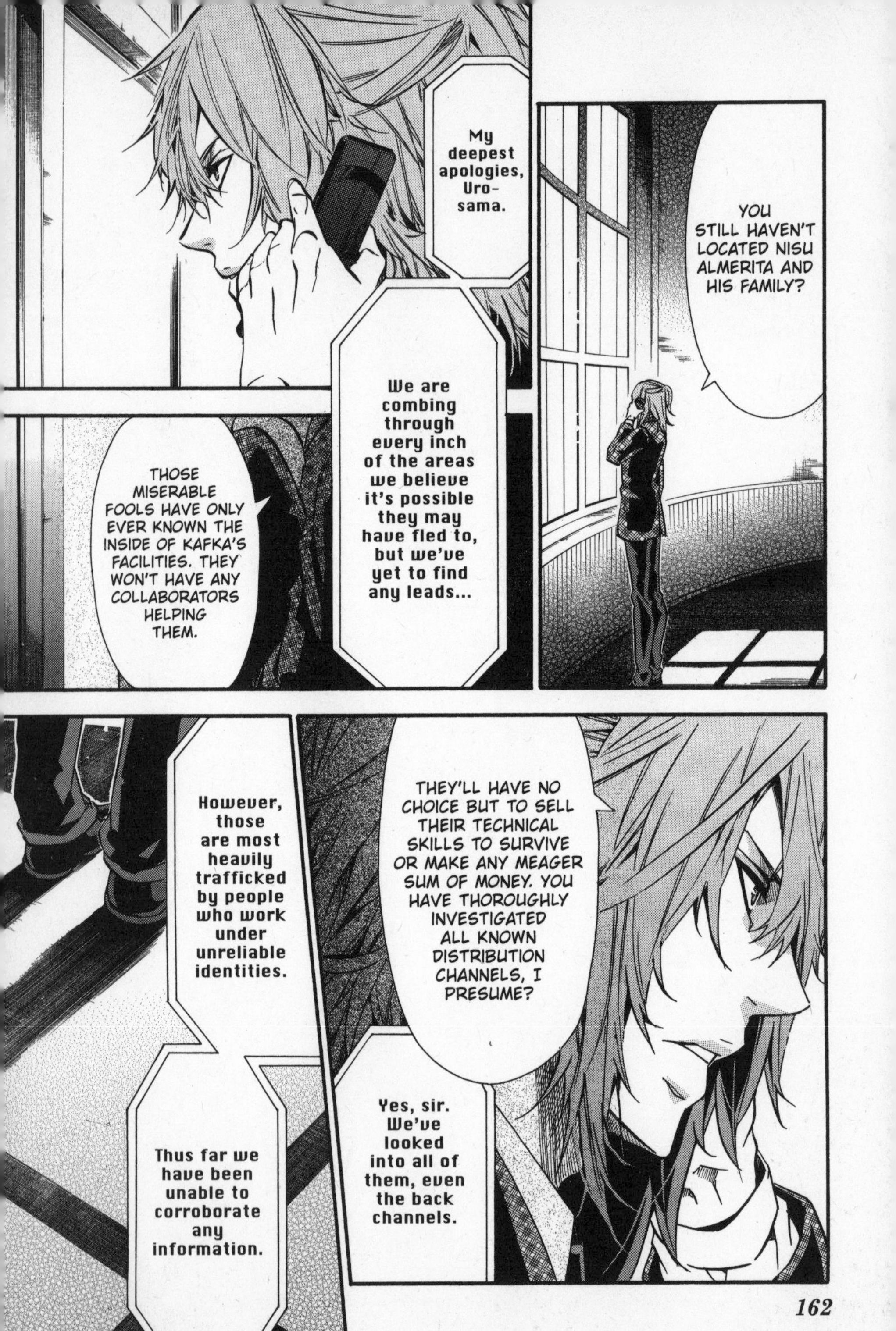
YOU STILL HAVEN'T LOCATED NISU ALMERITA AND HIS FAMILY?
My deepest apologies, Uro-sama.
We are combing through every inch of the areas we believe it's possible they may have fled to, but we've yet to find any leads...
THOSE MISERABLE FOOLS HAVE ONLY EVER KNOWN THE INSIDE OF KAFKA'S FACILITIES. THEY WON'T HAVE ANY COLLABORATORS HELPING THEM.
THEY'LL HAVE NO CHOICE BUT TO SELL THEIR TECHNICAL SKILLS TO SURVIVE OR MAKE ANY MEAGER SUM OF MONEY. YOU HAVE THOROUGHLY INVESTIGATED ALL KNOWN DISTRIBUTION CHANNELS, I PRESUME?
Yes, sir. We've looked into all of them, even the back channels.
However, those are most heavily trafficked by people who work under unreliable identities.
Thus far we have been unable to corroborate any information.

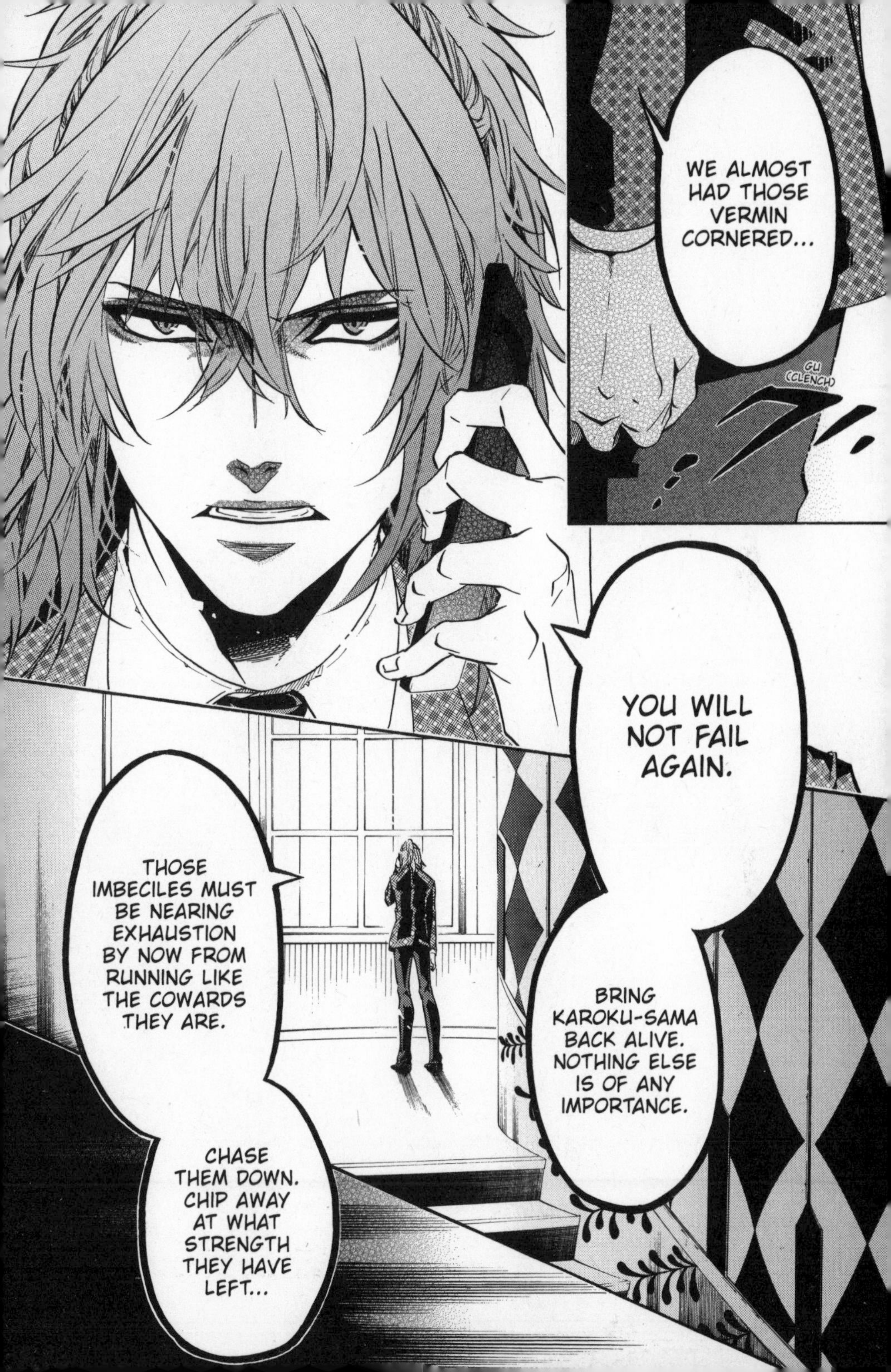
WE ALMOST HAD THOSE VERMIN CORNERED...
GU (CLENCH)
YOU WILL NOT FAIL AGAIN.
BRING KAROKU-SAMA BACK ALIVE. NOTHING ELSE IS OF ANY IMPORTANCE.
THOSE IMBECILES MUST BE NEARING EXHAUSTION BY NOW FROM RUNNING LIKE THE COWARDS THEY ARE.
CHASE THEM DOWN. CHIP AWAY AT WHAT STRENGTH THEY HAVE LEFT...

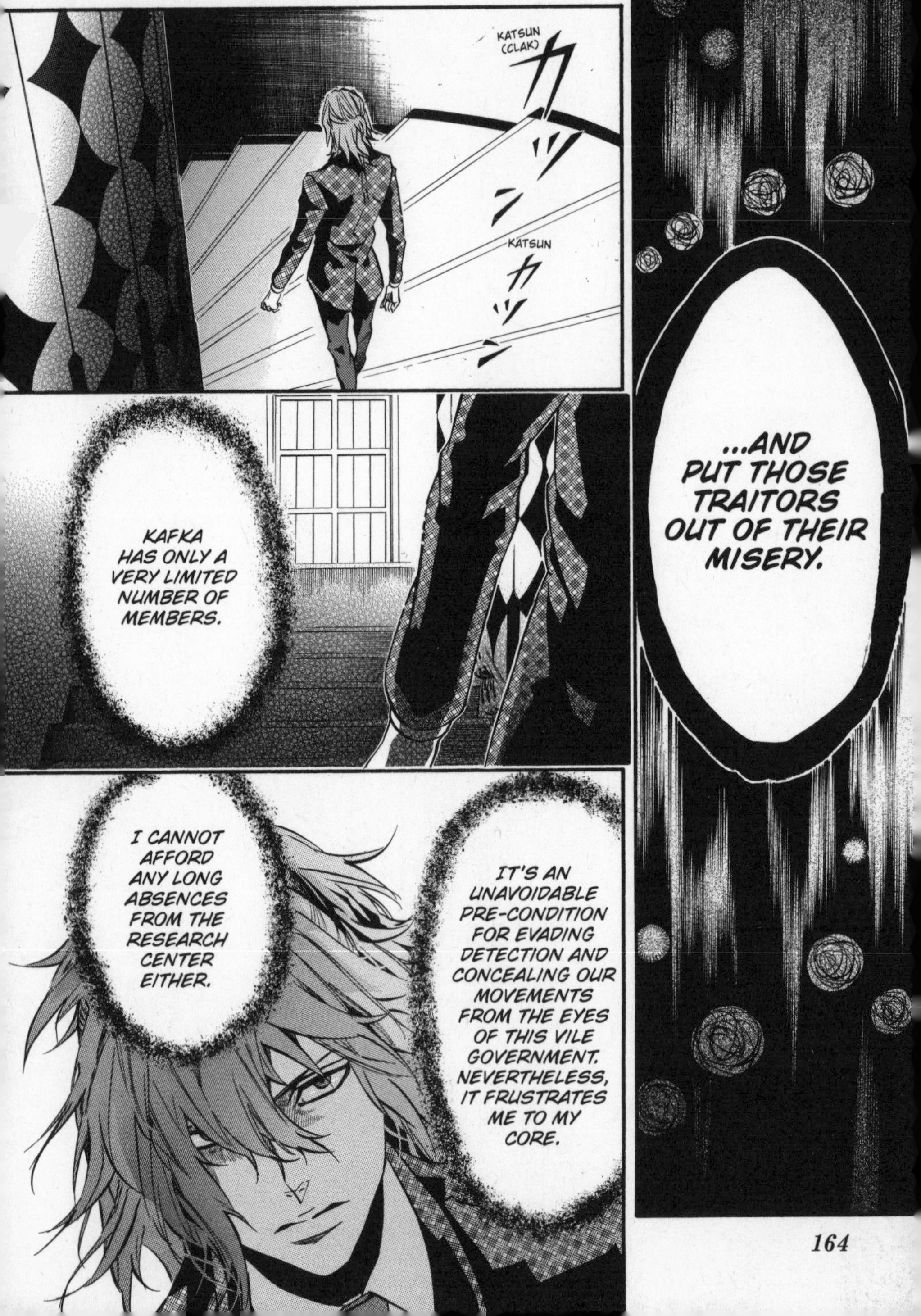
...AND PUT THOSE TRAITORS OUT OF THEIR MISERY.
KATSUN (CLAK)
カツン
KATSUN
カツン
KAFKA HAS ONLY A VERY LIMITED NUMBER OF MEMBERS.
IT'S AN UNAVOIDABLE PRE-CONDITION FOR EVADING DETECTION AND CONCEALING OUR MOVEMENTS FROM THE EYES OF THIS VILE GOVERNMENT. NEVERTHELESS, IT FRUSTRATES ME TO MY CORE.
I CANNOT AFFORD ANY LONG ABSENCES FROM THE RESEARCH CENTER EITHER.

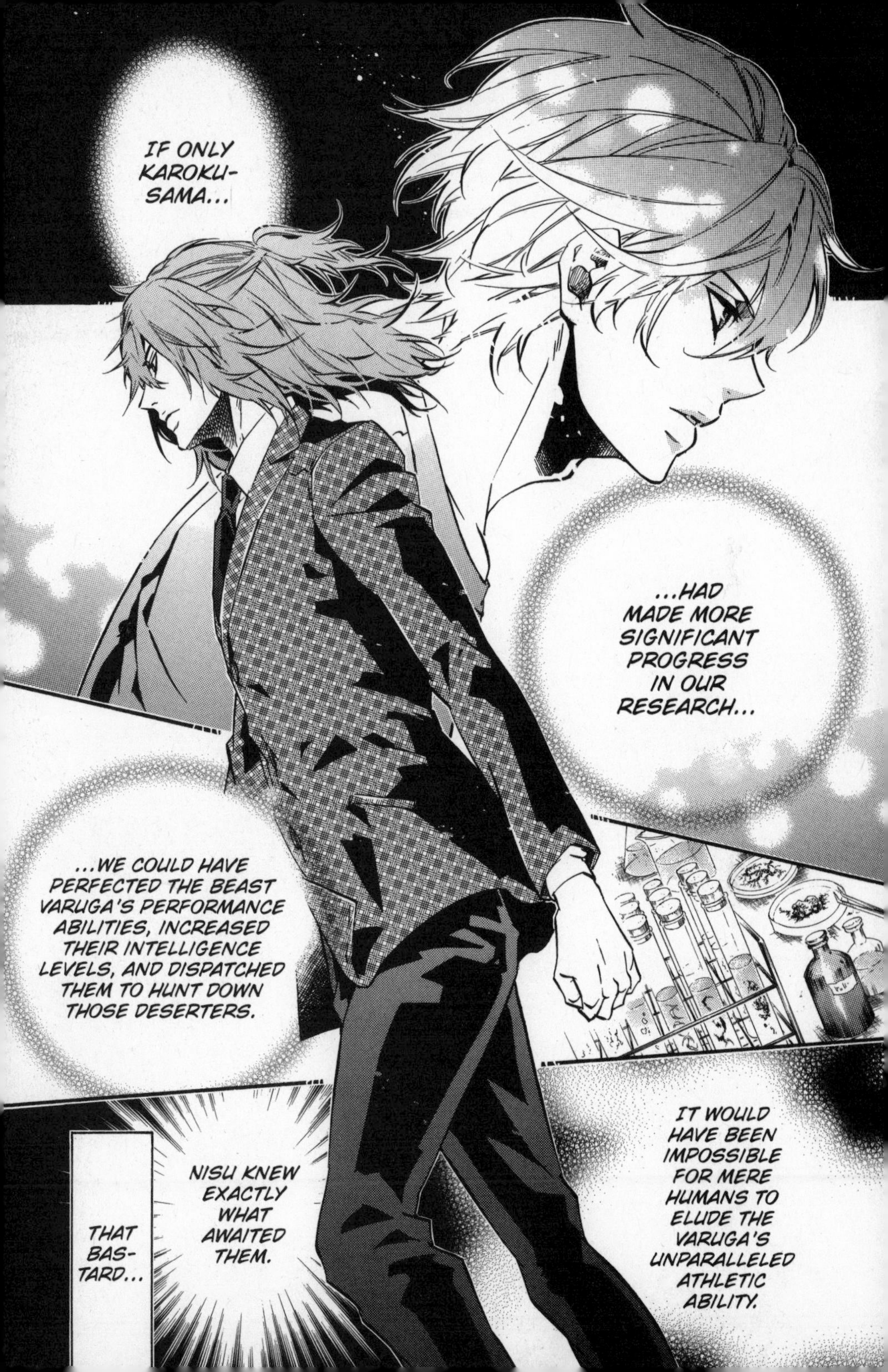
IF ONLY KAROKU-SAMA...
...HAD MADE MORE SIGNIFICANT PROGRESS IN OUR RESEARCH...
...WE COULD HAVE PERFECTED THE BEAST VARUGA'S PERFORMANCE ABILITIES, INCREASED THEIR INTELLIGENCE LEVELS, AND DISPATCHED THEM TO HUNT DOWN THOSE DESERTERS.
IT WOULD HAVE BEEN IMPOSSIBLE FOR MERE HUMANS TO ELUDE THE VARUGA'S UNPARALLELED ATHLETIC ABILITY.
NISU KNEW EXACTLY WHAT AWAITED THEM.
THAT BAS-TARD...

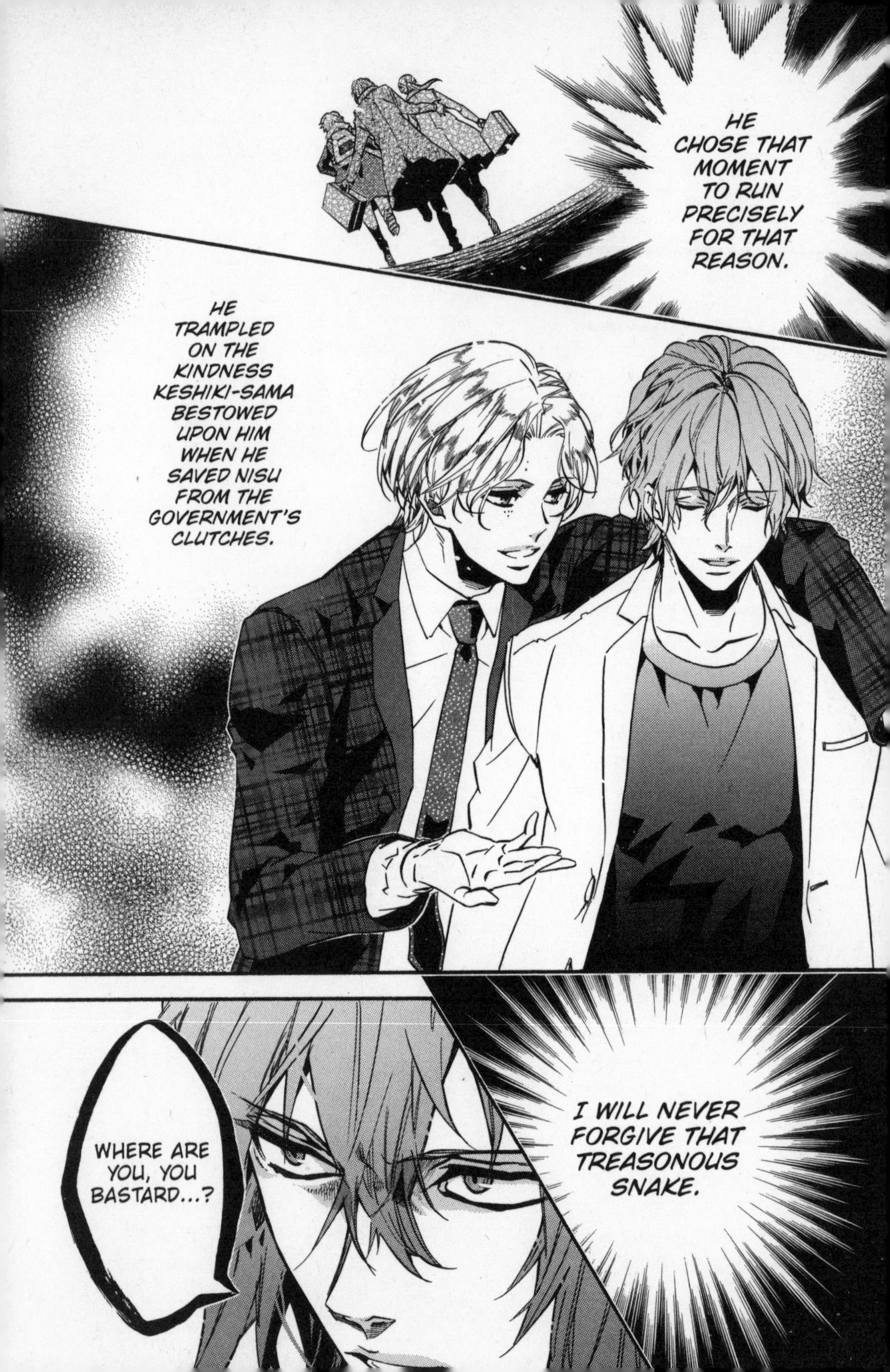
HE CHOSE THAT MOMENT TO RUN PRECISELY FOR THAT REASON.
HE TRAMPLED ON THE KINDNESS KESHIKI-SAMA BESTOWED UPON HIM WHEN HE SAVED NISU FROM THE GOVERNMENT'S CLUTCHES.
I WILL NEVER FORGIVE THAT TREASONOUS SNAKE.
WHERE ARE YOU, YOU BASTARD...?

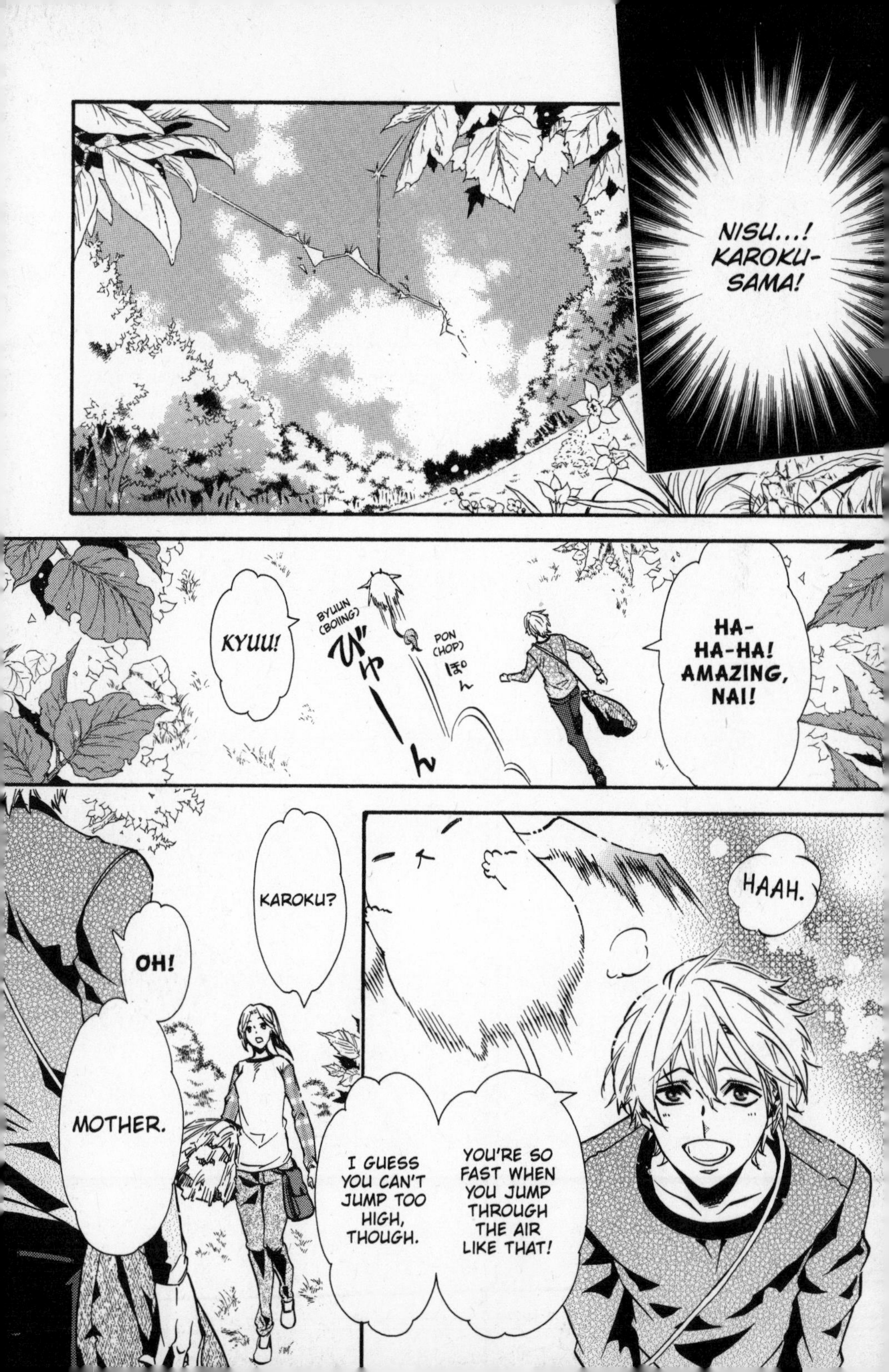
NISU...! KAROKU-SAMA!
HA-HA-HA! AMAZING, NAI!
PON (HOP) ぽん
BYUUN (BOIING) びゅーん
KYUU!
HAAH.
YOU'RE SO FAST WHEN YOU JUMP THROUGH THE AIR LIKE THAT!
I GUESS YOU CAN'T JUMP TOO HIGH, THOUGH.
KAROKU?
OH!
MOTHER.

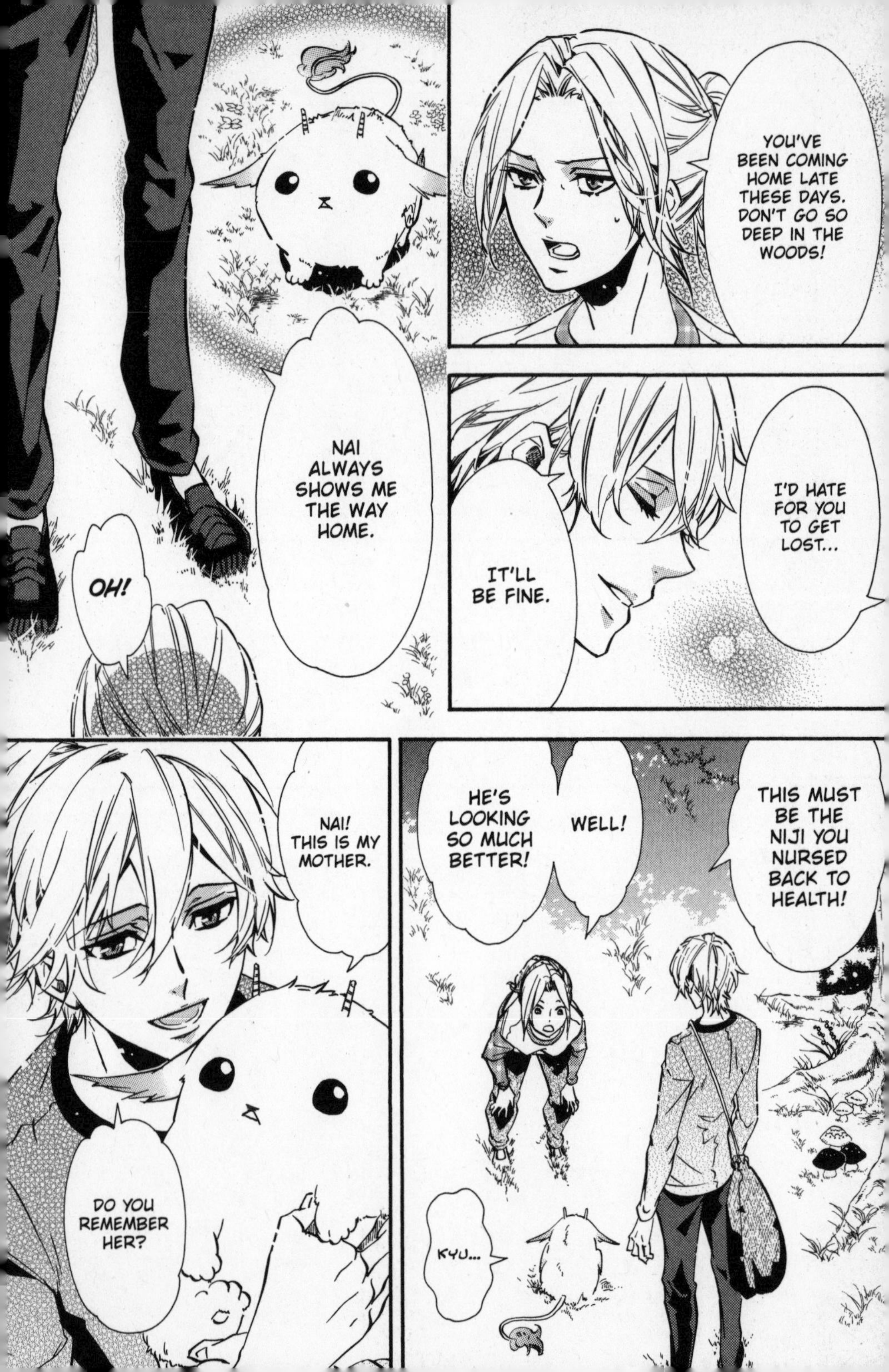
YOU'VE BEEN COMING HOME LATE THESE DAYS. DON'T GO SO DEEP IN THE WOODS!
I'D HATE FOR YOU TO GET LOST...
IT'LL BE FINE.
NAI ALWAYS SHOWS ME THE WAY HOME.
OH!
THIS MUST BE THE NIJI YOU NURSED BACK TO HEALTH!
WELL!
HE'S LOOKING SO MUCH BETTER!
KYU...
NAI! THIS IS MY MOTHER.
DO YOU REMEMBER HER?

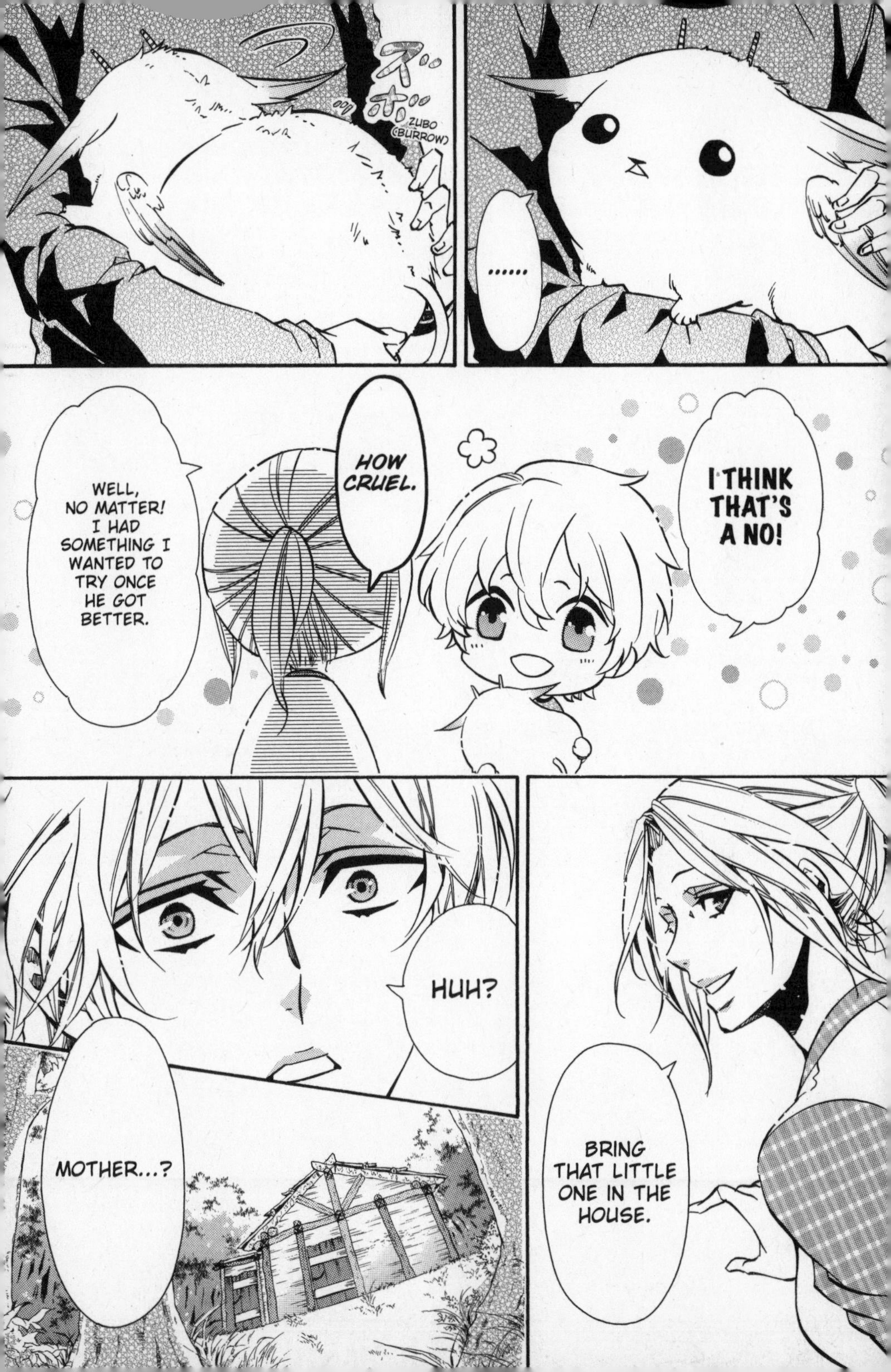
......
ZUBO (BURROW)
I THINK THAT'S A NO!
HOW CRUEL.
WELL, NO MATTER! I HAD SOMETHING I WANTED TO TRY ONCE HE GOT BETTER.
BRING THAT LITTLE ONE IN THE HOUSE.
HUH?
MOTHER...?

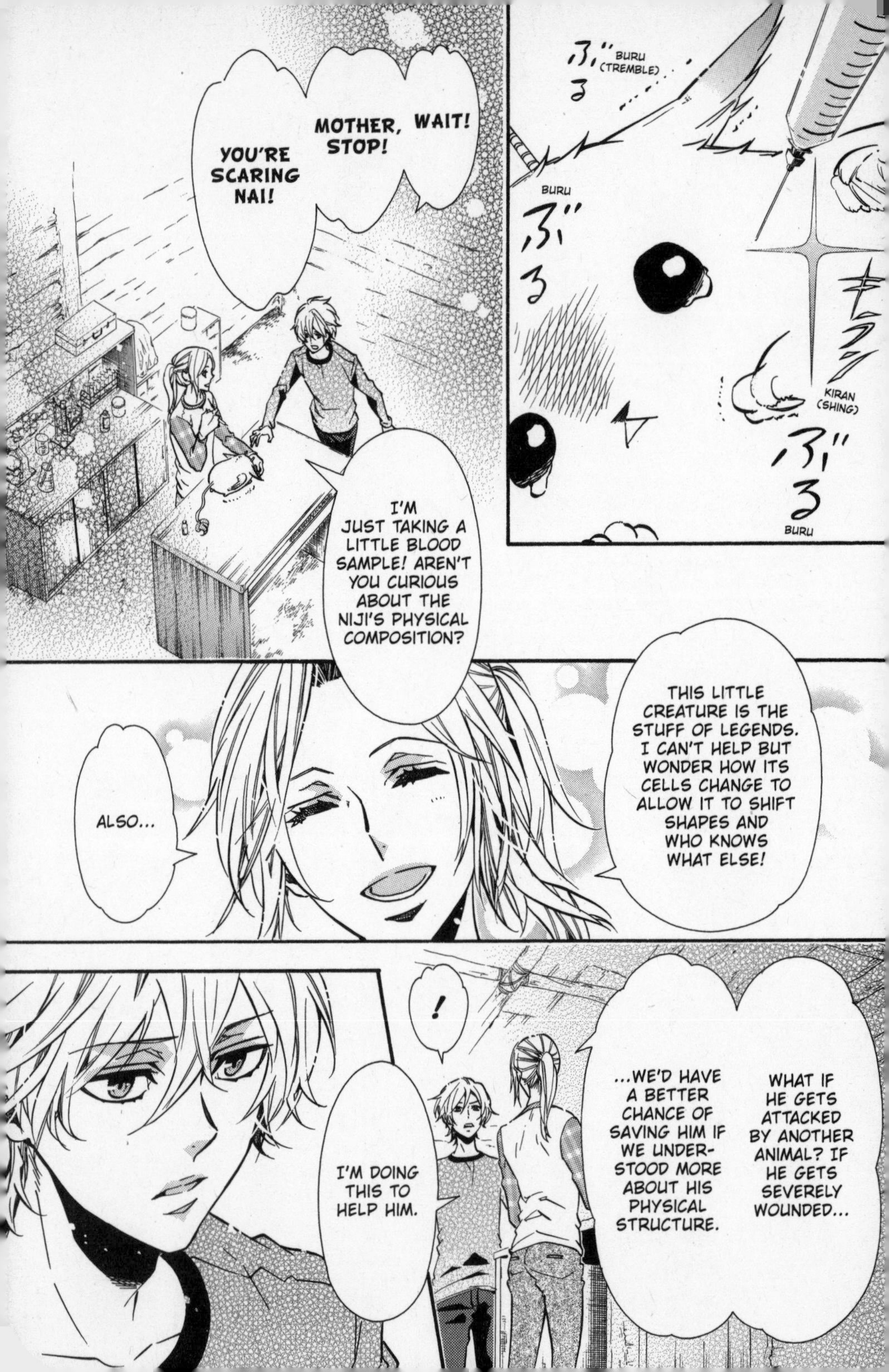
ぶる
BURU (TREMBLE)...
ぶる
BURU
キラン
KIRAN (SHING)
ぶる
BURU
MOTHER, WAIT! STOP!
YOU'RE SCARING NAI!
I'M JUST TAKING A LITTLE BLOOD SAMPLE! AREN'T YOU CURIOUS ABOUT THE NIJI'S PHYSICAL COMPOSITION?
THIS LITTLE CREATURE IS THE STUFF OF LEGENDS. I CAN'T HELP BUT WONDER HOW ITS CELLS CHANGE TO ALLOW IT TO SHIFT SHAPES AND WHO KNOWS WHAT ELSE!
...
ALSO...
WHAT IF HE GETS ATTACKED BY ANOTHER ANIMAL? IF HE GETS SEVERELY WOUNDED...
...WE'D HAVE A BETTER CHANCE OF SAVING HIM IF WE UNDER-STOOD MORE ABOUT HIS PHYSICAL STRUCTURE.
!
I'M DOING THIS TO HELP HIM.

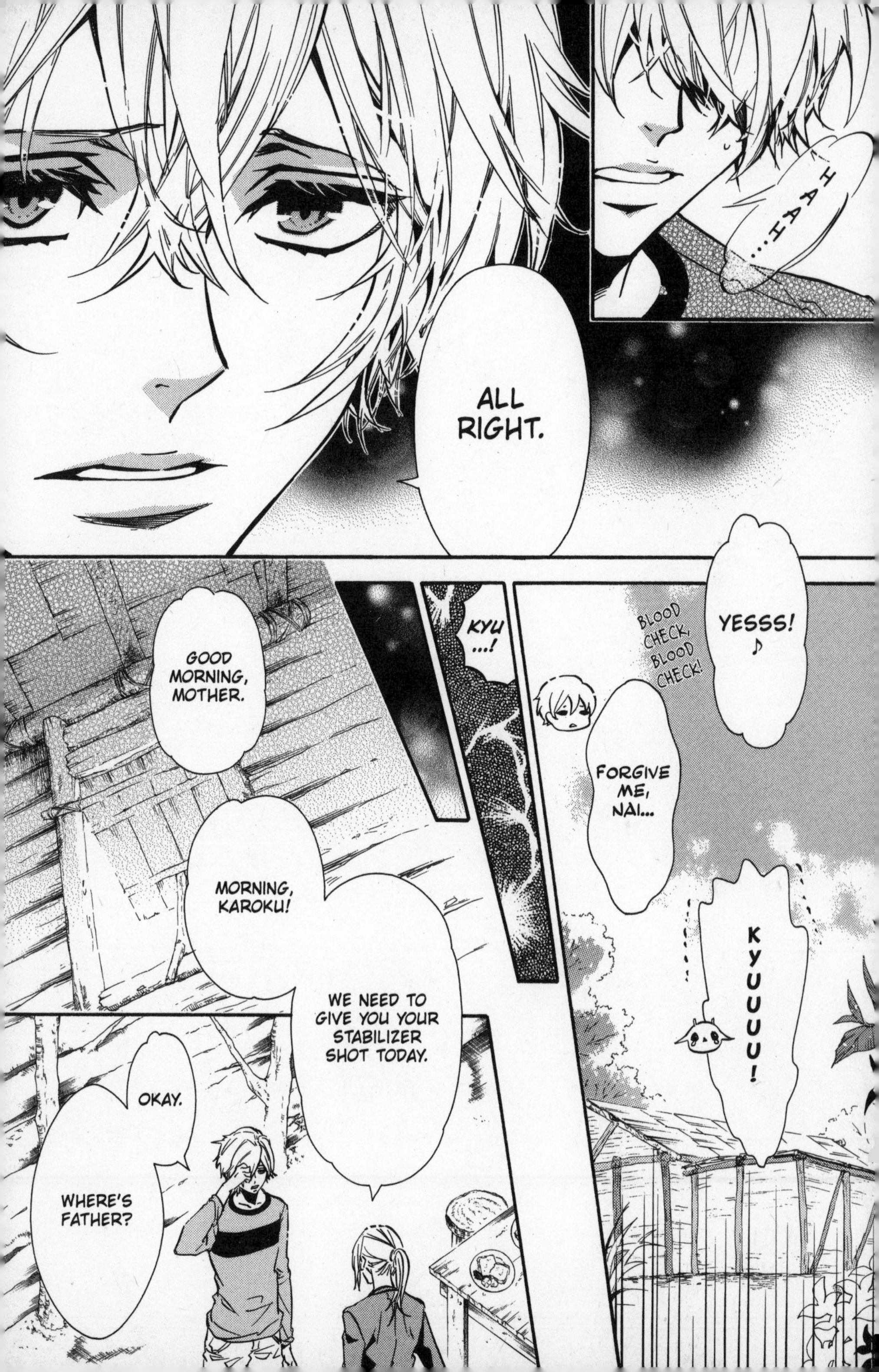
HAAH...
ALL RIGHT.
YESSS! ♪
BLOOD CHECK, BLOOD CHECK!
FORGIVE ME, NAI...
KYUUUU!
KYU ...!
GOOD MORNING, MOTHER.
MORNING, KAROKU!
WE NEED TO GIVE YOU YOUR STABILIZER SHOT TODAY.
OKAY.
WHERE'S FATHER?

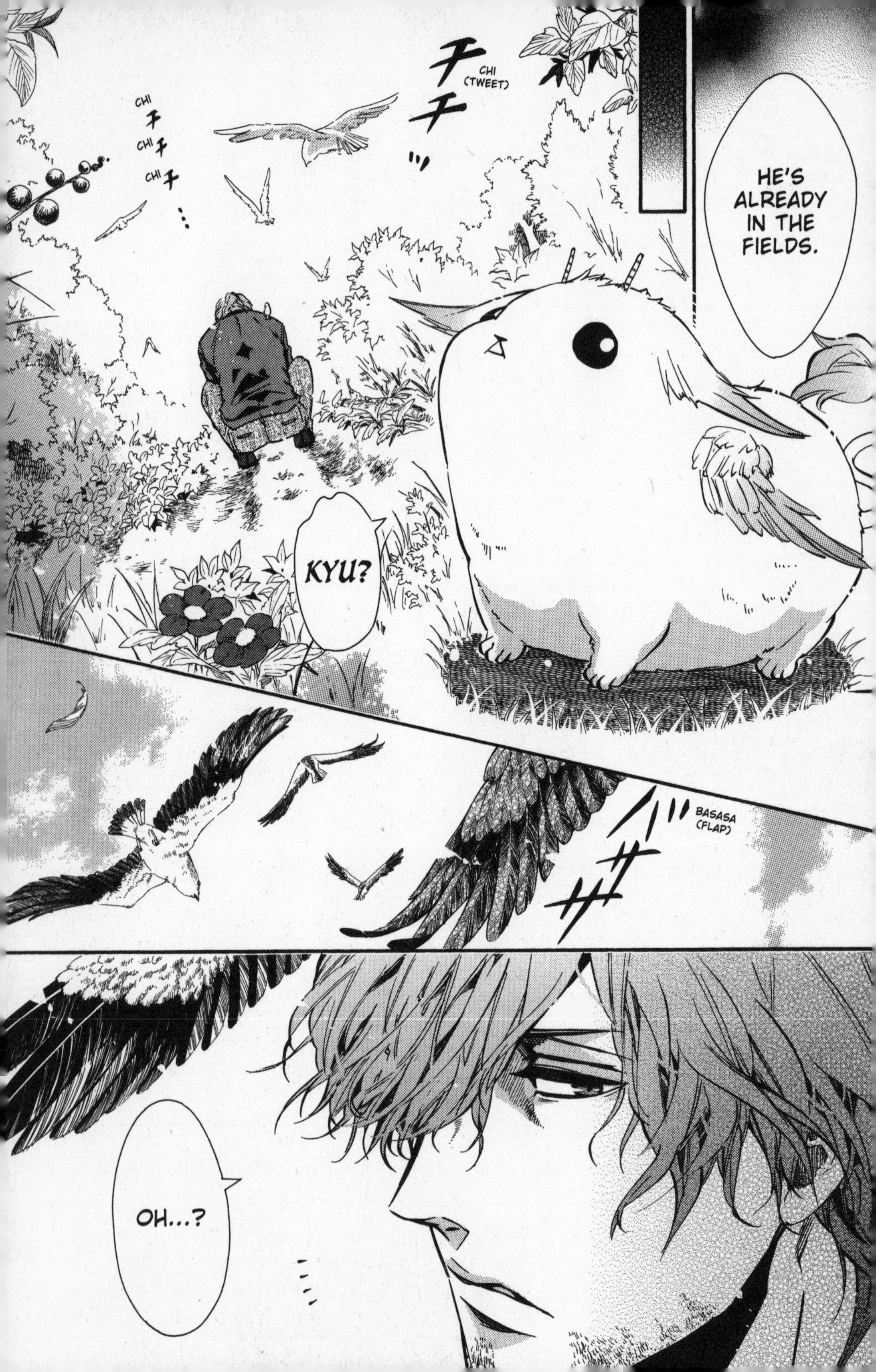
HE'S ALREADY IN THE FIELDS.
CHI (TWEET)
CHI CHI CHI
KYU?
BASASA (FLAP)
OH...?

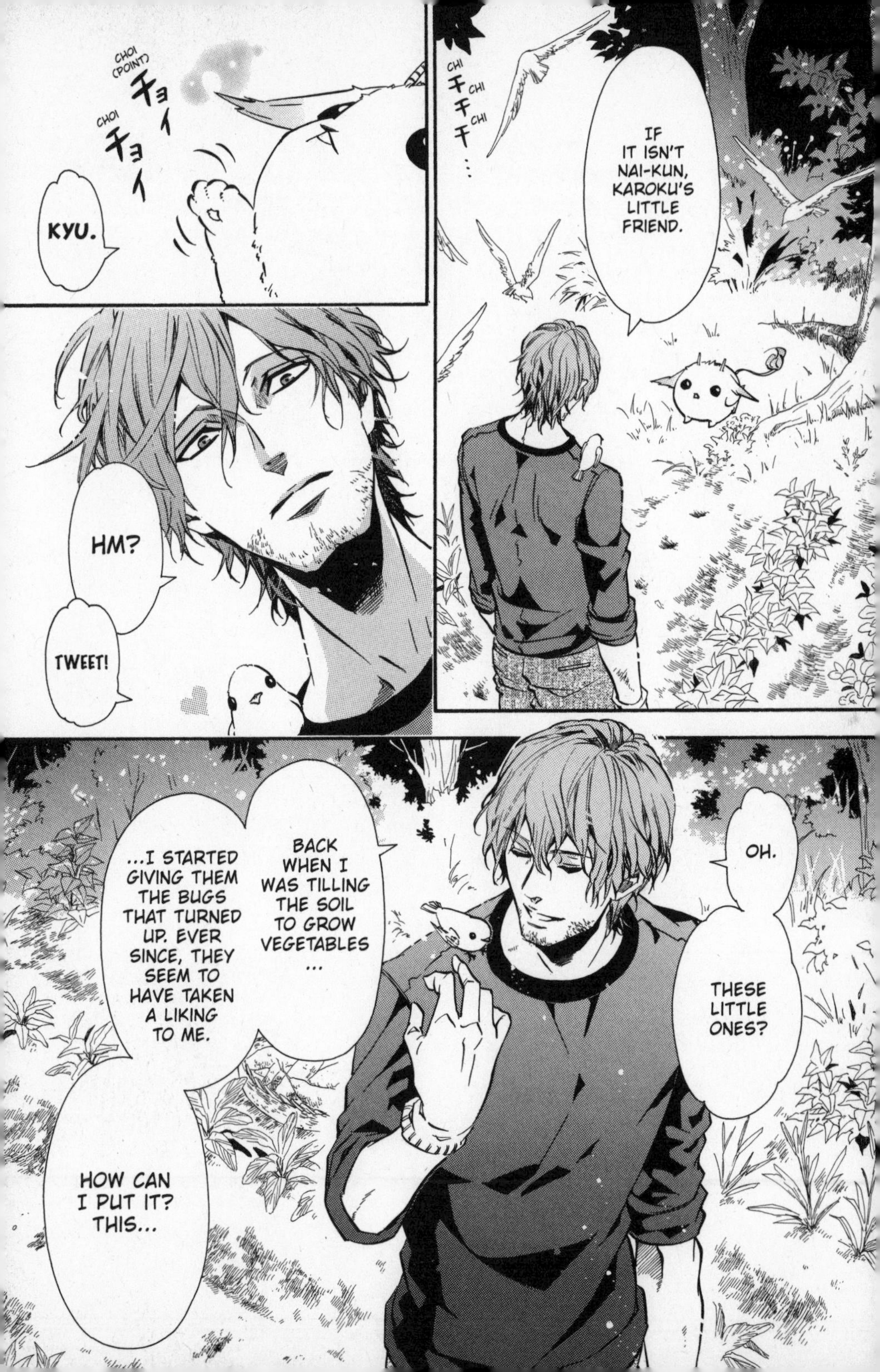
IF IT ISN'T NAI-KUN, KAROKU'S LITTLE FRIEND.
CHI チ CHI チ CHI チ...
CHOI (POINT) チョイ
CHOI チョイ
KYU.
HM?
TWEET!
OH.
THESE LITTLE ONES?
BACK WHEN I WAS TILLING THE SOIL TO GROW VEGETABLES...
...I STARTED GIVING THEM THE BUGS THAT TURNED UP. EVER SINCE, THEY SEEM TO HAVE TAKEN A LIKING TO ME.
HOW CAN I PUT IT? THIS...

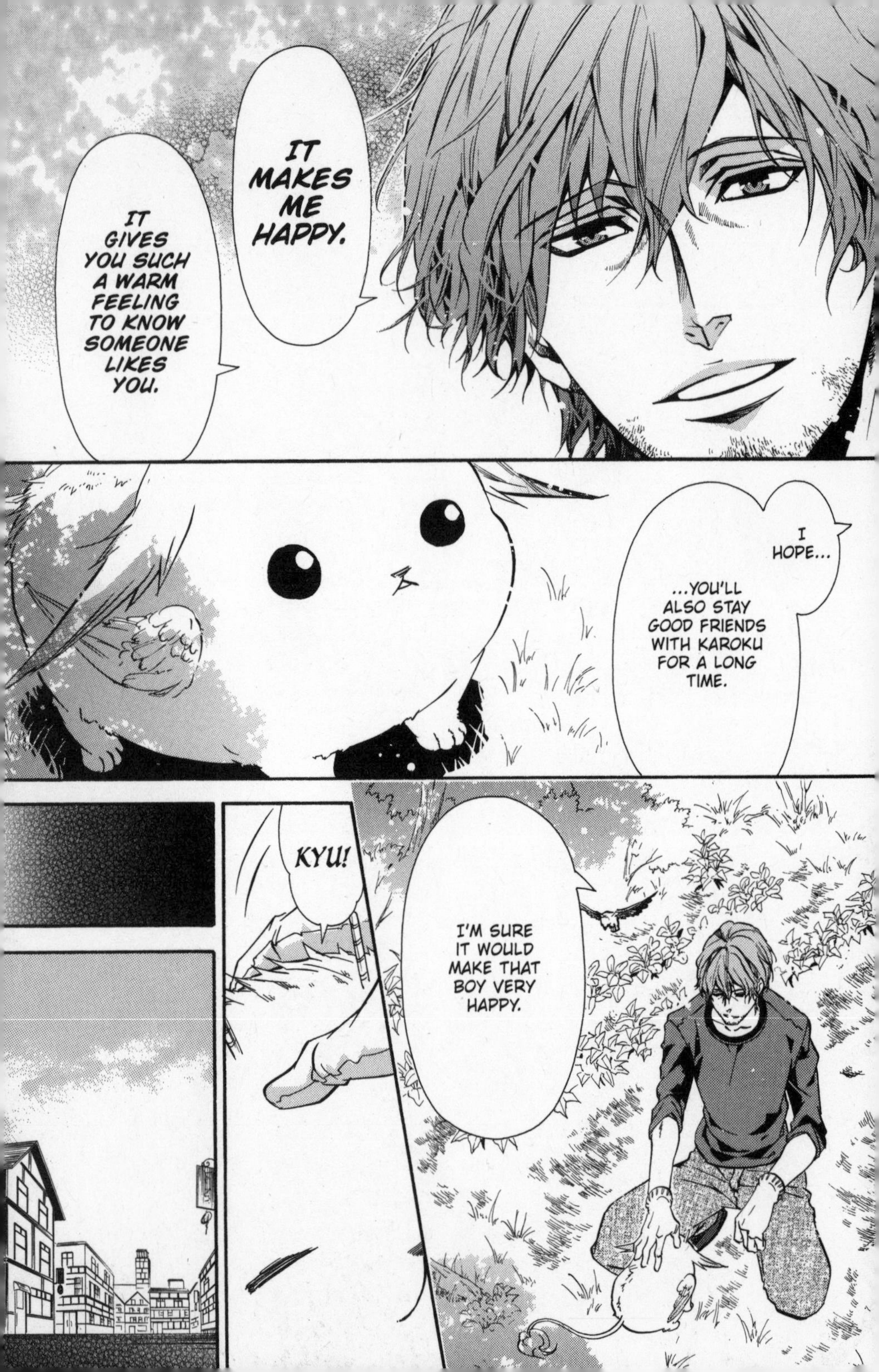
IT MAKES ME HAPPY.
IT GIVES YOU SUCH A WARM FEELING TO KNOW SOMEONE LIKES YOU.
I HOPE...
...YOU'LL ALSO STAY GOOD FRIENDS WITH KAROKU FOR A LONG TIME.
I'M SURE IT WOULD MAKE THAT BOY VERY HAPPY.
KYU!

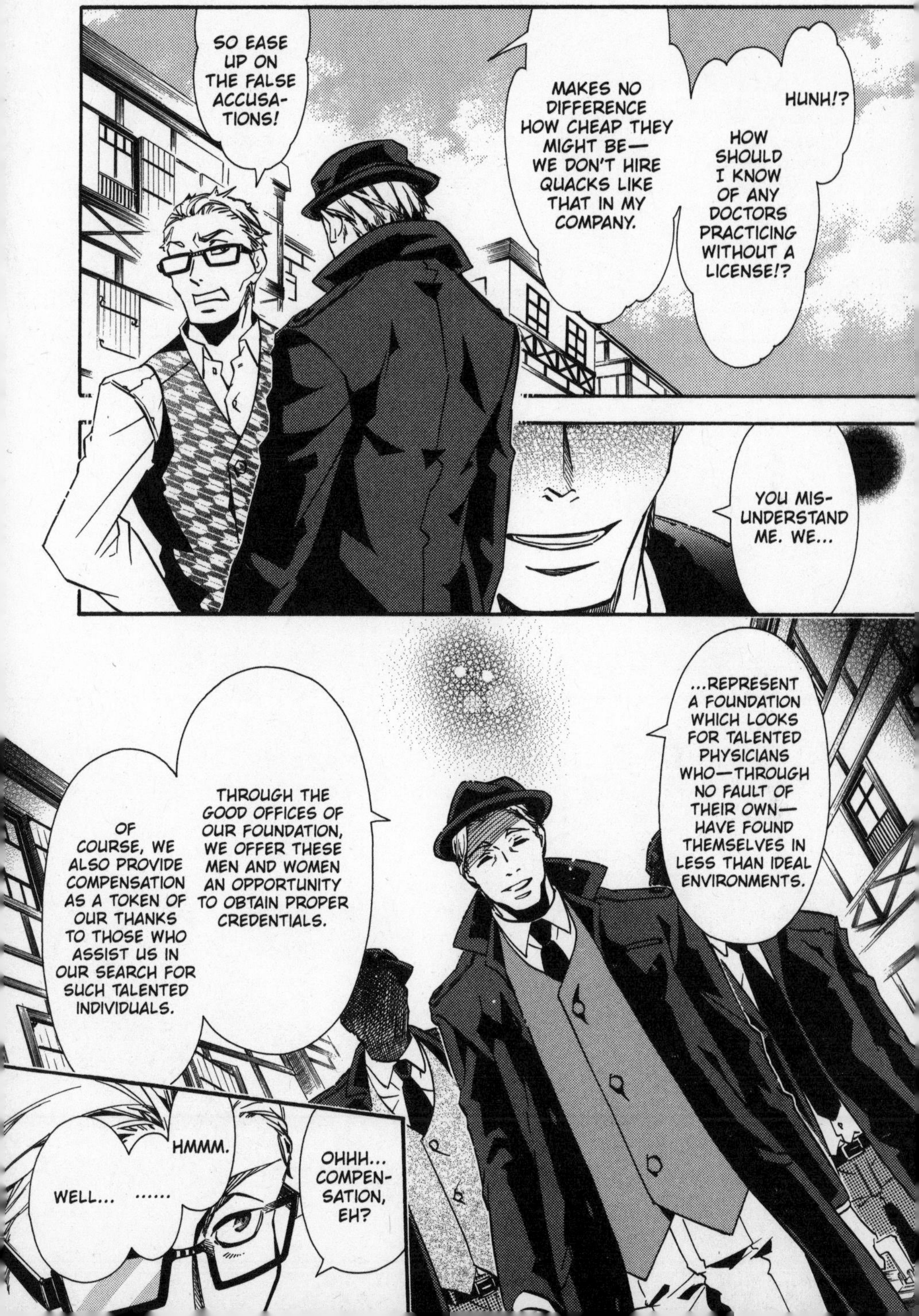
HUNH!?
HOW SHOULD I KNOW OF ANY DOCTORS PRACTICING WITHOUT A LICENSE!?
MAKES NO DIFFERENCE HOW CHEAP THEY MIGHT BE— WE DON'T HIRE QUACKS LIKE THAT IN MY COMPANY.
SO EASE UP ON THE FALSE ACCUSA- TIONS!
YOU MIS- UNDERSTAND ME. WE...
...REPRESENT A FOUNDATION WHICH LOOKS FOR TALENTED PHYSICIANS WHO—THROUGH NO FAULT OF THEIR OWN— HAVE FOUND THEMSELVES IN LESS THAN IDEAL ENVIRONMENTS.
THROUGH THE GOOD OFFICES OF OUR FOUNDATION, WE OFFER THESE MEN AND WOMEN AN OPPORTUNITY TO OBTAIN PROPER CREDENTIALS.
OF COURSE, WE ALSO PROVIDE COMPENSATION AS A TOKEN OF OUR THANKS TO THOSE WHO ASSIST US IN OUR SEARCH FOR SUCH TALENTED INDIVIDUALS.
OHHH... COMPEN- SATION, EH?
HMMM.
WELL... ......

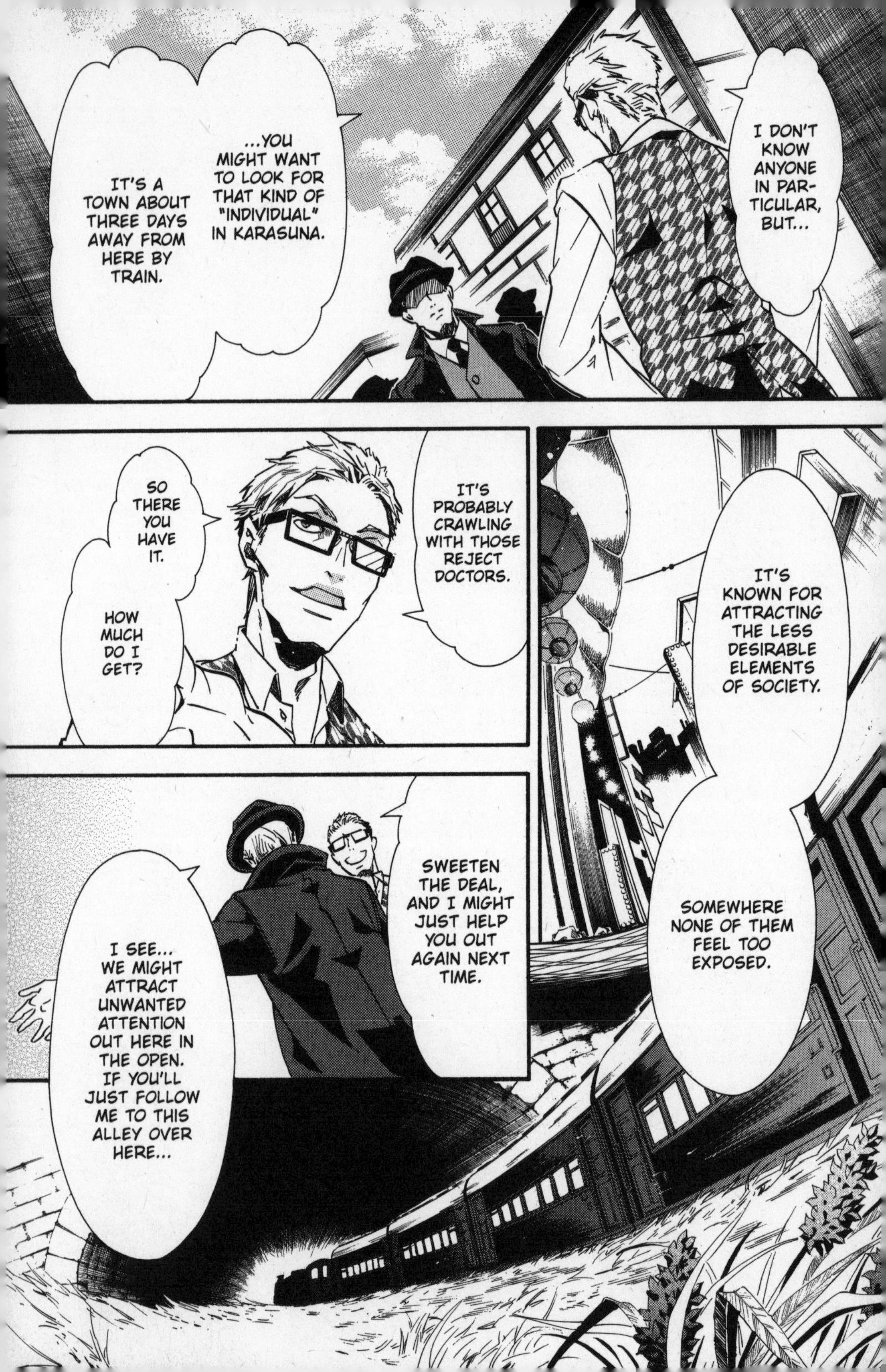
I DON'T KNOW ANYONE IN PARTICULAR, BUT...
...YOU MIGHT WANT TO LOOK FOR THAT KIND OF "INDIVIDUAL" IN KARASUNA.
IT'S A TOWN ABOUT THREE DAYS AWAY FROM HERE BY TRAIN.
IT'S KNOWN FOR ATTRACTING THE LESS DESIRABLE ELEMENTS OF SOCIETY.
SOMEWHERE NONE OF THEM FEEL TOO EXPOSED.
IT'S PROBABLY CRAWLING WITH THOSE REJECT DOCTORS.
SO THERE YOU HAVE IT.
HOW MUCH DO I GET?
SWEETEN THE DEAL, AND I MIGHT JUST HELP YOU OUT AGAIN NEXT TIME.
I SEE... WE MIGHT ATTRACT UNWANTED ATTENTION OUT HERE IN THE OPEN. IF YOU'LL JUST FOLLOW ME TO THIS ALLEY OVER HERE...

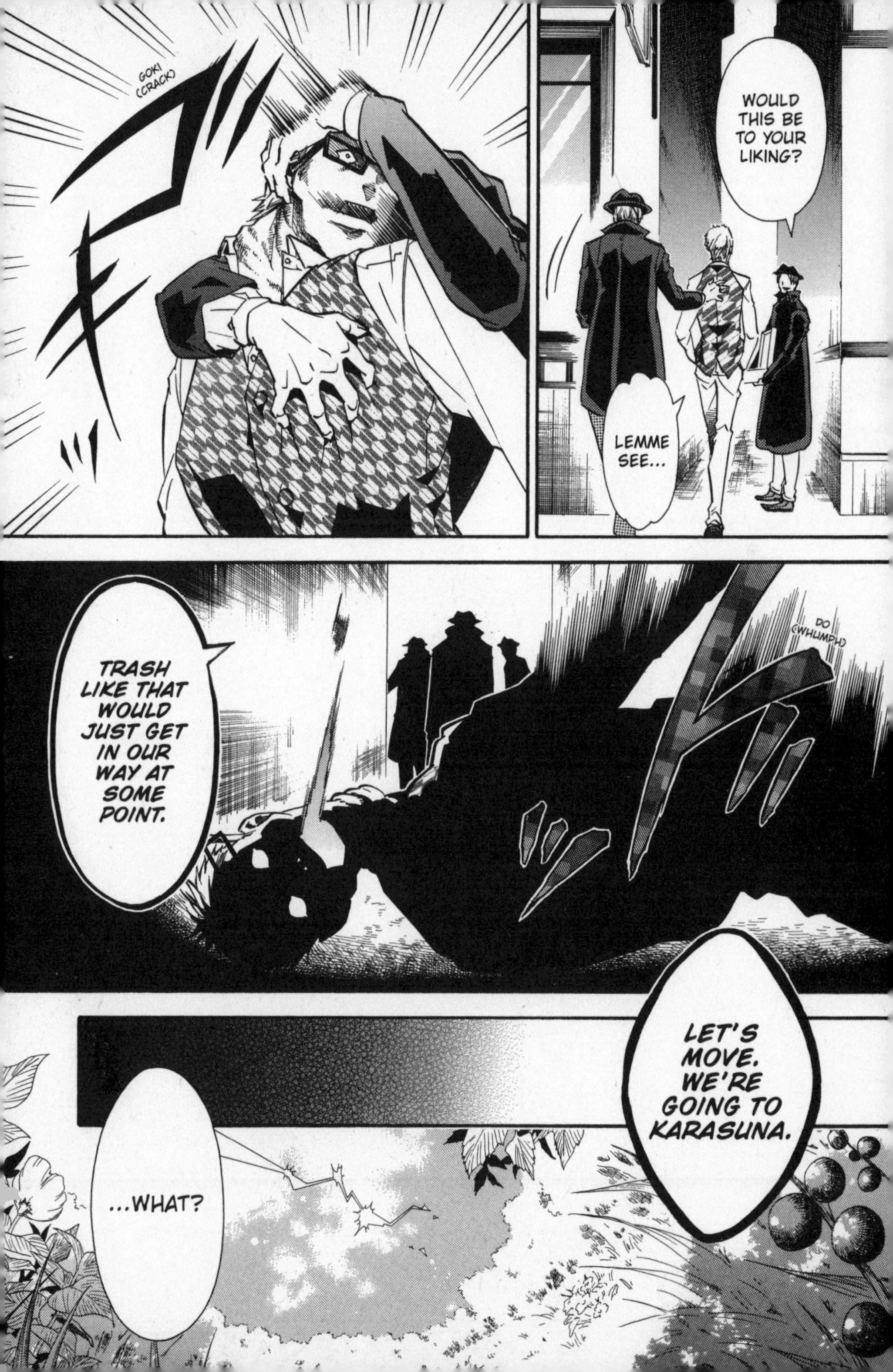
WOULD THIS BE TO YOUR LIKING?
LEMME SEE...
GOKI (CRACK)
DO (WHUMPH)
TRASH LIKE THAT WOULD JUST GET IN OUR WAY AT SOME POINT.
LET'S MOVE. WE'RE GOING TO KARASUNA.
...WHAT?

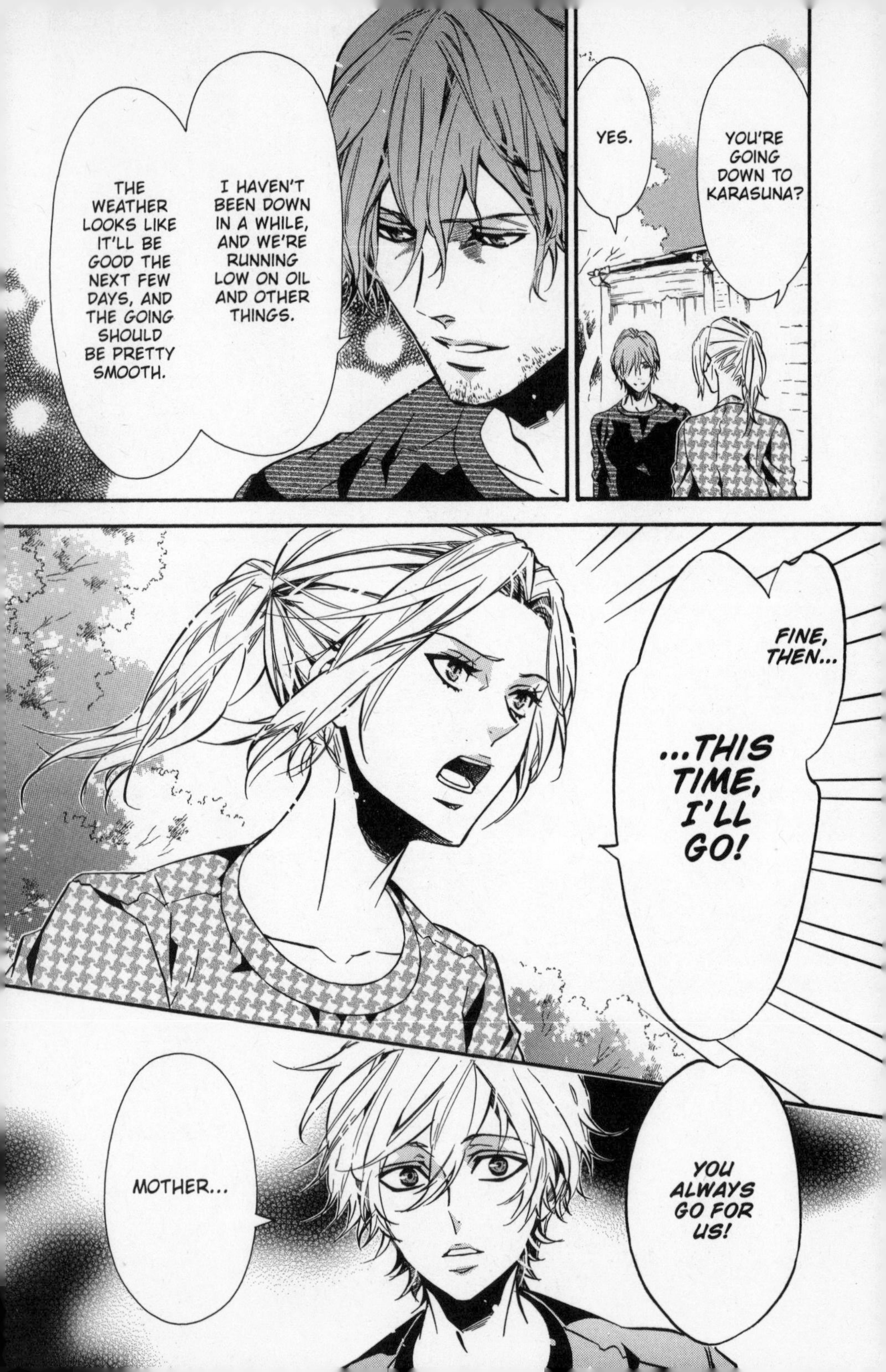
YOU'RE GOING DOWN TO KARASUNA?
YES.
I HAVEN'T BEEN DOWN IN A WHILE, AND WE'RE RUNNING LOW ON OIL AND OTHER THINGS.
THE WEATHER LOOKS LIKE IT'LL BE GOOD THE NEXT FEW DAYS, AND THE GOING SHOULD BE PRETTY SMOOTH.
FINE, THEN...
...THIS TIME, I'LL GO!
YOU ALWAYS GO FOR US!
MOTHER...

KARNEVAL

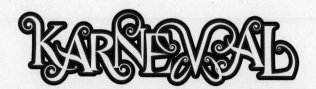

KARNEVAL

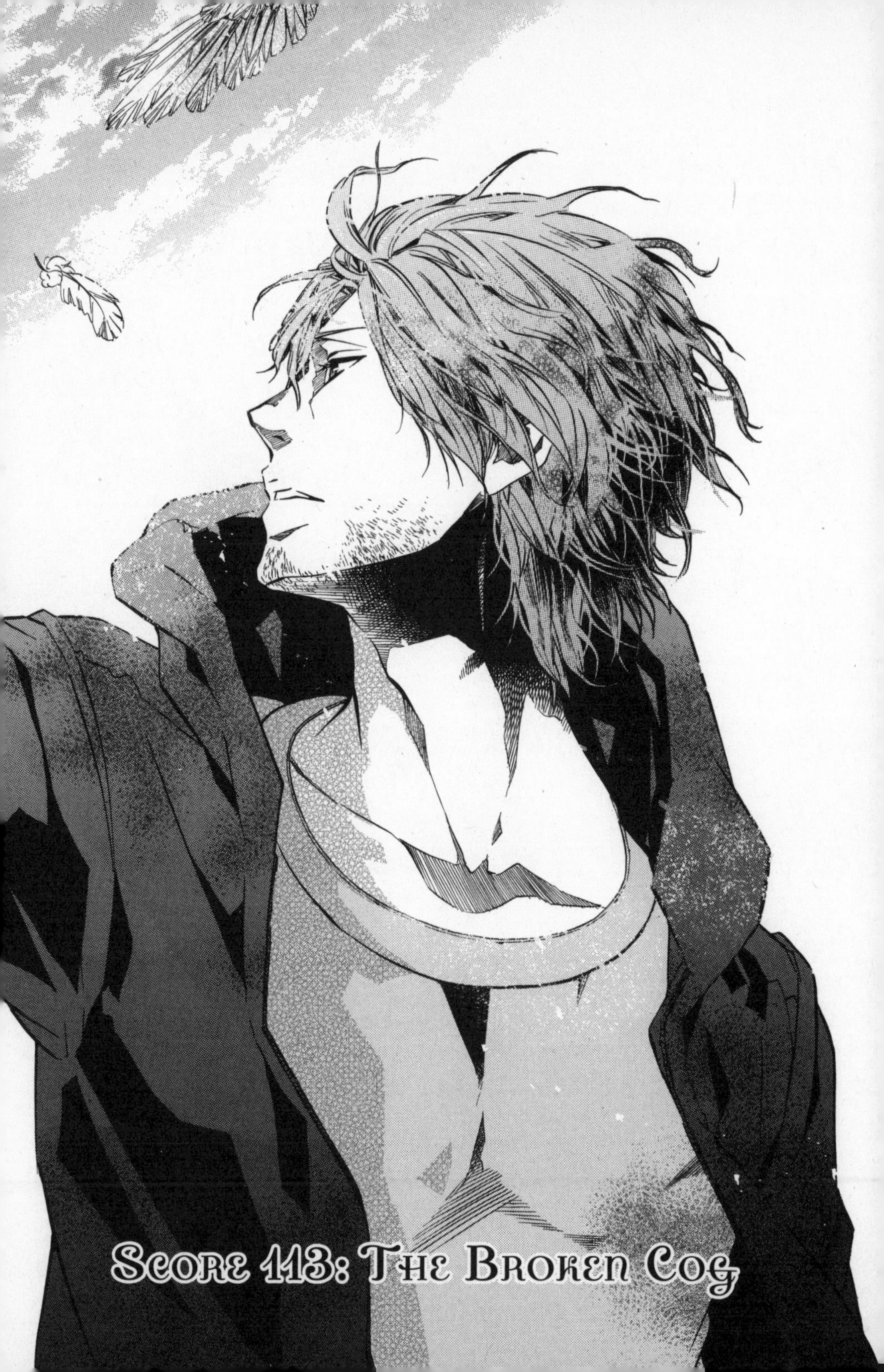
Score 113: The Broken Cog

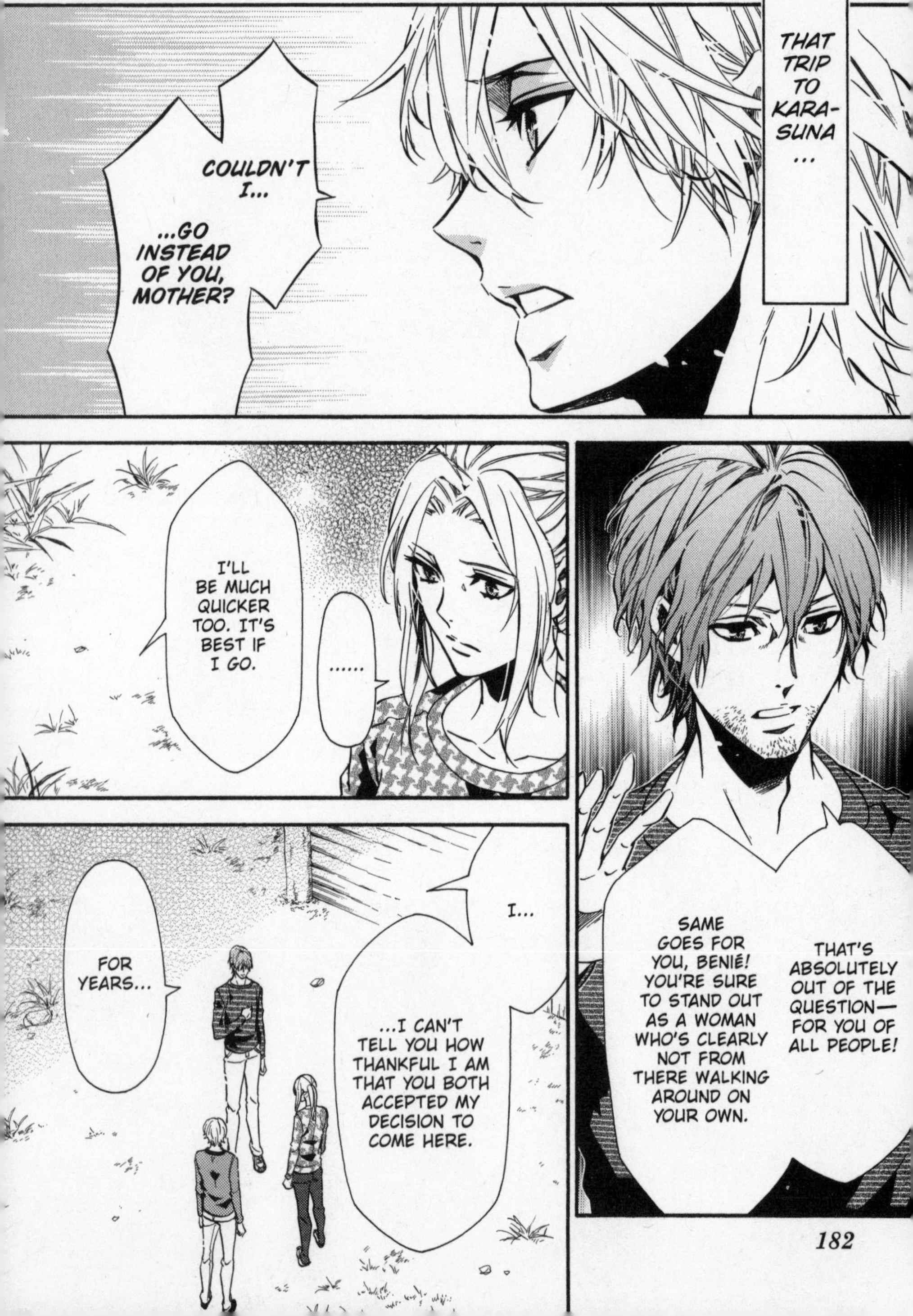
THAT TRIP TO KARA-SUNA...
COULDN'T I... ...GO INSTEAD OF YOU, MOTHER?
THAT'S ABSOLUTELY OUT OF THE QUESTION—FOR YOU OF ALL PEOPLE!
SAME GOES FOR YOU, BENIÉ! YOU'RE SURE TO STAND OUT AS A WOMAN WHO'S CLEARLY NOT FROM THERE WALKING AROUND ON YOUR OWN.
I'LL BE MUCH QUICKER TOO. IT'S BEST IF I GO.
......
I...
...I CAN'T TELL YOU HOW THANKFUL I AM THAT YOU BOTH ACCEPTED MY DECISION TO COME HERE.
FOR YEARS...

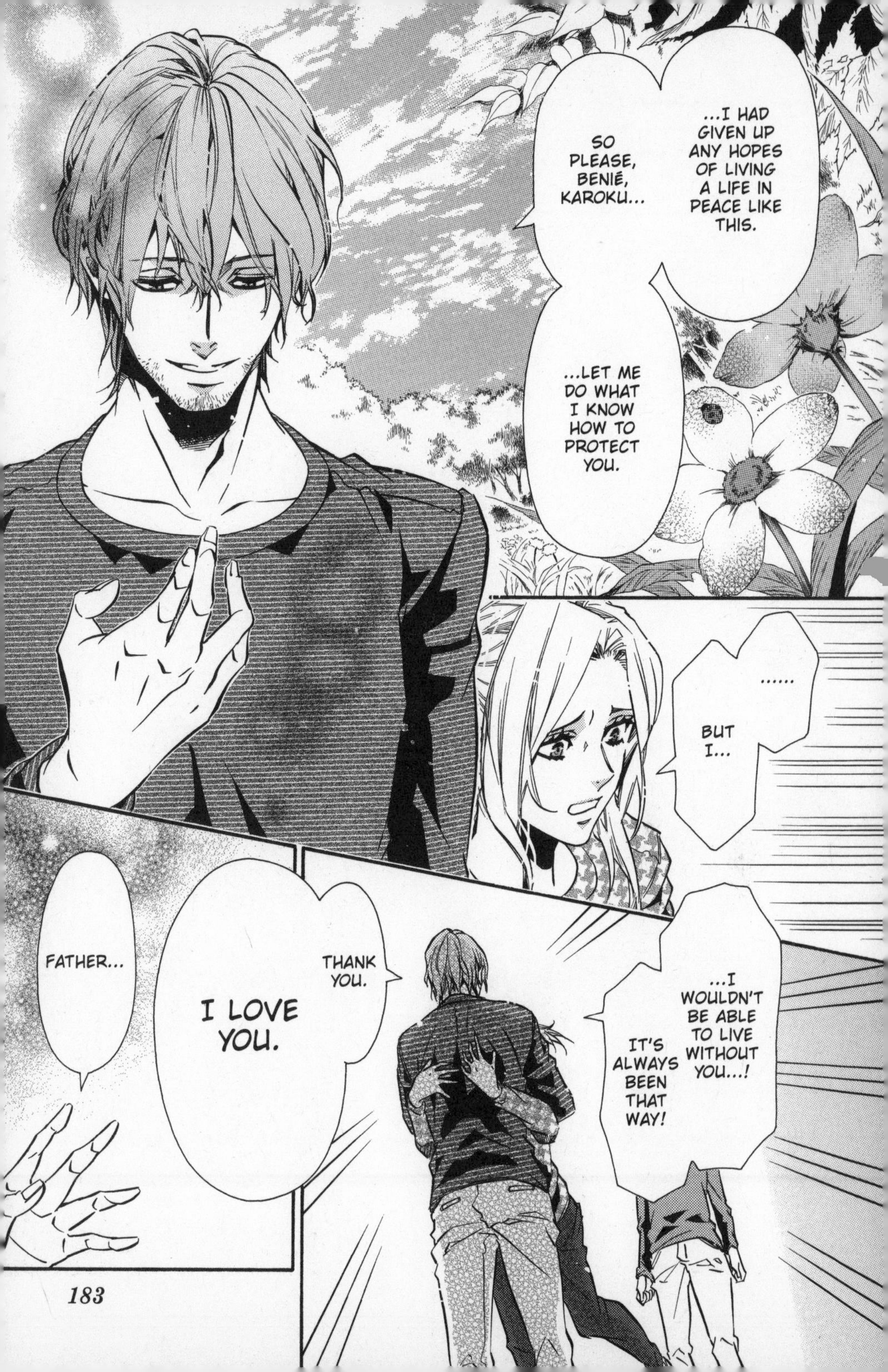
...I HAD GIVEN UP ANY HOPES OF LIVING A LIFE IN PEACE LIKE THIS.
SO PLEASE, BENIÉ, KAROKU...
...LET ME DO WHAT I KNOW HOW TO PROTECT YOU.
......
BUT I...
...I WOULDN'T BE ABLE TO LIVE WITHOUT YOU...!
IT'S ALWAYS BEEN THAT WAY!
THANK YOU.
I LOVE YOU.
FATHER...

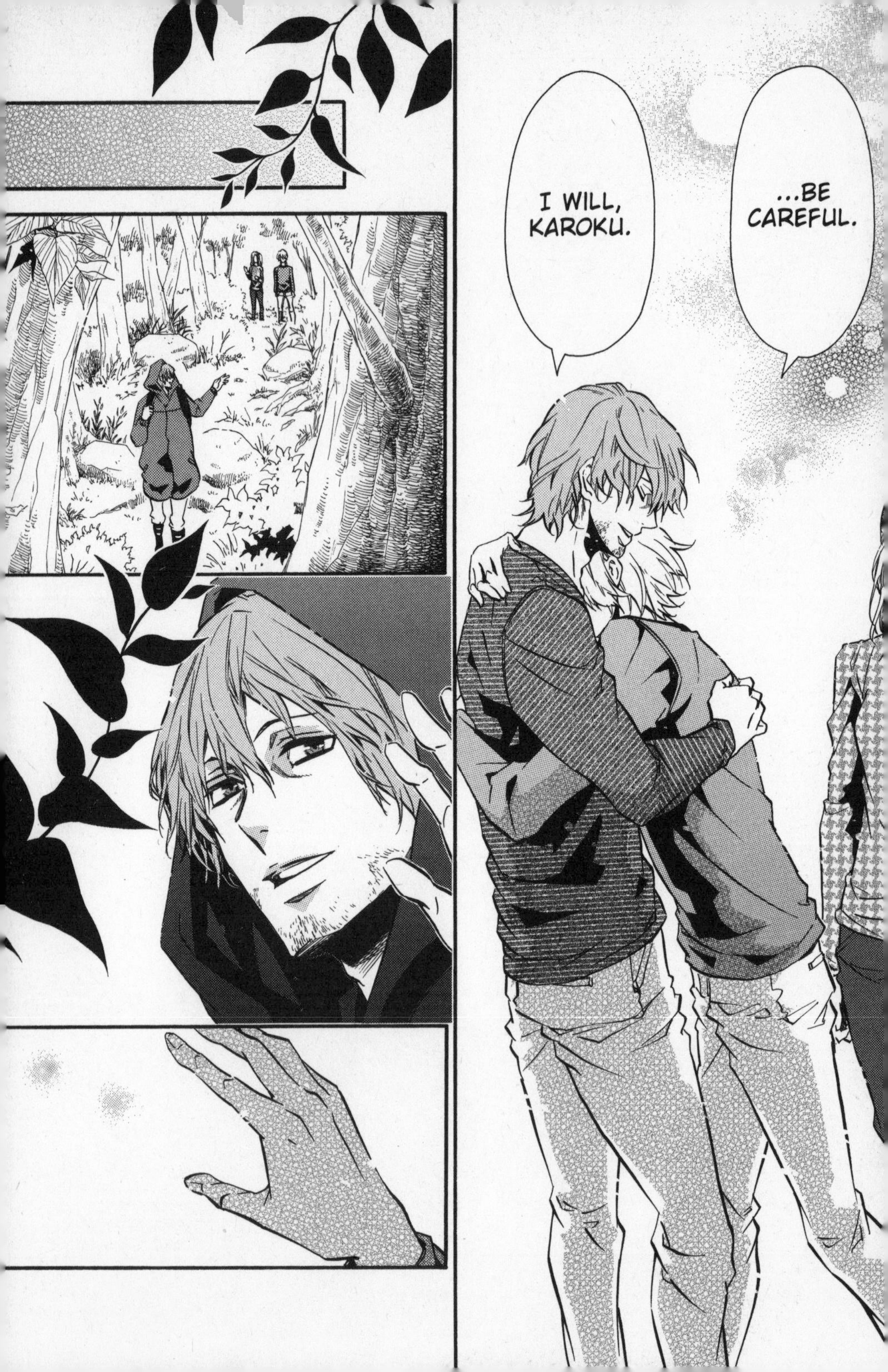
...BE CAREFUL.
I WILL, KAROKU.

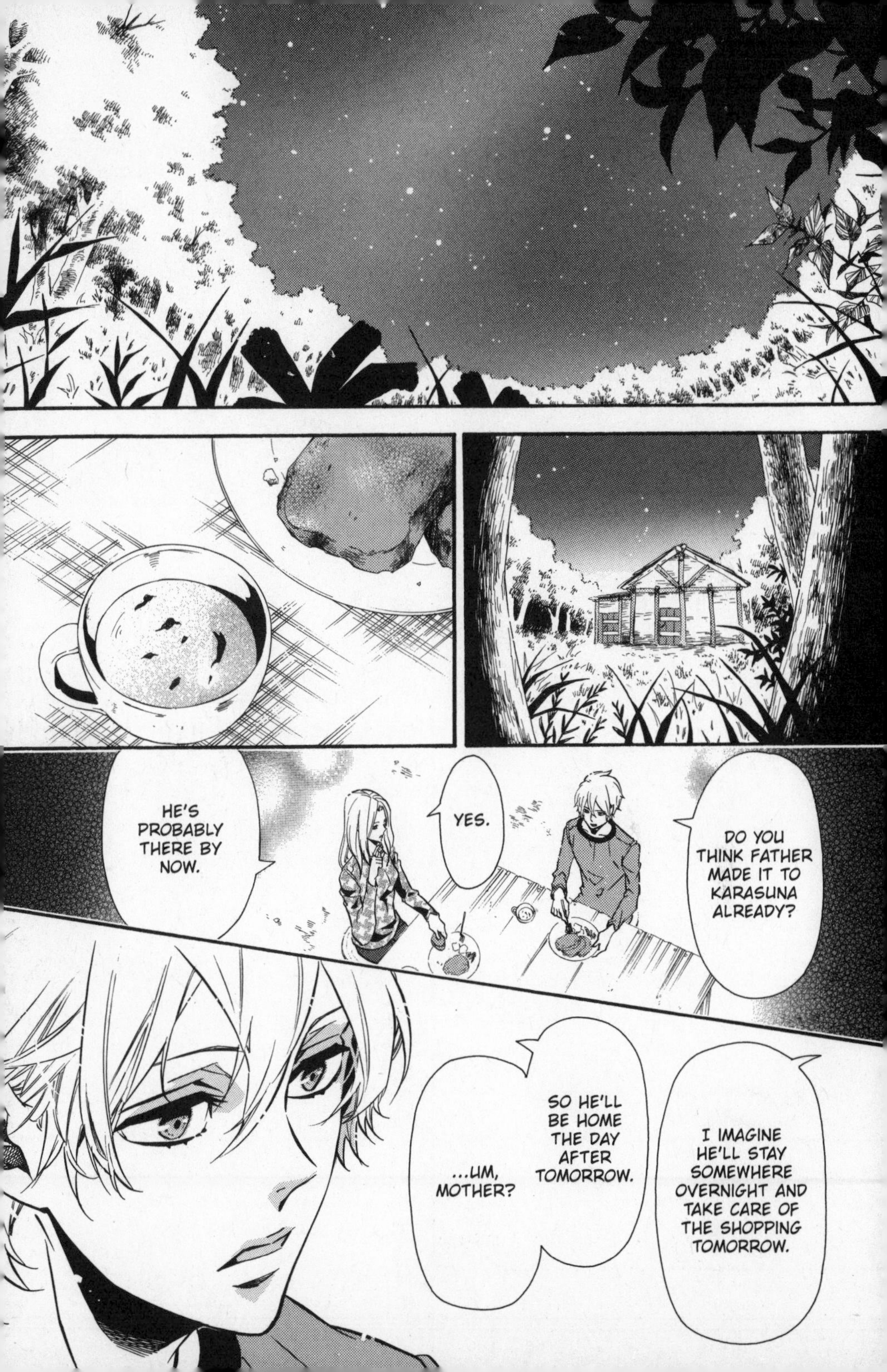
DO YOU THINK FATHER MADE IT TO KARASUNA ALREADY?
YES.
HE'S PROBABLY THERE BY NOW.
I IMAGINE HE'LL STAY SOMEWHERE OVERNIGHT AND TAKE CARE OF THE SHOPPING TOMORROW.
SO HE'LL BE HOME THE DAY AFTER TOMORROW.
...UM, MOTHER?

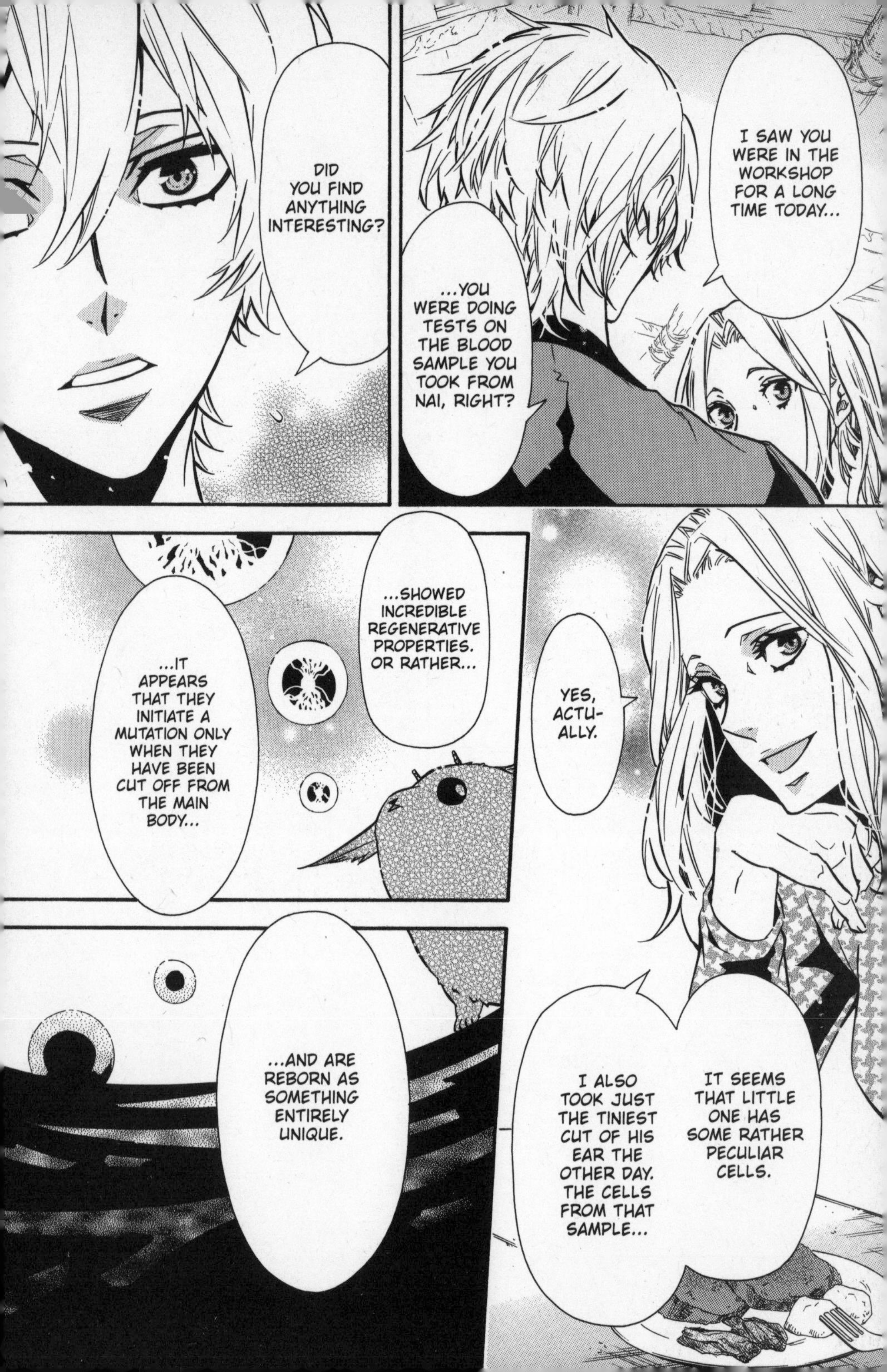
I SAW YOU WERE IN THE WORKSHOP FOR A LONG TIME TODAY...
...YOU WERE DOING TESTS ON THE BLOOD SAMPLE YOU TOOK FROM NAI, RIGHT?
DID YOU FIND ANYTHING INTERESTING?
YES, ACTU-ALLY.
IT SEEMS THAT LITTLE ONE HAS SOME RATHER PECULIAR CELLS.
I ALSO TOOK JUST THE TINIEST CUT OF HIS EAR THE OTHER DAY. THE CELLS FROM THAT SAMPLE...
...SHOWED INCREDIBLE REGENERATIVE PROPERTIES. OR RATHER...
...IT APPEARS THAT THEY INITIATE A MUTATION ONLY WHEN THEY HAVE BEEN CUT OFF FROM THE MAIN BODY...
...AND ARE REBORN AS SOMETHING ENTIRELY UNIQUE.

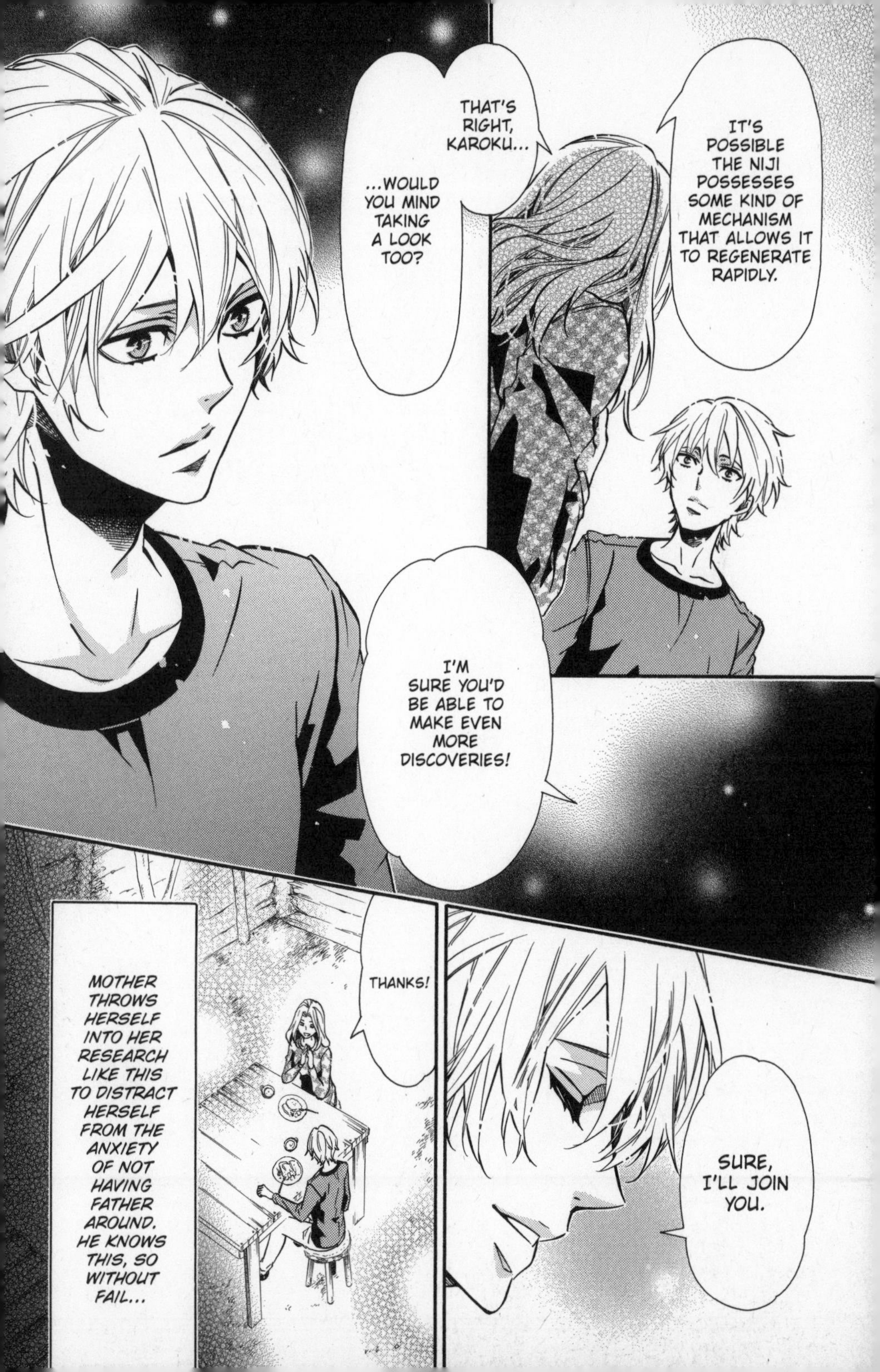
IT'S POSSIBLE THE NIJI POSSESSES SOME KIND OF MECHANISM THAT ALLOWS IT TO REGENERATE RAPIDLY.
THAT'S RIGHT, KAROKU...
...WOULD YOU MIND TAKING A LOOK TOO?
I'M SURE YOU'D BE ABLE TO MAKE EVEN MORE DISCOVERIES!
SURE, I'LL JOIN YOU.
THANKS!
MOTHER THROWS HERSELF INTO HER RESEARCH LIKE THIS TO DISTRACT HERSELF FROM THE ANXIETY OF NOT HAVING FATHER AROUND. HE KNOWS THIS, SO WITHOUT FAIL...

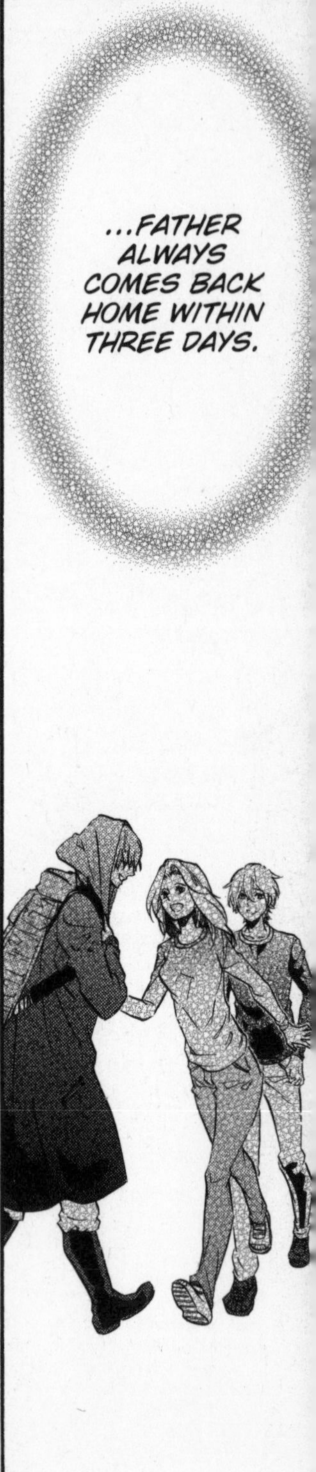
...FATHER ALWAYS COMES BACK HOME WITHIN THREE DAYS.

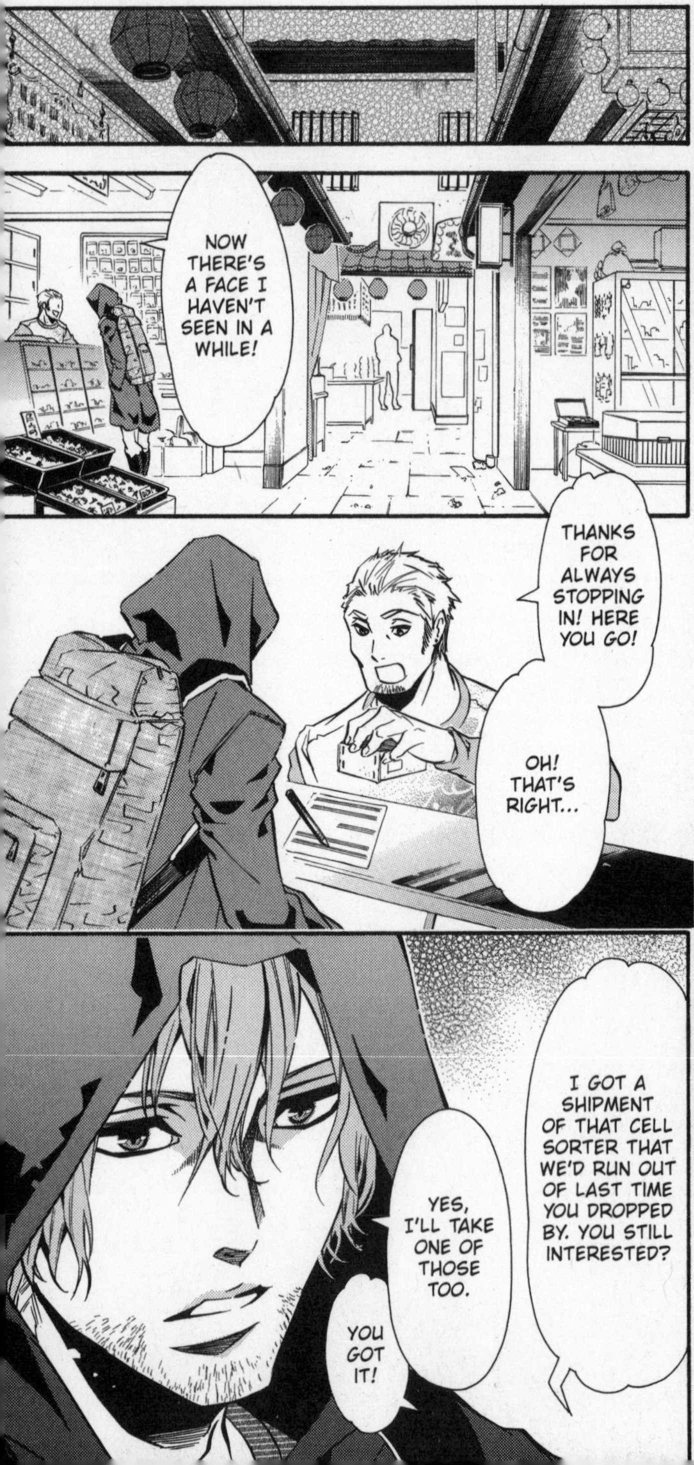
NOW THERE'S A FACE I HAVEN'T SEEN IN A WHILE!
THANKS FOR ALWAYS STOPPING IN! HERE YOU GO!
OH! THAT'S RIGHT...
I GOT A SHIPMENT OF THAT CELL SORTER THAT WE'D RUN OUT OF LAST TIME YOU DROPPED BY. YOU STILL INTERESTED?
YES, I'LL TAKE ONE OF THOSE TOO.
YOU GOT IT!

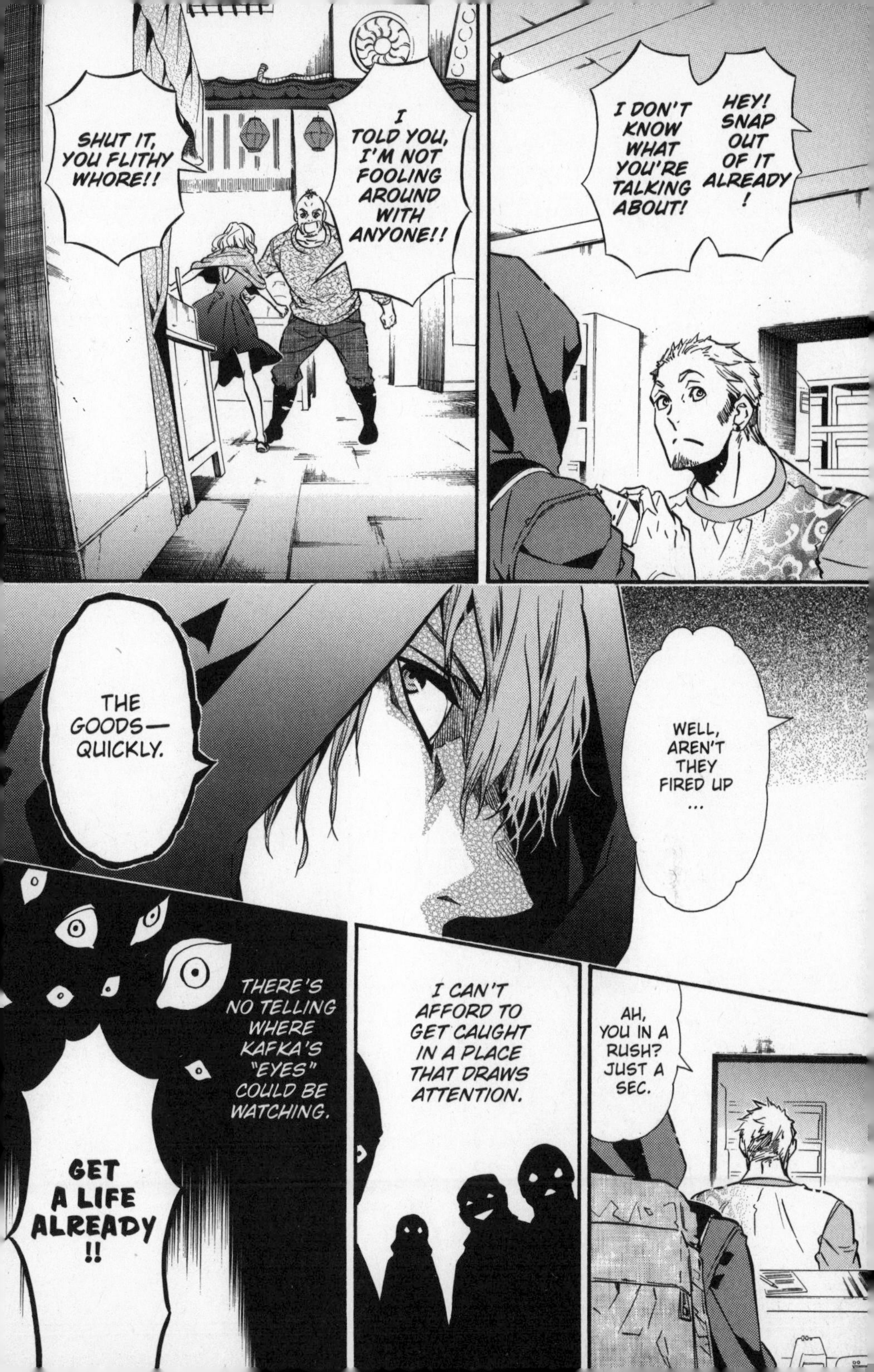
HEY! SNAP OUT OF IT ALREADY!
I DON'T KNOW WHAT YOU'RE TALKING ABOUT!
I TOLD YOU, I'M NOT FOOLING AROUND WITH ANYONE!!
SHUT IT, YOU FLITHY WHORE!!
WELL, AREN'T THEY FIRED UP ...
THE GOODS—QUICKLY.
AH, YOU IN A RUSH? JUST A SEC.
I CAN'T AFFORD TO GET CAUGHT IN A PLACE THAT DRAWS ATTENTION.
THERE'S NO TELLING WHERE KAFKA'S "EYES" COULD BE WATCHING.
GET A LIFE ALREADY!!

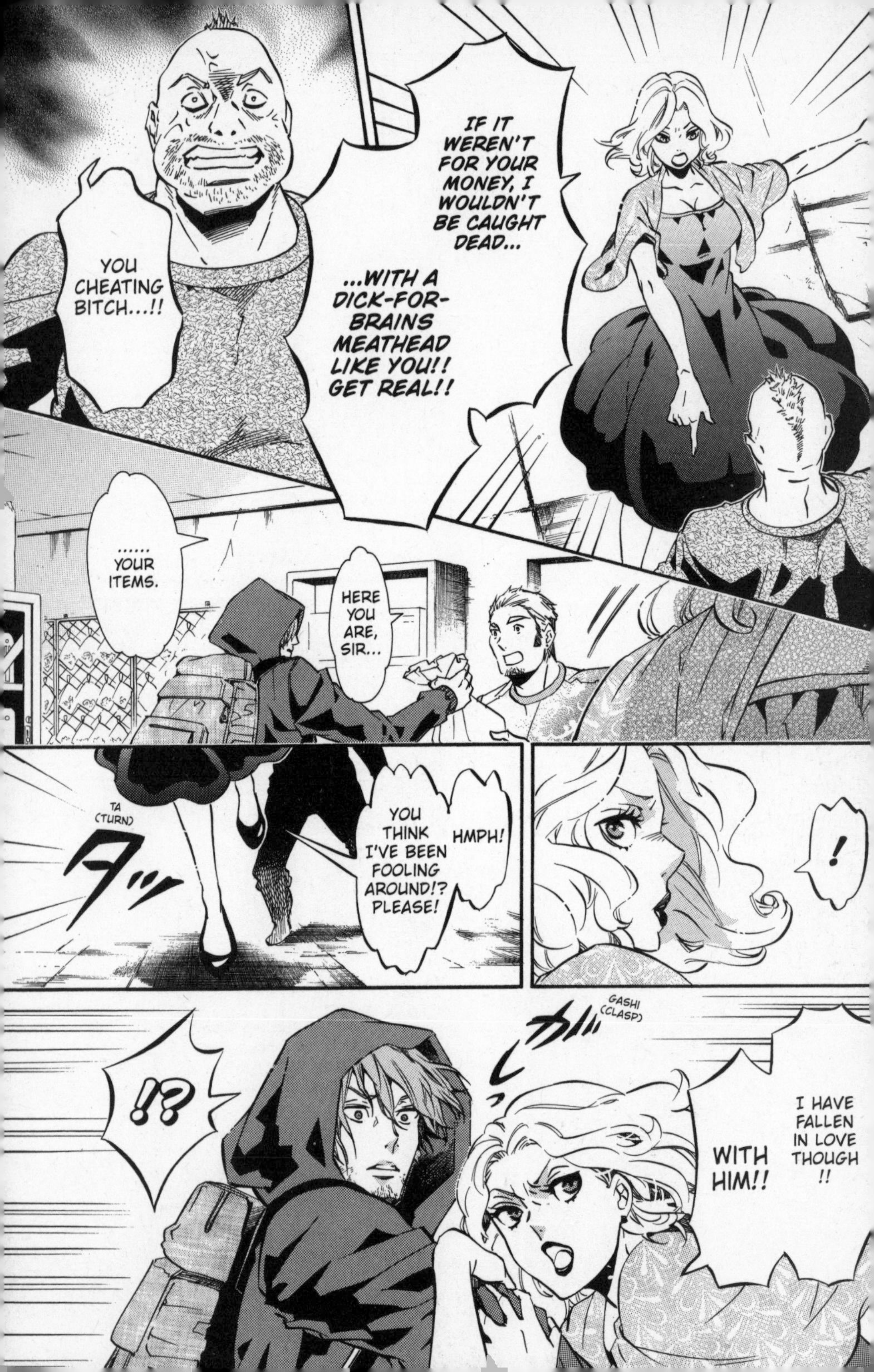
IF IT WEREN'T FOR YOUR MONEY, I WOULDN'T BE CAUGHT DEAD...
...WITH A DICK-FOR-BRAINS MEATHEAD LIKE YOU!! GET REAL!!
YOU CHEATING BITCH...!!
HERE YOU ARE, SIR...
...... YOUR ITEMS.
!
HMPH!
YOU THINK I'VE BEEN FOOLING AROUND!? PLEASE!
TA (TURN)
I HAVE FALLEN IN LOVE THOUGH!!
WITH HIM!!
GASHI (CLASP)
!?

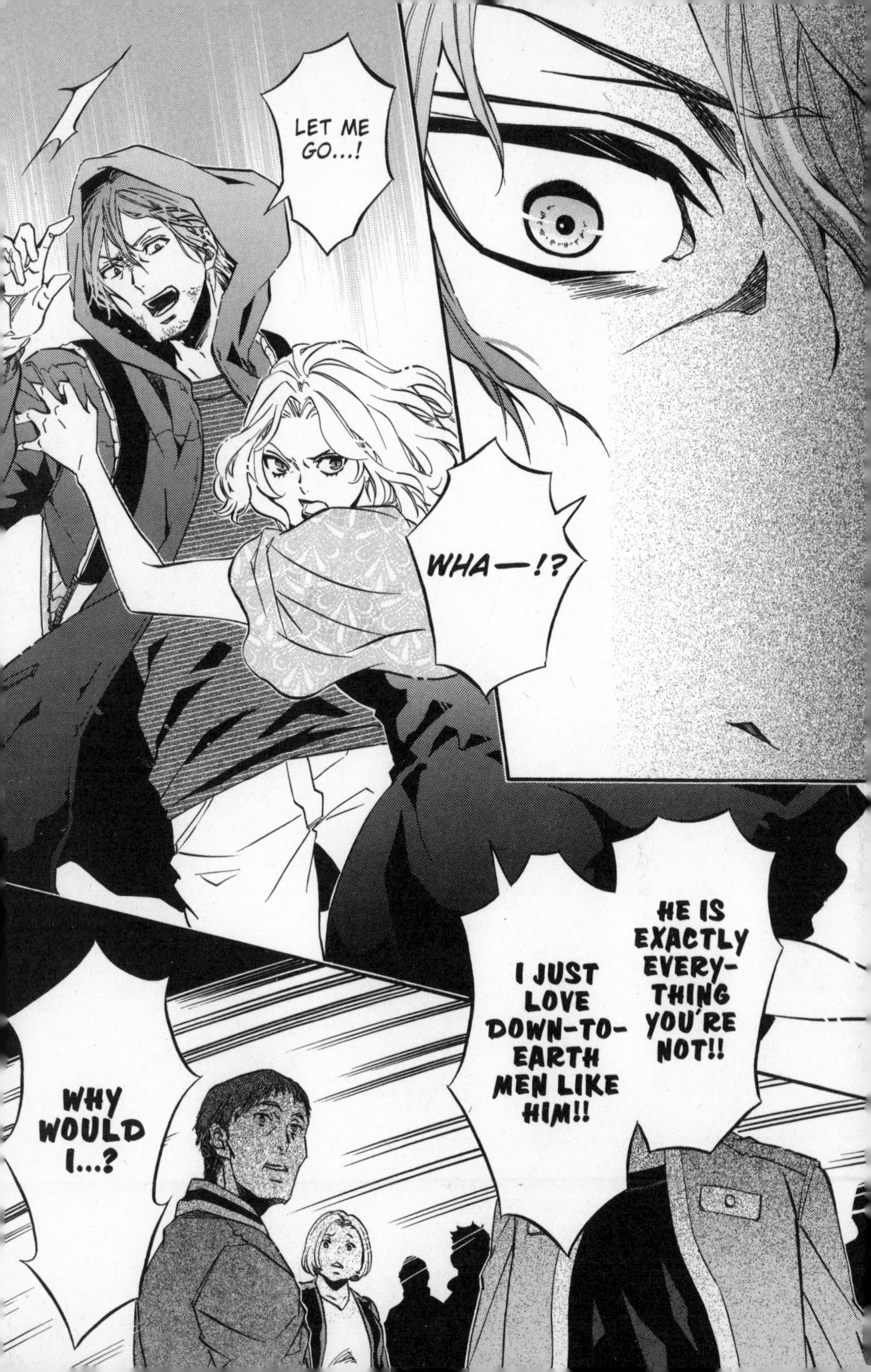
WHA—!?
LET ME GO...!
HE IS EXACTLY EVERY-THING YOU'RE NOT!!
I JUST LOVE DOWN-TO-EARTH MEN LIKE HIM!!
WHY WOULD I...?

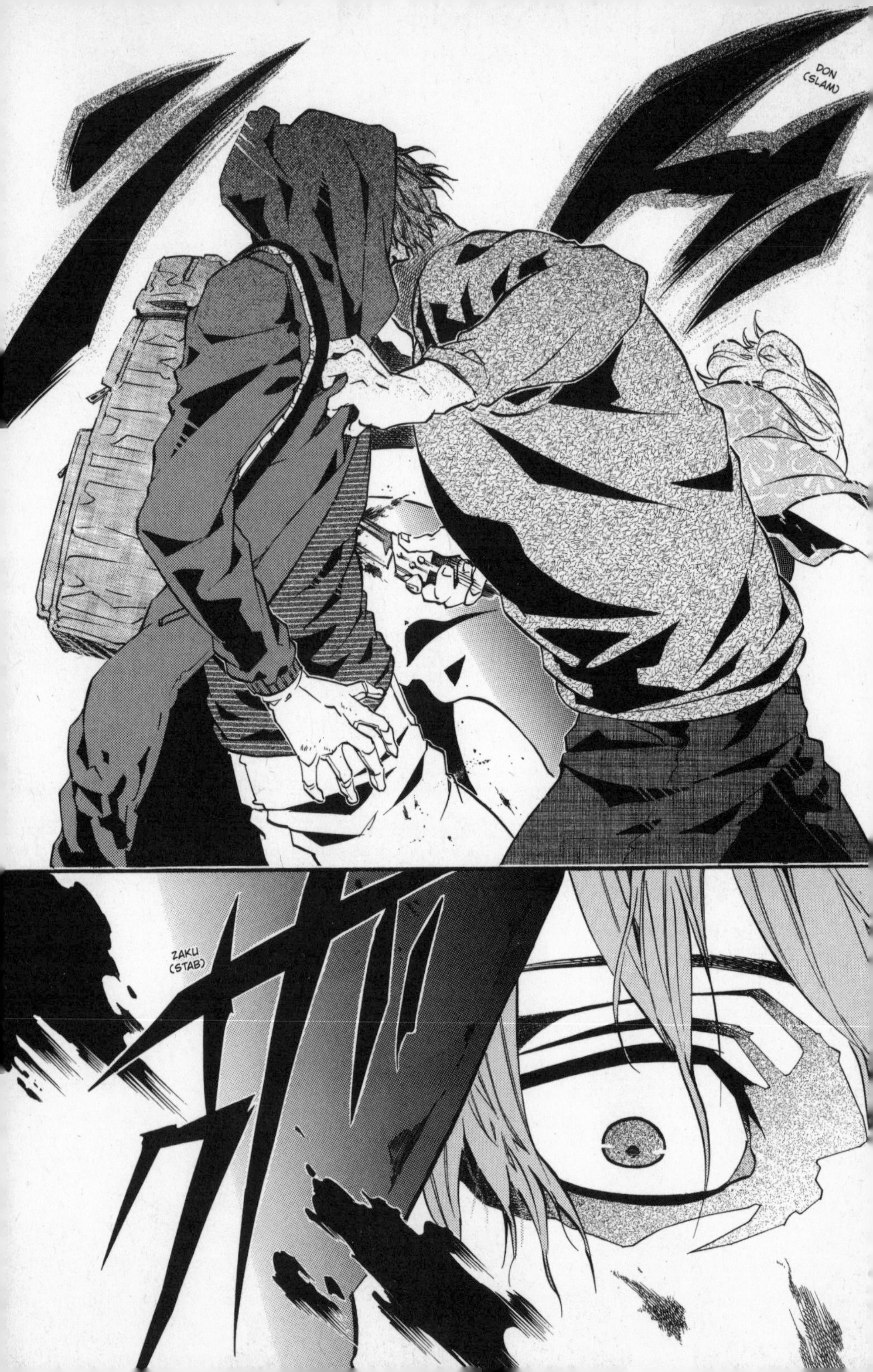
DON
(SLAM)
ZAKU
(STAB)

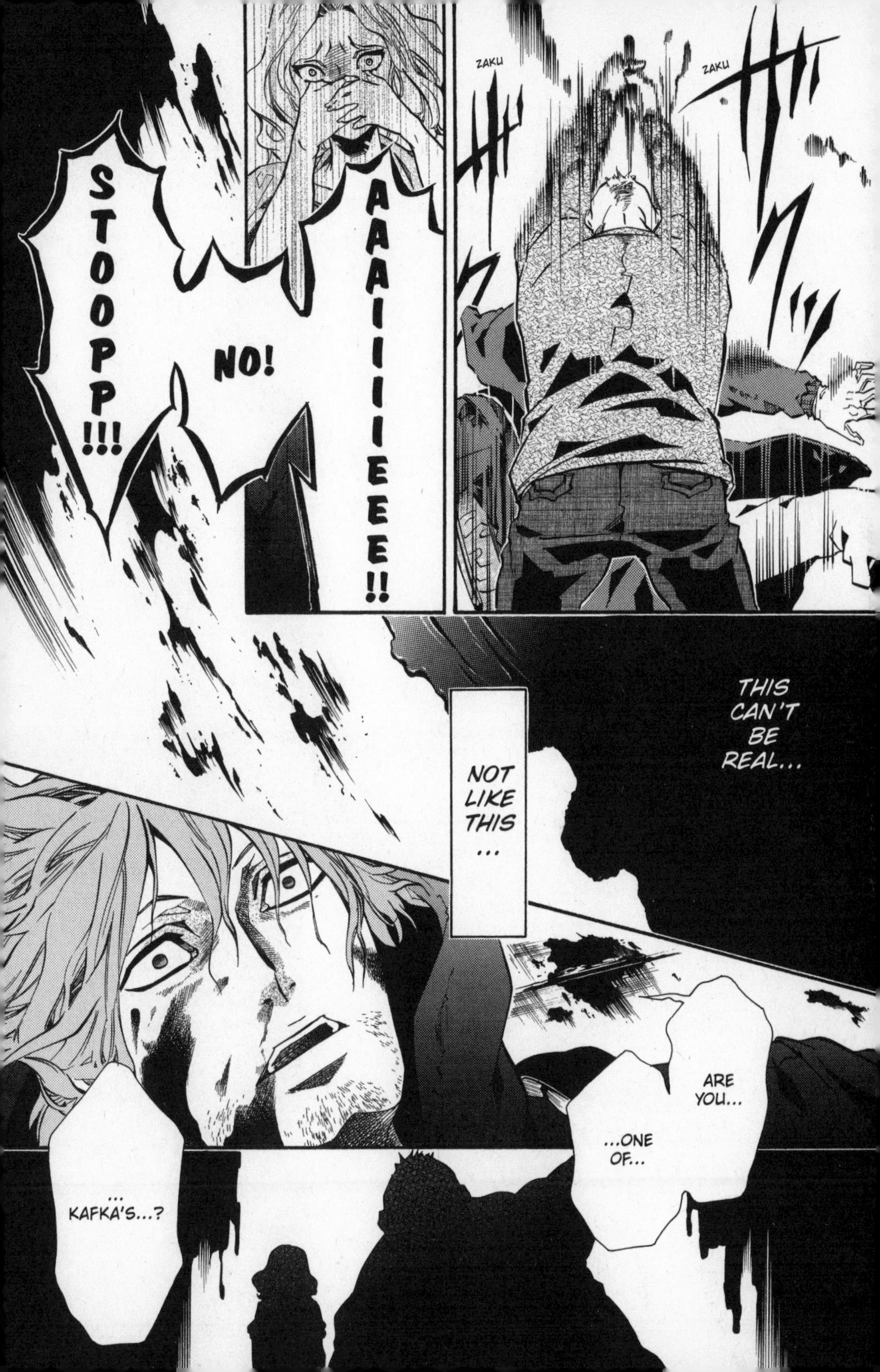
ZAKU
ZAKU
AAAIIIIEEE!!
NO!
STOOPP!!!
THIS CAN'T BE REAL...
NOT LIKE THIS...
ARE YOU...
...ONE OF...
...KAFKA'S...?

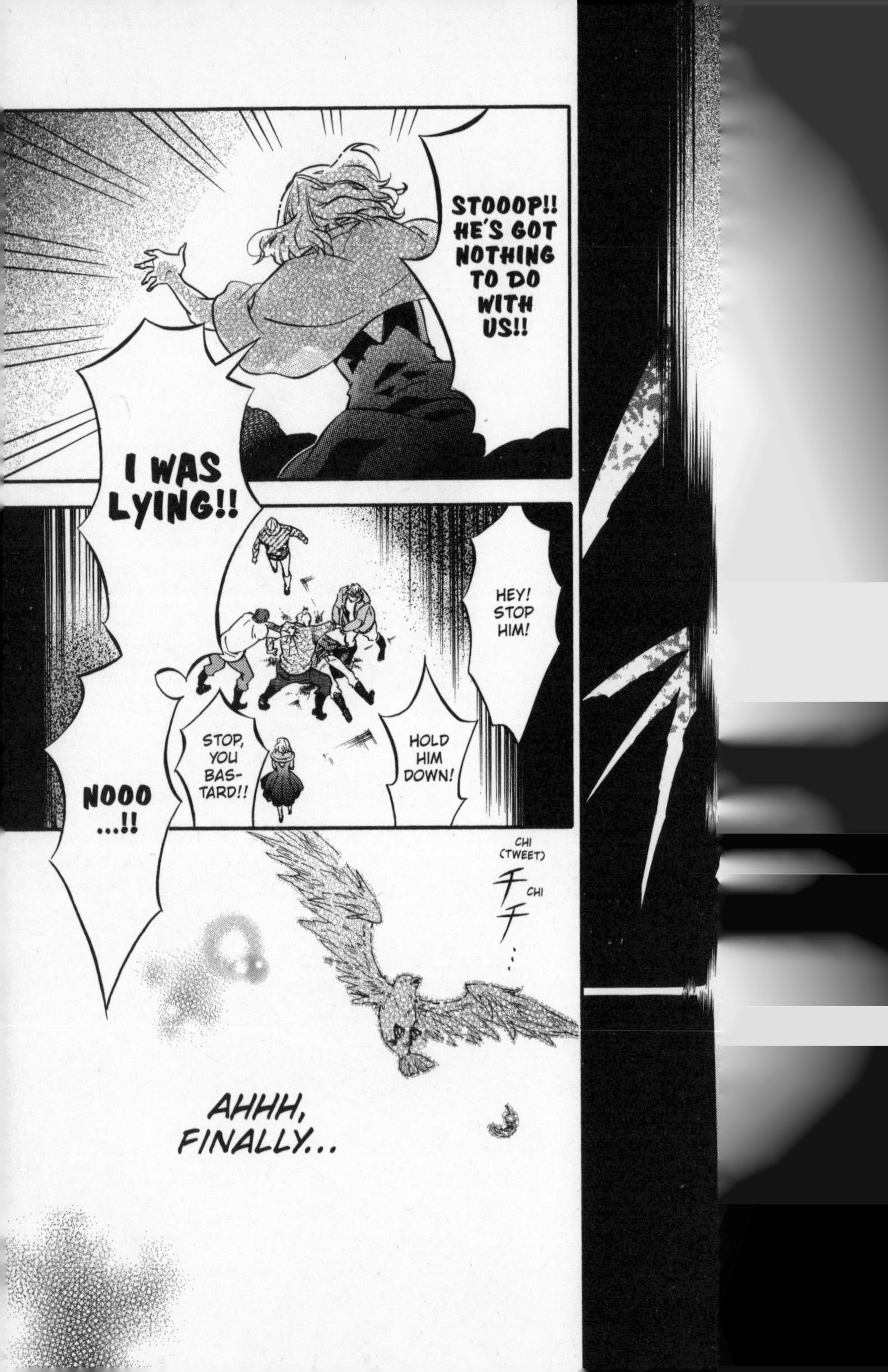
STOOOP!! HE'S GOT NOTHING TO DO WITH US!!
I WAS LYING!!
HEY! STOP HIM!
HOLD HIM DOWN!
STOP, YOU BAS-TARD!!
NOOO ...!!
CHI (TWEET)
チ CHI
チ...
AHHH, FINALLY...

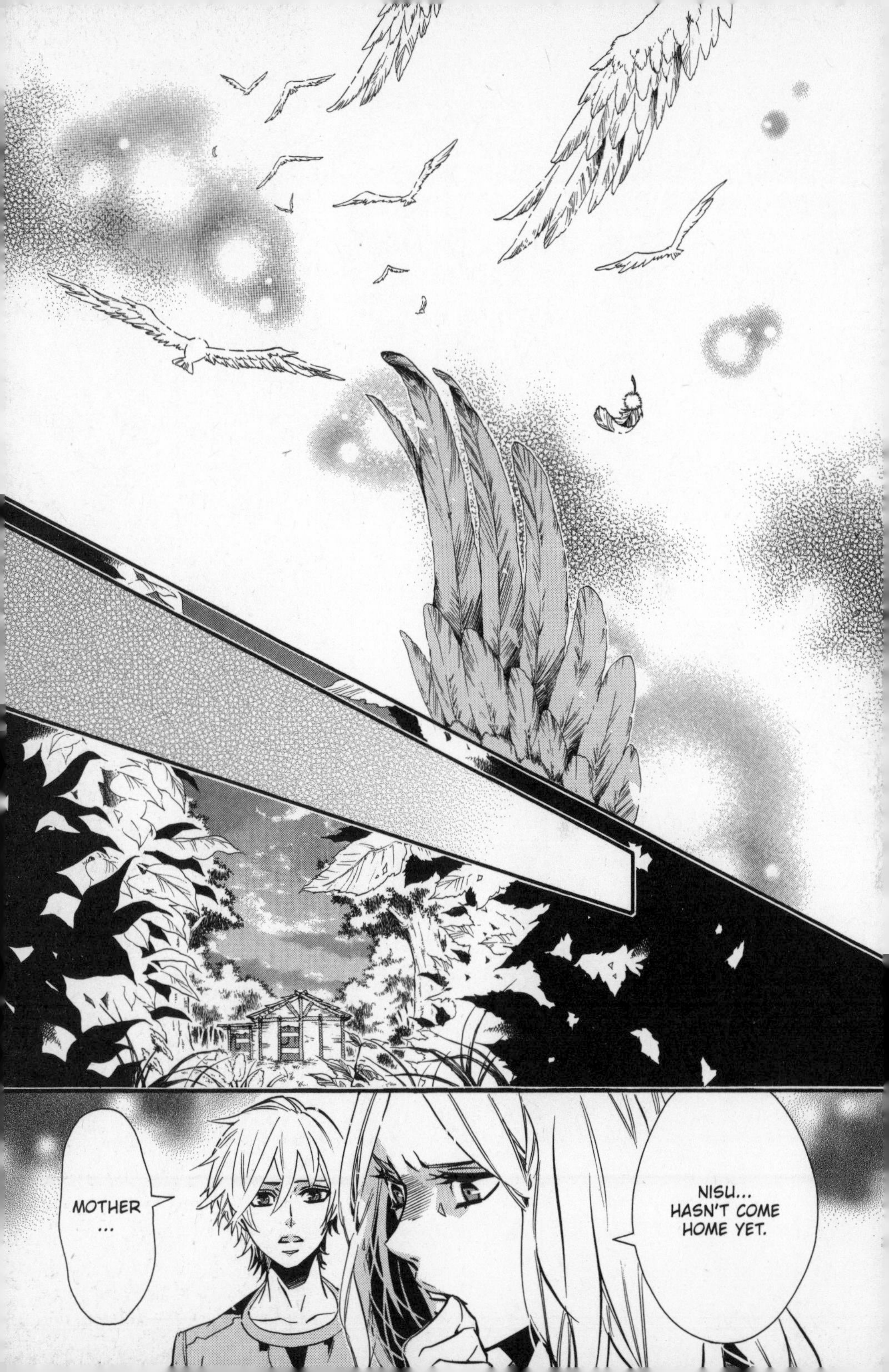
NISU... HASN'T COME HOME YET.
MOTHER ...

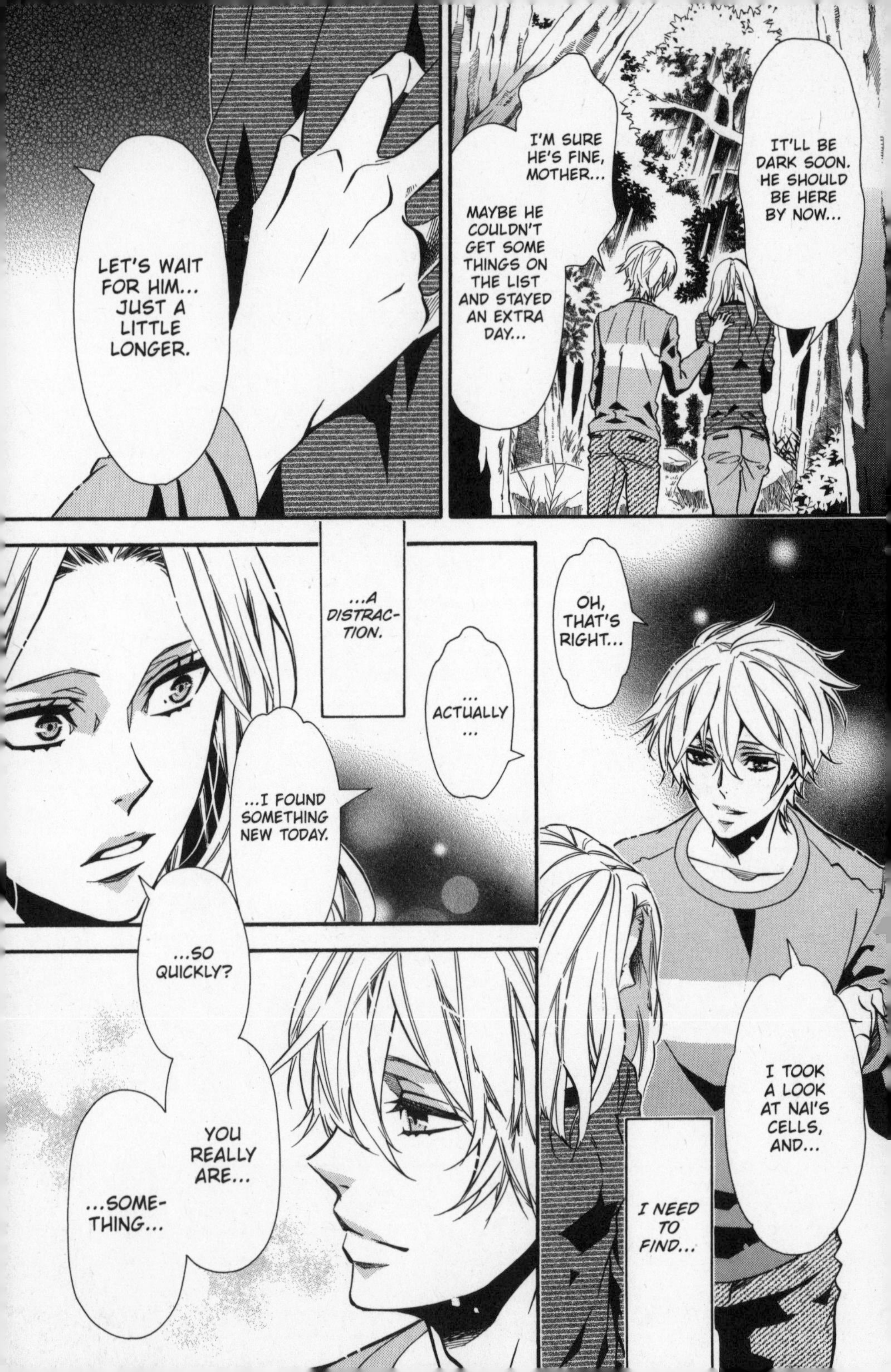
IT'LL BE DARK SOON. HE SHOULD BE HERE BY NOW...
I'M SURE HE'S FINE, MOTHER...
MAYBE HE COULDN'T GET SOME THINGS ON THE LIST AND STAYED AN EXTRA DAY...
LET'S WAIT FOR HIM... JUST A LITTLE LONGER.
OH, THAT'S RIGHT...
...ACTUALLY...
...I FOUND SOMETHING NEW TODAY.
I TOOK A LOOK AT NAI'S CELLS, AND...
I NEED TO FIND...
...A DISTRACTION.
...SO QUICKLY?
YOU REALLY ARE...
...SOME-THING...

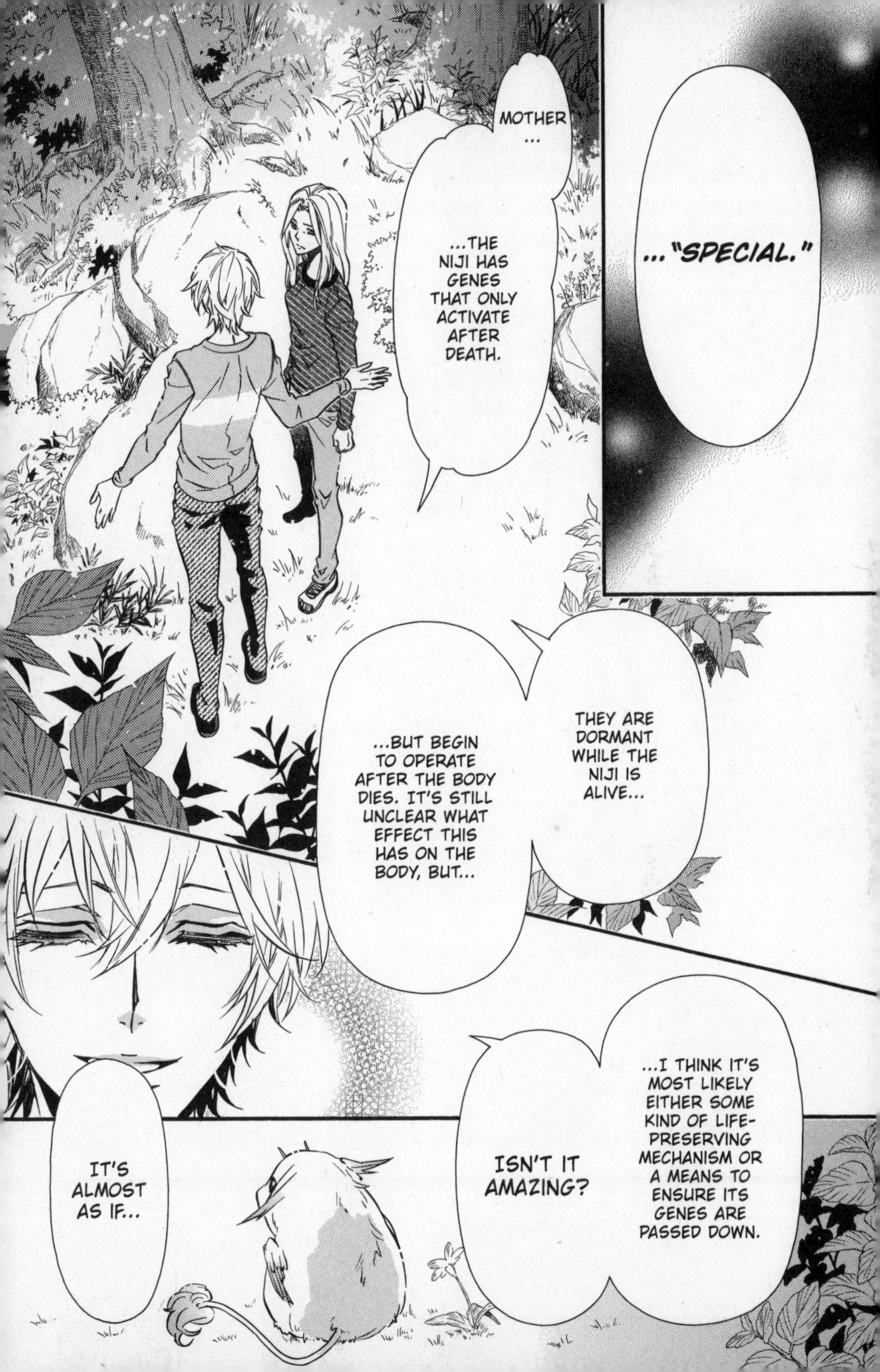
..."SPECIAL."
MOTHER...
...THE NIJI HAS GENES THAT ONLY ACTIVATE AFTER DEATH.
THEY ARE DORMANT WHILE THE NIJI IS ALIVE...
...BUT BEGIN TO OPERATE AFTER THE BODY DIES. IT'S STILL UNCLEAR WHAT EFFECT THIS HAS ON THE BODY, BUT...
...I THINK IT'S MOST LIKELY EITHER SOME KIND OF LIFE-PRESERVING MECHANISM OR A MEANS TO ENSURE ITS GENES ARE PASSED DOWN.
ISN'T IT AMAZING?
IT'S ALMOST AS IF...

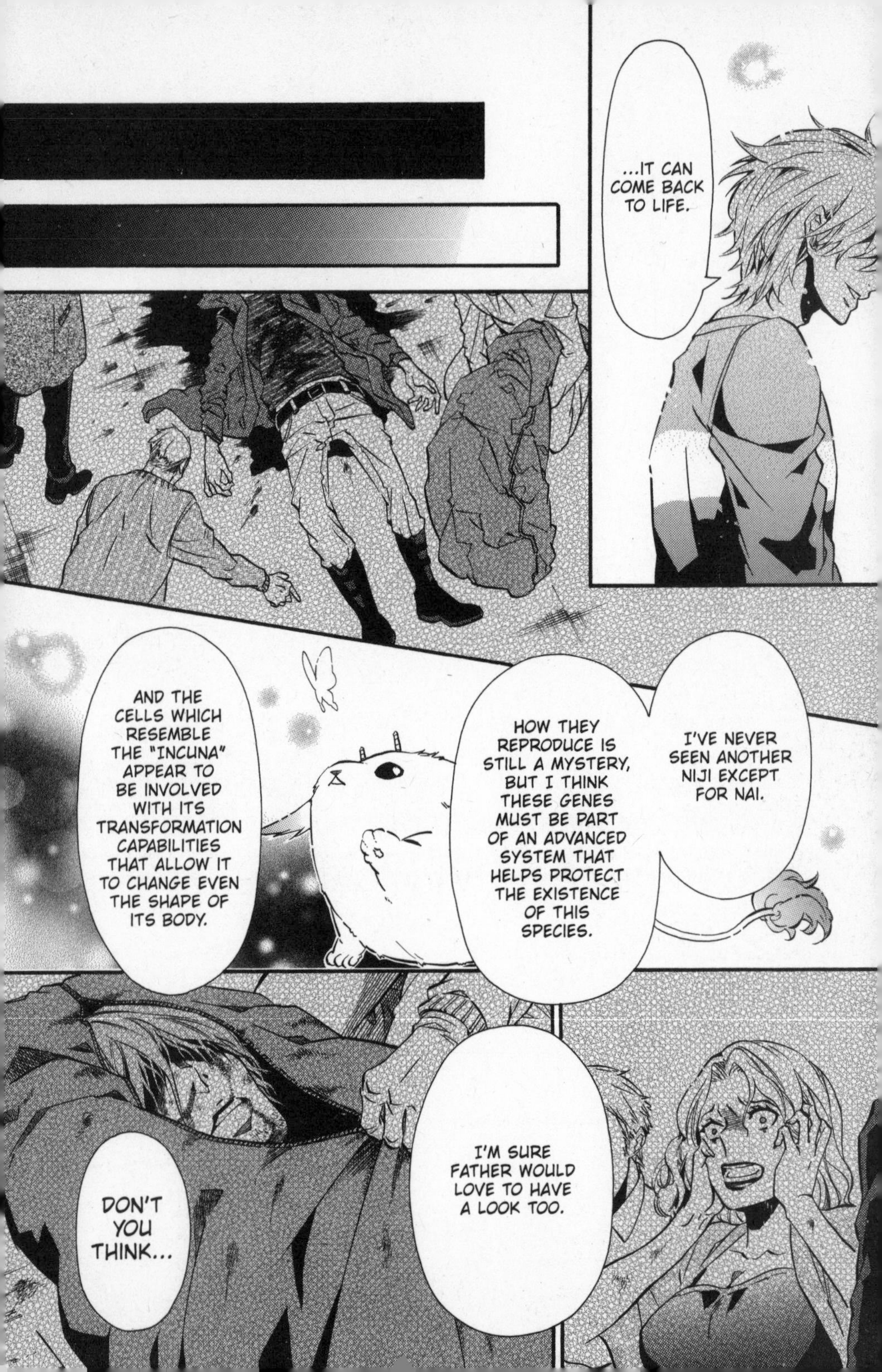
...IT CAN COME BACK TO LIFE.
I'VE NEVER SEEN ANOTHER NIJI EXCEPT FOR NAI.
HOW THEY REPRODUCE IS STILL A MYSTERY, BUT I THINK THESE GENES MUST BE PART OF AN ADVANCED SYSTEM THAT HELPS PROTECT THE EXISTENCE OF THIS SPECIES.
AND THE CELLS WHICH RESEMBLE THE "INCUNA" APPEAR TO BE INVOLVED WITH ITS TRANSFORMATION CAPABILITIES THAT ALLOW IT TO CHANGE EVEN THE SHAPE OF ITS BODY.
I'M SURE FATHER WOULD LOVE TO HAVE A LOOK TOO.
DON'T YOU THINK...

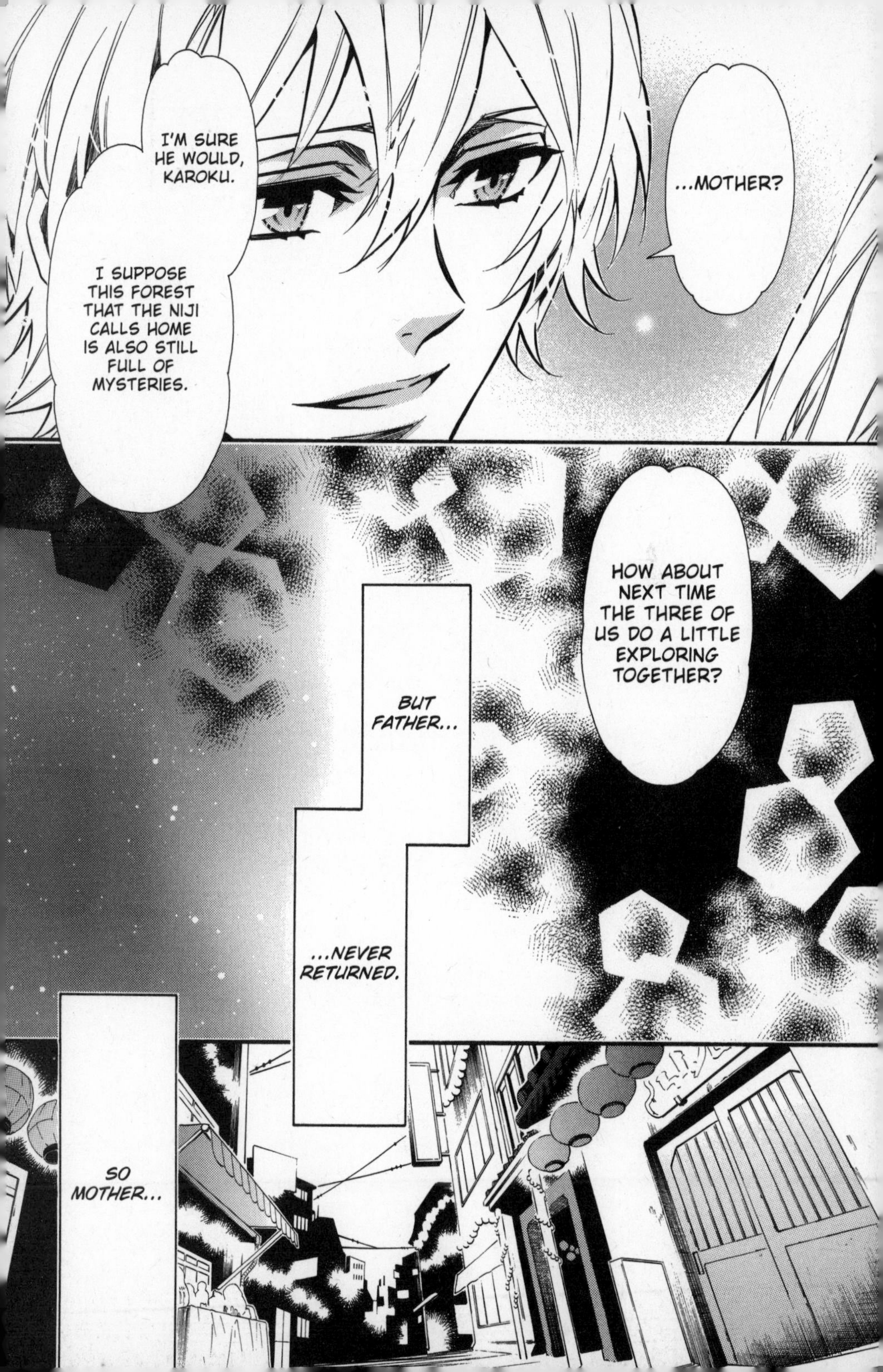
...MOTHER?
I'M SURE HE WOULD, KAROKU.
I SUPPOSE THIS FOREST THAT THE NIJI CALLS HOME IS ALSO STILL FULL OF MYSTERIES.
HOW ABOUT NEXT TIME THE THREE OF US DO A LITTLE EXPLORING TOGETHER?
BUT FATHER...
...NEVER RETURNED.
SO MOTHER...

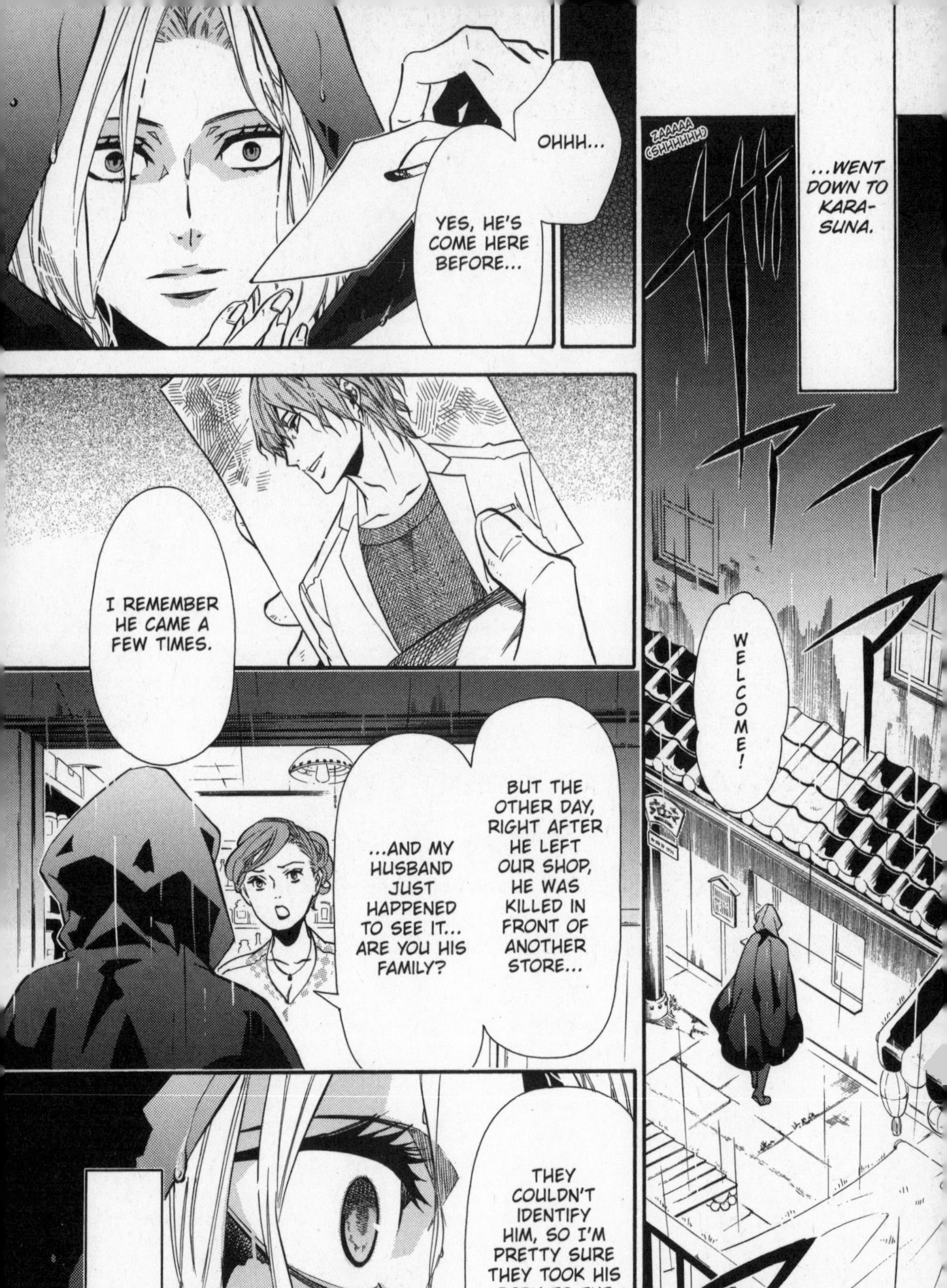
...WENT DOWN TO KARA-SUNA.
ZAAAAA (SHHHHHH)
WELCOME!
OHHH...
YES, HE'S COME HERE BEFORE...
I REMEMBER HE CAME A FEW TIMES.
BUT THE OTHER DAY, RIGHT AFTER HE LEFT OUR SHOP, HE WAS KILLED IN FRONT OF ANOTHER STORE...
...AND MY HUSBAND JUST HAPPENED TO SEE IT... ARE YOU HIS FAMILY?
THEY COULDN'T IDENTIFY HIM, SO I'M PRETTY SURE THEY TOOK HIS BODY TO THE "DISPOSAL SITE."
NISU...

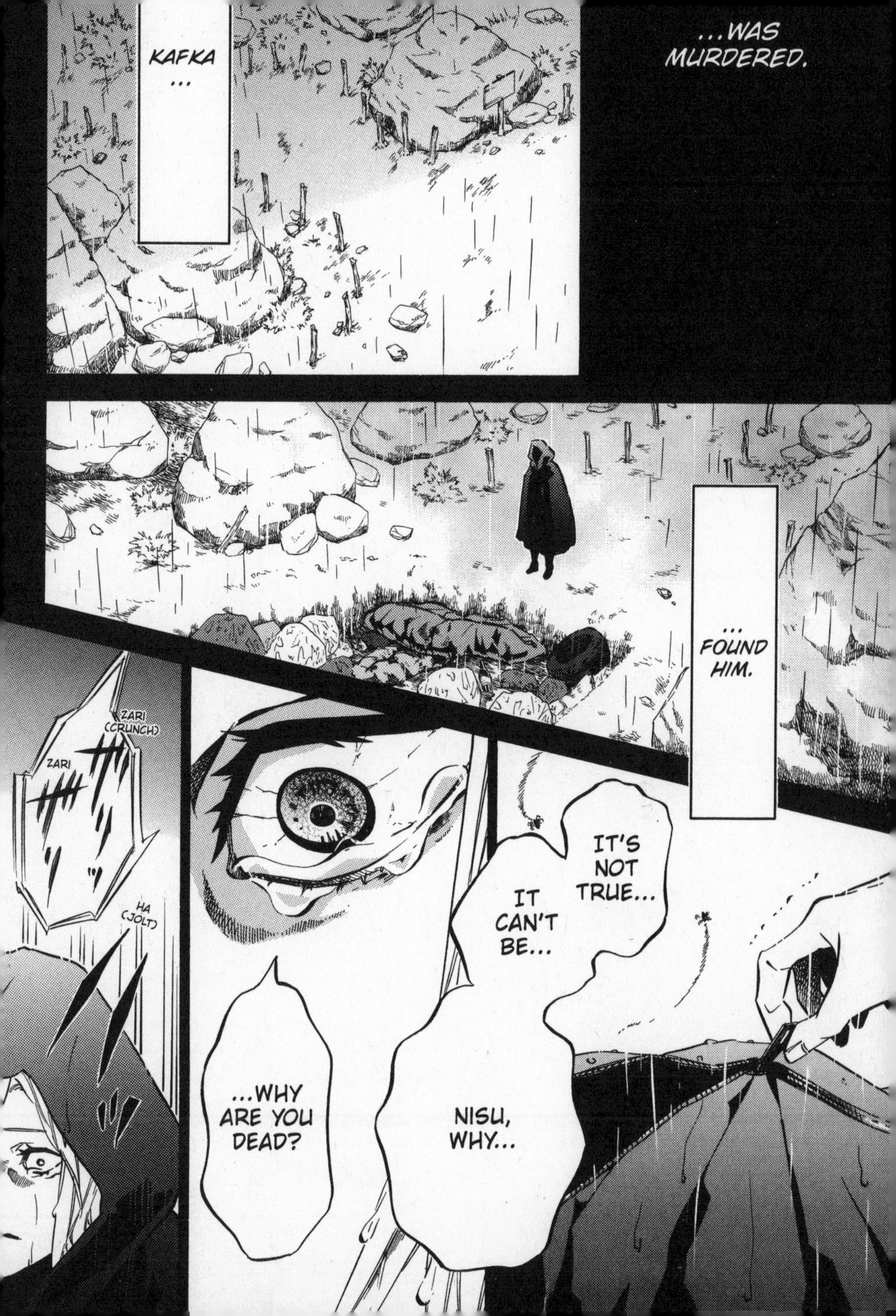
...WAS MURDERED.
KAFKA ...
... FOUND HIM.
IT'S NOT TRUE...
IT CAN'T BE...
NISU, WHY...
...WHY ARE YOU DEAD?
ZARI (CRUNCH)
ZARI
HA (JOLT)

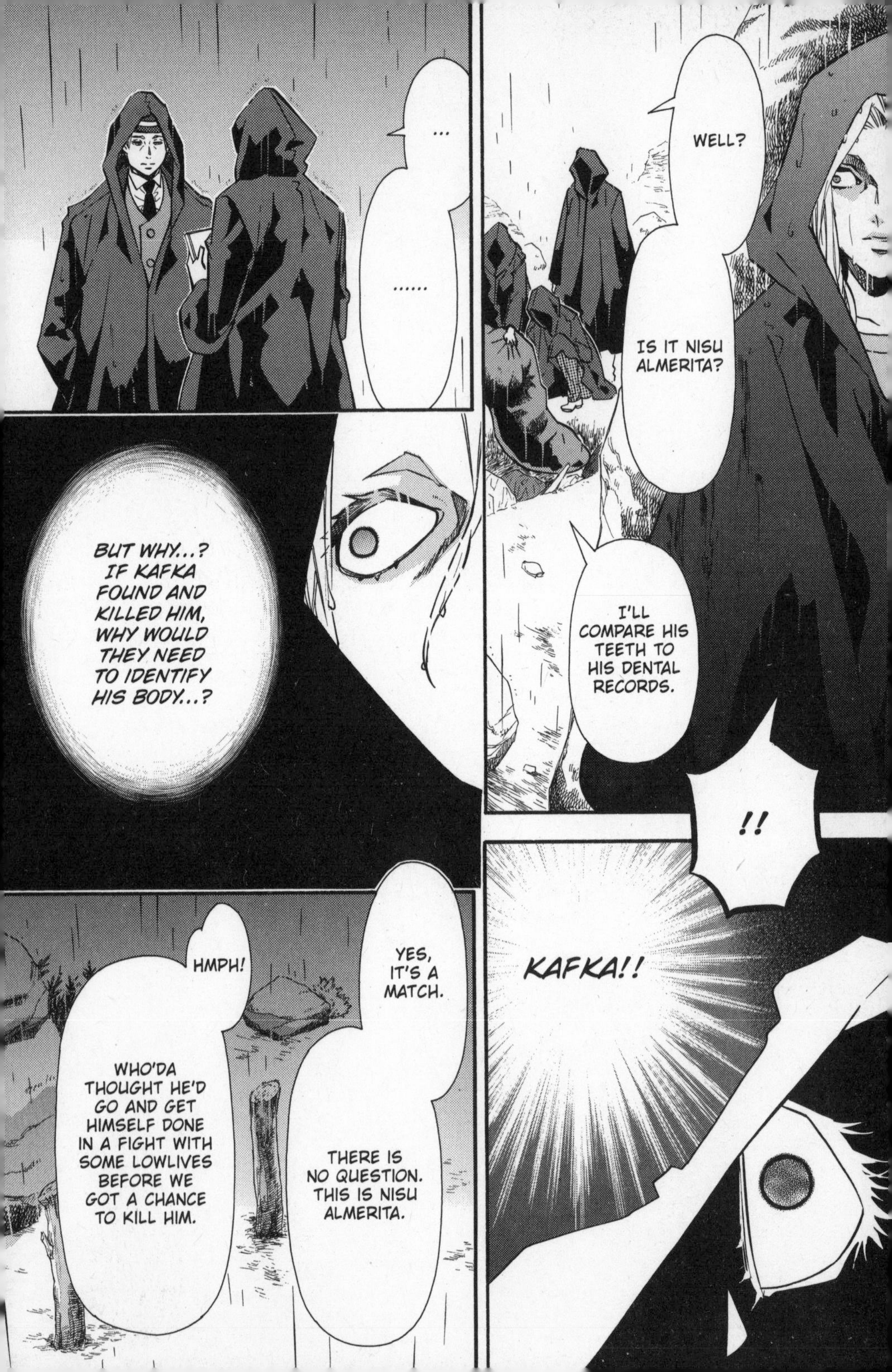
WELL?
IS IT NISU ALMERITA?
I'LL COMPARE HIS TEETH TO HIS DENTAL RECORDS.
...
......
BUT WHY...? IF KAFKA FOUND AND KILLED HIM, WHY WOULD THEY NEED TO IDENTIFY HIS BODY...?
!!
KAFKA!!
YES, IT'S A MATCH.
THERE IS NO QUESTION. THIS IS NISU ALMERITA.
HMPH!
WHO'DA THOUGHT HE'D GO AND GET HIMSELF DONE IN A FIGHT WITH SOME LOWLIVES BEFORE WE GOT A CHANCE TO KILL HIM.

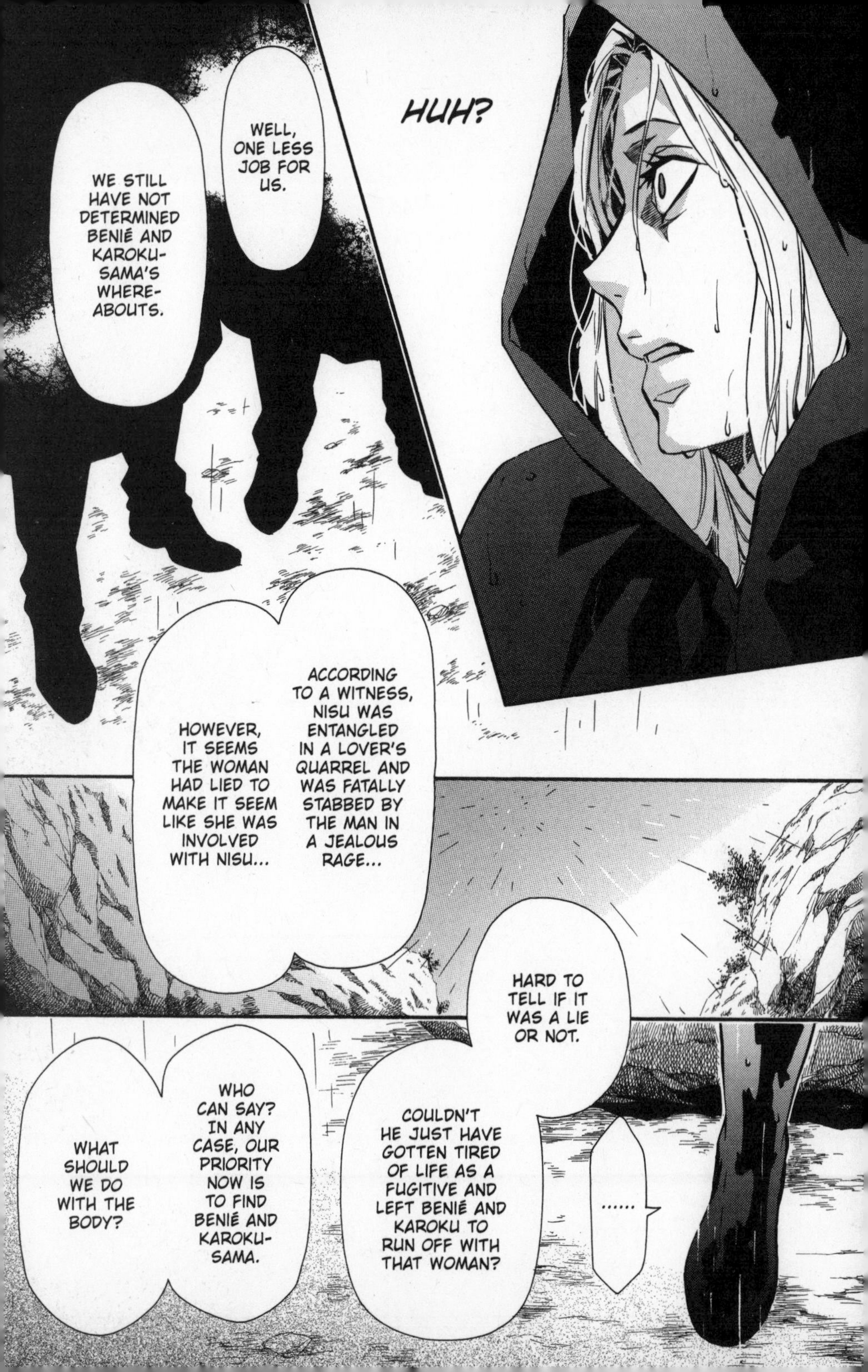
HUH?
WELL, ONE LESS JOB FOR US.
WE STILL HAVE NOT DETERMINED BENIÉ AND KAROKU-SAMA'S WHERE-ABOUTS.
ACCORDING TO A WITNESS, NISU WAS ENTANGLED IN A LOVER'S QUARREL AND WAS FATALLY STABBED BY THE MAN IN A JEALOUS RAGE...
HOWEVER, IT SEEMS THE WOMAN HAD LIED TO MAKE IT SEEM LIKE SHE WAS INVOLVED WITH NISU...
HARD TO TELL IF IT WAS A LIE OR NOT.
......
COULDN'T HE JUST HAVE GOTTEN TIRED OF LIFE AS A FUGITIVE AND LEFT BENIÉ AND KAROKU TO RUN OFF WITH THAT WOMAN?
WHO CAN SAY? IN ANY CASE, OUR PRIORITY NOW IS TO FIND BENIÉ AND KAROKU-SAMA.
WHAT SHOULD WE DO WITH THE BODY?

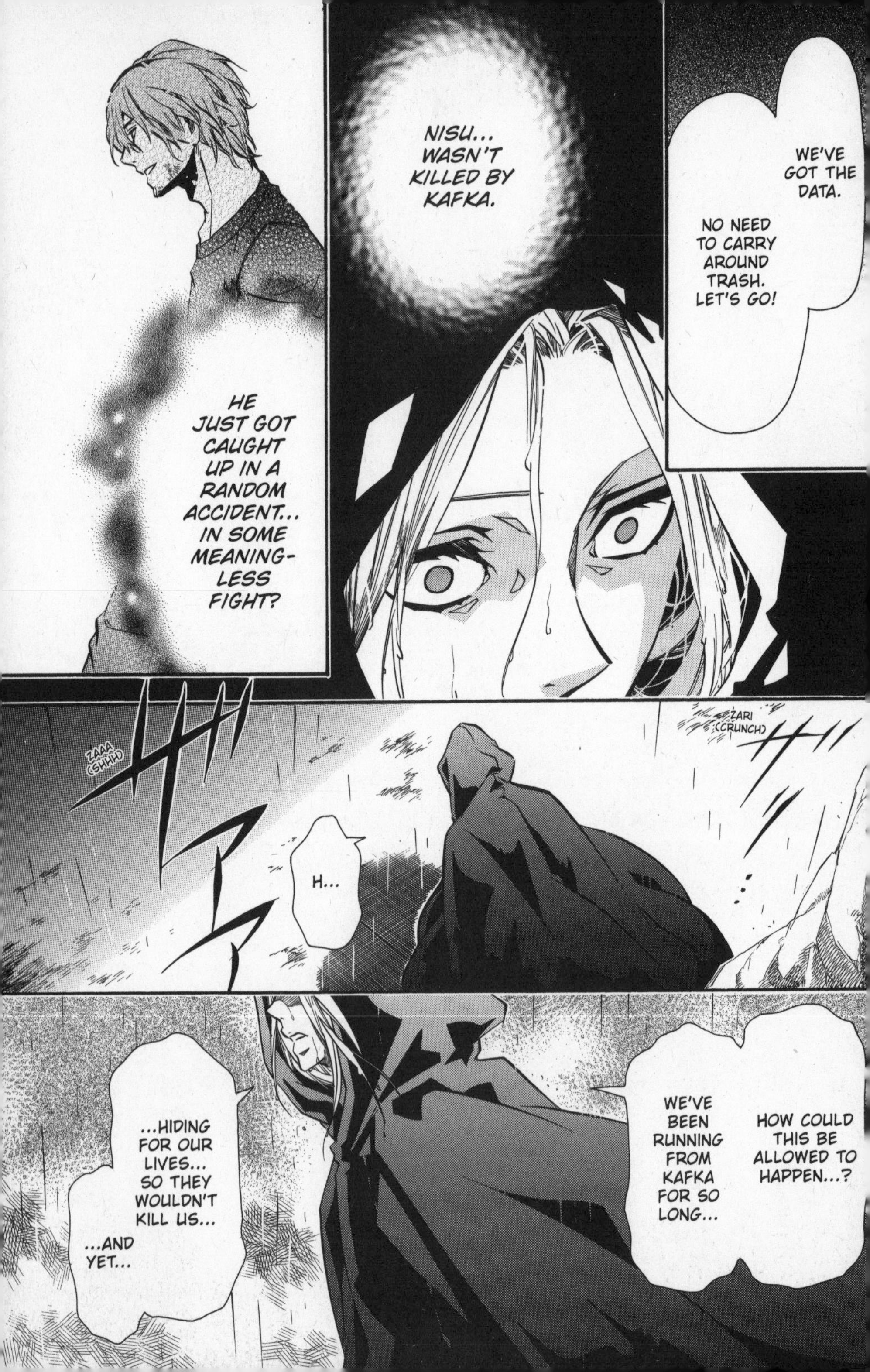
WE'VE GOT THE DATA.
NO NEED TO CARRY AROUND TRASH. LET'S GO!
NISU... WASN'T KILLED BY KAFKA.
HE JUST GOT CAUGHT UP IN A RANDOM ACCIDENT... IN SOME MEANING-LESS FIGHT?
ZARI (CRUNCH)
ZAAA (SHHH)
H...
HOW COULD THIS BE ALLOWED TO HAPPEN...?
WE'VE BEEN RUNNING FROM KAFKA FOR SO LONG...
...HIDING FOR OUR LIVES... SO THEY WOULDN'T KILL US...
...AND YET...

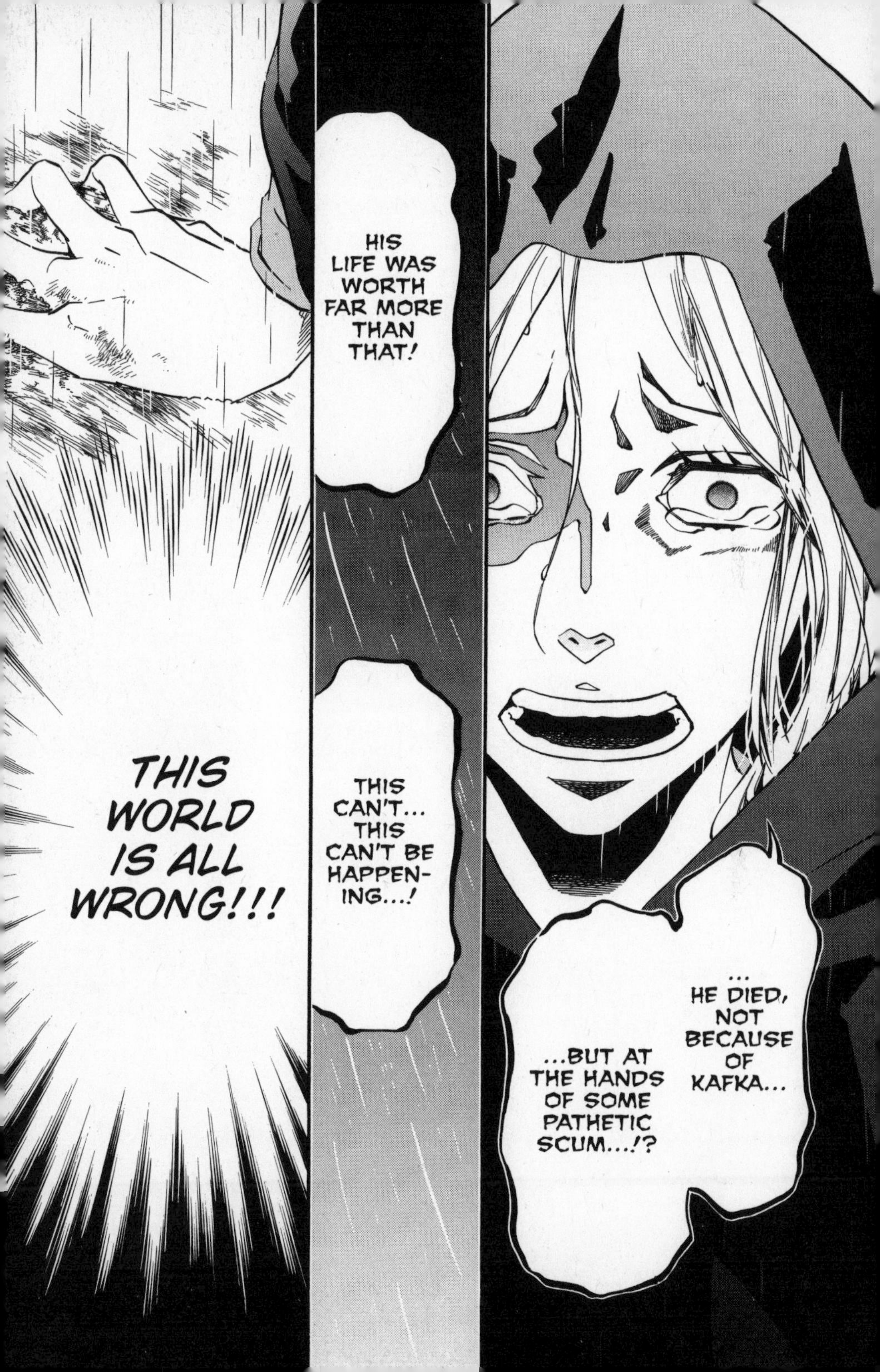
...HE DIED, NOT BECAUSE OF KAFKA...
...BUT AT THE HANDS OF SOME PATHETIC SCUM...!?
HIS LIFE WAS WORTH FAR MORE THAN THAT!
THIS CAN'T... THIS CAN'T BE HAPPEN-ING...!
THIS WORLD IS ALL WRONG!!!

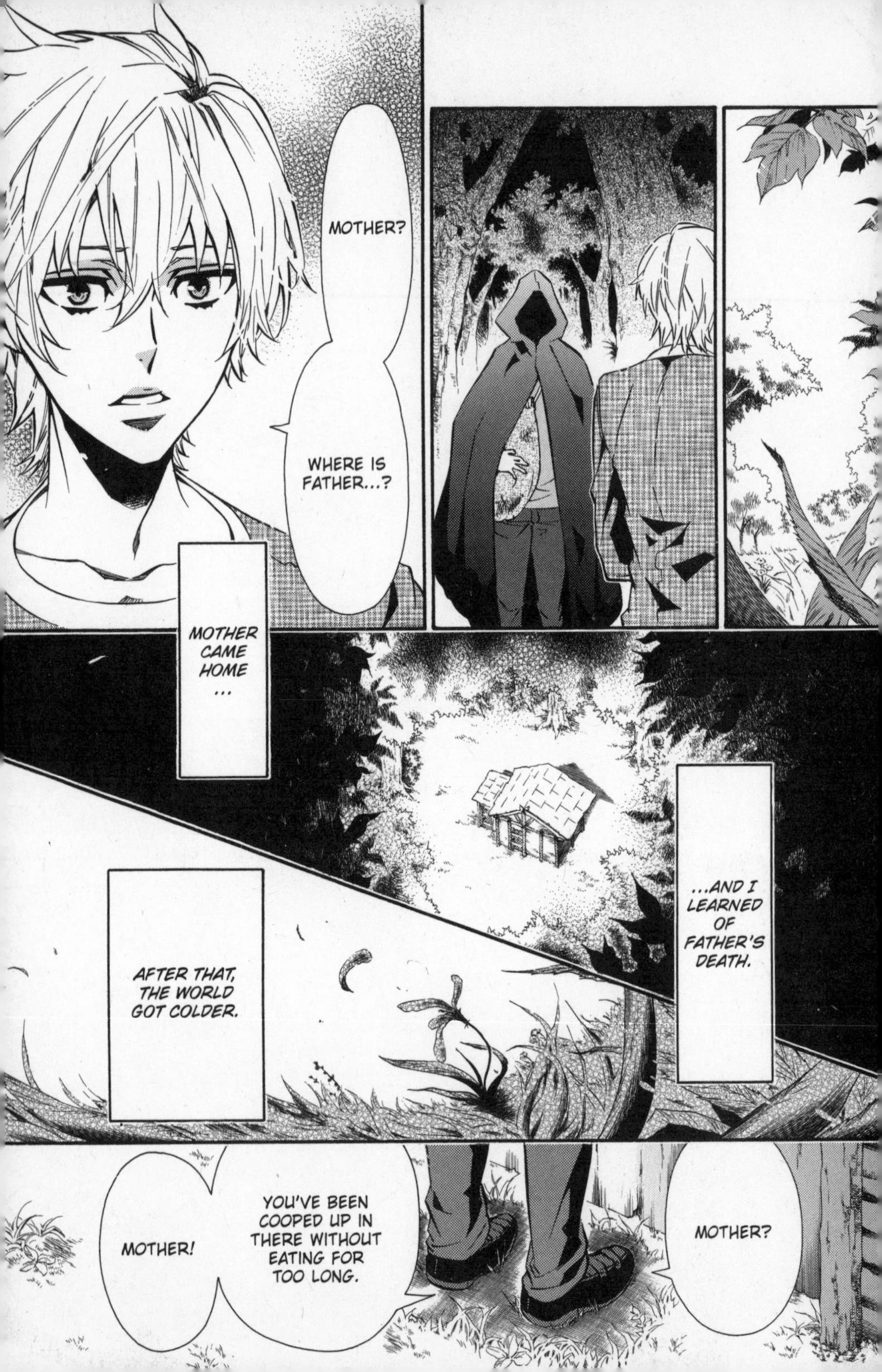
MOTHER?
WHERE IS FATHER...?
MOTHER CAME HOME ...
...AND I LEARNED OF FATHER'S DEATH.
AFTER THAT, THE WORLD GOT COLDER.
MOTHER?
YOU'VE BEEN COOPED UP IN THERE WITHOUT EATING FOR TOO LONG.
MOTHER!

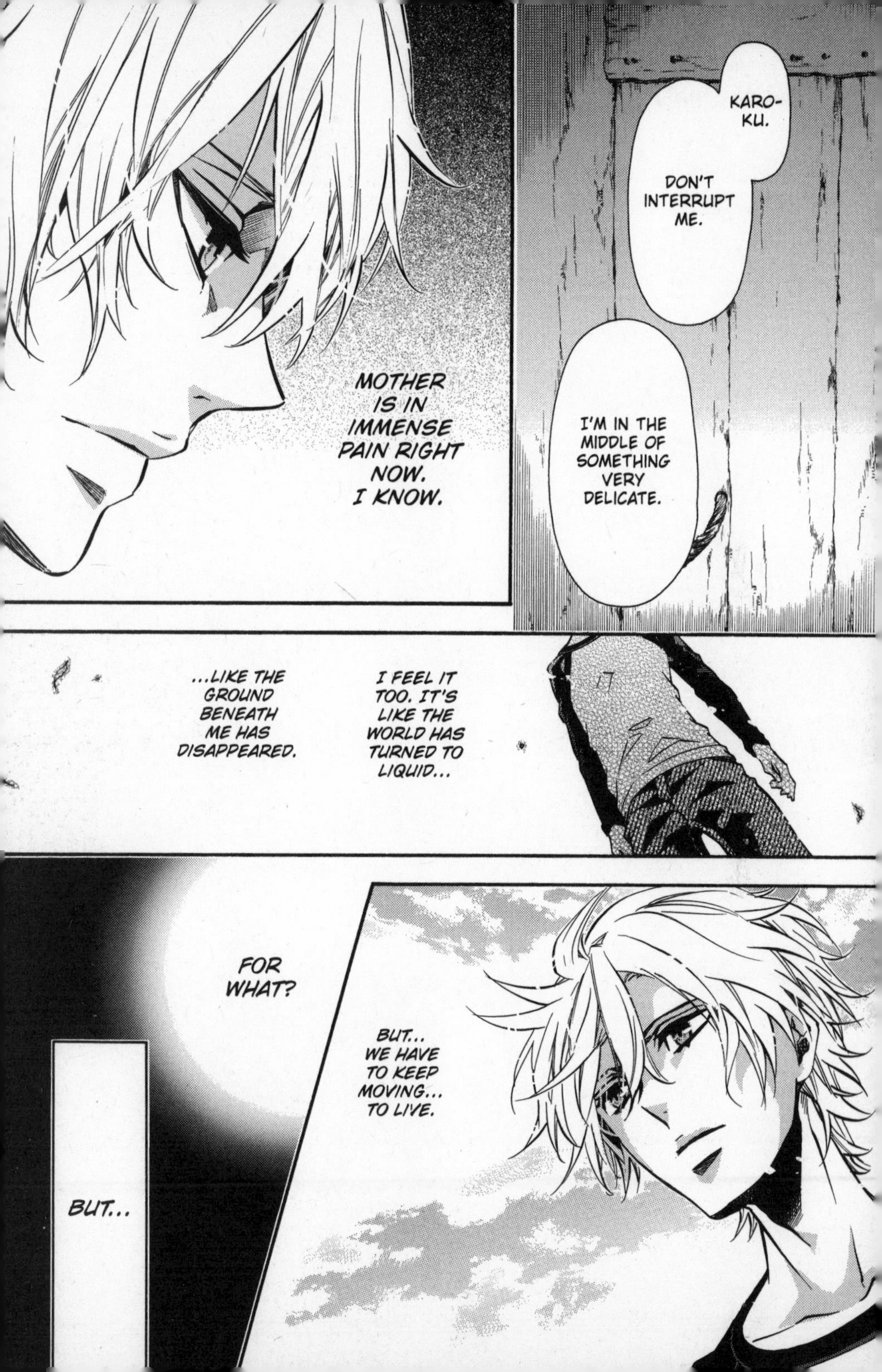
KARO-KU.
DON'T INTERRUPT ME.
I'M IN THE MIDDLE OF SOMETHING VERY DELICATE.
MOTHER IS IN IMMENSE PAIN RIGHT NOW. I KNOW.
I FEEL IT TOO. IT'S LIKE THE WORLD HAS TURNED TO LIQUID...
...LIKE THE GROUND BENEATH ME HAS DISAPPEARED.
BUT... WE HAVE TO KEEP MOVING... TO LIVE.
FOR WHAT?
BUT...

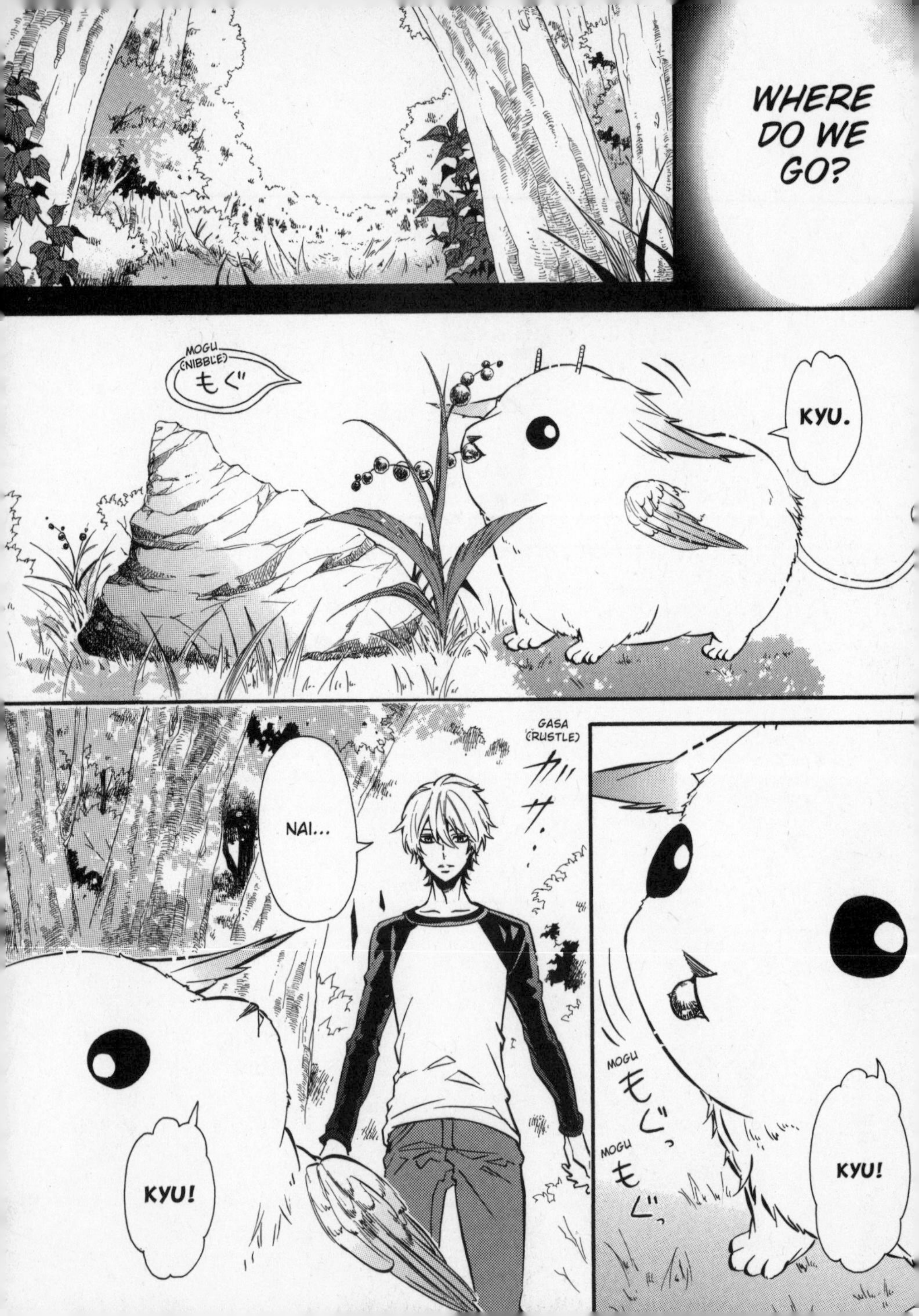
WHERE DO WE GO?
KYU.
MOGU (NIBBLE) もぐ
MOGU もぐっ
MOGU もぐっ
KYU!
GASA (RUSTLE) ガサ…
NAI…
KYU!

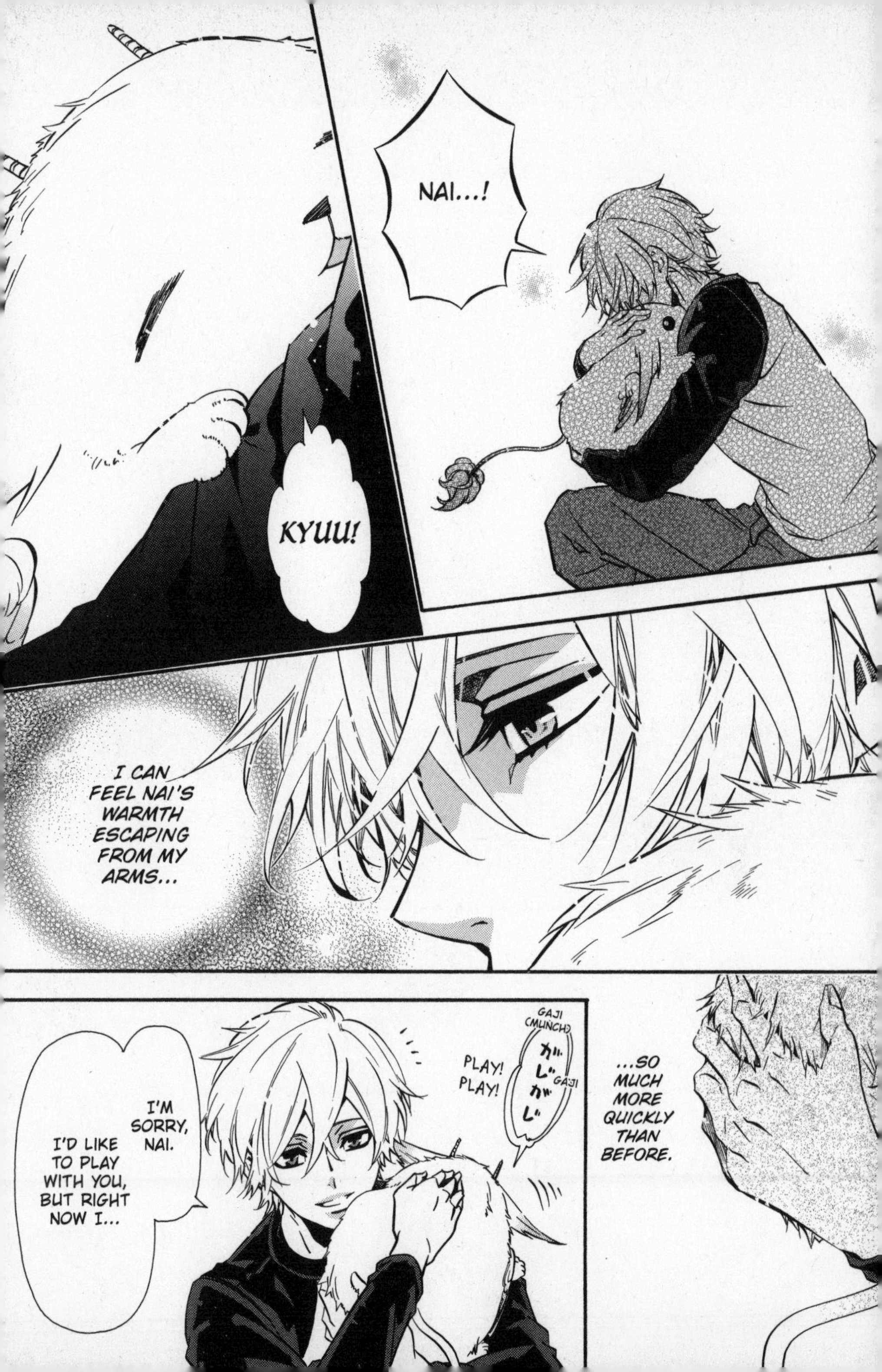
NAI...!
KYUU!
I CAN FEEL NAI'S WARMTH ESCAPING FROM MY ARMS...
...SO MUCH MORE QUICKLY THAN BEFORE.
GAJI (MUNCH) ガジ GAJI ガジ
PLAY! PLAY!
I'M SORRY, NAI.
I'D LIKE TO PLAY WITH YOU, BUT RIGHT NOW I...

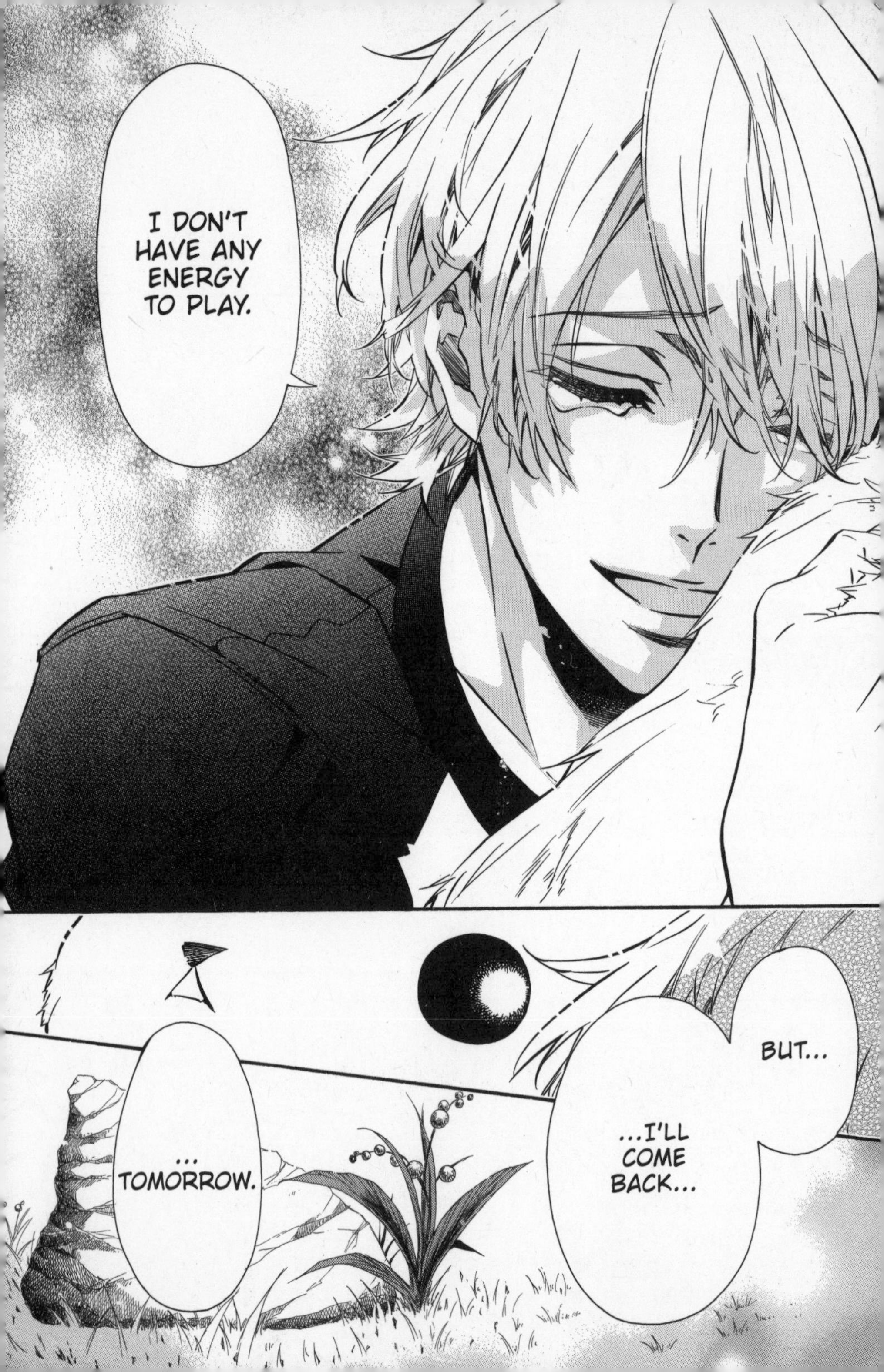
I DON'T HAVE ANY ENERGY TO PLAY.
BUT...
...I'LL COME BACK...
...TOMORROW.

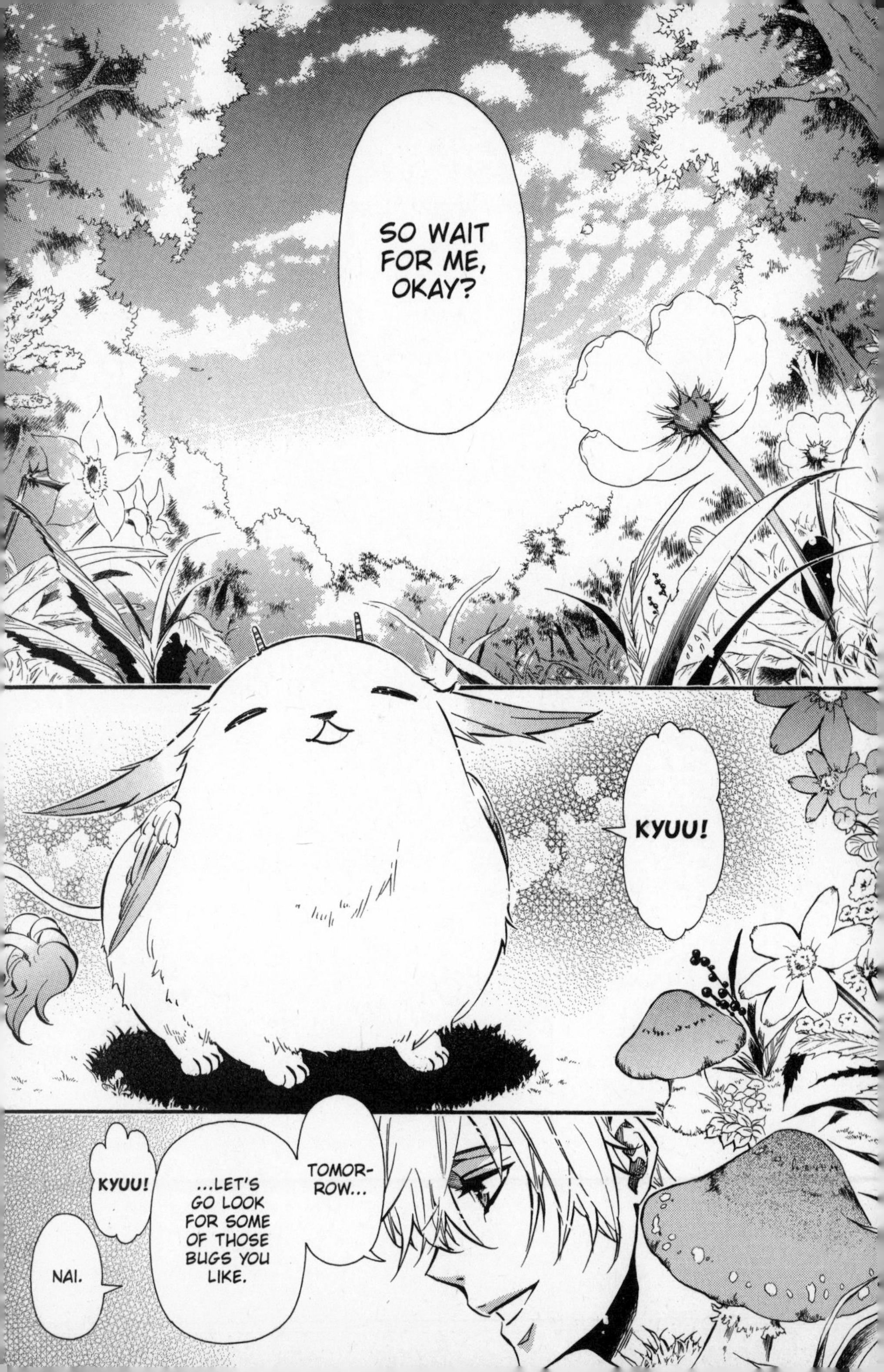
SO WAIT FOR ME, OKAY?
KYUU!
TOMOR-ROW...
...LET'S GO LOOK FOR SOME OF THOSE BUGS YOU LIKE.
KYUU!
NAI.

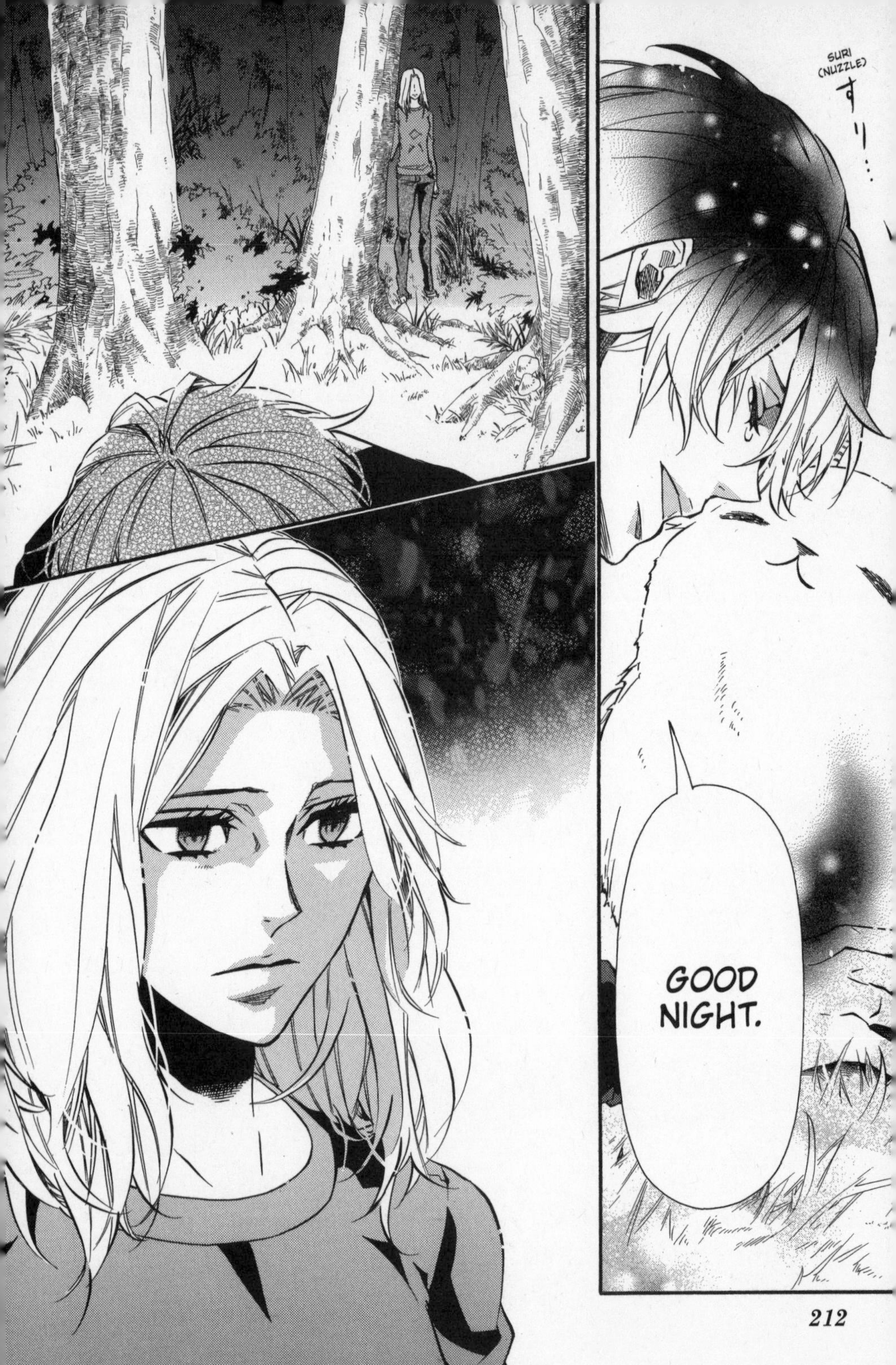
SURI (NUZZLE)
すり…
GOOD NIGHT.

KARNEVAL

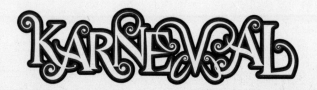

KARNEVAL

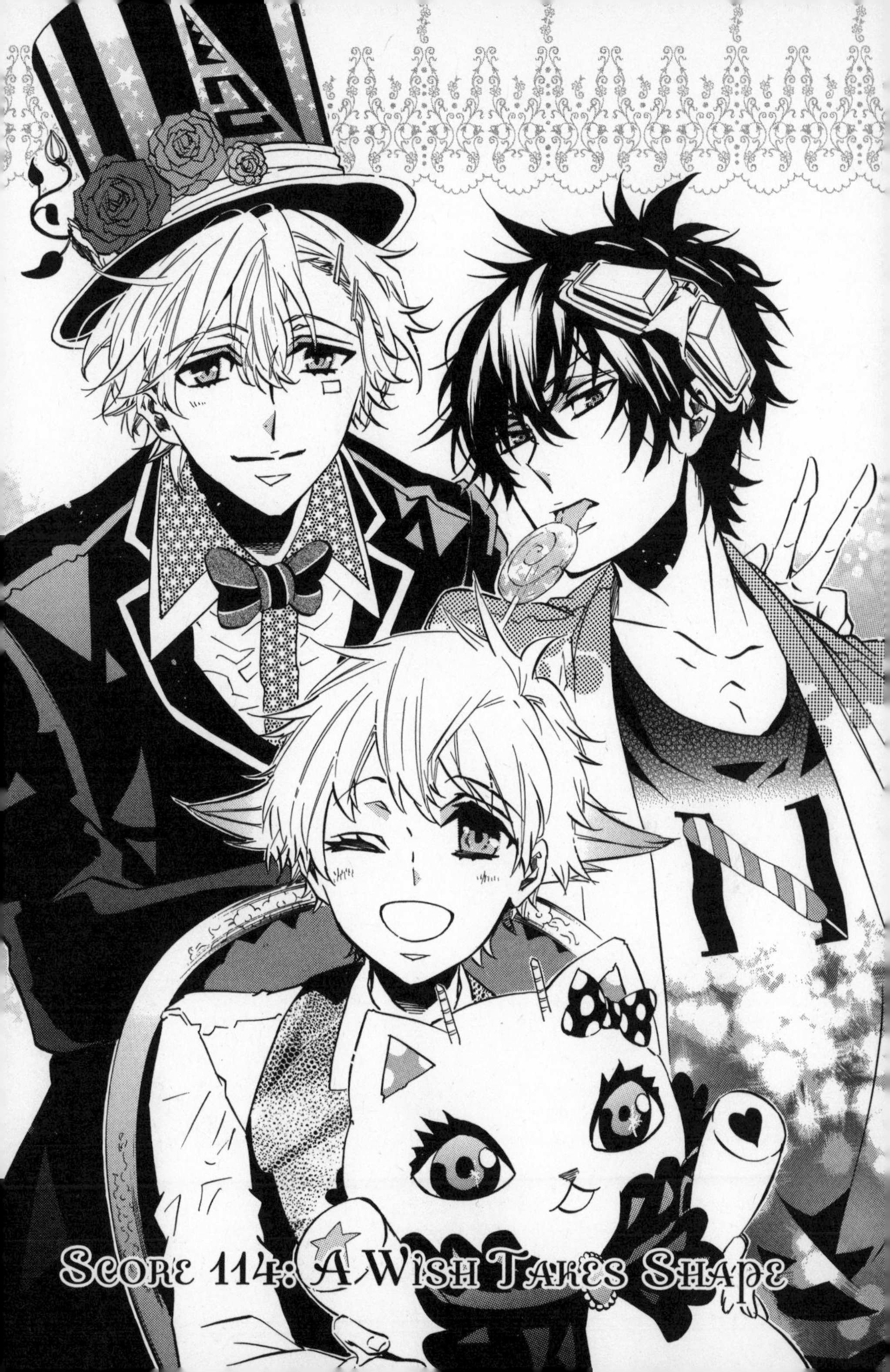
Score 114: A Wish Takes Shape

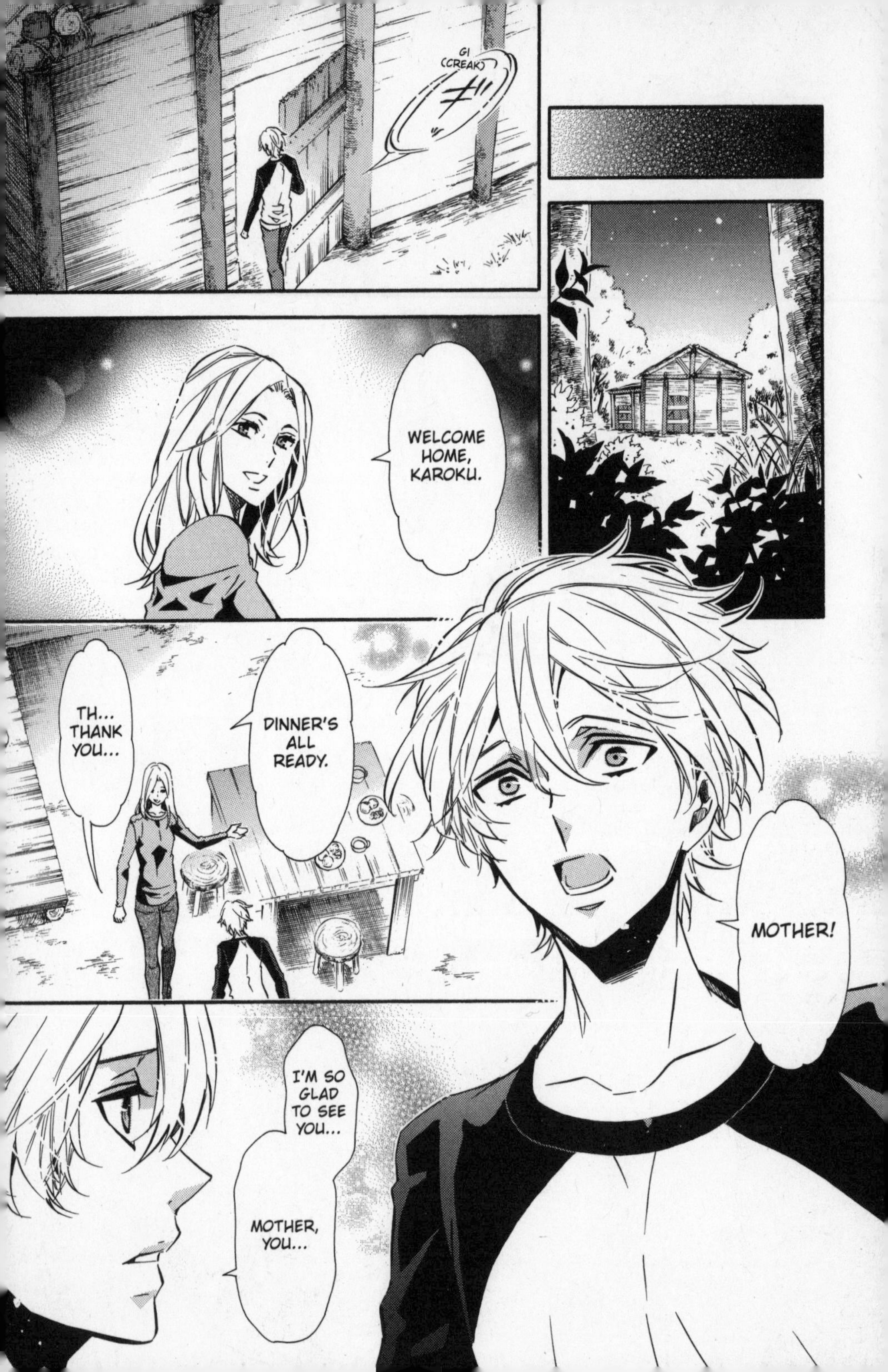
GI (CREAK)
WELCOME HOME, KAROKU.
MOTHER!
DINNER'S ALL READY.
TH... THANK YOU...
I'M SO GLAD TO SEE YOU...
MOTHER, YOU...

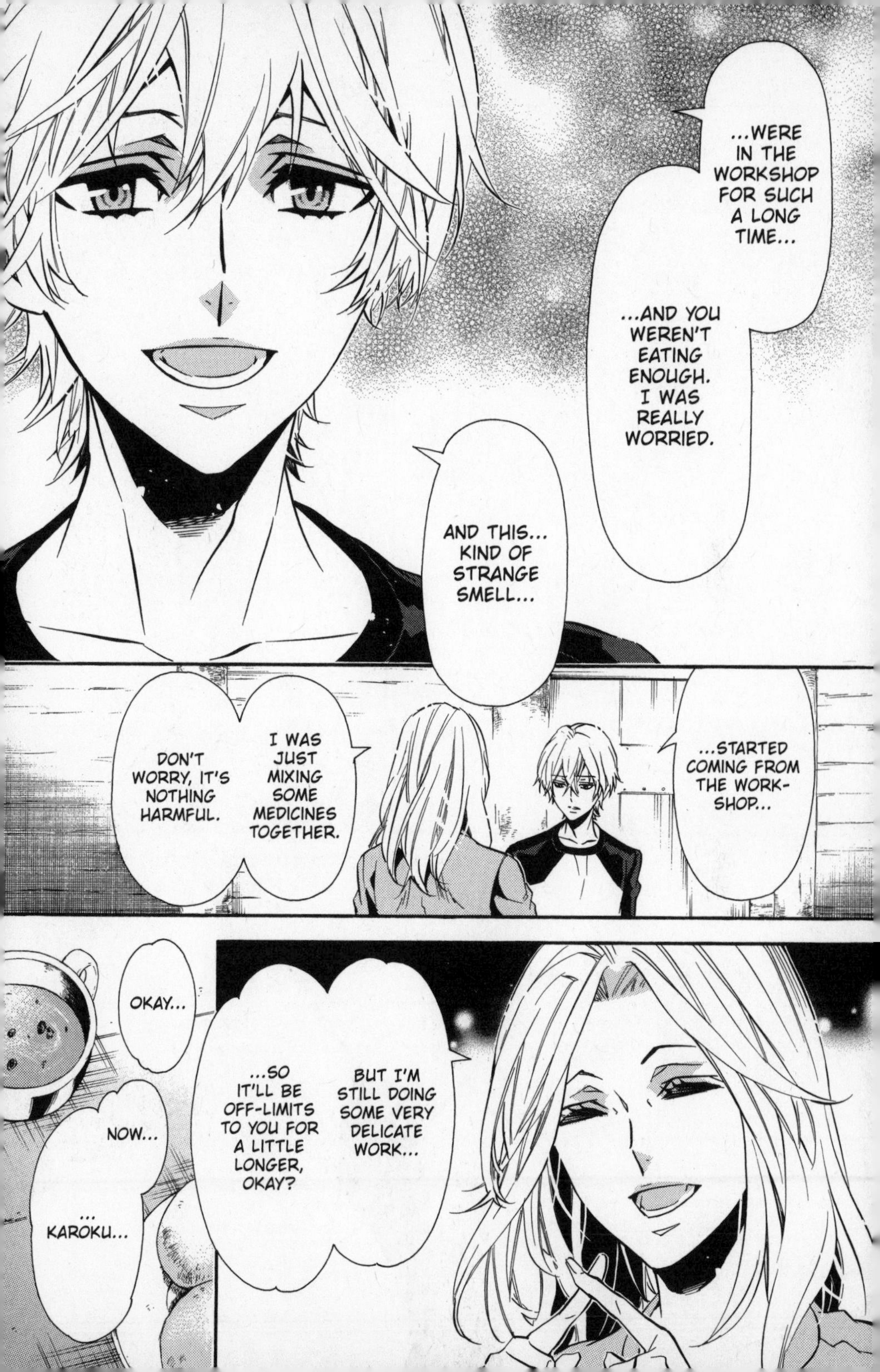
...WERE IN THE WORKSHOP FOR SUCH A LONG TIME...
...AND YOU WEREN'T EATING ENOUGH. I WAS REALLY WORRIED.
AND THIS... KIND OF STRANGE SMELL...
...STARTED COMING FROM THE WORK-SHOP...
I WAS JUST MIXING SOME MEDICINES TOGETHER.
DON'T WORRY, IT'S NOTHING HARMFUL.
BUT I'M STILL DOING SOME VERY DELICATE WORK...
...SO IT'LL BE OFF-LIMITS TO YOU FOR A LITTLE LONGER, OKAY?
OKAY...
NOW...
... KAROKU...

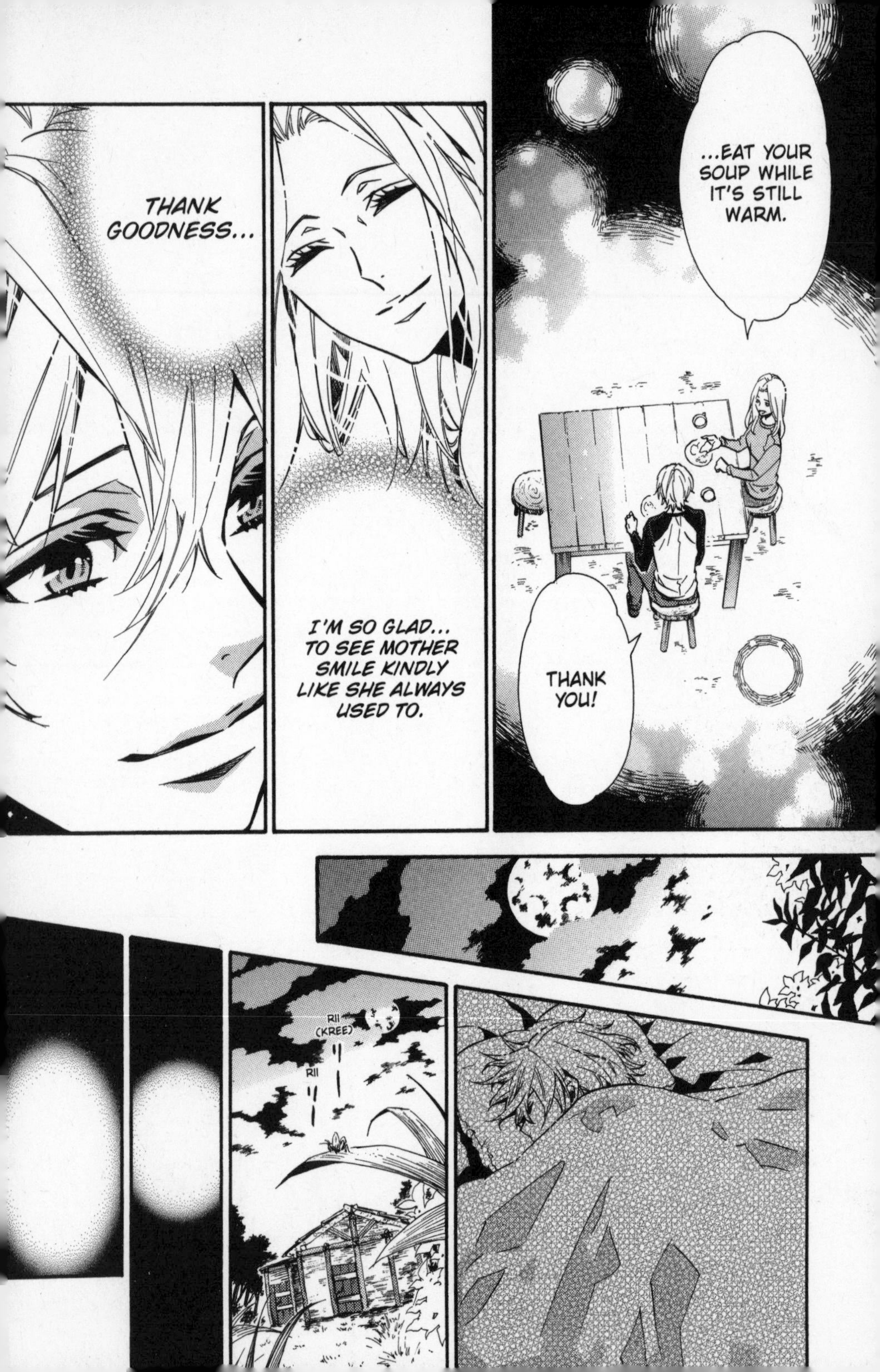
...EAT YOUR SOUP WHILE IT'S STILL WARM.
THANK YOU!
I'M SO GLAD... TO SEE MOTHER SMILE KINDLY LIKE SHE ALWAYS USED TO.
THANK GOODNESS...
RII (KREE)
RII

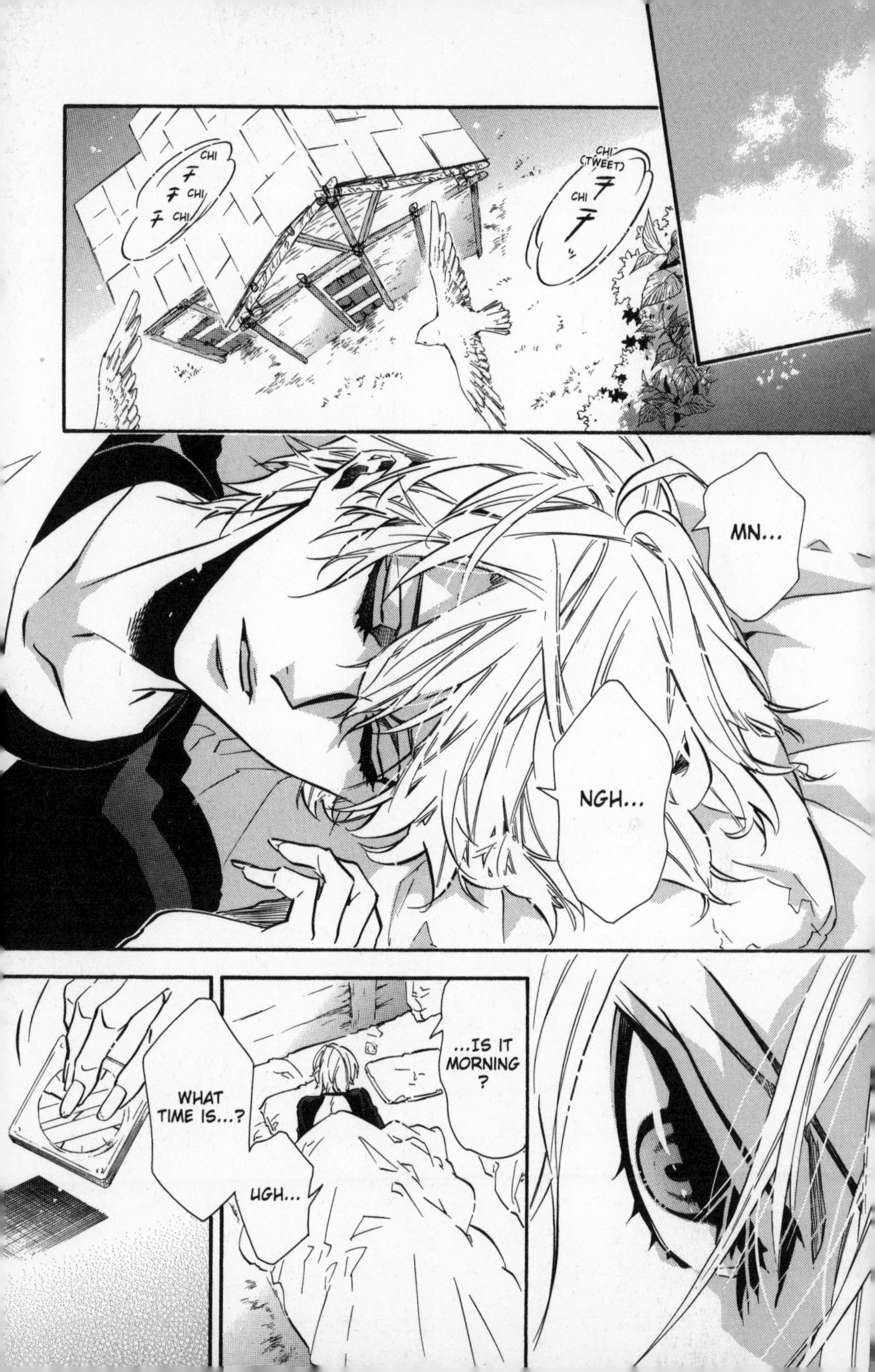
CHI (TWEET) CHI
チチッ
CHI CHI CHI
チチチ
MN...
NGH...
...IS IT MORNING?
UGH...
WHAT TIME IS...?

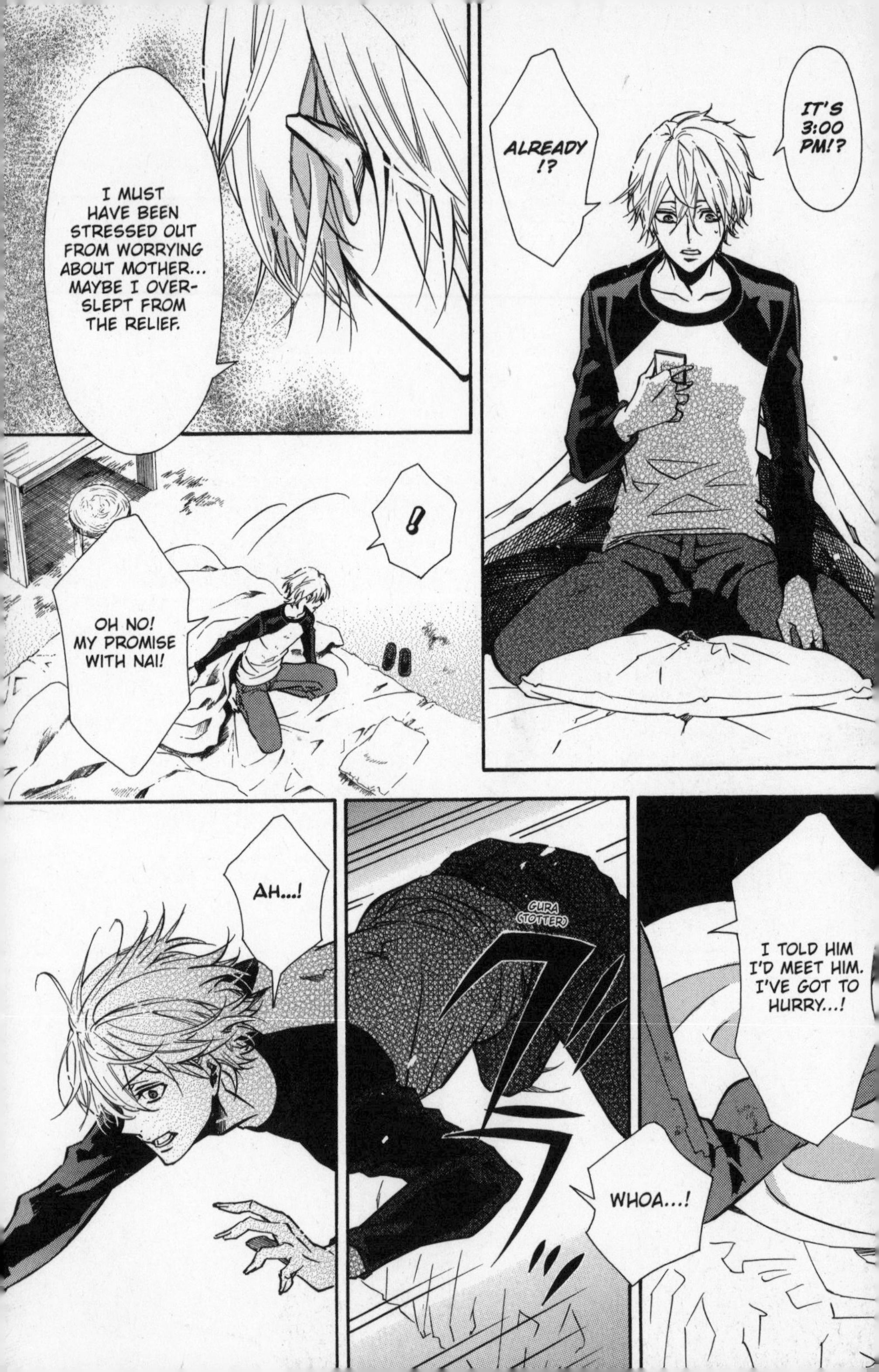
IT'S 3:00 PM!?
ALREADY!?
I MUST HAVE BEEN STRESSED OUT FROM WORRYING ABOUT MOTHER... MAYBE I OVER-SLEPT FROM THE RELIEF.
!
OH NO! MY PROMISE WITH NAI!
I TOLD HIM I'D MEET HIM. I'VE GOT TO HURRY...!
WHOA...!
GURA (TOTTER)
AH...!

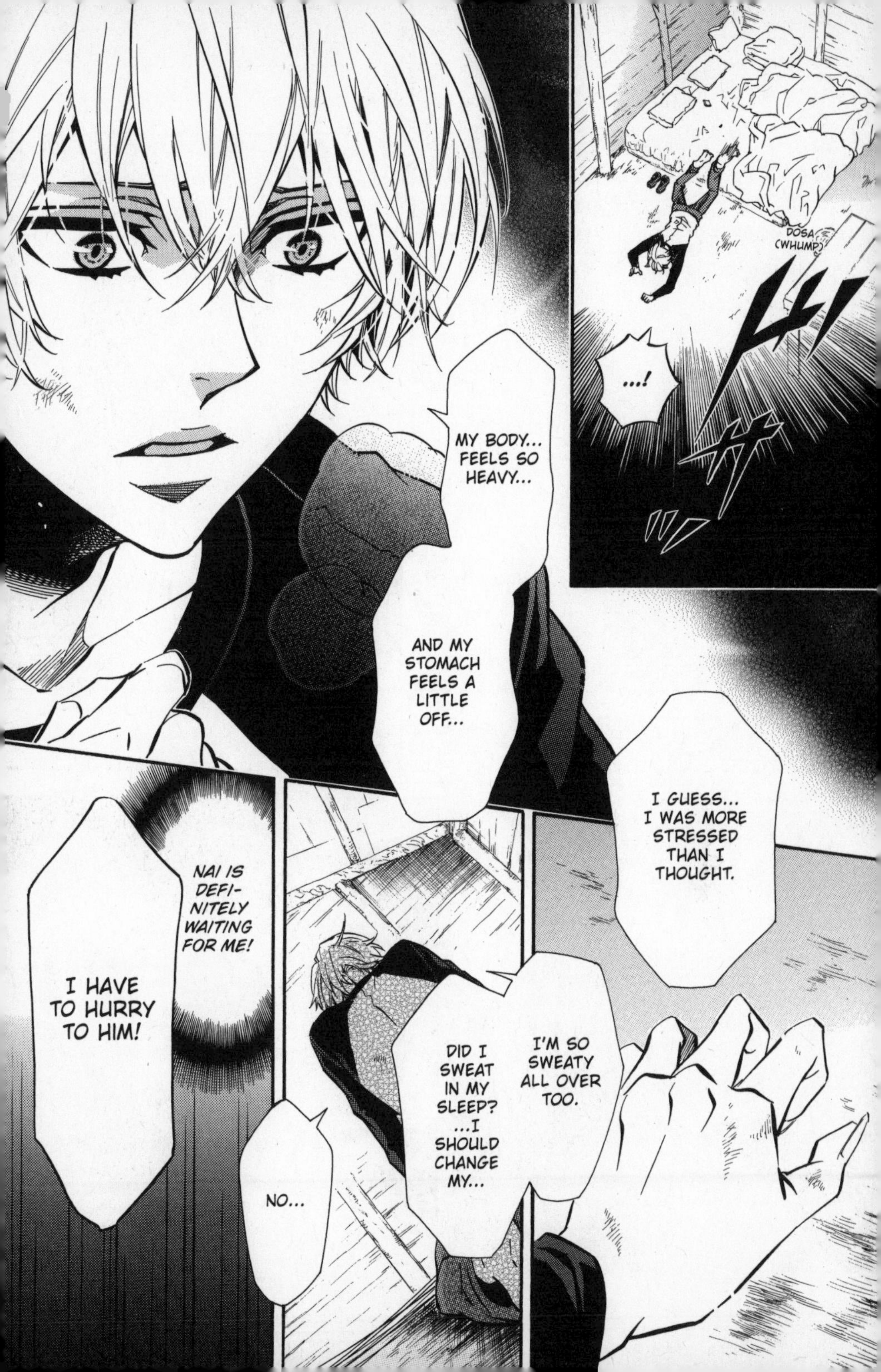
DOSA (WHUMP)
...!
MY BODY... FEELS SO HEAVY...
AND MY STOMACH FEELS A LITTLE OFF...
I GUESS... I WAS MORE STRESSED THAN I THOUGHT.
I'M SO SWEATY ALL OVER TOO.
DID I SWEAT IN MY SLEEP? ...I SHOULD CHANGE MY...
NO...
NAI IS DEFI- NITELY WAITING FOR ME!
I HAVE TO HURRY TO HIM!

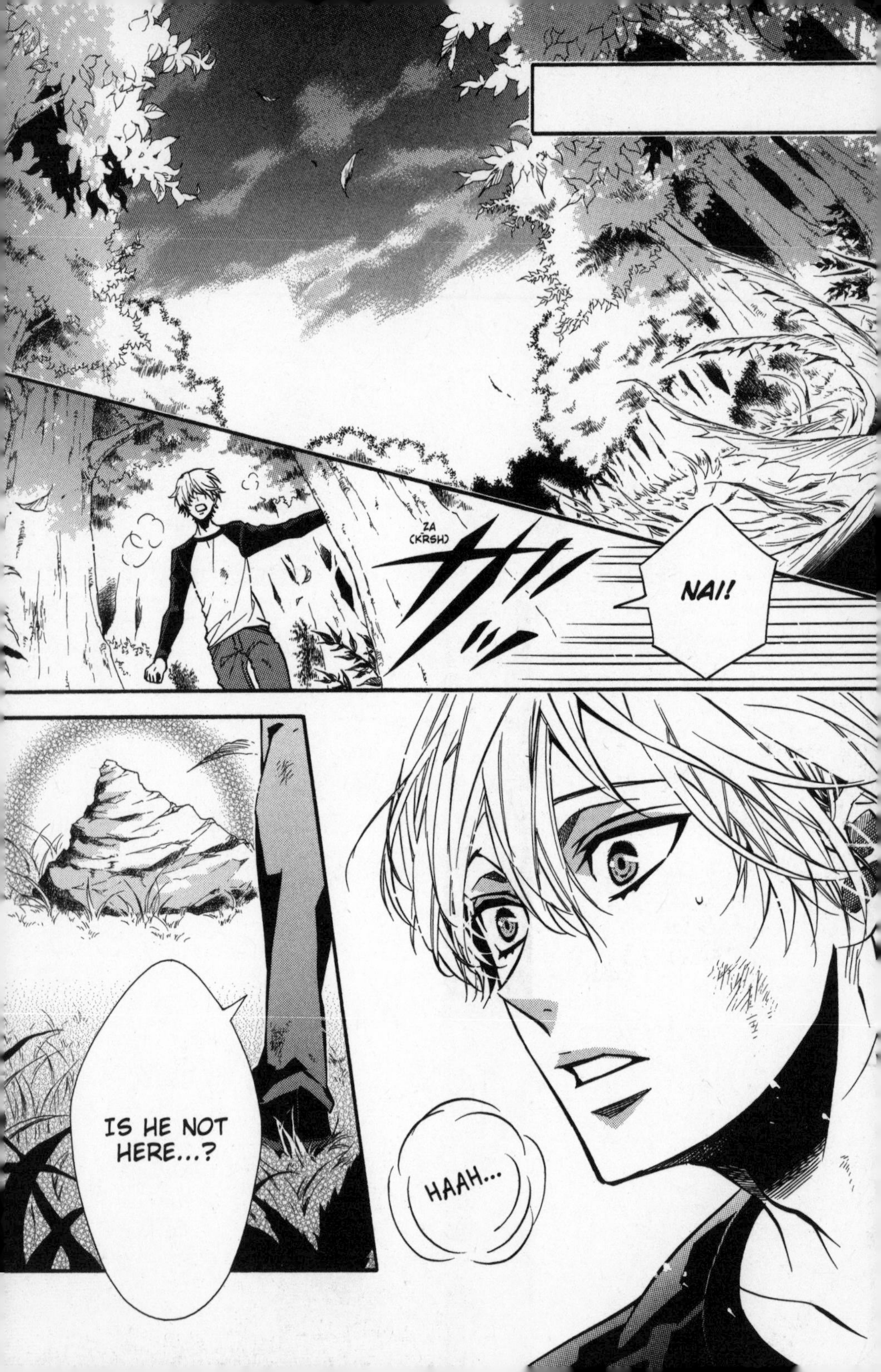
NAI!
ZA
(KRSH)
HAAH...
IS HE NOT HERE...?

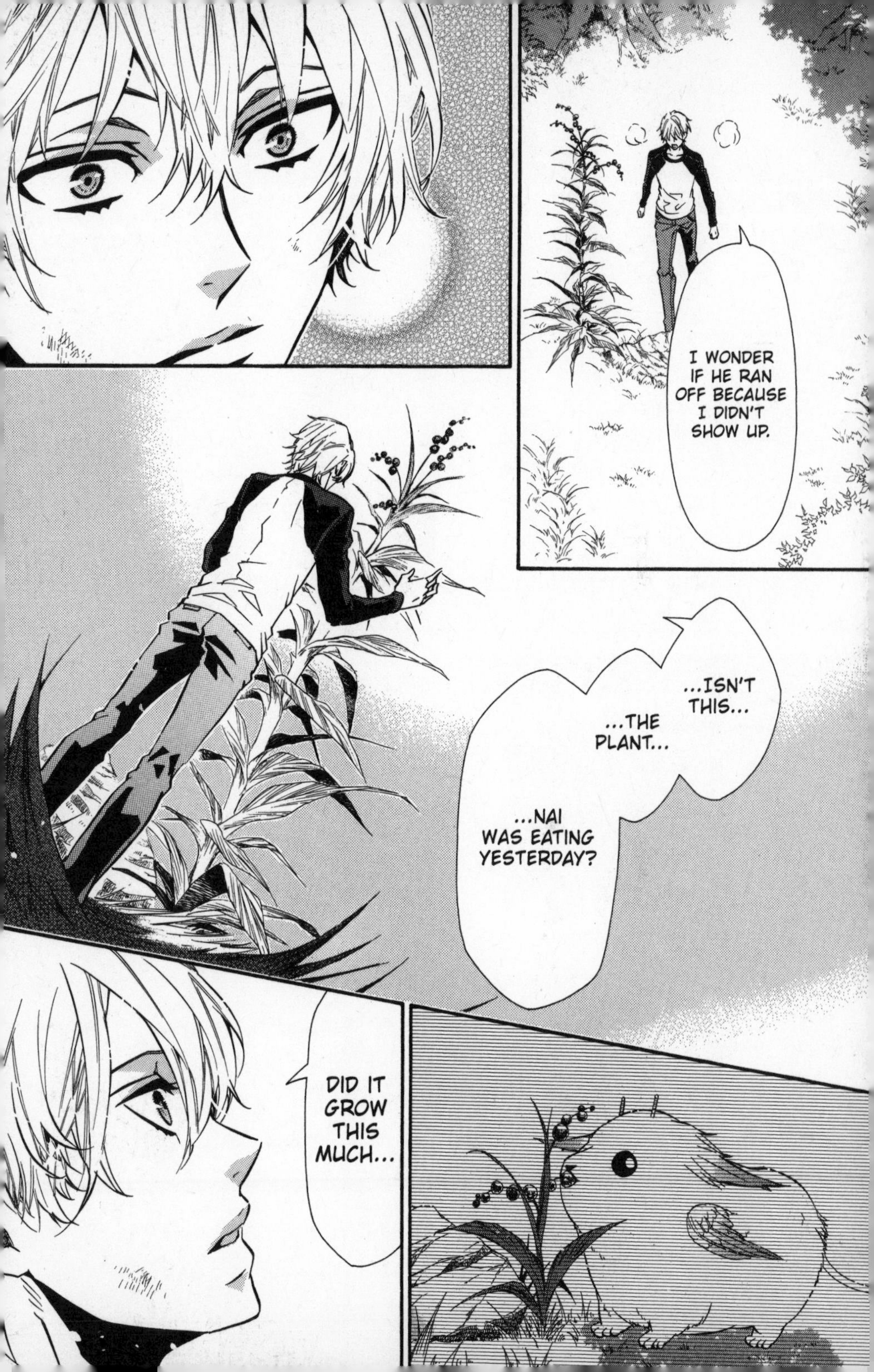
I WONDER IF HE RAN OFF BECAUSE I DIDN'T SHOW UP.
...ISN'T THIS...
...THE PLANT...
...NAI WAS EATING YESTERDAY?
DID IT GROW THIS MUCH...

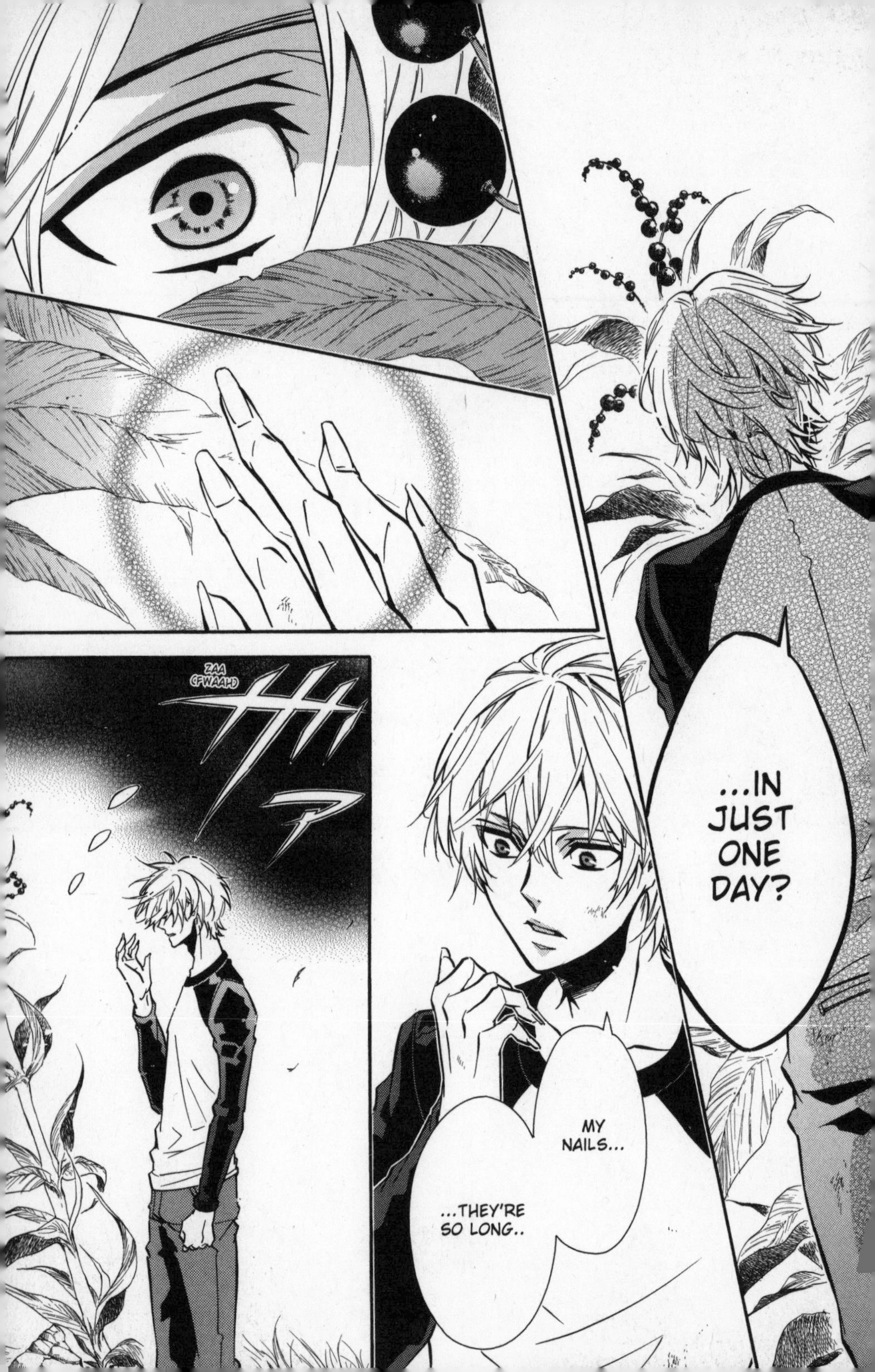
...IN JUST ONE DAY?
MY NAILS...
...THEY'RE SO LONG..
ZAA (FWAAH)

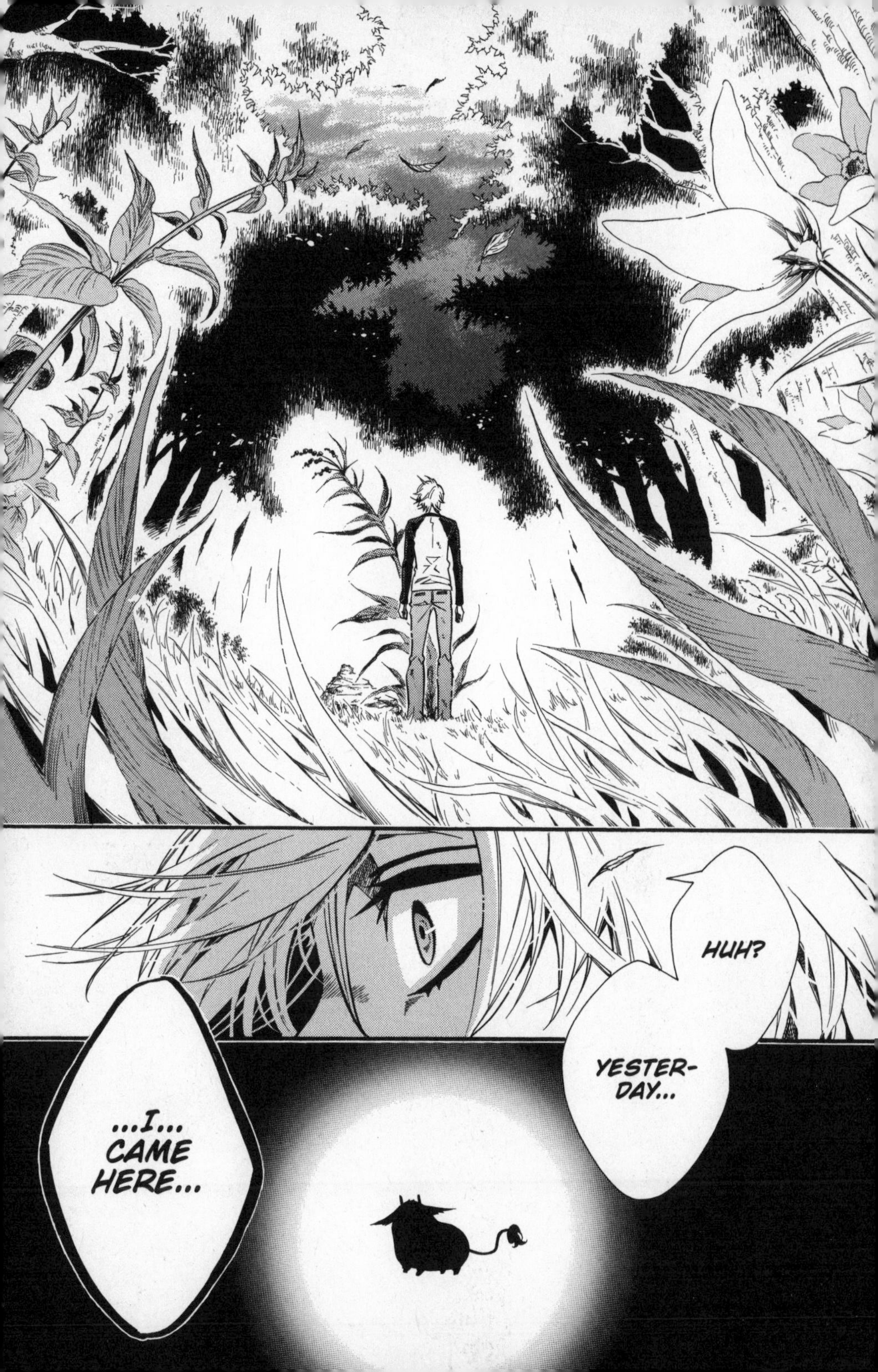
HUH?
YESTER-DAY...
...I... CAME HERE...

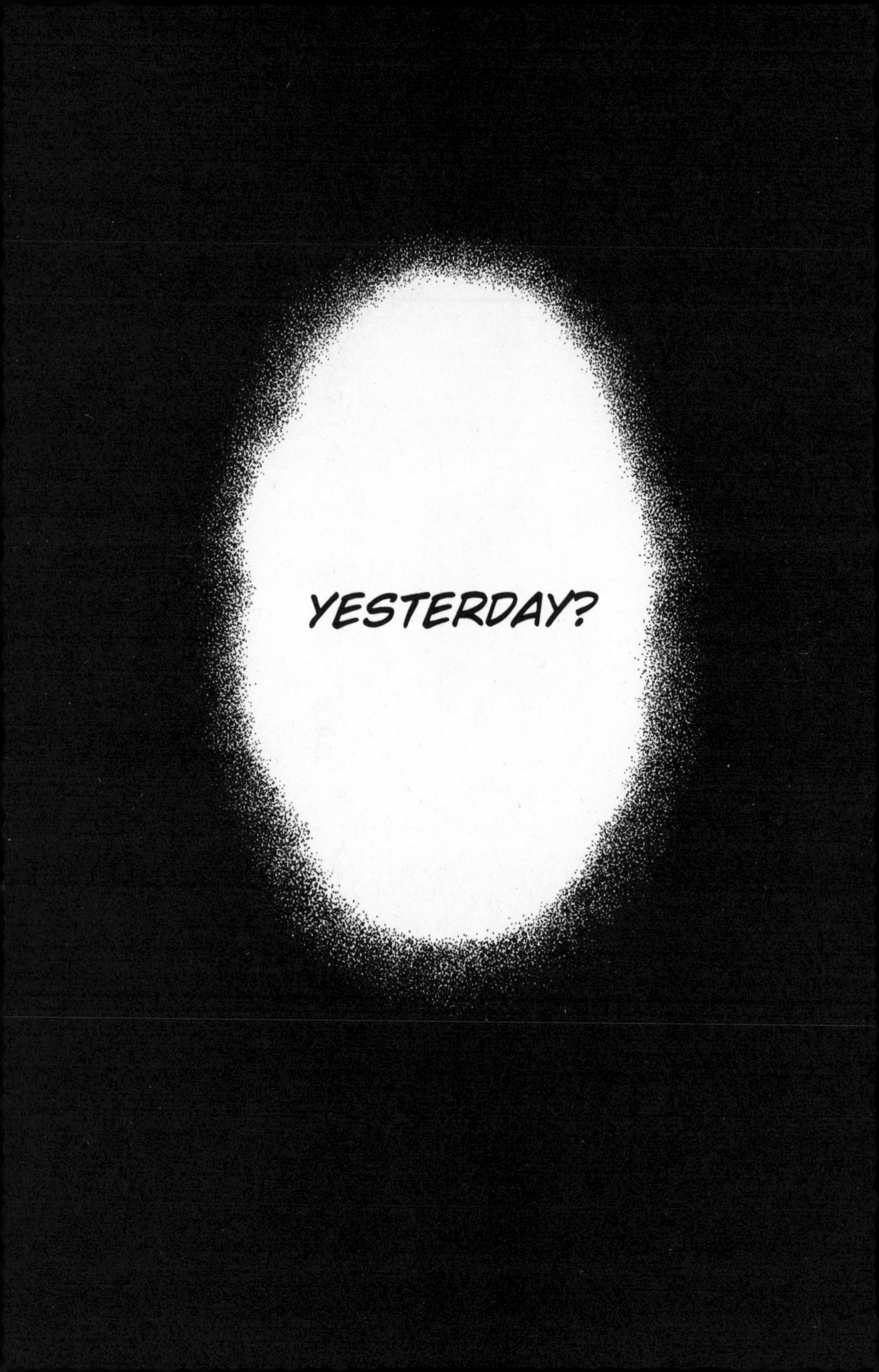
YESTERDAY?

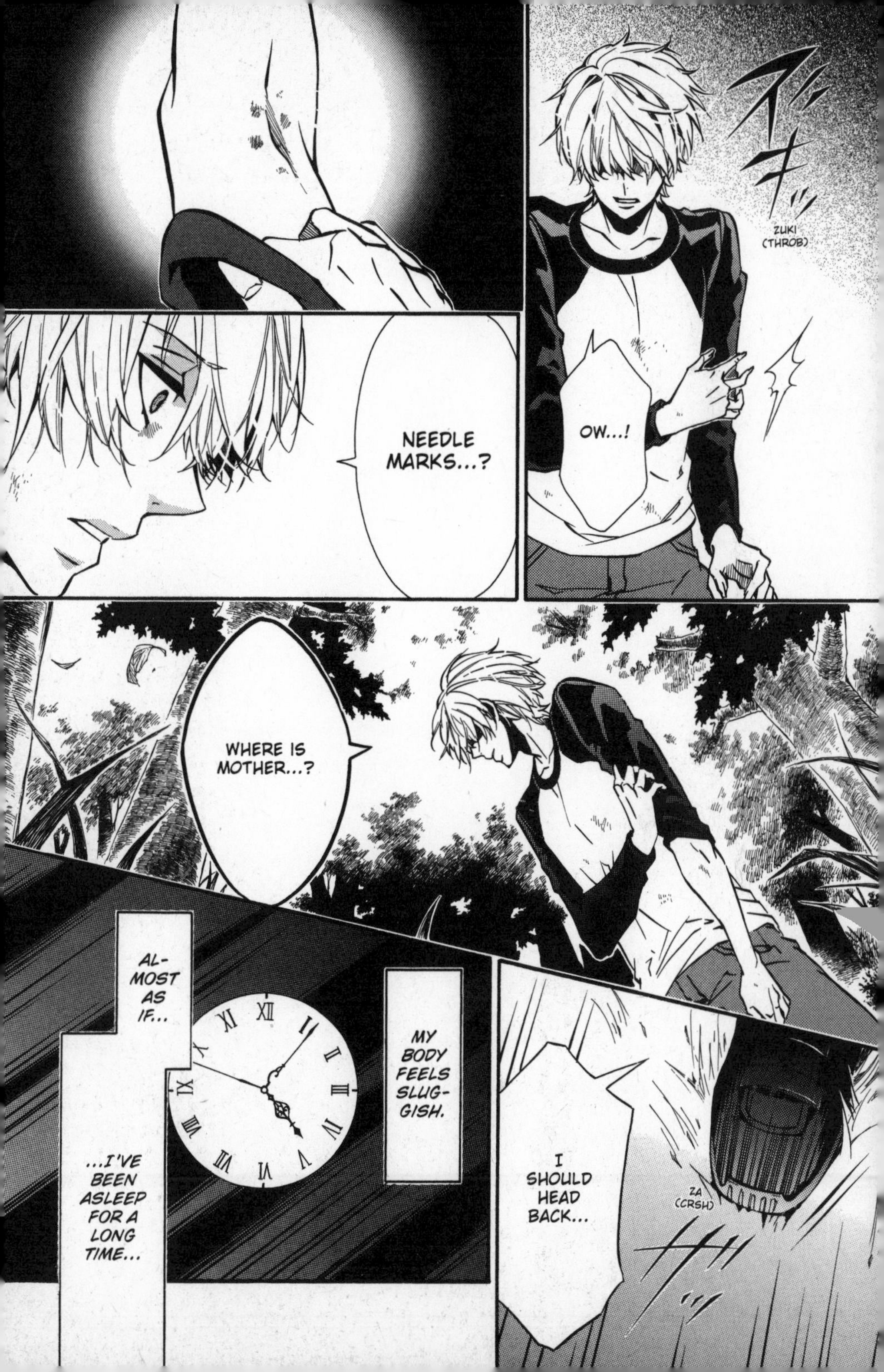
ZUKI (THROB)
OW...!
NEEDLE MARKS...?
WHERE IS MOTHER...?
I SHOULD HEAD BACK...
ZA (CRSH)
MY BODY FEELS SLUG-GISH.
AL-MOST AS IF...
...I'VE BEEN ASLEEP FOR A LONG TIME...

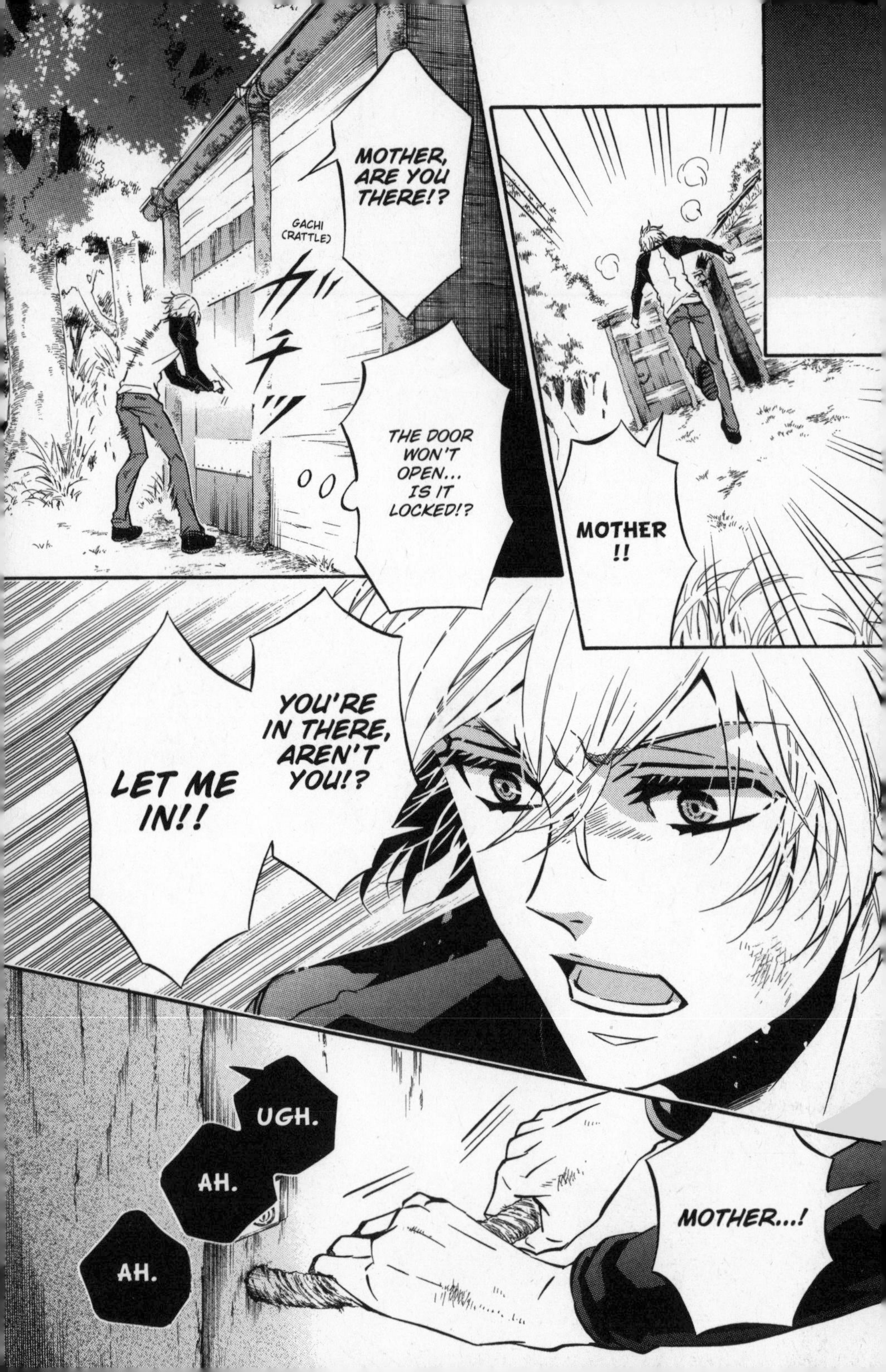
MOTHER !!
MOTHER, ARE YOU THERE!?
GACHI (RATTLE)
ガチッ
THE DOOR WON'T OPEN... IS IT LOCKED!?
YOU'RE IN THERE, AREN'T YOU!?
LET ME IN!!
MOTHER...!
UGH.
AH.
AH.

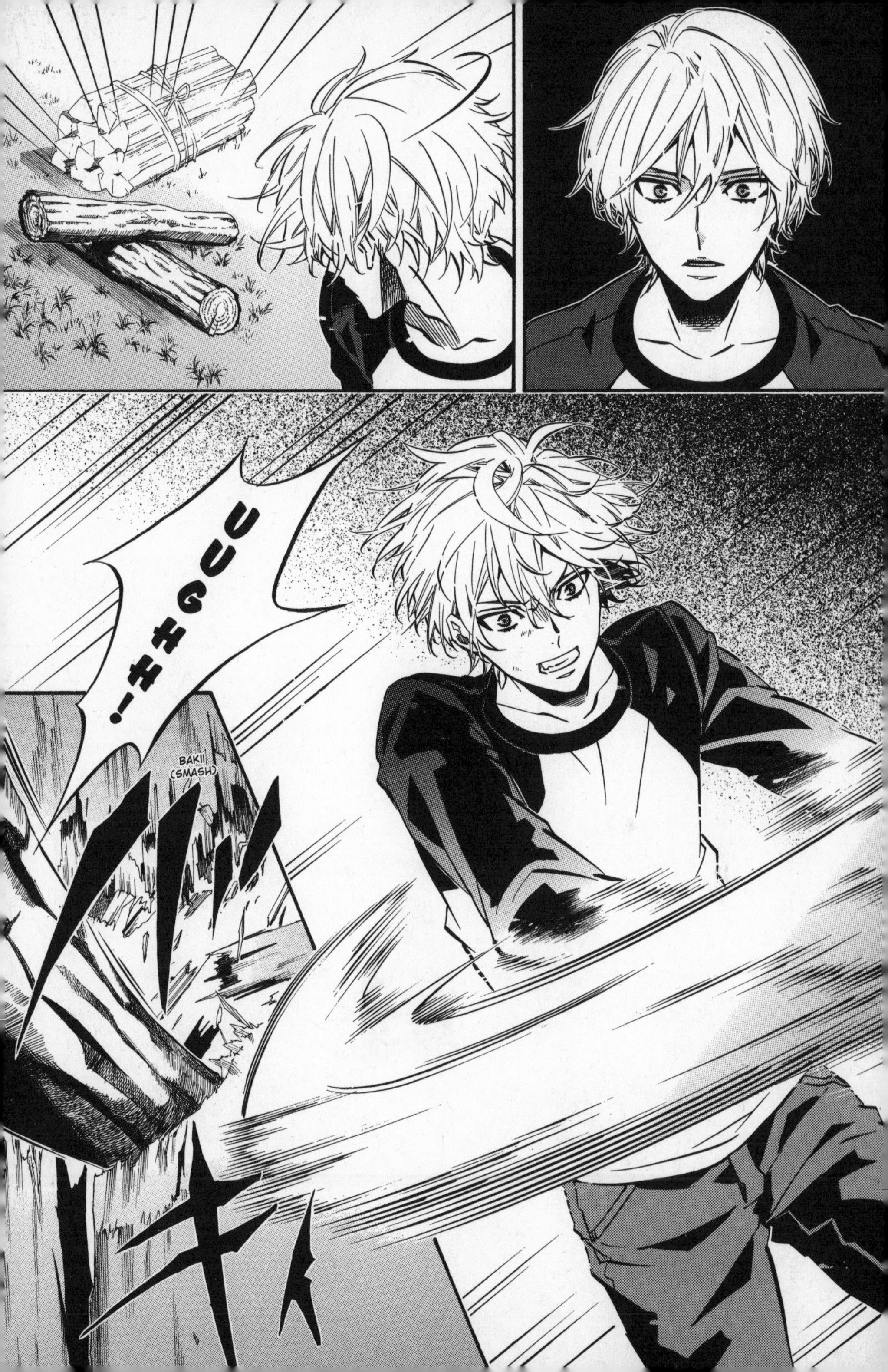
UUGHHH!
BAKI! (SMASH)

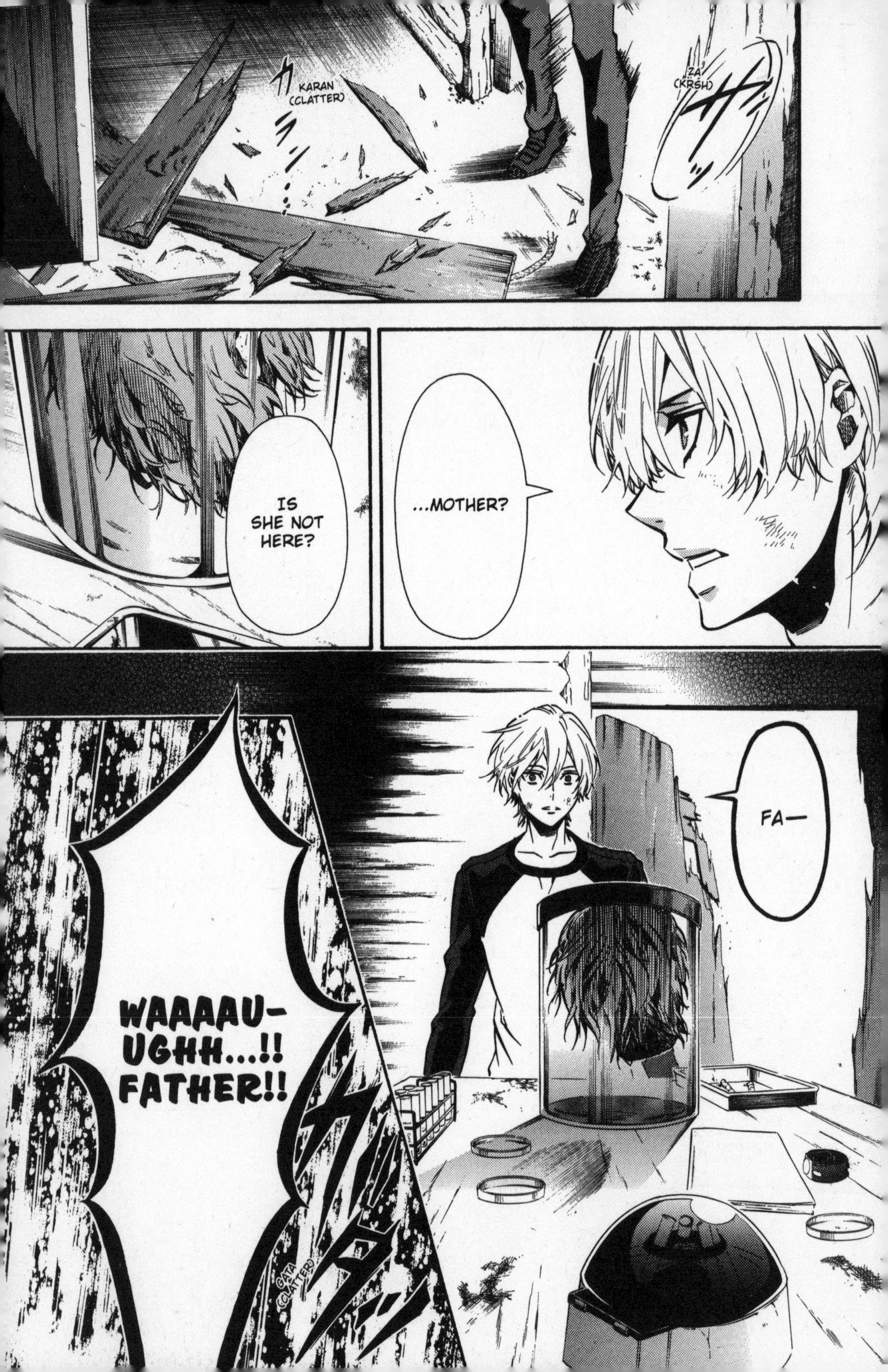
ZA (KRSH)
KARAN (CLATTER)
...MOTHER?
IS SHE NOT HERE?
FA—
WAAAAU-UGHH...!! FATHER!!
GATA (CLATTER)

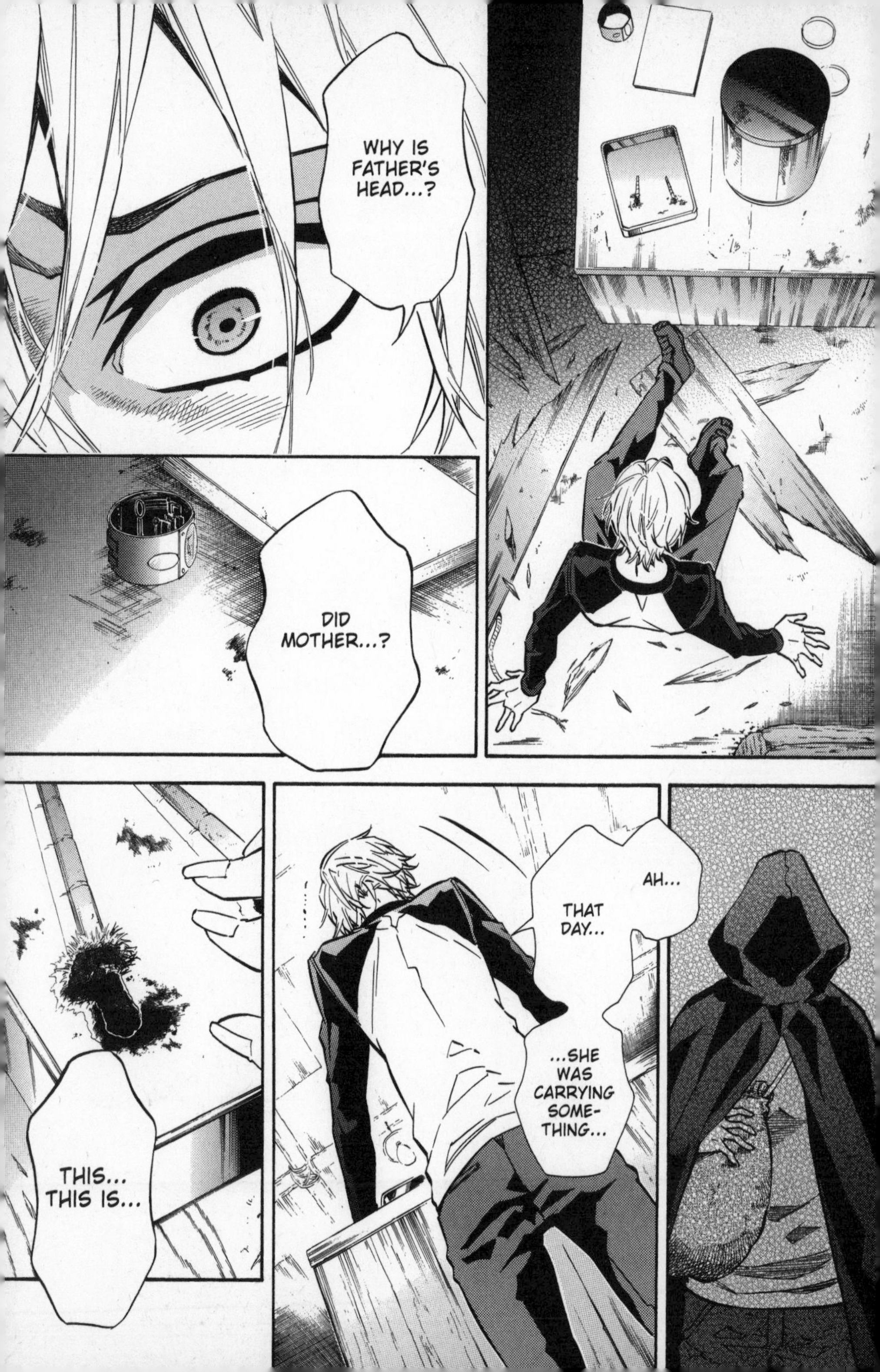
WHY IS FATHER'S HEAD...?
DID MOTHER...?
AH... THAT DAY...
...SHE WAS CARRYING SOME-THING...
THIS... THIS IS...

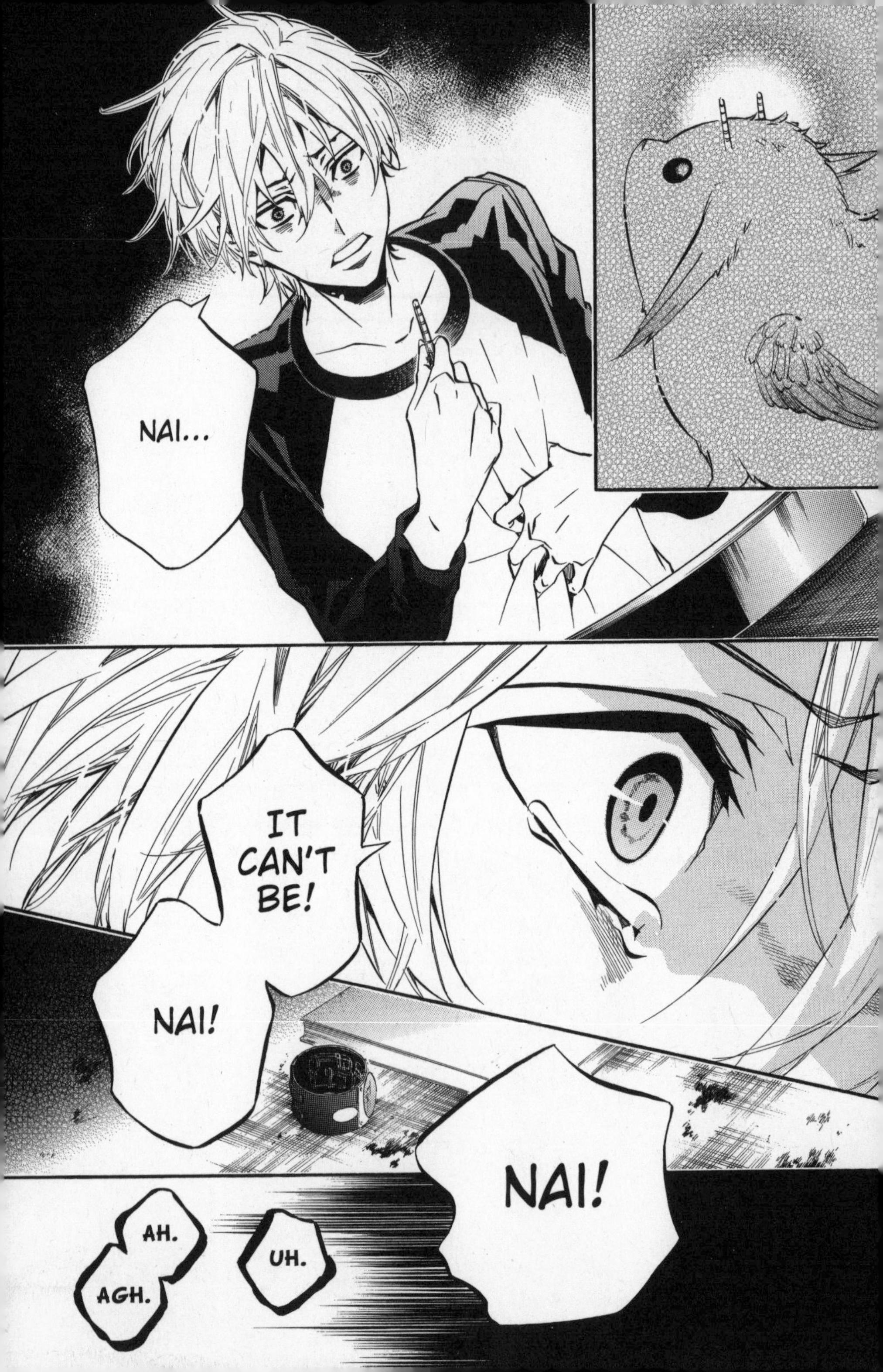
NAI...
IT CAN'T BE!
NAI!
NAI!
UH.
AH.
AGH.

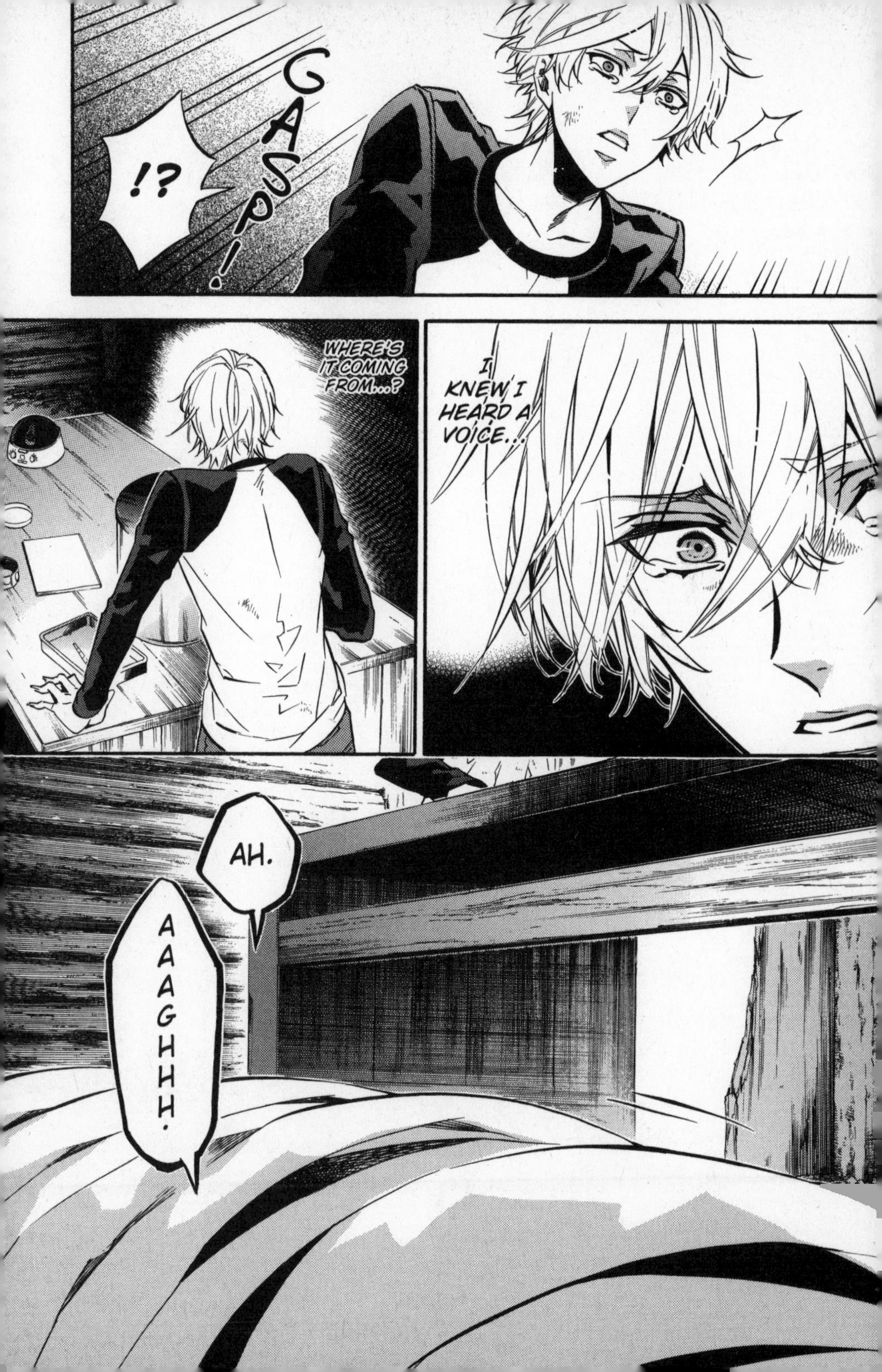
GASP!
!?
I KNEW I HEARD A VOICE...
WHERE'S IT COMING FROM...?
AH.
AAAAGHHH.

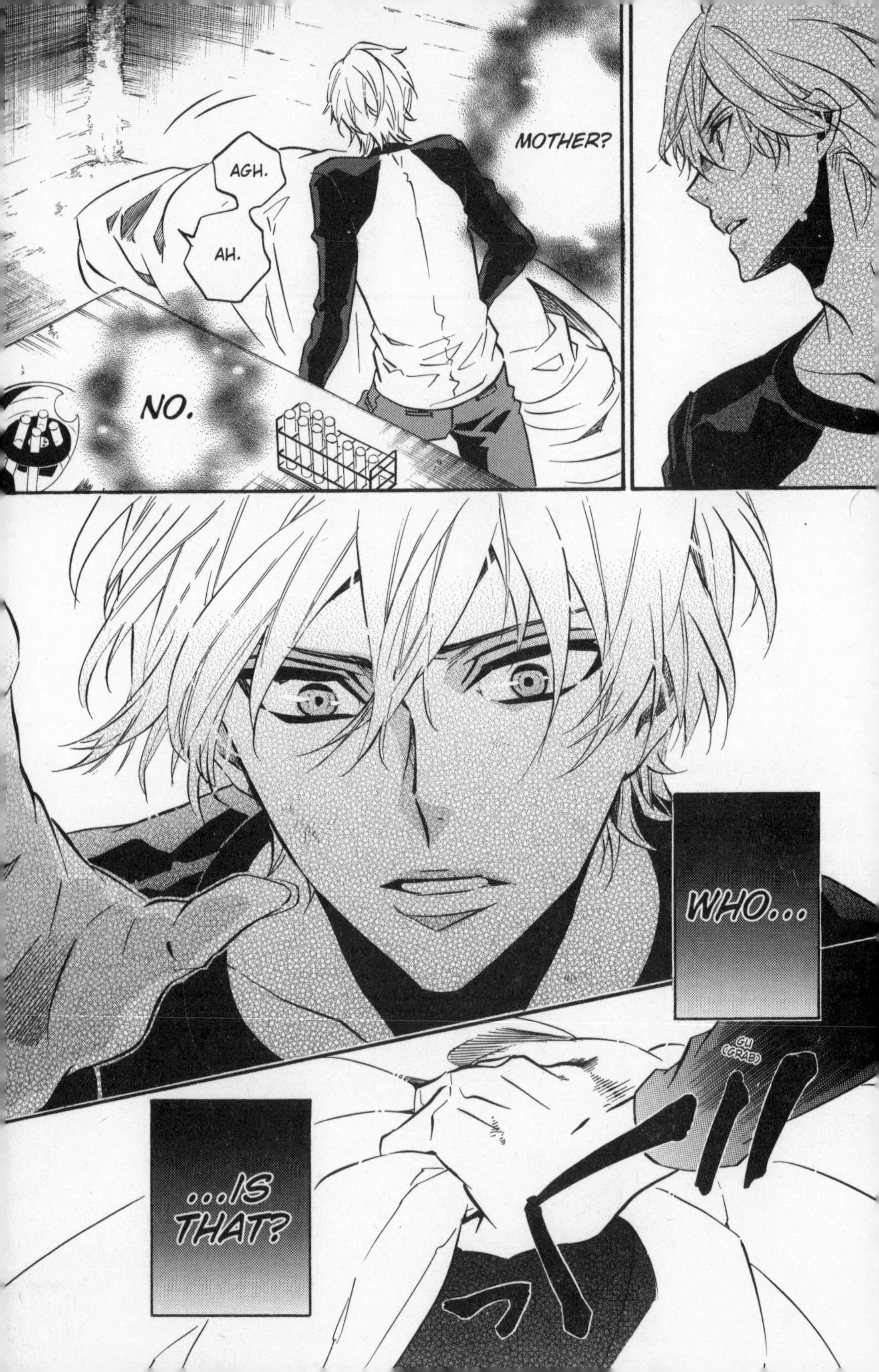
MOTHER?
AGH.
AH.
NO.
WHO...
GU (GRAB)
...IS THAT?

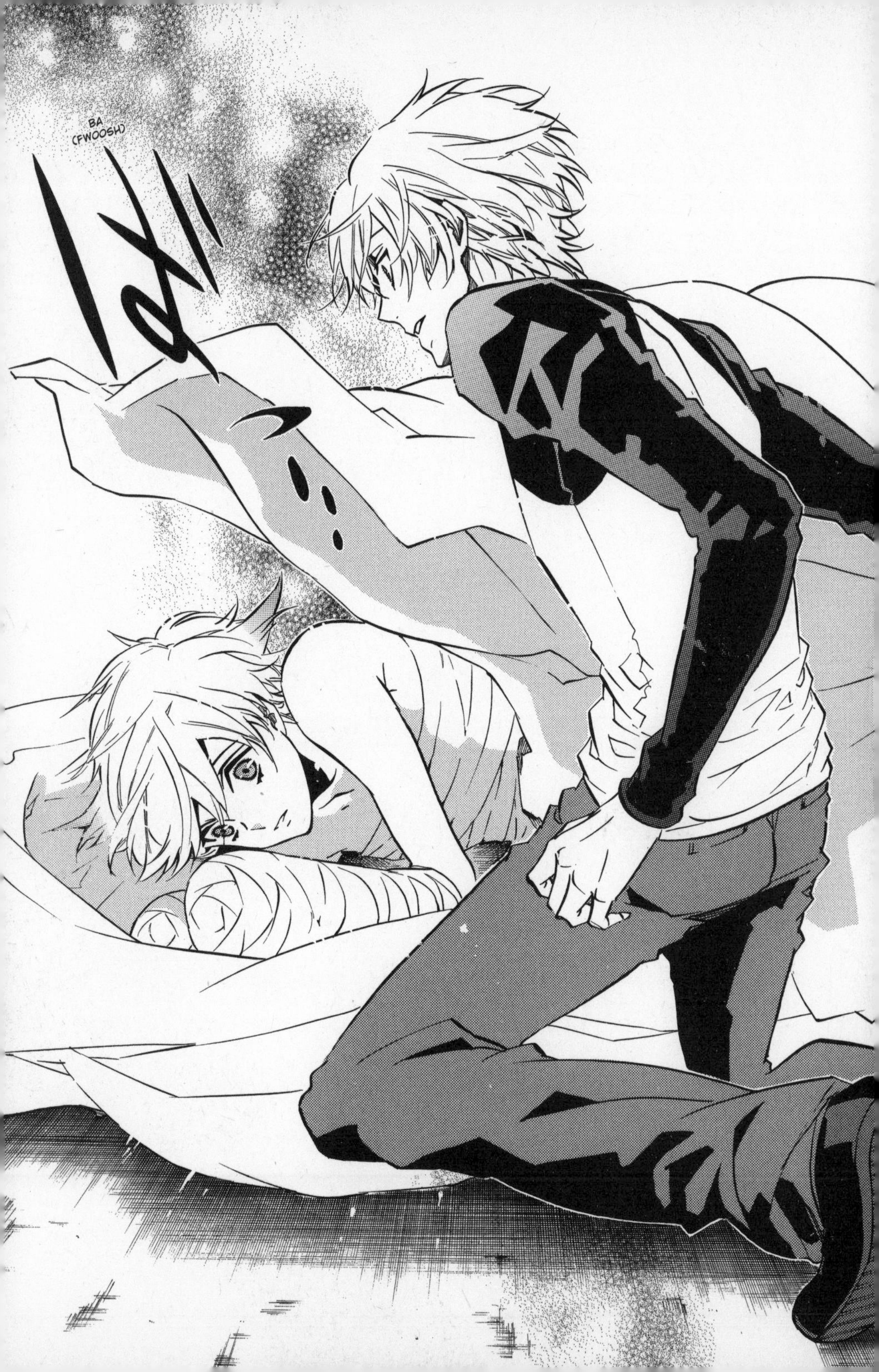
BA
(FWOOSH)

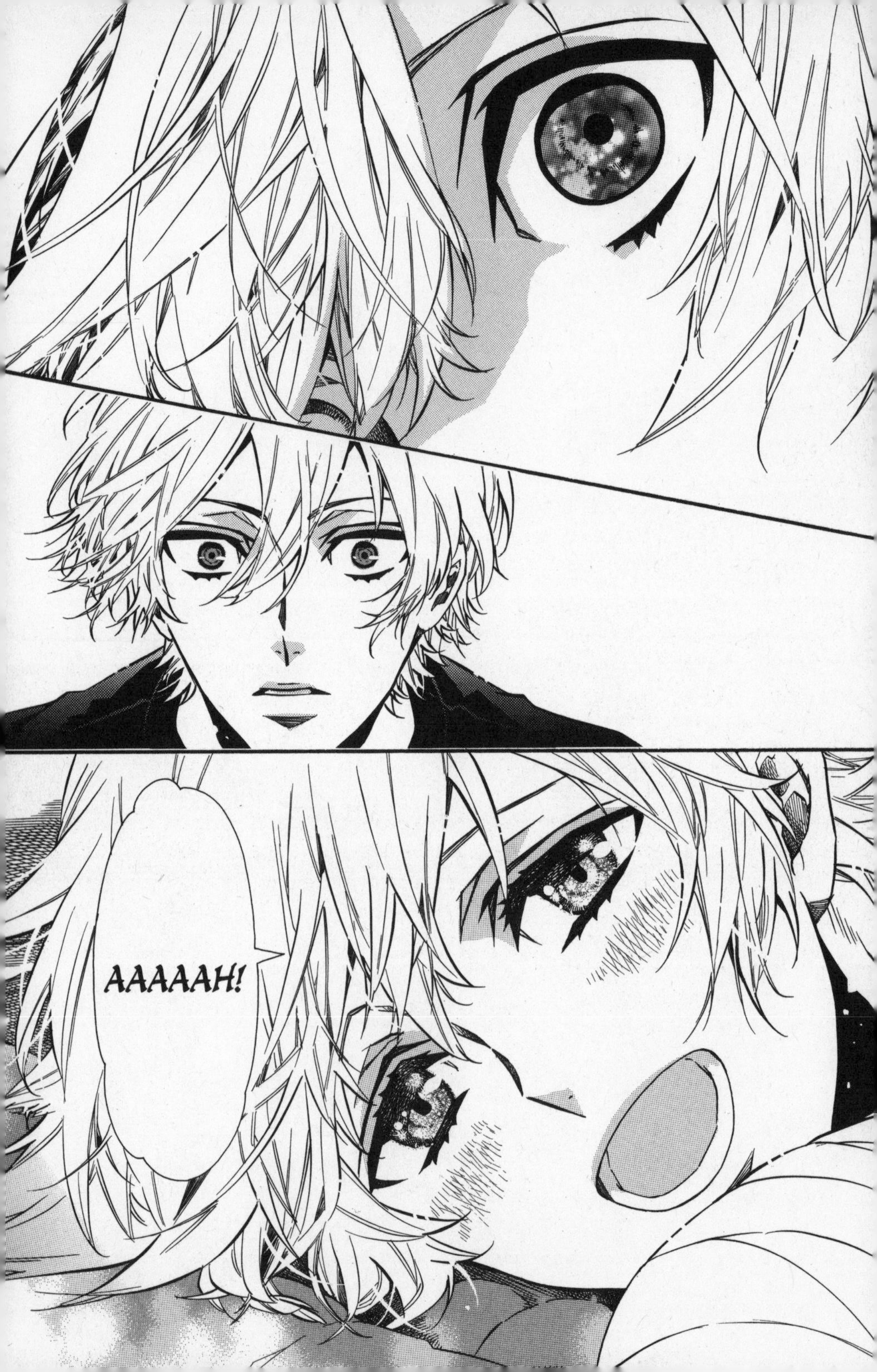
AAAAAH!

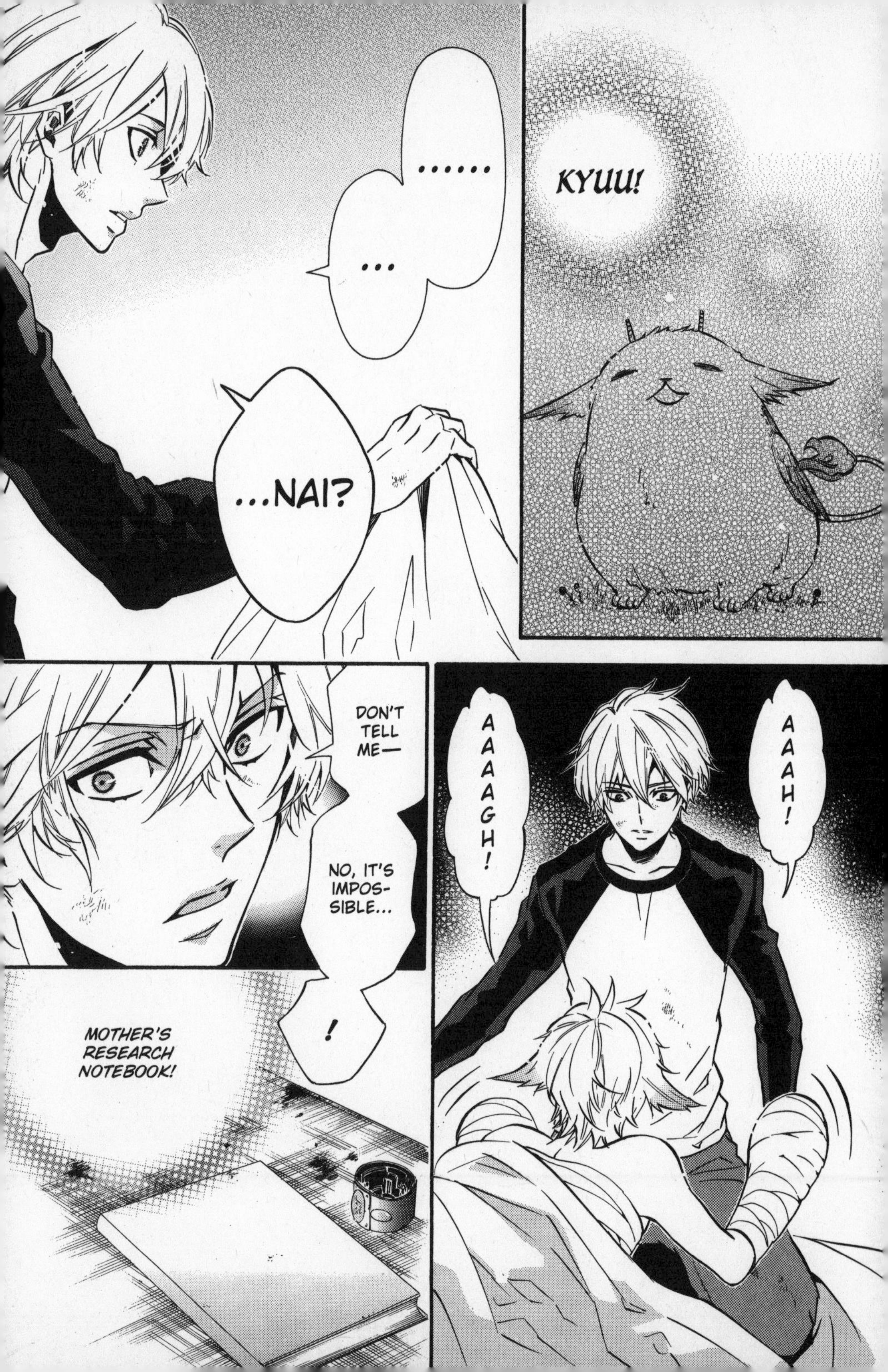
KYUU!
……
…
…NAI?
AAAH!
AAAAAGH!
DON'T TELL ME—
NO, IT'S IMPOSSIBLE…
!
MOTHER'S RESEARCH NOTEBOOK!

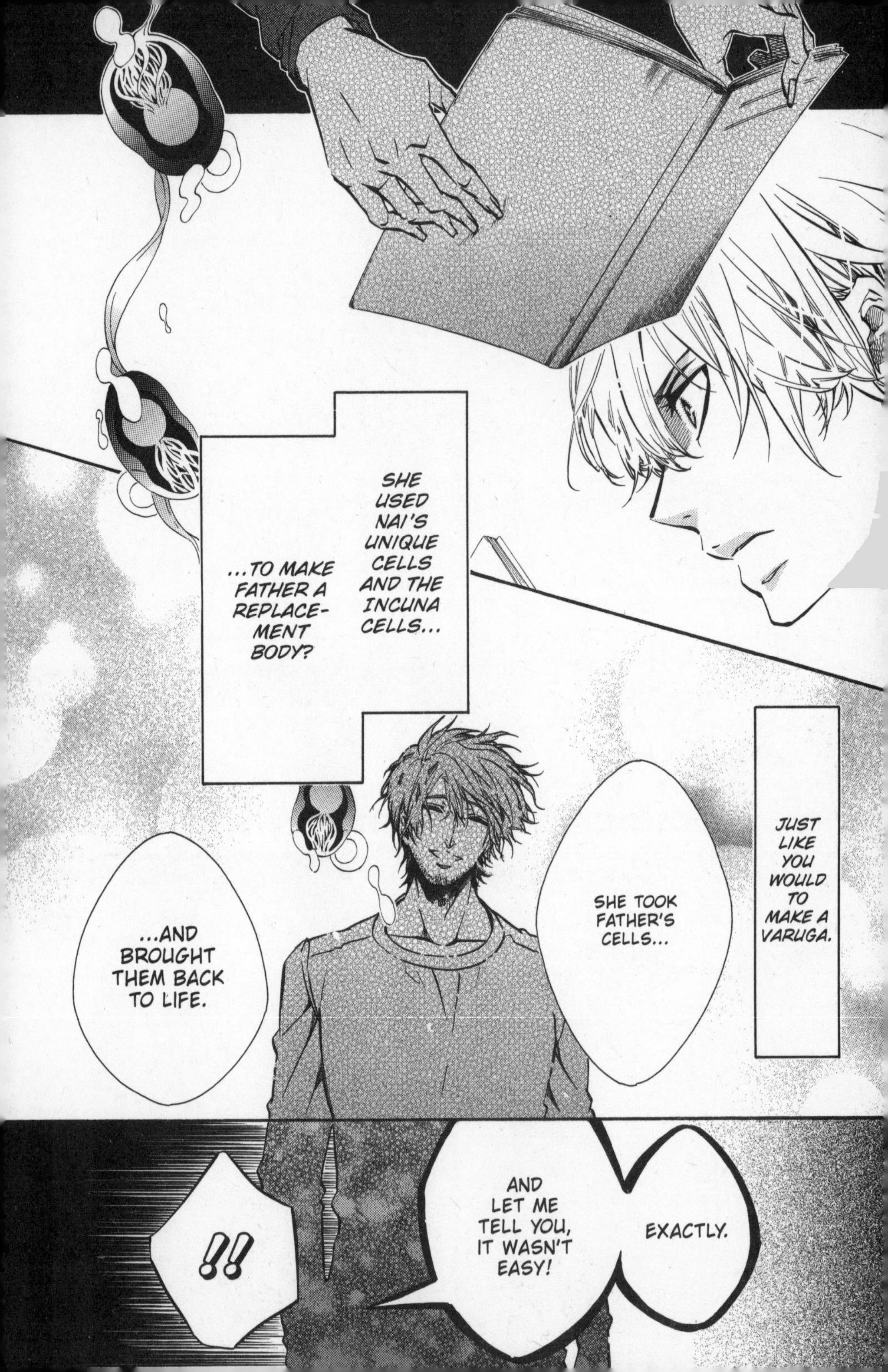
SHE USED NAI'S UNIQUE CELLS AND THE INCUNA CELLS...
...TO MAKE FATHER A REPLACEMENT BODY?
JUST LIKE YOU WOULD TO MAKE A VARUGA.
SHE TOOK FATHER'S CELLS...
...AND BROUGHT THEM BACK TO LIFE.
EXACTLY.
AND LET ME TELL YOU, IT WASN'T EASY!
!!

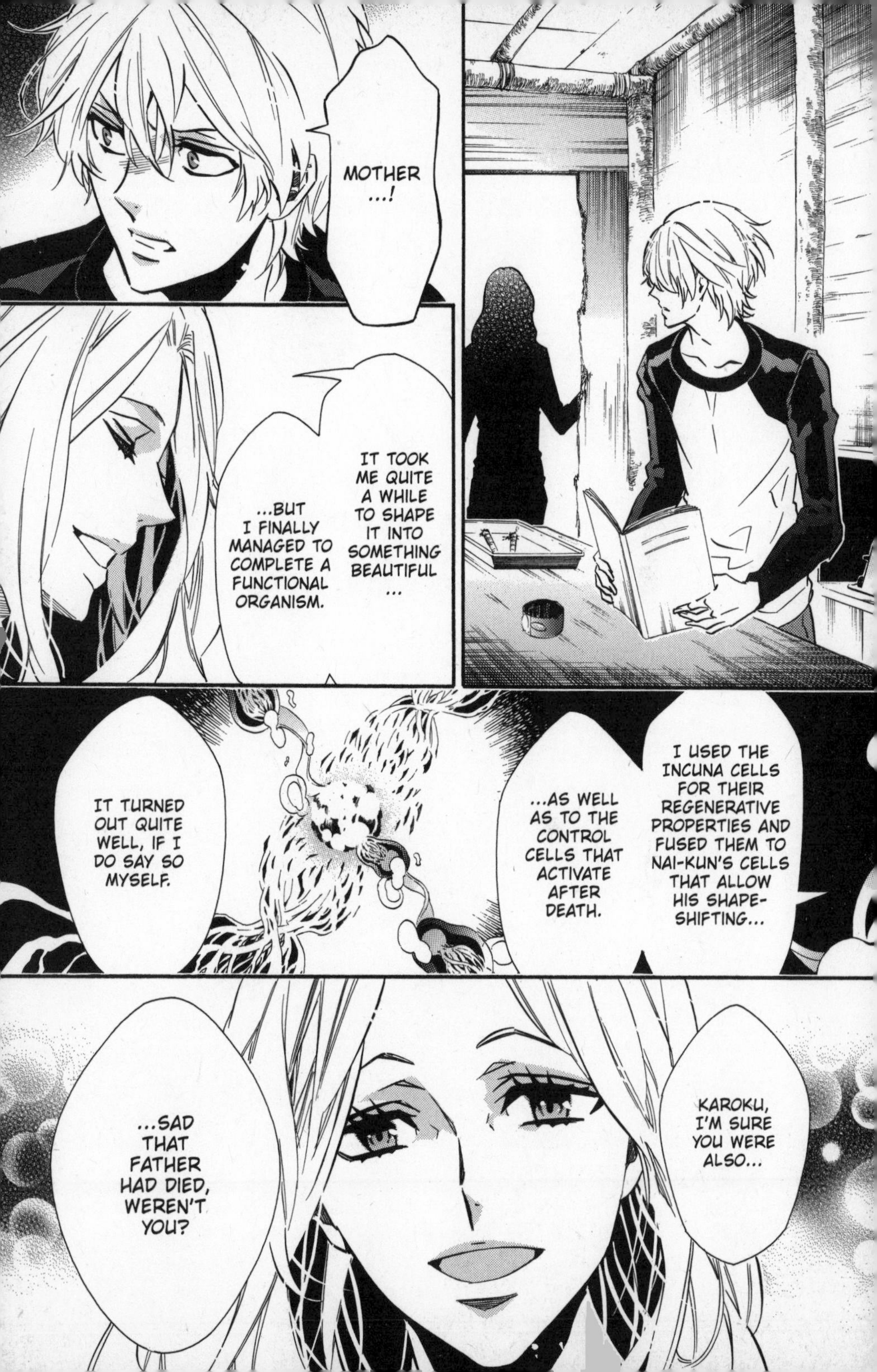
MOTHER ...!
IT TOOK ME QUITE A WHILE TO SHAPE IT INTO SOMETHING BEAUTIFUL ...
...BUT I FINALLY MANAGED TO COMPLETE A FUNCTIONAL ORGANISM.
I USED THE INCUNA CELLS FOR THEIR REGENERATIVE PROPERTIES AND FUSED THEM TO NAI-KUN'S CELLS THAT ALLOW HIS SHAPE-SHIFTING...
...AS WELL AS TO THE CONTROL CELLS THAT ACTIVATE AFTER DEATH.
IT TURNED OUT QUITE WELL, IF I DO SAY SO MYSELF.
KAROKU, I'M SURE YOU WERE ALSO...
...SAD THAT FATHER HAD DIED, WEREN'T YOU?

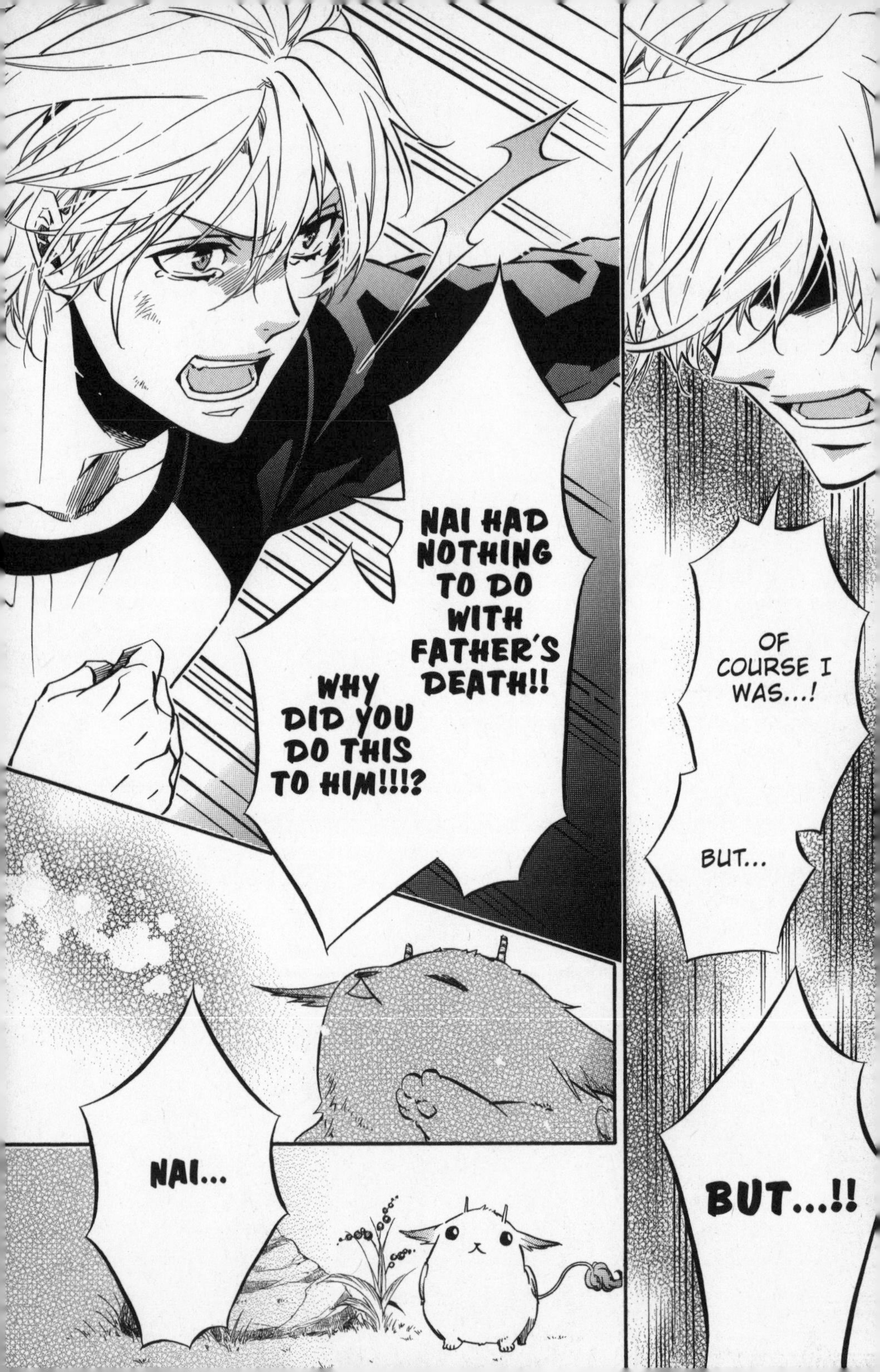
OF COURSE I WAS...!
BUT...
BUT...!!
NAI HAD NOTHING TO DO WITH FATHER'S DEATH!!
WHY DID YOU DO THIS TO HIM!!!?
NAI...

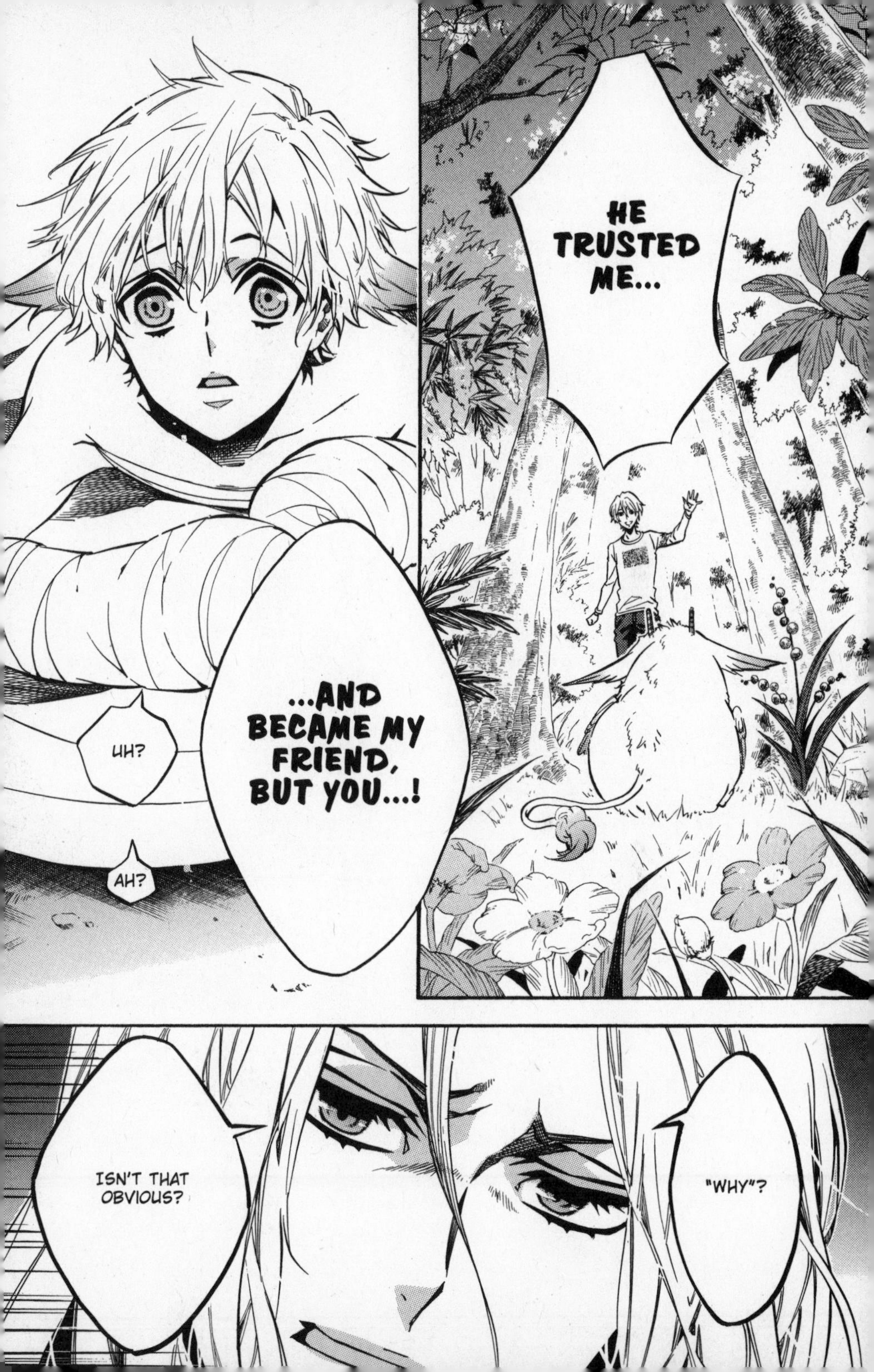
HE TRUSTED ME...
...AND BECAME MY FRIEND, BUT YOU...!
UH?
AH?
"WHY"?
ISN'T THAT OBVIOUS?

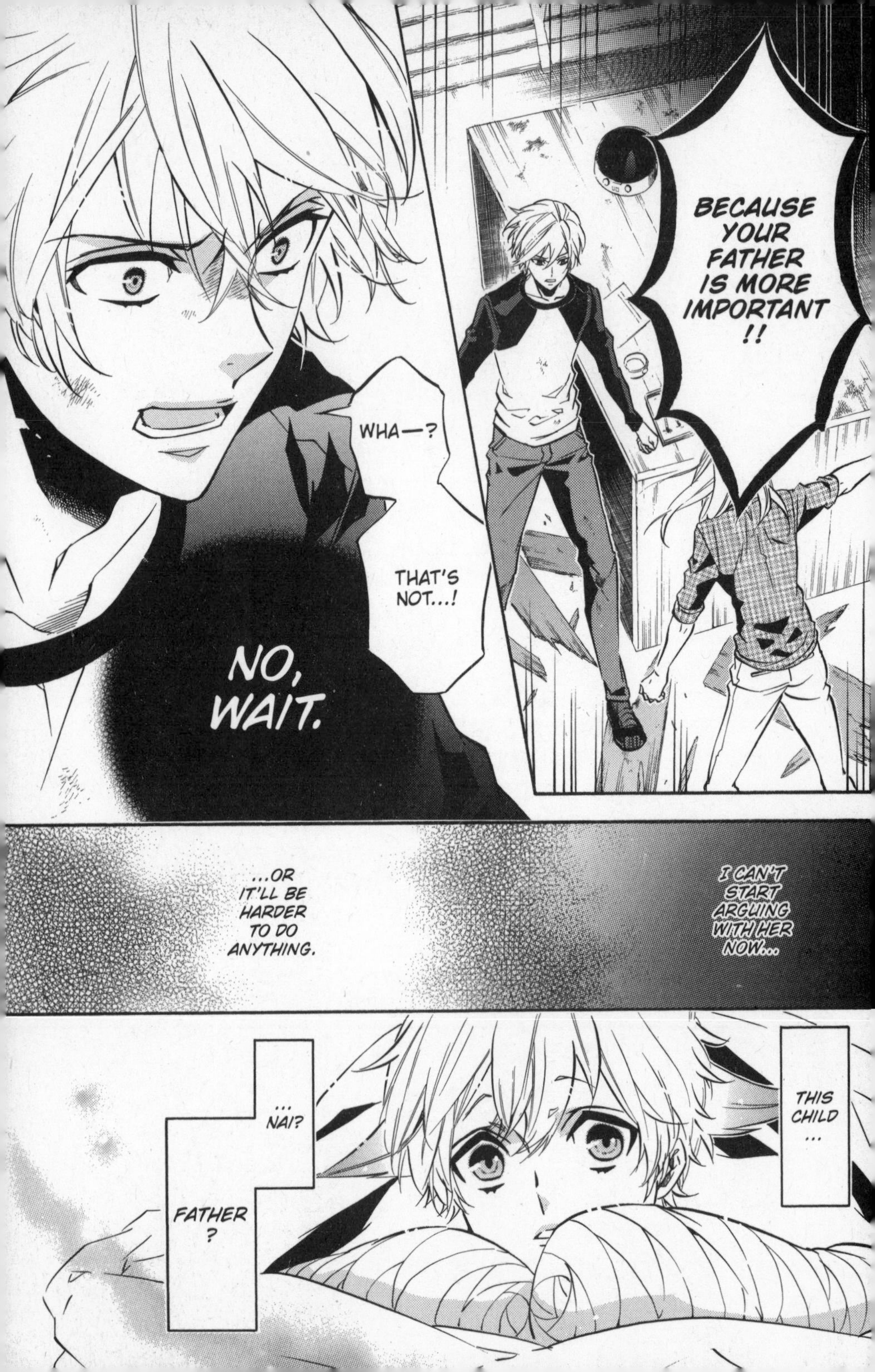
BECAUSE YOUR FATHER IS MORE IMPORTANT!!
WHA—?
THAT'S NOT...!
NO, WAIT.
I CAN'T START ARGUING WITH HER NOW...
...OR IT'LL BE HARDER TO DO ANYTHING.
THIS CHILD...
...NAI?
FATHER?

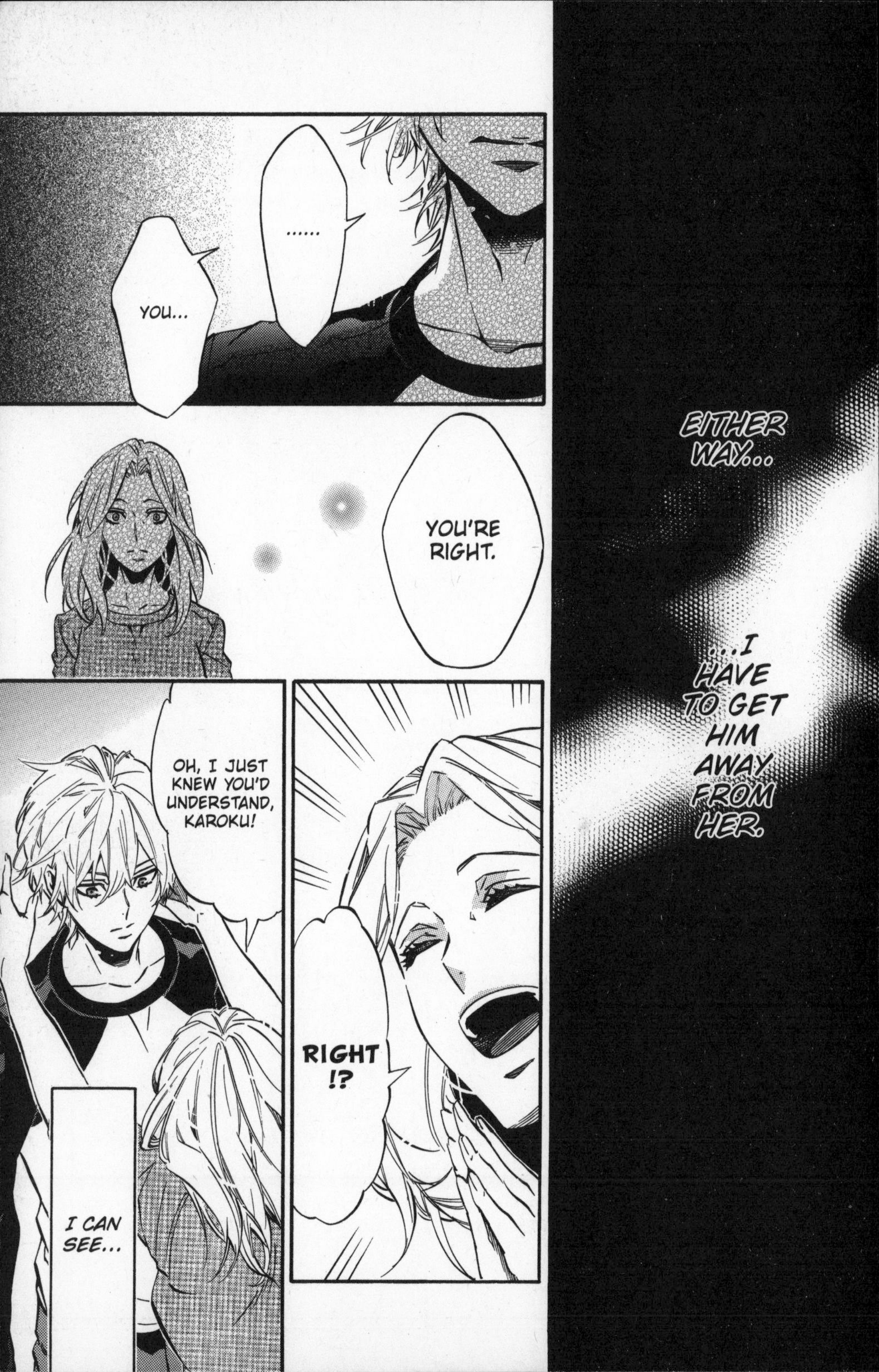
EITHER WAY...
...I HAVE TO GET HIM AWAY FROM HER.
......
YOU...
YOU'RE RIGHT.
RIGHT !?
OH, I JUST KNEW YOU'D UNDERSTAND, KAROKU!
I CAN SEE...

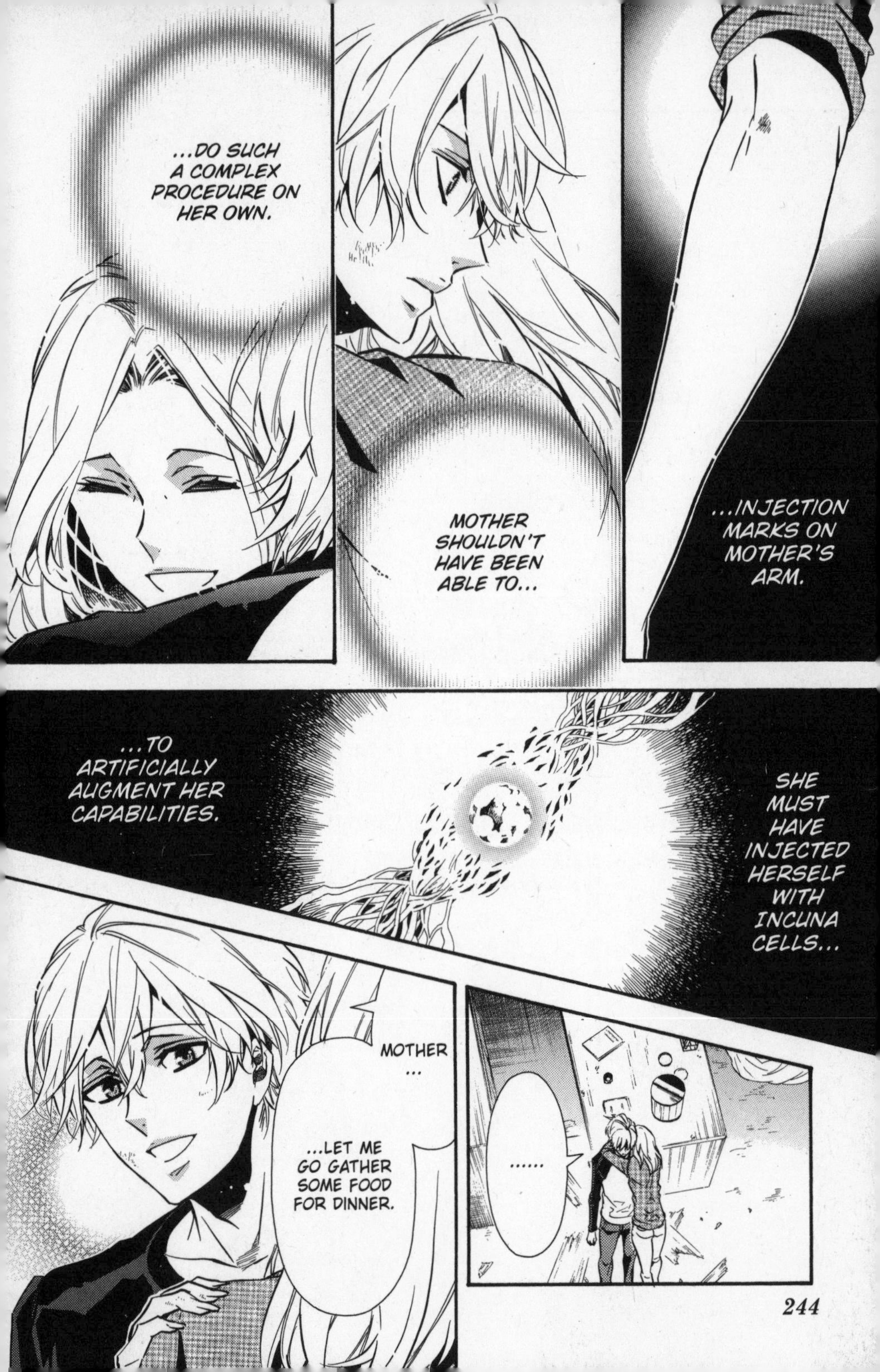
...INJECTION MARKS ON MOTHER'S ARM.
MOTHER SHOULDN'T HAVE BEEN ABLE TO...
...DO SUCH A COMPLEX PROCEDURE ON HER OWN.
SHE MUST HAVE INJECTED HERSELF WITH INCUNA CELLS...
...TO ARTIFICIALLY AUGMENT HER CAPABILITIES.
......
MOTHER ...
...LET ME GO GATHER SOME FOOD FOR DINNER.

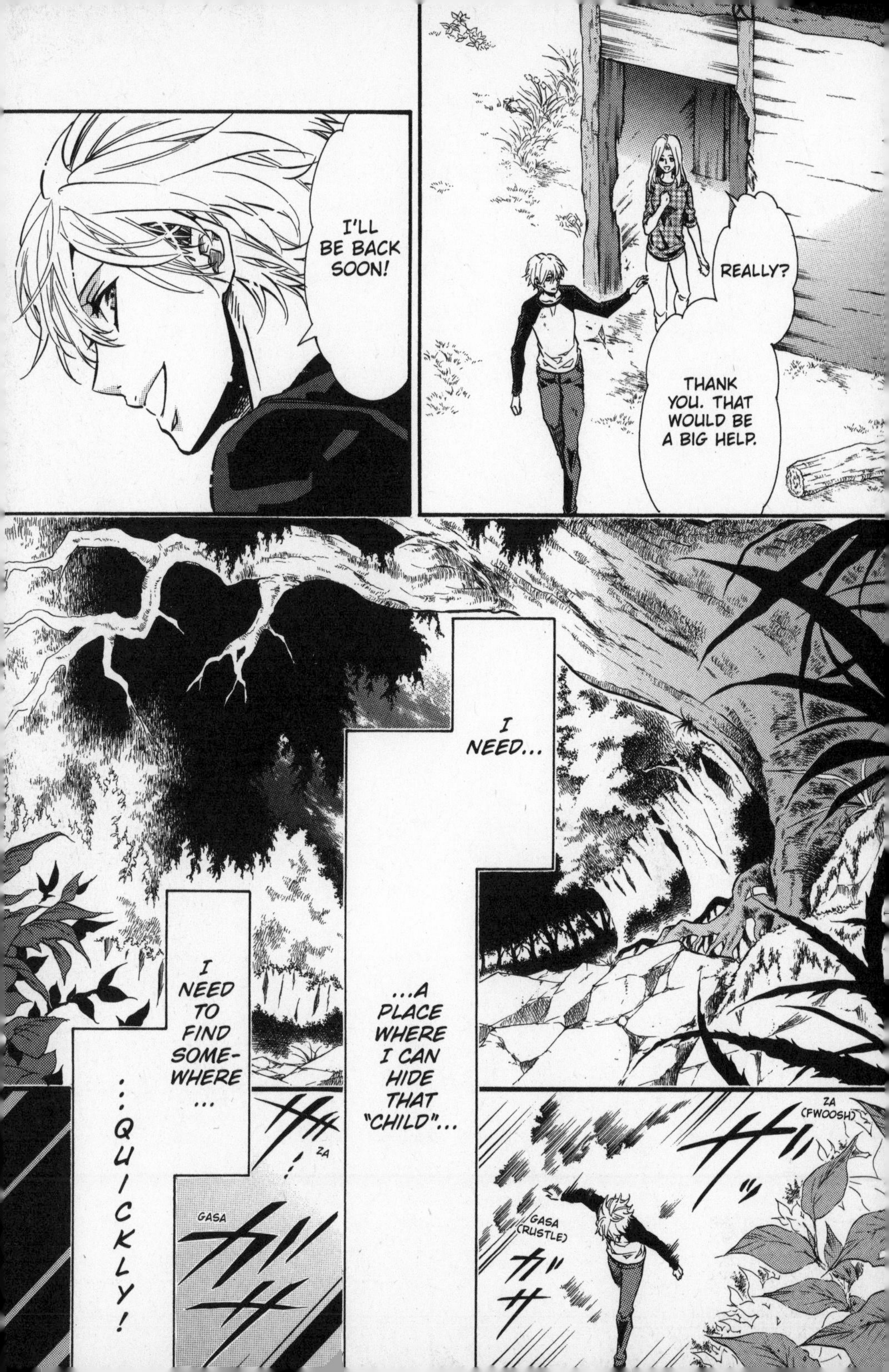
REALLY?
THANK YOU. THAT WOULD BE A BIG HELP.
I'LL BE BACK SOON!
I NEED...
...A PLACE WHERE I CAN HIDE THAT "CHILD"...
I NEED TO FIND SOME-WHERE...
...QUICKLY!
ZA (FWOOSH)
GASA (RUSTLE)
ZA
GASA

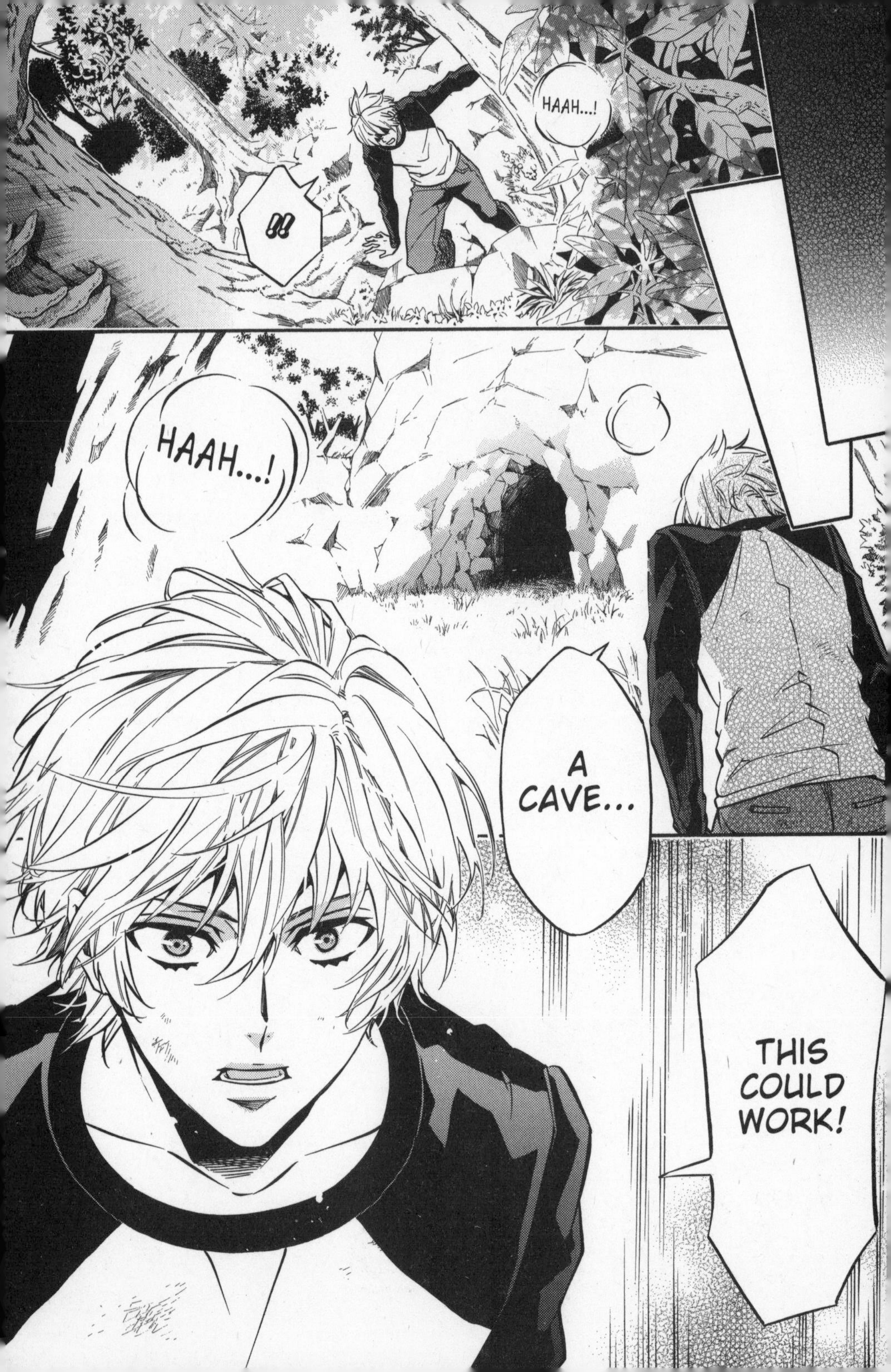
HAAH...!
!!
HAAH...!
A CAVE...
THIS COULD WORK!

KARNEVAL

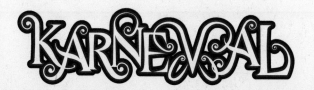

KARNEVAL

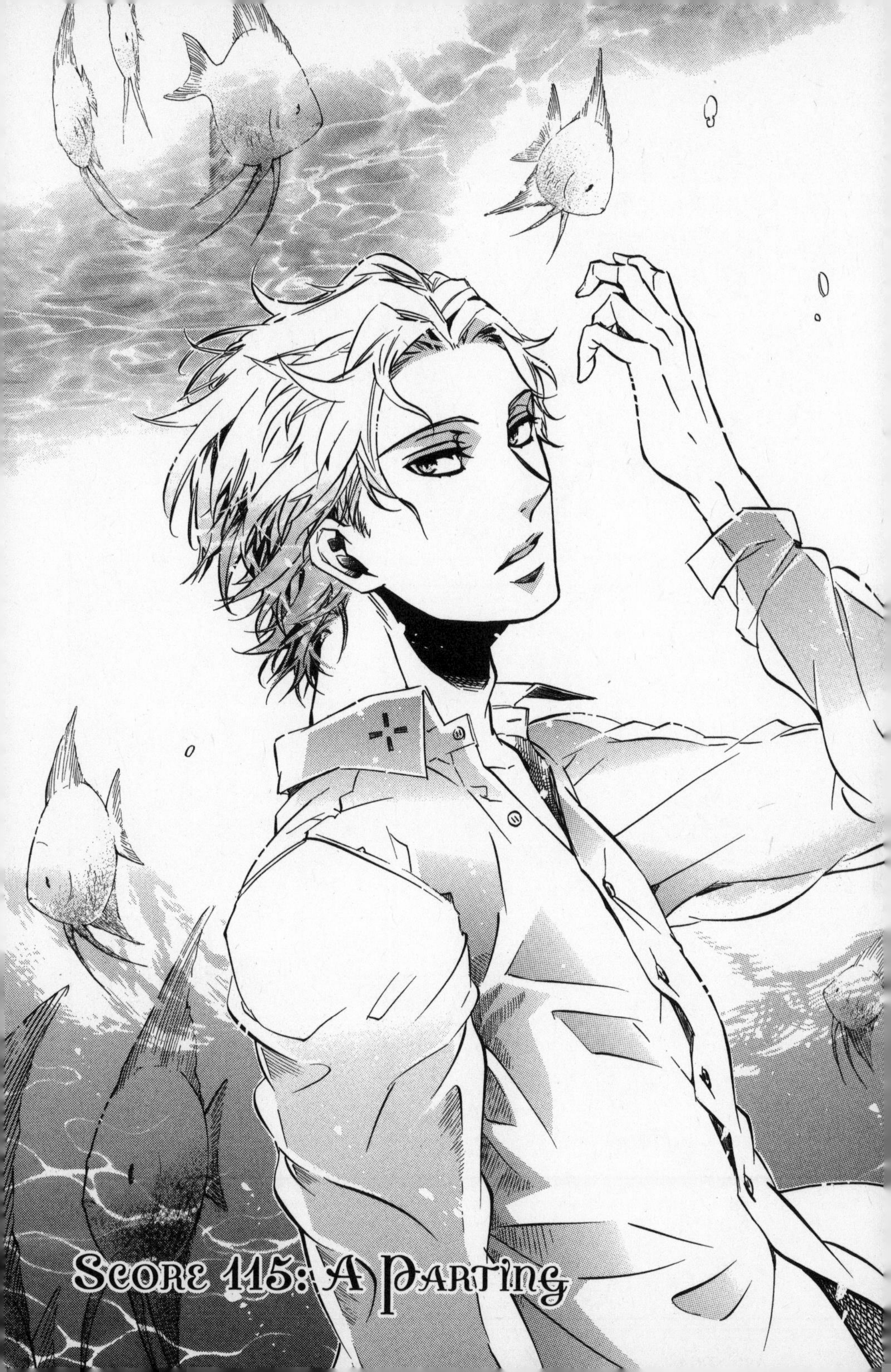
Score 115: A Parting

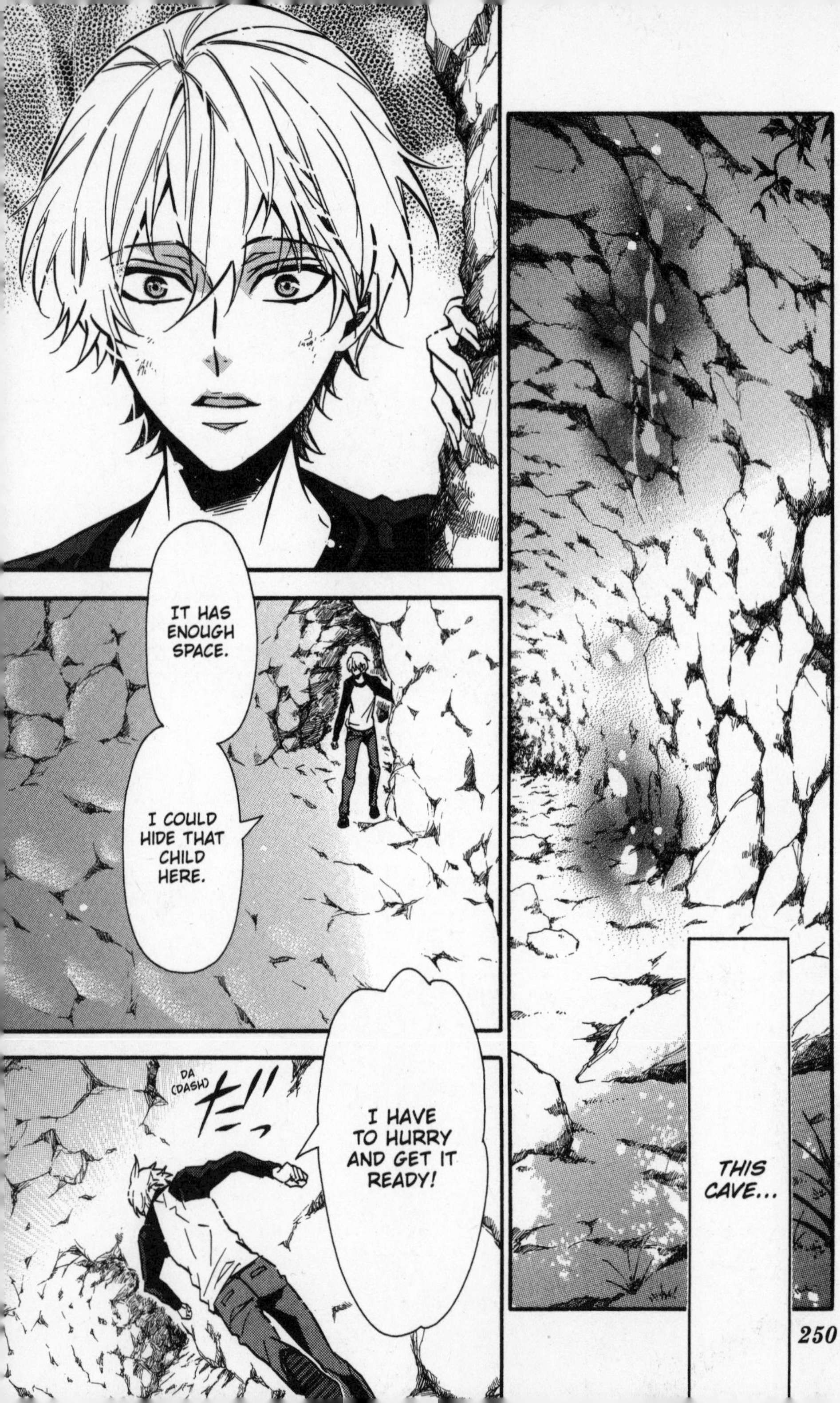
THIS CAVE...
IT HAS ENOUGH SPACE.
I COULD HIDE THAT CHILD HERE.
I HAVE TO HURRY AND GET IT READY!
DA (DASH)

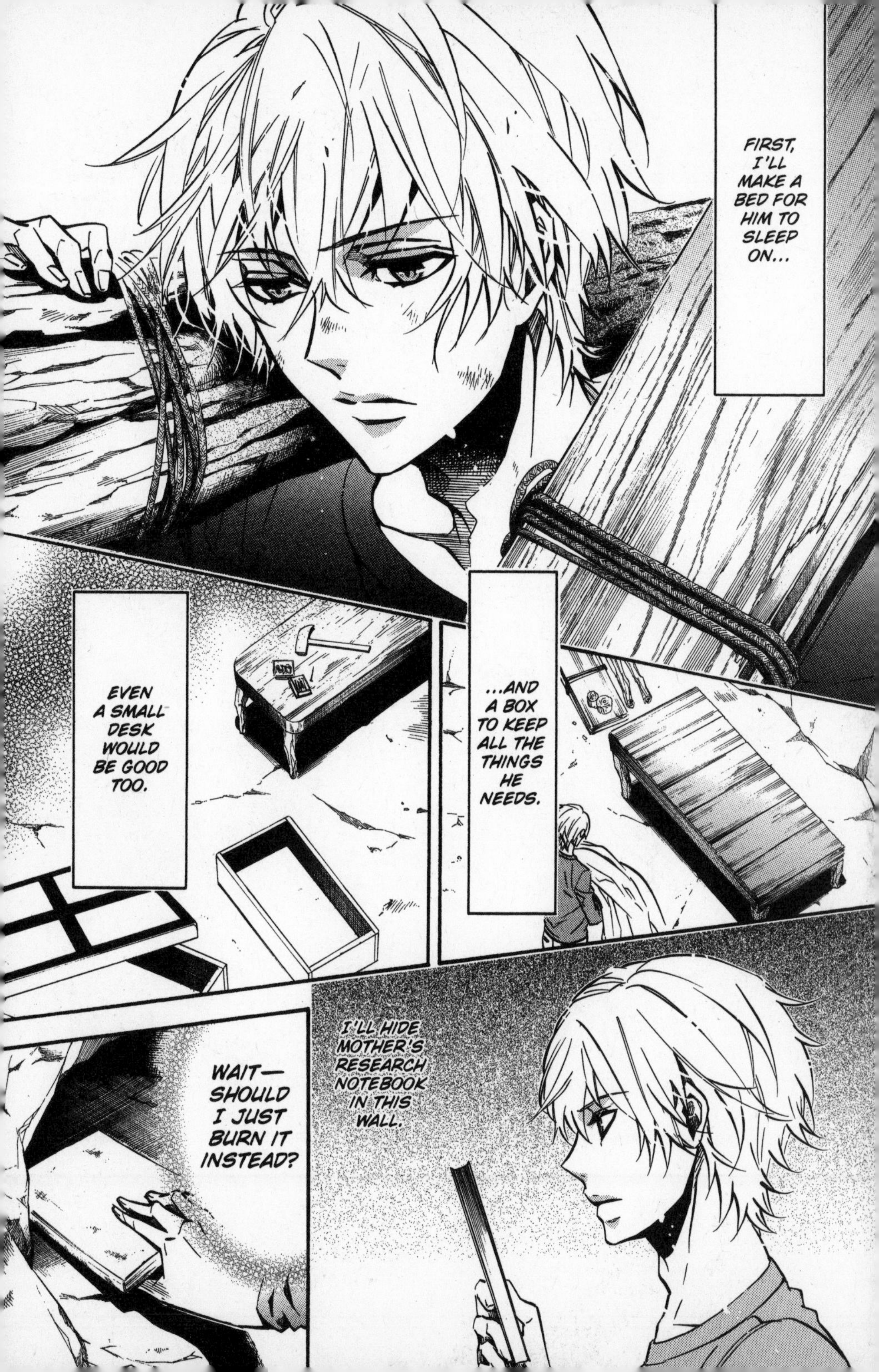
FIRST, I'LL MAKE A BED FOR HIM TO SLEEP ON...
...AND A BOX TO KEEP ALL THE THINGS HE NEEDS.
EVEN A SMALL DESK WOULD BE GOOD TOO.
I'LL HIDE MOTHER'S RESEARCH NOTEBOOK IN THIS WALL.
WAIT—SHOULD I JUST BURN IT INSTEAD?

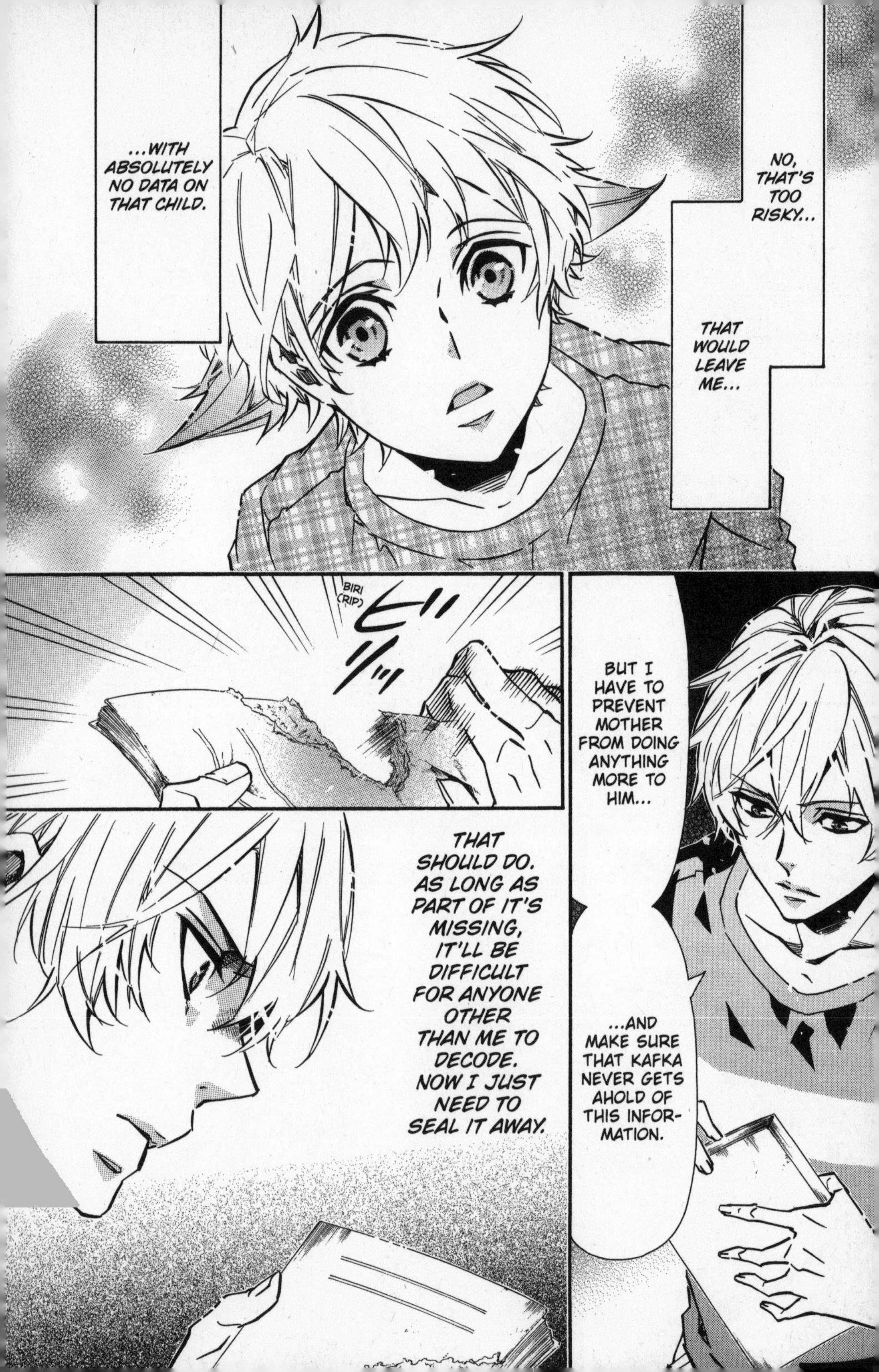
NO, THAT'S TOO RISKY...
THAT WOULD LEAVE ME...
...WITH ABSOLUTELY NO DATA ON THAT CHILD.
BUT I HAVE TO PREVENT MOTHER FROM DOING ANYTHING MORE TO HIM...
...AND MAKE SURE THAT KAFKA NEVER GETS AHOLD OF THIS INFORMATION.
BIRI (RIP)
THAT SHOULD DO. AS LONG AS PART OF IT'S MISSING, IT'LL BE DIFFICULT FOR ANYONE OTHER THAN ME TO DECODE. NOW I JUST NEED TO SEAL IT AWAY.

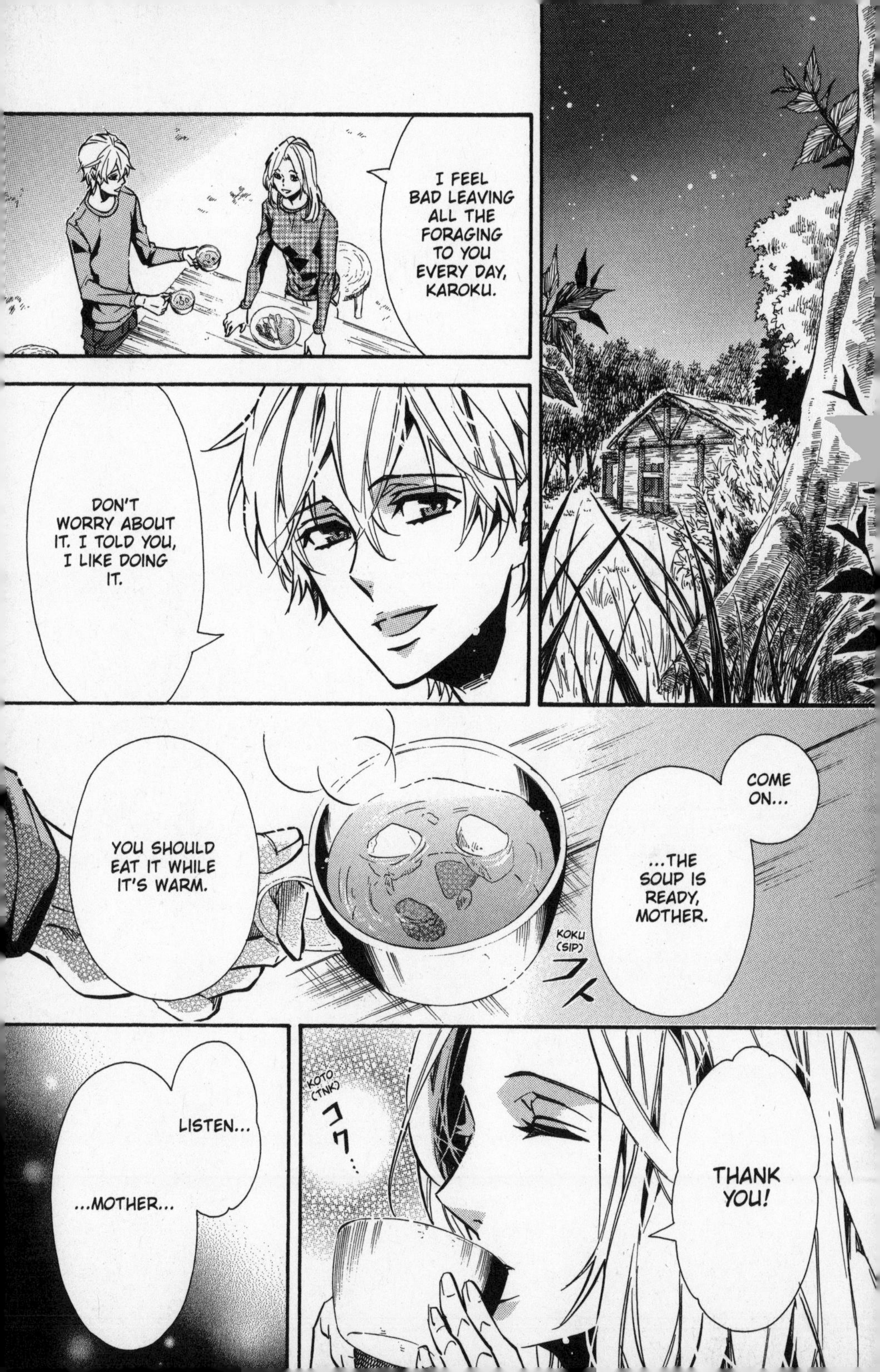
I FEEL BAD LEAVING ALL THE FORAGING TO YOU EVERY DAY, KAROKU.
DON'T WORRY ABOUT IT. I TOLD YOU, I LIKE DOING IT.
COME ON...
...THE SOUP IS READY, MOTHER.
KOKU (SIP)
コト
YOU SHOULD EAT IT WHILE IT'S WARM.
THANK YOU!
KOTO (TNK)
コク...
LISTEN...
...MOTHER...

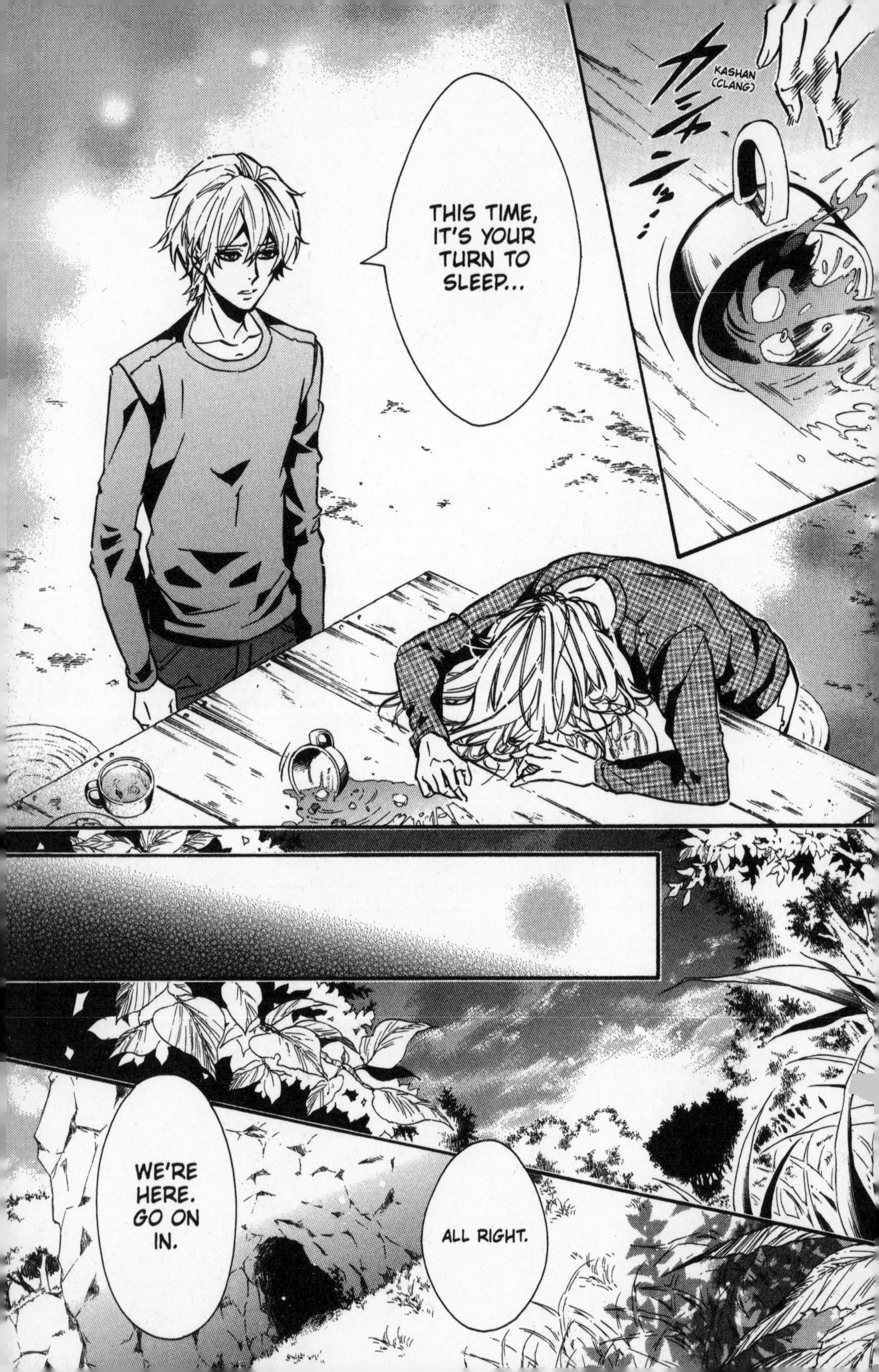
KASHAN (CLANG)
THIS TIME, IT'S YOUR TURN TO SLEEP...
WE'RE HERE. GO ON IN.
ALL RIGHT.

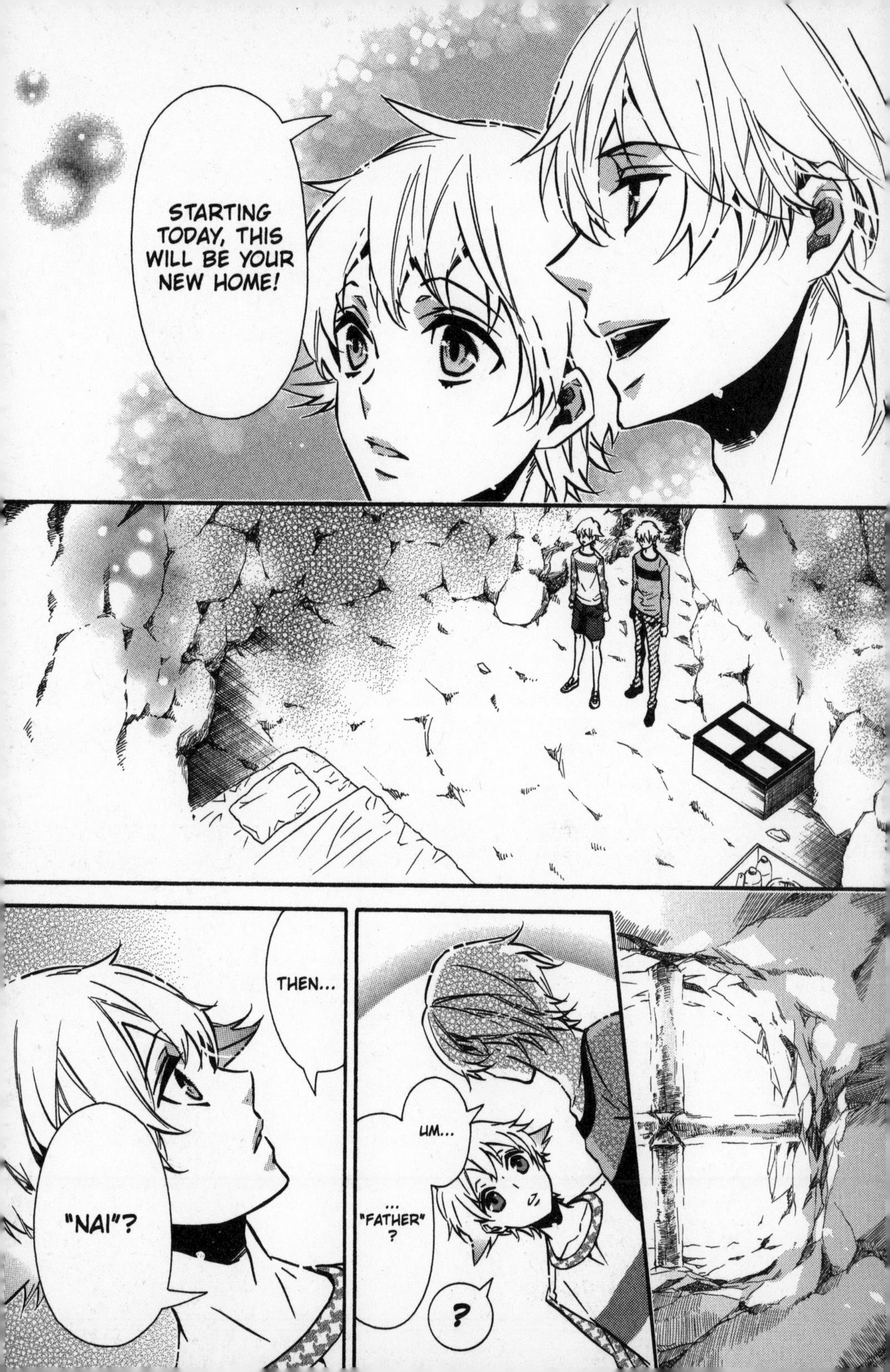
STARTING TODAY, THIS WILL BE YOUR NEW HOME!
UM...
... "FATHER"?
?
THEN...
"NAI"?

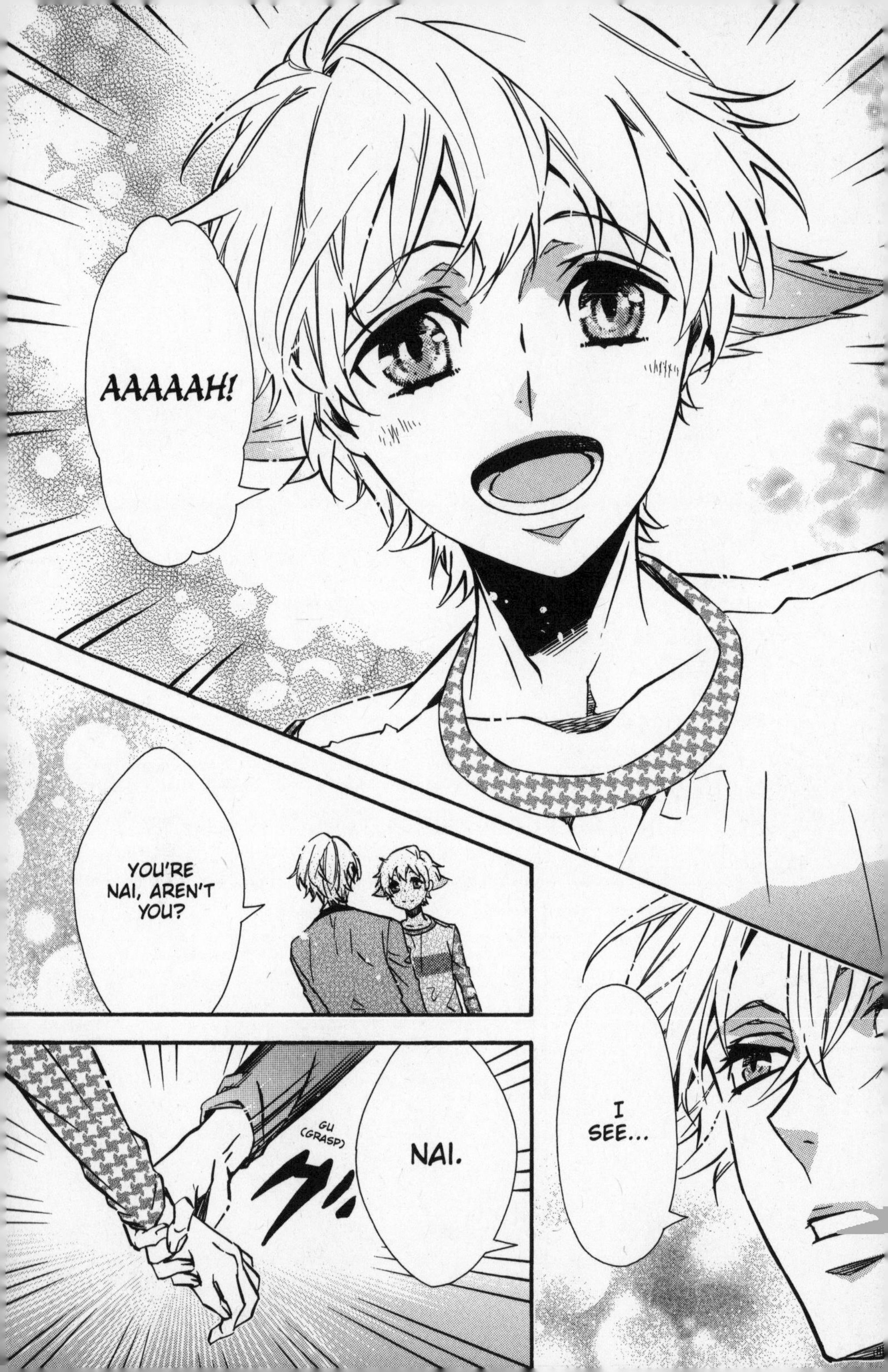
AAAAAH!
I SEE...
YOU'RE NAI, AREN'T YOU?
NAI.
GU (GRASP)

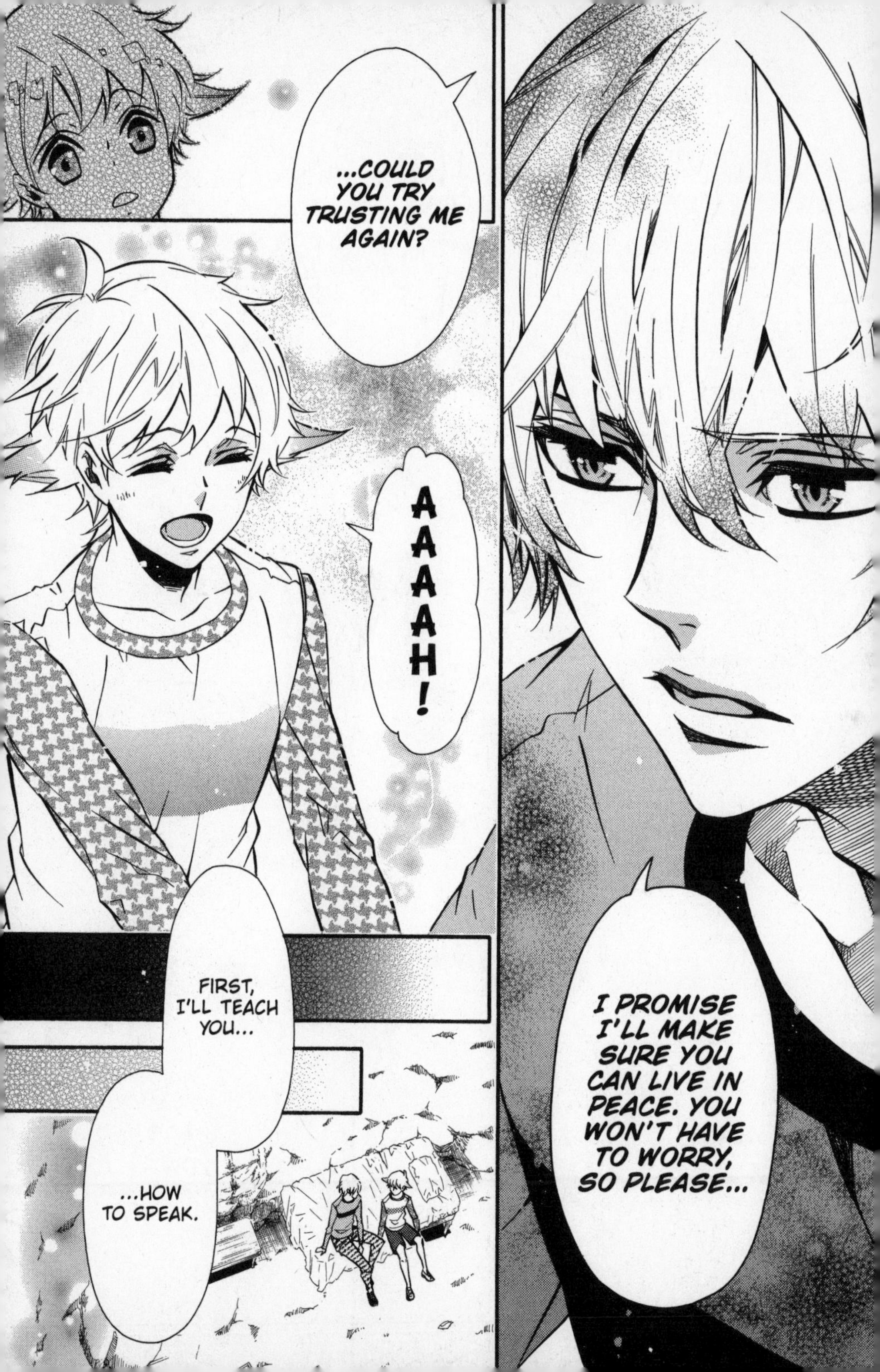
I PROMISE I'LL MAKE SURE YOU CAN LIVE IN PEACE. YOU WON'T HAVE TO WORRY, SO PLEASE...
...COULD YOU TRY TRUSTING ME AGAIN?
AAAAAH!
FIRST, I'LL TEACH YOU...
...HOW TO SPEAK.

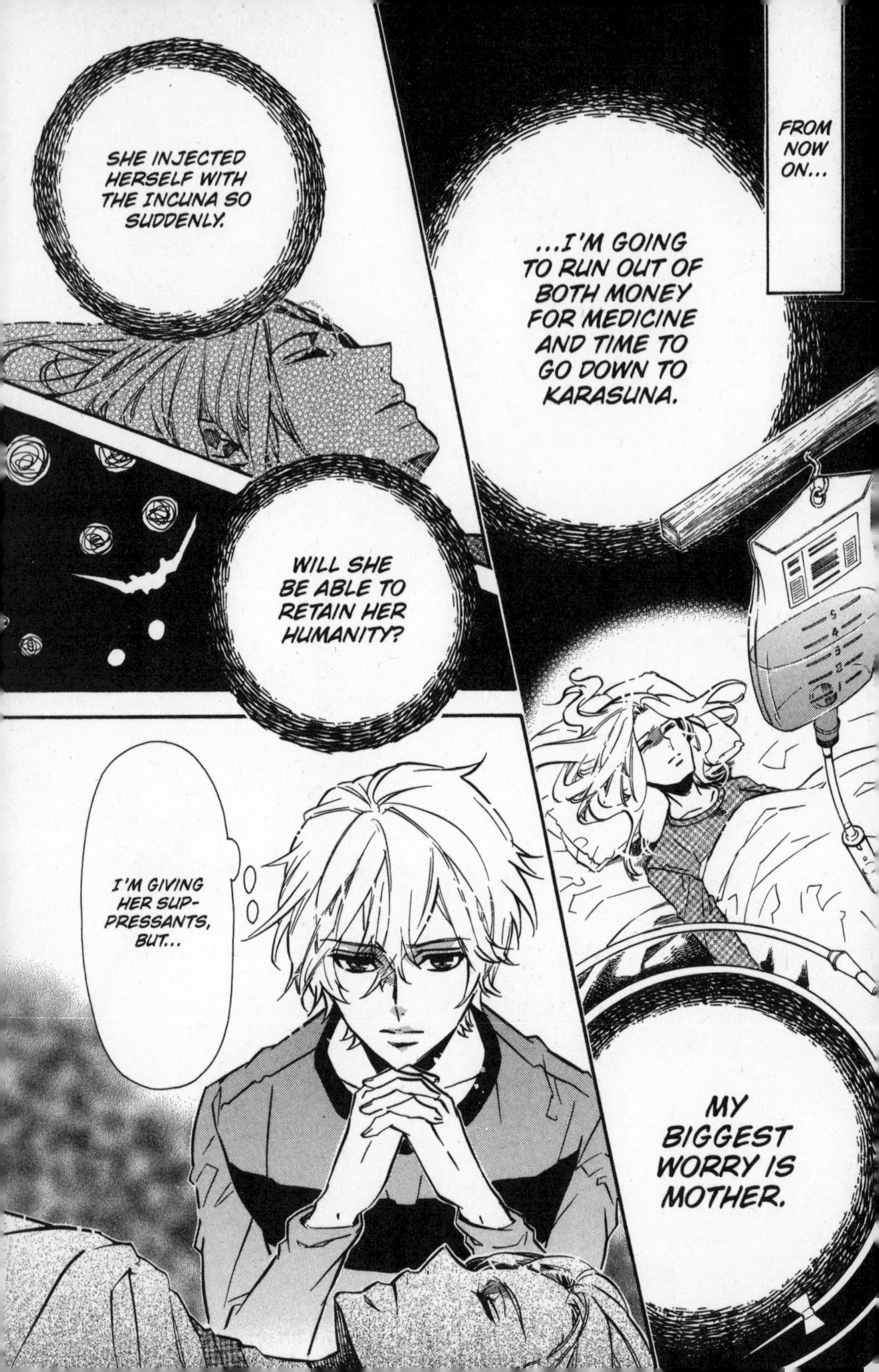
FROM NOW ON...
...I'M GOING TO RUN OUT OF BOTH MONEY FOR MEDICINE AND TIME TO GO DOWN TO KARASUNA.
MY BIGGEST WORRY IS MOTHER.
SHE INJECTED HERSELF WITH THE INCUNA SO SUDDENLY.
WILL SHE BE ABLE TO RETAIN HER HUMANITY?
I'M GIVING HER SUP-PRESSANTS, BUT...

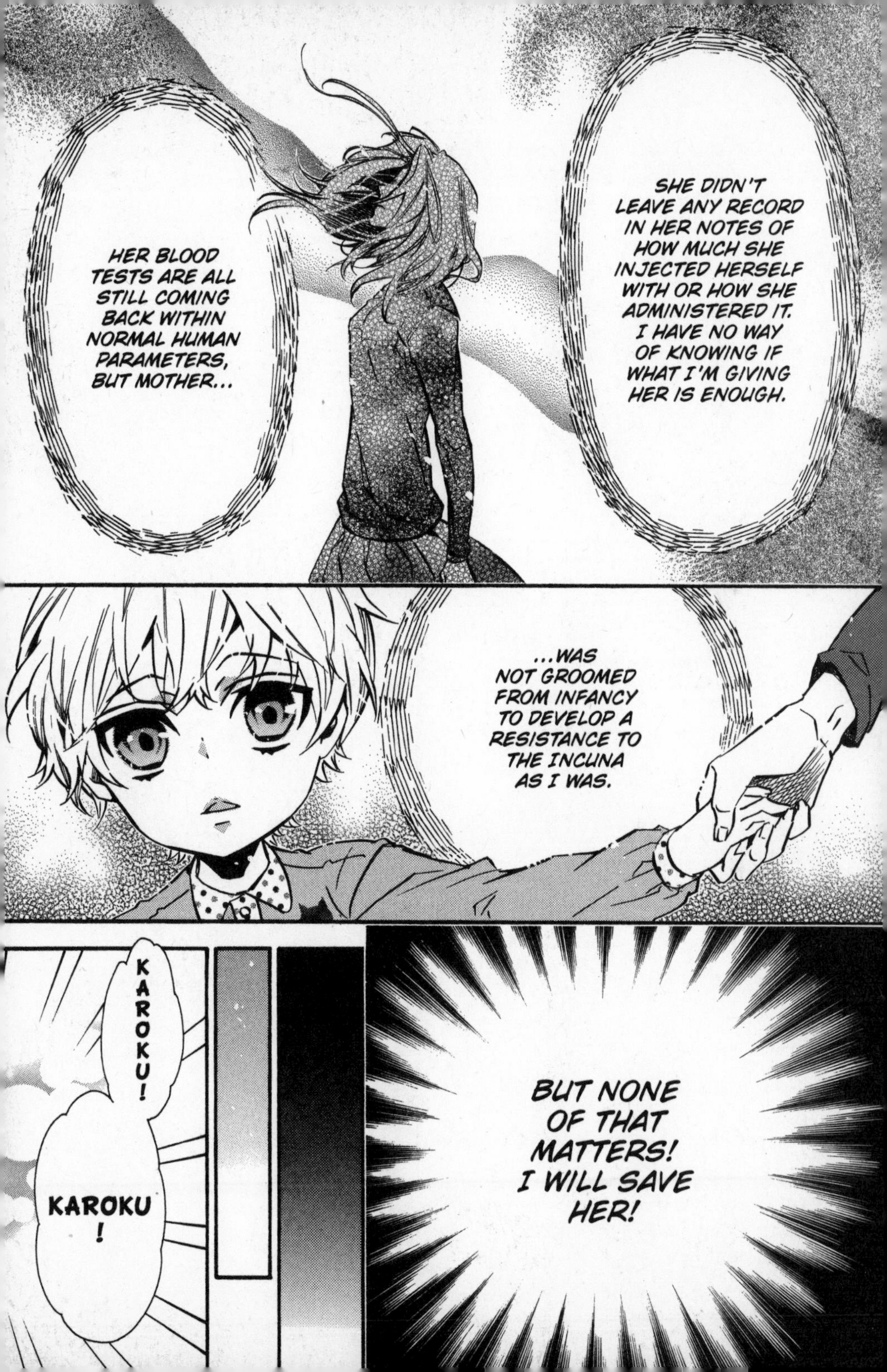
SHE DIDN'T LEAVE ANY RECORD IN HER NOTES OF HOW MUCH SHE INJECTED HERSELF WITH OR HOW SHE ADMINISTERED IT. I HAVE NO WAY OF KNOWING IF WHAT I'M GIVING HER IS ENOUGH.
HER BLOOD TESTS ARE ALL STILL COMING BACK WITHIN NORMAL HUMAN PARAMETERS, BUT MOTHER...
...WAS NOT GROOMED FROM INFANCY TO DEVELOP A RESISTANCE TO THE INCUNA AS I WAS.
BUT NONE OF THAT MATTERS! I WILL SAVE HER!
KAROKU!
KAROKU!

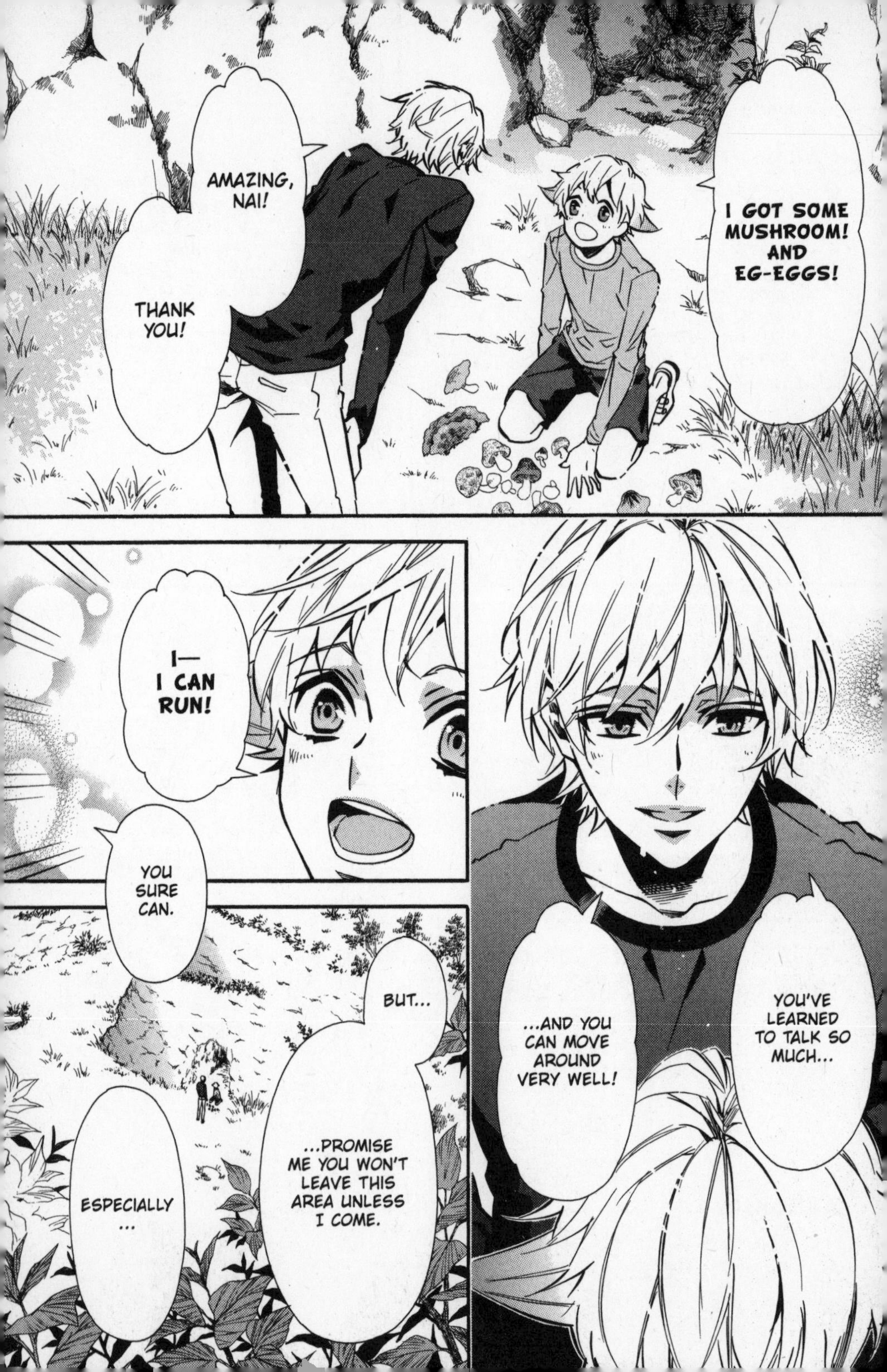
I GOT SOME MUSHROOM! AND EG-EGGS!
AMAZING, NAI!
THANK YOU!
YOU'VE LEARNED TO TALK SO MUCH...
...AND YOU CAN MOVE AROUND VERY WELL!
I— I CAN RUN!
YOU SURE CAN.
BUT...
...PROMISE ME YOU WON'T LEAVE THIS AREA UNLESS I COME.
ESPECIALLY ...

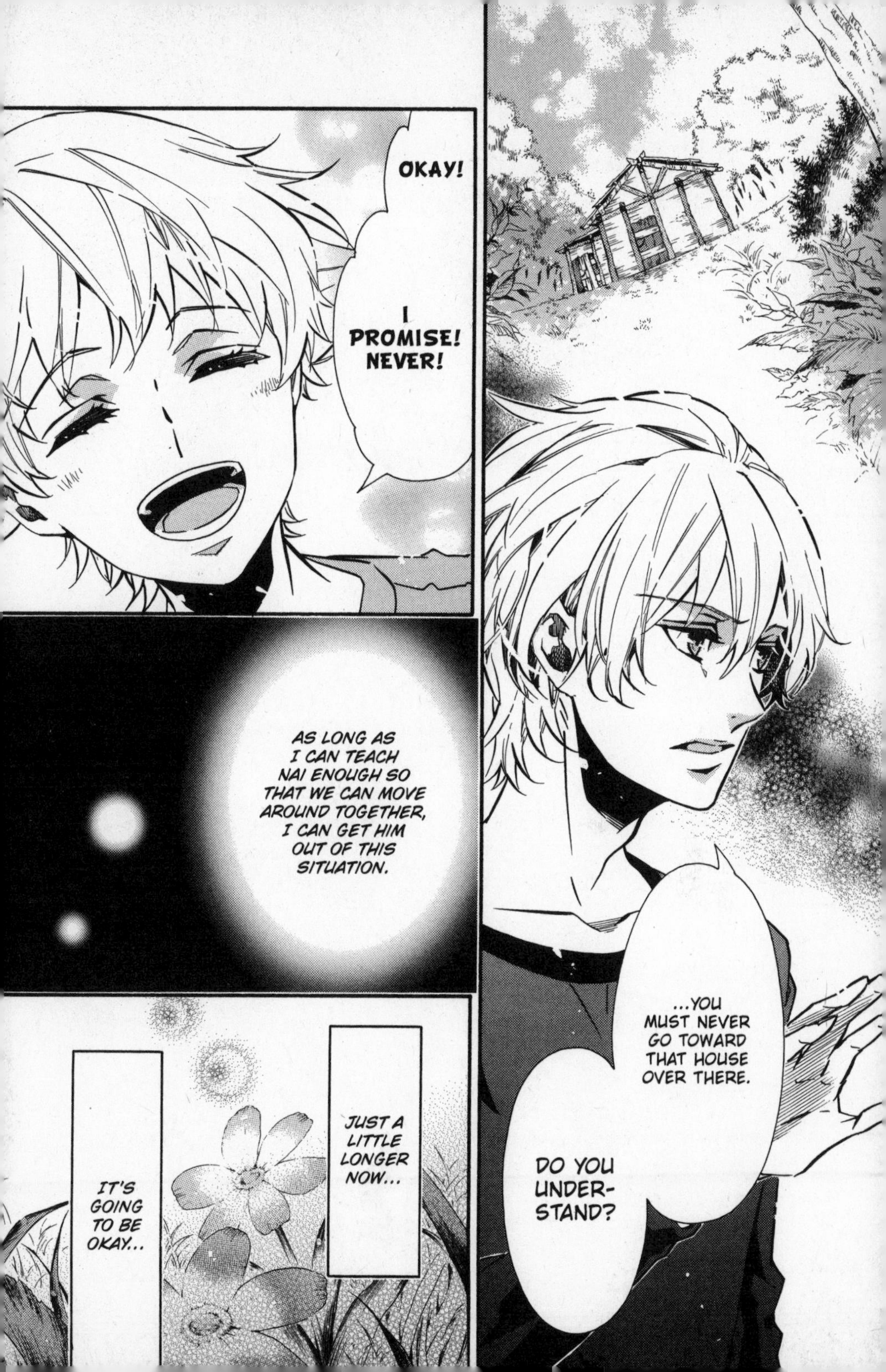
...YOU MUST NEVER GO TOWARD THAT HOUSE OVER THERE.
DO YOU UNDER-STAND?
OKAY!
I PROMISE! NEVER!
AS LONG AS I CAN TEACH NAI ENOUGH SO THAT WE CAN MOVE AROUND TOGETHER, I CAN GET HIM OUT OF THIS SITUATION.
JUST A LITTLE LONGER NOW...
IT'S GOING TO BE OKAY...

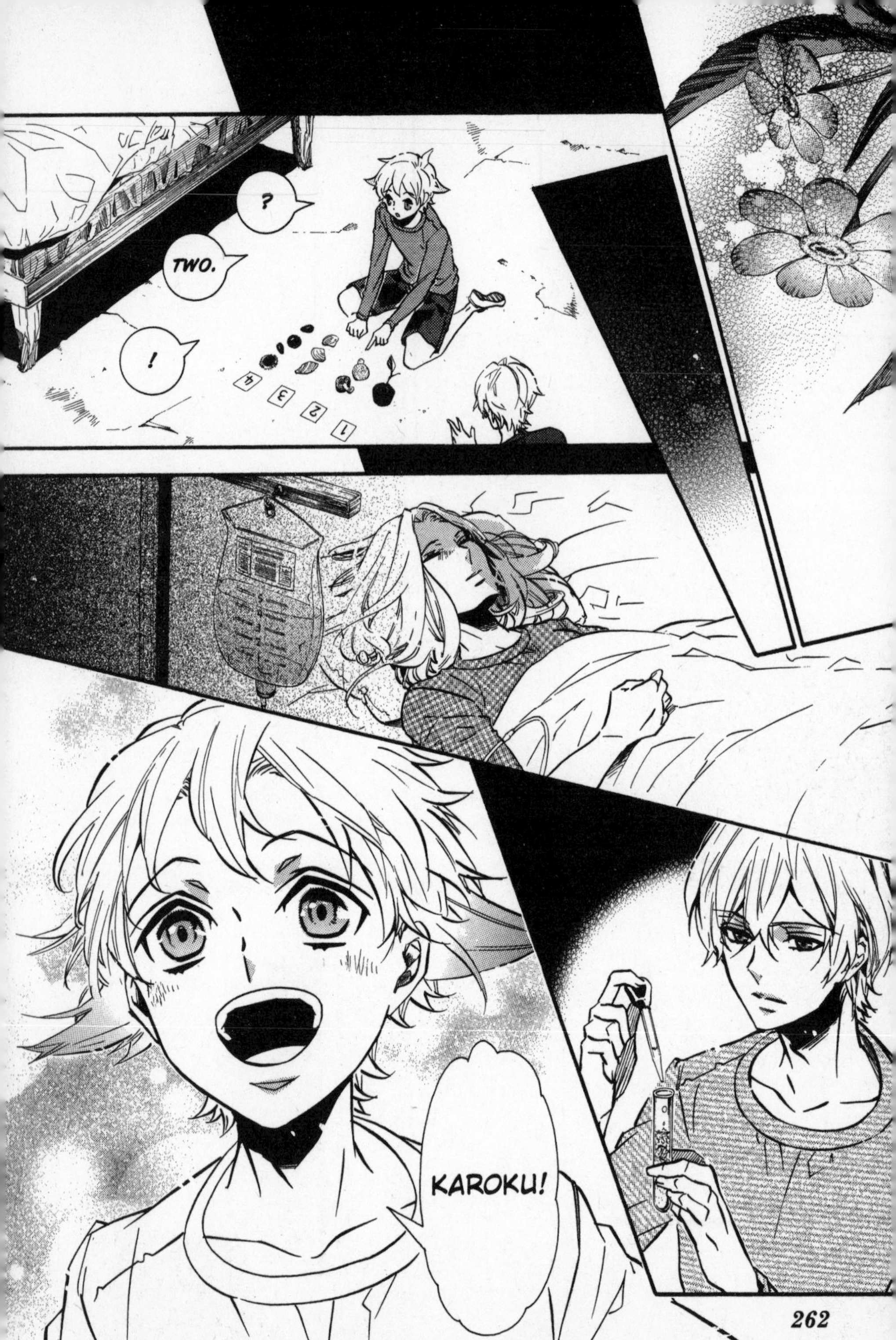
?
TWO.
!
KAROKU!

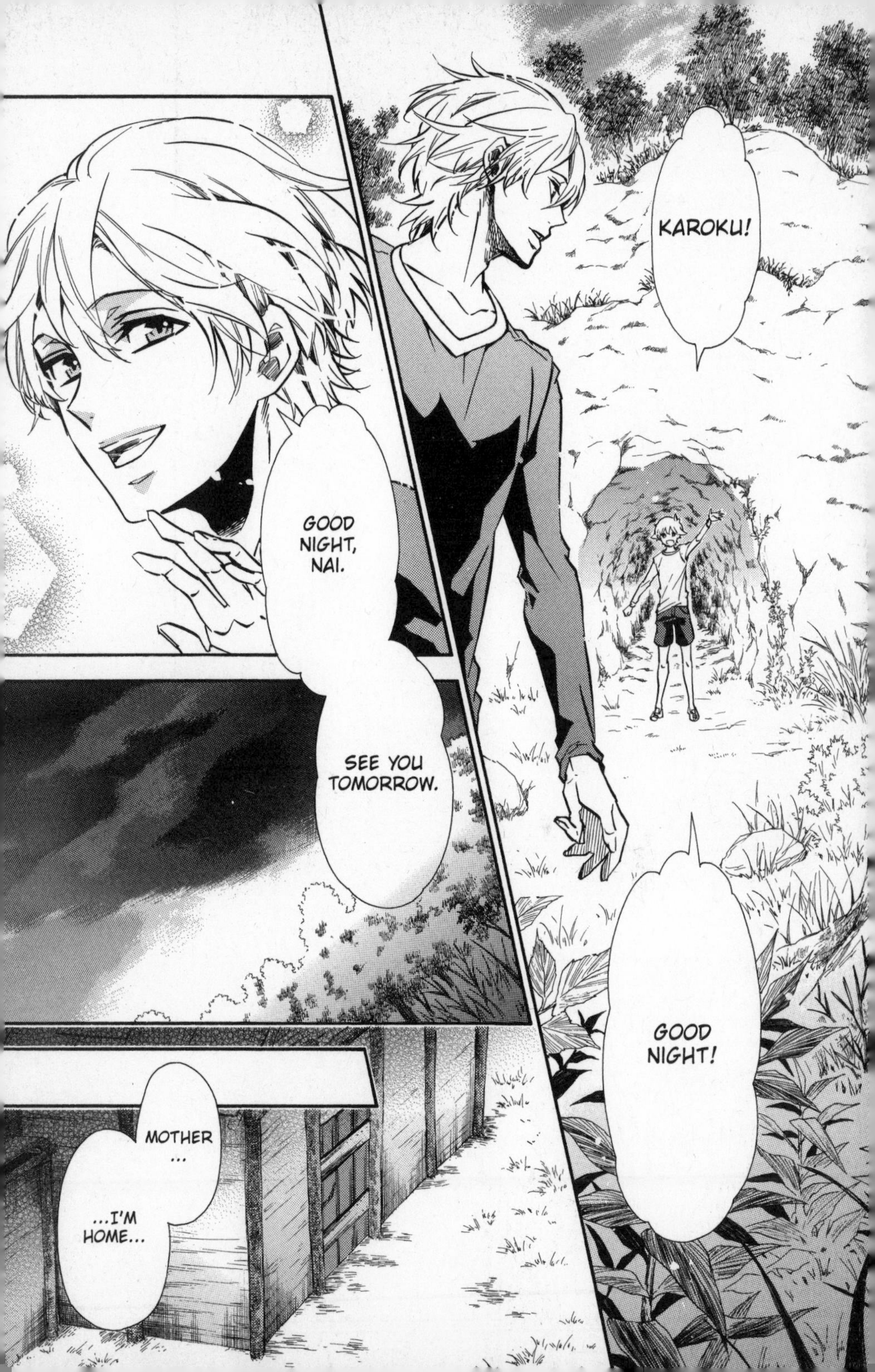
KAROKU!
GOOD NIGHT!
GOOD NIGHT, NAI.
SEE YOU TOMORROW.
MOTHER ...
...I'M HOME...

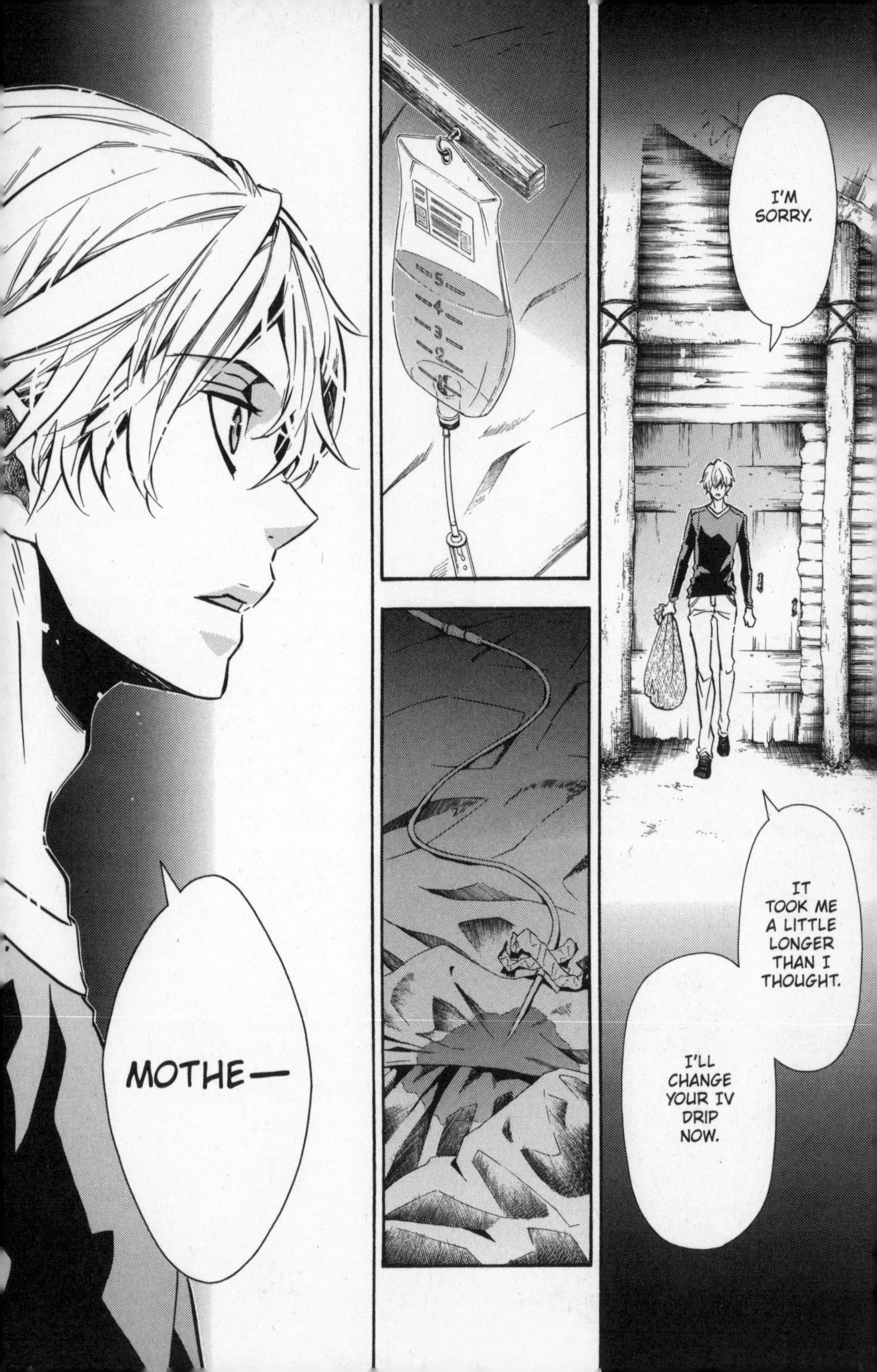
I'M SORRY.
IT TOOK ME A LITTLE LONGER THAN I THOUGHT.
I'LL CHANGE YOUR IV DRIP NOW.
MOTHE—

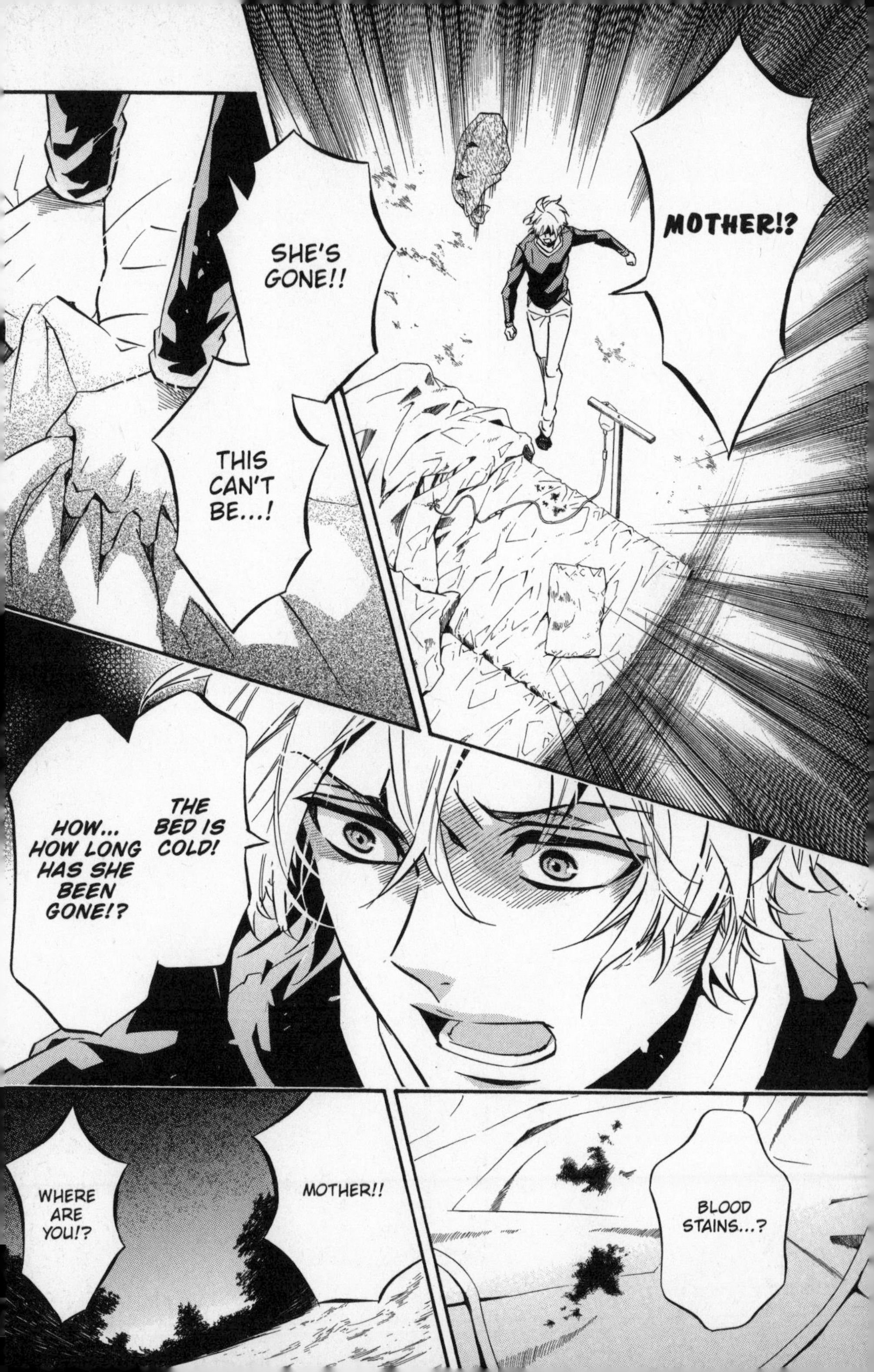
MOTHER!?
SHE'S GONE!!
THIS CAN'T BE...!
THE BED IS COLD!
HOW... HOW LONG HAS SHE BEEN GONE!?
BLOOD STAINS...?
MOTHER!!
WHERE ARE YOU!?

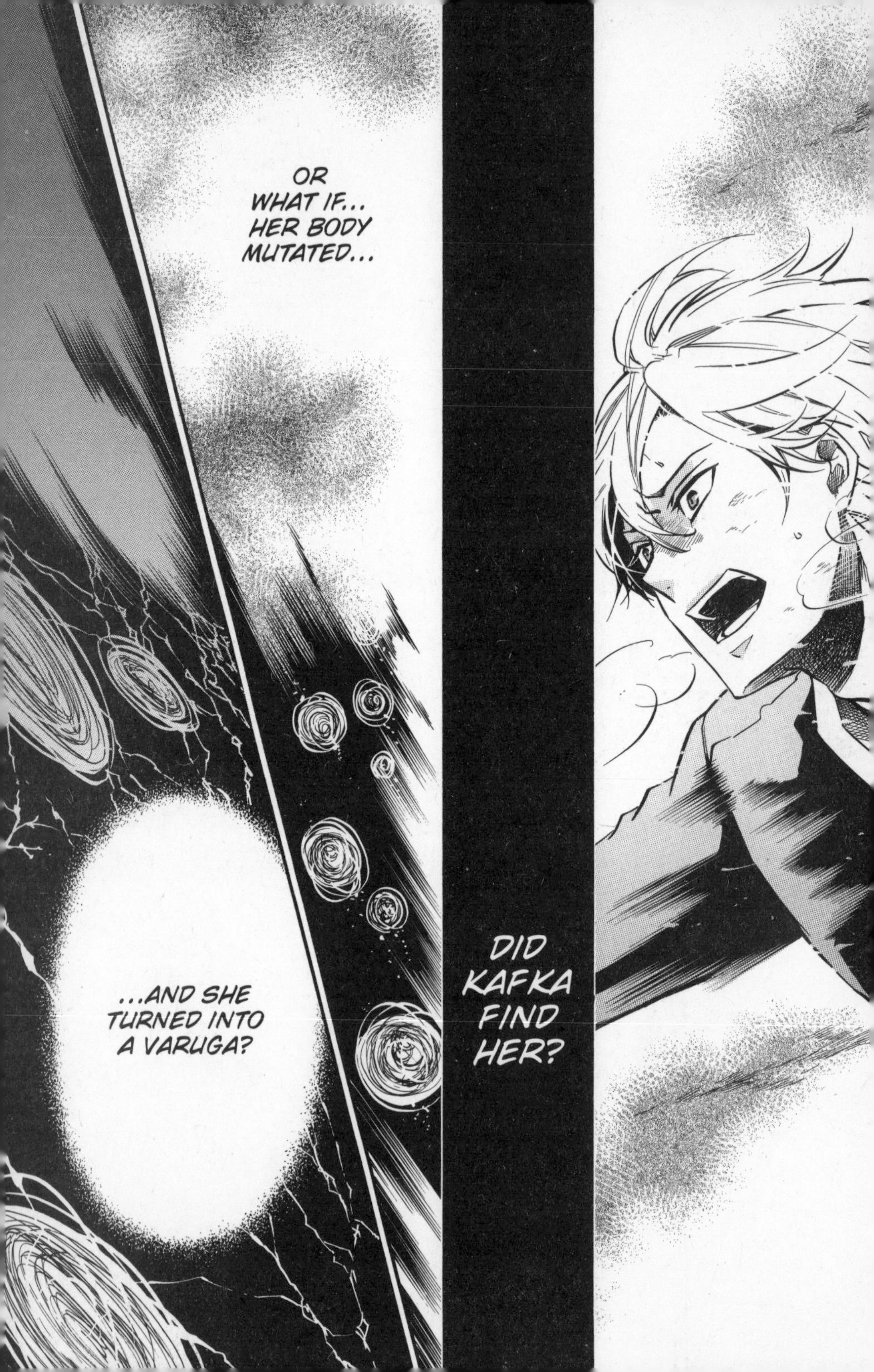
DID KAFKA FIND HER?
OR WHAT IF... HER BODY MUTATED...
...AND SHE TURNED INTO A VARUGA?

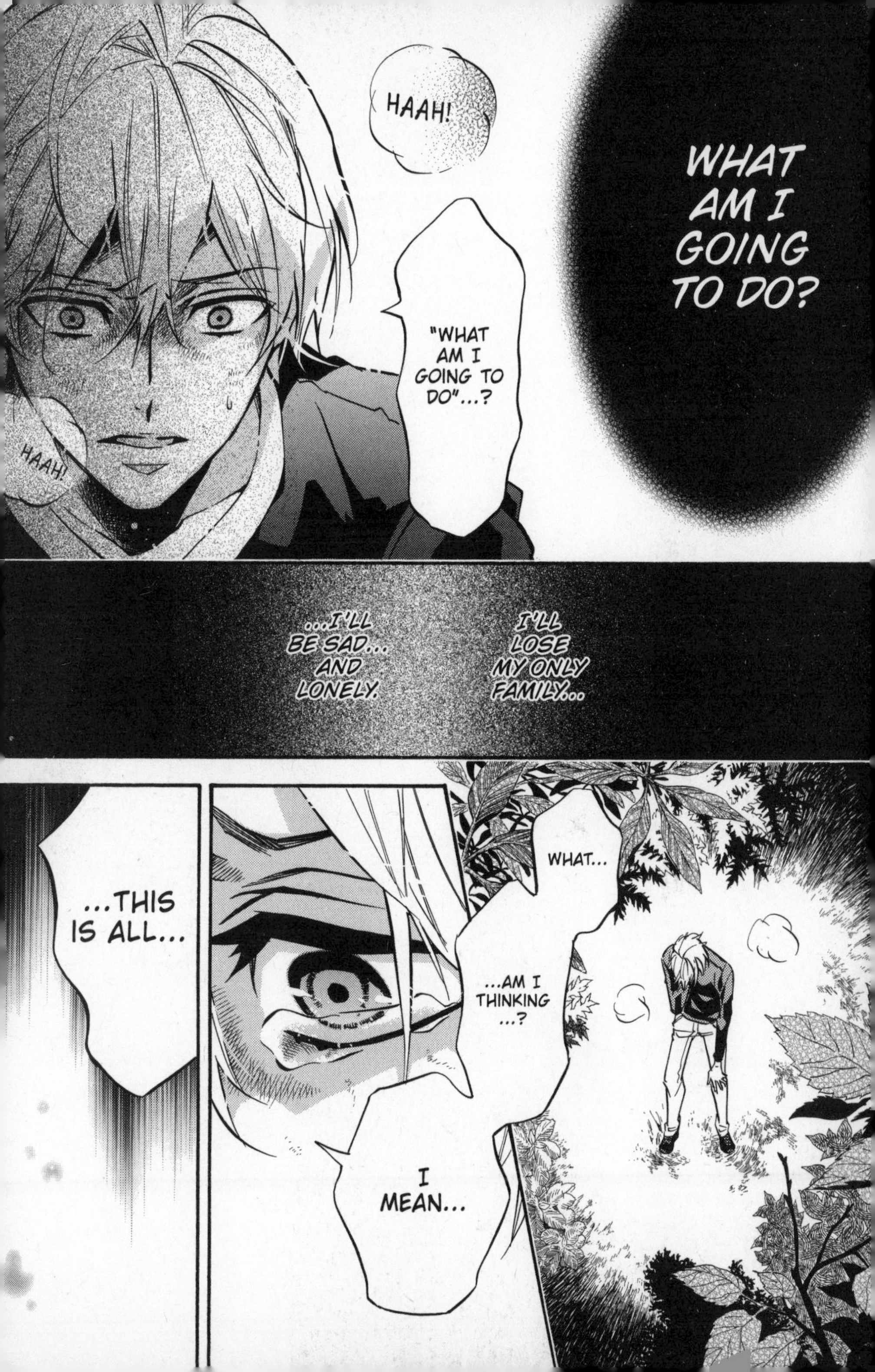
WHAT AM I GOING TO DO?
HAAH!
"WHAT AM I GOING TO DO"...?
HAAH!
I'LL LOSE MY ONLY FAMILY...
...I'LL BE SAD... AND LONELY.
WHAT...
...AM I THINKING...?
I MEAN...
...THIS IS ALL...

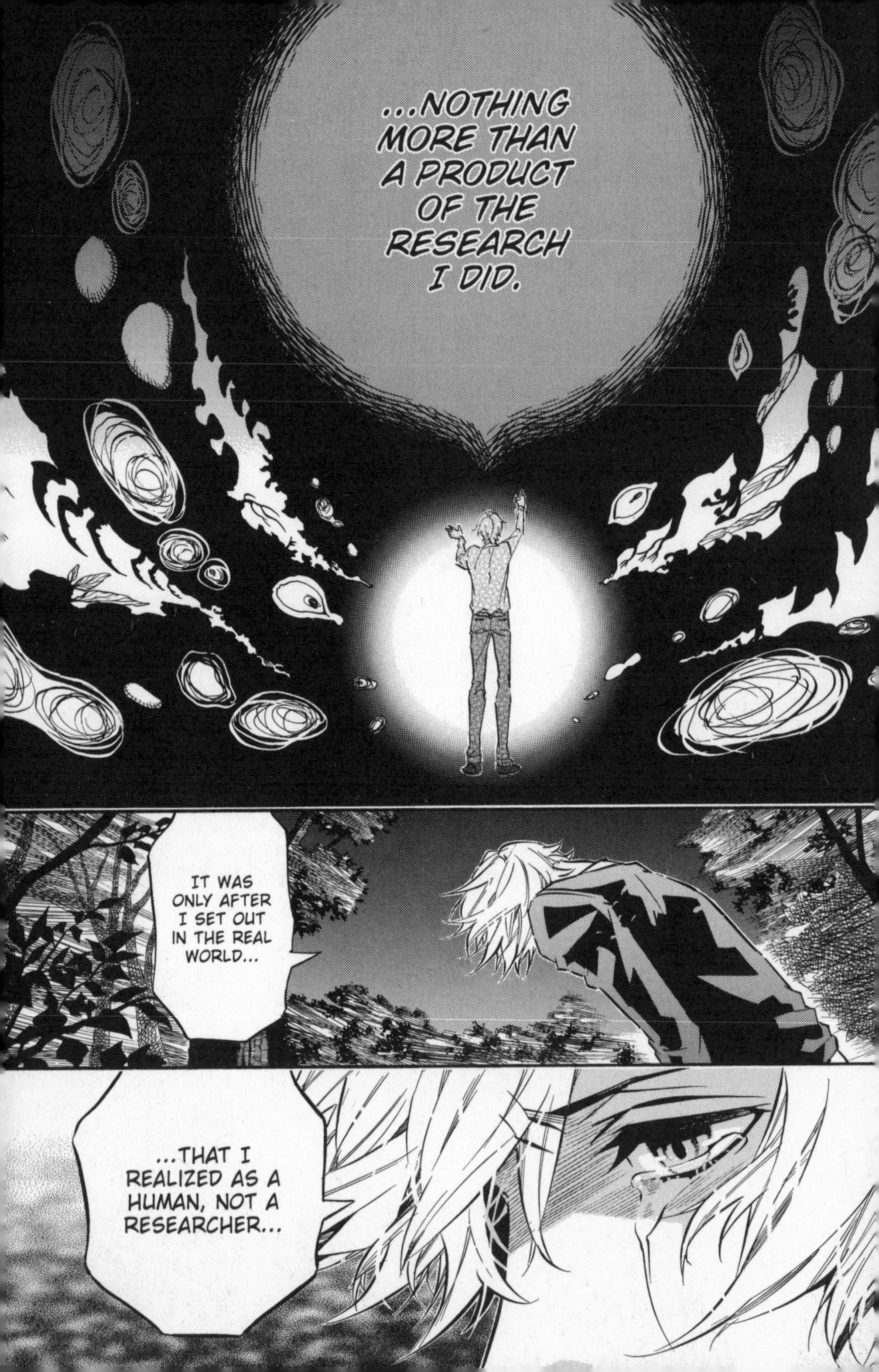
...NOTHING MORE THAN A PRODUCT OF THE RESEARCH I DID.
IT WAS ONLY AFTER I SET OUT IN THE REAL WORLD...
...THAT I REALIZED AS A HUMAN, NOT A RESEARCHER...

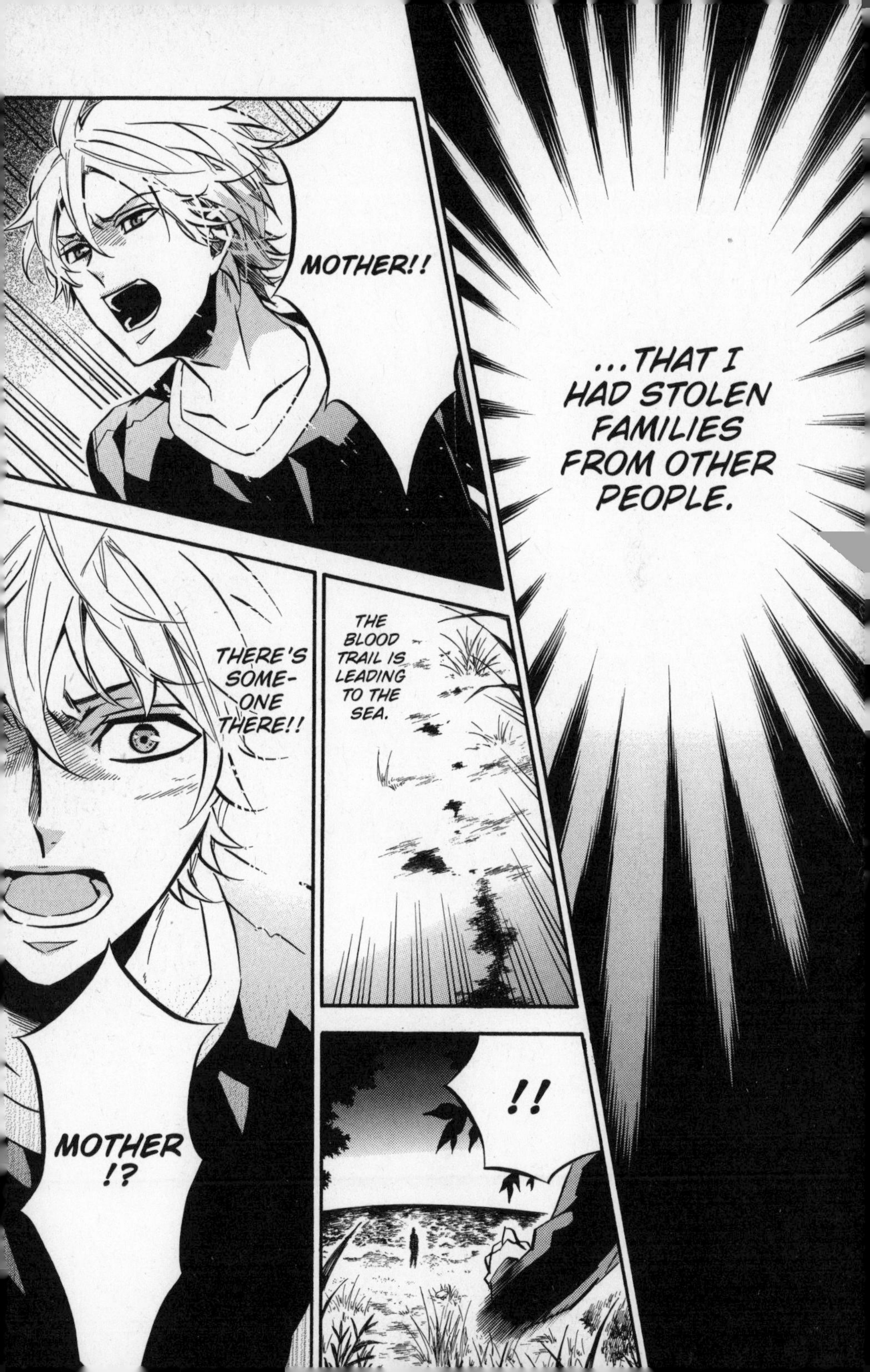
...THAT I HAD STOLEN FAMILIES FROM OTHER PEOPLE.
MOTHER!!
THE BLOOD TRAIL IS LEADING TO THE SEA.
!!
THERE'S SOME-ONE THERE!!
MOTHER !?

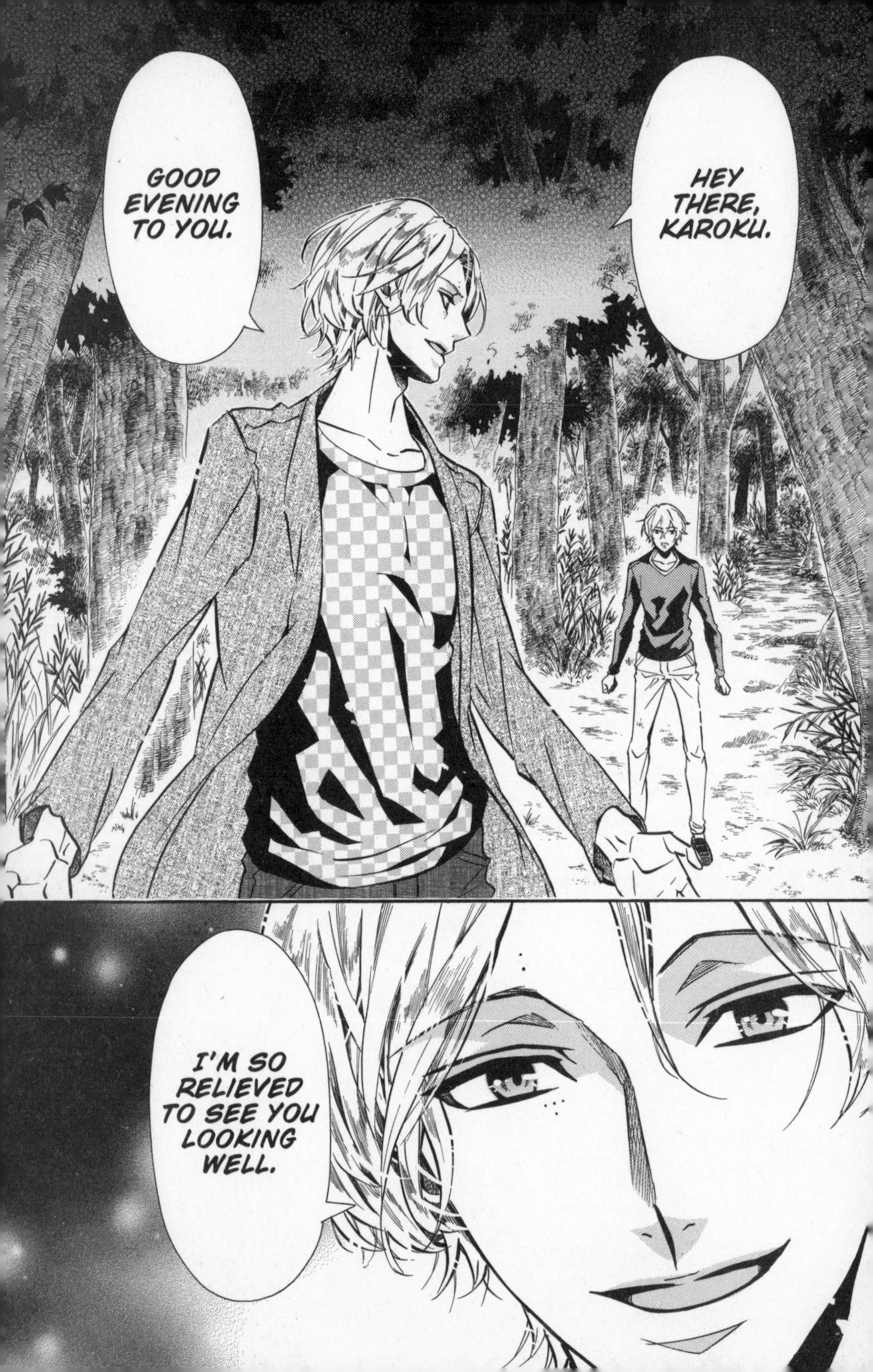
HEY THERE, KAROKU.
GOOD EVENING TO YOU.
I'M SO RELIEVED TO SEE YOU LOOKING WELL.

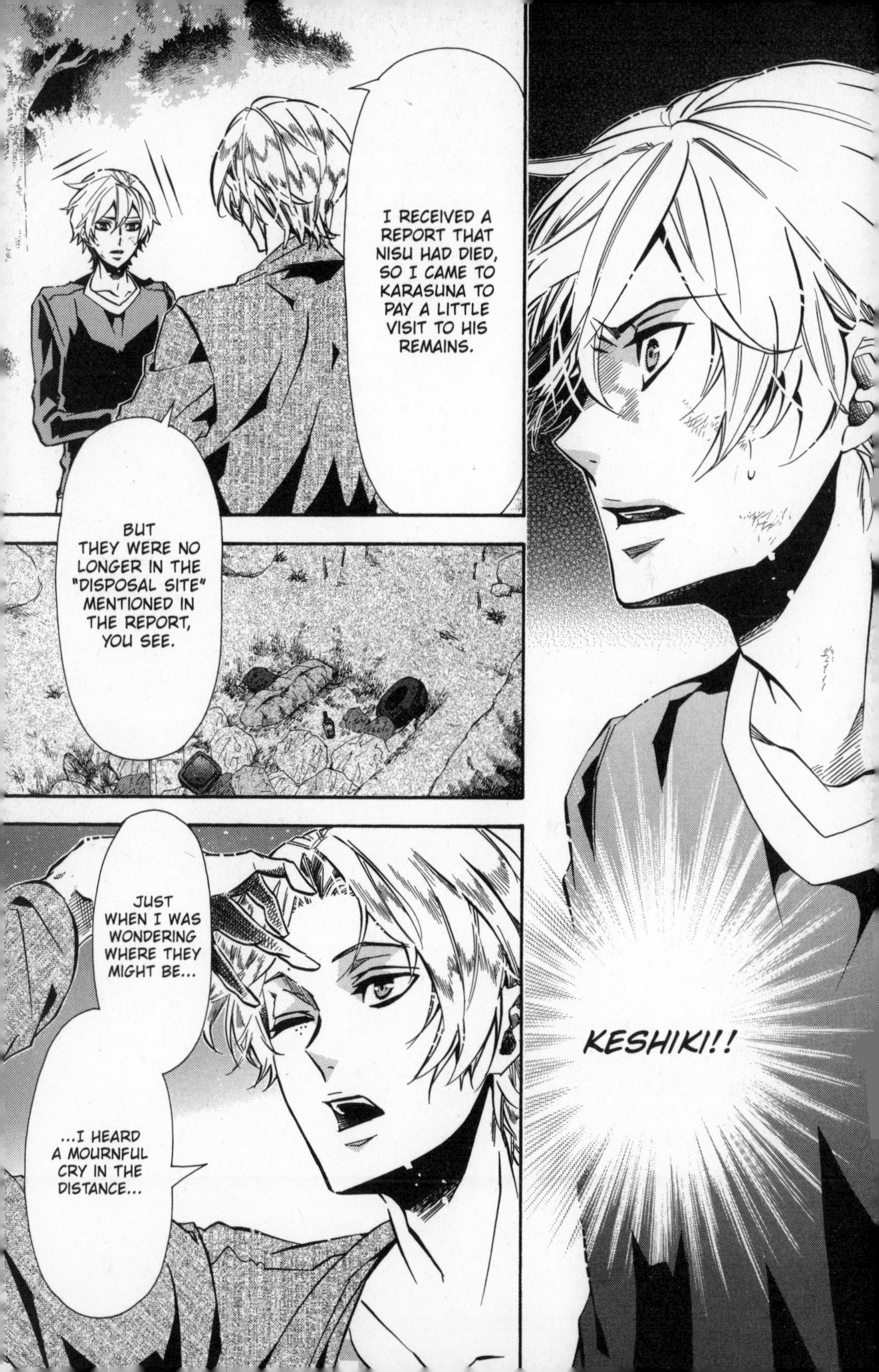
KESHIKI!!
I RECEIVED A REPORT THAT NISU HAD DIED, SO I CAME TO KARASUNA TO PAY A LITTLE VISIT TO HIS REMAINS.
BUT THEY WERE NO LONGER IN THE "DISPOSAL SITE" MENTIONED IN THE REPORT, YOU SEE.
JUST WHEN I WAS WONDERING WHERE THEY MIGHT BE...
...I HEARD A MOURNFUL CRY IN THE DISTANCE...

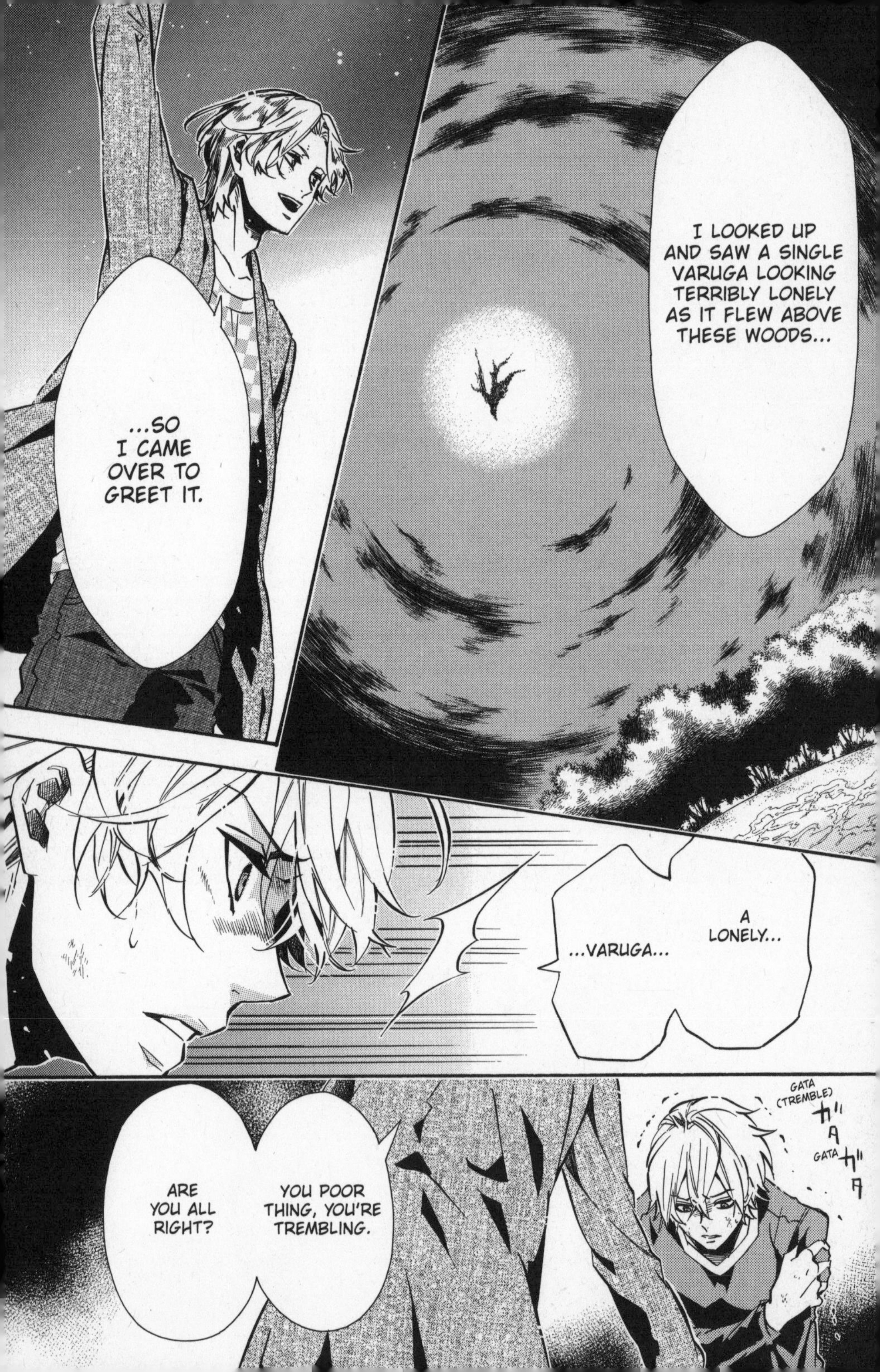
I LOOKED UP AND SAW A SINGLE VARUGA LOOKING TERRIBLY LONELY AS IT FLEW ABOVE THESE WOODS...
...SO I CAME OVER TO GREET IT.
A LONELY...
...VARUGA...
GATA (TREMBLE)
ガタ
GATA
ガタ
YOU POOR THING, YOU'RE TREMBLING.
ARE YOU ALL RIGHT?

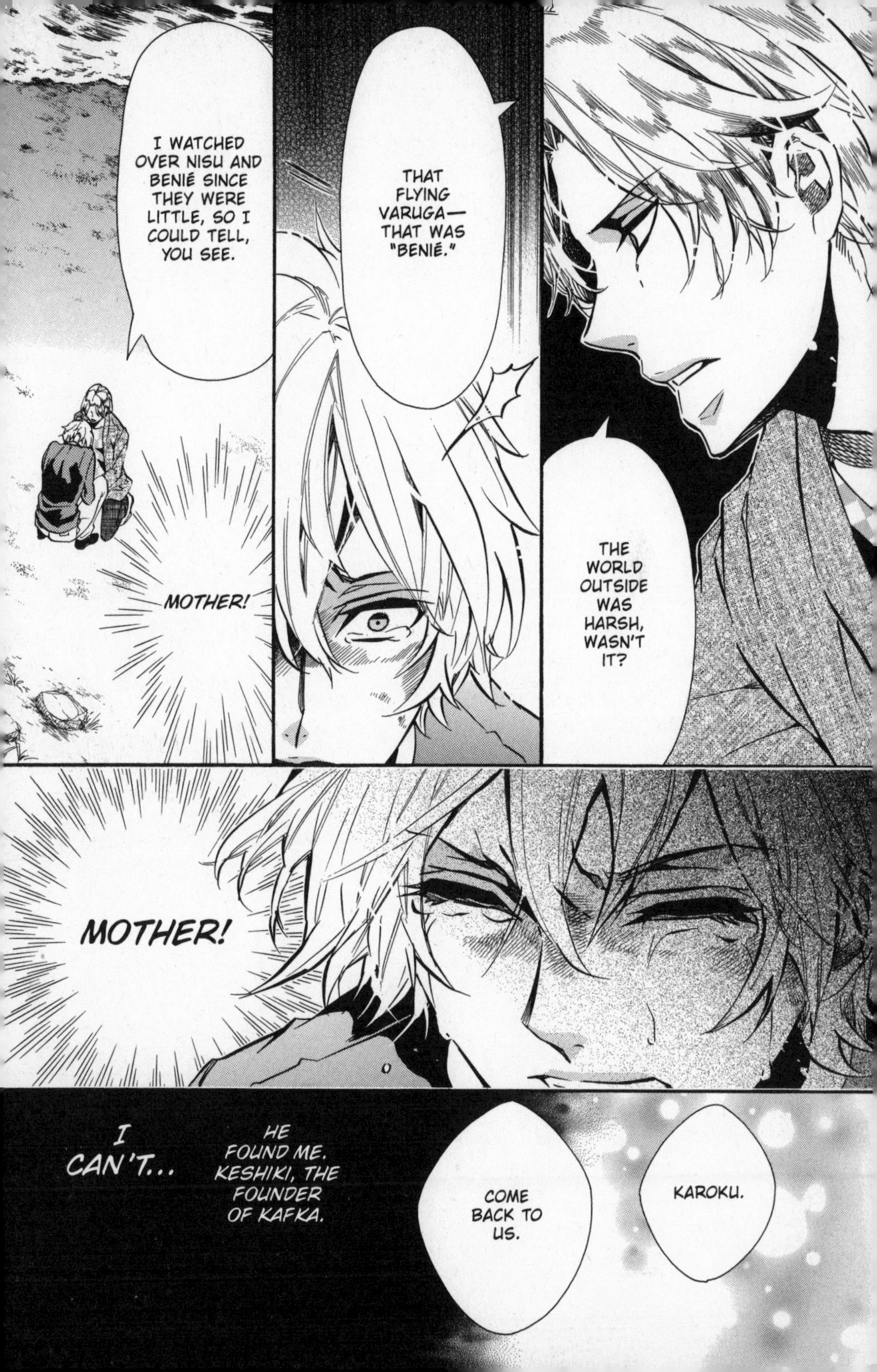
THE WORLD OUTSIDE WAS HARSH, WASN'T IT?
THAT FLYING VARUGA—THAT WAS "BENIÉ."
I WATCHED OVER NISU AND BENIÉ SINCE THEY WERE LITTLE, SO I COULD TELL, YOU SEE.
MOTHER!
MOTHER!
KAROKU.
COME BACK TO US.
HE FOUND ME. KESHIKI, THE FOUNDER OF KAFKA.
I CAN'T...

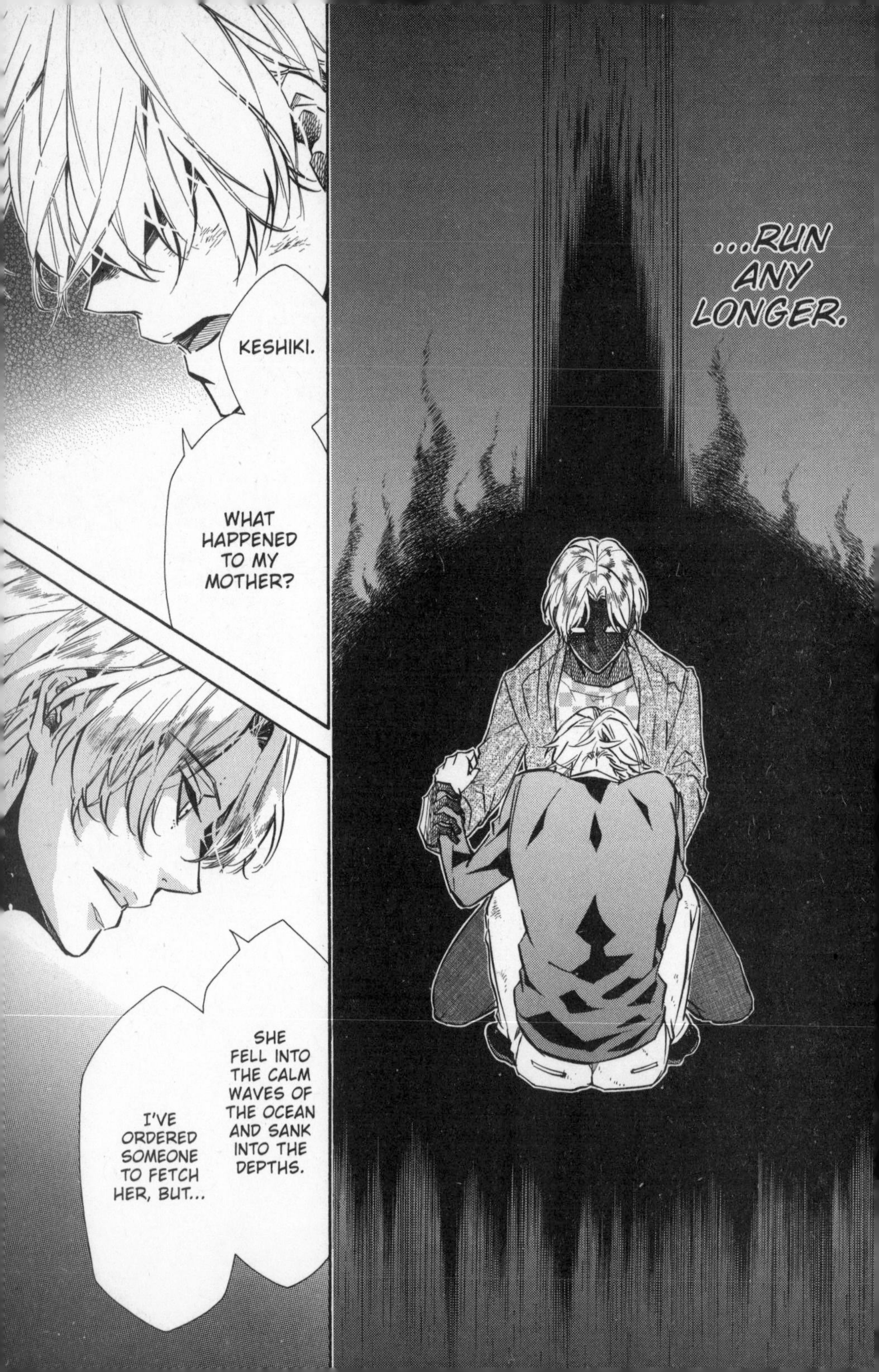
...RUN ANY LONGER.
KESHIKI.
WHAT HAPPENED TO MY MOTHER?
SHE FELL INTO THE CALM WAVES OF THE OCEAN AND SANK INTO THE DEPTHS.
I'VE ORDERED SOMEONE TO FETCH HER, BUT...

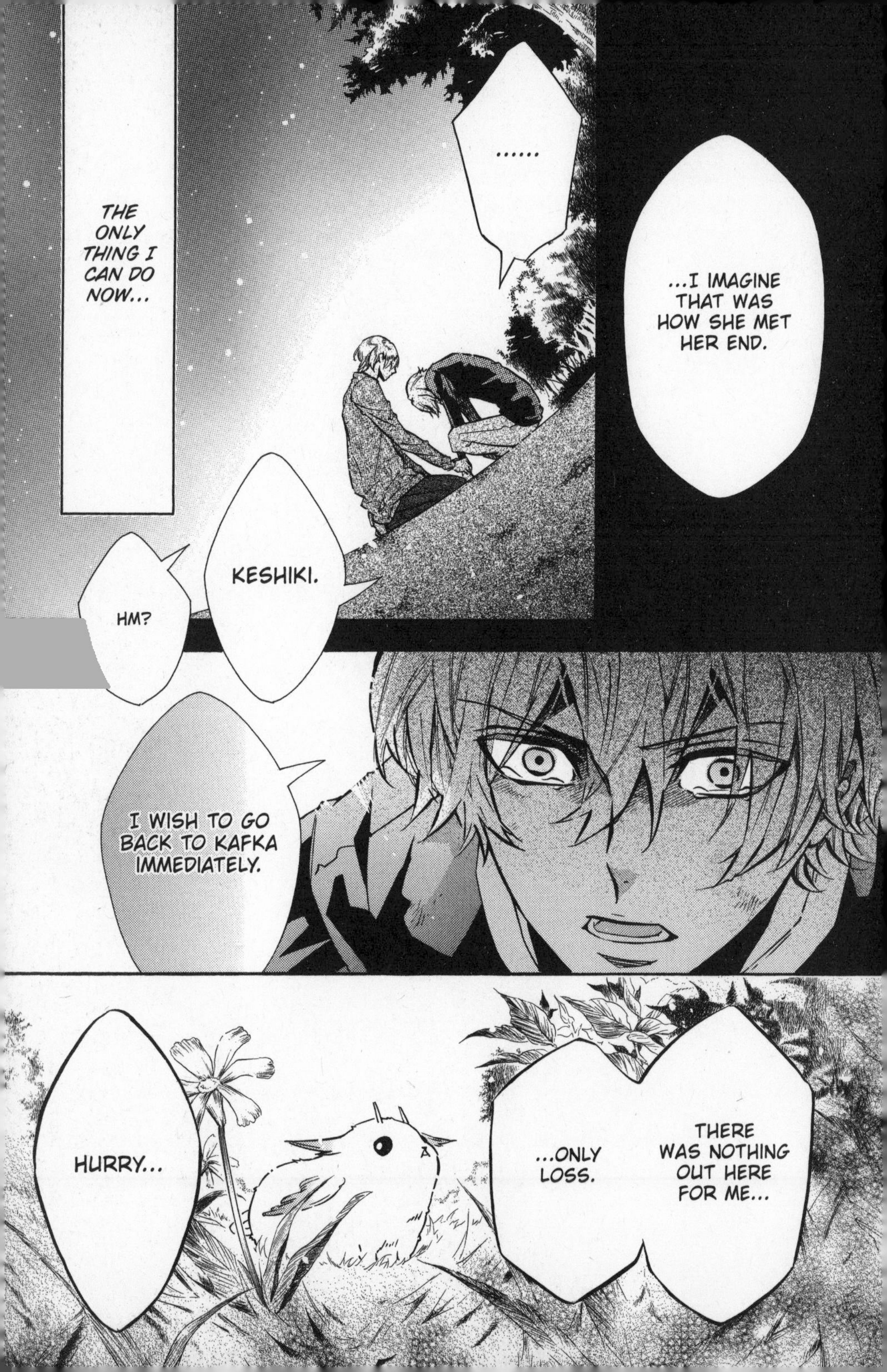
...I IMAGINE THAT WAS HOW SHE MET HER END.
......
THE ONLY THING I CAN DO NOW...
KESHIKI.
HM?
I WISH TO GO BACK TO KAFKA IMMEDIATELY.
THERE WAS NOTHING OUT HERE FOR ME...
...ONLY LOSS.
HURRY...

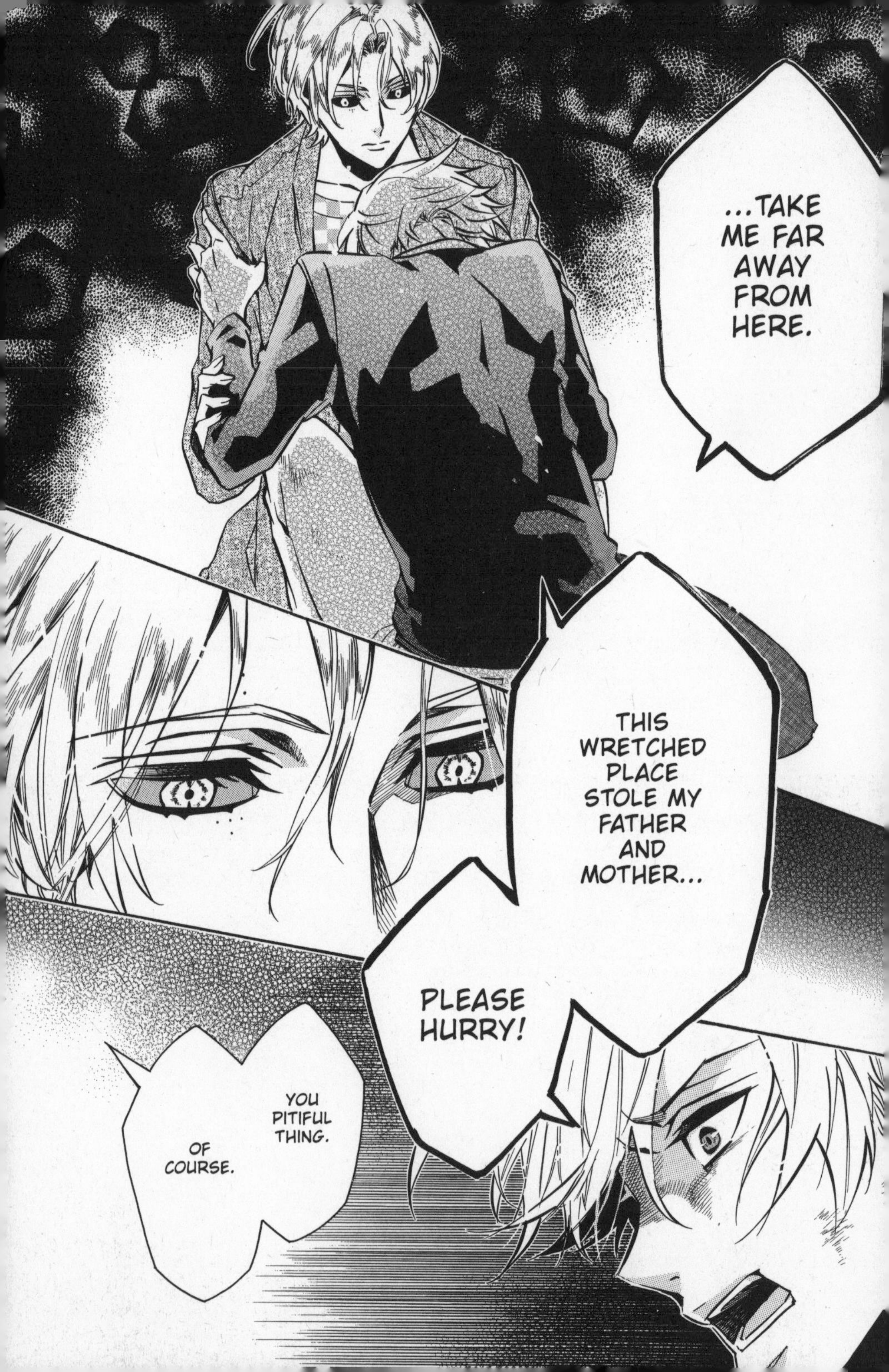
...TAKE ME FAR AWAY FROM HERE.
THIS WRETCHED PLACE STOLE MY FATHER AND MOTHER...
PLEASE HURRY!
YOU PITIFUL THING.
OF COURSE.

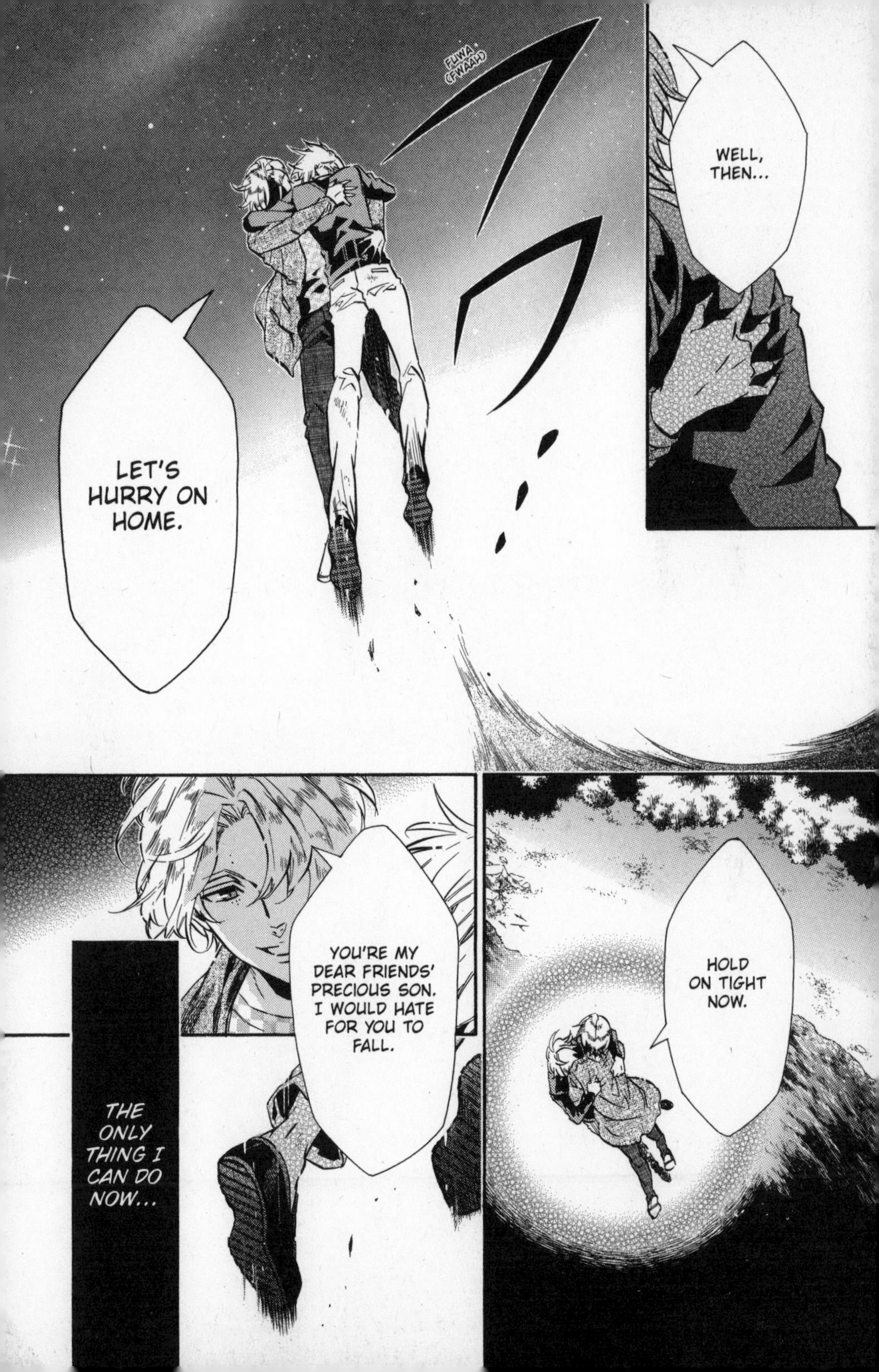
WELL, THEN...
FUWA (FWAAH)
LET'S HURRY ON HOME.
HOLD ON TIGHT NOW.
YOU'RE MY DEAR FRIENDS' PRECIOUS SON. I WOULD HATE FOR YOU TO FALL.
THE ONLY THING I CAN DO NOW...

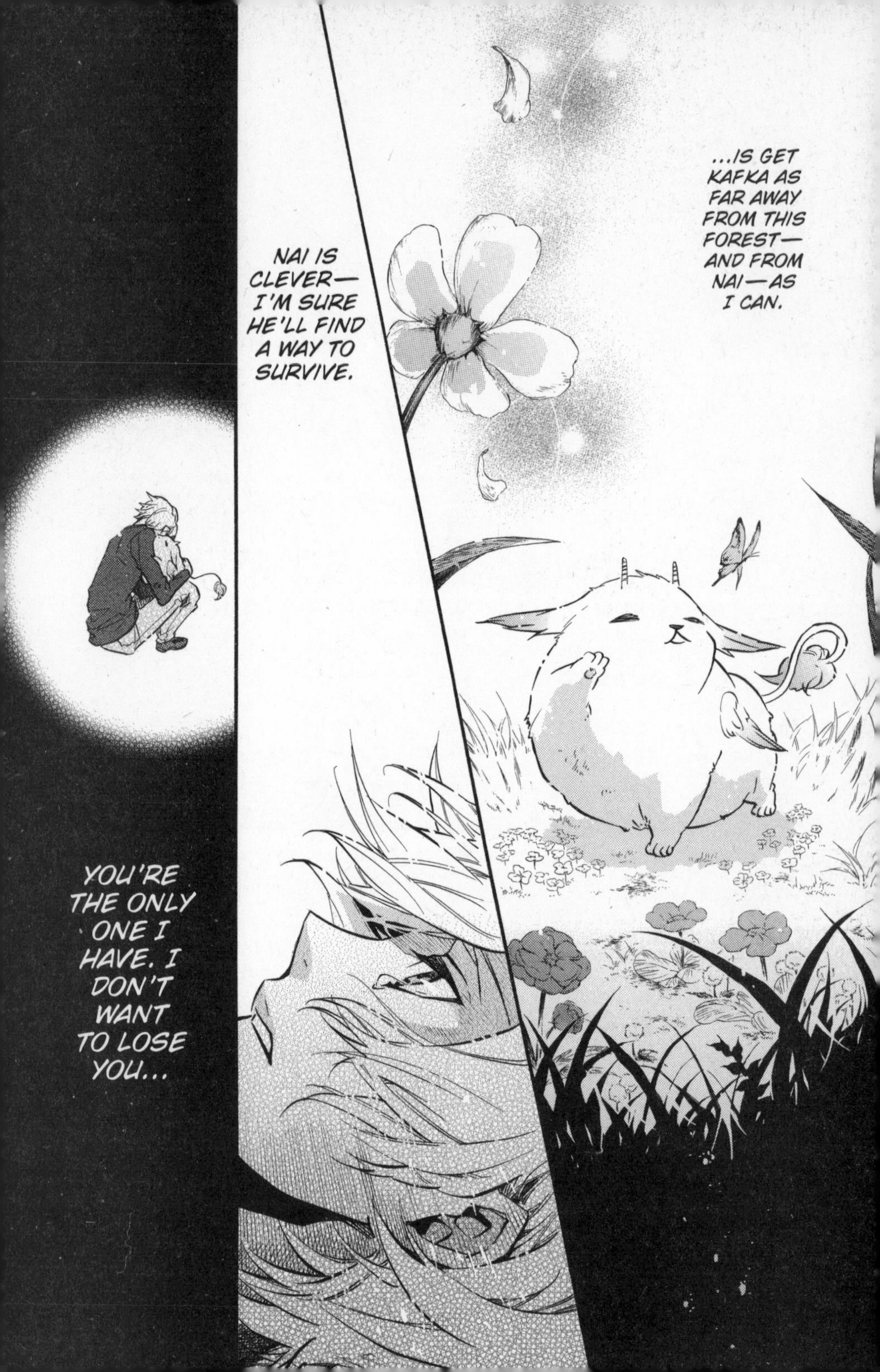
...IS GET KAFKA AS FAR AWAY FROM THIS FOREST—AND FROM NAI—AS I CAN.
NAI IS CLEVER—I'M SURE HE'LL FIND A WAY TO SURVIVE.
YOU'RE THE ONLY ONE I HAVE. I DON'T WANT TO LOSE YOU...

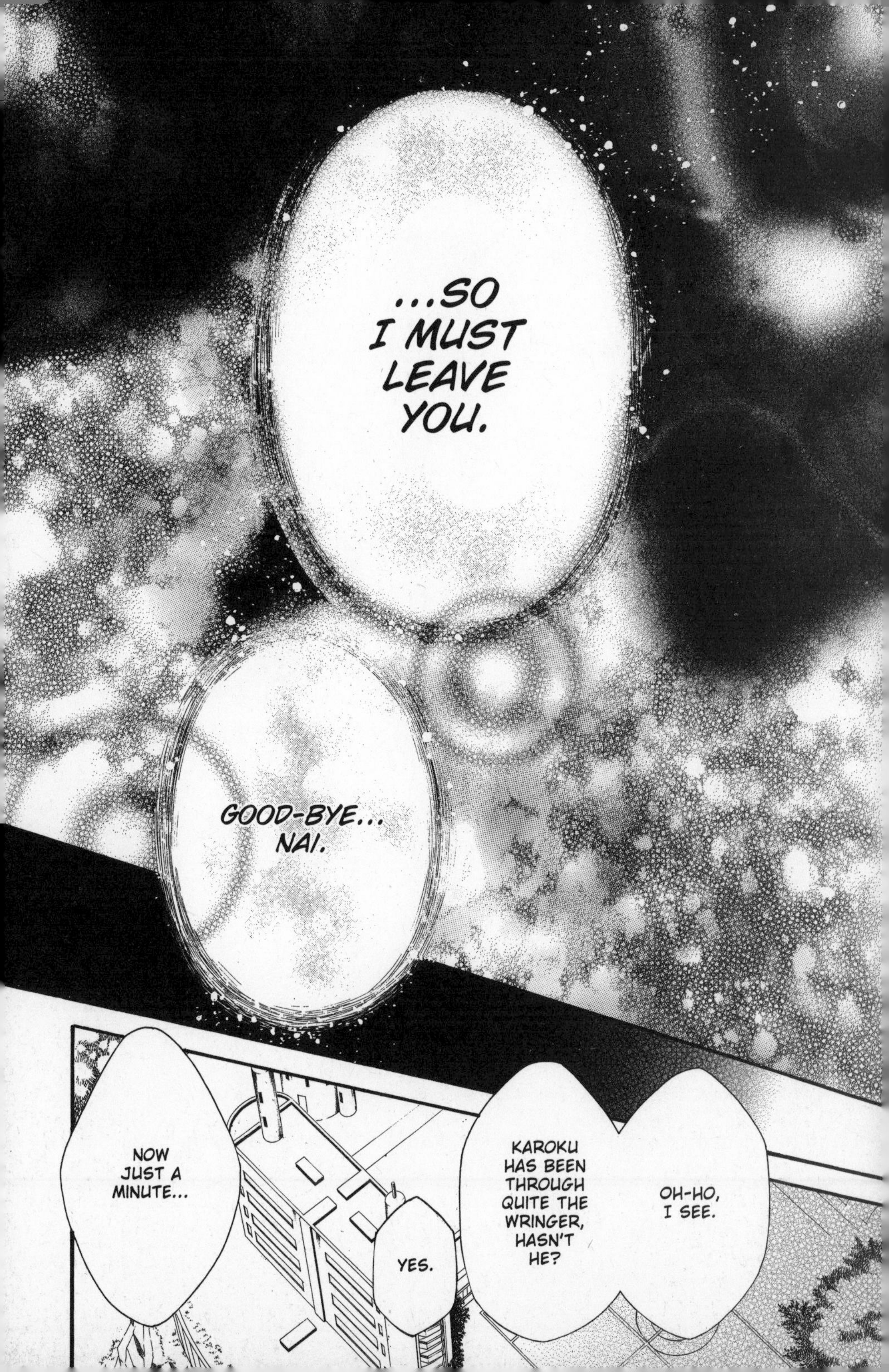
...SO I MUST LEAVE YOU.
GOOD-BYE... NAI.
OH-HO, I SEE.
KAROKU HAS BEEN THROUGH QUITE THE WRINGER, HASN'T HE?
YES.
NOW JUST A MINUTE...

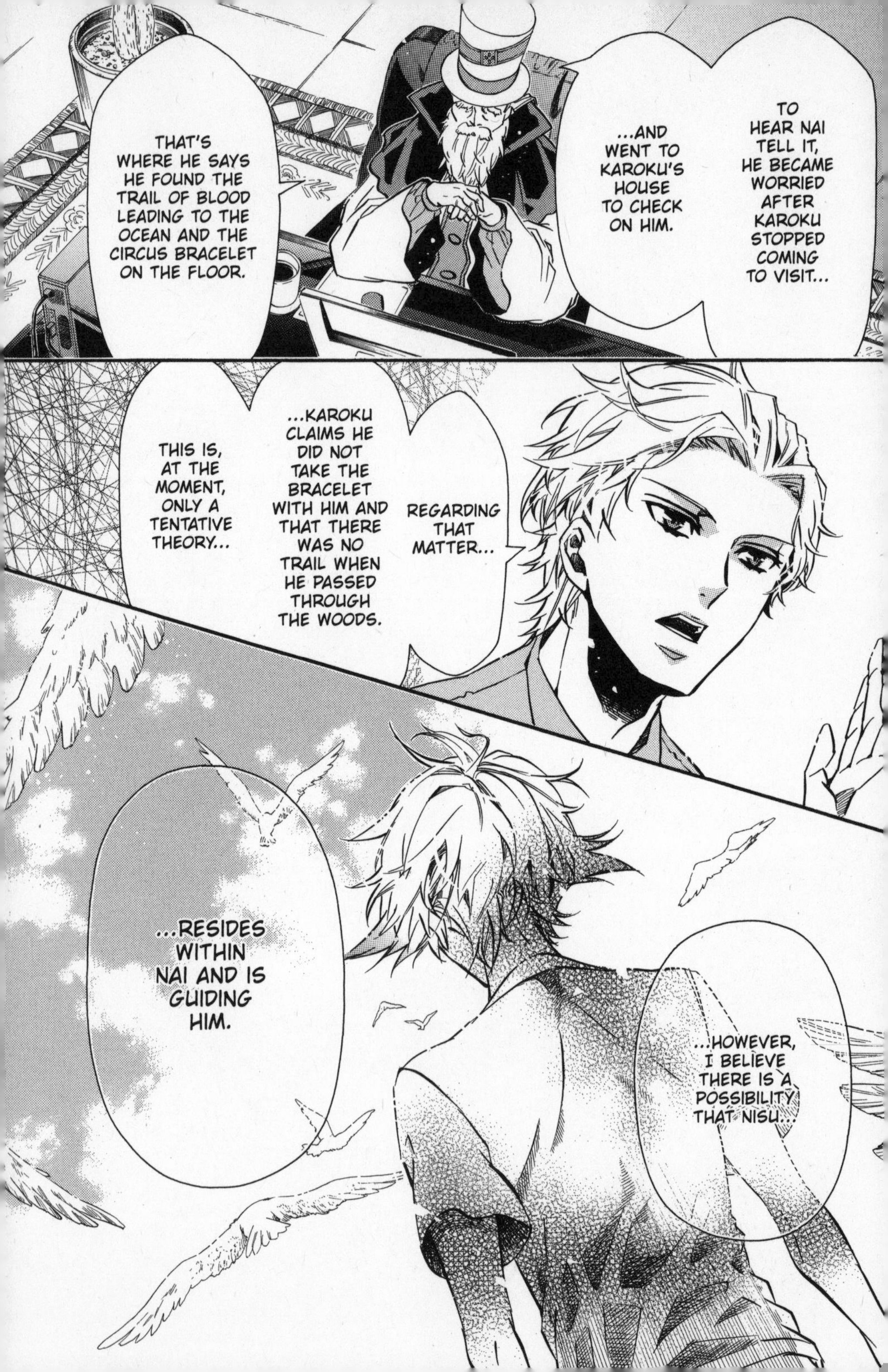
TO HEAR NAI TELL IT, HE BECAME WORRIED AFTER KAROKU STOPPED COMING TO VISIT...
...AND WENT TO KAROKU'S HOUSE TO CHECK ON HIM.
THAT'S WHERE HE SAYS HE FOUND THE TRAIL OF BLOOD LEADING TO THE OCEAN AND THE CIRCUS BRACELET ON THE FLOOR.
REGARDING THAT MATTER...
...KAROKU CLAIMS HE DID NOT TAKE THE BRACELET WITH HIM AND THAT THERE WAS NO TRAIL WHEN HE PASSED THROUGH THE WOODS.
THIS IS, AT THE MOMENT, ONLY A TENTATIVE THEORY...
...HOWEVER, I BELIEVE THERE IS A POSSIBILITY THAT NISU...
...RESIDES WITHIN NAI AND IS GUIDING HIM.

KARNEVAL

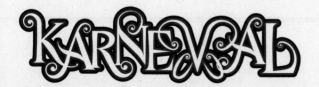

KARNEVAL

Score 116: Punishment

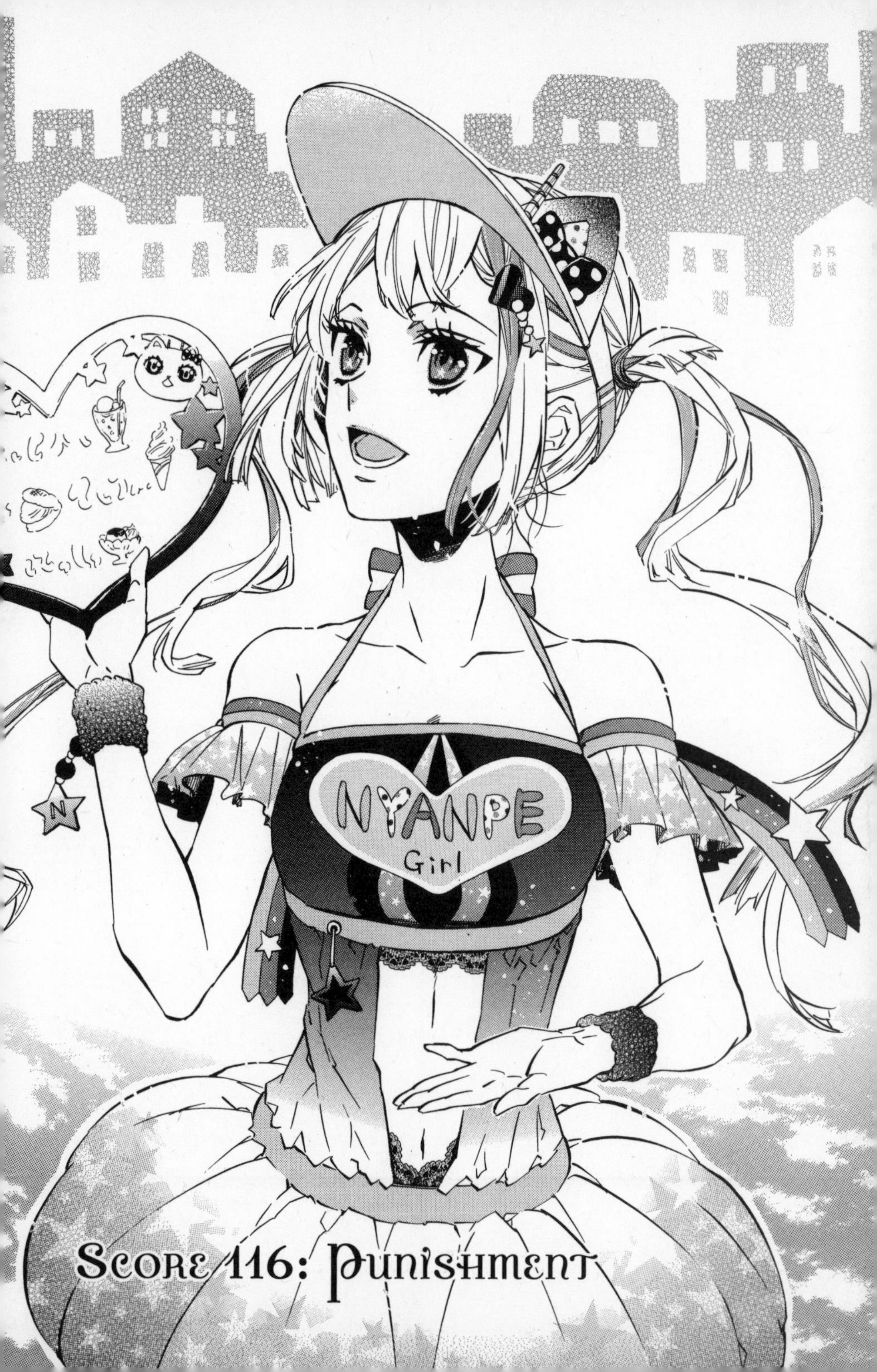
NYANPE
Girl

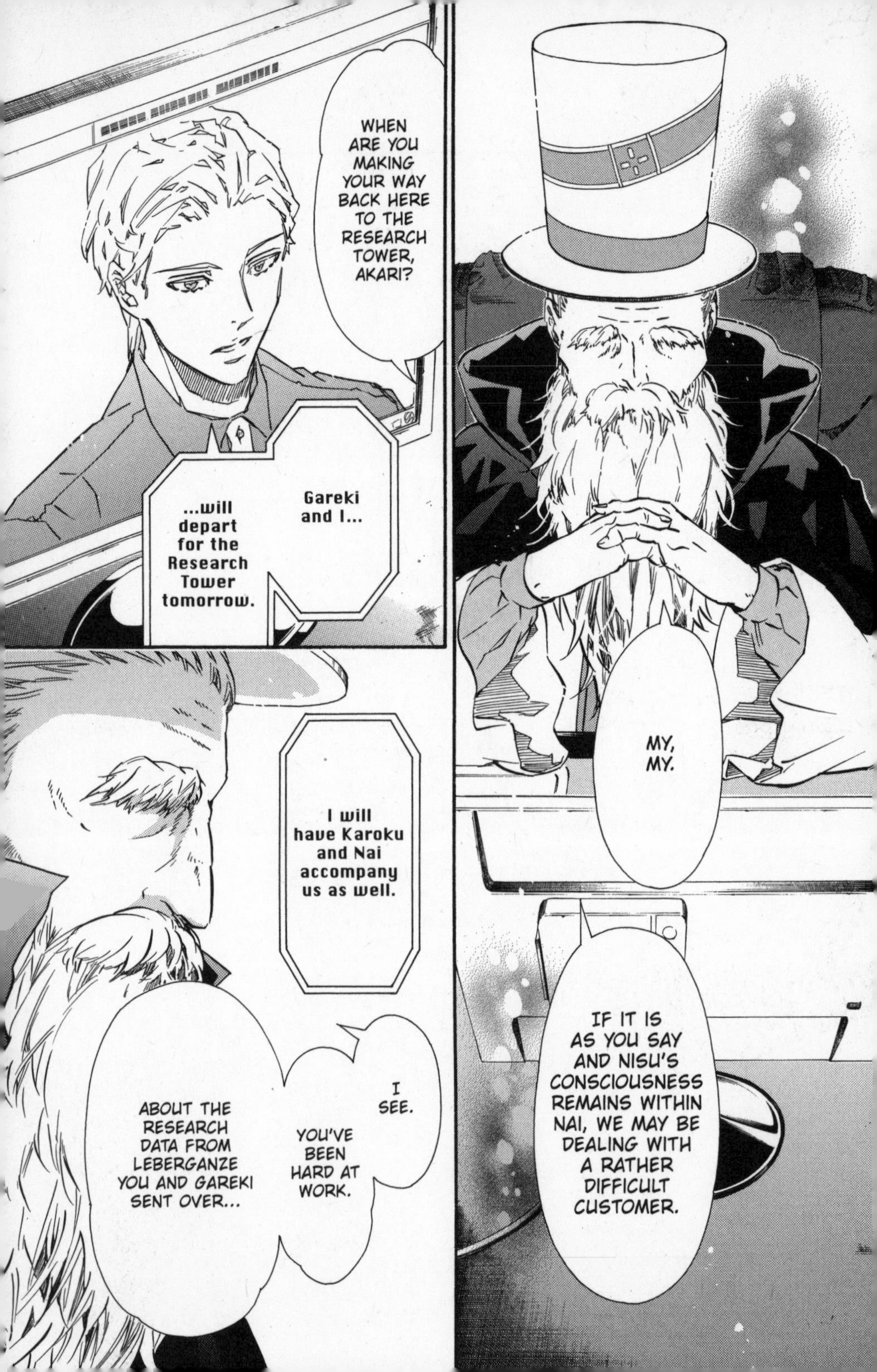
WHEN ARE YOU MAKING YOUR WAY BACK HERE TO THE RESEARCH TOWER, AKARI?
Gareki and I...
...will depart for the Research Tower tomorrow.
I will have Karoku and Nai accompany us as well.
I SEE.
YOU'VE BEEN HARD AT WORK.
ABOUT THE RESEARCH DATA FROM LEBERGANZE YOU AND GAREKI SENT OVER...
MY, MY.
IF IT IS AS YOU SAY AND NISU'S CONSCIOUSNESS REMAINS WITHIN NAI, WE MAY BE DEALING WITH A RATHER DIFFICULT CUSTOMER.

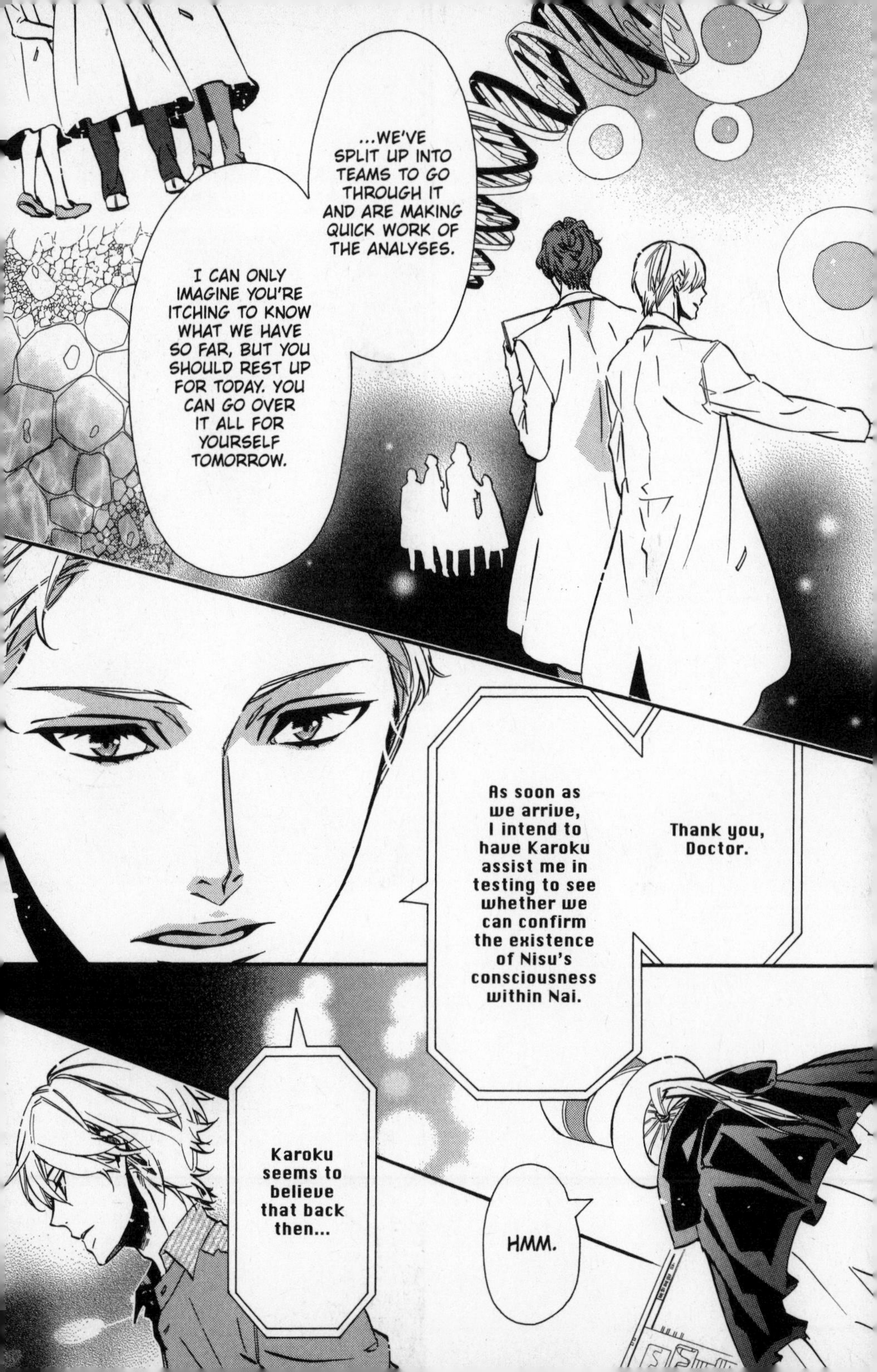
...WE'VE SPLIT UP INTO TEAMS TO GO THROUGH IT AND ARE MAKING QUICK WORK OF THE ANALYSES.
I CAN ONLY IMAGINE YOU'RE ITCHING TO KNOW WHAT WE HAVE SO FAR, BUT YOU SHOULD REST UP FOR TODAY. YOU CAN GO OVER IT ALL FOR YOURSELF TOMORROW.
Thank you, Doctor.
As soon as we arrive, I intend to have Karoku assist me in testing to see whether we can confirm the existence of Nisu's consciousness within Nai.
HMM.
Karoku seems to believe that back then...

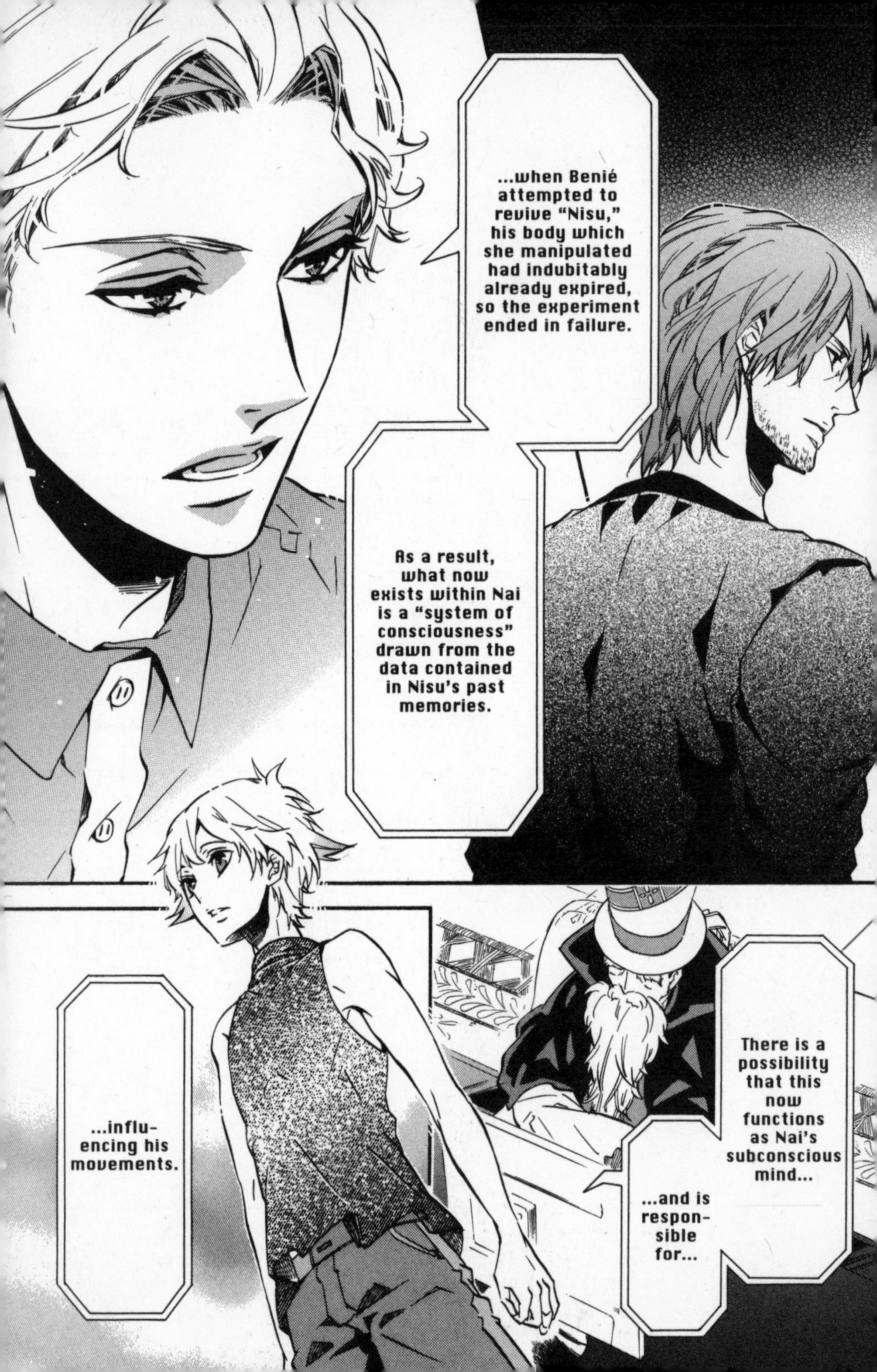
...when Benié attempted to revive "Nisu," his body which she manipulated had indubitably already expired, so the experiment ended in failure.
As a result, what now exists within Nai is a "system of consciousness" drawn from the data contained in Nisu's past memories.
There is a possibility that this now functions as Nai's subconscious mind...
...and is respon-sible for...
...influ-encing his movements.

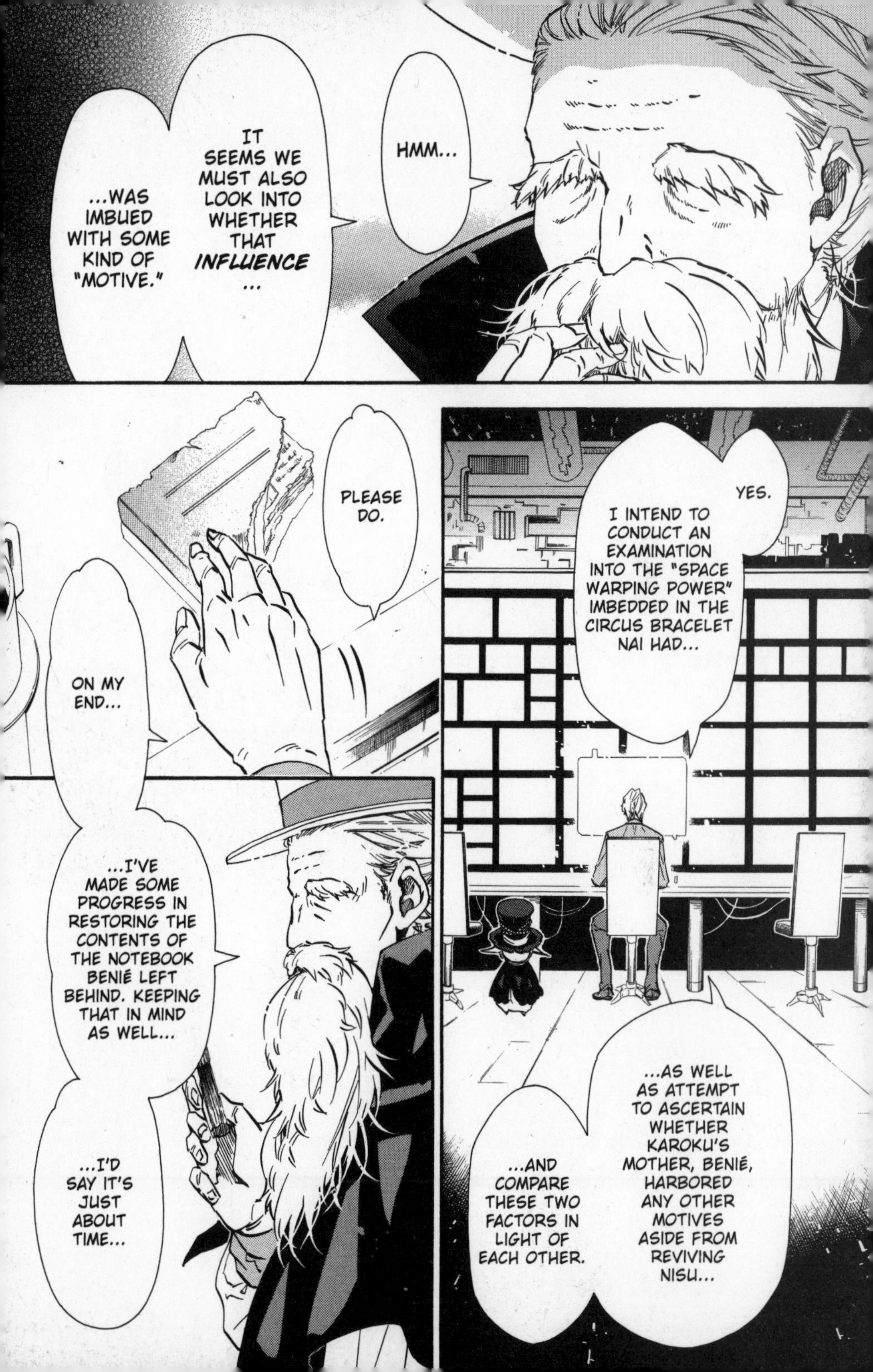
HMM...
IT SEEMS WE MUST ALSO LOOK INTO WHETHER THAT *INFLUENCE* ...
...WAS IMBUED WITH SOME KIND OF "MOTIVE."
YES.
I INTEND TO CONDUCT AN EXAMINATION INTO THE "SPACE WARPING POWER" IMBEDDED IN THE CIRCUS BRACELET NAI HAD...
...AS WELL AS ATTEMPT TO ASCERTAIN WHETHER KAROKU'S MOTHER, BENIÉ, HARBORED ANY OTHER MOTIVES ASIDE FROM REVIVING NISU...
...AND COMPARE THESE TWO FACTORS IN LIGHT OF EACH OTHER.
PLEASE DO.
ON MY END...
...I'VE MADE SOME PROGRESS IN RESTORING THE CONTENTS OF THE NOTEBOOK BENIÉ LEFT BEHIND. KEEPING THAT IN MIND AS WELL...
...I'D SAY IT'S JUST ABOUT TIME...

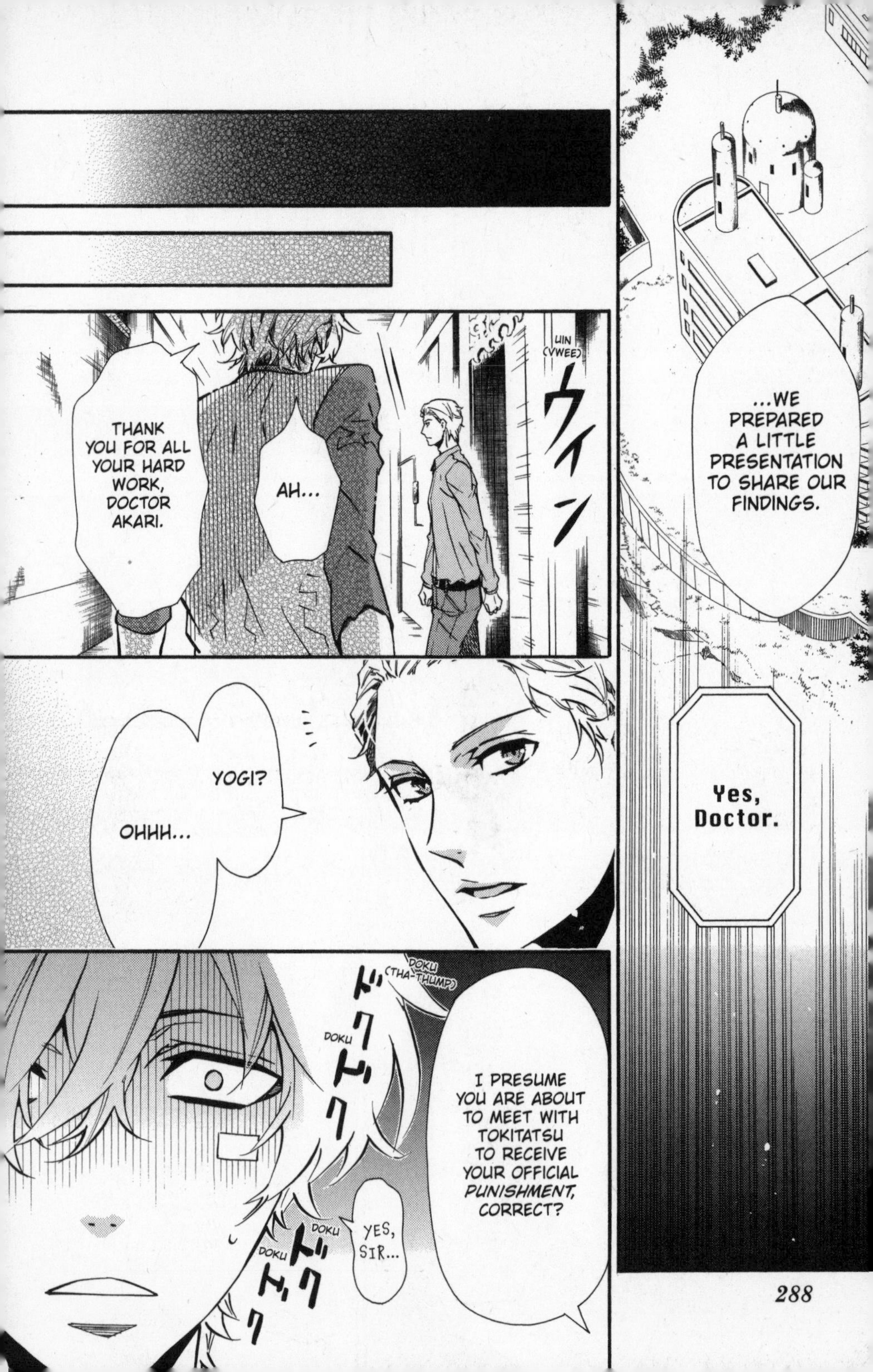
...WE PREPARED A LITTLE PRESENTATION TO SHARE OUR FINDINGS.
Yes, Doctor.
UIN (VWEE)
ウィン
AH...
THANK YOU FOR ALL YOUR HARD WORK, DOCTOR AKARI.
YOGI?
OHHH...
DOKU (THA-THUMP)
I PRESUME YOU ARE ABOUT TO MEET WITH TOKITATSU TO RECEIVE YOUR OFFICIAL *PUNISHMENT*, CORRECT?
DOKU
YES, SIR...
DOKU
DOKU

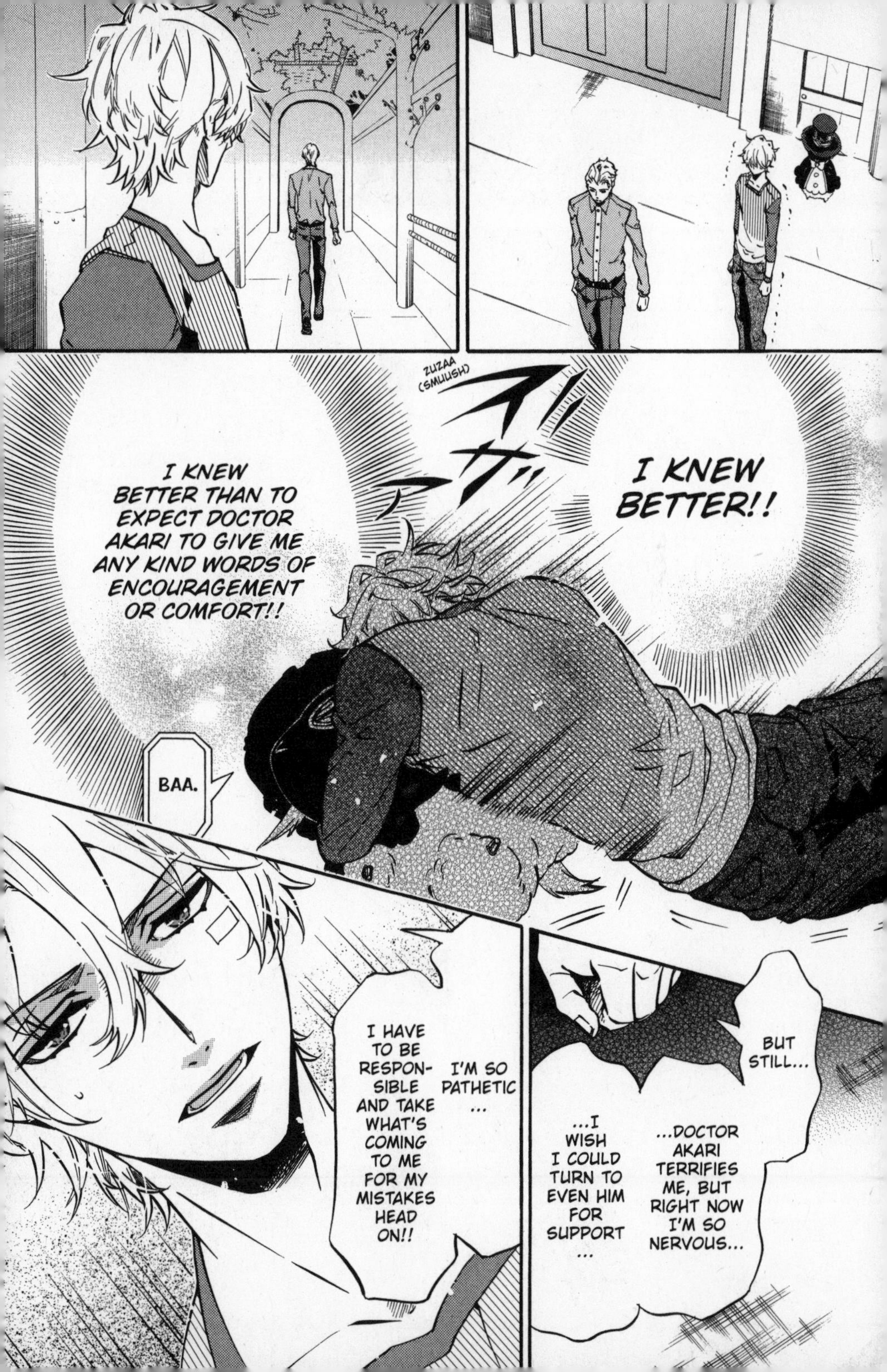
ZUZAA (SMUUSH)
I KNEW BETTER!!
I KNEW BETTER THAN TO EXPECT DOCTOR AKARI TO GIVE ME ANY KIND WORDS OF ENCOURAGEMENT OR COMFORT!!
BAA.
BUT STILL...
...DOCTOR AKARI TERRIFIES ME, BUT RIGHT NOW I'M SO NERVOUS...
...I WISH I COULD TURN TO EVEN HIM FOR SUPPORT...
I'M SO PATHETIC...
I HAVE TO BE RESPON-SIBLE AND TAKE WHAT'S COMING TO ME FOR MY MISTAKES HEAD ON!!

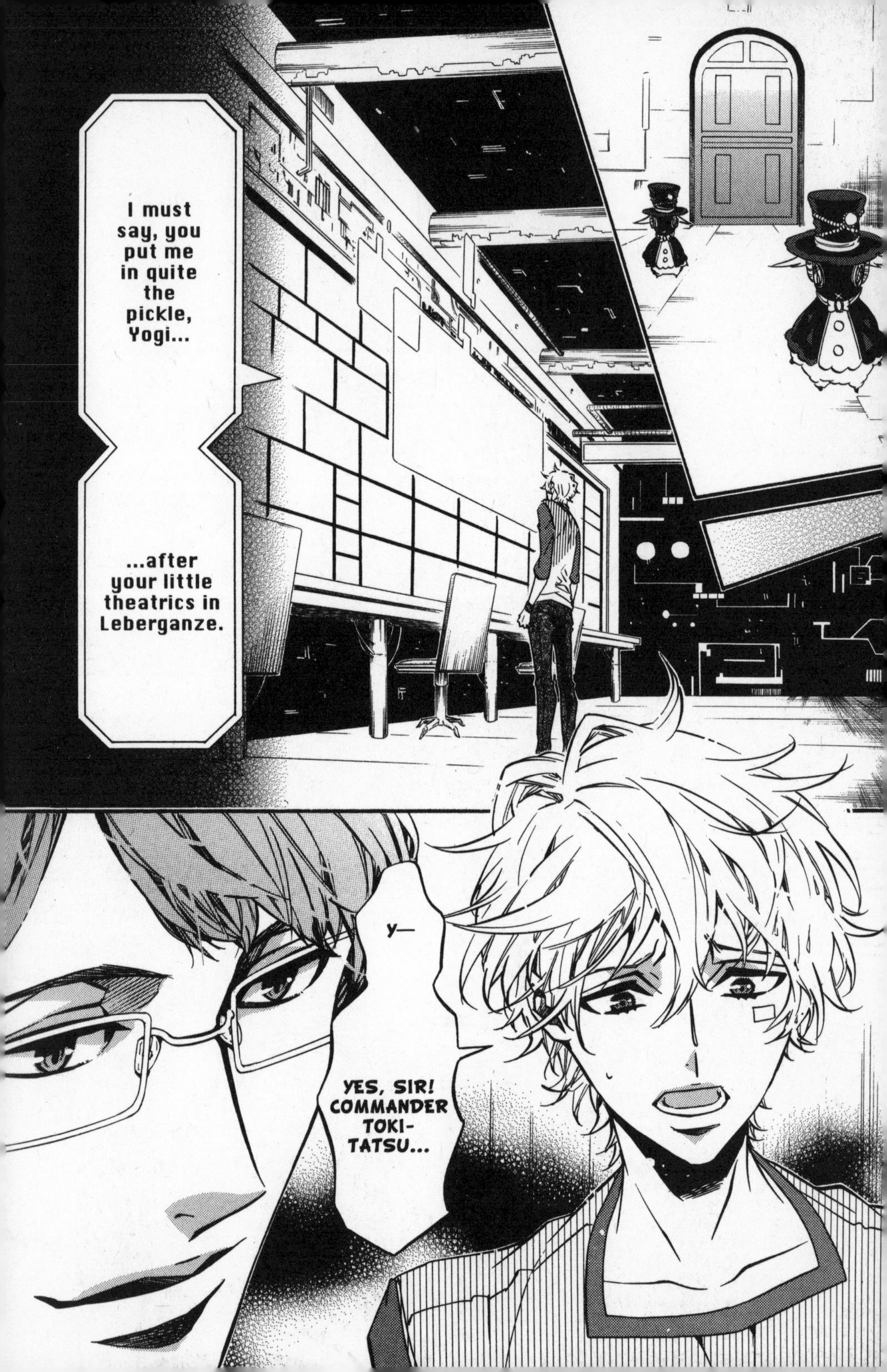
I must say, you put me in quite the pickle, Yogi...
...after your little theatrics in Leberganze.
y—
YES, SIR! COMMANDER TOKI-TATSU...

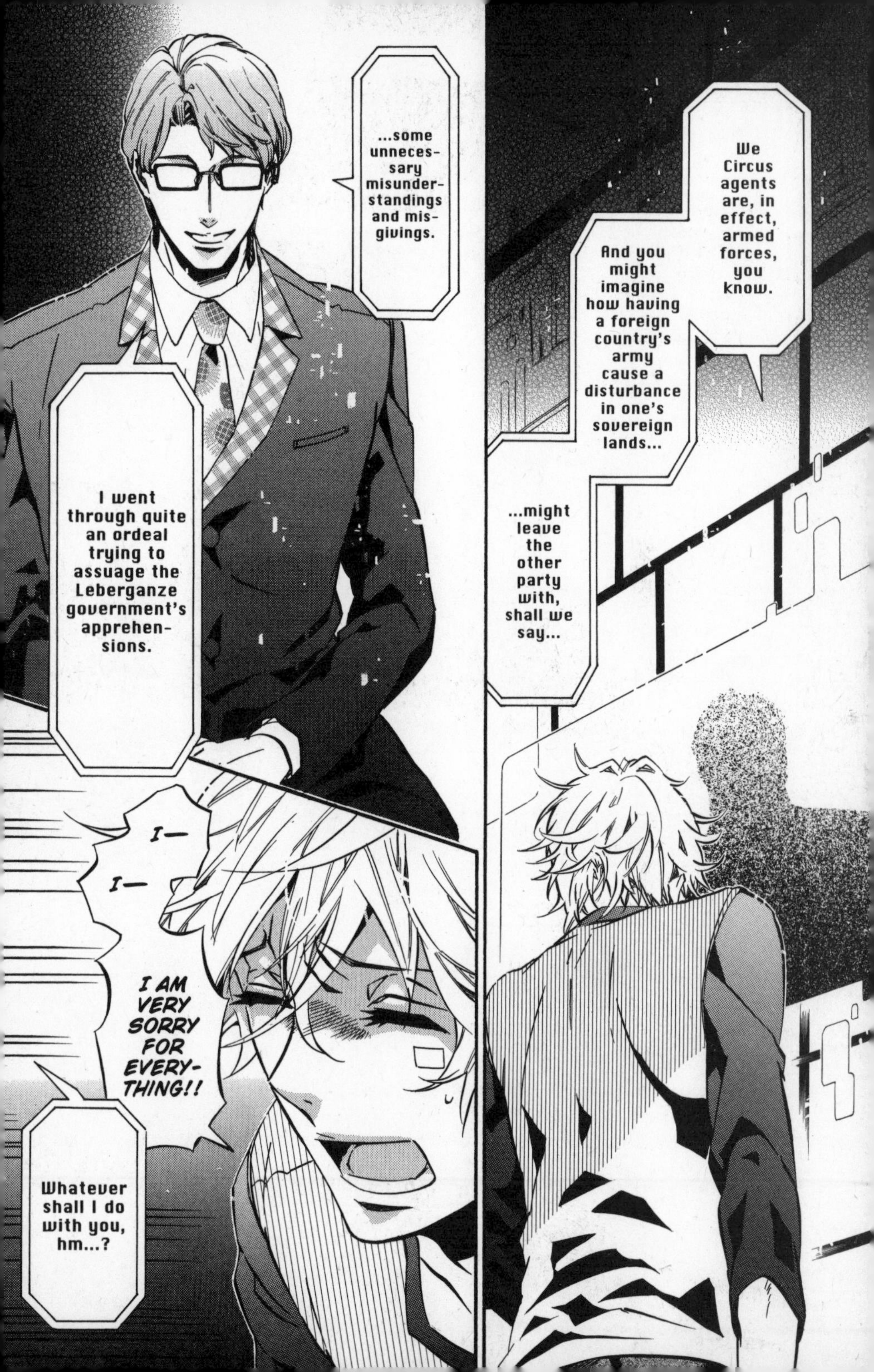
We Circus agents are, in effect, armed forces, you know.
And you might imagine how having a foreign country's army cause a disturbance in one's sovereign lands...
...might leave the other party with, shall we say...
...some unnecessary misunderstandings and misgivings.
I went through quite an ordeal trying to assuage the Leberganze government's apprehensions.
I— I—
I AM VERY SORRY FOR EVERYTHING!!
Whatever shall I do with you, hm...?

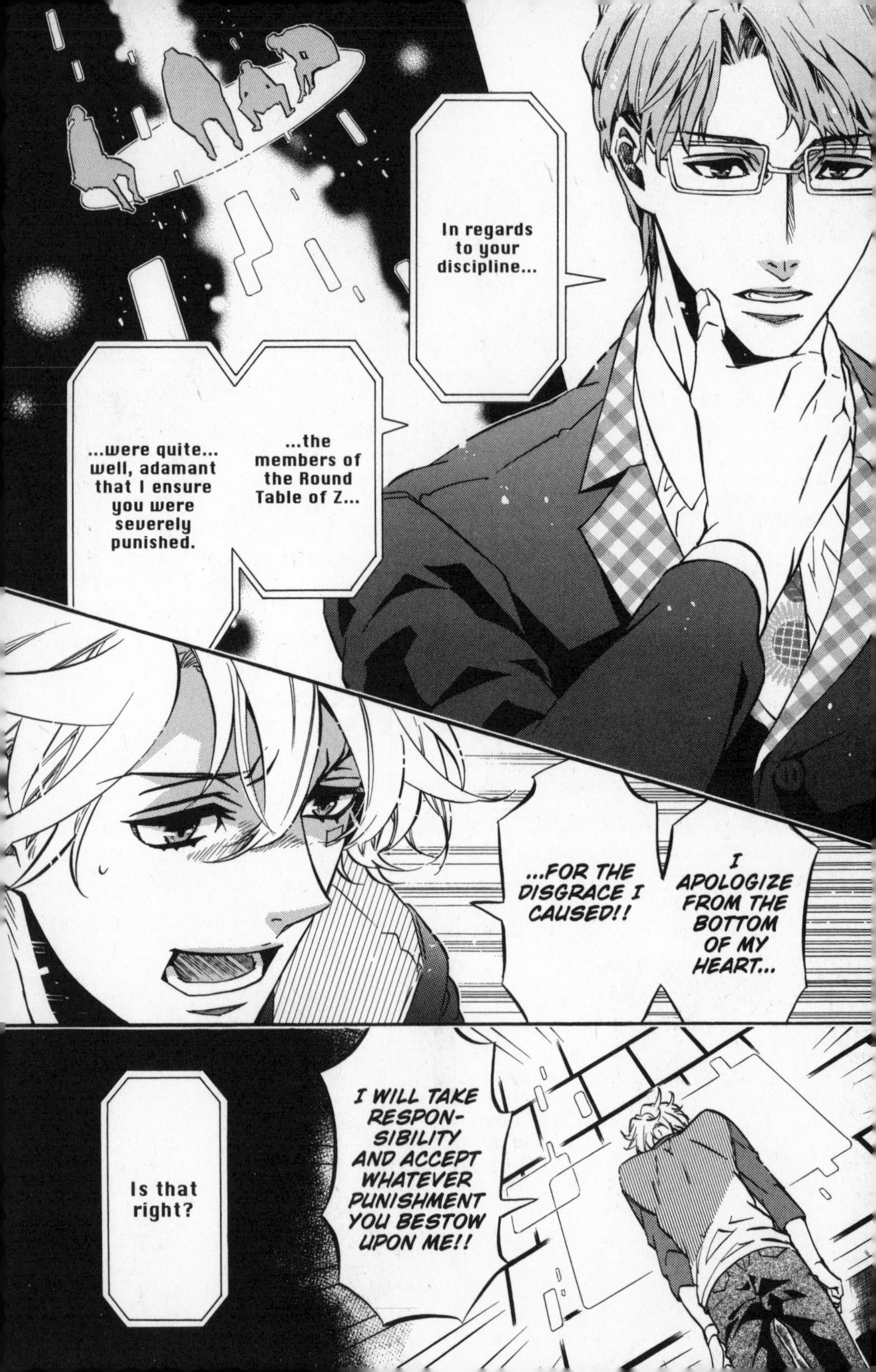
In regards to your discipline...
...the members of the Round Table of Z...
...were quite... well, adamant that I ensure you were severely punished.
I APOLOGIZE FROM THE BOTTOM OF MY HEART...
...FOR THE DISGRACE I CAUSED!!
I WILL TAKE RESPON-SIBILITY AND ACCEPT WHATEVER PUNISHMENT YOU BESTOW UPON ME!!
Is that right?

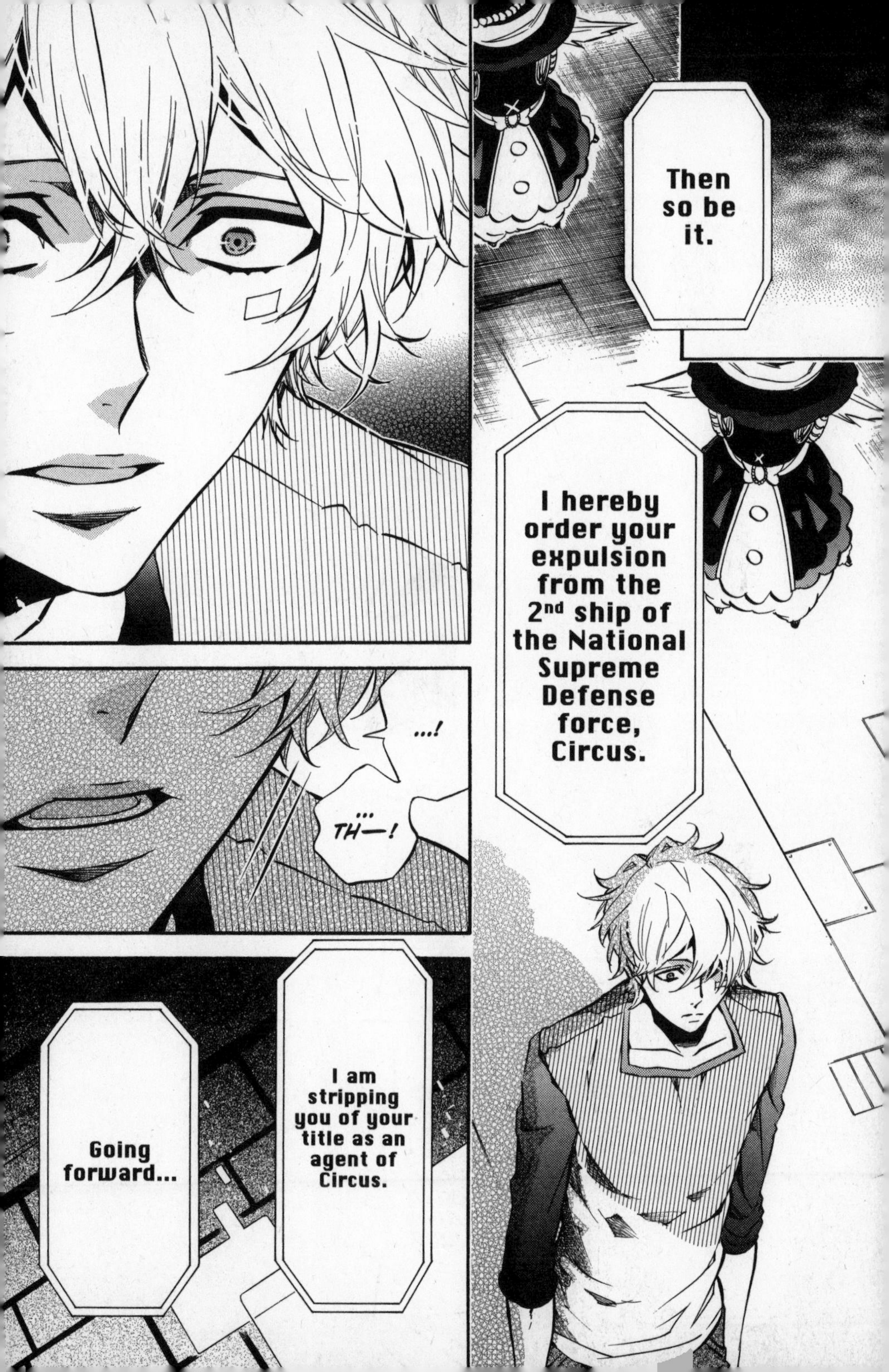
Then so be it.
I hereby order your expulsion from the 2nd ship of the National Supreme Defense force, Circus.
...!
... TH—!
I am stripping you of your title as an agent of Circus.
Going forward...

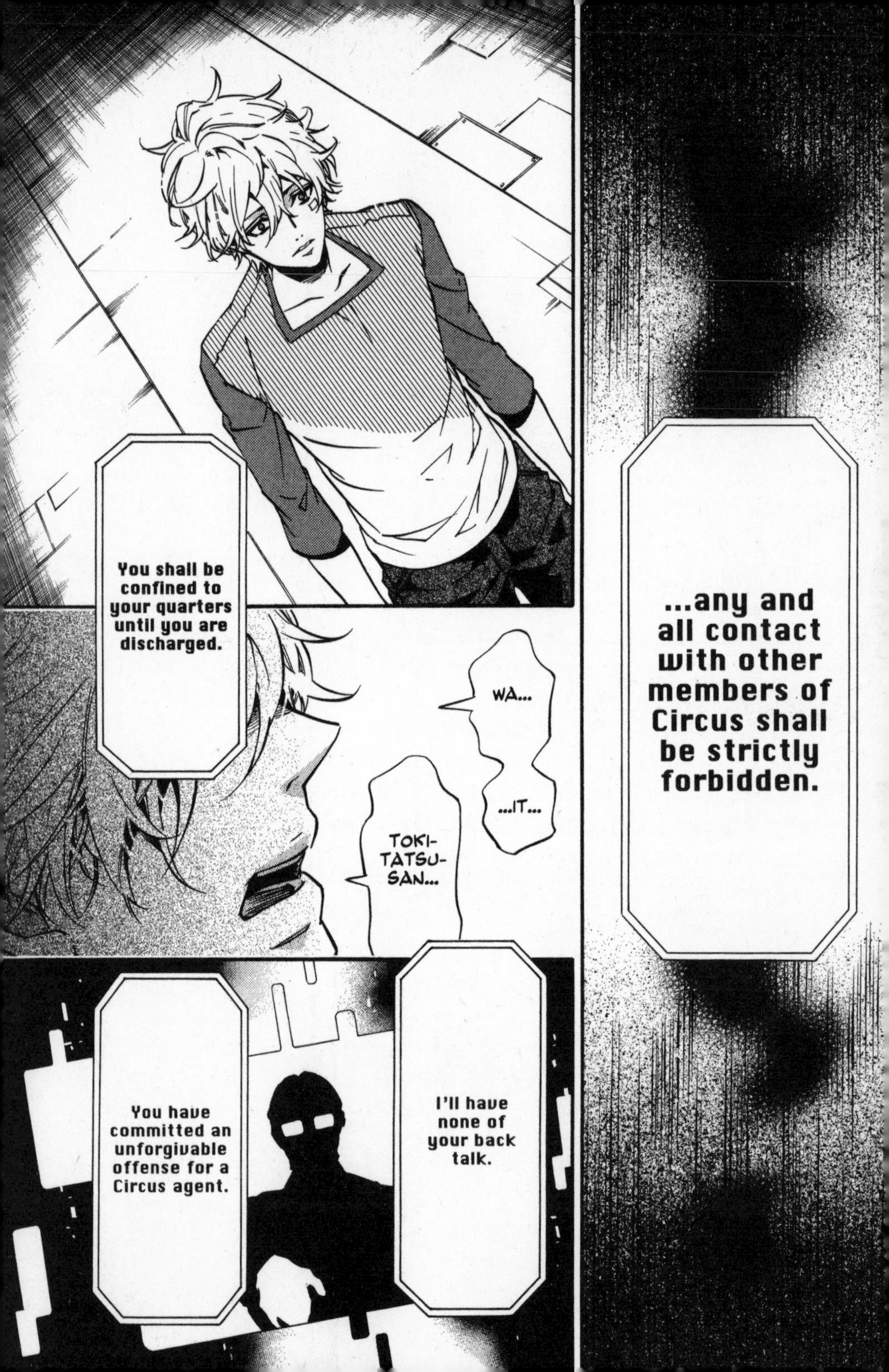
...any and all contact with other members of Circus shall be strictly forbidden.
You shall be confined to your quarters until you are discharged.
WA...
...IT...
TOKI-TATSU-SAN...
I'll have none of your back talk.
You have committed an unforgivable offense for a Circus agent.

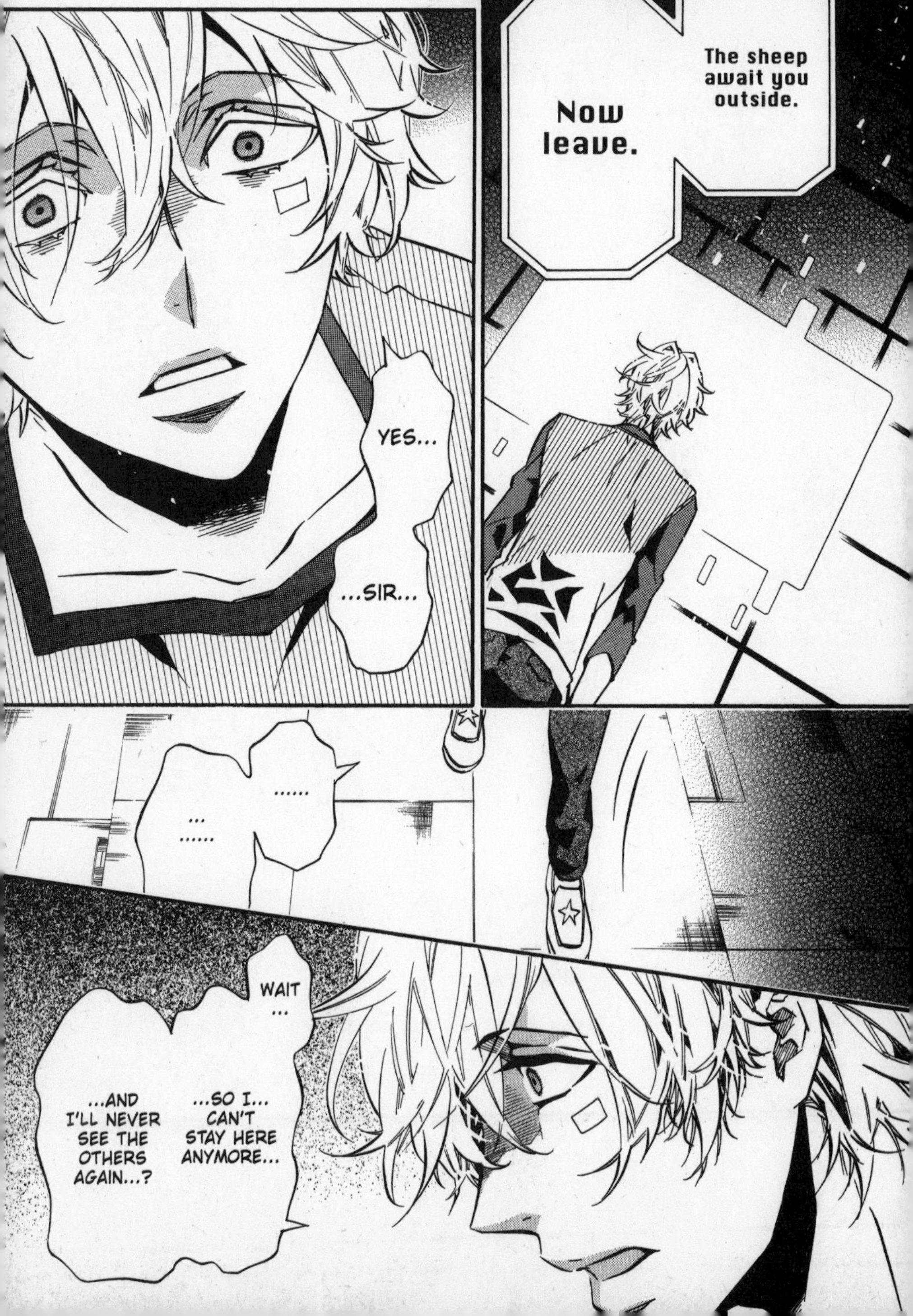
The sheep await you outside.
Now leave.
YES...
...SIR...
......
... .
WAIT ...
...SO I... CAN'T STAY HERE ANYMORE...
...AND I'LL NEVER SEE THE OTHERS AGAIN...?

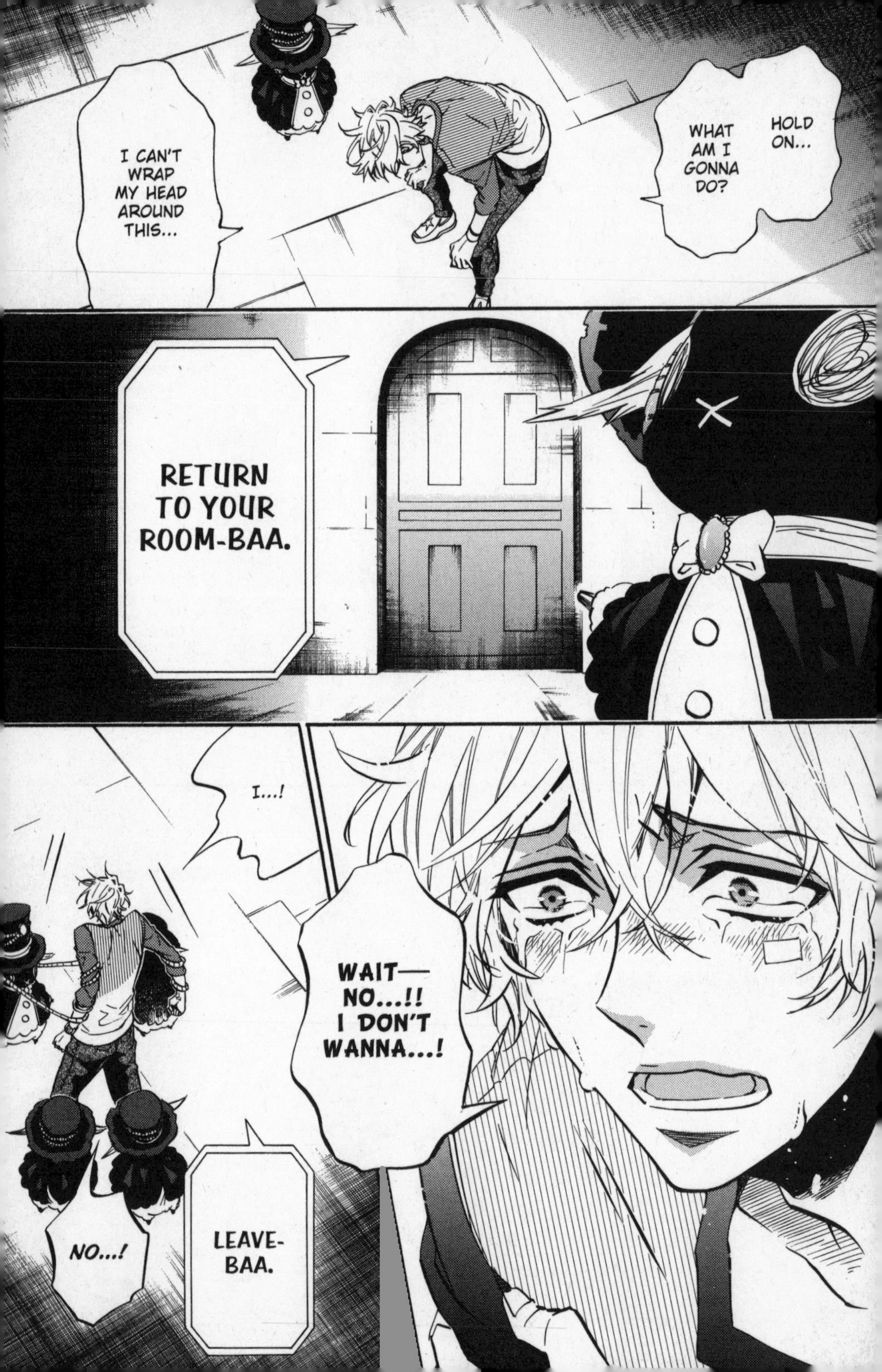
HOLD ON...
WHAT AM I GONNA DO?
I CAN'T WRAP MY HEAD AROUND THIS...
RETURN TO YOUR ROOM-BAA.
WAIT— NO...!! I DON'T WANNA...!
I...!
LEAVE-BAA.
NO...!

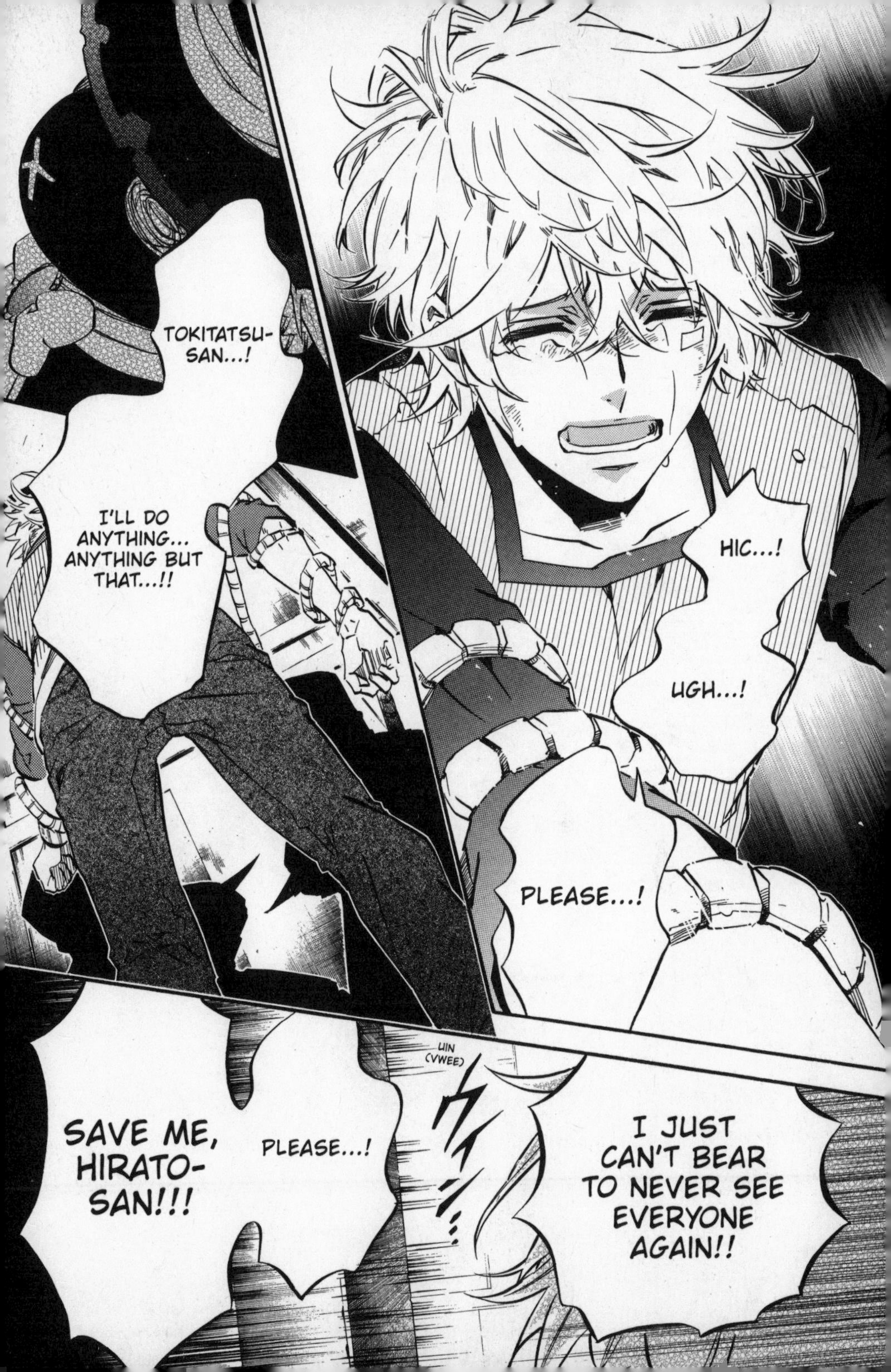
HIC...!
UGH...!
PLEASE...!
TOKITATSU-SAN...!
I'LL DO ANYTHING... ANYTHING BUT THAT...!!
I JUST CAN'T BEAR TO NEVER SEE EVERYONE AGAIN!!
UIN (VWEE)
PLEASE...!
SAVE ME, HIRATO-SAN!!!

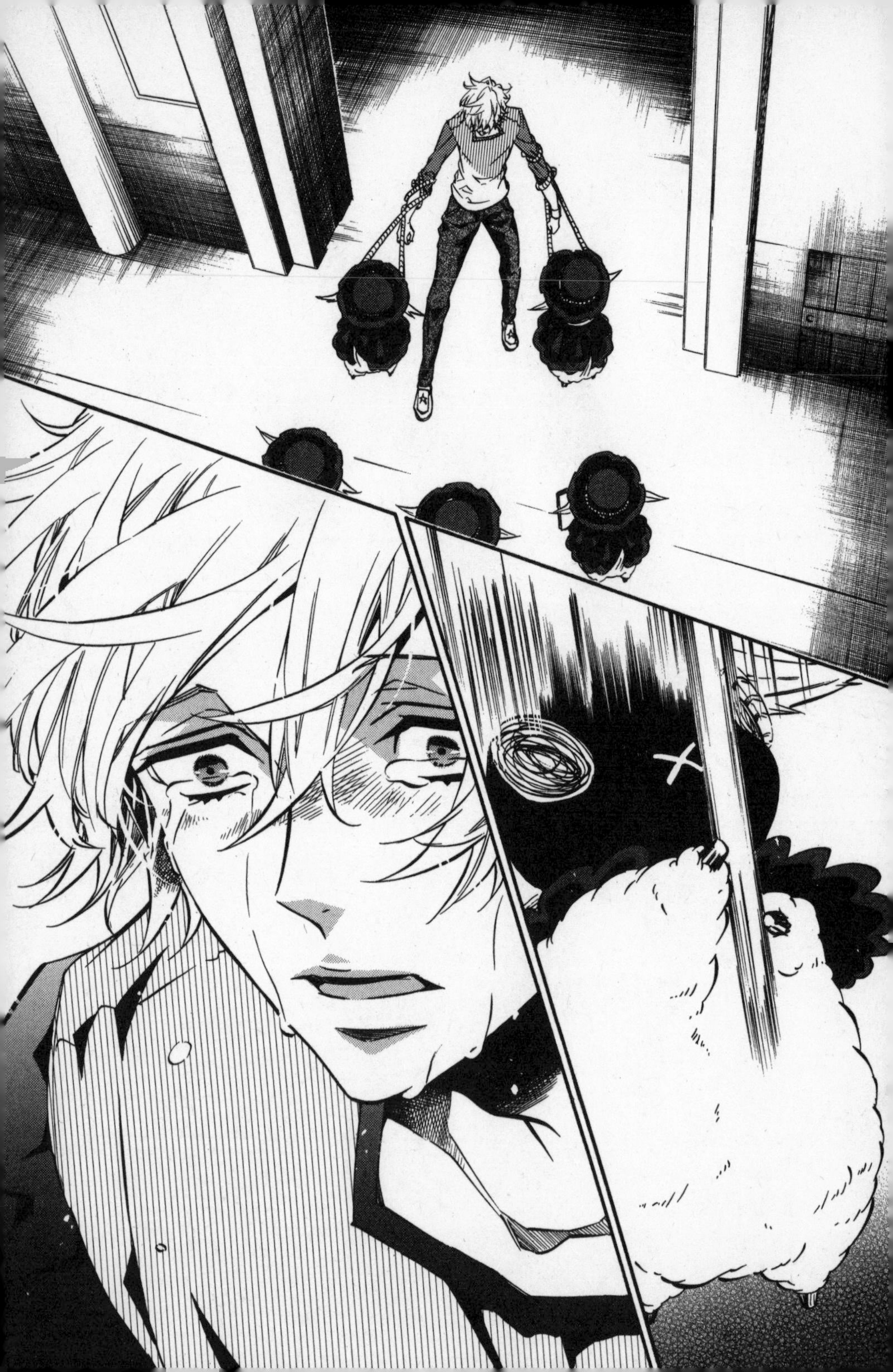

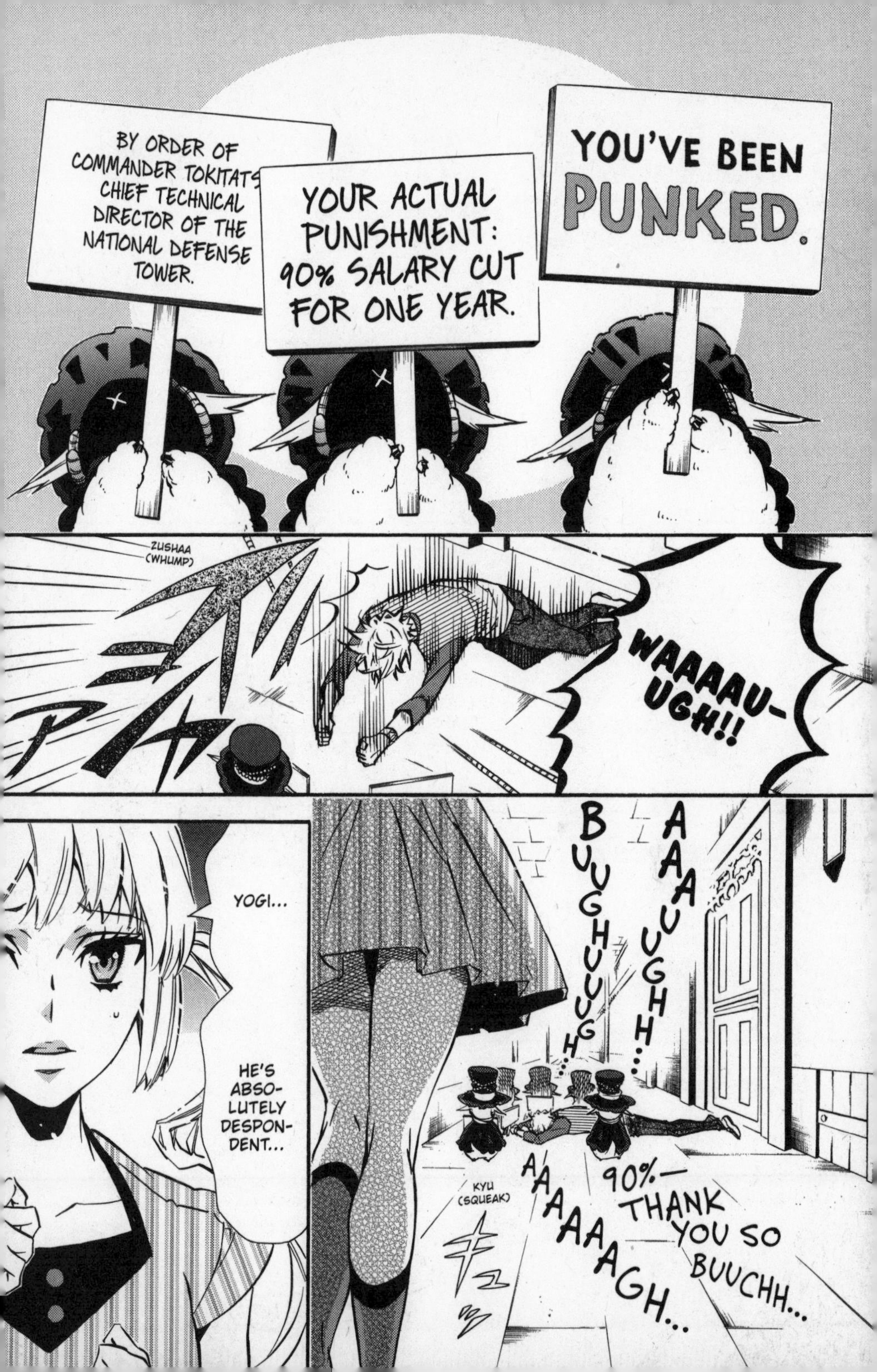
YOU'VE BEEN PUNKED.
YOUR ACTUAL PUNISHMENT: 90% SALARY CUT FOR ONE YEAR.
BY ORDER OF COMMANDER TOKITATSU CHIEF TECHNICAL DIRECTOR OF THE NATIONAL DEFENSE TOWER.
WAAAAAUGH!!
ZUSHAA (WHUMP)
AAAAUUGHH...
BUUGHUUUUGH...
90%— THANK YOU SO BUUCHH...
AAAAAAAGH...
KYU (SQUEAK)
YOGI...
HE'S ABSOLUTELY DESPONDENT...

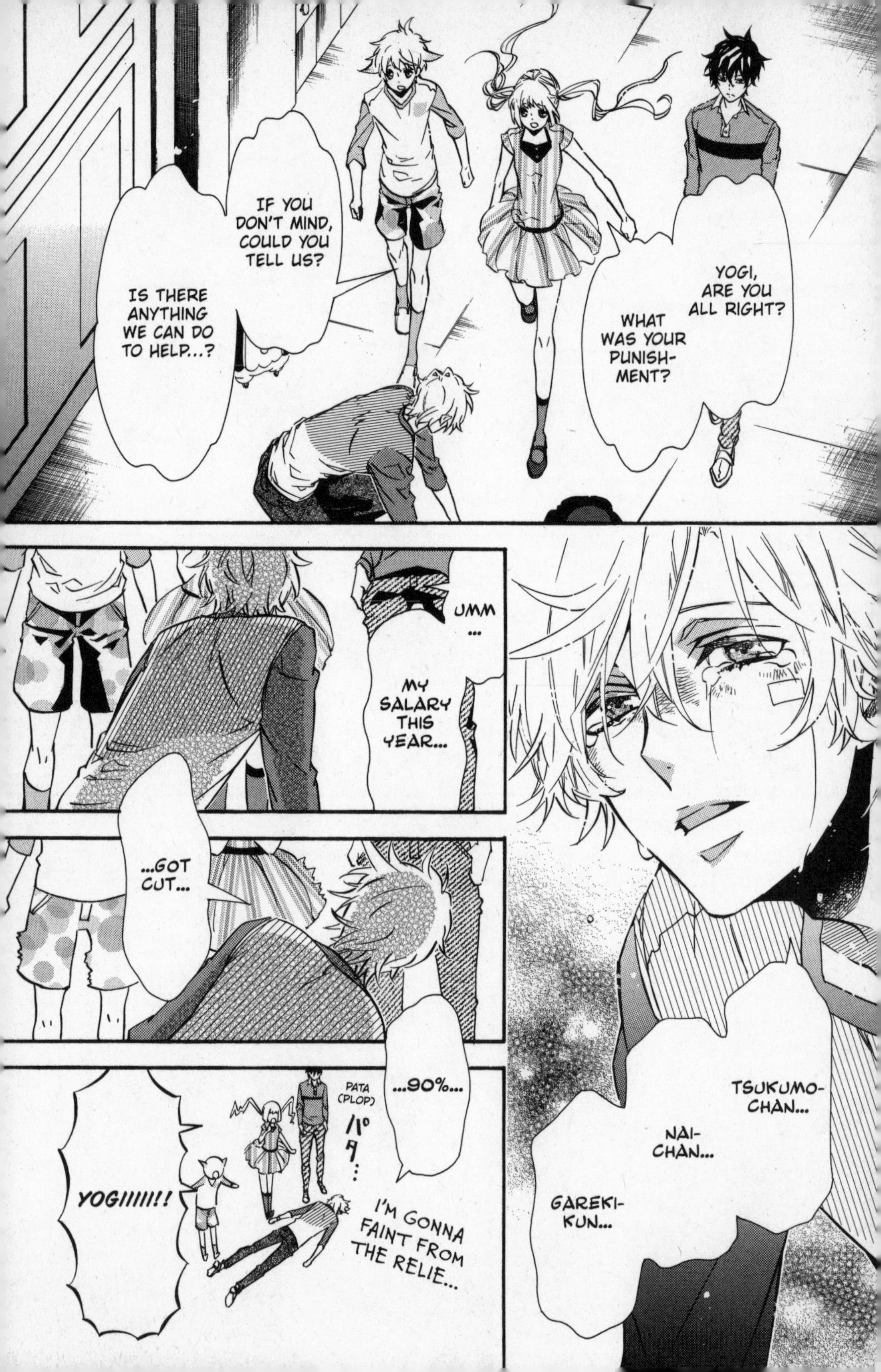
YOGI, ARE YOU ALL RIGHT?
WHAT WAS YOUR PUNISHMENT?
IF YOU DON'T MIND, COULD YOU TELL US?
IS THERE ANYTHING WE CAN DO TO HELP...?
TSUKUMO-CHAN...
NAI-CHAN...
GAREKI-KUN...
UMM...
MY SALARY THIS YEAR...
...GOT CUT...
...90%...
PATA (PLOP)
パタ
I'M GONNA FAINT FROM THE RELIE...
YOGI!!!!!!!

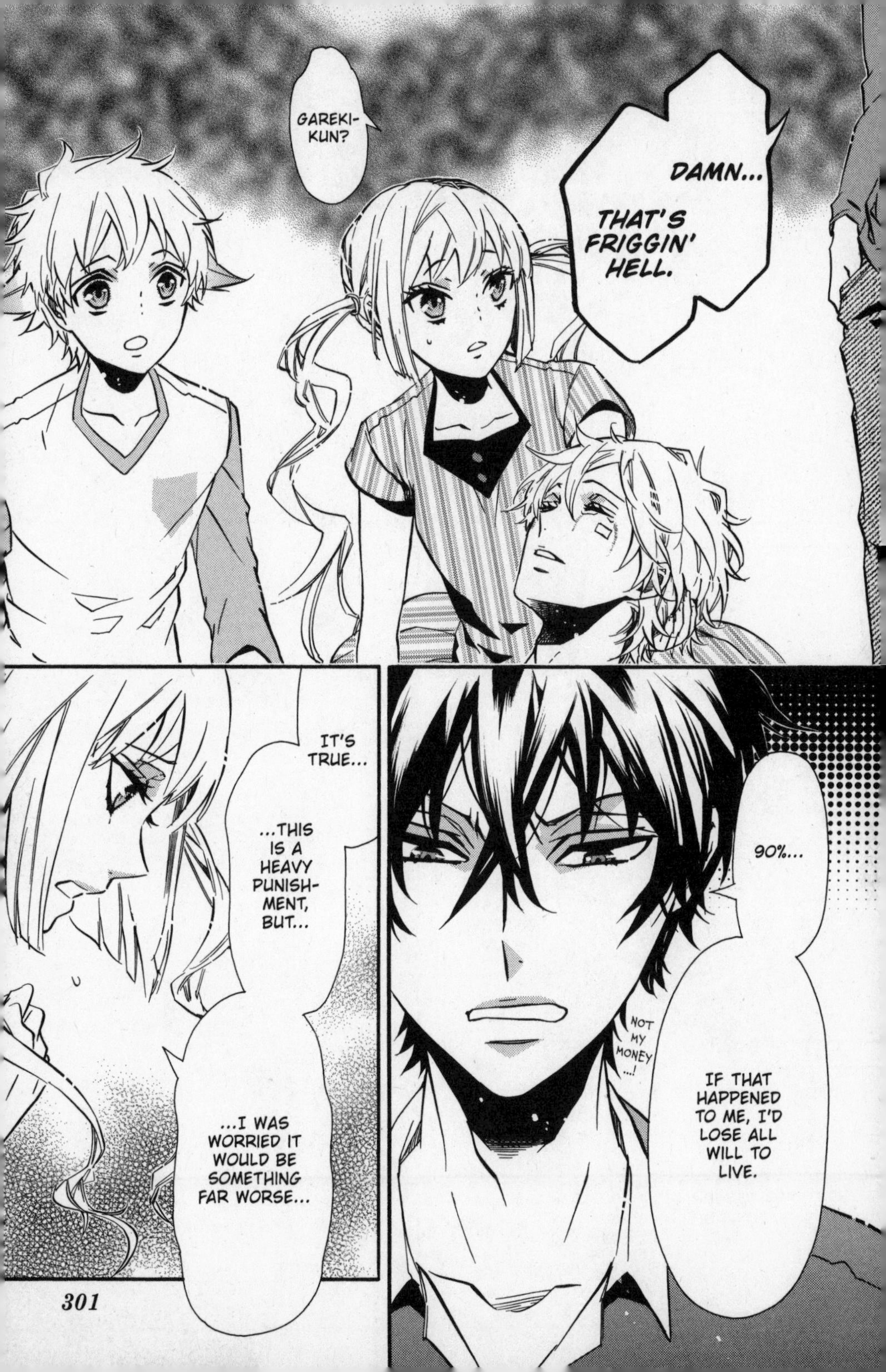
DAMN... THAT'S FRIGGIN' HELL.
GAREKI-KUN?
90%...
IF THAT HAPPENED TO ME, I'D LOSE ALL WILL TO LIVE.
NOT MY MONEY ...!
IT'S TRUE...
...THIS IS A HEAVY PUNISHMENT, BUT...
...I WAS WORRIED IT WOULD BE SOMETHING FAR WORSE...

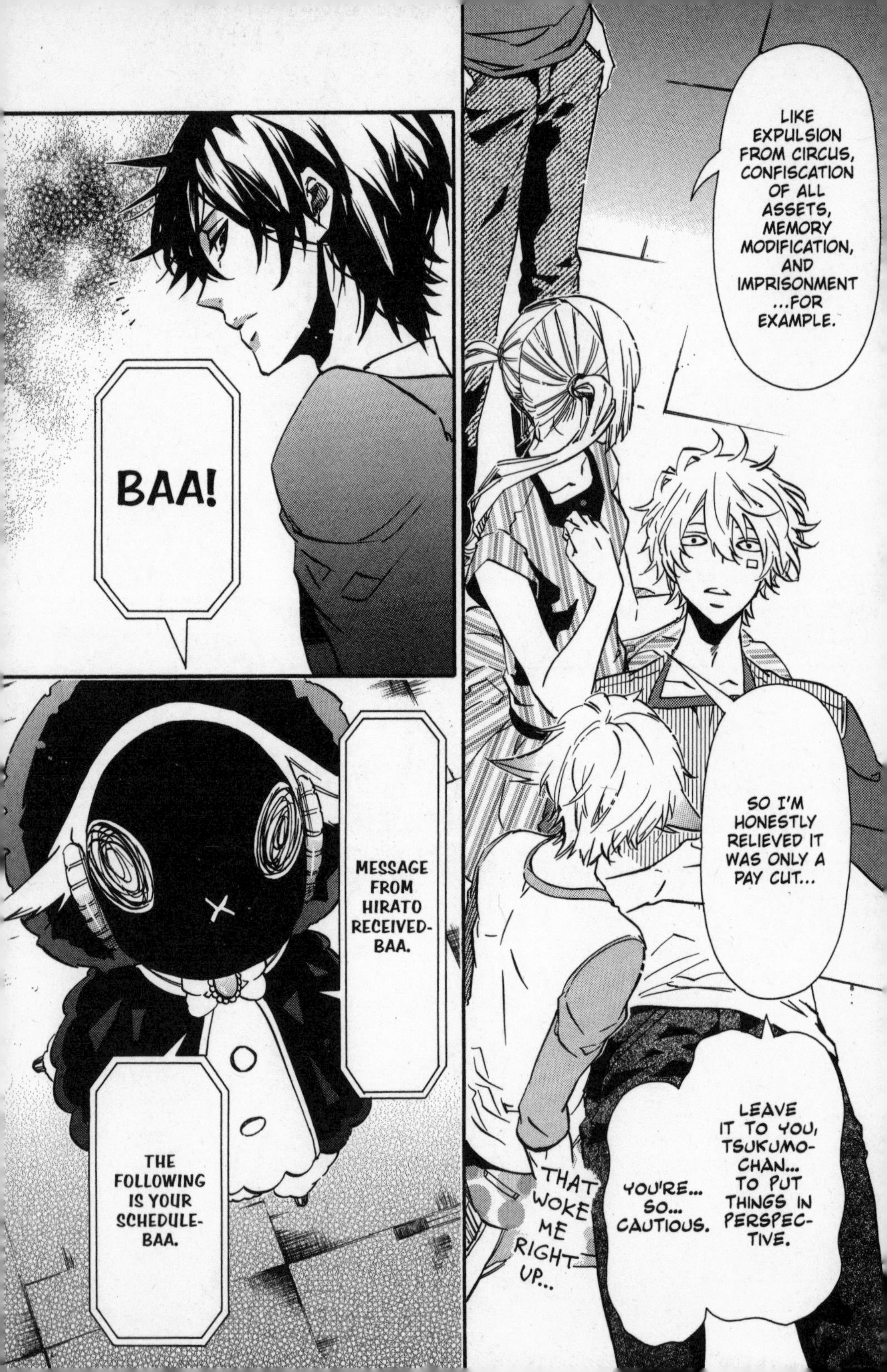
LIKE EXPULSION FROM CIRCUS, CONFISCATION OF ALL ASSETS, MEMORY MODIFICATION, AND IMPRISONMENT ...FOR EXAMPLE.
SO I'M HONESTLY RELIEVED IT WAS ONLY A PAY CUT...
LEAVE IT TO YOU, TSUKUMO-CHAN... TO PUT THINGS IN PERSPECTIVE.
YOU'RE... SO... CAUTIOUS.
THAT WOKE ME RIGHT UP...
BAA!
MESSAGE FROM HIRATO RECEIVED-BAA.
THE FOLLOWING IS YOUR SCHEDULE-BAA.

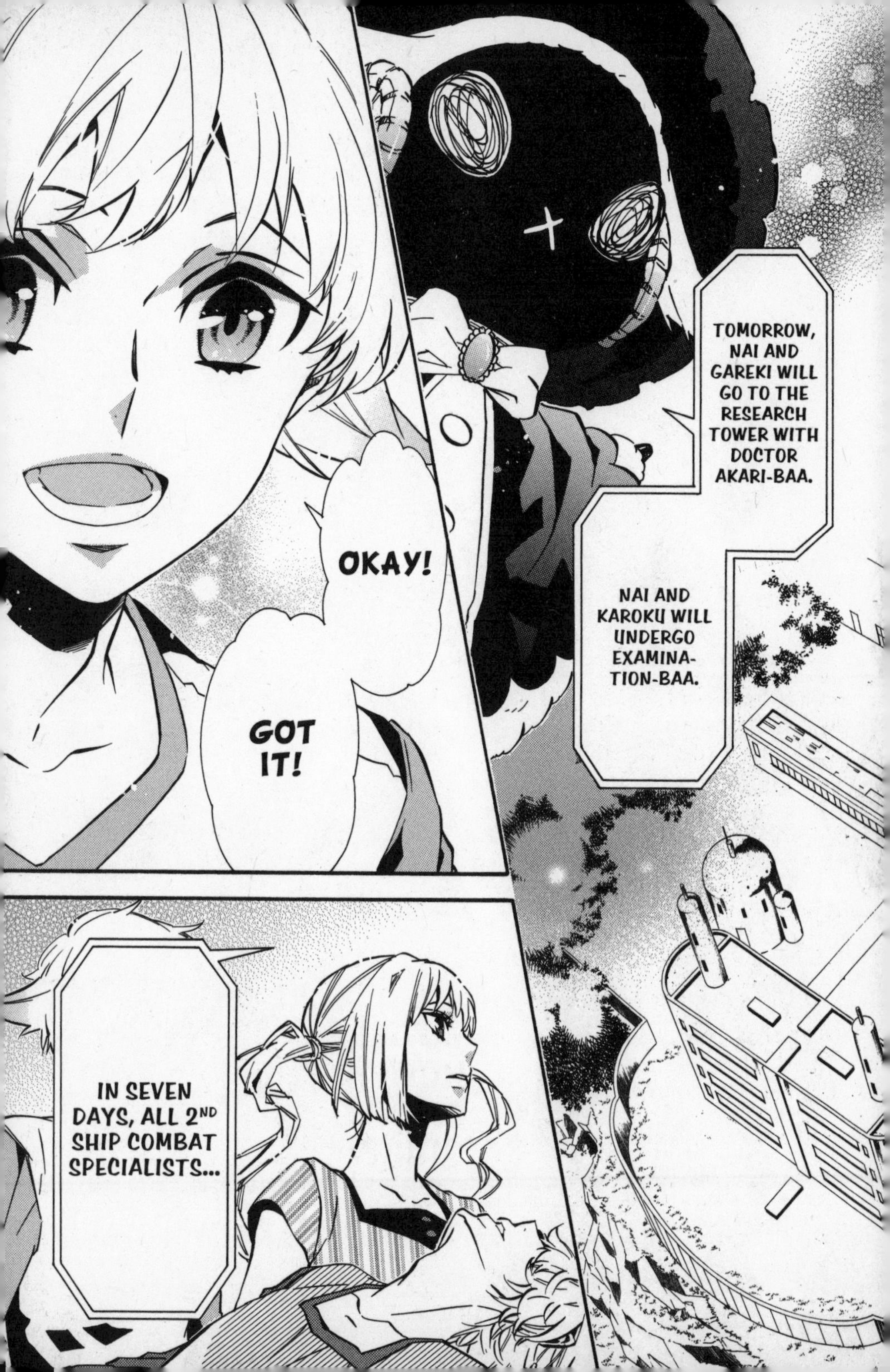
TOMORROW, NAI AND GAREKI WILL GO TO THE RESEARCH TOWER WITH DOCTOR AKARI-BAA.
NAI AND KAROKU WILL UNDERGO EXAMINATION-BAA.
OKAY!
GOT IT!
IN SEVEN DAYS, ALL 2ND SHIP COMBAT SPECIALISTS...

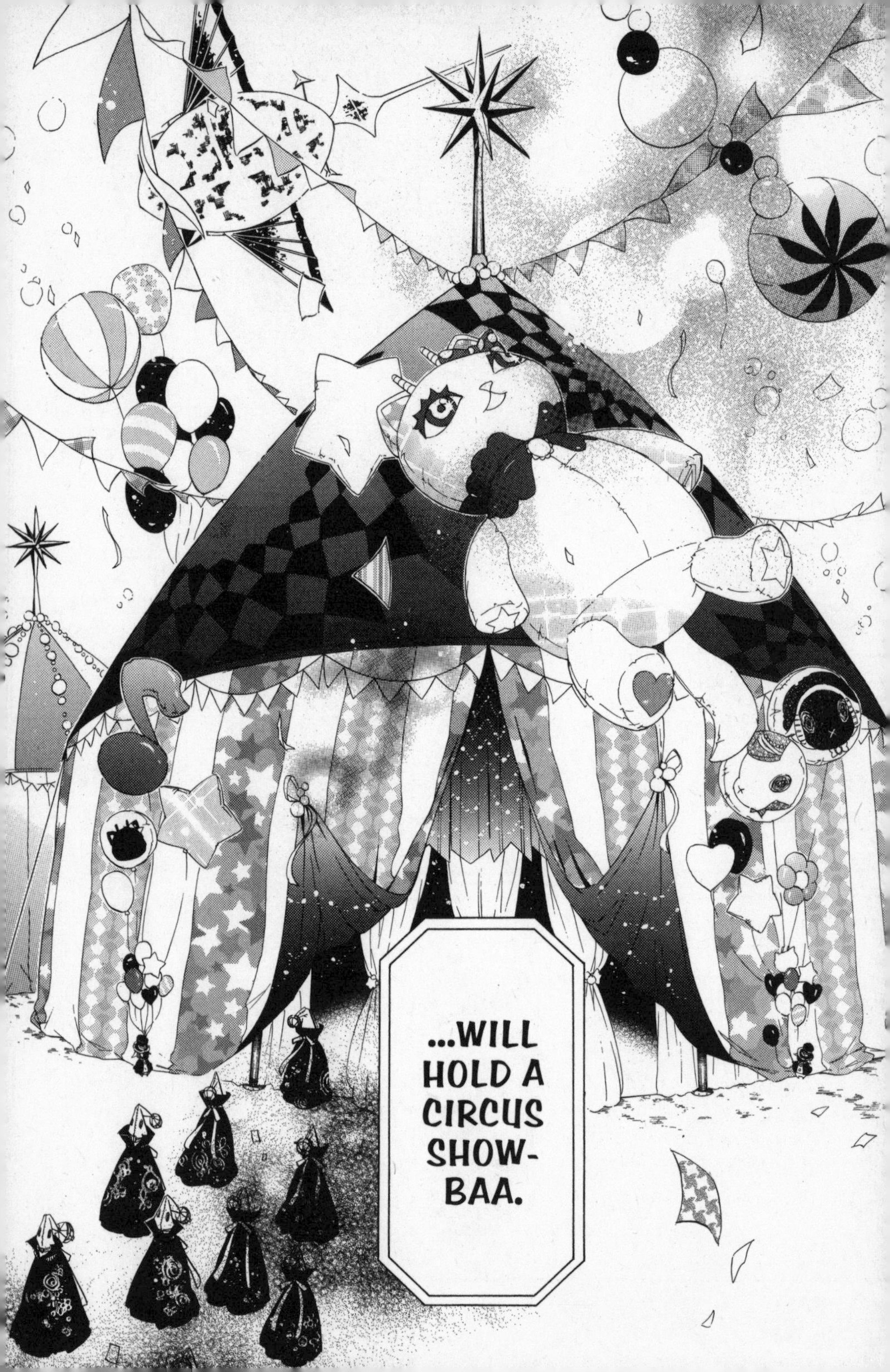
...WILL HOLD A CIRCUS SHOW-BAA.

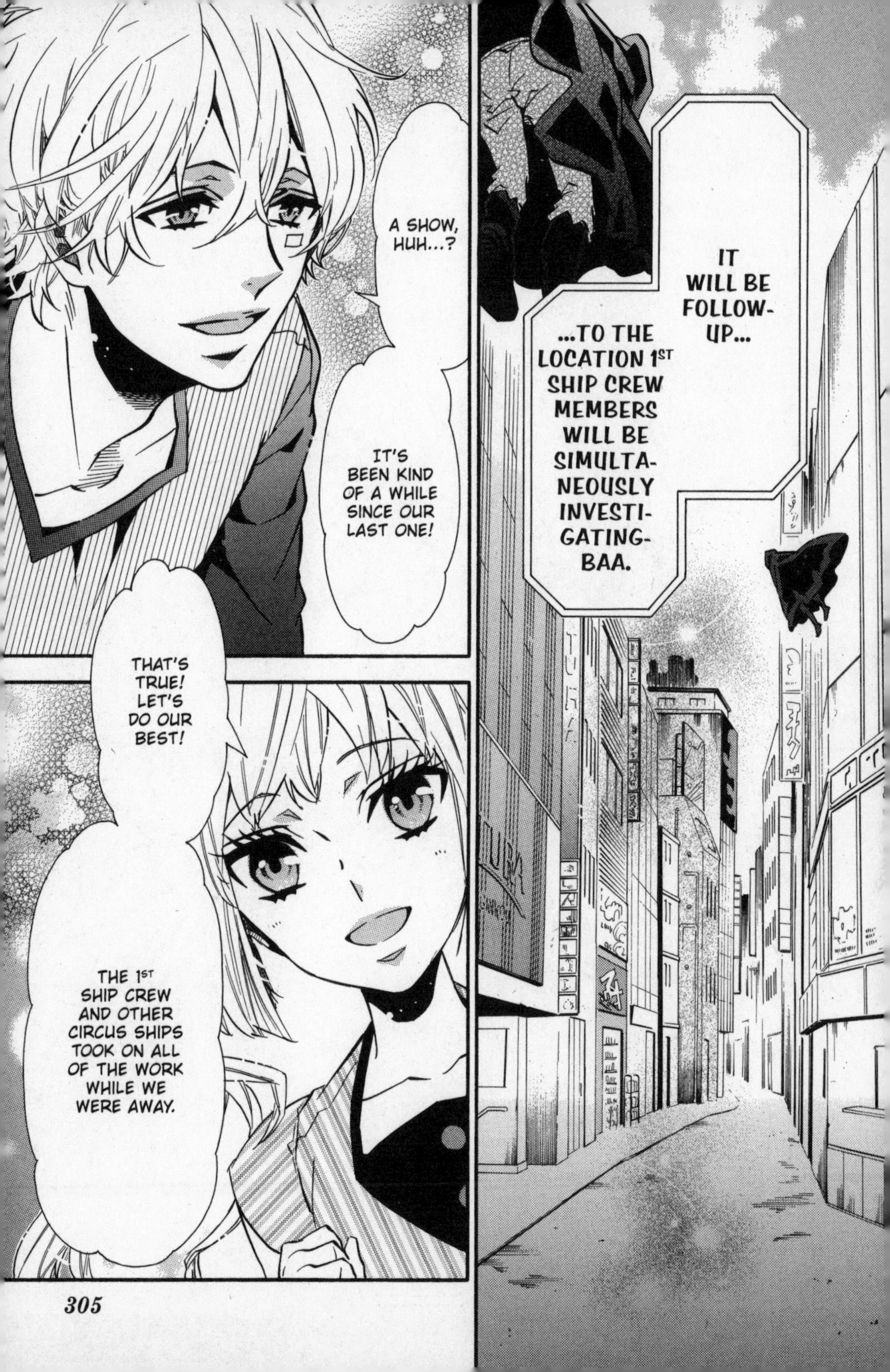
IT WILL BE FOLLOW-UP...
...TO THE LOCATION 1ST SHIP CREW MEMBERS WILL BE SIMULTANEOUSLY INVESTIGATING-BAA.
A SHOW, HUH...?
IT'S BEEN KIND OF A WHILE SINCE OUR LAST ONE!
THAT'S TRUE! LET'S DO OUR BEST!
THE 1ST SHIP CREW AND OTHER CIRCUS SHIPS TOOK ON ALL OF THE WORK WHILE WE WERE AWAY.

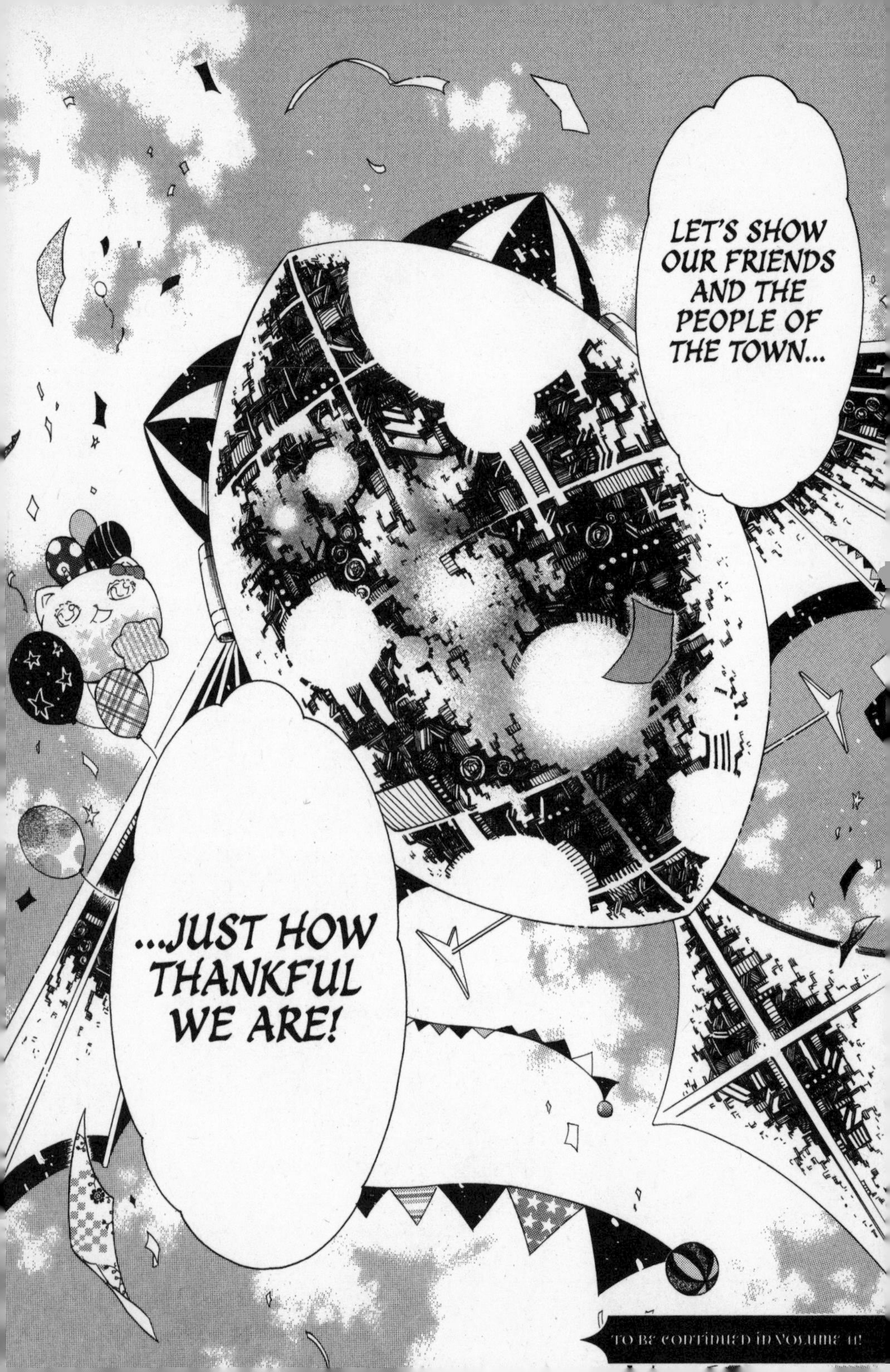
LET'S SHOW OUR FRIENDS AND THE PEOPLE OF THE TOWN...
...JUST HOW THANKFUL WE ARE!
TO BE CONTINUED IN VOLUME 11!

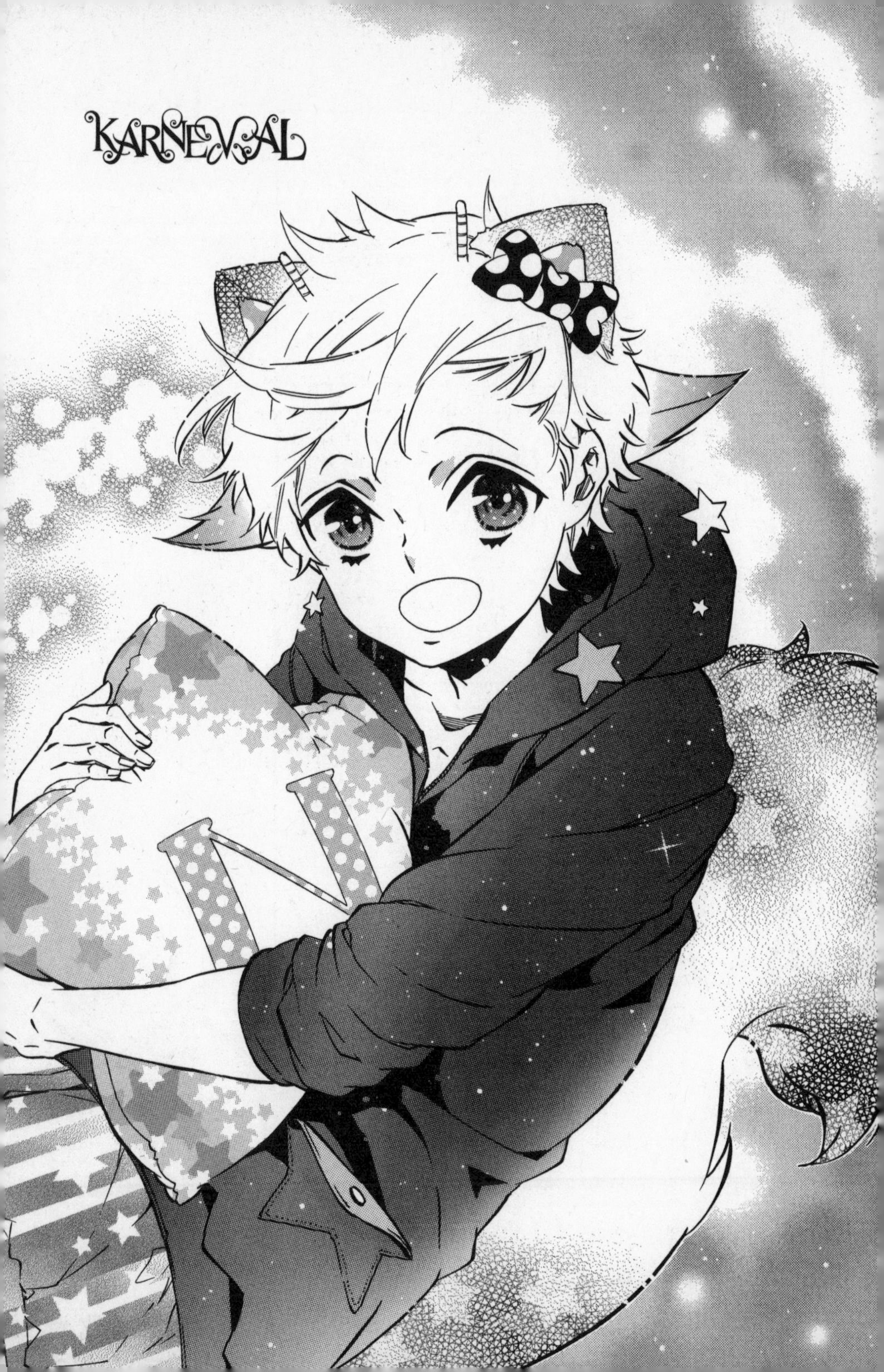
KARNEVAL

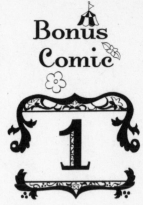

Bonus Comic 1

Nyanperona's Many Flavors

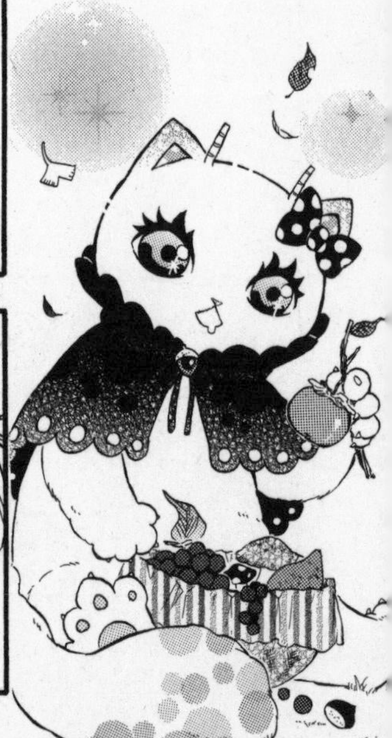

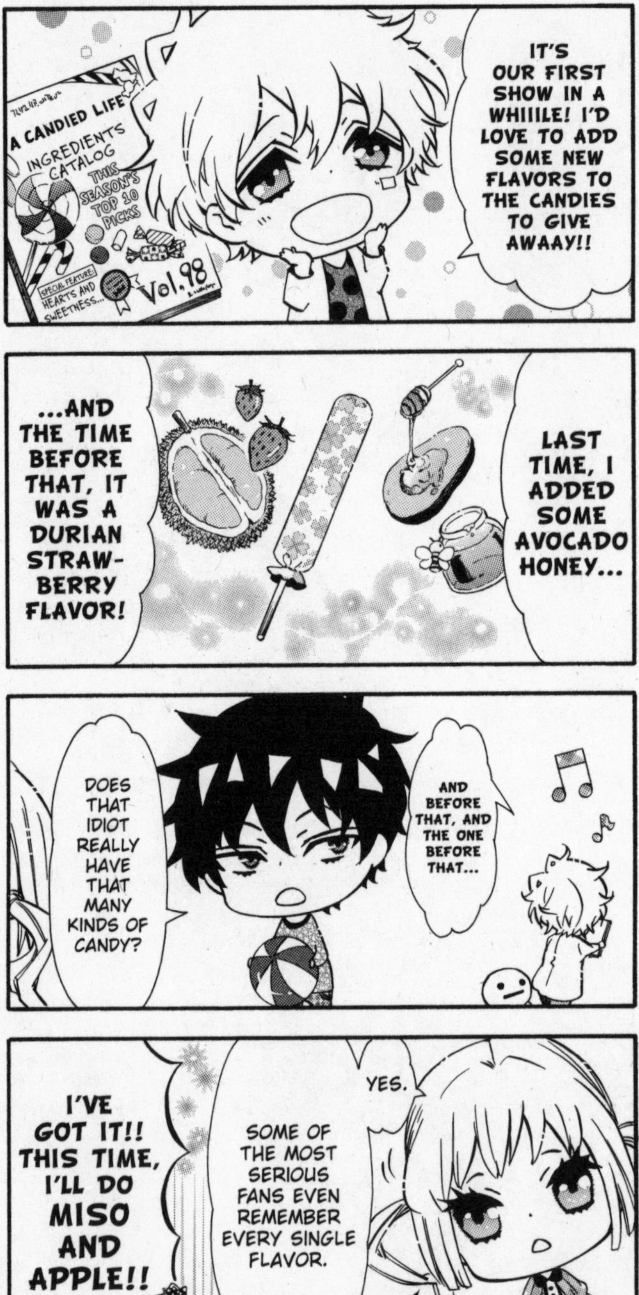
IT'S OUR FIRST SHOW IN A WHIIILE! I'D LOVE TO ADD SOME NEW FLAVORS TO THE CANDIES TO GIVE AWAAY!!
A CANDIED LIFE
INGREDIENTS CATALOG
THIS SEASON'S TOP 10 PICKS
SPECIAL FEATURE: HEARTS AND SWEETNESS...
Vol.98
LAST TIME, I ADDED SOME AVOCADO HONEY...
...AND THE TIME BEFORE THAT, IT WAS A DURIAN STRAW-BERRY FLAVOR!
AND BEFORE THAT, AND THE ONE BEFORE THAT...
DOES THAT IDIOT REALLY HAVE THAT MANY KINDS OF CANDY?
YES.
SOME OF THE MOST SERIOUS FANS EVEN REMEMBER EVERY SINGLE FLAVOR.
I'VE GOT IT!! THIS TIME, I'LL DO MISO AND APPLE!!

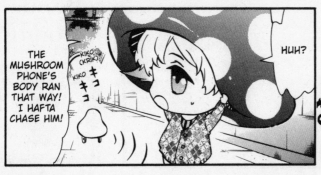

Bonus Comic 2

The Look in His Eyes

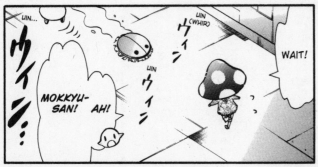

HUH?
KIKO (KRIK) キコ
KIKO キコ
THE MUSHROOM PHONE'S BODY RAN THAT WAY! I HAFTA CHASE HIM!
WAIT!
UIN (WHIR) ウィン
UIN ウィン
AH!
MOKKYU-SAN!
UIN...
ウィン...
NEED A RIDE...?
HUH?
UIN ウィン
UIN ウィン
WHAT THE—!?
IS THIS DEJA-VU!?

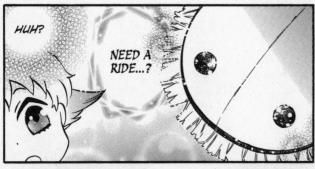

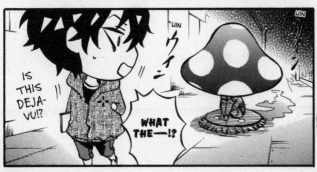

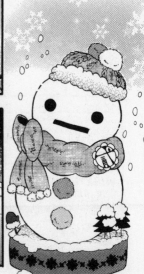

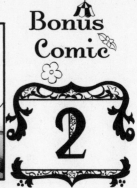

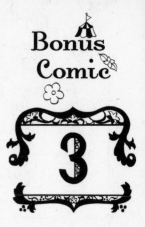

Bonus Comic 3

Thank You for 10 Years!

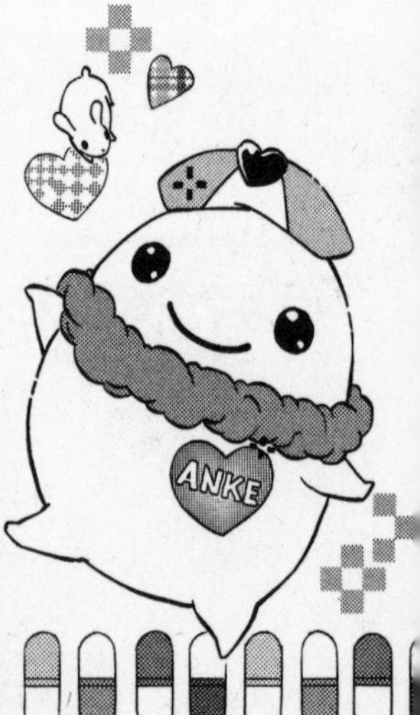
ANKE

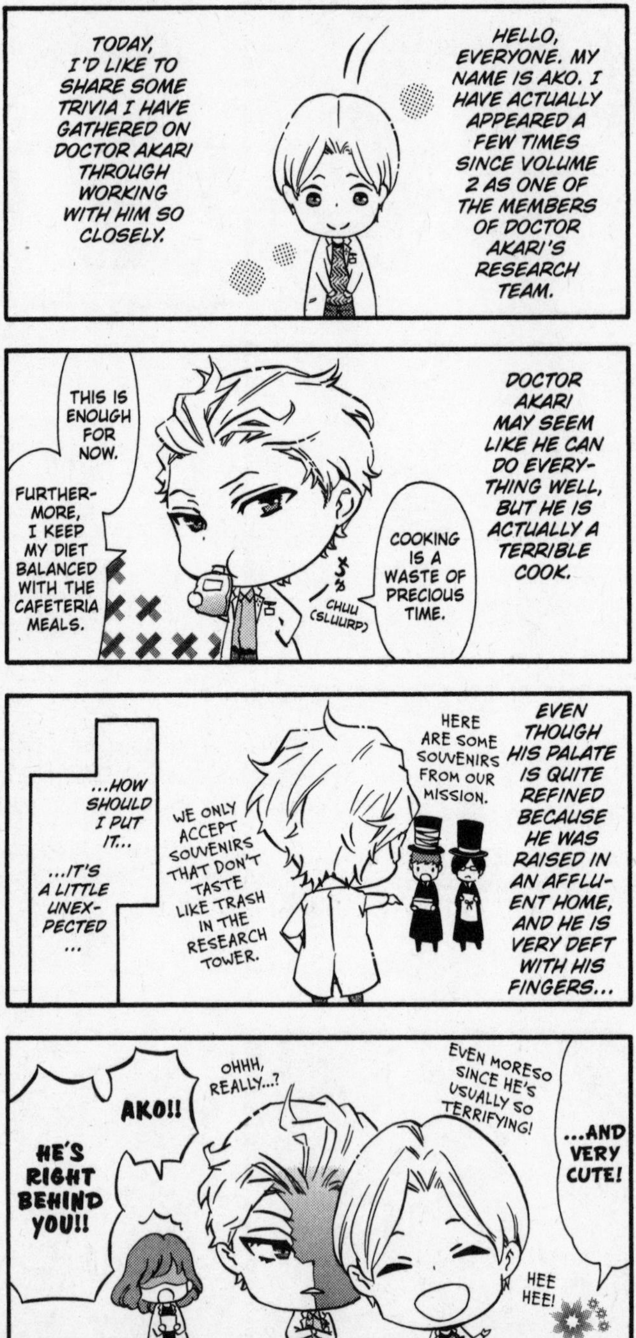
HELLO, EVERYONE. MY NAME IS AKO. I HAVE ACTUALLY APPEARED A FEW TIMES SINCE VOLUME 2 AS ONE OF THE MEMBERS OF DOCTOR AKARI'S RESEARCH TEAM.
TODAY, I'D LIKE TO SHARE SOME TRIVIA I HAVE GATHERED ON DOCTOR AKARI THROUGH WORKING WITH HIM SO CLOSELY.
DOCTOR AKARI MAY SEEM LIKE HE CAN DO EVERY-THING WELL, BUT HE IS ACTUALLY A TERRIBLE COOK.
COOKING IS A WASTE OF PRECIOUS TIME.
CHUU (SLUURP)
THIS IS ENOUGH FOR NOW.
FURTHER-MORE, I KEEP MY DIET BALANCED WITH THE CAFETERIA MEALS.
EVEN THOUGH HIS PALATE IS QUITE REFINED BECAUSE HE WAS RAISED IN AN AFFLU-ENT HOME, AND HE IS VERY DEFT WITH HIS FINGERS...
HERE ARE SOME SOUVENIRS FROM OUR MISSION.
WE ONLY ACCEPT SOUVENIRS THAT DON'T TASTE LIKE TRASH IN THE RESEARCH TOWER.
...HOW SHOULD I PUT IT...
...IT'S A LITTLE UNEX-PECTED...
...AND VERY CUTE!
EVEN MORESO SINCE HE'S USUALLY SO TERRIFYING!
HEE HEE!
OHHH, REALLY...?
AKO!!
HE'S RIGHT BEHIND YOU!!

SEE YOU NEXT TIME, IF I'M STILL ALIVE. BY AKO.

10th
Anniversary
ILLUSTRATIONS BY SUAMA

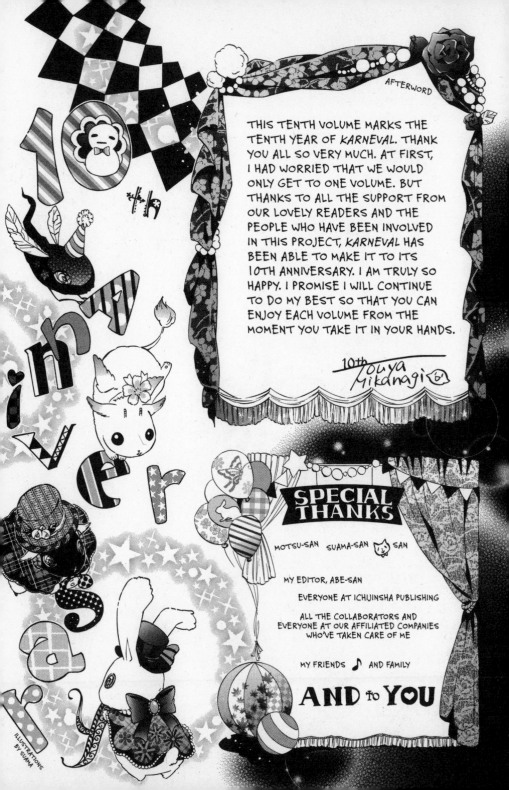

AFTERWORD

THIS TENTH VOLUME MARKS THE TENTH YEAR OF *KARNEVAL*. THANK YOU ALL SO VERY MUCH. AT FIRST, I HAD WORRIED THAT WE WOULD ONLY GET TO ONE VOLUME. BUT THANKS TO ALL THE SUPPORT FROM OUR LOVELY READERS AND THE PEOPLE WHO HAVE BEEN INVOLVED IN THIS PROJECT, *KARNEVAL* HAS BEEN ABLE TO MAKE IT TO ITS 10TH ANNIVERSARY. I AM TRULY SO HAPPY. I PROMISE I WILL CONTINUE TO DO MY BEST SO THAT YOU CAN ENJOY EACH VOLUME FROM THE MOMENT YOU TAKE IT IN YOUR HANDS.

10th Touya Mikanagi

SPECIAL THANKS

MOTSU-SAN SUAMA-SAN SAN

MY EDITOR, ABE-SAN

EVERYONE AT ICHIJINSHA PUBLISHING

ALL THE COLLABORATORS AND EVERYONE AT OUR AFFILIATED COMPANIES WHO'VE TAKEN CARE OF ME

MY FRIENDS ♪ AND FAMILY

AND to YOU

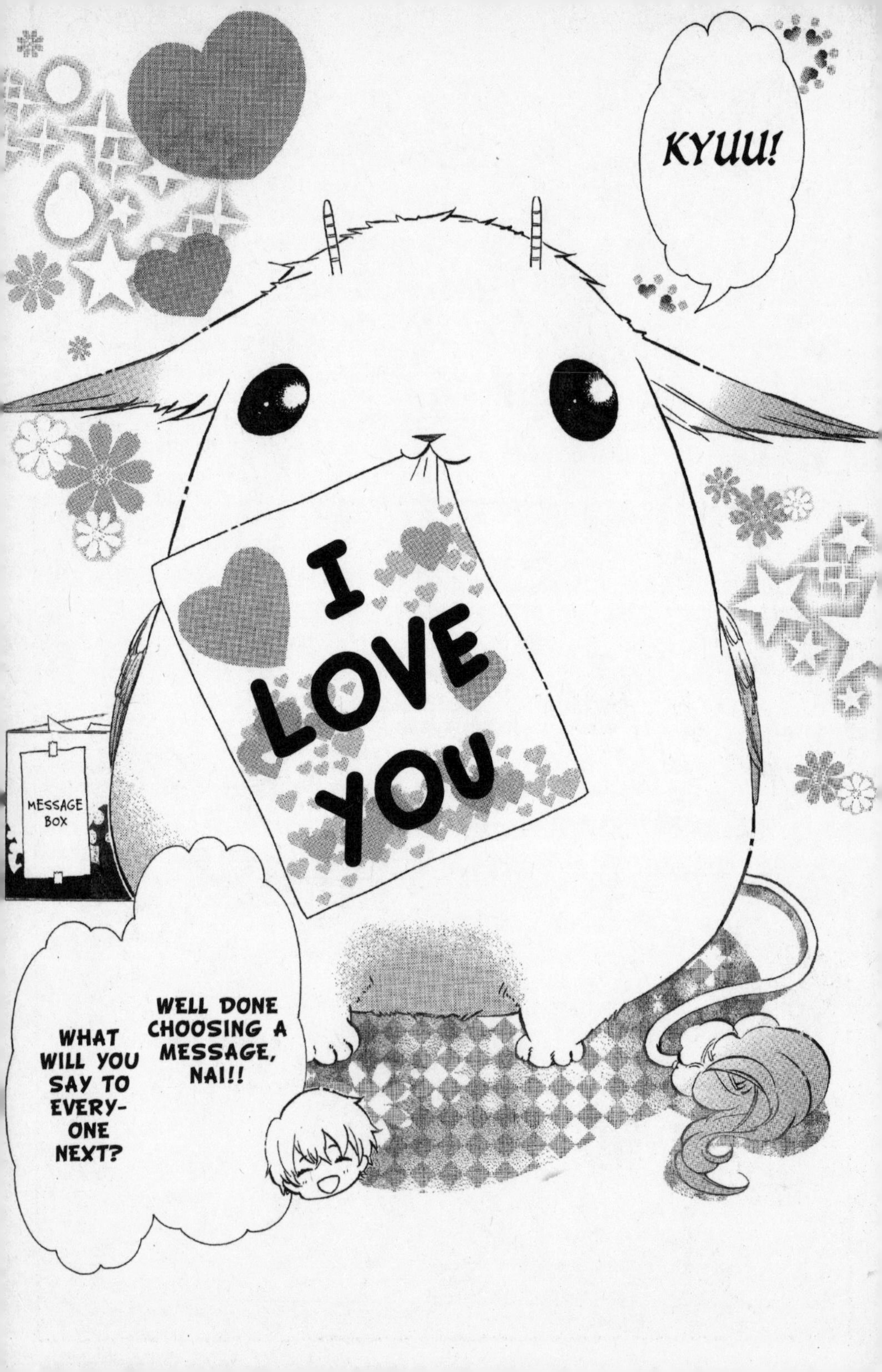
KYUU!
I LOVE YOU
MESSAGE BOX
WELL DONE CHOOSING A MESSAGE, NAI!!
WHAT WILL YOU SAY TO EVERY-ONE NEXT?

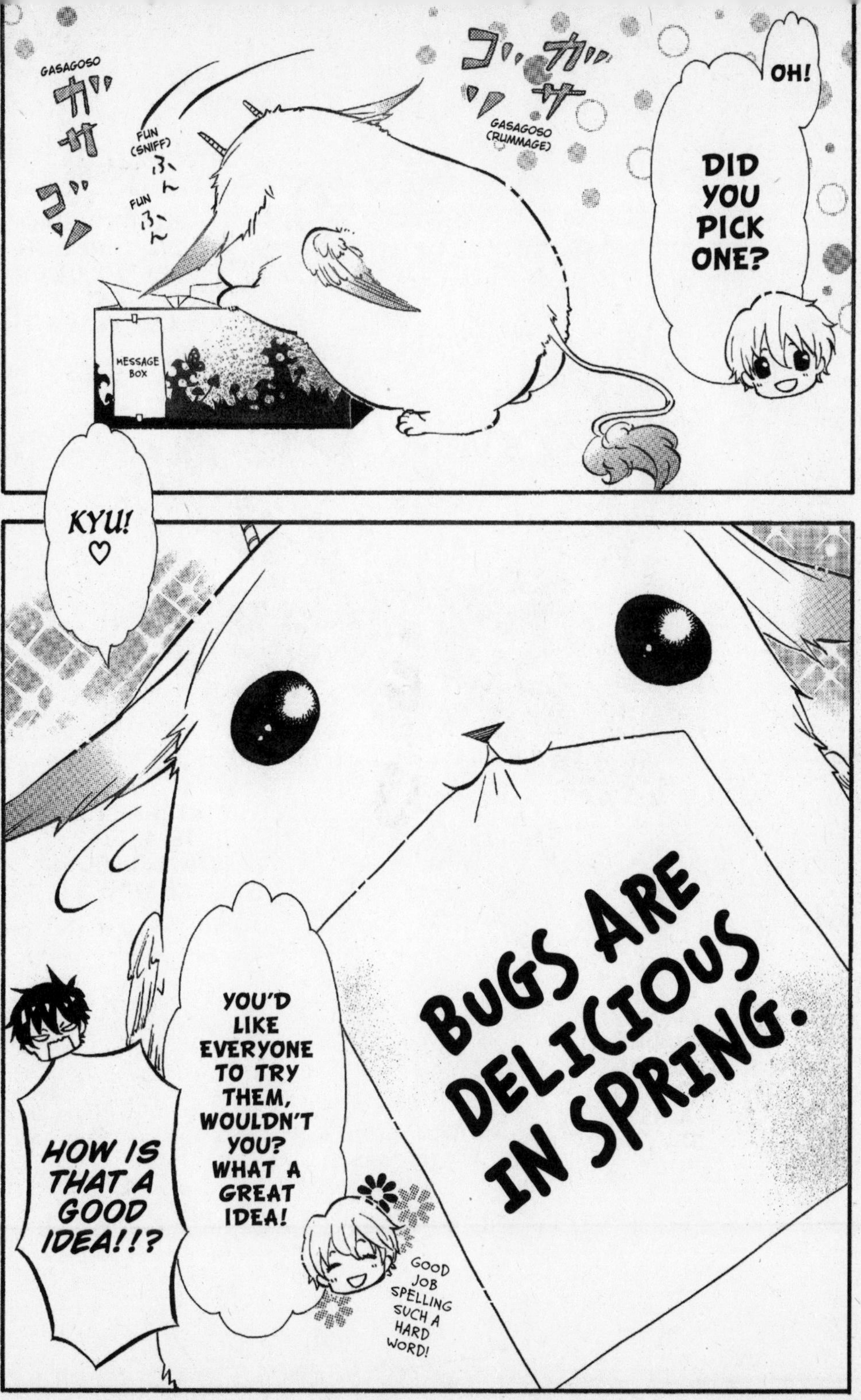
OH!
DID YOU PICK ONE?
GASAGOSO (RUMMAGE)
FUN (SNIFF) ふん
FUN ふん
GASAGOSO
MESSAGE BOX
KYU! ♡
BUGS ARE DELICIOUS IN SPRING.
YOU'D LIKE EVERYONE TO TRY THEM, WOULDN'T YOU? WHAT A GREAT IDEA!
GOOD JOB SPELLING SUCH A HARD WORD!
HOW IS THAT A GOOD IDEA!!?

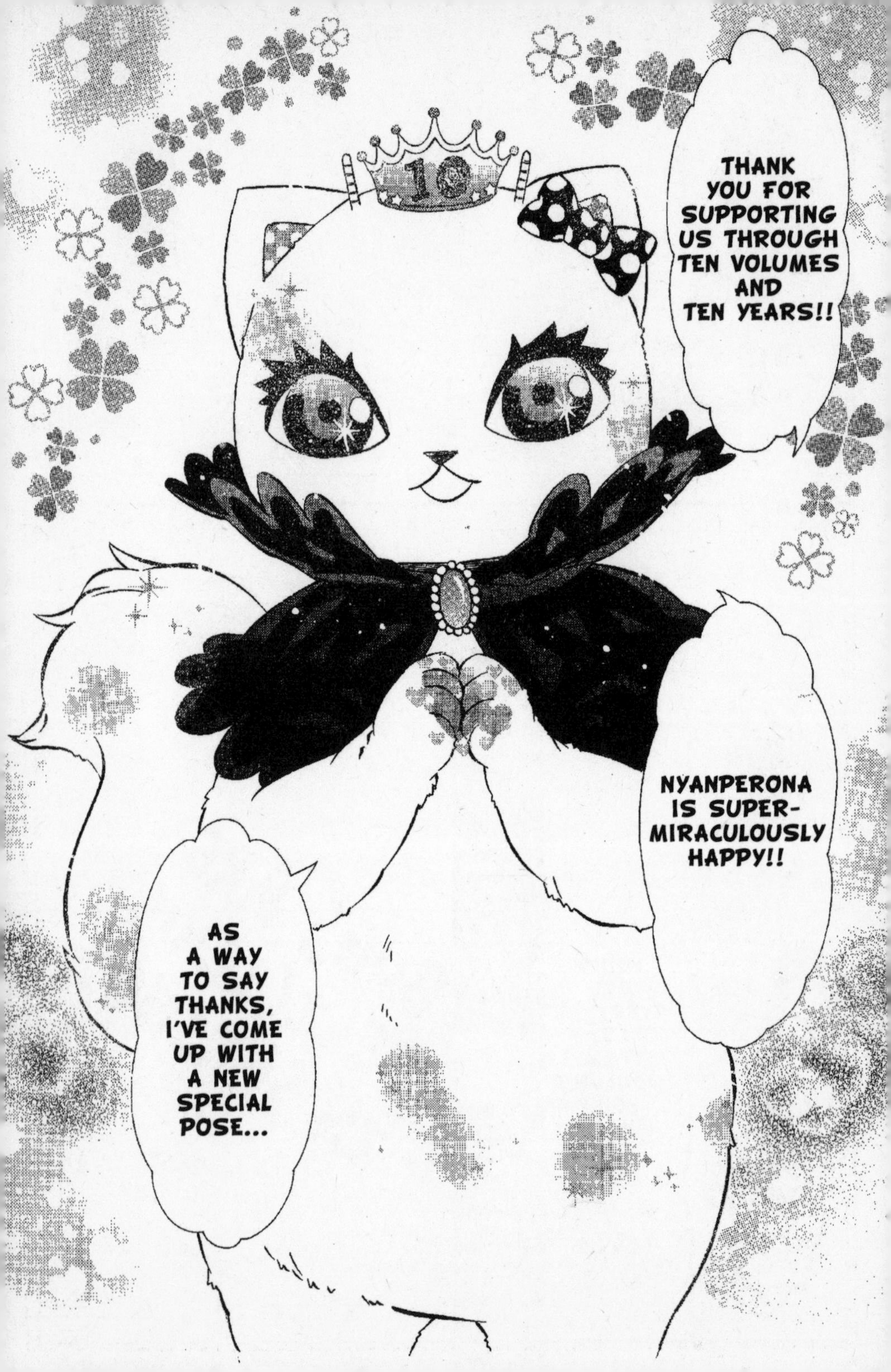
THANK YOU FOR SUPPORTING US THROUGH TEN VOLUMES AND TEN YEARS!!
NYANPERONA IS SUPER-MIRACULOUSLY HAPPY!!
AS A WAY TO SAY THANKS, I'VE COME UP WITH A NEW SPECIAL POSE...

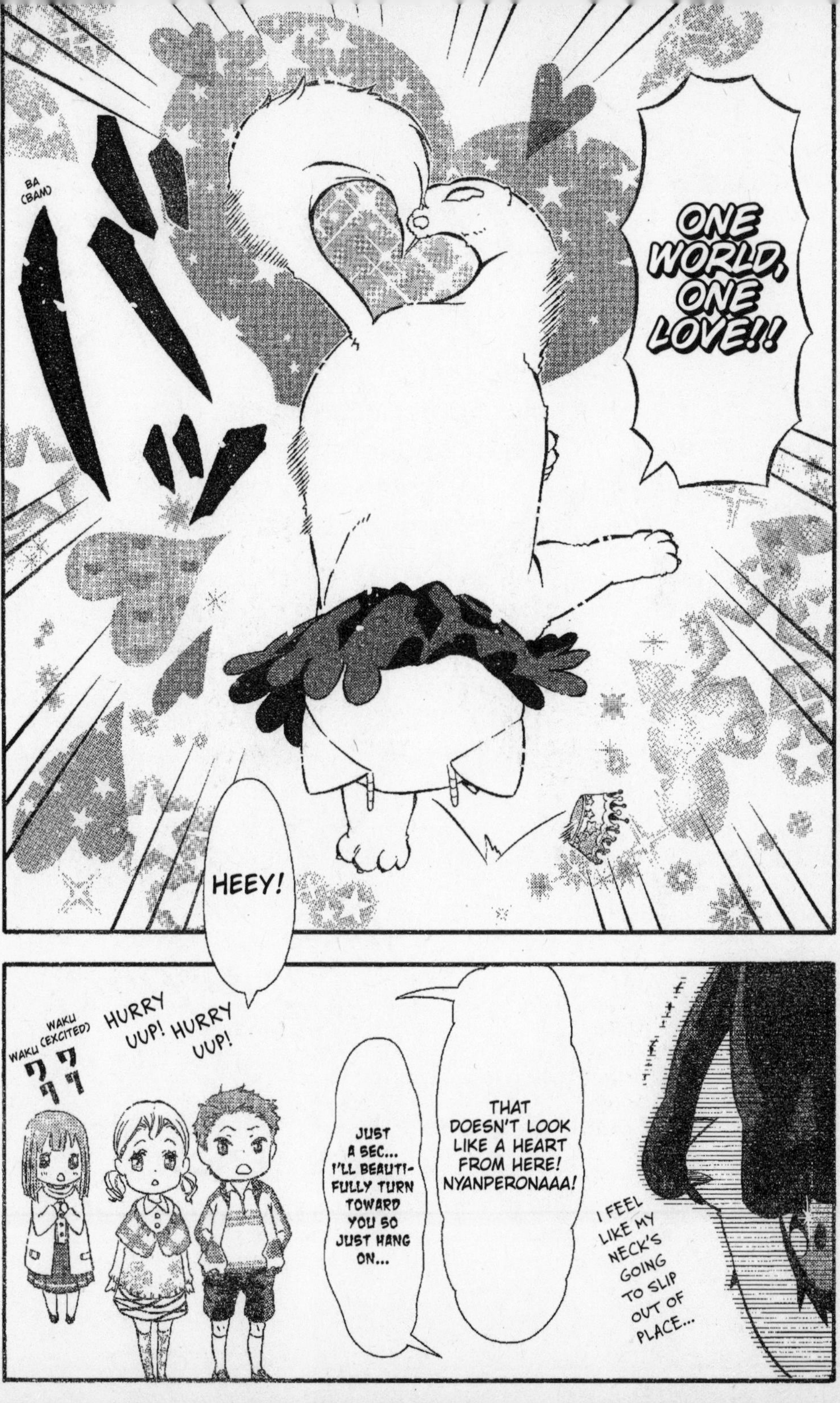
ONE WORLD, ONE LOVE!!
BA (BAM)
HEEY!
I FEEL LIKE MY NECK'S GOING TO SLIP OUT OF PLACE...
THAT DOESN'T LOOK LIKE A HEART FROM HERE! NYANPERONAAA!
JUST A SEC... I'LL BEAUTI-FULLY TURN TOWARD YOU SO JUST HANG ON...
HURRY UUP!
HURRY UUP!
WAKU WAKU (EXCITED)

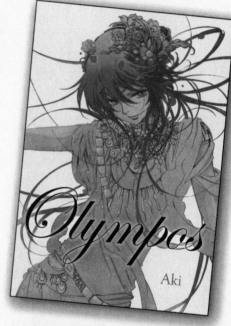

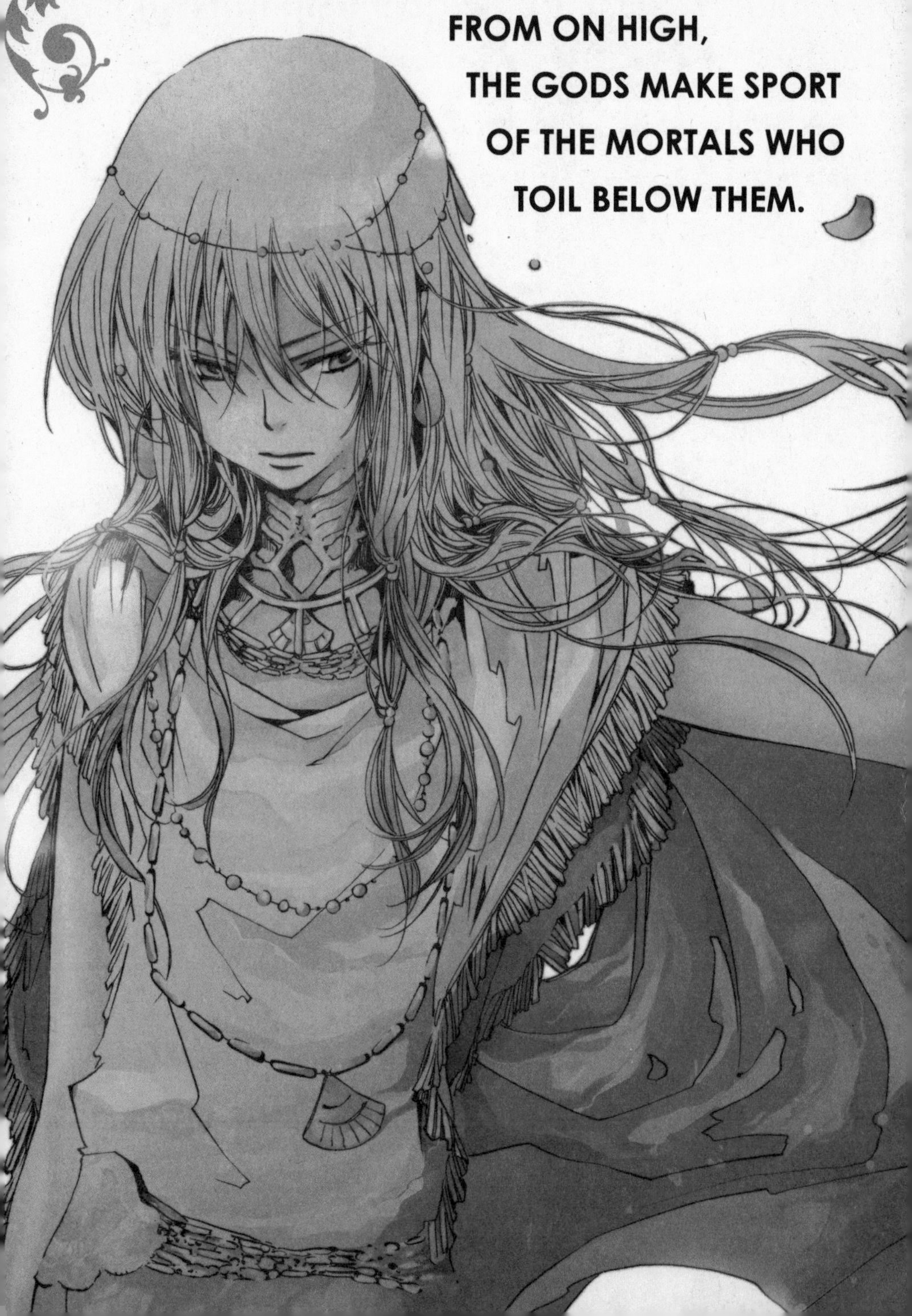
FROM ON HIGH,
THE GODS MAKE SPORT
OF THE MORTALS WHO
TOIL BELOW THEM.

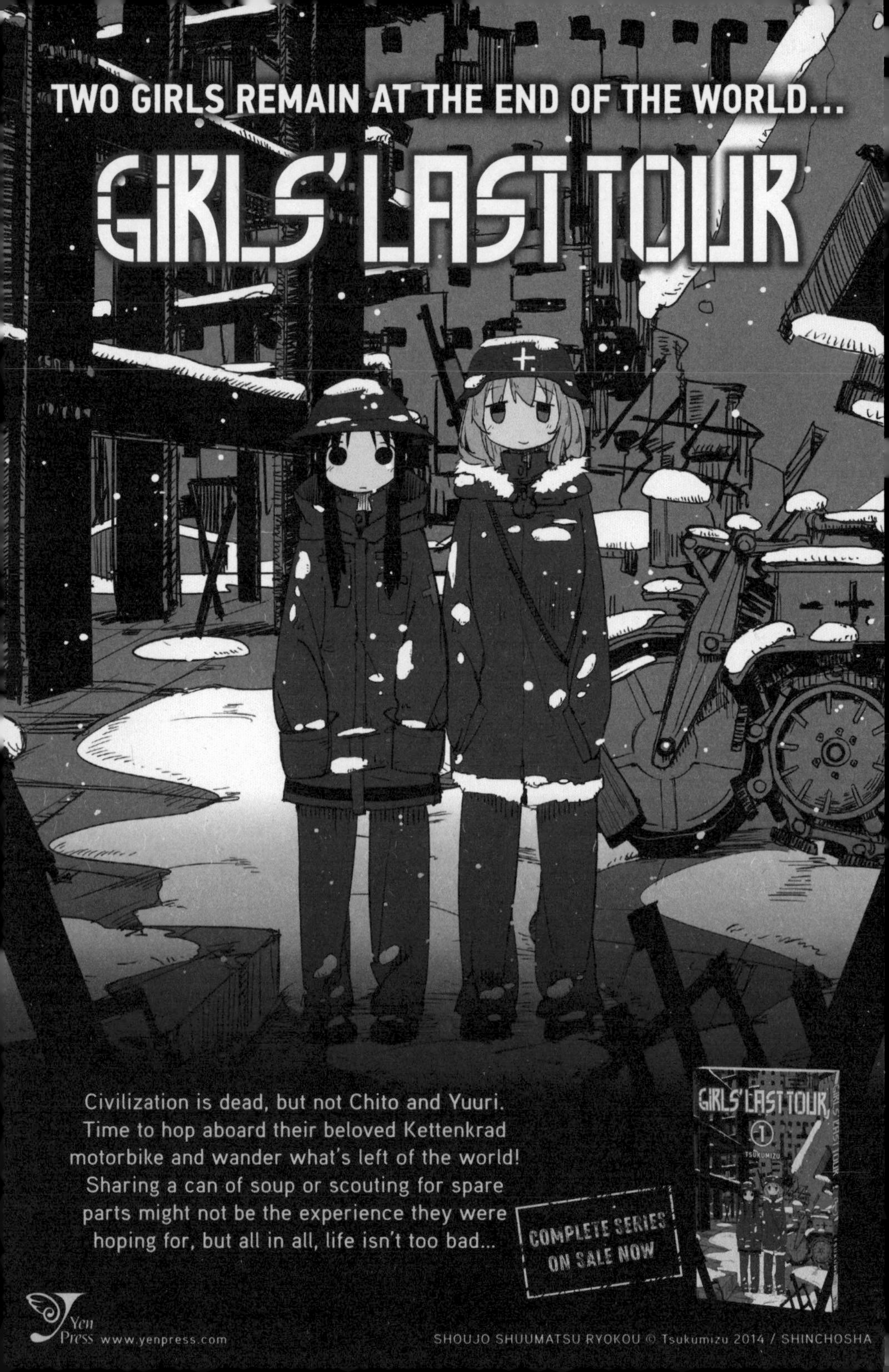
TWO GIRLS REMAIN AT THE END OF THE WORLD...
GIRLS' LAST TOUR
Civilization is dead, but not Chito and Yuuri. Time to hop aboard their beloved Kettenkrad motorbike and wander what's left of the world! Sharing a can of soup or scouting for spare parts might not be the experience they were hoping for, but all in all, life isn't too bad...
COMPLETE SERIES ON SALE NOW
GIRLS' LAST TOUR 1
TSUKUMIZU
Yen Press www.yenpress.com
SHOUJO SHUUMATSU RYOKOU © Tsukumizu 2014 / SHINCHOSHA

The legends foretold of six heroes awakening to save the world...

BUT IT NEVER SPECIFIED WHAT TO DO WITH SEVEN!

The manga adaptation of the super-popular light novel series!

When the world is threatened with destruction, six chosen heroes will rise to save it. One of them is Adlet Meyer, who calls himself "the strongest man in the world." But when he answers the call to assemble with the other heroes and face the darkness, there are not six heroes but seven. Who is the traitor in their midst?

ROKKA: Braves of the Six Flowers

Hello! This is YOTSUBA!

Guess what? Guess what? Yotsuba and Daddy just moved here from waaaay over there!

And Yotsuba met these nice people next door and made new friends to play with!

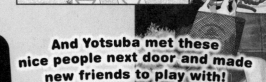

The pretty one took Yotsuba on a bike ride!
(Whoooa! There was a big hill!)

And Ena's a good drawer!
(Almost as good as Yotsuba!)

And their mom always gives Yotsuba ice cream!
(Yummy!)

And...
          And... OHHHH!

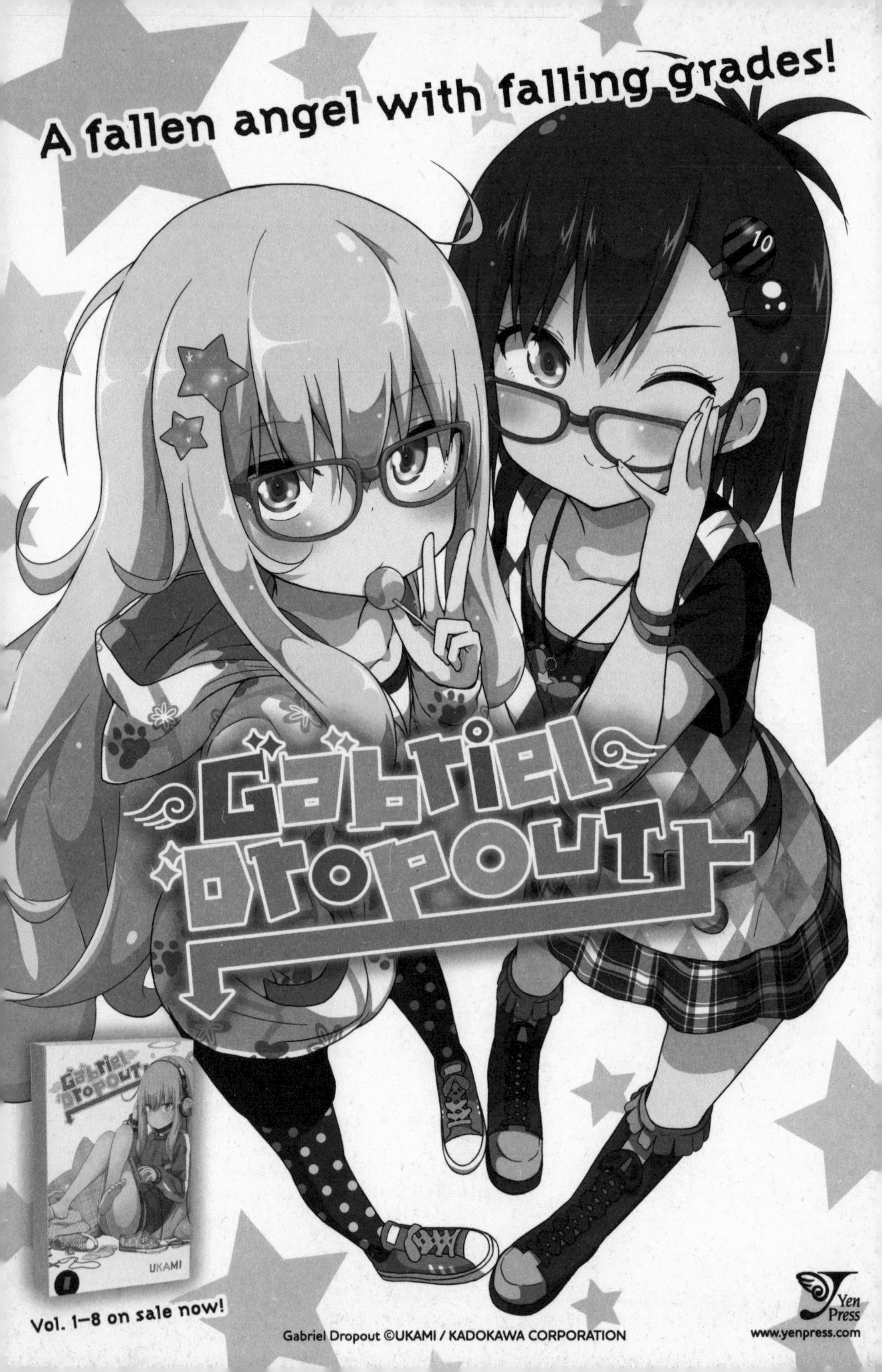
A fallen angel with falling grades!
Gabriel Dropout
Gabriel Dropout
UKAMI
1
Vol. 1–8 on sale now!
Gabriel Dropout ©UKAMI / KADOKAWA CORPORATION
Yen Press
www.yenpress.com

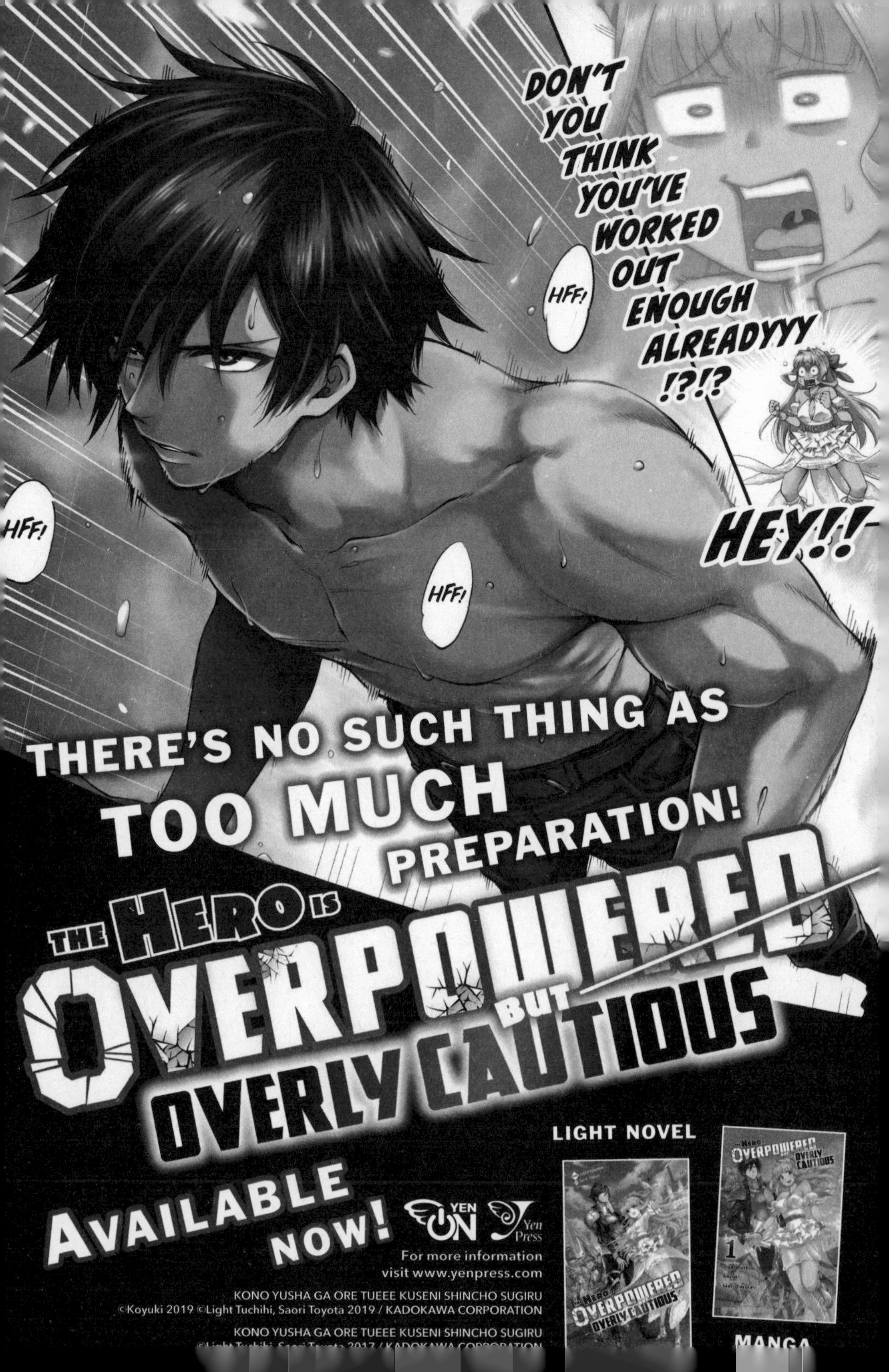

DON'T YOU THINK YOU'VE WORKED OUT ENOUGH ALREADYYY !?!?
HFF!
HEY!!
HFF!
HFF!
THERE'S NO SUCH THING AS TOO MUCH PREPARATION!
THE HERO IS OVERPOWERED BUT OVERLY CAUTIOUS
LIGHT NOVEL
AVAILABLE NOW!
YEN ON
Yen Press
For more information visit www.yenpress.com
KONO YUSHA GA ORE TUEEE KUSENI SHINCHO SUGIRU
©Koyuki 2019 ©Light Tuchihi, Saori Toyota 2019 / KADOKAWA CORPORATION
KONO YUSHA GA ORE TUEEE KUSENI SHINCHO SUGIRU
©Light Tuchihi, Saori Toyota 2017 / KADOKAWA CORPORATION
MANGA

Read the light novel that inspired the hit anime series!

Re:ZeRo
-Starting Life in Another World-

Also be sure to check out the manga series!

AVAILABLE NOW!

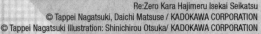

Death doesn't stop a video game–loving shut-in from going on adventures and fighting monsters!

KONOSUBA: GOD'S BLESSING ON THIS WONDERFUL WORLD!

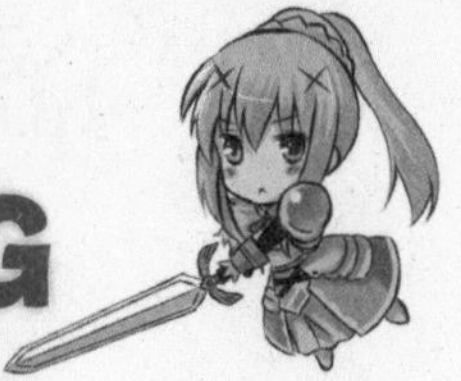

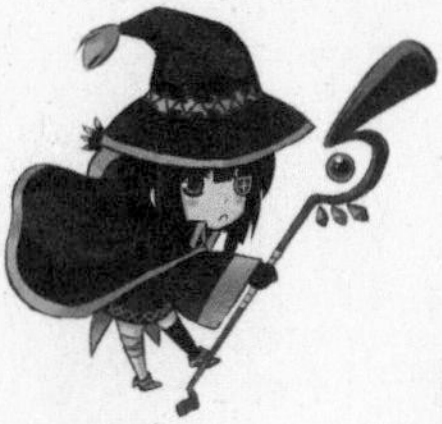

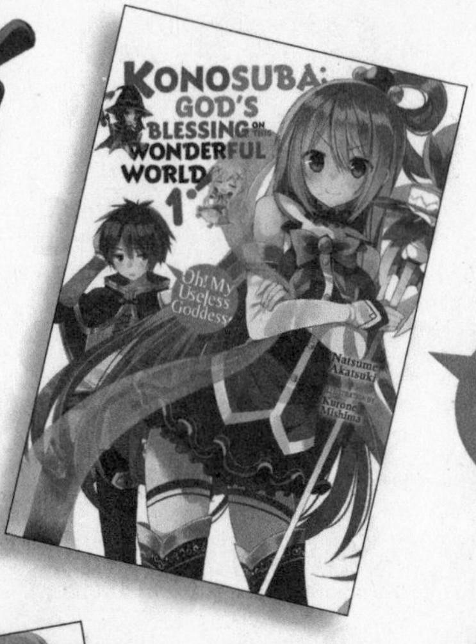
KONOSUBA: GOD'S BLESSING ON THIS WONDERFUL WORLD
1
Oh! My Useless Goddess!
Natsume Akatsuki
Kurone Mishima

IN STORES NOW

Yen ON

LIGHT NOVEL

Yen Press

MANGA

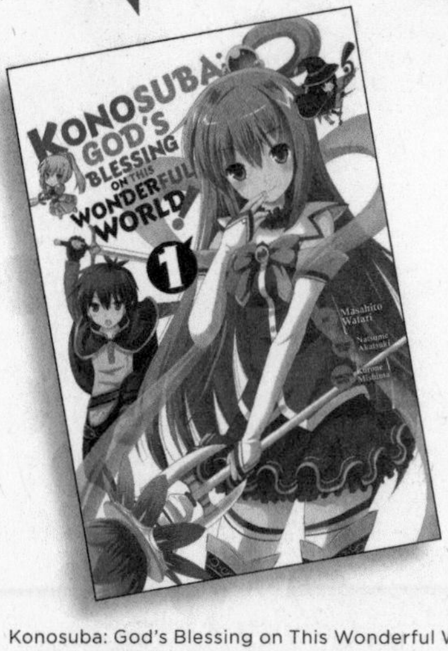
KONOSUBA: GOD'S BLESSING ON THIS WONDERFUL WORLD!
1
Masahito Watari
Natsume Akatsuki

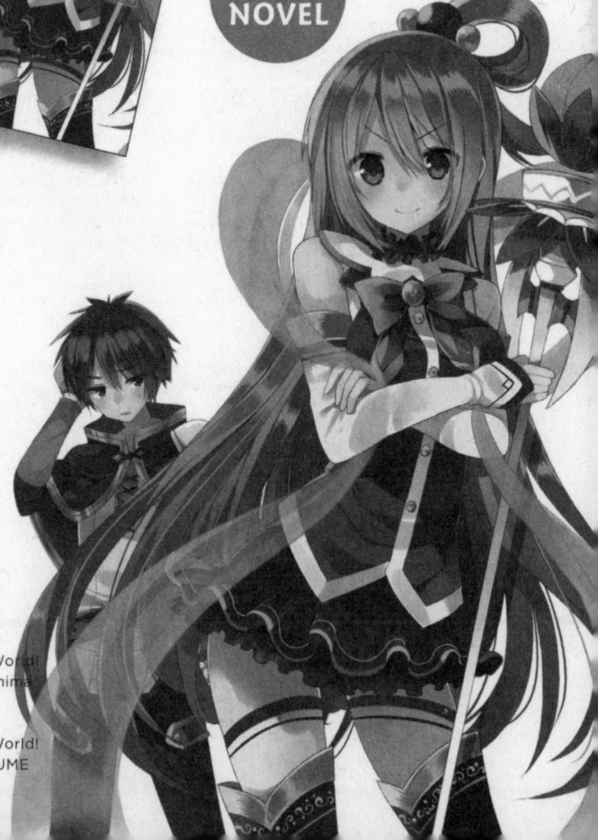

KARNEVAL 10

Touya Mikanagi

Translation: Su Mon Han   Lettering: Phil Christie

This book is a work of fiction. Names, characters, places, and incidents are the product of the author's imagination or are used fictitiously. Any resemblance to actual events, locales, or persons, living or dead, is coincidental.

Karneval vols. 19-20 © 2017 by Touya Mikanagi. All rights reserved. First published in Japan in 2017 by Ichijinsha Inc. Tokyo. Publication rights for this English edition arranged through Kodansha Ltd., Tokyo.

English translation © 2020 by Yen Press, LLC

Yen Press
150 West 30th Street, 19th Floor
New York, NY 10001

Visit us at yenpress.com • facebook.com/yenpress • twitter.com/yenpress • yenpress.tumblr.com • instagram.com/yenpress

First Yen Press Edition: May 2020

Yen Press is an imprint of Yen Press, LLC.
The Yen Press name and logo are trademarks of Yen Press, LLC.

Library of Congress Control Number: 2016936531

ISBNs: 978-1-9753-0644-1 (paperback)
978-1-9753-0835-3 (ebook)

10 9 8 7 6 5 4 3 2 1

WOR

Printed in the United States of America